AIRFRAME & POWERPLANT
MECHANICS
GENERAL HANDBOOK

U.S. DEPARTMENT OF TRANSPORTATION

FEDERAL AVIATION ADMINISTRATION

Flight Standards Service

First Edition 1970

First Revision 1976

Printed in U.S.A.

PREFACE

This handbook was developed and first printed in 1970 as one of a series of three handbooks for persons preparing for mechanic certification with airframe or powerplant ratings, or both. It is intended that this handbook will provide basic information on principles, fundamentals, and technical procedures in the subject matter areas common to both the airframe and powerplant ratings. Emphasis in this volume is on theory and methods of application.

The handbook is designed to aid students enrolled in a formal course of instruction as well as the individual who is studying on his own. Since the knowledge requirements for the airframe and powerplant ratings closely parallel each other in some subject areas, the chapters which discuss fire protection systems and electrical systems contain some material which is also duplicated in the Airframe and Powerplant Mechanics Powerplant Handbook, AC 65–12A, and the Airframe and Powerplant Mechanics Airframe Handbook, AC 65–15A.

This volume contains information on aircraft drawings, weight and balance, aircraft materials and processes, physics, electricity, inspection, ground support, and tools. Knowledge gained from the study of this handbook is essential before proceeding in a course of study in either the airframe or powerplant handbooks.

Because there are so many different types of airframes and powerplants in use today, it is reasonable to expect that differences exist in the components and systems of each. To avoid undue repetition, the practice of using representative systems and units is carried out throughout the handbook. Subject matter treatment is from a generalized point of view, and should be supplemented by reference to manufacturers' manuals or other textbooks if more detail is desired. This handbook is not intended to replace, substitute for, or supersede official regulations or the manufacturers' instructions.

Grateful acknowledgement is extended to the manufacturers of airframe and airframe components for their cooperation in making material available for inclusion.

Copyright material is used by special permission of the following organizations and may not be extracted or reproduced without permission of the copyright owner.

Monsanto Chemical	Skydrol ® Fluids
Townsend Corporation	Cherry Rivets
	Acres Sleeves
J. O. King, Inc.	Acres Sleeves
Gravines, Inc.	Fire Extinguishers
Walter Kidde	Fire Extinguishers
DuPont DeNemours	Fire Extinguishants
National Fire Protection	Fire Extinguisher and
Association	Extinguishant Specifications
National Association of	
Fire Extinguisher Distributors	Fire Extinguishers
Flight Safety Foundation	Refueling Data
American Petroleum Institute	Aviation Fuels
Exxon	Aviation Fuels
Parker Hannifin	Aircraft Fittings

The advancements in aeronautical technology dictate that an instructional handbook must be under continuous review and brought up to date periodically to be valid. Flight Standards requested comments, from the certificated aviation maintenance technician schools, on the three handbooks. As a result of this survey, the handbooks have been updated to this extent: new material has been added in the areas which were indicated as being deficient, and some material has been rearranged to improve the teachability of the handbooks.

We would appreciate having errors brought to our attention, as well as receiving suggestions for improving the usefulness of the handbooks. Comments and suggestions will be retained in our files until such time as the next revision will be accomplished.

Address all correspondence relating to these handbooks to:

U.S. Department of Transportation
Federal Aviation Administration
Flight Standards National Field Office
P.O. Box 25082
Oklahoma City, Oklahoma 73125

The companion handbooks to AC 65–9A are the Airframe and Powerplant Mechanics Powerplant Handbook, AC 65–12A, and the Airframe and Powerplant Mechanics Airframe Handbook, AC 65–15A.

CONTENTS

INTRODUCTION

The use of mathematics is so woven into every area of everyday life that seldom if ever does one fully realize how very helpless we would be in the performance of most of our daily work without the knowledge of even the simplest form of mathematics. Many persons have difficulty with relatively simple computations involving only elementary mathematics. Performing mathematical computations with success requires an understanding of the correct procedures and continued practice in the use of mathematical manipulations.

A person entering the aviation field will be required to perform with accuracy. The aviation mechanic is often involved in tasks that require mathematical computations of some sort. Tolerances in aircraft and engine components are often critical, making it necessary to measure within a thousandth or ten-thousandth of an inch. Because of the close tolerances to which he must adhere, it is important that the aviation mechanic be able to make accurate measurements and mathematical calculations.

Mathematics may be thought of as a kit of tools, each mathematical operation being compared to the use of one of the tools in the solving of a problem. The basic operations of addition, subtraction, multiplication, and division are the tools available to aid us in solving a particular problem.

WHOLE NUMBERS

Addition of Whole Numbers

The process of finding the combined amount of two or more numbers is called addition. The answer is called the sum.

When adding several whole numbers, such as 4567, 832, 93122, and 65, place them under each other with their digits in columns so that the last, or right hand, digits are in the same column.

When adding decimals such as 45.67, 8.32, 9.8122, and .65, place them under each other so that the decimal points are in a straight "up-and-down" line.

To check addition, either add the figures again in the same order, or add them in reverse order.

Subtraction of Whole Numbers

Subtraction is the process of finding the difference between two numbers by taking the smaller from the larger of the two numbers. The number which is subtracted is called the subtrahend, the other number the minuend, and their difference is called the remainder. To find the remainder, write the subtrahend under the minuend, as in addition. Beginning at the right, subtract each figure in the subtrahend from the figure above it and write the individual remainder below in the same column. When the process is completed, the number below the subtrahend is the remainder.

To check subtraction, add the remainder and the subtrahend together. The sum of the two should equal the minuend.

Multiplication of Whole Numbers

The process of finding the quantity obtained by repeating a given number a specified number of times is called multiplication. More simply stated, the process of multiplication is, in effect, a case of repeated addition in which all the numbers being added are identical. Thus, the sum of $6 + 6 + 6 + 6 = 24$ can be expressed by multiplication as $6 \times 4 = 24$. The numbers 6 and 4 are known as the factors of the multiplication, and 24 as the product.

In multiplication, the product is formed by multiplying the factors. When one of the factors is a single-digit integer (whole number), the product is formed by multiplying the single-digit integer with each digit of the other factor from right to left, carrying when necessary.

1

When both factors are multiple-digit integers, the product is formed by multiplying each digit in the multiplying factor with the other factor. Exercise care, when writing down the partial products formed, to make certain that the extreme right digit lines up under the multiplying digit. It is then a matter of simple addition to find the final product.

EXAMPLE

Determine the cost of 18 spark plugs that cost $3.25 each.

$$
\begin{array}{r}
3.25 \\
\times 18 \\
\hline
2600 \\
325 \\
\hline
58.50
\end{array}
$$

When multiplying a series of numbers together, the final product will be the same regardless of the order in which the numbers are arranged.

EXAMPLE

MULTIPLY: $(7)(3)(5)(2) = 210$

$$
\begin{array}{ccc}
7 & 21 & 105 \\
\times 3 & \times 5 & \times 2 \\
\hline
21 & 105 & 210
\end{array}
\quad \text{or} \quad
\begin{array}{ccc}
7 & 3 & 35 \\
\times 5 & \times 2 & \times 6 \\
\hline
35 & 6 & 210
\end{array}
$$

Division of Whole Numbers

The process of finding how many times one number is contained in a second number is called division. The first number is called the divisor, the second the dividend, and the result is the quotient.

Of the four basic operations with integers, division is the only one that involves trial and error in its solution. It is necessary to guess at the proper quotient digits, and though experience will tend to lessen the number of trials, everyone will guess incorrectly at some time or another.

Placing the decimal point correctly in the quotient quite often presents a problem. When dividing a decimal by a decimal, an important step is to first remove the decimal from the divisor. This is accomplished by shifting the decimal point to the right the number of places needed to eliminate it. Next, move the decimal point to the right as many places in the dividend as was necessary to move it in the divisor, and then proceed as in ordinary division.

FRACTIONS

A fraction is an indicated division that expresses one or more of the equal parts into which a unit is divided. For example, the fraction $\frac{2}{3}$ indicates that the whole has been divided into 3 equal parts and that 2 of these parts are being used or considered. The number above the line is the numerator; and the number below the line is the denominator.

If the numerator of a fraction is equal to or larger than the denominator, the fraction is known as an improper fraction. In the fraction $\frac{15}{8}$, if the indicated division is performed, the improper fraction is changed to a mixed number, which is a whole number and a fraction:

$$
\frac{15}{8} = 1\frac{7}{8}
$$

A complex fraction is one that contains one or more fractions or mixed numbers in either the numerator or denominator. The following fractions are examples:

$$
\frac{\frac{1}{2}}{\frac{2}{3}}; \quad \frac{\frac{5}{8}}{2}; \quad \frac{\frac{3}{4}}{\frac{5}{8}}; \quad \frac{3\frac{1}{2}}{\frac{2}{3}}
$$

A decimal fraction is obtained by dividing the numerator of a fraction by the denominator and showing the quotient as a decimal. The fraction $\frac{5}{8}$ equals $5 \div 8 = .625$.

A fraction does not change its value if both numerator and denominator are multiplied or divided by the same number.

$$
\frac{1}{4} \times \frac{3}{3} = \frac{3}{12} = \frac{1}{4}
$$

The same fundamental operations performed with whole numbers can also be performed with fractions. These are addition, subtraction, multiplication, and division.

Addition and Subtraction of Common Fractions

In order to add or subtract fractions, all the denominators must be alike. In working with fractions, as in whole numbers, the rule of likeness applies. That is, only like fractions may be added or subtracted.

When adding or subtracting fractions that have like denominators, it is only necessary to add or subtract the numerators and express the result as the numerator of a fraction whose denominator is the common denominator. When the denominators are unlike, it is necessary to first reduce the fractions to a common denominator before proceeding with the addition or subtraction process.

EXAMPLES

1. A certain switch installation requires $\frac{5}{8}$-inch plunger travel before switch actuation occurs. If $\frac{1}{8}$-inch travel is required after actuation, what will be the total plunger travel?

FIRST: Add the numerators.

$$5 + 1 = 6$$

NEXT: Express the result as the numerator of a fraction whose denominator is the common denominator.

$$\frac{5}{8} + \frac{1}{8} = \frac{6}{8}$$

2. The total travel of a jackscrew is $\frac{13}{16}$ of an inch. If the travel in one direction from the neutral position is $\frac{7}{16}$ of an inch, what is the travel in the opposite direction?

FIRST: Subtract the numerators.

$$13 - 7 = 6$$

NEXT: Express the result as the numerator of a fraction whose denominator is the common denominator.

$$\frac{13}{16} - \frac{7}{16} = \frac{6}{16}$$

3. Find the outside diameter of a section of tubing that has a $\frac{1}{4}$-inch inside diameter and a combined wall thickness of $\frac{5}{8}$ inch.

FIRST: Reduce the fractions to a common denominator.

$$\frac{1}{4} = \frac{2}{8}; \quad \frac{5}{8} = \frac{5}{8}$$

NEXT: Add the numerators, and express the result as the numerator of a fraction whose denominator is the common denominator.

$$\frac{2}{8} + \frac{5}{8} = \frac{7}{8}$$

4. The tolerance for rigging the aileron droop of an airplane is $\frac{7}{8}$ inch plus or minus $\frac{1}{5}$ inch.

What is the minimum droop to which the aileron can be rigged?

FIRST: Reduce the fractions to a common denominator.

$$\frac{7}{8} = \frac{35}{40}; \quad \frac{1}{5} = \frac{8}{40}$$

NEXT: Subtract the numerators, and express the result as in the above examples.

$$\frac{35}{40} - \frac{8}{40} = \frac{27}{40}$$

Finding the Least Common Denominator

When the denominators of fractions to be added or subtracted are such that a common denominator cannot be determined readily, the LCD (least common denominator) can be found by the continued division method.

To find the LCD of a group of fractions, write the denominators in a horizontal row. Next, divide the denominators in this row by the smallest integer that will exactly divide two or more of the denominators. Bring down to a new row all the quotients and numbers that were not divisible. Continue this process until there are no two numbers in the resulting row that are divisible by any integer other than one. Multiply together all the divisors and the remaining terms in the last row to obtain the least common denominator.

EXAMPLE

What is the LCD for $\frac{7}{8}$, $\frac{11}{20}$, $\frac{8}{36}$, $\frac{21}{45}$?

FIRST: Write the denominators in a horizontal row and divide this row by the smallest integer that will exactly divide two or more of the numbers.

2	8	20	36	45
	4	10	18	45

NEXT: Continue this process until there are no two numbers in the resulting row that are divisible by any integer other than one.

2	8	20	36	45
2	4	10	18	45
3	2	5	9	45
3	2	5	3	15
5	2	5	1	5
	2	1	1	1

THEN: Multiply together all the divisors and remaining terms in the last row to obtain the LCD.

$$LCD = 2 \times 2 \times 3 \times 3 \times 5 \times 2 = 360$$

Multiplication of Fractions

The product of two or more fractions is obtained by multiplying the numerators to form the numerator of the product and by multiplying the denominators to form the denominator of the product. The resulting fraction is then reduced to its lowest terms. A common denominator need not be found for this operation, as the new denominator in most cases will be different from that of all the original fractions.

EXAMPLE

What is the product of $\frac{3}{5} \times \frac{12}{22} \times \frac{1}{2}$?

FIRST: Multiply the numerators together.

$$3 \times 12 \times 1 = 36$$

NEXT: Multiply the denominators together.

$$5 \times 22 \times 2 = 220$$

THEN: Reduce the resulting fraction to its lowest terms.

$$\frac{36}{220} = \frac{9}{55}$$

Cancellation

Cancellation is a technique of dividing out or cancelling all common factors that exist between numerators and denominators. This aids in locating the ultimate product by eliminating much of the burdensome multiplication.

EXAMPLE

What is the product of $\frac{18}{10} \times \frac{5}{3}$?

The product could be found by multiplying 18×5 and 10×3, then dividing the product of the numerators by the product of the denominators. However, a much easier method of solution is by cancellation. It is apparent that the 10 in the denominator and the 5 in the numerator can both be divided an exact number of times by 5.

$$\frac{18}{\cancel{10}} \times \frac{\cancel{5}^{1}}{3} =$$

Also, the 18 and 3 are both exactly divisible by 3.

$$\frac{\cancel{18}^{6}}{\cancel{10}_{2}} \times \frac{\cancel{5}^{1}}{\cancel{3}_{1}} =$$

The resulting 6 in the numerator and the 2 in the denominator are both divisible by 2.

$$\frac{\cancel{18}^{6^{3}}}{\cancel{10}_{2_{1}}} \times \frac{\cancel{5}^{1}}{\cancel{3}_{1}} = \frac{3 \times 1}{1 \times 1} = \frac{3}{1} = 3$$

The fraction is thus reduced to its lowest terms, and the final multiplication and division steps are performed with ease when compared with the task of multiplying and dividing the larger fractions.

Division of Common Fractions

The division of common fractions is accomplished most conveniently by converting the problem into a multiplication of two common fractions. To divide one fraction by another fraction, invert the divisor fraction and multiply the numerators together and the denominators together. This is known as the inverted divisor method.

Always keep in mind the order in which the fractions are written. It is important in division that the operations be performed in the order indicated. Also, remember that it is always the divisor that is inverted, never the dividend.

MIXED NUMBERS

Mixed numbers can be added, subtracted, multiplied, or divided by changing them to improper fractions and proceeding as when performing the operations with other fractions.

EXAMPLE

A piece of tubing $6\frac{3}{16}$ inches long is cut from a piece $24\frac{1}{2}$ inches long. Allowing $\frac{1}{16}$ inch for the cut, what is the length of the remaining piece?

FIRST: Reduce the fractional parts to like fractions and complete the subtraction process.

$$\frac{1}{2} - \frac{3}{16} - \frac{1}{16} = \frac{8}{16} - \frac{3}{16} - \frac{1}{16} = \frac{4}{16} = \frac{1}{4}$$

NEXT: Subtract the integer parts.

$$24 - 6 = 18$$

THEN: Combine the results obtained in each step.

$$18 + \frac{1}{4} = 18\frac{1}{4} \text{ inches.}$$

DECIMALS

Decimals are fractions whose denominators are 10 or some multiple of 10, such as 100, 1,000, 10,000, etc. They are indicated by writing one or more digits to the right of a reference mark called a decimal point. Thus:

$$\frac{6}{10} = .6, \text{ both read six tenths.}$$

$$\frac{6}{100} = .06, \text{ both read six hundredths.}$$

$$\frac{6}{1,000} = .006, \text{ both read six thousandths.}$$

When writing a decimal, any number of zeros may be written at the right end without changing the value of the decimal. This may be illustrated in the following manner:

$$.5 = \frac{5}{10} = \frac{1}{2}; \ .50 = \frac{50}{100} = \frac{1}{2}; \ .500 = \frac{500}{1,000} = \frac{1}{2}.$$

A decimal fraction that is written where there is no whole number as .6, .06, etc., is called a pure decimal. When a whole number and a decimal fraction are written together as 3.6, 12.2, 131.12, etc., the number is known as a mixed decimal.

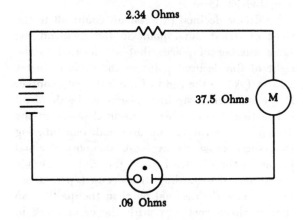

2.34 Ohms

37.5 Ohms (M)

.09 Ohms

FIGURE 1-1. A series circuit.

Addition of Decimals

When computing decimals, the rule of likeness requires that we add or subtract only like denominations. This rule was discussed previously under addition and subtraction of whole numbers. To add or subtract decimal expressions, arrange the decimals so that the decimal points align vertically, and add or subtract as with integers. Place the decimal point in the result directly below the decimal points in the addends or minuend and subtrahend.

EXAMPLES

The total resistance of series circuit (figure 1-1) is equal to the sum of the individual resistances. What is the total resistance for the diagram shown in this example?

FIRST: Arrange the decimals in a vertical column so that the decimal points are in alinement.

$$\begin{array}{r} 2.34 \\ 37.5 \\ .09 \end{array}$$

NEXT: Complete the addition following the technique used in adding whole numbers. Place the decimal point in the result directly below the other decimal points.

$$\begin{array}{r} 2.34 \\ 37.5 \\ .09 \\ \hline 39.93 \text{ ohms} \end{array}$$

Subtraction of Decimals

A series circuit containing two resistors has a total resistance of 37.27 ohms. One of the resistors has a value of 14.88 ohms. What is the value of the remaining resistor?

FIRST: Arrange the decimals in a vertical column so that the decimal points are in alinement.

$$\begin{array}{r} 37.27 \\ -14.88 \end{array}$$

NEXT: Perform the subtraction process using the procedure for subtracting whole numbers. Place the decimal point in the result directly below the other decimal points.

$$\begin{array}{r} 37.27 \\ -14.88 \\ \hline 22.39 \text{ ohms} \end{array}$$

5

Multiplication of Decimals

The multiplication of a decimal by another decimal will always produce an answer smaller than either of the two numbers. When a decimal is multiplied by a whole number or by a mixed decimal, the answer will lie between the two numbers.

When multiplying a decimal fraction by an integer or another decimal, establishing the position of the decimal point in the product causes the greatest amount of difficulty.

To multiply decimals, ignore the decimal points and multiply the terms as though they were whole numbers. To locate the decimal point in the product, begin at the right of the product and point off toward the left the number of decimal places that will equal the sum of the decimal places in the quantities multiplied.

EXAMPLE

Using the formula, Watts = Amperes × Voltage, what is the wattage of an electric heater that uses 9.45 amperes from a 120-volt source?

FIRST: Arrange the terms and multiply. Ignore the decimal point.

$$\begin{array}{r} 9.45 \\ \times 120 \\ \hline 000 \\ 1890 \\ 945 \\ \hline 113400 \end{array}$$

NEXT: Locate the decimal point. Begin at the right of the product and point off toward the left the number of places that will equal the sum of the decimal places in the quantities multiplied.

$$\begin{array}{r} 9.45 \\ \times 120 \\ \hline 18900 \\ 945 \\ \hline 1134.00 \end{array}$$

In some problems the number of digits in the product will be less than the sum of the decimal places in the quantities multiplied. Where this occurs, merely add zeros to the left of the product until the number of digits equals the sum of the decimal places in the quantities multiplied.

EXAMPLE

Multiply .218 by .203.

FIRST: Arrange the terms and multiply, ignoring the decimal point.

$$\begin{array}{r} .218 \\ .203 \\ \hline 654 \\ 4360 \\ \hline 44254 \end{array}$$

NEXT: Locate the decimal point. Add a zero to the left of the product so that the number of places will equal the sum of the decimal places in the quantities multiplied.

$$\begin{array}{r} .218 \\ \times .203 \\ \hline 654 \\ 4360 \\ \hline .044254 \end{array}$$

Division of Decimals

When one or both of the terms of a division problem involve decimal expressions, the quotient is found by converting the problem to one involving a whole number.

Two facts relating to division of decimals that must be borne in mind are: (1) When the dividend and divisor are multiplied by the same number, the quotient remains unchanged; and (2) if the divisor is a whole number, the decimal place in the quotient will align vertically with the decimal in the dividend when the problem is expressed in long division form.

To divide decimal expressions, count off to the right of the decimal point in the dividend the same number of places that are located to the right of the decimal point in the divisor. Insert a caret (∧) to the right of the last digit counted. If the number of decimal places in the dividend is less than the number of decimal places in the divisor, add zeros to the dividend, remembering that there must be at least as many decimal places in the dividend as in the divisor. Divide the terms, disregarding the decimal points entirely. Place the decimal point in the quotient so that it alines vertically with the caret mark in the dividend.

EXAMPLE

The wing area of a certain airplane is 245 square feet; its span is 40.33 feet. What is the mean chord of its wings?

FIRST: Arrange the terms as in long division and move the decimal point to the right, adding zeros as necessary, and insert a caret.

$$40.33_\wedge \overline{)245.00_\wedge}$$

NEXT: Divide the terms, disregarding the decimal points entirely. Add additional zeros to the right to permit carrying the quotient to the desired accuracy.

```
            6 07
40.33 |245.00 00
       241 98
         3 020
         0 000
         3 0200
         2 8221
           1979
```

THEN: Place the decimal point in the quotient so that it alines vertically with the caret mark in the dividend.

```
           6.07 feet
40.33 |24500 00
       24198
        3020
        0000
       30200
       28221
        1979
```

Rounding Off Decimals

There is a general tendency to think of all numbers as being precise. Actually the whole realm of measurement involves numbers that are only approximations of precise numbers. For example, measurements of length, area, and volume are at best approximations. The degree of accuracy of these measurements depends on the refinement of the measuring instruments.

Occasionally it is necessary to round a number to some value that is practical to use. For example, a measurement is computed to be 29.4948 inches. It is impractical, if not impossible, to measure this accurately with steel rule which is accurate only to $\frac{1}{64}$ of an inch.

To use this measurement, we can use the process of "rounding." A decimal expression is "rounded off" by retaining the digits for a certain number of places and discarding the rest. The retained number is an approximation of the computed or exact number. The degree of accuracy desired determines the number of digits to be retained. When the digit immediately to the right of the last retained digit is a 5, or greater than 5, increase the last retained digit by 1. When the digit immediately to the right of the last retained digit is less than 5, leave the last retained digit unchanged.

EXAMPLE

Round 29.4948 to the nearest tenth.

FIRST: Determine the number of digits to retain. In this case one—tenths being the first place to the right of the decimal point.

29.4948

NEXT: Change the value of the last retained digit, if required. In this case, since 9 is greater than 5, the final decimal is expressed thus:

29.4948 becomes 29.5 inches.

Converting Decimals to Common Fractions

To change a decimal fraction to a common fraction, count the number of digits to the right of the decimal point. Express the number as the numerator of a fraction whose denominator is 1 followed by the number of zeros that will equal the number of digits to the right of the decimal point.

EXAMPLE

Express .375 as a common fraction.

FIRST: Count the number of digits to the right of the decimal point.

```
.375
/ | \
1 2 3
```

NEXT: Express the number as the numerator of a fraction whose denominator is 1 followed by the number of zeros that will equal the number of digits to the right of the decimal point.

$$.375 = \frac{375}{1000}$$

7

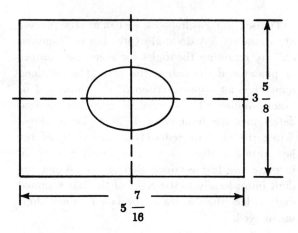

FIGURE 1–2. Locating the hole center.

Many times a dimension appearing in a maintenance manual or on a blueprint is expressed in decimal fractions. In order to use the dimension, it must be converted to some equivalent approximation applicable to the available measuring device. From the mechanic's standpoint, the steel rule will be the device most frequently used.

To change a decimal to the nearest equivalent fraction having a desired denominator, multiply the decimal by the desired denominator. The result will be the numerator of the desired fraction.

EXAMPLE

When accurate holes of uniform diameter are required, they are first drilled $\frac{1}{64}$ inch undersize and reamed to the desired diameter. What size drill would be used before reaming a hole to .763?

FIRST: Multiply the decimal by the desired denominator of 64.

$$
\begin{array}{r}
.763 \\
\times 64 \\
\hline
3052 \\
4578 \\
\hline
48832
\end{array}
$$

NEXT: Round the product to a whole number and express it as the numerator of the desired denominator.

$$48.832 = \frac{49}{64}$$

THEN: To determine the drill size, subtract $\frac{1}{64}$ inch from the finished hole size.

$$\frac{49}{64} - \frac{1}{64} = \frac{48}{64} = \frac{3}{4}\text{-inch drill.}$$

Converting Common Fractions to Decimals

To convert a common fraction, whether proper or improper, to a decimal, divide the numerator by the denominator. Add zeros to the right to permit carrying the quotient to the desired accuracy.

EXAMPLE

Find the distance the center of the hole (figure 1–2) is from the plate edges when the center of the hole is in the center of the plate. Express the length and width of the plate in decimal forms, and then divide each by 2. Express the final result to the nearest 32nd.

FIRST: Change the mixed numbers to improper fractions.

$$5\frac{7}{16} = \frac{87}{16}; \quad 3\frac{5}{8} = \frac{29}{8}$$

NEXT: Convert the improper fractions to decimal expressions.

$$\frac{87}{16} = 5.4375; \quad \frac{29}{8} = 3.625$$

THEN: Divide the decimal expressions by 2 to find the center of the plate.

$$\frac{5.4375}{2} = 2.7188; \quad \frac{3.625}{2} = 1.813$$

FINALLY: Express the final results to the nearest 32nd.

$$2.7188 = 2\frac{23}{32}; \quad 1.813 = 1\frac{26}{32}$$

PERCENTAGE

There are many problems that arise every day involving the percent expression. The greatest number of percentage problems involve some kind of comparison of a part to the whole. Such comparisons become percentage problems when the ratio fraction is expressed as a percent.

A fraction having the specific power of 100 for the denominator is given the name percent. When writing these fractions, the percent symbol (%) is substituted for the denominator. Any common fraction or decimal can be expressed as a percent. The fraction $\frac{1}{5}$ can thus be expressed as .20 or as 20 percent or simply as 20%. Note that the percent is the same as the decimal fraction except that the decimal point has been moved two places to the right and deleted after "percent" or the symbol "%" has been added.

Expressing a Decimal as a Percent

To express a decimal as a percent, move the decimal point two places to the right (add a zero if necessary) and affix the percent symbol.

EXAMPLE

Express .90 as a percent.

FIRST: Move the decimal point two places to the right.

90.

NEXT: Affix the percent symbol to the right after dropping the decimal point.

90%

Expressing a Percent as a Decimal

Sometimes it may be necessary to express a percent as a decimal. Keeping in mind that a percent is simply a decimal with the decimal point moved two places to the right, all that is necessary to express a percent as a decimal is to move the decimal point two places to the left.

Expressing a Common Fraction as a Percent

The technique involved in expressing a common fraction as a percent is essentially the same as that for a decimal fraction. The one difference is the procedure necessary to convert the fraction to a decimal.

EXAMPLE

Express $\frac{5}{8}$ as a percent.

FIRST: Convert the fraction to a decimal.

$$\frac{5}{8} = 5 \div 8 = .625$$

NEXT: Move the decimal point two places to the right and affix the percent symbol.

$$.625 = 62.5\%$$

Finding What Percent One Number is of Another

Determining what percent one number is of another is done by writing the part number as the numerator of a fraction and the whole number as the denominator of that fraction, and expressing this fraction as a percentage.

EXAMPLE

A motor rated as 12 horsepower is found to be delivering 10.75 horsepower. What is the motor efficiency expressed in percent?

FIRST: Write the part number, 10.75, as the numerator of a fraction whose denominator is the whole number, 12.

$$\frac{10.75}{12}$$

NEXT: Convert the fraction to its decimal equivalent.

$$10.75 \div 12 = .8958$$

THEN: Express the decimal as a percent.

$$.8958 = 89.58\% \text{ efficient.}$$

Finding a Percent of a Given Number

The technique used in determining a percent of a given number is based on the fundamental process of multiplication. It is necessary to state the desired percent as a decimal or common fraction and multiply the given number by the percent expressed as a decimal or other fraction.

EXAMPLE

The cruising speed of an airplane at an altitude of 7,500 feet is 290 knots. What is the cruising speed at 9,000 feet if it has increased 6 percent?

FIRST: State the desired percent as a decimal.

$$6\% = .06$$

NEXT: Multiply the given number by the decimal expression.

$$290 \times .06 = 17.40$$

THEN: Add the new product to the given number. This is the new cruising speed.

$$290 + 17.4 = 307.4 \text{ knots.}$$

Finding a Number When a Percent of It is Known

To determine a number when a percent of it is known, express the percent as a decimal and divide the known number by the decimal expression.

EXAMPLE

Eighty ohms represent 52 percent of a circuit's total resistance. Find the total resistance of this circuit.

FIRST: Express the percent as a decimal.

$$52\% = .52$$

NEXT: Divide the known number by the decimal expression.

$$80 \div .52 = 153.8 \text{ ohms total resistance.}$$

RATIO

An important application of the common fraction is that of ratio. A ratio represents the comparison of one number to another number. Comparison by the use of ratios has widespread application in the field of aviation. A ratio is used to express the comparison of the volume of a cylinder when the piston is at bottom center to the volume of a cylinder when the piston is at top center. This is referred to as the compression ratio. The aspect ratio of an aircraft wing is a comparison of the wing span to the wing chord. The relationship of maximum speed, wing area, wing span, loaded weight, and horsepower of different makes and models of aircraft may be compared through the use of ratios.

A ratio is the quotient of one number divided by another number, expressed in like terms. A ratio, therefore, is the fractional part that one number is of another. A ratio may be expressed as a fraction, or it may be written using the colon (:) as the symbol for expressing ratio; thus the ratio $\frac{7}{8}$ can be written 7:8.

Finding the Ratio of Two Quantitites

To find a ratio, the first term is divided by the second term. Both quantities of both terms must be expressed in the same units, and reduced to their lowest terms.

EXAMPLES

1. What is the weight ratio of a fuel load of 800 gallons to one of 10,080 pounds? Assume that the fuel weighs 7.2 pounds per gallon.

FIRST: Express the fuel load in gallons as the numerator of a fraction whose denominator is the fuel load in pounds.

$$R = \frac{800 \text{ gal.}}{10,080 \text{ lb.}}$$

NEXT: Express both quantities in the same unit (pounds).

$$R = \frac{(800 \times 7.2) \text{ lb.}}{10,080 \text{ lb.}}$$

THEN: Perform the indicated mathematical manipulations and reduce to lowest terms.

$$R = \frac{(800 \times 7.2)}{10,080} = \frac{5760}{10,080} = \frac{4}{7}, \text{ or } 4:7$$

What is the ratio in gallons?

FIRST: Express the ratio in fractional form.

$$R = \frac{800 \text{ gal.}}{10,080 \text{ lb.}}$$

NEXT: Express both quantities in the same unit (gallons).

$$R = \frac{800 \text{ gal.}}{\dfrac{10,080}{7.2}}$$

THEN: Perform the indicated mathematical manipulations and reduce to lowest terms.

$$R = \frac{800}{\dfrac{10,080}{7.2}} = \frac{800}{1,400} = \frac{4}{7}, \text{ or } 4:7$$

2. If the cruising speed of an airplane is 200 knots and its maximum speed is 250 knots, what is the ratio of cruising speed to maximum speed?

FIRST: Express the cruising speed as the numerator of a fraction whose denominator is the maximum speed.

$$R = \frac{200}{250}$$

NEXT: Reduce the resulting fraction to its lowest terms.

$$R = \frac{200}{250} = \frac{4}{5}$$

THEN: Express the result as a ratio of one.

$$R = \frac{4}{5}, \text{ or } .8:1 \text{ (Read 8/10ths to one)}$$

Finding the Quantity of the First Term

Now consider the situation when the ratio and the quantity that corresponds to the second term are given, and it is required to find the quantity that corresponds to the first term. To solve this type problem, multiply the term that corresponds to the second term by the fraction that represents the ratio.

EXAMPLE

The given ratio is 5/7 and the quantity that corresponds to the second term is 35. Find the quantity that corresponds to the first term.

FIRST: Express the problem as the product of the second term times the ratio.

$$35 \times 5/7 =$$

NEXT: Perform the indicated operation.

$$\overset{5}{\cancel{35}} \times 5/\cancel{7} = 25$$
$$1$$

The first term is 25. The proof of this can be demonstrated by showing that the ratio of 25 to 35 is 5:7, reduced to lowest terms.

$$25/35 = 5/7$$

Finding the Quantity of the Second Term

To solve a problem of this type, the ratio of the two quantities and the quantity that corresponds to the first term must be known. The solution is obtained by dividing the known number by the fraction that represents the ratio.

EXAMPLE

The ratio of two quantities is 2/3; the quantity that corresponds to the first term is 100. Find the quantity that corresponds to the second term.

FIRST: Express the problem as the quotient of the first term divided by the ratio.

$$100 \div 2/3 =$$

NEXT: Perform the indicated operation.

$$100 \div 2/3 =$$
$$\overset{50}{\cancel{100}} \times 3/\cancel{2} = 150$$
$$1$$

The second term is 150. Again, this can be proved by expressing 100 as a ratio of 150.

$$100/150 = 2/3$$

PROPORTION

A proportion is a statement of equality between two or more ratios. Thus,

$$\frac{3}{4} = \frac{6}{8}; \text{ or } 3:4 = 6:8.$$

This is read 3 is to 4 as 6 is to 8. The first and last terms of the proportion are called the *extremes*. The second and third terms are called the *means*.

In any proportion, the product of the *extremes* is equal to the product of the *means*. In the proportion

$$2:3 = 4:6$$

the product of the *extremes*, 2×6, is 12; the product of the *means*, 3×4, also is 12. An inspection of *any* proportion will show this to be true. This rule simplifies the solution of many practical problems.

An airplane flying a distance of 300 miles used 24 gallons of gasoline. How many gallons will it need to travel 750 miles?

$$300:750 = 24:x$$
$$(300)(x) = (750)(24)$$
$$300x = 18,000$$
$$x = 60$$

Sixty gallons of gasoline will be required to travel a distance of 750 miles.

POSITIVE AND NEGATIVE NUMBERS

Positive and negative numbers are numbers that have directional value from a given starting point or from zero. Numbers above or to one side, usually right, of zero are designated as positive $(+)$; those below or to the opposite side, usually left, of zero are designated as negative $(-)$. Figure 1–3 is representative of signed numbers on a horizontal scale.

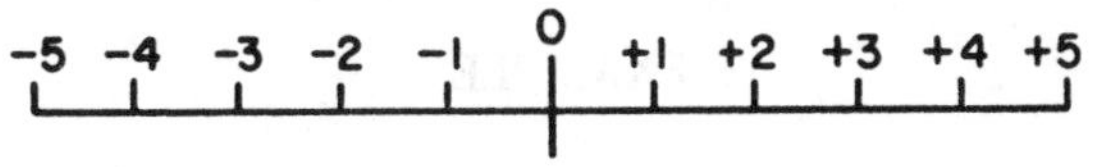

FIGURE 1–3. A scale of signed numbers.

The sum of positive numbers is positive.
The sum of negative numbers is negative.

Addition

To add a positive and a negative number, find the difference in their actual values and give this difference the sign (+ or −) of the larger number.

EXAMPLE

The weight of an aircraft is 2,000 pounds. A radio rack weighing 3 pounds and a transceiver weighing 10 pounds are removed from the aircraft. What is the new weight? For weight and balance purposes, all weight removed from an aircraft is given a minus sign, and all weight added is given a plus sign.

FIRST: Add the values for the removed weights.

$$10 + 3 = 13$$

NEXT: Prefix the sign for removed weights.

$$-13$$

THEN: Add the sum of the removed weights to the total weight, following the rule for unlike signs.

$$+2000 - 13 = +1987 \text{ pounds.}$$

Subtraction

To subtract positive and negative numbers, change the sign of the subtrahend (the number to be subtracted from another) and proceed as in addition.

EXAMPLE

What is the temperature difference between a temperature reading of +20 at 5,000 feet and a reading of −6 at 25,000 feet? Follow the rule, "a change in temperature is equal to the first reading, subtracted from the second reading."

FIRST: Change the sign of the number to be subtracted. +20 becomes −20.

NEXT: Combine the two terms, following the rule for adding like signs.

$$(-6) + (-20) = -26 \text{ degrees.}$$

Multiplication

The product of two positive numbers is positive (+). The product of two negative numbers is positive (+). The product of a positive and a negative number is negative (−).

EXAMPLES

$$3 \times 6 = 18 \qquad -3 \times 6 = -18$$
$$-3 \times -6 = 18 \qquad 3 \times -6 = -18$$

Division

The quotient of two positive numbers is positive. The quotient of two negative numbers is positive. The quotient of a positive and negative number is negative.

EXAMPLES

$$6 \div 3 = 2 \qquad -6 \div 3 = -2$$
$$-6 \div -3 = 2 \qquad 6 \div -3 = -2$$

POWERS AND ROOTS

Power

When one number, the base, is used as a factor two or more times, the result is a power of the base. A positive integral exponent, written as a small number just to the right and slightly above the base number, indicates the number of times the base is used as a factor. Thus, 4 squared, or

4^2 means 4×4, which is 16. The 4 is the base, the 2 is the exponent, and the 16 is the power.

Roots

A root of a number is one of two or more equal numbers that, when multiplied together, will produce the number. Such a number is called an equal factor. Thus, two equal factors that will produce 9 when multiplied together are 3 and 3. Therefore, the square root of 9 equals 3. This may be written $\sqrt{9} = 3$. The symbol $\sqrt{}$ is called a radical sign. Another method of indicating the square root of a number is to use a fractional exponent such as $9^{1/2} = 3$. If the root to be taken is other than a square root, it may be shown in a similar manner; that is, the cube root of 9 may be written $9^{1/3}$. For example, the cube root of 8 equals 2 and may be written $\sqrt[3]{8} = 2$, or $8^{1/3} = 2$; the fourth root of 256 equals 4 and may be written $\sqrt[4]{256} = 4$, or $256^{1/4} = 4$.

Computation of Square Root

It is comparatively easy to determine the square root of such numbers as 4, 9, 16, and 144. The numbers are the perfect squares of small numbers. Unfortunately, all numbers are not perfect squares; neither are they small. The square of a number is the product of that number multiplied by itself. Extracting the square root of a number is the reverse process of squaring a number, and is essentially a special division process. A description of this process follows and is presented in example form.

EXAMPLE

Find the square root of 213.16

FIRST: Starting at the decimal point, and marking off in both directions from the decimal point, separate the number into periods of two figures each. The last period at the left end need not have two figures; all others must have two figures. A zero may be added to the right end so that the period will have two figures.

$$\sqrt{2\underline{13}.\underline{16}}$$

NEXT: Select the largest number that can be squared in the first period. Place the selected number above the radical sign, and place the square of this

number under the first period and subtract.

$$
\begin{array}{r}
1 \\
\sqrt{2\underline{13}.\underline{16}} \\
1\quad\\
\end{array}
$$

$$
\begin{array}{r}
1 \\
\sqrt{2\underline{13}.\underline{16}} \\
1\quad \underline{1}\\
\overline{1}
\end{array}
$$

THEN: Bring down the next pair.

(1) Multiply the root by 2 and place the product to the left of the remainder as the trial divisor.

(2) Determine the number of times the trial divisor will go into that portion of the remainder that is one digit more than the trial divisor. Write this number to the right of the digit in the trial divisor to form the final divisor and also to the right of the digit in the root.

(3) Multiply this number times the completed divisor. If the resulting product is larger than the remainder, reduce the number by one, both in the root and in the final divisor, and repeat the multiplication process.

(4) Subtract the product formed from the remainder and bring down the next pair to form a new remainder.

(5) To complete the solution of extracting the square root, simply repeat the procedure set forth in this step for each period of numbers remaining. It is unnecessary to carry the root beyond the number of digits possessed by the original number.

$$
\begin{array}{r}
1\ 4.\ \ 6 \\
\sqrt{2\underline{13}.\underline{16}} \\
1 \\
\end{array}
$$

$$
\begin{array}{rr}
24 & 113 \\
 & \underline{96} \\
286 & 17\ 16 \\
 & 17\ 16 \\
\end{array}
$$

Two will divide into 11, 5 times. However, 5×25 is greater than 113, so the 5 must be reduced to a 4.

The decimal is placed in the root so that the number of digits in the whole number portion of the root is equal to the sum of the periods, or pairs, in the whole number portion of the number from which the root was extracted.

Powers of Ten

The difficulty of performing mathematical problems with very large (or very small) numbers and the counting and writing of many decimal places are both an annoyance and a source of error. The problems of representation and calculation are simplified by the use of "powers of ten." (See figure 1-4.). This system, sometimes referred to as "Engineer's Shorthand," requires an understanding of the principles of the exponent. These are summarized as follows:

(1) The positive exponent (or power) of a number is a shorthand method of indicating how many times the number is multiplied by itself. For example, 2^3 (read as 2-cubed or 2 to the third power) means 2 is to be multiplied by itself 3 times: $2 \times 2 \times 2 = 8$. A number with a negative exponent may be defined as its inverse or reciprocal (1 divided by the number) with the same exponent made positive. For example, 2^{-3} (read as 2 to the minus 3 power) is the same as

$$\frac{1}{(2)^3} = \frac{1}{2 \times 2 \times 2} = \frac{1}{8}.$$

(2) Any number, except zero, to the zero power is equal to 1. When a number is written without an exponent, the value of the exponent is 1. When an exponent has no sign (+ or −) preceding it, the exponent is positive.

(3) The value of a number does not change when it is both multiplied and divided by the same factor ($5 \times 10 \div 10 = 5$). Moving the decimal point of a number to the left is the same as dividing the number by 10 for each place the decimal point moves. Conversely, moving the decimal point to the right is the same as multiplying the number by 10 for each place the decimal point moves.

POWER OF TEN	EXPANSION	VALUE
Positive Exponent		
10^6	$10 \times 10 \times 10 \times 10 \times 10 \times 10$	1,000,000
10^5	$10 \times 10 \times 10 \times 10 \times 10$	100,000
10^4	$10 \times 10 \times 10 \times 10$	10,000
10^3	$10 \times 10 \times 10$	1,000
10^2	10×10	100
10^1	10	10
10^0		1

The velocity of light, 30, 000, 000, 000 centimeters per second, simplifies to 3×10^{10} centimeters per second.

Negative Exponent		
$10^{-1} = \frac{1}{10}$	$\frac{1}{10}$	$\frac{1}{10} = 0.1$
$10^{-2} = \frac{1}{10^2}$	$\frac{1}{10 \times 10}$	$\frac{1}{100} = 0.01$
$10^{-3} = \frac{1}{10^3}$	$\frac{1}{10 \times 10 \times 10}$	$\frac{1}{1,000} = 0.001$
$10^{-4} = \frac{1}{10^4}$	$\frac{1}{10 \times 10 \times 10 \times 10}$	$\frac{1}{10,000} = 0.0001$
$10^{-5} = \frac{1}{10^5}$	$\frac{1}{10 \times 10 \times 10 \times 10 \times 10}$	$\frac{1}{100,000} = 0.00001$
$10^{-6} = \frac{1}{10^6}$	$\frac{1}{10 \times 10 \times 10 \times 10 \times 10 \times 10}$	$\frac{1}{1,000,000} = 0.000001$

The mass of an electron, 0.000. 000, 000, 000, 000, 000, 000, 000, 911 gram, becomes 9.11×10^{-28} gram.

FIGURE 1–4. Powers of ten and their equivalents.

The procedure for use of powers of ten may be summarized as follows:

(1) Move the decimal point to the place desired. Count the number of places the decimal point is moved.

(2) Multiply the altered number by 10 to a power equal to the number of places the decimal point was moved.

(3) The exponent of 10 is negative if the decimal point is moved to the right, and it is positive if the decimal point is moved to the left. An aid for remembering the sign to be used is: L,

A, R, D. When the decimal point moves Left, you Add; and when the decimal point moves Right, you Deduct.

In most instances, you will find it convenient to reduce the numbers used to numbers between 1 and 10 times 10 to the proper power. Unless otherwise specified, all answers to problems using powers of ten will conform to that requirement.

Powers of Ten Added and Subtracted

Before using powers of ten in mathematical operations, it will be beneficial to review a few more principles governing exponents:

If two or more numbers are written with the same base, their product is equal to the base raised to a power equal to the algebraic sum of their exponents.

$$3^4 \times 3^5 \times 3^3 = 3^{4+5+3} = 3^{12}$$

If two numbers are written with the same base, their quotient is equal to the base raised to a power equal to the algebraic difference of their exponents (numerator's exponent minus denominator's exponent).

$$\frac{4^5}{4^3} = 4^{5-3} = 4^2$$

A factor may be moved from numerator to denominator or from denominator to numerator by changing the sign of its exponent. Thus we have

$$\frac{3^2}{4^{-3}} = 3^2 \times 4^3 = \frac{4^3}{3^{-2}} = \frac{1}{4^{-3} \times 3^{-2}}.$$

The bases must be the same before numbers can be multiplied or divided by the addition or subtraction of their exponents. Thus, $a^5 \times b^6$ cannot be combined because the bases (a and b) are not the same.

Note particularly that the rules specify algebraic addition and algebraic subtraction of the powers. Here are some summarizing examples:

$$3^7 \times 3^{-11} = 3^{7+(-11)} = 3^{7-11} = 3^{-4} = \frac{1}{3^4}.$$

$$4^{-5} \times 4^3 = 4^{-5+3} = 4^{-2} = \frac{1}{4^2}.$$

$$\frac{5^8}{5^{-6}} = 5^{8-(-6)} = 5^{8+6} = 5^{14}.$$

$$\frac{6^8}{6^{12}} = 6^{8-12} = 6^{-4} = \frac{1}{6^4}.$$

Multiplication and division employing powers of ten may be performed in three simple steps as follows:

(1) Reduce all numbers to values between 1 and 10 multiplied by 10 to the proper power.
(2) Perform the indicated operations.
(3) Change the result to a number between 1 to 10 multiplied by 10 multiplied by 10 to the proper power.

COMPUTING AREA

Mensuration formulas deal with the dimensions, areas, and volumes of geometric figures. There are five geometric figures with which you should be familiar, and there is a separate formula for finding the area of each. The area of a plane figure is equal to the number of square units it contains. Areas are measured in different units as compared to measuring length. An area that is square and 1 inch on each side is called a square inch. All area units are square units, such as square inch, square foot, square yard, square rod, and square mile. Other area units are the square centimeter, the square meter, et cetera, found in the metric system of measurement.

TABLES OF AREAS

144 square inches (sq. in.) = 1 square foot (sq. ft.).
9 square feet = 1 square yard (sq. yd.).
$30\frac{1}{4}$ square yards = 1 square rod (sq. rd.).
160 square rods = 1 acre (A).
640 acres = 1 square mile (sq. mile).

The technique for determining the area of any geometric shape is based upon the use of formulas. To solve a problem by formula, it is necessary to—

(1) select the formula that covers the problem situation,
(2) insert the known values in the selected formula, and

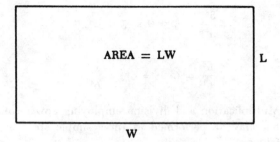

FIGURE 1–5. A rectangle.

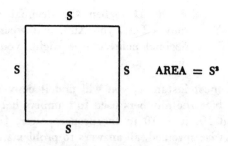

FIGURE 1–6. A square.

(3) then make the necessary mathematical manipulations to find the unknown quantity.

The Rectangle

A rectangle is a four-sided plane figure whose opposite sides are equal and all of whose angles are right angles (90°). The rectangle is a very familiar area in mechanics. It is the cross-sectional area of many beams, rods, fittings, etc. (See figure 1–5.)

The area of a rectangle is the product of the measures of the length and width when they are expressed in the same units of linear measure. The area may be expressed by the formula:

$$A = LW$$

where: A = area.

L = length of rectangle.

W = width of rectangle.

EXAMPLE

A certain aircraft panel is in the form of a rectangle having a length of 24 inches and a width of 12 inches. What is the area of the panel expressed in square inches?

FIRST: Determine the known values and substitute them in the formula.

$$A = LW$$

$$A = 24 \times 12$$

NEXT: Perform the indicated multiplication; the answer will be the total area in square inches.

$$A = 24 \times 12 = 288 \text{ sq. in.}$$

The Square

A square is a plane figure having four equal sides and four right angles (figure 1–6).

To determine the area of a square, find the product of the length of any two sides. Since a square is a figure whose sides are equal, the formula can be expressed as the square of the sides or:

$$A = S^2$$

where A is the area and S is the length of a side.

EXAMPLE

What is the area of a square plate whose side measures 25 inches?

FIRST: Determine the known value and substitute it in the formula

$$A = S^2$$

$$A = 25^2.$$

NEXT: Perform the indicated multiplication; the answer will be the total area in square inches.

$$A = 25 \times 25 = 625 \text{ sq. in.}$$

Triangles

A triangle is a three-sided polygon. There are three basic types of triangle: scalene, equilateral or equiangular, and isosceles. A scalene triangle is one in which all sides and angles are unequal, whereas the equilateral triangle, being just the opposite, has equal sides and equal angles. A triangle that has two equal sides and angles is known as an isosceles triangle.

Triangles may be further classified as to right, obtuse, or acute. These terms are descriptive of the included angles of the triangle. A right triangle is one that has one angle measuring 90°. In an obtuse triangle, one angle is greater than 90°,

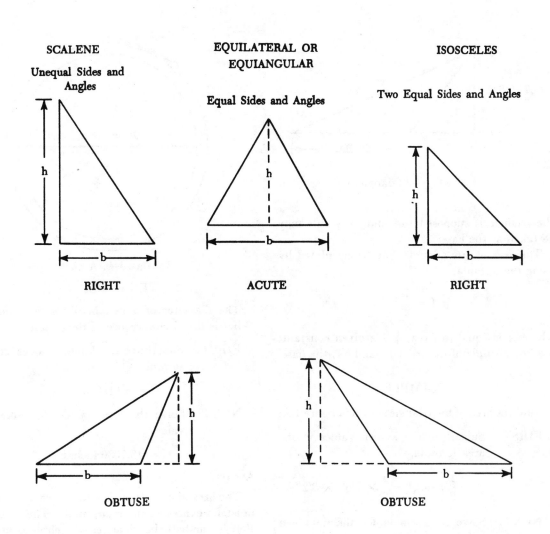

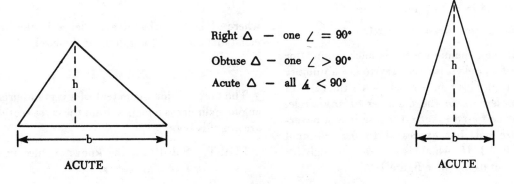

FIGURE 1–7. Types of triangles.

while in an acute triangle all the angles are less than 90°. The various types of triangles are shown in figure 1–7.

The altitude of a triangle is the perpendicular line drawn from the vertex to the base. In some triangles, as in figure 1–8, it may be necessary to extend the base so that the altitude will meet it.

The base of a triangle is the side upon which

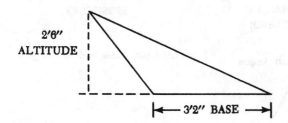

2'6"
ALTITUDE

|← 3'2" BASE →|

FIGURE 1-8. Triangle.

the triangle is supposed to stand. Any side may be taken as the base.

The area of any triangle may be calculated by using the formula:

$$A = \frac{1}{2}ab$$

where A is equal to Area; $\frac{1}{2}$ is a given constant; a is the altitude of the triangle; and b is the base.

EXAMPLE

Find the area of the triangle shown in figure 1-8.

FIRST: Substitute the known values in the area formula.

$$A = \frac{1}{2}ab = A = \frac{1}{2} \times 2'6'' \times 3'2''$$

NEXT: Solve the formula for the unknown value.

$$A = \frac{1}{2} \times 30 \times 38 = \frac{1140}{2}$$

$$A = 570 \text{ sq. in.}$$

Circumference and Area of a Circle

To find the circumference (distance around) or the area of a circle it is necessary to use a number called pi (π). This number represents the ratio of the circumference to the diameter of any circle. Pi cannot be found exactly because it is a never-ending decimal, but expressed to four decimal places it is 3.1416, which is accurate enough for most computations. (See figure 1-9.)

Circumference

The circumference of a circle may be found by using the formula:

$$C = \pi d$$

where C is the circumference; π is the given constant, 3.1416; and d is the diameter of the circle.

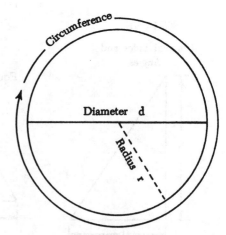

FIGURE 1-9. A circle.

EXAMPLE

The diameter of a certain piston is 5 inches. What is the circumference of the piston?

FIRST: Substitute the known values in the formula, $C = \pi d$.

$$C = 3.1416 \times 5$$

NEXT: Solve the formula for the unknown value.

$$C = 15.7080 \text{ inches.}$$

Area

The area of a circle, as in a rectangle or triangle, must be expressed in square units. The distance that is one-half the diameter of a circle is known as the radius. The area of any circle is found by squaring the radius and multiplying by π. The formula is expressed thus:

$$A = \pi r^2$$

where A is the area of a circle; π is the given constant; and r is the radius of the circle.

EXAMPLE

The bore (inside diameter) of a certain aircraft engine cylinder is 5 inches. Find the cross sectional area of this bore.

FIRST: Substitute the known values in the formula, $A = \pi r^2$.

$$A = 3.1416 \times 2.5^2$$

NEXT: Solve the formula for the unknown value.

$$A = 3.1416 \times 6.25$$

$$A = 19.635 \text{ sq. in.}$$

18

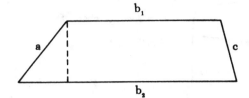

FIGURE 1–10. A trapezoid.

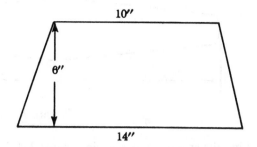

FIGURE 1–11. Computing the area of a trapezoid.

The Trapezoid

A trapezoid (figure 1–10) is a quadrilateral having one pair of parallel sides. The area of a trapezoid is determined by using the formula:

$$A = \frac{1}{2}(b_1 + b_2)h$$

where A is the area; $\frac{1}{2}$ is the given constant; b_1 and b_2 are the lengths of the two parallel sides; and h is the height.

EXAMPLE

What is the area of a trapezoid whose bases are 14 inches and 10 inches, and whose altitude is 6 inches? (See fig. 1–11.)

FIRST: Substitute the known values in the formula.

$$A = \frac{1}{2}(b_1 + b_2)h$$

$$A = \frac{1}{2}(10 + 14)6.$$

NEXT: Solve the formula for the unknown value.

$$A = \frac{1}{2}(24)6$$

$$A = \frac{1}{2} \times 144$$

$$A = 72 \text{ sq. in.}$$

Wing Area

To describe the planform of a wing (figure 1–12), several terms are required. To calculate wing area, it will be necessary to consider the meaning of the terms—span and chord. The wing *span* is the length of the wing from wing tip to wing tip. The *chord* is the width of the wing from leading edge to trailing edge. If the wing is a tapered wing, the average width or chord, known as the mean chord, must be known in finding the area. The formula for calculating wing area is:

$$A = SC$$

where A is the area expressed in square feet, S is the wing span, and C is the average chord.

The process used in calculating wing area will depend upon the shape of the wing. In some instances it will be necessary to use the formula for finding wing area in conjunction with one of the formulas for the area of a quadrilateral or a circle.

EXAMPLES

1. Find the area of the wing illustrated in figure 1–13.

To determine the area, it is necessary to decide what formula to use. It can be seen that the wing tips would form a 7-foot-diameter circle; the remainder of the wing planform is then in the shape of a rectangle. By combining the formulas for wing area and area of a circle, the area of a wing having circular tips can be calculated.

FIRST: Substitute the known value in the formula.

$$A = SC + \pi R^2$$

$$A = (25 - 7)(7) + (3.1416)(3.5^2).$$

The value for S is represented by the original wing span less the diameter of the circular tips.

NEXT: Solve the formula for the unknown value.

$$A = (18 \times 7) + (3.1416 \times 12.25)$$

$$A = 126 + 38.5$$

$$A = 164.5 \text{ sq. ft.}$$

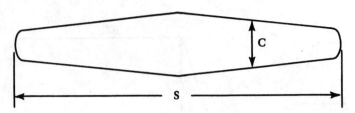

A = Wing Area, ft.²

C = Average chord, ft.

S = Span, ft.

FIGURE 1–12. Wing planform.

2. Find the area of a tapered wing (figure 1–14) whose structural span is 50 feet and whose mean chord is 6′8″.

FIRST: Substitute the known values in the formula.

$$A = SC$$

$$A = 50' \times 6'8''.$$

NEXT: Solve the formula for the unknown value.

$$A = 50' \times 6.67'$$

$$A = 333.5 \text{ sq. ft.}$$

3. Find the area of a trapezoidal wing (shown in figure 1–15) whose leading edge span measures 30 feet, whose trailing edge span measures 34 feet, and whose chord is 5 feet.

FIRST: Substitute the known values in the formula.

$$A = \frac{1}{2}(b_1 + b_2)h$$

$$A = \frac{1}{2}(30 + 34)5.$$

NEXT: Solve the formula for the unknown value.

$$A = \frac{1}{2}(64)5$$

$$A = \frac{1}{2}(320)$$

$$A = 160 \text{ sq. ft.}$$

COMPUTING THE VOLUME OF SOLIDS

Solids are objects with three dimensions—length, breadth, and thickness. They are of many shapes, the most common of which are prisms, cylinders, pyramids, cones, and spheres. Occasionally, it is necessary to determine the volume of a rectangle, a cube, a cylinder, or a sphere.

Since all volumes are not measured in the same units, it is necessary to know all the common units of volume and how they are related to each other. For example, the mechanic may know the volume of a tank in cubic feet or cubic inches, but when the tank is full of gasoline, he will be interested in how many gallons it contains. The following table shows the relationship between some of the common units of volume.

UNITS OF SPACE MEASURE

1,728 cu. in. = 1 cu. ft.

27 cu. ft. = 1 cu. yd.

231 cu. in. = 1 gal.

7.5 gals. = 1 cu. ft.

2 pts. = 1 qt.

4 qts. = 1 gal.

Volume of a Rectangular Solid

A rectangular solid is a solid bounded by rectangles. In other words, it is a square-cornered

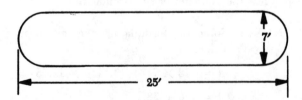

FIGURE 1–13. Wing with circular tips.

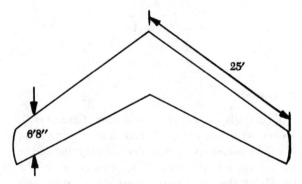

FIGURE 1–14. Tapered wing with sweepback.

20

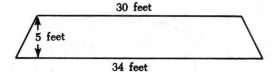

30 feet

5 feet

34 feet

FIGURE 1–15. Trapezoid wing.

volume such as a box (figure 1–16). If the solid has equal dimensions, it is called a cube.

The formula for determining the volume of a rectangular solid may be expressed thus:

$$V = lwh$$

where: V = Volume.

l = length.

w = width.

h = height.

EXAMPLE

A rectangular-shaped baggage compartment measures 5 feet 6 inches in length, 3 feet 4 inches in width, and 2 feet 3 inches in height. How many cubic feet of baggage will it hold?

FIRST: Substitute the known values into the formula.

$$V = lwh$$

$$V = 5'6'' \times 3'4'' \times 2'3''.$$

NEXT: Solve the formula for the unknown value.

$$V = 5\frac{1}{2} \times 3\frac{1}{3} \times 2\frac{1}{4}$$

$$V = \frac{11}{2} \times \frac{10}{3} \times \frac{9}{4}$$

$$V = \frac{165}{4} = 41.25 \text{ cu. ft.}$$

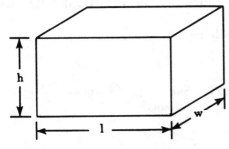

h

l

w

FIGURE 1–16. A rectangular solid.

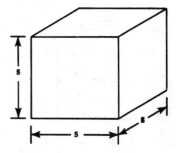

s

s

s

FIGURE 1–17. A cube.

If the rectangular solid is in the shape of a cube (figure 1–17), the formula can be expressed as the cube of the sides:

$$V = S^3$$

where V is the volume and S is the side measurement of the cube.

Area and Volume of a Cylinder

A solid having the shape of a can, length of pipe, or other such object is called a cylinder. The ends of a cylinder are identical circles as shown in figure 1–18.

Surface Area

The surface area of a cylinder is found by multiplying the circumference of the base by the altitude. The formula may be expressed as:

$$A = \pi dh$$

where A is the area, π is the given constant, d is the diameter, and h is the height of the cylinder.

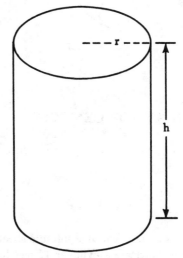

r

h

FIGURE 1–18. A cylinder.

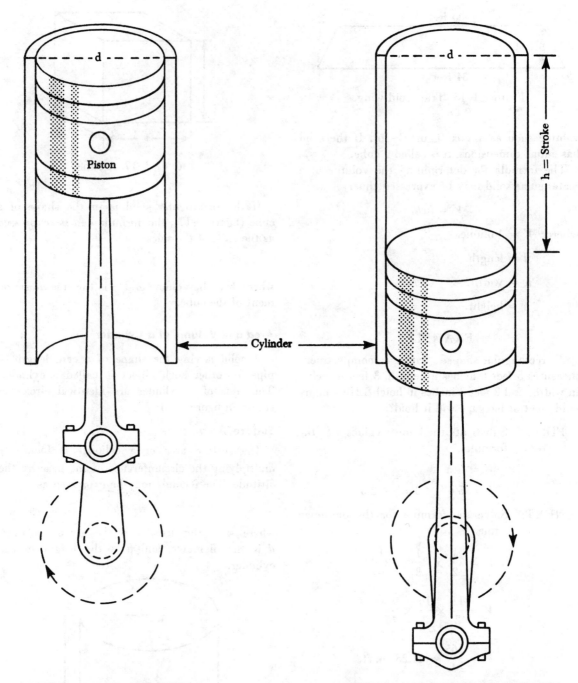

PISTON AT TOP CENTER   PISTON AT BOTTOM CENTER

FIGURE 1–19. Cylinder displacement.

EXAMPLE

How many square feet of aluminum sheet would be needed to fabricate a cylinder 12 feet long and 3 feet 6 inches in diameter?

FIRST: Substitute the known values in the formula.

$$A = \pi dh$$

$$A = 3.1416 \times 3'6'' \times 12'.$$

NEXT: Solve the formula for the unknown value.

$$A = 3.1416 \times 3.5' \times 12'$$

$$A = 132.95, \text{ or } 133 \text{ sq. ft.}$$

Volume

The volume of a cylinder may be found by multiplying the cross-sectional area by the height of the cylinder. The formula may be expressed as:

$$V = \pi r^2 h$$

where V is the volume; π is the given constant; r^2 is the square of the radius of the cylinder; and h is the height of the cylinder (figure 1–19).

EXAMPLE

The cylinder of an aircraft engine has a bore (inside diameter) of 5.5 inches, and the engine has a stroke of 5.5 inches. What is the piston displacement of one cylinder? The stroke represents the height of the cylinder to be measured, because the volume displaced by the piston depends on the length of the stroke.

FIRST: Substitute the known values in the formula.

$$V = \pi r^2 h$$

$$V = (3.1416)(2.75^2)(5.5).$$

NEXT: Solve the formula for the unknown value.

$$V = 17.28 \times 7.56$$

$$V = 130.64 \text{ cu. in.}$$

GRAPHS AND CHARTS

Graphs and charts are pictorial presentations of data, equations, and formulas. Through their use the relationship between two or more quantities may be more clearly understood. Also, a person can see certain conditions or relationships at a glance, while it would require considerable time to obtain the same information from a written description. Graphs may be used in a number of ways, such as representing a single equation or formula, or they may be used to solve two equations for a common value.

Graphs and charts take many forms. A few of the more common forms are called bar graphs, pictographs, broken-line graphs, continuous-curved-line graphs, and circle graphs. An example of each is shown in figure 1–20. The most useful

of these graphs in technical work is the continuous-curved-line graph.

Interpreting or Reading Graphs and Charts

It is more important, from the mechanic's viewpoint, to be able to read a graph properly than it is to draw one. The relationship between the horsepower of a certain engine at sea level and at any altitude up to 10,000 feet can be determined by use of the chart in figure 1–21. To use this type of chart, simply find the point on the horizontal axis that represents the desired altitude; move upward along this line to the point where it intersects the curved line; then move to the left, reading the percent of sea level horsepower available on the vertical axis.

EXAMPLE

What percent of the sea level horsepower is available at an altitude of 5,000 feet?

FIRST: Locate the point on the horizontal axis that represents 5,000 feet. Move upward to the point where the line intersects the curved line.

NEXT: Move to the left, reading the percent of sea level horsepower available at 5,000 feet. The available horsepower is 80%.

Nomograms

It is often necessary to make calculations using the same formula, but using different sets of values for the variables. It is possible to obtain a solution by use of a slide rule or by preparing a table giving the solution of the formula resulting from successive changes of each variable. However, in the case of formulas involving several mathematical operations, the labor entailed would usually be very great.

It is possible to avoid all this labor by using a diagram representing the formula, in which each variable is represented by one or more graduated lines. From this diagram, the solution of the formula for any given variable may be read by means of an index line. A diagram of this type is known as a nomogram.

Much of the information needed to solve aeronautical problems will be presented in nomogram form. Instruction manuals for the various aircraft contain numerous nomograms, many of which

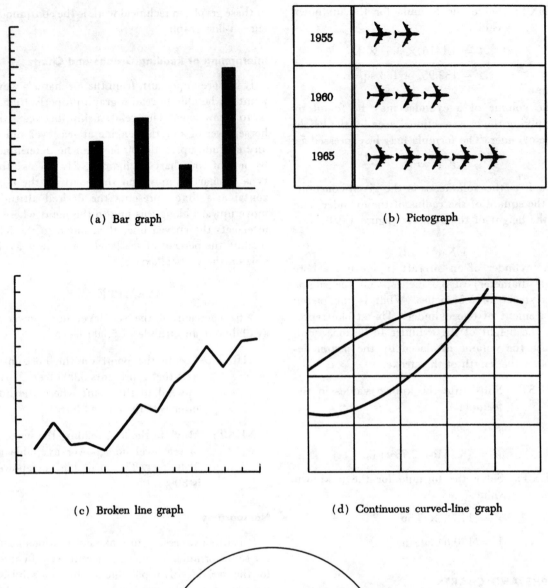

(a) Bar graph

(b) Pictograph

(c) Broken line graph

(d) Continuous curved-line graph

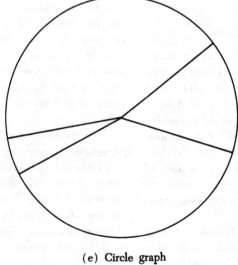

(e) Circle graph

FIGURE 1–20. Types of graphs.

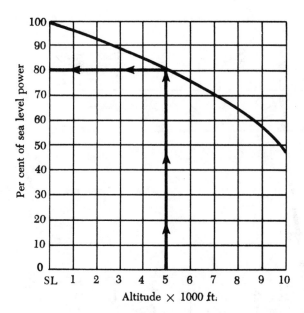

FIGURE 1–21. Horsepower vs. altitude chart.

appear quite complex. Many of the presentations will possess several curves on the same coordinate axis, each curve drawn for different constants in the equation. In the latter case, it is essential to select the proper curve for the desired conditions.

Again, as with the simpler graphs, it is more important for the mechanic to be able to read nomograms than it is to draw them.

The following example is taken from the maintenance manual for the Allison 501–D13 turboprop engine. A nomogram (figure 1–22) is used to determine the power requirements when the engine is operating at minimum torque. The OAT (outside air temperature), station barometric pressure, and engine r.p.m. are three factors that must be known to use this particular nomogram.

EXAMPLE

Determine the calculated horsepower of a certain engine, using the nomogram in figure 1–22. Assume that the OAT is 10° C., the barometric pressure is 28.5 in. Hg, and the engine is operating at 10,000 r.p.m.

FIRST: Locate the reference points on the OAT scale and on the barometric pressure scale that correspond to the given temperature and pressure readings. These are identified as ① and ②, respectively, on the chart. With the aid of a straightedge, connect these two points and establish point ③ on the pivot line.

NEXT: Locate the engine speed, identified as ④, on the engine speed r.p.m. scale. Using a straightedge, connect points ③ and ④ and establish point ⑤ on the calculated horsepower scale. The calculated horsepower is read at point ⑤. The calculated horsepower is 98%.

MODEL 501-D13 ENGINE AND MODEL 606 PROPELLER

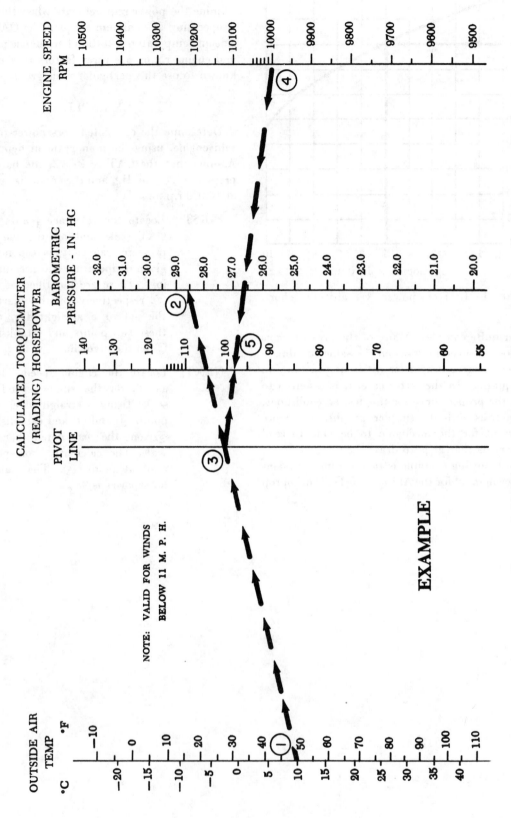

FIGURE 1-22. Power requirements at minimum torque.

26

MEASUREMENT SYSTEMS

Our customary system of measurement (figure 1–23) is part of our cultural heritage from the days when the thirteen colonies were under British rule. It started as a hodge-podge of Anglo-Saxon, Roman, and Norman-French weights and measures. Since medieval times, commissions appointed by various English monarchs had reduced the chaos of measurement by setting specific standards for some of the most important units. Early records, for instance, indicate that an inch was defined as the length of "three barleycorns, round and dry" when laid together; a pennyweight, or one-twentieth of a Tower ounce, was equal to 32 wheatcorns from the "midst of the ear."

The U.S. gallon is the British wine gallon, standardized at the beginning of the 18th century (and about 20 percent smaller than the Imperial gallon that the British adopted in 1824 and have since used to measure most liquids).

In short, as some of the founders of this country realized, the customary system was a makeshift based largely on folkways.

Metric System

The metric system is the dominant language of measurement in use today. Most of the world countries used the metric system prior to World War II. Since the war, more countries have converted or are in the process of converting to the metric system. Only the United States and 13 smaller countries have not made the conversion.

Congress has the power to define the standard of weights and measures. Repeatedly the metric system has been proposed and each time the question has been voted down.

The metric system was developed by a French statesman, Talleyrand, Bishop of Autum, using a "meter" as a standard; the meter being a specific portion of the circumference of the earth at the equator. From this base measurement the meter was developed and accepted as the standard. Divisions and multiples of the meter are based on the decimal system.

LENGTH	MASS	VOLUME	TEMPERATURE	ELECTRIC CURRENT	TIME
METRIC					
Meter	Kilogram	Liter	Celsius (Centigrade)	Ampere	Second
CUSTOMARY					
inch	ounce	fluid ounce	Fahrenheit	ampere	second
foot	pound	teaspoon			
year	ton	tablespoon			
fathom	grain	cup			
rod	dram	pint			
mile		quart			
		gallon			
		barrell			
		peck			
		bushel			

FIGURE 1–23. Some common units.

The Logic of Metric

No other system of measurement that has been actually used can match the inherent simplicity of International Metric. It was designed deliberately to fill all the needs of scientists and engineers. Laymen need only know and use a few simple parts of it. It is logically streamlined, whereas other systems developed more or less haphazardly. At this time there are only six base units in the International Metric System. The unit of length is the meter. The unit of mass is the kilogram. The unit of time is the second. The unit of electric current is the ampere. The unit of temperature is the kelvin (which in common use is translated into the degree Celsius, formerly called degree centigrade). The unit of luminous intensity is the candela.

All the other units of measurement in the International Metric System are derived from these six base units. *Area* is measured in square meters; *speed* in meters per second; *density* in kilograms per cubic meter. The *newton*, the unit of force, is a simple relationship involving meters, kilograms, and seconds; and the pascal, unit of *pressure*, is defined as one newton per square meter. In some other cases, the relationship between the derived and base units must be expressed by rather more complicated formulas—which is inevitable in any measurement system, owing to the innate complexity of some of the things we measure. Similar relationships among mass, area, time and other quantities in the customary system usually require similar formulas, made all the more complicated because they can contain arbitrary constants. For example, one horsepower is defined as 550 foot-pounds per second.

The third intrinsic advantage is that metric is based on the decimal system. Multiples and submultiples of any given unit are always related by powers of 10. For instance, there are 10 millimeters in one centimeter; 100 centimeters in one meter; and 1,000 meters in one kilometer. This greatly simplifies converting larger to smaller measurements. For example, in order to calculate the number of meters in 3.794 kilometers, multiply by 1,000 (move the decimal point three places to the right) and the answer is 3,794. For comparison, in order to find the number of inches in 3.794 miles, it is necessary to multiply first by 5,280 and then by 12.

Moreover, multiples and submultiples of all the International Metric units follow a consistent naming scheme, which consists of attaching a prefix to the unit, whatever it may be. For example, kilo stands for 1,000: one kilometer equals 1,000 meters, and one kilogram equals 1,000 grams. Micro is the prefix for one millionth: one meter equals one million micrometers, and one gram equals one million micrograms (figure 1–24).

PREFIX	MEANS
tera (10^{12})	One trillion times
giga (10^{9})	One billion times
mega (10^{6})	One million times
kilo (10^{3})	One thousand times
hecto (10^{2})	One hundred times
deca (10)	Ten times
deci (10^{-1})	One tenth of
centi (10^{-2})	One hundredth of
milli (10^{-3})	One thousandth of
micro (10^{-6})	One millionth of
nano (10^{-9})	One billionth of
pico (10^{-12})	One trillionth of

FIGURE 1–24. Names and symbols for metric prefixes.

Conversion: Metric To Conventional

People tend to resist changes, usually because they do not understand either the purpose of the change or the new order. Terminology for customary units and metric units have been discussed. A conversion table also has been included. Examples of its use follow:

To convert inches to millimeters, multiply the number of inches by 25. (Ex. 25 into mm = 25 × 25 = 625 mm)

To convert millimeters to inches multiply millimeters by .04. (Ex. 625 mm × .04 = 25 inches.)

To convert square inches to square centimeters multiply by 6.5. (Ex. 100 sq. in. × 6.5 = 650 sq. cm.)

To convert square centimeters to square inches multiply by .16. (Ex. 100 × .16 = 16 sq. in.)

	WHEN YOU KNOW:	YOU CAN FIND:	IF YOU MULTIPLY BY:
LENGTH	inches	millimeters	25
	feet	centimeters	30
	yards	meters	0.9
	miles	kilometers	1.6
	millimeters	inches	0.04
	centimeters	inches	0.4
	meters	yards	1.1
	kilometer	miles	0.6
AREA	square inches	square centimeters	6.5
	square feet	square meters	0.09
	square yards	square meters	0.8
	square miles	square kilometers	2.6
	acres	square hectometers (hectares)	0.4
	square centimeters	square inches	0.16
	square meters	square yards	1.2
	square kilometers	square miles	0.4
	square hectometers (hectares)	acres	2.5
MASS	ounces	grams	28
	pounds	kilograms	0.45
	short tons	megagrams (metric tons)	0.9
	grams	ounces	0.035
	kilograms	pounds	2.2
	megagrams (metric tons)	short tons	1.1
LIQUID VOLUME	ounces	milliliters	30
	pints	liters	0.47
	quarts	liters	0.95
	gallons	liters	3.8
	milliliters	ounces	0.034
	liters	pints	2.1
	liters	quarts	1.06
	liters	gallons	0.26
TEMPERATURE	degrees Fahrenheit	degrees Celsius	5/9 (after subtracting 32)
	degrees Celsius	degrees Fahrenheit	9/5 (then add 32)

FIGURE 1–25. Converting customary to metric.

Figure 1–26 is practically self explanatory. Measurements starting at 1/64 inch up to 20 inches have been converted to decimal divisions of inches and to millimeters.

| Inches | | M M | Inches | | M M | Inches | | M M | Inches | | M M |
Fractions	Decimals		Fractions	Decimals		Fractions	Decimals		Fractions	Decimals	
-	.0004	.01	25/32	.781	19.844	-	2.165	55.	3-11/16	3.6875	93.663
-	.004	.10	-	.7874	20.	2-3/16	2.1875	55.563	-	3.7008	94.
-	.01	.25	51/64	.797	20.241	-	2.2047	56.	3-23/32	3.719	94.456
1/64	.0156	.397	13/16	.8125	20.638	2-7/32	2.219	56.356	-	3.7401	95.
-	.0197	.50	-	.8268	21.	-	2.244	57.	3-3/4	3.750	95.250
-	.0295	.75	53/64	.828	21.034	2-1/4	2.250	57.150	-	3.7795	96.
1/32	.03125	.794	27/32	.844	21.431	2-9/32	2.281	57.944	3-25/32	3.781	96.044
-	.0394	1.	55/64	.859	21.828	-	2.2835	58.	3-13/16	3.8125	96.838
3/64	.0469	1.191	-	.8661	22.	2-5/16	2.312	58.738	-	3.8189	97.
-	.059	1.5	7/8	.875	22.225	-	2.3228	59.	3-27/32	3.844	97.631
1/16	.062	1.588	57/64	.8906	22.622	2-11/32	2.344	59.531	-	3.8583	98.
5/64	.0781	1.984	-	.9055	23.	-	2.3622	60.	3-7/8	3.875	98.425
-	.0787	2.	29/32	.9062	23.019	2-3/8	2.375	60.325	-	3.8976	99.
3/32	.094	2.381	59/64	.922	23.416	-	2.4016	61.	3-29/32	3.9062	99.219
-	.0984	2.5	15/16	.9375	23.813	2-13/32	2.406	61.119	-	3.9370	100.
7/64	.109	2.778	-	.9449	24.	2-7/16	2.438	61.913	3-15/16	3.9375	100.013
-	.1181	3.	61/64	.953	24.209	-	2.4409	62.	3-31/32	3.969	100.806
1/8	.125	3.175	31/32	.969	24.606	2-15/32	2.469	62.706	-	3.9764	101.
-	.1378	3.5	-	.9843	25.	-	2.4803	63.	4	4.000	101.600
9/64	.141	3.572	63/64	.9844	25.003	2-1/2	2.500	63.500	4-1/16	4.062	103.188
5/32	.156	3.969	1	1.000	25.400	-	2.5197	64.	4-1/8	4.125	104.775
-	.1575	4.	-	1.0236	26.	2-17/32	2.531	64.294	-	4.1338	105.
11/64	.172	4.366	1-1/32	1.0312	26.194	-	2.559	65.	4-3/16	4.1875	106.363
-	.177	4.5	1-1/16	1.062	26.988	2-9/16	2.562	65.088	4-1/4	4.250	107.950
3/16	.1875	4.763	-	1.063	27.	2-19/32	2.594	65.881	4-5/16	4.312	109.538
-	.1969	5.	1-3/32	1.094	27.781	-	2.5984	66.	-	4.3307	110.
13/64	.203	5.159	-	1.1024	28.	2-5/8	2.625	66.675	4-3/8	4.375	111.125
-	.2165	5.5	1-1/8	1.125	28.575	-	2.638	67.	4-7/16	4.438	112.713
7/32	.219	5.556	-	1.1417	29.	2-21/32	2.656	67.469	4-1/2	4.500	114.300
15/64	.234	5.953	1-5/32	1.156	29.369	-	2.6772	68.	-	4.5275	115.
-	.2362	6.	-	1.1811	30.	2-11/16	2.6875	68.263	4-9/16	4.562	115.888
1/4	.250	6.350	1-3/16	1.1875	30.163	-	2.7165	69.	4-5/8	4.625	117.475
-	.2559	6.5	1-7/32	1.219	30.956	2-23/32	2.719	69.056	4-11/16	4.6875	119.063
17/64	.2656	6.747	-	1.2205	31.	2-3/4	2.750	69.850	-	4.7244	120.
-	.2756	7.	1-1/4	1.250	31.750	-	2.7559	70.	4-3/4	4.750	120.650
9/32	.281	7.144	-	1.2598	32.	2-25/32	2.781	70.6439	4-13/16	4.8125	122.238
-	.2953	7.5	1-9/32	1.281	32.544	-	2.7953	71.	4-7/8	4.875	123.825
19/64	.297	7.541	-	1.2992	33.	2-13/16	2.8125	71.4376	-	4.9212	125.
5/16	.312	7.938	1-5/16	1.312	33.338	-	2.8346	72.	4-15/16	4.9375	125.413
-	.315	8.	-	1.3386	34.	2-27/32	2.844	72.2314	5	5.000	127.000
21/64	.328	8.334	1-11/32	1.344	34.131	-	2.8740	73.	-	5.1181	130.
-	.335	8.5	1-3/8	1.375	34.925	2-7/8	2.875	73.025	5-1/4	5.250	133.350
11/32	.344	8.731	-	1.3779	35.	2-29/32	2.9062	73.819	5-1/2	5.500	139.700
-	.3543	9.	1-13/32	1.406	35.719	-	2.9134	74.	-	5.518	140.
23/64	.359	9.128	-	1.4173	36.	2-15/16	2.9375	74.613	5-3/4	5.750	146.050
-	.374	9.5	1-7/16	1.438	36.513	-	2.9527	75.	-	5.9055	150.
3/8	.375	9.525	-	1.4567	37.	2-31/32	2.969	75.406	6	6.000	152.400
25/64	.391	9.922	1-15/32	1.469	37.306	-	2.9921	76.	6-1/4	6.250	158.750
-	.3937	10.	-	1.4961	38.	3	3.000	76.200	-	6.2992	160.
13/32	.406	10.319	1-1/2	1.500	38.100	3-1/32	3.0312	76.994	6-1/2	6.500	165.100
-	.413	10.5	1-17/32	1.531	38.894	-	3.0315	77.	-	6.6929	170.
27/64	.422	10.716	-	1.5354	39.	3-1/16	3.062	77.788	6-3/4	6.750	171.450
-	.4331	11.	1-9/16	1.562	39.688	-	3.0709	78.	7	7.000	177.800
7/16	.438	11.113	-	1.5748	40.	3-3/32	3.094	78.581	-	7.0866	180.
29/64	.453	11.509	1-19/32	1.594	40.481	-	3.1102	79.	-	7.4803	190
15/32	.469	11.906	-	1.6142	41.	3-1/8	3.125	79.375	7-1/2	7.500	190.500
-	.4724	12.	1-5/8	1.625	41.275	-	3.1496	80.	-	7.8740	200.
31/64	.484	12.303	-	1.6535	42.	3-5/32	3.156	80.169	8	8.000	203.200
-	.492	12.5	1-21/32	1.6562	42.069	3-3/16	3.1875	80.963	-	8.2677	210.
1/2	.500	12.700	1-11/16	1.6875	42.863	-	3.1890	81.	8-1/2	8.500	215.900
-	.5118	13.	-	1.6929	43.	3-7/32	3.219	81.756	-	8.6614	220.
33/64	.5156	13.097	1-23/32	1.719	43.656	-	3.2283	82.	9	9.000	228.600
17/32	.531	13.494	-	1.7323	44.	3-1/4	3.250	82.550	-	9.0551	230.
35/64	.547	13.891	1-3/4	1.750	44.450	-	3.2677	83.	-	9.4488	240.
-	.5512	14.	-	1.7717	45.	3-9/32	3.281	83.344	9-1/2	9.500	241.300
9/16	.563	14.288	1-25/32	1.781	45.244	-	3.3071	84.	-	9.8425	250.
-	.571	14.5	-	1.8110	46.	3-5/16	3.312	84.1377	10	10.000	254.001
37/64	.578	14.684	1-13/16	1.8125	46.038	3-11/32	3.344	84.9314	-	10.2362	260.
-	.5906	15.	1-27/32	1.844	46.831	-	3.3464	85.	-	10.6299	270.
19/32	.594	15.081	-	1.8504	47.	3-3/8	3.375	85.725	11	11.000	279.401
39/64	.609	15.478	1-7/8	1.875	47.625	-	3.3858	86.	-	11.0236	280.
5/8	.625	15.875	-	1.8898	48.	3-13/32	3.406	86.519	-	11.4173	290.
-	.6299	16.	1-29/32	1.9062	48.419	-	3.4252	87.	-	11.8110	300.
41/64	.6406	16.272	1-15/16	1.9375	49.213	3-7/16	3.438	87.313	12	12.000	304.801
-	.6496	16.5	-	1.9685	50.	-	3.4646	88.	13	13.000	330.201
21/32	.656	16.669	1-31/32	1.969	50.006	3-15/32	3.469	88.106	-	13.7795	350.
-	.6693	17.	2	2.000	50.800	3-1/2	3.500	88.900	14	14.000	355.601
43/64	.672	17.066	-	2.0079	51.	-	3.5039	89.	15	15.000	381.001
11/16	.6875	17.463	2-1/32	2.03125	51.594	3-17/32	3.531	89.694	-	15.7480	400.
45/64	.703	17.859	-	2.0472	52.	-	3.5433	90.	16	16.000	406.401
-	.7087	18.	2-1/16	2.062	52.388	3-9/16	3.562	90.4877	17	17.000	431.801
23/32	.719	18.256	-	2.0868	53.	-	3.5827	91.	-	17.7165	450.
-	.7283	18.5	2-3/32	2.094	53.181	3-19/32	3.594	91.281	18	18.000	457.201
47/64	.734	18.653	2-1/8	2.125	53.975	-	3.622	92.	19	19.000	482.601
-	.7480	19.	-	2.126	54.	3-5/8	3.625	92.075	-	19.6350	500.
3/4	.750	19.050	2-5/32	2.156	54.769	3-21/32	3.656	92.869	20	20.000	508.001
49/64	.7656	19.447				-	3.6614	93.			

FIGURE 1–26. Fractions, decimals, and millimeters.

FUNCTIONS OF NUMBERS

The Functions of Numbers chart (figure 1–27) is included in this chapter for convenience in making computations. Familiarization with the various parts of this chart will illustrate the advantages of using "ready-made" computations.

No.	Square	Cube	Square Root	Cube Root	Circumference	Area
1	1	1	1.0000	1.0000	3.1416	0.7854
2	4	8	1.4142	1.2599	6.2832	3.1416
3	9	27	1.7321	1.4422	9.4248	7.0686
4	16	64	2.0000	1.5874	12.5664	12.5664
5	25	125	2.2361	1.7100	15.7080	19.635
6	36	216	2.4495	1.8171	18.850	28.274
7	49	343	2.6458	1.9129	21.991	38.485
8	64	512	2.8284	2.0000	25.133	50.266
9	81	729	3.0000	2.0801	28.274	63.617
10	100	1,000	3.1623	2.1544	31.416	78.540
11	121	1,331	3.3166	2.2240	34.558	95.033
12	144	1,728	3.4641	2.2894	37.699	113.10
13	169	2,197	3.6056	2.3513	40.841	132.73
14	196	2,744	3.7417	2.4101	43.982	153.94
15	225	3,375	3.8730	2.4662	47.124	176.71
16	256	4,096	4.0000	2.5198	50.265	201.06
17	289	4,913	4.1231	2.5713	53.407	226.98
18	324	5,832	4.2426	2.6207	56.549	254.47
19	361	6,859	4.3589	2.6684	59.690	283.53
20	400	8,000	4.4721	2.7144	62.832	314.16
21	441	9,261	4.5826	2.7589	65.973	346.36
22	484	10,648	4.6904	2.8020	69.115	380.13
23	529	12,167	4.7958	2.8439	72.257	415.48
24	576	13,824	4.8990	2.8845	75.398	452.39
25	625	15,625	5.0000	2.9240	78.540	490.87
26	676	17,576	5.0990	2.9625	81.681	530.93
27	729	19,683	5.1962	3.0000	84.823	572.56
28	784	21,952	5.2915	3.0366	87.965	615.75
29	841	24,389	5.3852	3.0723	91.106	660.52
30	900	27,000	5.4772	3.1072	94.248	706.86
31	1,961	29,791	5.5678	3.1414	97.389	754.77
32	1,024	32,768	5.6569	3.1748	100.53	804.25
33	1,089	35,937	5.7446	3.2075	103.67	855.30
34	1,156	39,304	5.8310	3.2396	106.81	907.92
35	1,225	42,875	5.9161	3.2717	109.96	962.11
36	1,296	46,656	6.0000	3.3019	113.10	1,017.88
37	1,369	50,653	6.0828	3.3322	116.24	1,075.21
38	1,444	54,872	6.1644	3.3620	119.38	1,134.11
39	1,521	59,319	6.2450	3.3912	122.52	1,194.59
40	1,600	64,000	6.3246	3.4200	125.66	1,256.64
41	1,681	68,921	6.4031	3.4482	128.81	1,320.25
42	1,764	74,088	6.4807	3.4760	131.95	1,385.44
43	1,849	79,507	6.5574	3.5034	135.09	1,452.20
44	1,936	85,184	6.6332	3.5303	138.23	1,520.53
45	2,025	91,125	6.7082	3.5569	141.37	1,590.43
46	2,116	97,336	6.7823	3.5830	144.51	1,661.90
47	2,209	103,823	6.8557	3.6088	147.65	1,734.94
48	2,304	110,592	6.9282	3.6342	150.80	1,809.56
49	2,401	117,649	7.0000	3.6593	153.94	1,885.74
50	2,500	125,000	7.0711	3.6840	157.08	1,963.50

FIGURE 1–27. Functions of numbers.

Numbers

The number column contains the numbers 1 through 100. The other columns contain computations for each number.

No.	Square	Cube	Square Root	Cube Root	Circum- ference	Area
51	2,601	132,651	7.1414	3.7084	160.22	2,042.82
52	2,704	140,608	7.2111	3.7325	163.36	2,123.72
53	2,809	148,877	7.2801	3.7563	166.50	2,206.18
54	2,916	157,464	7.3485	3.7798	169.65	2,290.22
55	3,025	166,375	7.4162	3.8030	172.79	2,375.83
56	3,136	175,616	7.4833	3.8259	175.93	2,463.01
57	3,249	185,193	7.5498	3.8485	179.07	2,551.76
58	3,364	195,112	7.6158	3.8709	182.21	2,642.08
59	3,481	205,379	7.6811	3.8930	185.35	2,733.97
60	3,600	216,000	7.7460	3.9149	188.50	2,827.43
61	3,721	226,981	7.8102	3.9365	191.64	2,922.47
62	3,844	238,328	7.8740	3.9579	194.78	3,019.07
63	3,969	250,047	7.9373	3.9791	197.92	3,117.25
64	4,096	262,144	8.0000	4.0000	201.06	3,126.99
65	4,225	274,625	8.0623	4.0207	204.20	3,381.31
66	4,356	287,496	8.1240	4.0412	207.34	3,421.19
67	4,489	300,763	8.1854	4.0615	210.49	3,525.65
68	4,624	314,432	8.2462	4.0817	213.63	3,631.68
69	4,761	328,509	8.3066	4.1016	216.77	3,739.28
70	4,900	343,000	8.3666	4.1213	219.91	3,848.45
71	5,041	357,911	8.4261	4.1408	233.05	3,959.19
72	5,184	373,248	8.4853	4.1602	226.19	4,071.50
73	5,329	389,017	8.5440	4.1793	229.34	4,185.39
74	5,476	405,224	8.6023	4.1983	232.48	4,300.84
75	5,625	421,875	8.6603	4.2172	235.62	4,417.86
76	5,776	438,976	8.7178	4.2358	238.76	4,536.46
77	5,929	456,533	8.7750	4.2543	241.90	4,656.63
78	6,084	474,552	8.8318	4.2727	245.05	4,778.36
79	6,214	493,039	8.8882	4.2908	248.19	4,901.67
80	6,400	512,000	8.9443	4.3089	251.33	5,026.55
81	6,561	531,441	9.0000	4.3267	254.47	5,153.00
82	6,724	551,368	9.0554	4.3445	257.61	5,281.02
83	6,889	571,787	9.1104	4.3621	260.75	5,410.61
84	7,056	592,704	9.1652	4.3795	263.89	5,541.77
85	7,225	614,125	9.2195	4.3968	267.04	5,674.50
86	7,396	636,056	9.2376	4.4140	270.18	5,808.80
87	7,569	638,503	9.3274	4.4310	273.32	5,944.68
88	7,744	681,472	9.3808	4.4480	276.46	6,082.12
89	7,921	704,969	9.4340	4.4647	279.60	6,221.14
90	8,100	729,000	9.4868	4.4814	282.74	6,361.73
91	8,281	753,571	9.5394	4.4979	285.88	6,503.88
92	8,464	778,688	9.5917	4.5144	289.03	6,647.61
93	8,649	804,357	9.6437	4.5307	292.17	6,792.91
94	8,836	830,584	9.6954	4.5468	295.31	6,939.78
95	9,025	857,375	9.7468	4.5629	298.45	7,088.22
96	9,216	884,736	9.7980	4.5789	301.59	7,283.23
97	9,409	912,673	9.8489	4.5947	304.73	7,389.81
98	9,604	941,192	9.8995	4.6104	307.88	7,542.96
99	9,801	970,299	9.9499	4.6261	311.02	7,697.69
100	10,000	1,000,000	10.0000	4.6416	314.16	7,853.98

FIGURE 1-27. Functions of numbers (continued).

Square

Square is the product obtained by multiplying a number by itself: $1 \times 1 = 1$, $2 \times 2 = 4$, $17 \times 17 = 289$. Squaring may be considered a special form of area computation: Area=Length multiplied by Width, $A = L \times W$.

Cube

Cube is the product obtained by multiplying a number by itself, then multiplying that product by the number again: $1 \times 1 \times 1 = 1$, $2 \times 2 \times 2 = 8$, $13 \times 13 \times 13 = 2,197$. Cubing may be considered a specialized form of volumn computation: Volume=Length multiplied by Width by Heighth, $V = L \times W \times H$.

Square Root

Square root is the opposite of a "squared" number. The square root of a number is, that number which when multiplied by itself (squared) will produce the original or desired number: For example, the square root of 1 is 1, $1 \times 1 = 1$. The square root of 4 is 2. The square root of 24 is 4.8990. If an area of 24 square inches must be a perfect square, the length of each side would be 4.8990 inches.

Cube Root

A cube root is the opposite of a "cubed" number. The cube root of a number is that number which when multiplied by itself (cubed) will produce the original or desired number. The cube root of 1 is 1, $1 \times 1 \times 1 = 1$. The cube root of 27 is 3, $3 \times 3 \times 3 = 27$. If a container of 100 cubic inches and cubic in shape is desired, then the length of each side would be 4.6416.

Circumference of A Circle

Circumference is the linear measurement of the distance around a circle. The circumference is calculated by multiplying the diameter of the circle by the constant 3.1416 (π). This constant was calculated by dividing the circumference of circles by their diameter. For example, diameter=1, circumference=3.1416, $1 \times 3.1416 = 3.1416$. Diameter=10, $10 \times 3.1416 = 31.4160$, diameter=12, $12 \times 3.1416 = 37.699$.

Area of A Circle

Area of a circle is the number of square units of measurement contained in the area circumscribed by a circle of the diameter of the listed number. This is calculated by the formula $(\pi) \times r^2 = a$, (π) multiplied by the radius squared equals area. The radius is equal to one half the diameter. For example, diameter=2, radius=1. $3.1416 \times 1 = 3.1416$ square units in a circle which has a diameter of 2. Another example, diameter=4, radius= 2. $3.1416 \times 2^2 = 3.1416 \times 4 = 12.5664$ square units. lion micrograms.

CHAPTER 2

AIRCRAFT DRAWINGS

PRINTS

The exchange of ideas is essential to everyone, regardless of his vocation or position. Usually, this exchange is carried on by the oral or written word; but under some conditions the use of these alone is impractical. Industry discovered that it could not depend entirely upon written or spoken words for the exchange of ideas because misunderstanding and misinterpretation arose frequently. A written description of an object can be changed in meaning just by misplacing a comma; the meaning of an oral description can be completely changed by the use of a wrong word. To avoid these possible errors, industry uses drawings to describe objects. For this reason, drawing is called the Draftsman's Language.

Drawing, as we use it, is a method of conveying ideas concerning the construction or assembly of objects. This is done with the help of lines, notes, abbreviations, and symbols. It is very important that the aviation mechanic who is to make or assemble the object understand the meaning of the different lines, notes, abbreviations, and symbols that are used in a drawing. (See especially "The Meaning of Lines" section of this chapter.)

Prints are the link between the engineers who design an aircraft and the men who build, maintain, and repair it. A print may be a copy of a working drawing for an aircraft part or group of parts, or for a design of a system or group of systems. They are made by placing a tracing of the drawing over a sheet of chemically treated paper and exposing it to a strong light for a short period of time. When the exposed paper is developed, it turns blue where the light has penetrated the transparent tracing. The inked lines of the tracing, having blocked out the light, show as white lines on a blue background. Other types of sensitized paper have been developed; prints may have a white background with colored lines or a colored background with white lines.

A print shows the various steps required in building anything from a simple component to a complete aircraft.

WORKING DRAWINGS

Working drawings must give such information as size of the object and all of its parts, its shape and that of all of its parts, specifications as to the material to be used, how the material is to be finished, how the parts are to be assembled, and any other information essential to making and assembling the particular object.

Working drawings may be divided into three classes: (1) Detail drawings, (2) assembly drawings, and (3) installation drawings.

Detail Drawing

A detail drawing is a description of a single part, given in such a manner as to describe by lines, notes, and symbols the specifications as to size, shape, material, and methods of manufacture that are to be used in making the part. Detail drawings are usually rather simple; and, when single parts are small, several detail drawings may be shown on the same sheet or print. (See detail drawing at the top of figure 2–1.)

Assembly Drawing

An assembly drawing is a description of an object made up of two or more parts. Examine the assembly drawing in the center of figure 2–1. It describes the object by giving, in a general way, the size and shape. Its primary purpose is to show the relationship of the various parts. An assembly drawing is usually more complex than a detail drawing, and is often accompanied by detail drawings of various parts.

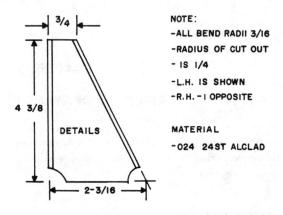

NOTE:
-ALL BEND RADII 3/16
-RADIUS OF CUT OUT
- IS 1/4
-L.H. IS SHOWN
-R.H. -I OPPOSITE

MATERIAL
-024 24ST ALCLAD

DETAILS

4 3/8

3/4

2-3/16

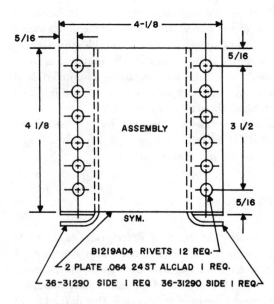

4-1/8

5/16

5/16

4 1/8

3 1/2

ASSEMBLY

5/16

SYM.

B1219AD4 RIVETS 12 REQ.
2 PLATE .064 24ST ALCLAD I REQ.
36-31290 SIDE I REQ   36-31290 SIDE I REQ.

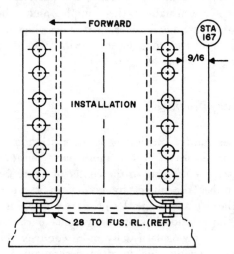

FORWARD

STA 167

9/16

INSTALLATION

28 TO FUS. RL. (REF)

FIGURE 2-1. Working drawings.

Installation Drawing

An installation drawing is one which includes all necessary information for a part or an assembly of parts in the final position in the aircraft. It shows the dimensions necessary for the location of specific parts with relation to the other parts and reference dimensions that are helpful in later work in the shop. (See installation drawing at the bottom of figure 2–1.)

CARE AND USE OF DRAWINGS

Drawings are both expensive and valuable; consequently, they should be handled carefully. Open drawings slowly and carefully to prevent tearing the paper. When the drawing is open, smooth out the fold lines instead of bending them backward.

To protect drawings from damage, never spread them on the floor or lay them on a surface covered with tools or other objects that may make holes in the paper. Hands should be free of oil, grease, or other unclean matter than can soil or smudge the print.

Never make notes or marks on a print, as they may confuse other persons and lead to incorrect work. Only authorized persons are permitted to make notes or changes on prints, and they must sign and date any changes they make.

When finished with a drawing, fold and return it to its proper place. Prints are folded originally in a proper size for filing, and care should be taken so that the original folds are always used.

TITLE BLOCKS

Every print must have some means of identification. This is provided by a title block (see figure 2–2). The title block consists of a drawing number and certain other data concerning the drawing and the object it represents. This information is grouped in a prominent place on the print, usually in the lower right-hand corner. Sometimes the title block is in the form of a strip extending almost the entire distance across the bottom of the sheet.

Although title blocks do not follow a standard form, insofar as layout is concerned, all of them will present essentially the following information:

1. A drawing number to identify the print for filing purposes and to prevent confusing it with any other print.

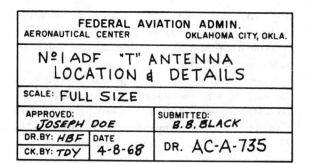

FIGURE 2–2. Title block.

2. The name of the part or assembly.
3. The scale to which it is drawn.
4. The date.
5. The name of the firm.
6. The name of the draftsmen, the checker, and the person approving the drawing.

Drawing or Print Numbers

All prints are identified by a number, which appears in a number block in the lower right-hand corner of the title block. It may also be shown in other places—such as near the top border line, in the upper right-hand corner, or on the reverse side of the print at both ends—so that the number will show when the print is folded or rolled. The purpose of the number is for quick identification of a print. If a print has more than one sheet and each sheet has the same number, this information is included in the number block, indicating the sheet number and the number of sheets in the series.

Reference and Dash Numbers

Reference numbers that appear in the title block refer a person to the numbers of other prints. When more than one detail is shown on a drawing, dash numbers are used. Both parts would have the same drawing number plus an individual number, such as 40267–1 and 40267–2.

In addition to appearing in the title block, dash numbers may appear on the face of the drawing near the parts they identify. Dash numbers are also used to identify right-hand and left-hand parts.

In aircraft, many parts on the left side are like the corresponding parts on the right side but in reverse. The left-hand part is always shown in the drawing. The right-hand part is called for in the title block. Above the title block will be found a notation such as: 470204–1LH shown; 470204–2RH opposite. Both parts carry the same number, but the part called for is distinguished by a dash number. Some prints have odd numbers for left-hand parts and even numbers for right-hand parts.

Universal Numbering System

The universal numbering system provides a means of identifying standard drawing sizes. In the universal numbering system, each drawing number consists of six or seven digits. The first digit is always 1, 2, 4, or 5 (figure 2–3), and indicates the size of the drawing. The remaining digits identify the drawing. Many firms have modified this basic system to conform to their particular needs. Letters may be used instead of numbers. The letter or number depicting the standard drawing size may be prefixed to the number, separated from it by a dash. Other numbering systems provide a separate box preceding the drawing number for the drawing size identifier. In other modification of this system the part number of the depicted assembly is assigned as the drawing number.

SIZE	1	2	4	5
LENGTH	11"	17"	22"	INDEFINITE (ROLL)
WIDTH	8-1/2"	11"	17"	17, 22, 25.50, 34, and 36 inches

FIGURE 2–3. Standard blueprint paper sizes.

BILL OF MATERIAL

A list of the materials and parts necessary for the fabrication or assembly of a component or system is often included on the drawing. The list usually will be in ruled columns in which are listed the part number, name of the part, material from which the part is to be constructed, the quantity required, and the source of the part or material. A typical bill of material is shown in figure 2–4. On drawings that do not have a bill of material, the data may be indicated directly on the drawing.

On assembly drawings, each item is identified by a number in a circle or square. An arrow connecting the number with the item assists in locating it in the bill of material.

BILL OF MATERIAL			
ITEM	PART NO.	REQUIRED	SOURCE
CONNECTOR	UG-21D/U	2	STOCK

FIGURE 2–4. A typical bill of material.

OTHER DATA

Revision Block

Revisions to a drawing are necessitated by changes in dimensions, design, or materials. The changes are usually listed in ruled columns either adjacent to the title block or at one corner of the drawing. All changes to approved drawings must be carefully noted on all existing prints of the drawing.

When drawings contain such corrections, attention is directed to the changes by lettering or numbering them and listing those changes against the symbol in a revision block (figure 2–5). The revision block contains the identification symbol, the date, the nature of the revision, the authority for the change, and the name of the draftsman who made the change.

To distinguish the corrected drawing from its previous version, many firms are including, as part of the title block, a space for entering the appropriate symbol to designate that the drawing has been changed or revised.

2	CHANGED PART NO. 5	E.O.1	2/3/70	B.K.
1	REVISED DIMENSIONS	J.L.M.	7/1/69	E.K.P.
NO.	REVISION	AUTH.	DATE	SIGN.

FIGURE 2–5. Revision block.

Notes

Notes are added to drawings for various reasons. Some of these notes refer to methods of attachment or construction. Others give alternatives, so that the drawing can be used for different styles of the same object. Still others list modifications that are available.

Notes may be found alongside the item to which they refer. If the notes are lengthy, they may be placed elsewhere on the drawing and identified by letters or numbers. Notes are used only when the information cannot be conveyed in the conventional manner or when it is desirable to avoid crowding the drawing. Figure 2–1 illustrates one method of depicting notes.

When the note refers to a specific part, a light line with an arrowhead leads from the note to the part. If it applies to more than one part, the note is so worded that no mistake can be made as to the parts to which it pertains. When there are several notes, they are generally grouped together and numbered consecutively.

Zone Numbers

Zone numbers on drawings are similar to the numbers and letters printed on the borders of a map. They are there to help locate a particular point. To find a point, mentally draw horizontal and vertical lines from the letters and numerals specified; the point where these lines would intersect is the area sought.

Use the same method to locate parts, sections, and views on large drawings, particularly assembly drawings. Parts numbered in the title block can be located on the drawing by finding the numbers in squares along the lower border. Zone numbers read from right to left.

Station Numbers

A numbering system is used on large assemblies for aircraft to locate stations such as fuselage frames. Fuselage Frame-Sta 185 indicates that the frame is 185 inches from the datum of the aircraft. The measurement is usually taken from the nose or zero station, but in some instances it may be taken from the fire wall or some other point chosen by the manufacturer.

The same station numbering system is used for wing and stabilizer frames. The measurement is taken from the center line or zero station of the aircraft.

Finish Marks

Finish marks are used to indicate the surface that must be machine finished. Such finished surfaces have a better appearance and allow a closer fit with adjoining parts. During the finishing process the required limits and tolerances must be observed. Do not confuse machined finishes with those of paint, enamel, chromium plating, and similar coating.

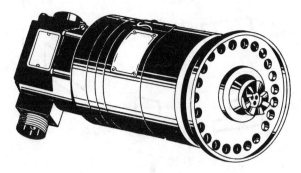

FIGURE 2–6. Pictorial drawing.

Tolerances

When a given dimension on a print shows an allowable variation, the plus (+) figure indicates the maximum, and the minus (−) figure the minimum, allowable variation. The sum of the plus and minus allowance figures is called tolerance. For example, using .225 + .0025 − .0005, the plus and minus figures indicate the part will be acceptable if it is not more than .0025 larger than the .225 given dimension, or not more than .0005 smaller than the .225 dimension. Tolerance in this example is .0030 (.0025 max. plus .005 min.).

If the plus and minus allowances are the same, you will find them presented as .224 ± .0025. The tolerance would then be .0050. Allowance can be indicated in either fractional or decimal form. When very accurate dimensions are necessary, decimal allowances are used. Fractional allowances are sufficient when close dimensions are not required. Standard tolerances of −.010 or −1/32 may be given in the title block of many drawings, to apply throughout the drawing.

METHODS OF ILLUSTRATING OBJECTS

A number of methods are used to illustrate objects graphically. The most common are pictorial drawings, orthographic projections, and diagrams.

Pictorial Drawings

A pictorial drawing, figure 2–6, is similar to a photograph. It shows an object as it appears to the eye, but it is not satisfactory for showing complex forms and shapes. Pictorial drawings are useful in showing the general appearance of an object and are used extensively with orthographic projection drawings. Pictorial drawings are used in maintenance, overhaul, and part numbers.

Orthographic Projection Drawings

In order to show the exact size and shape of all the parts of complex objects, a number of views are necessary. This is the system used in orthographic projection.

In orthographic projection there are six possible views of an object, because all objects have six sides—front, top, bottom, rear, right side, and left side. Figure 2–7(a) shows an object placed in a transparent box, hinged at the edges. The projections on the sides of the box are the views as seen looking straight at the object through each side. If the outlines of the object are drawn on each surface and the box opened as shown in (b), then laid flat as shown in (c), the result is a six-view orthographic projection.

It is seldom necessary to show all six views to portray an object clearly; therefore, only those views necessary to illustrate the required characteristics of the object are drawn. One-view, two-view, and three-view drawings are the most common. Regardless of the number of views used, the arrangement is generally as shown in figure 2–7, with the front view being the principal one. If the right-side view is shown, it will be to the right of the front view. If the left-side view is shown, it will be to the left of the front view. The top and bottom views, if included, will be shown in their respective positions relative to the front view.

One-view drawings are commonly used for objects of uniform thickness, such as gaskets, shims, and plates. A dimensional note gives the thickness as shown in figure 2–8. One-view drawings are also commonly used for cylindrical, spherical, or square parts if all the necessary dimensions can be properly shown in one view.

When space is limited and two views must be shown, symmetrical objects are often represented by half views, as illustrated in figure 2–9.

Aircraft drawings seldom show more than two principal, or complete, views of an object. Instead, generally there will be one complete view and one or more detail views or sectional views.

Detail View

A detail view shows only a part of the object but in greater detail and to a larger scale than the principal view. The part that is shown in detail elsewhere on the drawing is usually encircled by a heavy line on the principal view. Figure 2–10 is an example of the use of detail views. The

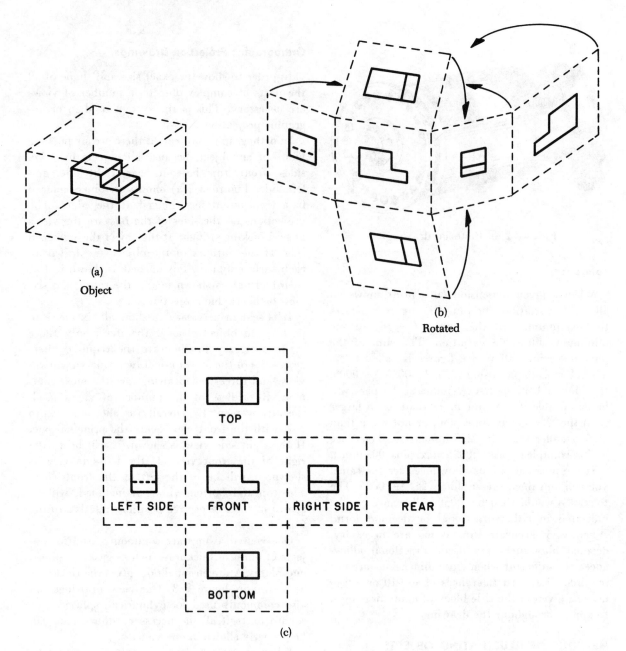

(a)
Object

(b)
Rotated

TOP

LEFT SIDE | FRONT | RIGHT SIDE | REAR

BOTTOM

(c)

FIGURE 2–7. Orthographic projection.

principal view shows the complete control wheel, while the detail view is an enlarged drawing of a portion of the control wheel.

Sectional Views

A section or sectional view is obtained by cutting away part of an object to show the shape and construction at the cutting plane. The part or parts cut away are shown by the use of section (cross-hatching) lines.

Sectional views are used when the interior construction or hidden features of an object cannot be shown clearly by exterior views. For example, figure 2–11, a sectional view of a coaxial cable connector, shows the internal construction of the connector. This is known as a full section. Other types of sections are described in the following paragraphs.

Half Sections

In a half section, the cutting plane extends only halfway across the object, leaving the other half of the object as an exterior view. Half sections are

40

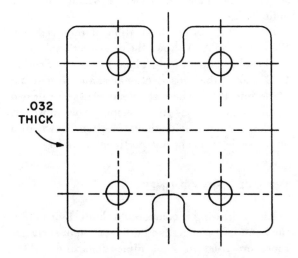

FIGURE 2–8. One-view drawing.

FIGURE 2–9. Symmetrical object with exterior half view.

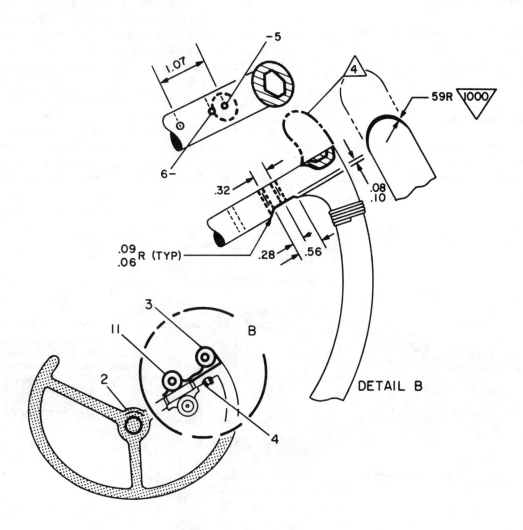

FIGURE 2–10. Detail view.

41

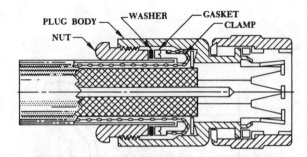

PLUG BODY — WASHER — GASKET CLAMP
NUT

FIGURE 2–11. Sectional view of a cable connector.

used to advantage with symmetrical objects to show both the interior and exterior.

Figure 2–12 is a half-sectional view of a quick disconnect used in aircraft fluid systems.

Revolved Sections

A revolved section drawn directly on the exterior view shows the shape of the cross section of a part, such as the spoke of a wheel. An example of a revolved section is shown in figure 2–13.

Removed Sections

Removed sections illustrate particular parts of an object. They are drawn like revolved sections, except that they are placed at one side and, to bring out pertinent details, are often drawn to a larger scale than the view on which they are indicated.

Figure 2–14 is an illustration of removed sections. Section A–A shows the cross-sectional shape of the object at cutting plane line A–A. Section B–B shows the cross-sectional shape at cutting plane line B–B. These sectional views are drawn to the same scale as the principal view; however, as already mentioned, they are often drawn to a larger scale to bring out pertinent details.

THE MEANING OF LINES

Every drawing is composed of lines. Lines mark the boundaries, edges, and intersection of surfaces. Lines are used to show dimensions and hidden surfaces, and to indicate centers. Obviously, if the same kind of line is used to show all of these things, a drawing becomes a meaningless collection of lines. For this reason, various kinds of standardized lines are used on aircraft drawings. These are illustrated in figure 2–15, and their correct uses are shown in figure 2–16.

Most drawings use three widths, or intensities, of lines: thin, medium, or thick. These lines may vary somewhat on different drawings, but there will always be a noticeable difference between a thin and a thick line, with the width of the medium line somewhere between the two.

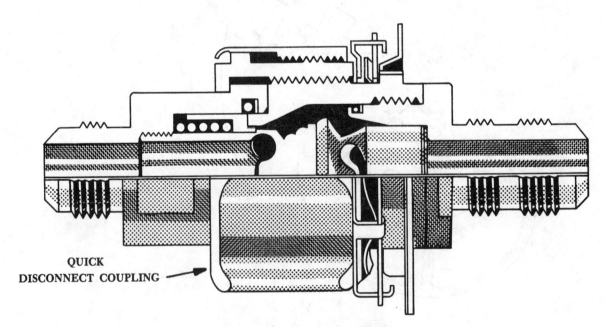

QUICK
DISCONNECT COUPLING →

FIGURE 2–12. Half section.

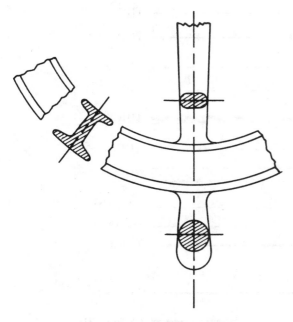

FIGURE 2-13. Revolved sections.

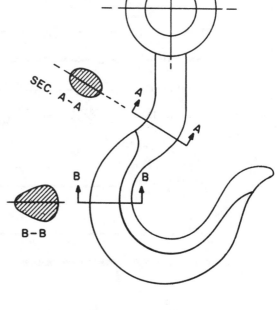

FIGURE 2-14. Removed sections.

Center Lines

Center lines are made up of alternate long and short dashes. They indicate the center of an object or part of an object. Where center lines cross, the short dashes intersect symmetrically. In the case of very small circles, the center lines may be shown unbroken.

Dimension Lines

A dimension line is a light solid line, broken at the midpoint for insertion of measurement indications, and having opposite pointing arrowheads at each end to show origin and termination of a measurement. They are generally parallel to the line for which the dimension is given, and are usually placed outside the outline of the object and between views if more than one view is shown.

All dimensions and lettering are placed so that they will read from left to right. The dimension of an angle is indicated by placing the degree of the angle in its arc. The dimensions of circular parts are always given in terms of the diameter of the circle and are usually marked with the letter D or the abbreviation DIA following the dimension. The dimension of an arc is given in terms of its radius and is marked with the letter R following the dimension. Parallel dimensions are placed so that the longest dimension is farthest from the outline and the shortest dimension is closest to

the outline of the object. On a drawing showing several views, the dimensions will be placed upon each view to show its details to the best advantage.

In dimensioning distances between holes in an object, dimensions are usually given from center to center rather than from outside to outside of the holes. When a number of holes of various sizes are shown, the desired diameters are given on a leader followed by notes indicating the machining operations for each hole. If a part is to have three holes of equal size, equally spaced, this information is given. For precision work, sizes are given in decimals. Diameters and depths are given for counterbored holes. For countersunk holes the angle of countersinking and the diameters are given. Study the examples shown in figure 2-17.

The dimensions given for fits signify the amount of clearance allowable between moving parts. A positive allowance is indicated for a part that is to slide or revolve upon another part. A negative allowance is one given for a force fit. Whenever possible, the tolerance and allowances for desired fits conform to those set up in the American Standard for Tolerances, Allowances, and Gages for Metal Fits. The classes of fits specified in the standard may be indicated on assembly drawings.

43

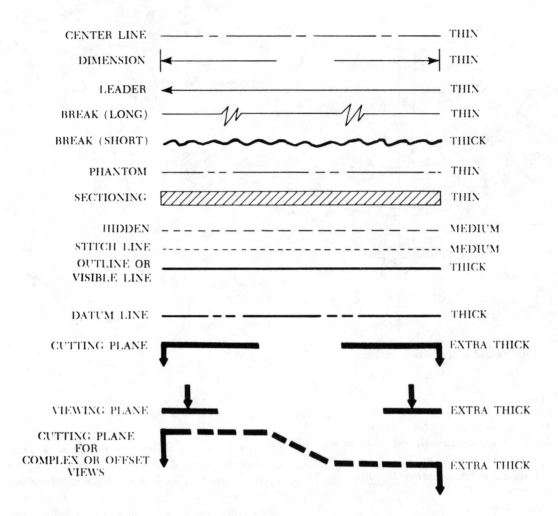

CENTER LINE		THIN
DIMENSION		THIN
LEADER		THIN
BREAK (LONG)		THIN
BREAK (SHORT)		THICK
PHANTOM		THIN
SECTIONING		THIN
HIDDEN		MEDIUM
STITCH LINE		MEDIUM
OUTLINE OR VISIBLE LINE		THICK
DATUM LINE		THICK
CUTTING PLANE		EXTRA THICK
VIEWING PLANE		EXTRA THICK
CUTTING PLANE FOR COMPLEX OR OFFSET VIEWS		EXTRA THICK

FIGURE 2-15. The meaning of lines.

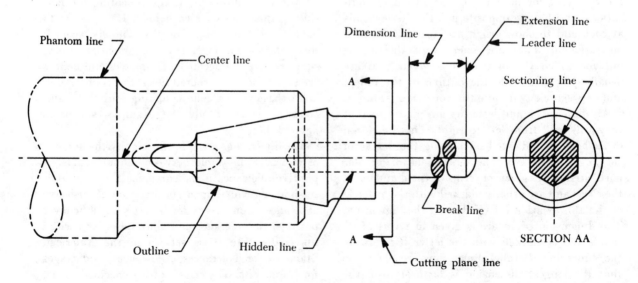

FIGURE 2-16. Correct uses of lines.

44

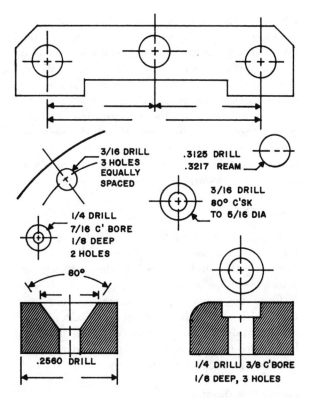

3/16 DRILL
3 HOLES
EQUALLY
SPACED

.3125 DRILL
.3217 REAM

3/16 DRILL
80° C'SK
TO 5/16 DIA

1/4 DRILL
7/16 C' BORE
1/8 DEEP
2 HOLES

80°

.2560 DRILL

1/4 DRILL 3/8 C'BORE
1/8 DEEP, 3 HOLES

FIGURE 2–17. Dimensioning holes.

Leader Lines

Leaders are solid lines with one arrowhead and indicate a part or portion to which a note, number, or other reference applies.

Break Lines

Break lines indicate that a portion of the object is not shown on the drawing. Short breaks are made by solid, freehand lines. For long breaks, solid ruled lines with zigzags are used. Shafts, rods, tubes, and other such parts which have a portion of their length broken out, have the ends of the break drawn as indicated in figure 2–16.

Phantom Lines

Phantom lines indicate the alternate position of parts of the object or the relative position of a missing part. Phantom lines are composed of one long and two short evenly spaced dashes.

Sectioning Lines

Sectioning lines indicate the exposed surfaces of an object in sectional view. They are generally thin, full lines, but may vary with the kind of material shown in section.

Hidden Lines

Hidden lines indicate invisible edges or contours. Hidden lines consist of short dashes evenly spaced and are frequently referred to as dash lines.

Outline or Visible Lines

The outline or visible line is used for all lines on the drawing representing visible lines on the object.

Stitch Lines

Stitch lines indicate stitching or sewing lines and consist of a series of evenly spaced dashes.

Cutting Plane and Viewing Plane Lines

Cutting plane lines indicate the plane in which a sectional view of the object is taken. In figure 2–16, plane line A–A indicates the plane in which section A–A is taken.

Viewing plane lines indicate the plane from which a surface is viewed.

READING DRAWINGS

A drawing cannot be read all at once any more than a whole page of print can be read at a glance. Both must be read a line at a time. To read a drawing effectively, follow a systematic procedure.

Upon opening a drawing, read the drawing number and the description of the article. Next, check the model affected, the latest change letter, and the next assembly listed. Having determined that the drawing is the correct one, proceed to read the illustration(s).

In reading a multiview drawing, first get a general idea of the shape of the object by scanning all the views; then select one view for a more careful study. By referring back and forth to the adjacent view, it will be possible to determine what each line represents.

Each line on a view represents a change in the direction of a surface, but another view must be consulted to determine what the change is. For example, a circle on one view may mean either a hole or a protruding boss, as in the top view of the object in figure 2–18. Looking at the top view, we see two circles; however, the other view must be consulted to determine what each circle represents. A glance at the other view tells us that the smaller circle represents a hole, and the larger

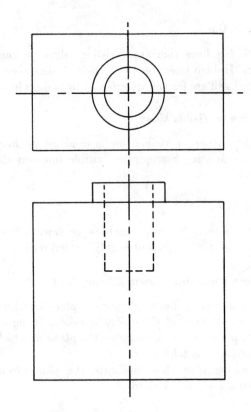

FIGURE 2–18. Reading views.

circle represents a protruding boss. In the same way, the top view must be consulted to determine the shape of the hole and the protruding boss.

It can be seen from this example that one cannot read a print by looking at a single view, when more than one view is given. Two views will not always describe an object, and when three views are given, all three must be consulted to be sure the shape has been read correctly.

After determining the shape of an object, determine its size. Information on dimensions and tolerances is given so that certain design requirements may be met. Dimensions are indicated by figures either with or without the inch mark. If no inch mark is used, the dimension is in inches. It is customary to give part dimensions and an overall dimension that gives the greatest length of the part. If the overall dimension is missing, it can be determined by adding the separate part dimensions.

Drawings may be dimensioned in decimals or fractions. This is especially true in reference to tolerances. Many firms, instead of using plus and minus signs for tolerances, give the complete dimension for both tolerances. For example, if a dimension is 2 inches with a plus or minus toler-

ance of 0.01, the drawing would show the total dimensions as: $\frac{2.01}{1.99}$. A print tolerance (usually found in the title block) is a general tolerance that can be applied to parts where the dimensions are noncritical. Where a tolerance is not shown on a dimension line, the print tolerance applies.

To complete the reading of a drawing, read the general notes and the contents of the material block, check and find the various changes incorporated, and read the special information given in or near views and sections.

DIAGRAMS

A diagram may be defined as a graphic representation of an assembly or system, indicating the various parts and expressing the methods or principles of operation.

There are many types of diagrams; however, those with which the aviation mechanic will be concerned during the performance of his job may be grouped into two classes or types— installation diagrams and schematic diagrams.

Installation Diagrams

Figure 2–19 is an example of an installation diagram. This is a diagram of the gust lock systems of an aircraft. It identifies each of the components in the systems and shows their location in the aircraft. Each letter (A, B, C, etc.) on the principal view refers to a detail view located elsewhere on the diagram. Each detail view is an enlarged drawing of a portion of a system. The numbers on the various views are referred to as call outs, and serve to identify each component.

Installation diagrams are used extensively in aircraft maintenance and repair manuals and are invaluable in identifying and locating components and understanding the operation of various systems.

Schematic Diagram

Schematic diagrams do not indicate the location of individual components in the aircraft, but do locate components with respect to each other within the system. Figure 2–20 illustrates a schematic diagram of an aircraft hydraulic system. The hydraulic pressure gage is not necessarily located above the landing gear selector valve in the aircraft; however, it is connected to the pressure line that leads to the selector valve.

Schematic diagrams of this type are used mainly in trouble-shooting. Note that each line is coded

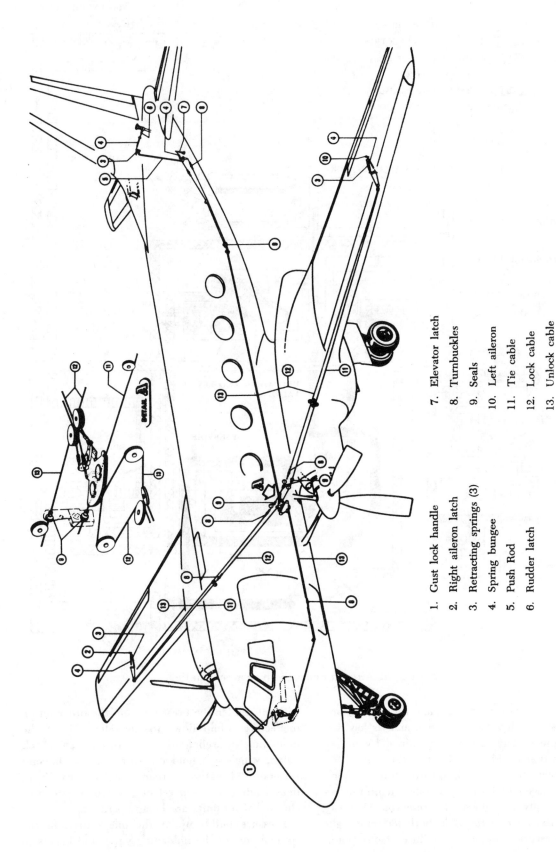

1. Gust lock handle
2. Right aileron latch
3. Retracting springs (3)
4. Spring bungee
5. Push Rod
6. Rudder latch
7. Elevator latch
8. Turnbuckles
9. Seals
10. Left aileron
11. Tie cable
12. Lock cable
13. Unlock cable

FIGURE 2–19. Example of installation diagram (gust lock system).

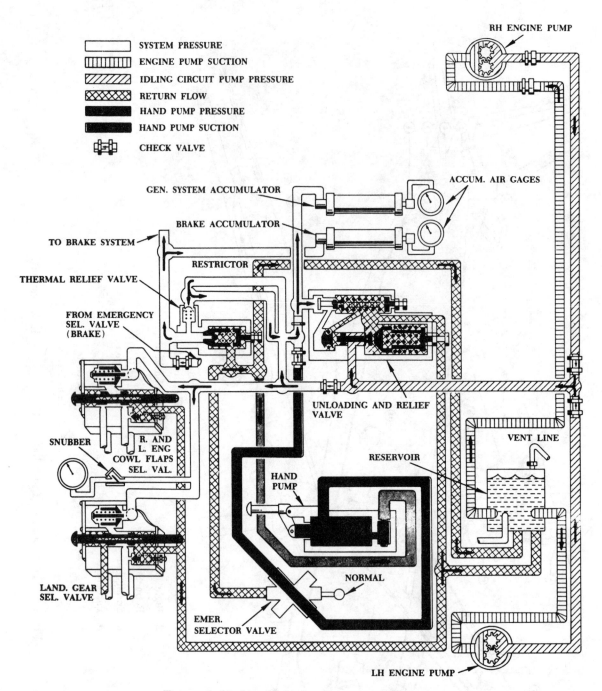

SYSTEM PRESSURE
ENGINE PUMP SUCTION
IDLING CIRCUIT PUMP PRESSURE
RETURN FLOW
HAND PUMP PRESSURE
HAND PUMP SUCTION
CHECK VALVE

RH ENGINE PUMP

GEN. SYSTEM ACCUMULATOR

BRAKE ACCUMULATOR

ACCUM. AIR GAGES

TO BRAKE SYSTEM

THERMAL RELIEF VALVE

RESTRICTOR

FROM EMERGENCY
SEL. VALVE
(BRAKE)

UNLOADING AND RELIEF
VALVE

VENT LINE

SNUBBER

R. AND
L. ENG
COWL FLAPS
SEL. VAL.

RESERVOIR

HAND
PUMP

LAND. GEAR
SEL. VALVE

NORMAL

EMER.
SELECTOR VALVE

LH ENGINE PUMP

FIGURE 2–20. Aircraft hydraulic system schematic.

for ease of reading and tracing the flow. Each component is identified by name, and its location within the system can be ascertained by noting the lines that lead into and out of the unit.

In tracing the flow of fluid through the system, it can be seen that the engine-driven pumps receive a supply of fluid from the reservoir. One-way check valves are installed in both left and right pump pressure lines so that failure of one pump will not render the pressure from the other pump ineffective. Fluid flows to the relief side of the unloading and relief valve, and through the check valve, which will hold pressure built up beyond this point. Pressure is then directed through all lines leading to each selector valve, where it is checked if no units are being operated.

Pressure builds up in the line routed to the control port of the unloading valve and begins to

48

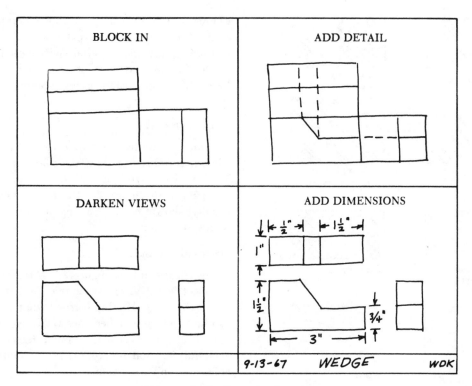

FIGURE 2–21. Steps in sketching.

charge the system accumulator. Pressure to charge the brake accumulator is routed through a check valve incorporated in the thermal relief valve; this prevents the pressure from returning to the general system.

Although the general system accumulator starts charging at the same time, it will not charge as fast, because the fluid passes through a restrictor valve. The general system pressure will bleed into the brake system whenever the brake pressure drops below system pressure.

As soon as the pressure reaches the relief valve setting, the valve will open slightly. General system pressure increases until it reaches the value established as the system operating pressure. At this point, through the line leading to the control part of the unloading valve, the pressure will force the unloading and relief valve completely open. The pressure trapped in the system by the one-way check valve holds the value open to create an idling circuit, which prevails until some unit of the hydraulic system is operated.

Schematic diagrams, like installation diagrams, are used extensively in aircraft manuals.

DRAWING SKETCHES

A sketch is a simple, rough drawing that is made rapidly and without much detail. Sketches may take many forms—from a simple pictorial presentation to a multiview orthographic projection.

A sketch is frequently drawn for use in manufacturing a replacement part. Such a sketch must provide all necessary information to those persons who must manufacture the part.

A mechanic need not be an accomplished artist. However, in many situations, he will need to prepare a drawing to present an idea for a new design, a modification, or a repair method. The medium of sketching is an excellent way of accomplishing this.

The rules and conventional practices for making mechanical drawings are followed to the extent that all views needed to portray an object accurately are shown in their proper relationship. It is also necessary to observe the rules for correct line use (figures 2–15 and 2–16) and dimensioning.

To make a sketch, first determine what views are necessary to portray the object; then block in the views, using light construction lines. Next, complete the details, darken the object outline, and sketch extension and dimension lines. Complete the drawing by adding notes, dimensions, title, date and, when necessary, the sketcher's name. The steps in making a sketch of an object are illustrated in figure 2–21.

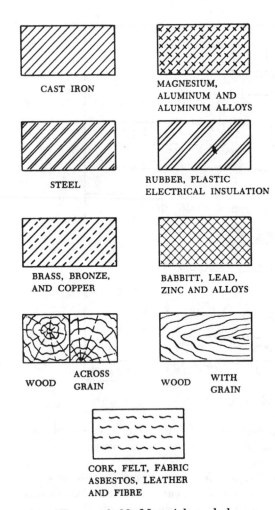

FIGURE 2-22. Material symbols.

The degree to which a sketch is complete will depend on its intended use. Obviously, a sketch used only to represent an object pictorially need not be dimensioned. If a part is to be manufactured from the sketch, it should show all the necessary construction details.

DRAWING SYMBOLS

The drawings for a component are composed largely of symbols and conventions representing its shape and material. Symbols are the shorthand of drawing. They graphically portray the characteristics of a component, with a minimum amount of drawing.

Material Symbols

Section-line symbols show the kind of material from which the part is to be constructed. The material may not be indicated symbolically when its exact specification must also be shown else-

where on the drawing. In this case, the more easily drawn symbol for cast iron is used for the sectioning, and the material specification is listed in the bill of materials or indicated in a note. Figure 2-22 illustrates a few standard material symbols.

Shape Symbols

Symbols can be used to excellent advantage, when it is desired to show the shape of an object. Typical shape symbols used on aircraft drawings are shown in figure 2-23. Shape symbols are usually shown on a drawing as a revolved or removed section.

Electrical Symbols

Electrical symbols (figure 2-24) represent various electrical devices rather than an actual drawing of the units. Having learned what the various symbols indicate, it becomes relatively simple to look at an electrical diagram and determine what each unit is, what function it serves, and how it is connected in the system.

CARE OF DRAFTING INSTRUMENTS

Good drawing instruments are expensive precision tools. Reasonable care given to them during their use and storage will prolong their service life.

T-squares, triangles, and scales should not be used, or placed, where their surfaces or edges may be damaged. Use a drawing board only for its intended purpose, and not in a manner that will mar the working surface.

Compasses, dividers, and pens will provide better results with less annoyance, if they are correctly shaped and sharpened, and they are not damaged by careless handling.

Store drawing instruments in a place where they are not likely to be damaged by contact with other tools or equipment. Protect compass and divider points by inserting them into a piece of soft rubber or similar material. Never store ink pens without first cleaning and drying them thoroughly.

MICROFILM

The practice of recording drawings, parts catalogs, and maintenance and overhaul manuals on microfilms was introduced in recent years. Microfilm is regular 16-mm. or 35-mm. film. Since 35-mm. film is larger, it provides a better reproduction of drawings. Depending on the size of

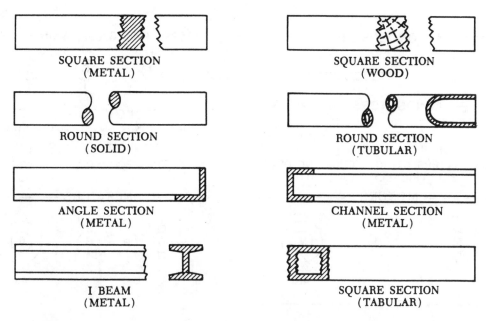

SQUARE SECTION
(METAL)

SQUARE SECTION
(WOOD)

ROUND SECTION
(SOLID)

ROUND SECTION
(TUBULAR)

ANGLE SECTION
(METAL)

CHANNEL SECTION
(METAL)

I BEAM
(METAL)

SQUARE SECTION
(TABULAR)

FIGURE 2–23. Shape symbols.

the drawing to be reproduced, a varying number of drawings can be photographed on one reel of 35-mm. film. To view or read drawings or manuals on a reel of film, you need either a portable 35-mm. film projector or a microfilm reader or viewer.

The advantage of microfilm is that several reels, which represent perhaps hundreds of drawings, require only a small amount of storage space. Too, a person working on an aircraft may need to refer to a specific dimension. He can place the reel of microfilm in a projector, locate the drawing or desired information, and read the dimension. If he has to study a detail of the drawing, or work with the drawing for a long period of time, an enlarged photographic reproduction can be made, using the microfilm as a negative.

Microfilm of drawings has many other uses and advantages. However, microfilm is not intended to replace the need for original drawings, especially where the originals are modified and kept current over a long period of time.

When drawings are filmed on continuous reels, corrections can be made by cutting out superseded drawings and splicing in the revised ones. When these corrections become numerous, the procedure becomes impractical and is discarded in favor of again filming all the related drawings.

A method that allows corrections to be made easily is to photograph the drawings and then cut up the film into individual slides. This has one disadvantage; it requires considerable time to convert the film into slides, insert them into transparent protective envelopes, and arrange them in sequence so that desired drawings can be located quickly.

A 70-mm. microfilm has become available very recently. With it, larger size drawings can be reproduced as individual frames or slides, and these can be inserted in regular paper envelopes and kept in an ordinary file. When held to the light, this large microfilm can be read with the naked eye.

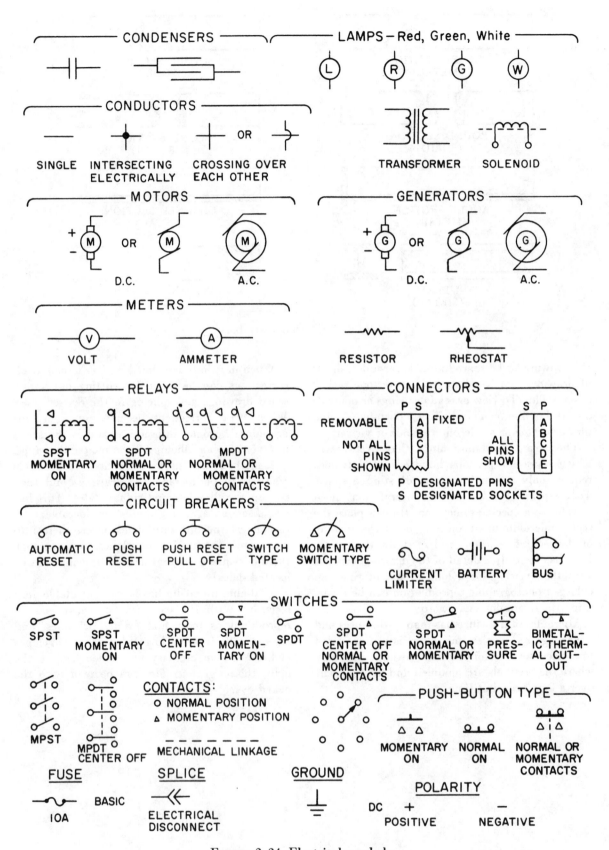

FIGURE 2–24. Electrical symbols.

CHAPTER 3

AIRCRAFT WEIGHT AND BALANCE

PURPOSE

The primary purpose of aircraft weight and balance control is safety. A secondary purpose is to achieve the utmost in efficiency during flight.

Improper loading reduces the efficiency of an aircraft from the standpoint of ceiling, maneuverability, rate of climb, speed, and fuel consumption. It can be the cause of failure to complete a flight, or even to start it. Possible loss of life and destruction of valuable equipment may result from overstressed structures or from a sudden shift in cargo and consequent change in flight characteristics.

The empty weight and the corresponding c.g. (center of gravity) of all civil aircraft must be determined at the time of certification. The manufacturer can weigh the aircraft, or he can compute the weight and balance report. A manufacturer is permitted to weigh one aircraft out of each 10 produced. The remaining nine aircraft are issued a computed weight and balance report based on the averaged figures of aircraft that are actually weighed. The condition of the aircraft at the time of determining empty weight must be one that is well defined and can be easily repeated.

NEED FOR REWEIGHING

Aircraft have a tendency to gain weight because of the accumulation of dirt, greases, etc., in areas not readily accessible for washing and cleaning. The weight gained in any given period of time will depend on the function of the aircraft, its hours in flight, atmospheric conditions, and the type landing field from which it is operating. For this reason, periodic aircraft weighings are desirable and, in the case of air carrier and air taxi aircraft, are required by Federal Aviation Regulations.

Privately owned and operated aircraft are not required by regulation to be weighed periodically. They are usually weighed when originally certificated, or after making major alterations that can affect the weight and balance. Even though the aircraft need not be weighed, it must be loaded so that the maximum weight and c.g. limits are not exceeded during operation.

Airline aircraft (scheduled and nonscheduled) carrying passengers or cargo are subject to certain rules that require owners to show that the aircraft is properly loaded and will not exceed the authorized weight and balance limitations during operation.

THEORY OF WEIGHT AND BALANCE

The theory of weight and balance is extremely simple. It is that of the familiar lever that is in equilibrium or balance when it rests on the fulcrum in a level position. The influence of weight is directly dependent upon its distance from the fulcrum. To balance the lever the weight must be distributed so that the turning effect is the same on one side of the fulcrum as on the other. In general, a lighter weight far out on the lever has the same effect as a heavy weight near the fulcrum. The distance of any object from the fulcrum is called the *lever arm*. The *lever arm* multiplied by the *weight* of the object is its turning effect about the fulcrum. This turning effect is known as the *moment*.

Similarly, an aircraft is balanced if it remains level when suspended from an imaginary point. This point is the location of its ideal c.g. An aircraft in balance does not have to be perfectly level, but it must be reasonably close to it. Obtaining this balance is simply a matter of placing loads so that the average arm of the loaded aircraft falls

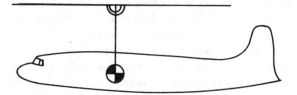

FIGURE 3–1. An airplane suspended from its center of gravity (c.g.).

within the c.g. range. The exact location of the range is specified for each type of airplane.

MATHEMATICAL PROOF

Weight and balance control consists of mathematical proof of the correct weight, balance, and loading within specified limits. These limits are set forth in the specifications for a particular aircraft. The removal or addition of equipment changes the aircraft empty weight and the c.g. The useful load is affected accordingly. The effects these changes produce on the balance of an aircraft must be investigated to determine the effect on the flight characteristics of the aircraft.

WEIGHT AND BALANCE DATA

Weight and balance data can be obtained from the following sources:

    a. The aircraft specifications.
    b. The aircraft operating limitations.
    c. The aircraft flight manual.
    d. The aircraft weight and balance report.

When weight and balance records have been lost and cannot be duplicated from any source, the aircraft must be re-weighed. A new set of weight and balance records must be computed and compiled.

TERMINOLOGY

In the study of weight and balance principles, computation, and control, it is necessary to know the meaning of the terms used. The following terminology is used in the practical application of weight and balance control, and should be thoroughly studied.

The Datum

The datum is an imaginary vertical plane from which all horizontal measurements are taken for balance purposes, with the aircraft in level flight attitude. It is a plane at right angles to the longitudinal axis of the aircraft. For each aircraft make and model, all locations of equipment, tanks, baggage compartments, seats, engines, propellers, etc., are listed in the Aircraft Specification or Type Certificate Data Sheets as being so many inches from the datum. There is no fixed rule for the location of the datum. In most cases it is located on the nose of the aircraft or some point on the aircraft structure itself. In a few cases,

it is located a certain distance forward of the nose section of the aircraft. The manufacturer has the choice of locating the datum where it is most convenient for measurement, locating equipment, and weight-and-balance computation.

The datum location is indicated on most aircraft specifications. On some of the older aircraft, where the datum is not indicated, any convenient datum may be selected. However, once the datum is selected, it must be properly identified so that anyone who reads the figures will have no doubt about the exact datum location. Figure 3–2 shows some datum locations used by manufacturers.

The Arm

The arm is the horizontal distance that an item of equipment is located from the datum. The arm's distance is always given or measured in inches, and, except for a location which might be exactly on the datum (0), it is preceded by the algebraic sign for plus (+) or minus (−). The plus (+) sign indicates a distance aft of the datum and the minus (−) sign indicates a distance forward of the datum. If the manufacturer chooses a datum that is at the most forward location on an aircraft (or some distance forward of the aircraft), all the arms will be plus (+) arms. Location of the datum at any other point on the aircraft will result in some arms being plus (+), or aft of the datum, and some arms minus (−), or forward of the datum.

The arm of each item is usually included in parentheses immediately after the item's name or weight in the specifications for the aircraft, e.g., seat (+23). When such information is not given, it must be obtained by actual measurement. Datum, arm, c.g., and the forward and aft c.g. limits are illustrated in figure 3–3.

The Moment

A moment is the product of a weight multiplied by its arm. The moment of an item about the datum is obtained by multiplying the weight of the item by its horizontal distance from the datum. Likewise, the moment of an item about the c.g. can be computed by multiplying its weight by the horizontal distance from the c.g.

A 20-pound weight located 30 inches from the datum would have a moment of 20 × 30 or 600 lb.-in. Whether the value of 600 lb.-in. is preceded by a plus (+) or minus (−) sign depends on

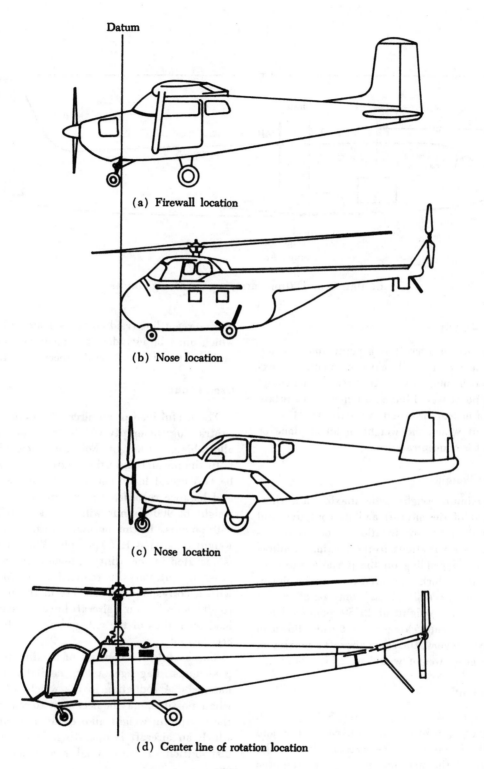

(a) Firewall location

(b) Nose location

(c) Nose location

(d) Center line of rotation location

FIGURE 3–2. Various datum locations.

whether the moment is the result of a weight being removed or added and its location in relation to the datum. Any item of weight added to the aircraft either side of the datum is plus weight. Any weight item removed is a minus weight. When multiplying a weight by an arm, the resulting moment is plus if the signs are alike and minus if the signs are unlike.

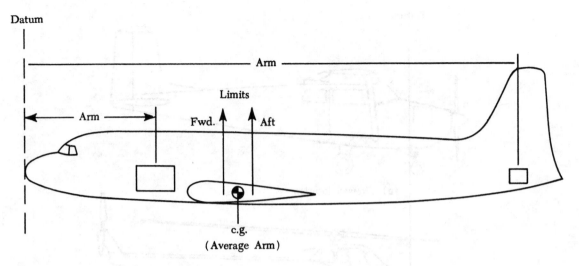

FIGURE 3–3. Datum, arm, c.g., and c.g. limits.

Center of Gravity

The c.g. of an aircraft is a point about which the nose-heavy and tail-heavy moments are exactly equal in magnitude. An aircraft suspended from this point would have no tendency to rotate in either a noseup or nosedown attitude. It is the point about which the weight of an airplane or any object is concentrated.

Maximum Weight

The maximum weight is the maximum authorized weight of the aircraft and its contents, and is indicated in the specifications. For many aircraft there are variations to the maximum allowable weight, depending on the purpose and conditions under which the aircraft is to be flown. For example, a certain aircraft may be allowed a maximum gross weight of 2,750 pounds when flown in the normal category, but when flown in the utility category, the same aircraft's maximum allowable gross weight would be 2,175 pounds.

Empty Weight

The empty weight of an aircraft includes all operating equipment that has a fixed location and is actually installed in the aircraft. It includes the weight of the airframe, powerplant, required equipment, optional or special equipment, fixed ballast, hydraulic fluid, and residual fuel and oil.

Residual fuel and oil are the fluids that will not normally drain out because they are trapped in the fuel lines, oil lines, and tanks. They must be included in the aircraft's empty weight. Infor-mation regarding residual fluids in aircraft systems which must be included in the empty weight will be indicated in the Aircraft Specification.

Useful Load

The useful load of an aircraft is determined by subtracting the empty weight from the maximum allowable gross weight. For aircraft certificated in both the normal and utility categories, there may be two useful loads listed in the aircraft weight and balance records. An aircraft with an empty weight of 900 pounds will have a useful load of 850 pounds, if the normal category maximum weight is listed as 1,750 pounds. When the aircraft is operated in the utility category, the maximum gross weight may be reduced to 1,500 pounds, with a corresponding decrease in the useful load to 600 pounds. Some aircraft have the same useful load regardless of the category in which they are certificated.

The useful load consists of maximum oil, fuel, passengers, baggage, pilot, copilot, and crewmembers. A reduction in the weight of an item, where possible, may be necessary to remain within the maximum weight allowed for the category in which an aircraft is operating. Determining the distribution of these weights is called a weight check.

Empty Weight Center of Gravity

The empty weight c.g., abbreviated EWCG, is the c.g. of an aircraft in its empty weight condition. It is an essential part of the weight and balance record of the aircraft. It has no usefulness in itself, but serves as a basis for other computations and not as an indication of what the loaded c.g. will be. The EWCG is computed at the time of weighing, using formulas established for tailwheel- and nosewheel-type aircraft.

Empty Weight Center of Gravity Range

The EWCG range is an allowable variation of travel within the c.g. limits. When the EWCG of the aircraft falls within this range, it is impossible to exceed the EWCG limits using standard specification loading arrangements. Not all aircraft have this range indicated on the Aircraft Specifications or Type Certificate Data Sheets. Where it is indicated, the range is valid only as long as the aircraft is loaded according to the standard specification. The installation of items not listed in the specification will not permit use of this range.

Operating Center of Gravity Range

The operating c.g. range is the distance between the forward and rearward c.g. limits indicated in the pertinent Aircraft Specification or Type Certificate Data Sheets. These limits, determined at the time of design and manufacture, are the extreme loaded c.g. positions allowable within the applicable regulations controlling the design of the aircraft. These limits are shown in either percent of MAC (mean aerodynamic chord) or inches from the datum of the aircraft.

The loaded aircraft c.g. location must remain within these limits at all times. Accordingly, detailed instructions for determining load distribution are provided on placards, loading charts, and load adjusters.

Mean Aerodynamic Chord

The MAC is the mean average chord of the wing. An airfoil section is a cross section of a wing from leading edge to trailing edge. A chord is usually defined as an imaginary straight line drawn parallel to the airfoil through the leading and trailing edges of the section. The MAC of a constant chord wing would be the same as the actual chord of the wing. Any departure from a rectangular wing plan form will affect the length of the MAC and the resulting distance from the MAC leading edge to the aircraft wing leading edge. Figure 3–4 shows the MAC for a sweptwing aircraft.

The aircraft c.g. is usually placed at the maximum forward position of the center of pressure on the MAC to obtain the desired stability. Because of the relationship between the c.g. location and the moments produced by aerodynamic forces, the greatest of which is lift, the c.g. location is generally expressed with respect to the wing. This is done by specifying c.g. in percent of the wing's MAC.

The location of the MAC, in relation to the datum, is given in the Aircraft Specifications or Type Certificate Data Sheets, the weight and balance report, or the aircraft flight manual. Compute the c.g. location in percent of MAC as follows:

(1) Find the difference between the distance to the empty weight c.g. location from the datum and the distance to the leading edge of MAC from the datum.
(2) Divide the difference by the length of the MAC.
(3) Multiply the answer by 100.
(4) The final answer is then expressed in percent.

An example problem that utilizes the equation for computing percent of MAC is shown in figure 3–5.

Aircraft Leveling Means

Reference points are provided for leveling the aircraft on the ground. They are designated by the manufacturer and are indicated in the pertinent Aircraft Specifications. The most common leveling procedure is to place a spirit level at designated points on the aircraft structure. Some aircraft have special leveling scales built into the airframe structure. The scale is used with a plumb bob to level the aircraft longitudinally and laterally.

Weighing Points

In weighing an aircraft, the point on the scale at which the weight is concentrated is called the weighing point. When weighing light- to medium-weight land planes, the wheels are usually placed on the scales. This means that the weighing point is, in effect, the same location obtained by extending a vertical line through the center line of the axle and onto the scale.

Other structural locations capable of supporting the aircraft, such as jack pads on the main spar,

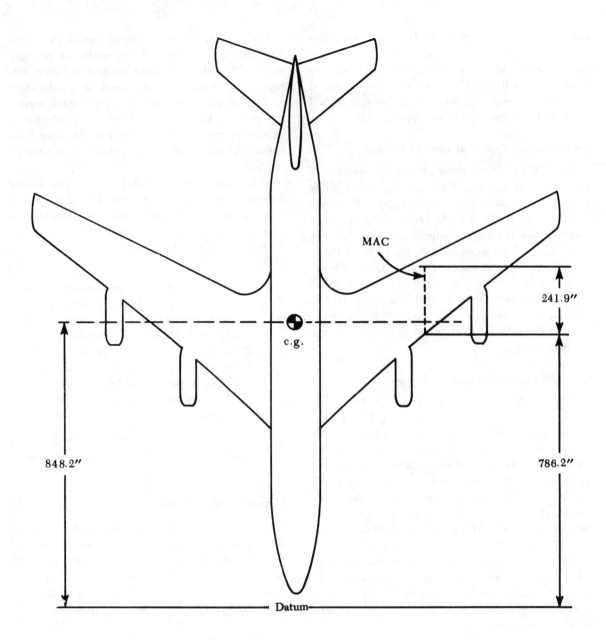

FIGURE 3–4. The c.g. shown in relation to MAC.

Zero Fuel Weight

The zero fuel weight is the maximum allowable weight of a loaded aircraft without fuel. Included in the zero fuel weight is the weight of cargo, passengers, and crew. All weights in excess of the zero fuel weight must consist of usable fuel.

may also be used if the aircraft weight is resting on the jack pads. The weighing points should be clearly indicated in the weight and balance report.

Minimum Fuel

The term "minimum fuel" should not be interpreted to mean the minimum amount of fuel required to fly an aircraft. Minimum fuel, as it applies to weight and balance, is the amount of fuel that must be shown on the weight and balance report when the airplane is loaded for an extreme-condition check.

The minimum fuel load for a small aircraft with a reciprocating engine for balance purposes is based on engine horsepower. It is calculated in the METO (maximum except take-off) horsepower and

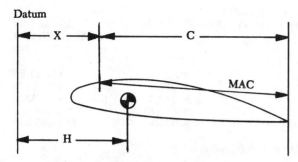

Datum

H = Distance from the datum to the EWCG = 170 inches.

X = Distance from the datum to the MAC leading edge = 150 inches.

C = Length of MAC = 80 inches.

$$\text{c.g. in } \% \text{ of MAC} = \frac{H - X}{C} \times 100$$

$$\% \text{ of MAC} = \frac{170 - 150}{80} \times 100 =$$

$$\frac{20}{80} \times 100 = 25\%$$

FIGURE 3–5. Finding percent of MAC.

is the figure used when the fuel load must be reduced to obtain the most critical loading on the c.g. limit being investigated. Either of 2 formulas may be used.

Formula 1:

Minimum fuel = 1/12 gallons per horsepower. hp × 1/12 × 6 lb.

1200 × 1/12 × 6 = 1200 × 1/12 × 6 = 600 lb. fuel.

Formula 2:

Minimum fuel = 1/2 lb. per engine horsepower. hp × 1/2 = minimum fuel.

1200 × 1/2 = 600 lb. fuel.

This will be the minimum pounds of fuel required for the forward or rearward weight check.

For turbine-engine powered aircraft, the minimum fuel load is specified by the aircraft manufacturer.

The fuel tank location in relation to the c.g. limit affected by the computation determines the use of minimum fuel. For example, when a forward weight check is performed, if the fuel tanks are located forward of the forward c.g. limit, they are assumed to be full. If they are located aft of the forward c.g. limit, they are assumed to be empty. If the minimum fuel required for a particular aircraft exceeds the capacity of the tanks located forward of the forward c.g. limit, the excess fuel must be loaded in the tanks that are aft of the forward c.g. limit. When a rearward weight check is conducted, the fuel loading conditions are opposite to those used for the forward check.

Full Oil

Full oil is the quantity of oil shown as oil capacity in the Aircraft Specifications. When weighing an aircraft, the oil tank may either contain the number of gallons of oil specified or be drained. When an aircraft with full oil tanks is weighed, the weight of the oil must be subtracted from the recorded readings to arrive at the actual empty weight. The weight and balance report must show whether weights include full oil or if the oil tanks were drained.

Tare Weight

Tare includes the weight of all extra items, such as jacks, blocks, and chocks on the weighing scale platform, except that of the item being weighed. The weight of these items, when included in the scale reading, is deducted to obtain the actual weight of the aircraft.

AIRCRAFT WEIGHING PROCEDURE

Before beginning a study of aircraft weighing procedure or attempting the actual weighing of an aircraft, it is necessary to become familiar with the weight and balance information in the applicable Aircraft Specification or Type Certificate Data Sheet.

The specification for Taylorcraft, model BC and BCS airplanes, illustrated in figure 3–6 has been reproduced in its entirety. A few of the items need explaining; the rest are self-explanatory.

The designation 2 PCLM is read "2-place, closed land monoplane" and indicates that the airplane seats two persons, has an enclosed cockpit, can be operated from the solid part of the earth's surface, and has only one wing. Two PCSM indicates that the airplane is a "2-place, closed sea monoplane." It should be noted that the c.g. range, EWCG range, and the maximum weight are different for the landplane and the seaplane. The location of the seats indicates a side-by-side arrangement. The datum and the leveling means are shown in the portion of the specification that is pertinent to all models. Since the datum and the leveling means are directly connected to weight and balance, they would be among the first items referred to in planning the weighing operation.

Although the location or arrangement of the

DEPARTMENT OF TRANSPORTATION
FEDERAL AVIATION ADMINISTRATION

A-696
Revision 16
TAYLORCRAFT

BC	BCS12-D
BCS	BC12-D1
BC-65	BCS12-D1
BCS-65	BC12D-85
BC12-65 (Army L-2H)	BCS12D-85
BCS12-65	BC12D-4-85
BC12-D	BCS12D-4-85

9 September 1969

AIRCRAFT SPECIFICATION NO. A-696

Type Certificate Holder. Taylorcraft Aviation Corporation
104 Prospect Street
Alliance, Ohio 44601

I—Model BC, 2 PCLM, Approved August 24, 1938; Model BCS, 2 PCSM, Approved April 5, 1939

Engine. Continental A-50-1 (see item 114(a) for optional engines)

Fuel. 73 min. grade aviation gasoline

Engine Limits. For all operations, 1900 r.p.m. (50 hp.)

Propeller Limits. Diameter: Maximum 83 in.

Airspeed Limits. (True Ind.)

Landplane:	Level flight or climb	105 m.p.h.	(91 knots)
	Glide or dive	131 m.p.h.	(114 knots)
Seaplane:	Level flight or climb	95 m.p.h.	(83 knots)
	Glide or dive	129 m.p.h.	(112 knots)

Center of Gravity (C.G.) Range.
Landplane: (+14.5) to (+19.7)
Seaplane: (+15.1) to (+19.4)

Empty Weight C.G. Range.
Landplane: (+15.3) to (+18.5)
Seaplane: (+15.9) to (+18.3)

When empty weight C.G. falls within pertinent range, computation of critical for and aft C.G. positions is unnecessary. Ranges are not valid for non-standard arrangements.

Maximum Weight.
Landplane: 1100 lb. (S/N 1407 and up are eligible at 1150 lb.)
Seaplane: 1228 lb.

Number of Seats. 2 (+23)

Maximum Baggage. 30 lb. (+40)

Fuel Capacity. 12 gal. (−9). See item 115 for auxiliary tank.

Oil Capacity. 4 quart. (−21)

Control Surface Movements.
Elevators: Up 25° Down 27°
Rudders: Right 26° Left 26°
Ailerons: (Not available)

Serial No. Eligible. 1001 and up

Required Equipment.
Landplane: 1 or 4, 104, 202, 203, 210(a), 401
Seaplane: 1 or 4, 104, 205, 401

Specifications Pertinent to All Models.

Datum. Leading edge of wing

Leveling Means. Upper surface of horizontal stabilizer

Certification Basis. Part 04 of the Civil Air Regulations effective as amended to May 1, 1938. Type Certificate No. 696 issued.

Production Basis. None. Prior to original certification, an FAA representative must perform a detailed inspection for workmanship, materials and conformity with the approved technical data, and a check of the flight characteristics.

FIGURE 3–6. A typical aircraft specification.

landing gear is not shown in figure 3–6, this information is given in the Aircraft Specification or Type Certificate Data Sheets and the maintenance manual. The location of the wheels has important significance, since this can be used as a doublecheck against actual measurements taken at the time of weighing.

Weighing an Aircraft

Weighing an aircraft is a very important and exacting phase of aircraft maintenance and must be carried out with accuracy and good workmanship. Thoughtful preparation saves time and prevents mistakes.

To begin, assemble all the necessary equipment, such as:

1. Scales, hoisting equipment, jacks, and leveling equipment.
2. Blocks, chocks, or sandbags for holding the airplane on the scales.
3. Straightedge, spirit level, plumb bobs, chalk line, and a measuring tape.
4. Applicable Aircraft Specifications and weight and balance computation forms.

If possible, aircraft should be weighed in a closed building where there are no air currents to cause incorrect scale readings. An outside weighing is permissible if wind and moisture are negligible.

Prepare Aircraft For Weighing

Drain the fuel system until the quantity indication reads zero, or empty, with the aircraft in a level attitude. If any fuel is left in the tanks, the aircraft will weigh more, and all later calculations for useful load and balance will be affected. Only trapped or unusable fuel (residual fuel) is considered part of the aircraft empty weight. Fuel tank caps should be on the tanks or placed as close as possible to their correct locations, so that the weight distribution will be correct.

In special cases, the aircraft may be weighed with the fuel tanks full, provided a means of determining the exact weight of the fuel is available. Consult the aircraft manufacturer's instructions to determine whether a particular model aircraft should be weighed with full fuel or with the fuel drained.

If possible, drain all engine oil from the oil tanks. The system should be drained with all drain valves open. Under these conditions, the amount of oil remaining in the oil tank, lines, and engine is termed residual oil and is included in the empty weight. If impractical to drain, the oil tanks should be completely filled.

The position of such items as spoilers, slats, flaps, and helicopter rotor systems is an important factor when weighing an aircraft. Always refer to the manufacturer's instructions for the proper position of these items.

Unless otherwise noted in the Aircraft Specifications or manufacturer's instructions, hydraulic reservoirs and systems should be filled; drinking and washing water reservoirs and lavatory tanks should be drained; and constant-speed-drive oil tanks should be filled.

Inspect the aircraft to see that all items included in the certificated empty weight are installed in the proper location. Remove items that are not regularly carried in flight. Also look in the baggage compartments to make sure they are empty.

Replace all inspection plates, oil and fuel tank caps, junction box covers, cowling, doors, emergency exits, and other parts that have been removed. All doors, windows, and sliding canopies should be in their normal flight position. Remove excessive dirt, oil, grease, and moisture from the aircraft.

Properly calibrate, zero, and use the weighing scales in accordance with the manufacturer's instructions.

Some aircraft are not weighed with the wheels on the scales, but are weighed with the scales placed either at the jacking points or at special weighing points. Regardless of what provisions are made for placing the aircraft on the scales or jacks, be careful to prevent it from falling or rolling off, thereby damaging the aircraft and equipment. When weighing an aircraft with the wheels placed on the scales, release the brakes to reduce the possibility of incorrect readings caused by side loads on the scales.

All aircraft have leveling points or lugs, and care must be taken to level the aircraft, especially along the longitudinal axis. With light, fixed-wing airplanes, the lateral level is not as critical as it is with heavier airplanes. However, a reasonable effort should be made to level the light airplanes around the lateral axis. Accuracy in leveling all aircraft longitudinally cannot be overemphasized.

Measurements

The distance from the datum to the main weighing point centerline, and the distance from the main weighing point centerline to the tail (or nose) weighing point centerline must be known to determine the c.g. relative to the main weighing point and the datum.

An example of main weighing point to datum and main weighing point to tail weighing point is shown in figure 3–7. See figure 3–8 for an example of main weighing point to datum and main weighing point to nosewheel measurements.

These distances may be calculated using information from the Aircraft Specifications or Type Certificate Data Sheets. However, it will often be necessary to determine them by actual measurement.

After the aircraft has been placed on the scales (figure 3–9) and leveled, hang plumb bobs from the datum, the main weighing point, and the tail or nose weighing point so that the points of the plumb bobs touch the floor. Make a chalk mark on the floor at the points of contact. If desired, a chalk line may be drawn connecting the chalk marks. This will make a clear pattern of the weighing point distances and their relation to the datum.

Record the weights indicated on each of the scales and make the necessary measurements while the aircraft is still level. After all weights

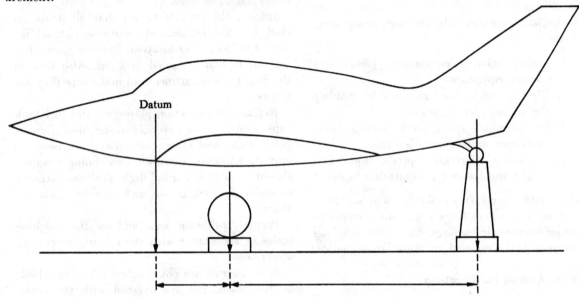

FIGURE 3–7. Main weighing point to datum and main weighing point to tail weighing point.

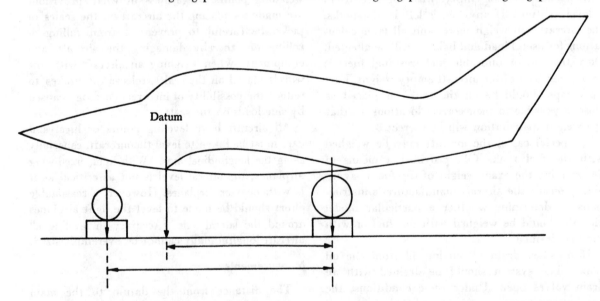

FIGURE 3–8. Main weighing point to datum and main weighing point to nose weighing point.

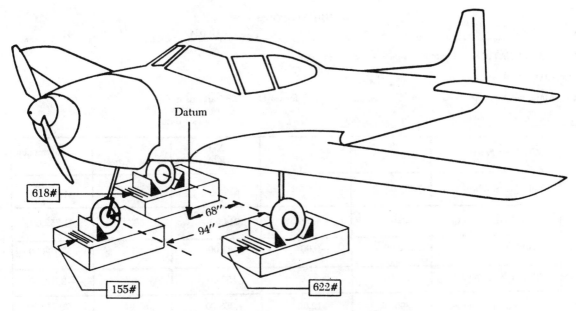

FIGURE 3–9. Weighing an aircraft using platform scales.

and measurements are obtained and recorded, the aircraft may be removed from the scales. Weigh the tare and deduct its weight from the scale reading at each respective weighing point where tare is involved.

Balance Computation

To obtain gross weight and the c.g. location of the loaded airplane, first determine the empty weight and the EWCG location. When these are known, it is easy to compute the effect of fuel, crew, passengers, cargo, and expendable weight as they are added. This is done by adding all the weights and moments of these additional items and re-calculating the c.g. for the loaded airplane.

The scale readings and measurements recorded on the sample form in figure 3–10 form the basis for the examples of computing the empty weight and the empty weight c.g.

Empty Weight

The empty weight of the aircraft is determined by adding the net weight on each weighing point. The net weight is the actual scale reading, less the tare weight.

Weighing scale point	Scale reading (lbs.)	Tare (lbs.)	Net weight (lbs.)
Left main wheel	622.00	−5.00	617.00
Right main wheel	618.00	−4.00	614.00
Nosewheel	155.00	−3.00	152.00
Total			1,383.00

This gives the aircraft weight as weighed.

Empty Weight C.G.

The c.g. location is found through the progressive use of two formulas. First calculate the total moments using the following formulas:

$$\text{Moment} = \text{Arm} \times \text{Weight}$$

Weight point	Net weight (lbs.)		Arm (in.)		Moment (lb.-in.)
Left main wheel	617.0	×	68″	=	41,956.0
Right main wheel	614.0	×	68″	=	41,752.0
Nosewheel	152.0	×	−26″	=	−3,952.0
	1,383.0				79,756.0

MAKE Rotary .... MODEL ...... A .... SERIAL ..... 0242 .... N ..... 411 ....

DATUM LOCATION   Leading edge of wing at root

Aircraft weighed with full oil.

1. Main weighing point is located (— ...." forward) (+68" aft) of datum.

2. Tail or nose weighing point is located (—26" forward) (+ ...." aft)of datum.

	Weighing Point	Scale Reading	— Tare	= Net Weight	× Arm	= Moment
3.	Left Main Wheel	622.00	—5.00	617.00	68"	41,956.00
4.	Right Main Wheel	618.00	—4.00	614.00	68"	41,752.00
5.	Sub-Total	1,240.00	—9.00	1,231.00	68"	83,708.00
6.	Tail or Nose Wheel	155.00	—3.00	152.00	—26"	—3,952.00
7.	Total as Weighed	1,395.00	—12.00	1,383.00	57.67	79,756.00

Space for listing of Items when Aircraft is not Weighed Empty.

	Item	Net Weight	Arm	Moment
8.	Oil – 8 gallons @ 7.5 p/p/g	—60.00	—30.00	1,800.00
9.	Aircraft Empty Weight & c.g.	1,323.00	61.64"	81,556.00

Maximum Allowable Gross Weight 1,773 pounds

Useful Load 450 pounds

Computed by: Frank A. Adams

A & P Number: 1366968

FIGURE 3–10. Sample weighing form.

then divide the sum of the moments by the total weights involved:

$$c.g. = \frac{\text{Total moment}}{\text{Total weight}} = \frac{79,756.0}{1,383}$$

$$= 57.67 \text{ in.}$$

Consequently, the c.g., as weighed, is 57.67 in. from the datum.

Since the aircraft was weighed with the oil tank full, it is necessary to remove the oil to obtain the empty weight and empty weight c.g.

Item	Net weight (lbs.)	Arm (in.)	Moment (lb.-in.)
Acft. total as weighed	1,383.0	57.67	79,756.0
Less oil, 8 gallons, @ 7.5 lbs. per gallon	—60.0	—30.00	1,800.0
Acft. empty weight and moment	1,323.0		81,556.0

Again using the formula:

$$c.g. = \frac{\text{Total moment}}{\text{Total weight}} = \frac{81,556.0}{1,323}$$

$$= 61.64 \text{ in.}$$

The EWCG is located 61.64 in. aft of the datum.

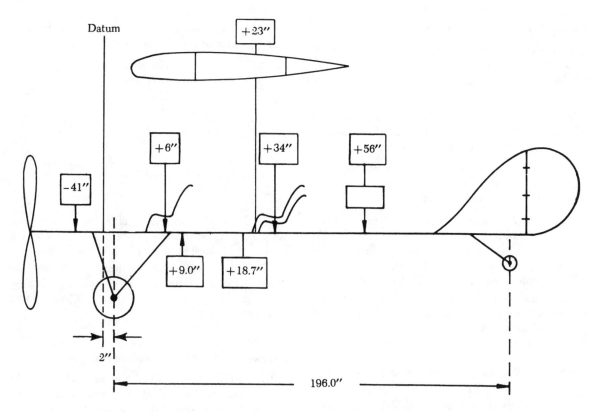

Tail wheel weight = 50 lbs.

Tail wheel arm = 198.0''

Empty weight (without oil) = 950 lbs.

Datum location = leading edge of wing.

Engine = 100 hp.

CG range = (+9.0'') to (+18.7'').

Fuel capacity = 40 gal @ +23''.

Number of seats = 3 (one @ + 6'' and two @ +34'').

Maximum gross weight = 1775 lbs.

Oil capacity = 8 qts @ −41''.

Maximum baggage = 50 lbs @ +56''.

Note: (This airplane can be flown from either the front or rear seat.)

FIGURE 3–11. Schematic diagram for forward weight and balance check.

The maximum allowable gross weight as shown in the Aircraft Specifications is 1,733 pounds. By subtracting the aircraft empty weight from this figure, the useful load is determined to be 450 pounds.

WEIGHT AND BALANCE EXTREME CONDITIONS

The weight and balance extreme conditions represent the maximum forward and rearward c.g. position for the aircraft.

An aircraft has certain fixed points, fore and aft, beyond which the c.g. should not be permitted at any time during flight. A check should be made to ensure that the c.g. will not shift out of limits when crew, passengers, cargo, and expendable weights are added or removed. If the limits are exceeded and the aircraft is flown in this condition, it may lead to insufficient stability, with resulting difficulty in controlling the aircraft.

Adverse loading checks are a deliberate attempt to load an aircraft in a manner that will create the most critical balance condition and still remain within the design c.g. limits of the aircraft.

It should be noted that when the EWCG falls within the EWCG range, it is unnecessary to perform a forward or rearward weight and balance check. In other words, it is impossible to load the aircraft to exceed the c.g. limits, provided standard loading and seating arrangements are used.

Forward Weight and Balance Check

To make this check, the following information is needed:

1. The weight, arm, and moment of the empty aircraft.

2. The maximum weights, arms, and moments of the items of useful load that are located ahead of the forward c.g. limit.

3. The minimum weights, arms, and moments of the items of useful load that are located aft of the forward c.g. limit.

The example shown in figure 3–11 presents one method of conducting an extreme-condition check. This method makes it easy to visualize exactly where the weights of various loading arrangements are distributed and how they affect c.g. location.

Using the data given in figure 3–11, determine if the airplane can be loaded to cause the c.g. to go beyond its limits.

FIRST STEP: Load the airplane as follows:

Oil—8 qts. @ −41 in.= (15.0 lbs.) (−41 in.).
Pilot—170 lbs. @ +6 in.= (170.0 lbs.) (+6 in.).
Fuel, minimum—50 lbs. @ +23 in.= (50.0 lbs.) (+23 in.).
No passengers.
No baggage.

Fill any fuel tanks which are ahead of the forward limit. If the fuel tanks are to the rear of the forward limit, use the minimum required amount of fuel.

SECOND STEP: Total all weights and moments.

Item	Weight (lbs.)	Arm (in.)	Moments (lb.-in.)
Acft. EW	950.0	+12.3	+11,685.0
Oil	15.0	−41.0	− 615.0
Pilot	170.0	+ 6.0	+ 1,020.0
Fuel (min.)	50.0	+23.0	+ 1,150.0
Total	1,185.0		13,240.0

The above figures require careful consideration. Notice that each weight is multiplied by its arm to obtain its moment. All the weights are added to obtain 1,185 lbs., the total weight. However, when adding the moments, all the plus moments are added:

$$\begin{array}{r} 11,685.0 \\ 1,020.0 \\ 1,150.0 \\ \hline 13,855.0 \end{array}$$

The minus moment of −615.0 is subtracted from the sum of the plus moments:

$$\begin{array}{r} 13,855.0 \\ - \ 615.0 \\ \hline 13,240.0 \end{array}$$

THIRD STEP: Find the most forward c.g. position by dividing the total moments by the total weight.

$$\frac{13,240.0}{1,185} = 11.17 \text{ in.}$$

Since the total moment is plus, the answer must be plus. Therefore, the forward extreme position of the c.g. is located at 11.17 aft of the datum.

The forward c.g. limit for this example airplane is +9.0 in. aft of the datum; therefore, it is easy to see that it can be safely flown with this loading arrangement.

Rearward Weight and Balance Check

To establish that neither the maximum weight nor the rearward c.g. limit is exceeded, the following information is needed:

1. The weight, arm, and moment of the empty aircraft.

2. The maximum weights, arms, and moments of the items of useful load that are located aft of the rearward c.g. limit.

3. The minimum weights, arms, and moments of the items of useful load that are located ahead of the rearward c.g. limit.

The most rearward c.g. position is found by repeating the three steps that were followed in making the most forward c.g. check, except in this case the airplane is loaded so that it will be tail-heavy.

FIRST STEP: Load the airplane in a manner that will make it most tail-heavy.

Oil—8 qts. @ −41 in.= (15.0 lbs.) (−41 in.).
Pilot—170 lbs. @ +6 in.= (170.0 lbs.) (+6 in.).
Fuel (max.)—40 gals. @ +23 in.= (240.0 lbs.) (+23 in.).
Passengers—two @ 170 lbs. each=340 lbs. @ +34 in.= (340.0 lbs.) (+34 in.).
Baggage (max.)—50 lbs. @ +56 in.= (50 lbs.) (+56 in.).

Fill any fuel tanks which are aft of the rear limit. If the fuel tanks are forward of the rear limit, use the minimum required amount of fuel.

SECOND STEP: Total all weights and moments as shown here:

Item	Weight (lbs.)	Arm (in.)	Moments (lb.-in.)
Acft. EW	950.0	+12.3	+11,685.0
Oil	15.0	−41.0	− 615.0
Pilot	170.0	+ 6.0	+ 1,020.0
Fuel (max.)	240.0	+23.0	+ 5,520.0
Passengers (two)	340.0	+34.0	+11,560.0
Baggage (max.)	50.0	+56.0	+ 2,800.0
Total	1,765.0		31,970.0

THIRD STEP: Find the most rearward c.g. position by dividing the total moments by the total weight.

Most rearward c.g. when loaded as shown in figure 3–11:

$$\frac{31,970.0}{1,765} = 18.11 \text{ in.}$$

The rearward c.g. limit for this example airplane is +18.7 in. aft of the datum; therefore, it can be flown safely with this loading arrangement.

INSTALLATION OF BALLAST

Ballast is used in an aircraft to attain the desired c.g. balance. It is usually located as far aft or as far forward as possible to bring the c.g. within limits using a minimum amount of weight. Ballast that is installed to compensate for the removal or installation of equipment items and that is to remain in the aircraft for long periods is called permanent ballast. It is generally lead bars or plates bolted to the aircraft structure. It may be painted red and placarded: PERMANENT BALLAST—DO NOT REMOVE. In most cases, the installation of permanent ballast results in an increase in the aircraft empty weight.

Temporary ballast, or removable ballast, is used to meet certain loading conditions that may vary from time to time. It generally takes the form of lead shot bags, sand bags, or other weight items that are not permanently installed. Temporary ballast should be placarded: BALLAST ____ LBS. REMOVAL REQUIRES WEIGHT AND BALANCE CHECK. The baggage compartment is usually the most convenient location for temporary ballast.

The places for carrying ballast should be properly designed, installed, and plainly marked. The aircraft operation manual must include instructions regarding the proper placement of the removable ballast under all loading conditions for which such ballast is necessary.

Controlling c.g. Position With Ballast

Figure 3–12 shows an example aircraft whose c.g. exceeds the forward c.g. limit under certain loading conditions. The forward weight and balance check proves that with only the pilot and minimum fuel aboard, the forward c.g. is exceeded.

Most forward c.g. check

Item	Weight (lbs.)	Arm (in.)	Moments (lb.-in.)
Acft. EW	1,600.0	+15.6	+24,960.0
Oil	22.5	−22.0	− 495.0
Fuel (min.)	115.0	+18.0	+ 2,070.0
Pilot	170.0	+10.0	+ 1,700.0
Total	1,907.5		+28,235.0

$$\text{Most forward c.g.} = \frac{\text{Total moment}}{\text{Total weight}}$$

$$= \frac{28,235}{1,907.5} = 14.8 \text{ in.}$$

Without ballast placed somewhere aft to bring the c.g. within the designated limits of +16.5 in. to +20.0 in., the aircraft is unsafe to fly when loaded with the pilot and minimum fuel. The problem of determining how many pounds of ballast are needed to move the c.g. within the approved limits can be solved by using the following formula:

Ballast weight needed:

$$\frac{(\text{Weight of acft as loaded}) \ (\text{Distance out of limits})}{\text{Arm from variable weight location to limit affected}}$$

Inserting in the formula the applicable values:

Weight of the aircraft as loaded = 1907.5
Distance out of limit = +1.7 in.
Arm from variable weight location to the limit affected = 53.5 in.

We obtain the following:

$$\frac{(1907.5) \ (1.7)}{53.5} = \begin{array}{l}\text{60.6 lbs., ballast weight} \\ \text{needed in the baggage} \\ \text{compartment.}\end{array}$$

When the mathematical computation ends in a fractional pound, use the next higher whole pound as the actual ballast weight. Consequently, 61.0 pounds must be placed in the baggage compartment to bring the c.g. safely within the c.g. range.

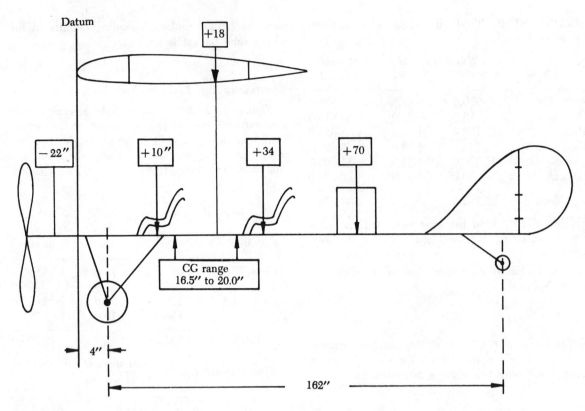

Datum

+18

−22″   +10″   +34   +70

CG range
16.5″ to 20.0″

4″

162″

Tail wheel arm = 166″.

Tail wheel weight = 115 lbs.

CG range = (+16.5″) to (+20.0″)

Fuel capacity = 38 gal @ 18″ (19 gal. in each wing

Maximum baggage = 100 lbs @ 70″

Maximum gross weight = 2620 lbs.

A/C EW (without oil) = 1600 lbs.

Datum = leading edge of wing.

Engine = 230 hp.

Oil capacity = 12 qts @ −22″.

Number of seats = 4 (two @ +10″ and two @ +34″).

Note: Flight controls in front seat only.

FIGURE 3–12. Example aircraft whose c.g. exceeds the forward c.g. limit.

A final forward weight and balance check should be made to prove that by adding 61.0 pounds of ballast in the baggage compartment, this aircraft could be safely flown with minimum fuel aboard. Place a placard in the cockpit in a conspicuous place for the pilot, or anyone concerned, to see. The placard should read: FOR SOLO FLIGHT CARRY A MINIMUM OF 61.0 POUNDS IN BAGGAGE COMPARTMENT.

Maximum Load Conditions

A rearward weight and balance check will determine whether the airplane shown in figure 3–12 can be flown safely when fully loaded without exceeding the aft c.g. limit or its maximum gross weight.

Most Rearward c.g. check.

Item	Weight (lbs.)	Arm (in.)	Moments (lb.-in.)
Acft. EW	1,600.0	+15.6	24,960.0
Oil	22.5	−22.0	− 495.0
Fuel (max.)	228.0	+18.0	4,104.0
Pilot	170.0	+10.0	1,700.0
Passenger	170.0	+10.0	1,700.0
Passengers (two)	340.0	+34.0	11,560.0
Baggage (max.)	100.0	+10.0	7,000.0
Total	2,630.5		50,529.0

$$\text{Most rearward c.g.} = \frac{\text{Total moments}}{\text{Total weight}}$$

$$= \frac{50,529.0}{2,630.5} = 19.21 \text{ in.}$$

68

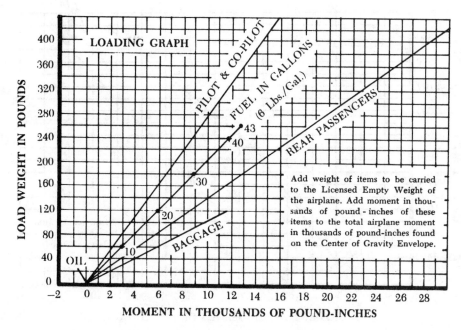

FIGURE 3–13. Typical loading graph.

The c.g. is well within the c.g. range when fully loaded; however, the maximum allowable gross weight is exceeded by 10.5 pounds. In this case a number of alternatives are available to remedy this overloaded condition without appreciably reducing the aircraft payload or flight range, as follows:

> Alternative No. 1—reduce baggage by 10.5 lbs.
>
> Alternative No. 2—reduce fuel by 10.5 lbs., or 1.75 gals.
>
> Alternative No. 3—reduce passenger load by one passenger.

Each alternative listed will require a placard stating the loading arrangement by which the gross weight and c.g. will be retained within their designated limits. Compute a new c.g. position for each alternate loading arrangement.

LOADING GRAPHS AND C.G. ENVELOPES

The weight and balance computation system, commonly called the loading graph and c.g. envelope system, is an excellent and rapid method for determining the c.g. location for various loading arrangements. This method can be applied to any make and model of aircraft.

Aircraft manufacturers using this method of weight and balance computation prepare graphs similar to those shown in figure 3–13 and 3–14 for each make and model aircraft at the time of original certification. The graphs become a permanent part of the aircraft records. Along with the graphs are the data for the empty weight arm and moment (index number) for that particular make and model aircraft.

The loading graph illustrated in figure 3–13 is used to determine the index number of any item or weight that may be involved in loading the aircraft. To use this graph, find the point on the vertical scale that represents the known weight. Project a horizontal line to the point where it intersects the proper diagonal weight line (i.e., pilot, copilot, baggage, etc.). From the point of intersection, read straight downward to the horizontal scale to find the moment or index number.

After the moment for each item of weight has been determined, all weights are added and all moments are added. With knowledge of the total weight and moment, project a line from the respective point on the c.g. envelope shown in figure 3–14, and place a point at the intersection of the two lines. If the point is within the diagonal lines, the loading arrangement meets all balance requirements.

The following is an actual weight and balance computation using the graphs in figure 3–13 and 3–14. For this example, assume that the aircraft has an empty weight of 1,386.0 pounds and a moment of 52,772.0 pound-inches. The index

69

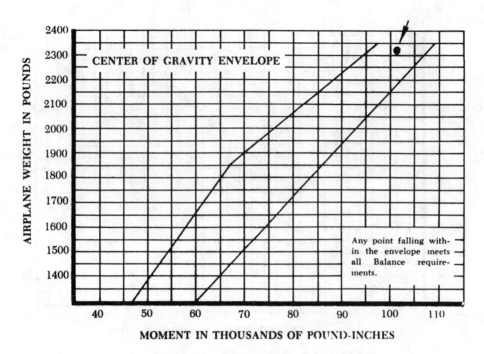

FIGURE 3–14. Center of gravity envelope.

number for the empty weight of the aircraft is developed by dividing the empty-weight moment by 1,000. This gives an index number of 52.8 for the airplane's empty-weight moment. Load the aircraft to determine whether the c.g. will fall within the diagonal lines of figure 3–14. Arrange item weights and index numbers in an orderly form to facilitate adding.

Item	Weight (lbs.)	Moment (thousands of lb.-in.)
Acft. EW	1,386.0	52.8
Oil	19.0	− 0.4
Pilot & copilot	340.0	12.2
Rear passengers (two)	340.0	24.1
Baggage	20.0	1.9
Fuel	245.0	11.8
Total	2,350.0	102.4

The total airplane weight in pounds is 2,350.0, and the moment is 102.4. Locate this point (2,350 @ 102.4) on the c.g. envelope illustrated in figure 3–14. Since the point falls within the diagonal lines, the loading arrangement meets all weight-and-balance requirements.

ELECTRONIC WEIGHING EQUIPMENT

Electronic weighing equipment greatly simplified the mechanics of weighing large, heavy aircraft. Figure 3–15 shows one type of electronic scales. The complete weighing kit is contained in a portable carrier. Included in the kit are a steel tape, plumb bobs, spirit level, straightedge, hydrometer (for determining the fuel specific gravity) and the load cells. The load cells are actually strain gages that reflect the load imposed upon them by the aircraft in terms of voltage change. This change is indicated on a scale that is calibrated to read in pounds.

One load cell is placed between the jack-pad and the jack at each weighing point. Each load cell must be balanced or "zeroed" before applying any load to the cell. After completing the weighing operation, remove all load from the cells and check to see if the cell reading is still zero. Any deviation from zero is referred to as the "zero scale shift" and constitutes the tare when using electronic weighing scales. The direction of shift is the factor that determines whether the tare is added to or subtracted from the scale reading. Always follow the instructions of the manufacture whose scales you are using.

HELICOPTER WEIGHT AND BALANCE

The weight and balance principles and procedures that have been described apply generally to

70

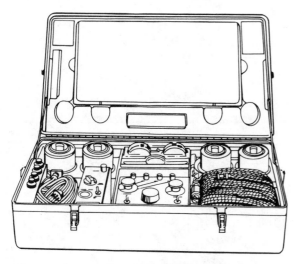

FIGURE 3–15. Aircraft electronic weighing kit.

helicopters. Each model helicopter is certificated for a specific maximum gross weight. However, it cannot be operated at this maximum weight under all conditions. Combinations of high altitude, high temperature, and high humidity determine the density altitude at a particular location. This, in turn, critically affects the hovering, takeoff, climb, autorotation, and landing performance of a helicopter. A heavily loaded helicopter has less ability to withstand shocks and additional loads caused by turbulent air. The heavier the load, the less the margin of safety for the supporting structures, such as the main rotor, fuselage, landing gear, etc.

Most helicopters have a much more restricted c.g. range than do airplanes. In some cases this range is less than 3 inches. The exact location and

length of the c.g. range is specified for each helicopter and usually extends a short distance fore and aft of the main rotor mast or the centroid of a dual rotor system. Ideally, the helicopter should have such perfect balance that the fuselage remains horizontal while in a hover, and the only cyclic adjustment required should be that made necessary by the wind. The fuselage acts as a pendulum suspended from the rotor. Any change in the center of gravity changes the angle at which it hangs from this point of support. More recently designed helicopters have loading compartments and fuel tanks located at or near the balance point. If the helicopter is not loaded properly and the c.g. is not very near the balance point, the fuselage does not hang horizontally in a hover. If the c.g. is too far aft, the nose tilts up, and excessive forward cyclic control is required to maintain a stationary hover. Conversely, if the c.g. is too far forward, the nose tilts down and excessive aft cyclic control is required. In extreme out-of-balance conditions, full fore or aft cyclic control may be insufficient to maintain control. Similar lateral balance problems may be encountered if external loads are carried.

Upon delivery by the manufacturer, the empty weight, empty weight c.g., and the useful load are noted on the weight and balance data sheet in the helicopter flight manual. If, after delivery, additional fixed equipment is added or removed, or if a major repair or alteration is made, which may affect the empty weight, empty weight c.g., or useful load, the weight and balance data must be revised. All weight and balance changes should be entered in the appropriate aircraft record.

GENERAL

Fuel is a substance that, when combined with oxygen, will burn and produce heat. Fuels may be classified according to their physical state as solid, gaseous, or liquid.

Solid Fuels

Solid fuels are used extensively for external-combustion engines, such as a steam engine, where the burning takes place under boilers or in furnaces. They include such fuels as wood and coal. Solid fuels are not used in reciprocating engines, where the burning takes place inside the cylinder, because of their slow rate of burning, low heat value, and numerous other disadvantages.

Gaseous Fuels

Gaseous fuels are used to some extent for internal-combustion engines, where a large supply of combustible gas is readily available. Natural gas and liquefied petroleum gas are two of the more common types. Gaseous fuels can be disregarded for use in aircraft engines. The large space they occupy limits the supply of fuel that can be carried.

Liquid Fuels

Liquid fuels, in many respects, are the ideal fuel for use in internal-combustion engines. Liquid fuels are classified as either nonvolatile or volatile. The nonvolatile fuels are the heavy oils used in diesel engines. The volatile class includes those fuels that are commonly used with a fuel metering device and are carried into the engine cylinder or combustion chamber in a vaporized or partially vaporized condition. Among these are alcohol, benzol, kerosene, and gasoline.

Aviation fuel is a liquid containing chemical energy that, through combustion, is released as heat energy and then converted to mechanical energy by the engine. This mechanical energy is used to produce thrust, which propels the aircraft. Gasoline and kerosene are the two most widely used aviation fuels.

CHARACTERISTICS AND PROPERTIES OF AVIATION GASOLINE

Aviation gasoline consists almost entirely of hydrocarbons, namely, compounds consisting of hydrogen and carbon. Some impurities in the form of sulphur and dissolved water will be present. The water cannot be avoided, since the gasoline is exposed to moisture in the atmosphere. A small amount of sulphur, always present in crude petroleum, is left in the process of manufacture.

Tetraethyl lead (TEL) is added to the gasoline to improve its performance in the engine. Organic bromides and chlorides are mixed with TEL so that during combustion volatile lead halides will be formed. These then are exhausted with the combustion products. TEL, if added alone, would burn to a solid lead oxide and remain in the engine cylinder. Inhibitors are added to gasoline to suppress the formation of substances that would be left as solids when the gasoline evaporates.

Certain properties of the fuel affect engine performance. These properties are volatility, the manner in which the fuel burns during the combustion process, and the heating value of the fuel. Also important is the corrosiveness of the gasoline as well as its tendency to form deposits in the engine during use. These latter two factors are important because of their effect on general cleanliness, which has a bearing on the time between engine overhauls.

Volatility

Volatility is a measure of the tendency of a liquid substance to vaporize under given conditions. Gasoline is a complex blend of volatile

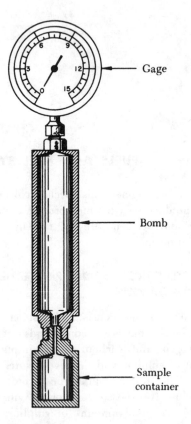

FIGURE 4-1. Vapor pressure test apparatus.

hydrocarbon compounds that have a wide range of boiling points and vapor pressures. It is blended in such a way that a straight chain of boiling points is obtained. This is necessary to obtain the required starting, acceleration, power, and fuel mixture characteristics for the engine.

If the gasoline vaporizes too readily, fuel lines may become filled with vapor and cause decreased fuel flow. If the fuel does not vaporize readily enough, it can result in hard starting, slow warm-up, poor acceleration, uneven fuel distribution to cylinders, and excessive crankcase dilution.

The lower grades of automobile fuel are not held within the tolerances required for aviation gasoline and usually contain a considerable amount of cracked gasoline, which may form excessive gum deposits. For these reasons, automobile fuels should not be used in aircraft engines, especially air-cooled engines operating at high cylinder temperatures.

Vapor Lock

Vaporization of gasoline in fuel lines results in a reduced supply of gasoline to the engine. In severe cases, it may result in engine stoppage.

This phenomenon is referred to as vapor locking. A measure of a gasoline's tendency to vapor lock is obtained from the Reid vapor pressure test. In this test a sample of the fuel is sealed in a "bomb" equipped with a pressure gage. The apparatus (see figure 4–1) is then immersed in a constant-temperature bath and the indicated pressure is noted. The higher the corrected vapor pressure of the sample under test, the more susceptible it is to vapor locking. Aviation gasolines are limited to a maximum of 7 p.s.i. because of their increased tendency to vapor lock at high altitudes.

Carburetor Icing

Carburetor icing is also related to volatility. When the fuel changes from a liquid to a vapor state, it extracts heat from its surroundings to make this change. The more volatile the fuel, the more rapid the heat extraction will be. As the gasoline leaving the carburetor discharge nozzle vaporizes, it can freeze water vapor contained in the incoming air. The moisture freezes on the walls of the induction system, the venturi throat, and the throttle valves. This type of ice formation restricts the fuel and air passages of the carburetor. It causes loss of power and, if not eliminated, eventual engine stoppage. Extreme icing conditions can make operation of the throttle controls impossible. This icing condition is most severe in the temperature range of 30° to 40° F. outside air temperature.

Aromatic Fuels

Some fuels may contain considerable quantities of aromatic hydrocarbons, which are added to increase the rich mixture performance rating of the fuel. Such fuels, known as aromatic fuels, have a strong solvent and swelling action on some types of hose and other rubber parts of the fuel system. For this reason, aromatic-resistant hose and rubber parts have been developed for use with aromatic fuels.

Detonation

In an engine that is operating in a normal manner, the flame front traverses the charge at a steady velocity of about 100 feet per second until the charge is consumed. When detonation occurs, the first portion of the charge burns in a normal manner but the last portion burns almost instantaneously, creating an excessive momentary pressure unbalance in the combustion chamber. This abnormal type of combustion is called detonation. This tremendous increase in the speed of burning causes the cylinder head temperature to rise. In severe cases, the increase in burning speed will decrease engine efficiency and may cause structural damage to the cylinder head or piston.

During normal combustion, the expansion of the burning gases presses the head of the piston down firmly and smoothly without excessive shock. The increased pressure of detonation exerted in a short period of time produces a heavy shock load to the walls of the combustion chamber and the piston head. It is this shock to the combustion chamber that is heard as an audible knock in an automobile engine. If other sounds could be filtered out, the knock would be equally audible in an aircraft engine. Generally, it is necessary to depend upon instruments to detect detonation in an aircraft engine.

Surface Ignition

Ignition of the fuel/air mixture by hot spots or surfaces in the combustion chamber is called surface ignition. If this occurs before the normal ignition event, the phenomenon is referred to as preignition. When it is prevalent, the result is power loss and engine roughness. Preignition is generally attributed to overheating of such parts as spark plug electrodes, exhaust valves, carbon deposits, etc. Where preignition is present, an engine may continue to operate even though the ignition has been turned off.

Present information indicates that gasoline high in aromatic hydrocarbon content is much more likely to cause surface ignition than fuels with a low content.

Octane and Performance Number Rating

Octane and performance numbers designate the antiknock value of the fuel mixture in an engine cylinder. Aircraft engines of high power output have been made possible principally as a result of blending to produce fuels of high octane ratings. The use of such fuels has permitted increases in compression ratio and manifold pressure, resulting in improved engine power and efficiency. However, even the high-octane fuels will detonate under severe operating conditions and when certain engine controls are improperly operated.

Antiknock qualities of aviation fuel are designated by grades. The higher the grade, the more compression the fuel can stand without detonating. For fuels that have two numbers, the first number indicates the lean-mixture rating and the second the rich-mixture rating. Thus, grade 100/130 fuel has a lean-mixture rating of 100 and a rich-mixture rating of 130. Two different scales are used to designate fuel grade. For fuels below grade 100, octane numbers are used to designate grade. The octane number system is based on a comparison of any fuel with mixtures of iso-octane and normal heptane. The octane number of a fuel is the percentage of iso-octane in the mixture that duplicates the knock characteristics of the particular fuel being rated. Thus, grade 91 fuel has the same knock characteristics as a blend of 91 percent iso-octane and 9 percent normal heptane.

With the advent of fuels having antiknock characteristics superior to iso-octane, another scale was adopted to designate the grade of fuels above the 100-octane number. This scale represents the performance rating of the fuel—its knock-free power available as compared with that available with pure iso-octane. It is arbitrarily assumed that 100 percent power is obtained from iso-octane alone. An engine that has a knock-limited horsepower of 1,000 with 100-octane fuel will have a knock-limited horsepower of 1.3 times as much (1,300 horsepower) with 130 performance number fuel.

The grade of an aviation gasoline is no indication of its fire hazard. Grade 91/96 gasoline is as easy to ignite as grade 115/145 and explodes with as much force. The grade indicates only the gasoline's performance in the aircraft's engine.

A convenient means of improving the antiknock characteristics of a fuel is to add a knock inhibitor. Such a fluid must have a minimum of corrosive or other undesirable qualities, and probably the best available inhibitor in general use at present is TEL (tetraethyl lead). The few difficulties encountered because of the corrosion tendencies of ethylized gasoline are insignificant when compared with the results obtained from the high antiknock value of the fuel. For most aviation fuels the addition of more than 6 ml. per gallon is not permitted. Amounts in excess of this have little effect on the antiknock value, but increase corrosion and spark plug trouble.

There are two distinct types of corrosion caused by the use of ethyl gasoline. The first is caused by the reaction of the lead bromide with hot metallic surfaces, and occurs when the engine is in operation; the second is caused by the condensed products of combustion, chiefly hydrobromic acid, when the engine is not running.

Purity

Aviation fuels must be free of impurities that would interfere with the operation of the engine or the units in the fuel and induction system.

Even though all precautions are observed in storing and handling gasoline, it is not uncommon to find a small amount of water and sediment in an aircraft fuel system. A small amount of such contamination is usually retained in the strainers in the fuel system. Generally, this is not considered a source of great danger, provided the strainers are drained and cleaned at frequent intervals. However, the water can present a serious problem because it settles to the bottom of the fuel tank and can then be circulated through the fuel system. A small quantity of water will flow with the gasoline through the carburetor metering jets and will not be especially harmful. An excessive amount of water will displace the fuel passing through the jets and restrict the flow of fuel; it will cause loss of power and can result in engine stoppage.

Under certain conditions of temperature and humidity, condensation of moisture (from the air) occurs on the inner surfaces of the fuel tanks. Since this condensation occurs on the portion of the tank above the fuel level, it is obvious that the practice of servicing an airplane immediately after flight will do much to minimize this hazard.

Fuel Identification

Gasolines containing TEL must be colored to conform with the law. In addition, gasoline may be colored for purposes of identification. For example, grade 100 low lead aviation gasoline is *blue*, grade 100 is *green* and grade 80 is *red*. See figure 4–2.

100/130 gasoline is manufactured (1975) in two grades—high-lead, up to 4.6 milliliters of lead per gallon and low-lead, not over 2.0 milliliters per gallon. The purpose being to eliminate two grades of lower octane fuel (80/87) and 91/96). The high-lead will continue to be colored green whereas the low-lead will be blue.

The low-lead will replace the 80/87 and 91/96 octane fuels as they are phased out. Engine manufacturers have prepared instructions to be followed in making adjustments necessary for changeover to the 100 octane fuel.

A change in color of an aviation gasoline usually indicates contamination with another product or a loss of fuel quality. A color change can also be caused by a chemical reaction that has weakened the lighter dye component. This color change in itself may not affect the quality of the fuel.

A color change can also be caused by the preservative in a new hose. Grade 115/145 gasoline that has been trapped for a short period of time in new hose may appear green. Flushing a small amount of gasoline through the hose usually removes all traces of color change.

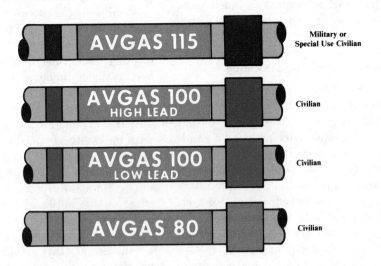

FIGURE 4–2. Identification of avgas.

76

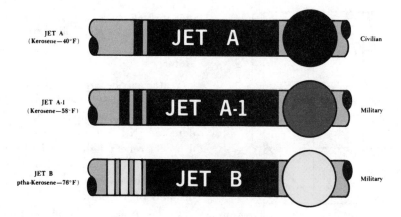

JET A (Kerosene—40°F)	JET A	Civilian
JET A-1 (Kerosene—58°F)	JET A-1	Military
JET B ptha-Kerosene—76°F)	JET B	Military

FIGURE 4–3. Identification of jet fuels.

Fuel Identification Markings

The most positive method of identifying the type and grade of fuel includes the following:

1. *Marking of Hose.* A color band not less than one foot wide painted adjacent to the fitting on each end of hose used to dispense fuel. The bands completely encircle the hose, and the name and grade of the product is stenciled longitudinally in one-inch letters of a contrasting color over the color band.

2. *Marking of Fuel Carriers, Pits and Fill Stands.* Tags identifying the name and grade of the product permanently affixed to each discharge meter and fill pipe. Porcelain tags (4″×6″) carrying the same information permanently bolted to the outside of the rear compartment of fuel servicing equipment. The delivery pipes of truck fill stands are banded with colors corresponding to that used on the dispensing hose.

TURBINE ENGINE FUELS

The aircraft gas turbine is designed to operate on a distillate fuel, commonly called jet fuel. Jet fuels are also composed of hydrocarbons with a little more carbon and usually a higher sulphur content than gasoline. Inhibitors may be added to reduce corrosion and oxidation. Anti-icing additives are also being blended to prevent fuel icing.

Two types of jet fuel in common use today are: (1) Kerosene grade turbine fuel, now named Jet A; and (2) a blend of gasoline and kerosene fractions, designated Jet B. There is a third type, called Jet A–1, which is made for operation at extremely low temperatures. See figure 4–3.

There is very little physical difference between Jet A (JP-5) fuel and commercial kerosene. Jet A was developed as a heavy kerosene having a higher flash point and lower freezing point than most kerosenes. It has a very low vapor pressure, so there is little loss of fuel from evaporation or boil-off at higher altitudes. It contains more heat energy per gallon than does Jet B (JP-4).

Jet B is similar to Jet A. It is a blend of gasoline and kerosene fractions. Most commercial turbine engines will operate on either Jet A or Jet B fuel. However, the difference in the specific gravity of the fuels may require fuel control adjustments. Therefore, the fuels cannot always be considered interchangeable.

Both Jet A and Jet B fuels are blends of heavy distillates and tend to absorb water. The specific gravity of jet fuels, especially kerosene, is closer to water than is aviation gasoline; thus, any water introduced into the fuel, either through refueling or condensation, will take an appreciable time to settle out. At high altitudes, where low temperatures are encountered, water droplets combine with the fuel to form a frozen substance referred to as "gel." The mass of "gel" or "icing" that may be generated from moisture held in suspension in jet fuel can be much greater than in gasoline.

Volatility

One of the most important characteristics of a jet fuel is its volatility. It must, of necessity, be a compromise between several opposing factors. A highly volatile fuel is desirable to aid in starting in cold weather and to make aerial restarts easier and surer. Low volatility is desirable to reduce

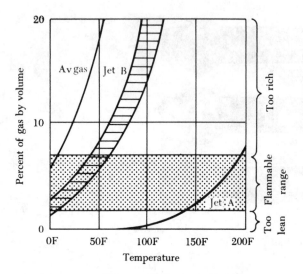

FIGURE 4–4. Vaporization of aviation fuels at atmospheric pressure.

the possibility of vapor lock and to reduce fuel losses by evaporation.

At normal temperatures, gasoline in a closed container or tank can give off so much vapor that the fuel/air mixture may be too rich to burn. Under the same conditions, the vapor given off by Jet B fuel can be in the flammable or explosive range. Jet A fuel has such a low volatility that at normal temperatures it gives off very little vapor and does not form flammable or explosive fuel/air mixtures. Figure 4–4 shows the vaporization of aviation fuels at atmospheric pressure.

Identification

Because jet fuels are not dyed, there is no on-sight identification for them. They range in color from a colorless liquid to a straw-colored (amber) liquid, depending on age or the crude petroleum source.

Jet fuel numbers are type numbers and have no relation to the fuel's performance in the aircraft engine.

FUEL SYSTEM CONTAMINATION

There are several forms of contamination in aviation fuel. The higher the viscosity of the fuel, the greater is its ability to hold contaminants in suspension. For this reason, jet fuels having a high viscosity are more susceptible to contamination than aviation gasoline. The principal contaminants that reduce the quality of both gasoline

and turbine fuels are other petroleum products, water, rust or scale, and dirt.

Water

Water can be present in the fuel in two forms: (1) Dissolved in the fuel or (2) entrained or suspended in the fuel. Entrained water can be detected with the naked eye. The finely divided droplets reflect light and in high concentrations give the fuel a dull, hazy, or cloudy appearance. Particles of entrained water may unite to form droplets of free water.

Fuel can be cloudy for a number of reasons. If the fuel is cloudy and the cloud disappears at the bottom, air is present. If the cloud disappears at the top, water is present. A cloud usually indicates a water-in-fuel suspension. Free water can cause icing of the aircraft fuel system, usually in the aircraft boost-pump screens and low-pressure filters. Fuel gage readings may become erratic because the water short-circuits the aircrafts electrical fuel cell quantity probe. Large amounts of water can cause engine stoppage. If the free water is saline, it can cause corrosion of the fuel system components.

Foreign Particles

Most foreign particles are found as sediment in the fuel. They are composed of almost any material with which the fuel comes into contact. The most common types are rust, sand, aluminum and magnesium compounds, brass shavings, and rubber.

Rust is found in two forms: (1) Red rust, which is nonmagnetic and (2) black rust, which is magnetic. They appear in the fuel as red or black powder (which may resemble a dye), rouge, or grains. Sand or dust appears in the fuel in a crystalline, granular, or glasslike form.

Aluminum or magnesium compounds appear in the fuel as a form of white or gray powder or paste. This powder or paste becomes very sticky or gelatinous when water is present. Brass is found in the fuel as bright gold-colored chips or dust. Rubber appears in the fuel as fairly large irregular bits. All of these forms of contamination can cause sticking or malfunctions of fuel metering devices, flow dividers, pumps, and nozzles.

Contamination with Other Types or Grades of Fuel

The unintentional mixing of petroleum products can result in fuels that give unacceptable performance in the aircraft. An aircraft engine is designed to operate most efficiently on fuel of definite specifications. The use of fuels that differ from these specifications reduces operating efficiency and can lead to complete engine failure.

Operators of turbine-powered aircraft are sometimes forced by circumstances to mix fuels. Such mixing, however, has very definite disadvantages. When aviation gasoline is mixed with jet fuel, the TEL in the gasoline forms deposits on the turbine blades and vanes. Continuous use of mixed fuels may cause a loss in engine efficiency. However, on a limited usage basis, they will have no detrimental effects on the engine.

Aviation gasoline containing by volume more than 0.5 percent of jet fuel may be reduced below the allowable limits in knock rating. Gasoline contaminated with turbine fuel is unsafe for use in reciprocating engines.

Microbial Growth

Microbial growth is produced by various forms of micro-organisms that live and multiply in the water interfaces of jet fuels. These organisms may form a slime similar in appearance to the deposits found in stagnent water. The color of this slime growth may be red, brown, gray, or black. If not properly controlled by frequent removal of free water, the growth of these organisms can become extensive. The organisms feed on the hydrocarbons that are found in fuels, but they need free water in order to multiply.

Micro-organisms have a tendency to mat, generally appearing as a brown blanket which acts as a blotter to absorb more moisture. This mixture or mat accelerates the growth of micro-organisms. The buildup of micro-organisms not only can interfere with fuel flow and quantity indication, but, more important, it can start electrolytic corrosive action.

Sediment

Sediment appears as dust, powder, fibrous material, grains, flakes, or stain. Specks or granules of sediment indicate particles in the visible size range, i.e., approximately 40 microns or larger in size. (See figure 4–5.) The presence of any appreciable number of such particles indicates either a malfunction of the filter/separators or a source of contamination downstream of the filter/ separator, or else an improperly cleaned sample container. Even with the most efficient filter/ separators and careful fuel handling, an occasional

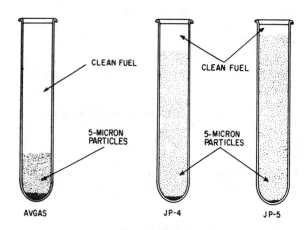

TIME : 1 HOUR

FIGURE 4–5. Comparison of particle's rate of settling in three types of fuel.

visible particle will be encountered. These strays are usually due to particle migration through the filter media and may represent no particular problem to the engine or fuel control. The sediment ordinarily encountered is an extremely fine powder, rouge, or silt. The two principle components of this fine sediment are normally sand and rust.

Sediment includes both organic and inorganic matter. The presence of appreciable quantities of fibrous materials (close to naked eye visibility) is usually indicative of filter element breakdown, either because of a ruptured element or mechanical disintegration of a component in the system. Usually, high metal content of relatively large particles suggest a mechanical failure somewhere in the system which is necessarily not limited to a metallic filter failure.

In a clean sample of fuel, sediment should not be visible except upon the most meticulous inspection. Persistent presence of sediment is suspect and requires that appropriate surveillance tests and corrective measures be applied to the fuel handling system.

Sediment or solid contamination can be separated into two categories: (1) coarse sediment and (2) fine sediment.

Course Sediment

Sediment that can be seen and that easily settles out of fuel or can be removed by adequate filteration is coarse sediment. Ordinarily, particles 10 microns in size and larger are regarded as coarse sediment. (See figure 4–6.)

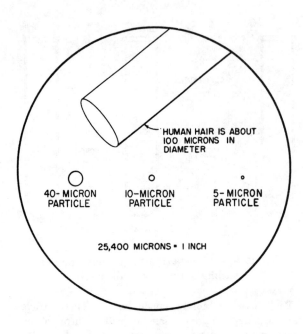

FIGURE 4–6. Enlargement of small particles and comparison to human hair.

Coarse particles clog orifices and wedge in sliding valve clearances and shoulders, causing malfunctions and excessive wear of fuel controls and metering equipment. They are also effective in clogging nozzle screens and other fine screens throughout the aircraft fuel system.

Fine Sediment

Particles smaller than 10 microns may be defined as fine sediment. (See figure 4–6.) Ninety eight percent of the fine sediment in fuel can be removed by proper settling, filtration, and centrifuging. Particles in this range accumulate throughout fuel controls, appearing as a dark shellac-like surface on sliding valves, and may also be centrifuged out in rotating chambers as sludge-like matter, causing sluggish operation of fuel metering equipment. Fine particles are not visible to the naked eye as distinct or separate particles; they will, however, scatter light and may appear as point flashes of light or a slight haze in fuel.

Maximum possible settling time should be allowed in fuel tanks after filling to allow reasonable settlement of water and sediment.

Contamination Detection

Coarse contamination can be detected visually. The major criterion for contamination detection is that the fuel be clean, bright, and contain no perceptible free water. Clean means the absence of any readily visible sediment or entrained water. Bright refers to the shiny appearance of clean, dry fuels. Free water is indicated by a cloud, haze, or a water slug. A cloud may or may not be present when the fuel is saturated with water. Perfectly clear fuel can contain as much as three times the volume of water considered to tolerable.

Several field methods for checking water content have been devised. One is the adding of a food color that is soluble in water, but not in fuel. Colorless fuel samples acquire a definite tint if water is present. Another method uses a gray chemical powder that changes color to pink through purple, if 30 or more p.p.m. (parts per million) of water are present in a fuel sample. In a third method a hypodermic needle is used to draw a fuel sample through a chemically treated filter. If the sample changes the color of the filter from yellow to blue, the fuel contains at least 30 p.p.m. of water.

Since fuel drained from tank sumps may have been cold-soaked, it should be realized that no method of water detection can be accurate while the fuel entrained water is frozen into ice crystals.

There is a good chance that water will not be drained or detected if the sumps are drained while the fuel is below 32° F. after being cooled in flight. The reason for this is that the sump drains may not be at the lowest point in the fuel tank while the airplane is in a flight attitude, and water may accumulate and freeze on other areas of the tank where it will remain undetected until it thaws.

Draining will be more effective if it is done after the fuel has been undisturbed for a period of time during which the free water can precipitate and settle to the drain point. The benefits of a settling period will be lost, however, unless the accumulated water is removed from the drains before the fuel is disturbed by internal pumps.

Contamination Control

The aircraft fuel system can be considered as being divided into three parts when discussing clean fuel. The manufacturer produces clean fuel. Contamination can occur at any time after the fuel is produced. The first part of the fuel system is the delivery and storage system between the refinery and the airport fuel service truck. Although this system is not physically a part of the aircraft, it is of equal importance in controlling contamination.

Anytime fuel is transferred it is susceptible to contamination. Therefore, all aviation maintenance personnel should be familiar with the following means of contamination control.

Fundamental in the control of contamination of turbine fuels are the methods followed by the industry in receiving and storing any bulk shipment of a petroleum product. These methods have long been established as sound, and they are too well known to need repetition here. The refueling facilities used by operators of turbine powered aircraft should incorporate the following features:

1. Fuel being pumped into airport storage should pass through a filter-separator. The filter should meet the requirements of U.S. Government Specification MIL–F–8508A.

2. Turbine fuels should be allowed to settle for a period of one hour per foot of depth of the fuel before being withdrawn for use. This means that ordinarily more than one storage tank must be provided for each grade of product.

3. Storage tanks should be checked with litmus paper after each new load of fuel is received and the fuel has settled. The litmus paper should remain submerged for a minimum of 15 seconds. During periods of heavy rain underground tanks should be checked with litmus paper more frequently.

4. Suction lines should be a minimum of 6 inches from the bottom of the tank. *Kerosene storage tanks* should be equipped with floating type suction lines. Floating suction does not remove the bottom product, which may not have settled sufficiently. It also prevents reintroduction into the fuel of any contamination at the bottom of the tank. Floating suction is the only logical way to take full advantage of gravity in removing water and particulate matter contamination. Its importance must not be minimized.

5. Fuel being withdrawn from storage should be passed through a filter-separator meeting the specification MIL–F–8508A.

6. Great care should be exercised in loading mobile fuelers to exclude airborne dust and dirt, rain or other foreign material.

7. To lessen the likelihood of rust and scale the tanks of mobile fuelers should be constructed of either stainless steel, nonferrous material or steel coated with a reliable, inert material.

8. As turbine fuel is being dispensed into the aircraft from truck or hydrant it should be filtered to a degree of 5 microns for solid particles and contain no more than 0.0015 per cent of free and entrained water. Bypass valves around the filter should not be permitted.

9. All the quality control procedures usually followed in handling aviation gasoline should be employed. These include regular and frequent check of filter-separators; frequent quality check such as the "clear and bright" test; and continual emphasis on cleanliness. Examples: "Don't let the hose nozzle drag on the apron." "Keep the dust cap on the nozzle at all times when nozzle is not in use."

FUEL SYSTEM

The aircraft fuel system stores fuel and delivers the proper amount of clean fuel at the right pressure to meet the demands of the engine. A well-designed fuel system ensures positive and reliable fuel flow throughout all phases of flight, which include changes in altitude, violent maneuvers and sudden acceleration and deceleration. Furthermore, the system must be reasonably free from tendency to vapor lock, which can result from changes in ground and in-flight climatic conditions. Such indicators as fuel pressure gages, warning signals, and tank quantity gages are provided to give continuous indications of how the system is functioning.

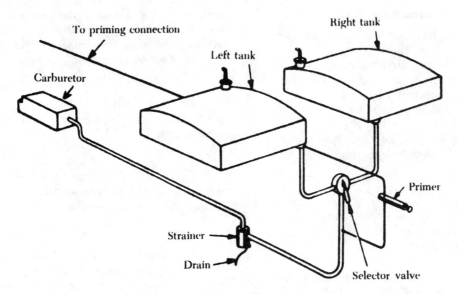

FIGURE 4–7. Gravity feed fuel system.

The simplest type of fuel system is the gravity feed, which is still in use on many low-powered airplanes. A gravity feed system is shown in figure 4–7. The fuel tanks are mounted above the carburetor, with gravity causing the fuel to flow from the tanks to the carburetor. A selector valve is provided to stop the fuel flow or to select a particular tank in the system from which to draw fuel. A strainer filters the fuel before it reaches the carburetor. A drain is provided for removing water and sediment trapped at the strainer. A primer furnishes the additional fuel required for engine starting.

Airplanes equipped with a high-output engine require a fuel system that supplies fuel to the carburetor at a positive pressure. The basic source for this pressure is an engine-driven fuel pump, but auxiliary fuel pumps or booster pumps are required in every pressure feed system to: (1) supply fuel pressure for starting the engine; (2) supply fuel to the primer system; and (3) to serve as an emergency pump in case the engine-driven pump fails.

FUEL SYSTEM COMPONENTS

The basic components of a fuel system include tanks, lines, valves, pumps, filtering units, gages, warning signal, and primer. Some systems will include central refueling provisions, fuel dump valves, and a means for transferring fuel. In order to clarify the operating principles of complex aircraft fuel systems, the various units are discussed in the following paragraphs.

Fuel Tanks

The location, size, shape, and construction of fuel tanks vary with the type and intended use of the aircraft. In some aircraft, the fuel tanks are integral with the wing or other structural portions of the aircraft.

Fuel tanks are made of materials that will not react chemically with any aviation fuel. Aluminum alloy is widely used, and synthetic rubber bladder-type fuel cells are used in some installations.

Usually a sump and a drain are provided at the lowest point in the tank as shown in figure 4–8. When a sump or low point is provided in the tank, the main fuel supply is not drawn from the bottom of the sump, but from a higher point in the tank.

The top of each tank is vented to the outside air in order to maintain atmospheric pressure within the tank. Air vents are designed to minimize the possibility of their stoppage by dirt and ice formation. In order to permit rapid changes in internal air pressure, the size of the vent is proportional to the size of the tank, thus preventing the collapse of the tank in a steep dive or glide. All except the very smallest of tanks are fitted with internal baffles to resist fuel surging caused by changes in the attitude of the aircraft. Usually an expansion space is provided in fuel tanks to allow for an increase in fuel volume due to expansion.

The filler neck and cap are usually located in a recessed well, equipped with a scupper and

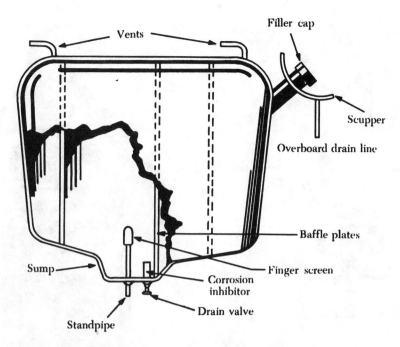

FIGURE 4–8. A typical metal fuel tank.

drain. The scupper is designed to prevent overflowing fuel from entering the wing or fuselage structure. Fuel caps have provisions for locking devices to prevent accidental loss during flight. Filler openings are clearly marked with the word "FUEL", the tank capacity, and the type of fuel to be used. Information concerning the capacity of each tank is usually posted near the fuel selector valves, as well as on the tank filler caps.

Some fuel tanks are equipped with dump valves that make it possible to jettison fuel during flight in order to reduce the weight of the aircraft to its specified maximum landing weight. In aircraft equipped with dump valves, the operating control is located within reach of the pilot, copilot, or flight engineer. Dump valves are designed and installed to afford safe, rapid discharge of fuel.

Fuel Cells

Present day aircraft may be equipped with one or more of the following types of fuel cells: the bladder-type fuel cell and the integral fuel cell.

Bladder-Type Fuel Cells

The bladder-type fuel cell is a nonself-sealing cell that is used to reduce weight. It depends entirely upon the structure of the cavity in which it sits to support the weight of the fuel within it. For this reason, the cell is made slightly larger than the cavity. The bladder cells in use are made either of rubber or of nylon.

Integral Fuel Cells

Since integral fuel cells are usually built into the wings of the aircraft structure, they are not removable. An integral cell is a part of the aircraft structure, which has been so built that after the seams, structural fasteners, and access doors have been properly sealed, the cell will hold fuel without leaking. This type of construction is usually referred to as a "wet wing."

Fuel Lines and Fittings

In an aircraft fuel system, the various tanks and other components are usually joined together by fuel lines made of metal tubing connected, where flexibility is necessary, by lengths of flexible hose. The metal tubing usually is made of aluminum alloy, and the flexible hose is made of synthetic rubber or Teflon. The diameter of the tubing is governed by the fuel flow requirements of the engine.

Each fuel line is identified by a color-coded band near each end. Except for short lines between flexible connections, tubing should be properly supported by clamping to structural members of the aircraft.

A special heat-resistant hose is used where the

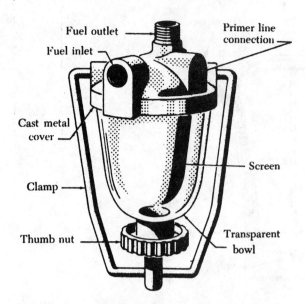

FIGURE 4–9. Main fuel strainer for light aircraft.

flexible lines will be subjected to intense heat. For all flexible fuel lines located forward of the firewall, fire-resistant hose is used.

In many installations, the fuel lines are designed to be located within the tanks. Therefore, minor leaks occurring within the tank are classified as internal leaks and will not cause fire hazards.

Fuel Strainers

Strainers are installed in the tank outlets and frequently in the tank filler necks. These are of fairly coarse mesh and prevent only the larger particles from entering the fuel system. Other, fine-mesh, strainers are provided in the carburetor fuel inlets and in the fuel lines.

The function of the main strainer is important: it not only prevents foreign matter from entering the carburetor, but also, because of its location at the low point of the fuel system, traps any small amount of water that may be present in the system. In multiengine aircraft, one main strainer is usually installed in each engine nacelle.

A main fuel strainer for a light airplane is shown in figure 4–9. It consists of a cast metal top, a screen, and a glass bowl. The bowl is attached to the cover by a clamp and thumb nut. Fuel enters the unit through the inlet port, filters through the screen, and exits through the outlet port. At regular intervals the glass bowl is drained, and the screen is removed for inspection and cleaning.

The main fuel strainer shown in figure 4–10 is so

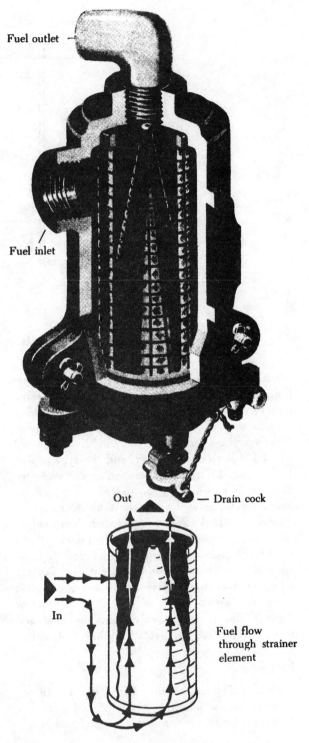

FIGURE 4–10. Main fuel strainer.

installed that the fuel flows through it before reaching the engine-driven pump. It is located at the lowest point in the fuel system. The shape and construction of the fine-mesh screen provides

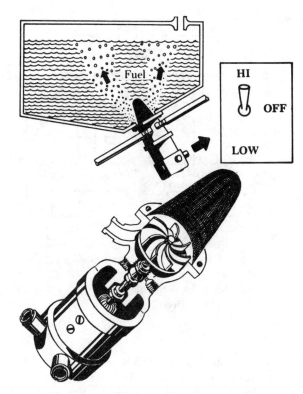

FIGURE 4–11. Centrifugal fuel booster pump.

a large screening surface encased in a compact housing. Reinforcing the screen is a coarse, heavy-wire mesh.

Auxiliary Fuel Pumps

The electrically driven centrifugal booster pump, shown in figure 4–11, supplies fuel under pressure to the inlet of the engine-driven fuel pump. This type of pump is an essential part of the fuel system, particularly at high altitudes, to keep the pressure on the suction side of the engine-driven pump from becoming low enough to permit the fuel to boil. This booster pump is also used to transfer fuel from one tank to another, to supply fuel under pressure for priming when starting the engine, and, as an emergency unit, to supply fuel to the carburetor in case the engine-driven pump fails. To increase the capacity of the pump under emergency conditions, many pumps are equipped with a two-speed or variable-speed control so that the recommended fuel inlet pressure to the carburetor can be maintained. As a precautionary measure, the booster pump is always turned on during takeoffs and landings to ensure a positive supply of fuel.

The booster pump is mounted at the tank outlet

within a detachable sump or is submerged in fuel at the bottom of the fuel tank. The seals between the impeller and the power section of the pump prevent leakage of fuel or fumes into the motor. If any liquid or vapor should leak past the seal, it is vented overboard through a drain. As an added precaution in nonsubmerged-type pumps, air is allowed to circulate around the motor to remove dangerous fuel vapor.

As fuel enters the pump from the tank, a high-speed impeller throws the fuel outward in all directions at high velocity. The high rotational speed swirls the fuel and produces a centrifuge action that separates air and vapor from the fuel before it enters the fuel line to the carburetor. This results in practically vapor-free fuel delivery to the carburetor and permits the separated vapors to rise through the fuel tank and escape through the tank vents. Since a centrifugal-type pump is not a positive-displacement pump, no relief valve is necessary.

Although the centrifugal type is the most common type of booster pump, there are still a few sliding-vane-type booster pumps in service. This type, too, is driven by an electric motor. Unlike the centrifugal type, it does not have the advantage of the centrifuge action to separate the vapor from the fuel. Since it is a positive-displacement-type pump, it must have a relief valve to prevent excessive pressure. Its construction and operation are identical to the engine-driven pump.

Hand Pump

The hand, or wobble, pump is frequently used on light aircraft. It is generally located near other fuel system components and operated from the cockpit by suitable controls. A diagram of a wobble pump is shown in figure 4–12. When the handle attached to the central blade is operated, the low pressure created on the chamber below the upward moving blade, permits the incoming fuel pressure to lift the lower flapper and allows fuel to flow into this chamber. At the same time fuel flows through a drilled passageway to fill the chamber above the downward moving blade. As the blade moves downward, the lower flapper closes, preventing fuel from escaping back into the inlet line. The fuel below the downward moving blade flows through a passageway into another chamber and is discharged through an outlet flapper valve to the carburetor. The cycle is re-

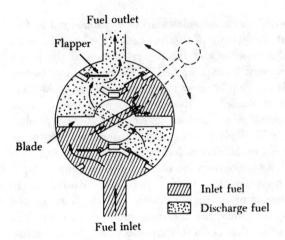

FIGURE 4-12. Schematic diagram of a wobble pump.

peated each time the handle is moved in either direction.

Engine-Driven Fuel Pump

The purpose of the engine-driven fuel pump is to deliver a continuous supply of fuel at the proper pressure at all times during engine operation. The pump widely used at the present time is the positive-displacement, rotary-vane-type pump.

A schematic diagram of a typical engine-driven pump (vane-type) is shown in figure 4-13. Regardless of variations in design, the operating principle of all vane-type fuel pumps is the same.

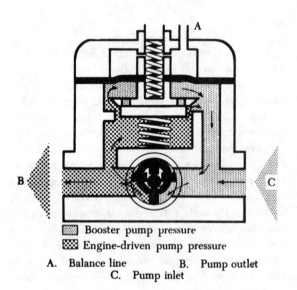

▨ Booster pump pressure
▩ Engine-driven pump pressure
A. Balance line   B. Pump outlet
          C. Pump inlet

FIGURE 4-13. Engine-driven fuel pump (pressure delivery).

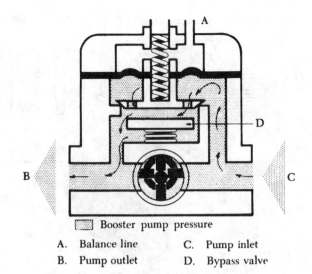

▨ Booster pump pressure
A. Balance line   C. Pump inlet
B. Pump outlet   D. Bypass valve

FIGURE 4-14. Engine-driven fuel pump (bypass flow).

The engine-driven pump is usually mounted on the accessory section of the engine. The rotor, with its sliding vanes, is driven by the crankshaft through the accessory gearing. Note how the vanes carry fuel from the inlet to the outlet as the rotor turns in the direction indicated. A seal prevents leakage at the point where the drive shaft enters the pump body, and a drain carries away any fuel that leaks past the seal. Since the fuel provides enough lubrication for the pump, no special lubrication is necessary.

Since the engine-driven fuel pump normally discharges more fuel than the engine requires, there must be some way of relieving excess fuel to prevent excessive fuel pressures at the fuel inlet of the carburetor. This is accomplished through the use of a spring-loaded relief valve that can be adjusted to deliver fuel at the recommended pressure for a particular carburetor. Figure 4-13, shows the pressure relief valve in operation, by-passing excess fuel back to the inlet side of the pump. Adjustment is made by increasing or decreasing the tension of the spring.

The relief valve of the engine-driven pump is designed to open at the set pressure regardless of the pressure of the fuel entering the pump. To maintain the proper relation between fuel pressure and carburetor inlet air pressure, the chamber above the fuel pump relief valve is vented either to the atmosphere or through a balance line to carburetor air inlet pressure. The combined pressures of spring tension and either atmospheric or

86

carburetor inlet air pressure determine the absolute pressure at which the relief valve opens. This balanced-type relief valve has certain objectionable features that must be investigated when encountering fuel system troubles. A sylphon or diaphragm failure will allow air to enter the fuel on the inlet side of the pump if the pump inlet pressure is less than atmospheric. Conversely, if the pump inlet pressure is above atmospheric pressure, fuel will be discharged from the vent. For proper altitude compensation the vent must be open. If it should become clogged by ice or foreign matter while at altitude, the fuel pressure will decrease during descent. If the vent becomes clogged during ascent, the fuel pressure will increase as the altitude is increased.

In addition to the relief valve, the fuel pump has a bypass valve that permits fuel to flow around the pump rotor whenever the pump is inoperative. This valve, shown in figure 4–14, consists of a disk that is lightly spring-loaded against a series of ports in the relief valve head. When fuel is needed for starting the engine, or in the event of engine-driven pump failure, fuel at booster-pump pressure is delivered to the fuel pump inlet. When the pressure is great enough to move the bypass disk from its seat, fuel is allowed to enter the carburetor for priming or metering. When the engine-driven pump is in operation, the pressure built up on the outlet side of the pump, together with the pressure of the bypass spring, holds the disk on its seat and prevents fuel flow through the ports.

Valves

Selector valves are installed in the fuel system to provide a means for shutting off the fuel flow, for tank and engine selection, for crossfeed, and for fuel transfer. The size and number of ports (openings) vary with the type of installation. For example, a single-engine aircraft with two fuel tanks and a reserve fuel supply requires a valve with four ports—three inlets from the tanks and a common outlet. The valve must accommodate the full flow capacity of the fuel line, must not leak, and must operate freely with a definite "feel" or "click" when it is in the correct position. Selector valves may be operated either manually or electrically. A tube, rod, or cable is attached to a manually operated valve so that it can be operated from the cockpit. Electrically operated valves have an actuator, or motor. The three main types of selector valves are the poppet, cone, and disk.

The poppet-type selector valve has an individual poppet valve at each inlet port. A cam and yoke on the same shaft act to open the selected poppet valve as the yoke is turned. Figure 4–15 shows how the cam lifts the upper poppet valve from its seat when the control handle is set to the "number 2" tank. This opens the passage from the "number 2" tank to the engine. At the same time, a raised portion of the index plate drops into a notch in the side of the cam. (See the detail of the index mechanism.) This produces the "feel" that indicates the valve is in the wide open position. The control handle should always be set by "feel" rather than by the marking on the indicator dial. The index mechanism also keeps the valve in the desired position and prevents creeping caused by vibration. Some valves have more than one raised portion on the cam to allow two or more ports to be opened at the same time.

The cone-type selector valve has either an all-metal or a cork-faced aluminum housing. The cone, which fits into the housing, is rotated by means of a cockpit control. To supply fuel from the desired tank, the cockpit control is turned until the passages in the cone align with the correct ports in the housing. An indexing mechanism aids in obtaining the desired setting and also holds the cone in the selected position. Some cone-type valves have a friction release mechanism that reduces the amount of turning torque required to make a tank selection and that can be adjusted to prevent leakage.

The rotor of the disk-type selector valve fits into a cylindrical hole in the valve body. A disk-type valve is shown in figure 4–16. Note that the rotor has one open port and several sealing disks— one for each port in the housing. To select a tank, the rotor is turned until the open port aligns with the port from which fuel flow is desired. At this time, all other ports are closed by the sealing disks. In this position, fuel will flow from the desired tank to the selector valve and out through the engine-feed port at the bottom of the valve. To ensure positive port alignment for full fuel flow, the indexing mechanism (shown in the center of figure 4–16 forces a spring-loaded ball into a ratchet ring. When the selector valve is placed in the closed position, the open port in the rotor is opposite a blank in the valve body, while each sealing disk covers a tank port.

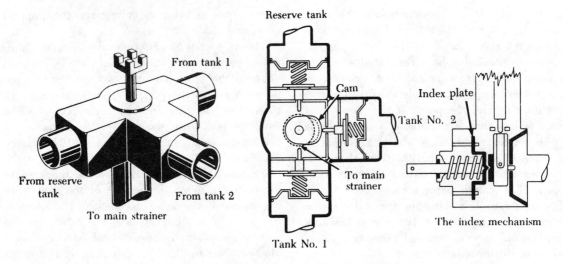

FIGURE 4–15. Poppet-type selector valve.

Fuel tank shutoff valves have two positions, open and closed. They are installed in the system to prevent fuel loss when a fuel system component is being removed or when a part of the system is damaged. In some installations they are used to control the fuel flow during fuel transfer. They are operated either manually or electrically. An electrically operated fuel shutoff valve includes a reversible electric motor linked to a sliding-valve assembly. The motor moves the valve gate in and out of the passage through which the fuel flows, thus, shutting off or turning on the fuel flow.

FUEL SYSTEM INDICATORS

Fuel Quantity Gages

Fuel quantity gages are necessary so that the operator may know the quantity of fuel remaining in the tanks during operation of the aircraft. The four general types of fuel gages are: (1) Sight glass, (2) mechanical, (3) electrical, and (4) electronic. The type of fuel gage installation depends on the size of the aircraft and the number and location of the fuel tanks. Since the sight glass and mechanical fuel gages are not suitable for aircraft where tanks are located an appreciable distance from the cockpit, larger aircraft use either electrical or electronic fuel quantity gages. On some aircraft, one fuel gage, called a totalizer, indicates the total amount of fuel remaining in all the fuel tanks.

The sight glass is the simplest form of fuel quantity gage. The indicator is a glass or plastic tube placed on the same level as the tank. It operates on the principle that a liquid seeks its

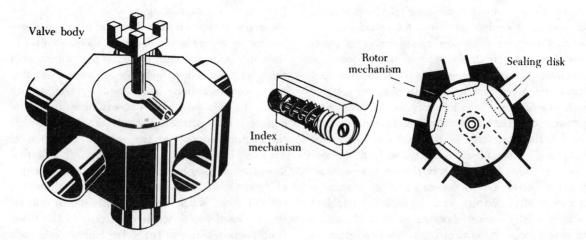

FIGURE 4–16. Disk-type selector valve.

88

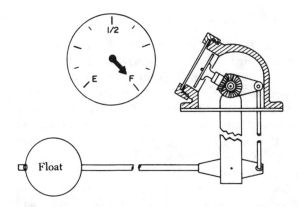

FIGURE 4–17.   Float-and-lever type fuel level gage.

own level. The tube is calibrated in gallons or has a metal scale near it. The sight glass may have a shutoff valve so that the fuel can be shut off for cleaning and for preventing loss of fuel if the tube is broken.

The mechanical-type fuel quantity gage is usually located in the tank and is known as a direct reading gage. It has an indicator connected to a float resting on the surface of the fuel. As the fuel level changes, the float mechanically operates the indicator, thus showing the level of fuel in the tank. One type of mechanical fuel gage is illustrated in figure 4–17.

The electrical-type quantity gage consists of an indicator in the cockpit and a float-operated transmitter installed in the tank. As the fuel level changes, the transmitter sends an electric signal to the indicator, which shows the changing fuel level. Two important advantages of this fuel quantity gage (and the electronic type discussed in the next paragraph) are that the indicator can be located any distance from the tank and the fuel levels of several tanks can be read on one indicator.

The electronic-type (capacitance) fuel quantity gage differs from the other types in that it has no movable devices in the fuel tank. Instead of floats and their attendant mechanical units, the dielectric qualities of fuel and air furnish a measurement of fuel quantity. Essentially, the tank transmitter is a simple electric condenser. The dielectric (or nonconducting material) of the condenser is fuel and air (vapor) above the fuel. The capacitance of the tank unit at any one time will depend on the existing proportion of fuel and vapors in the tank. The capacitance of the transmitter is compared to a reference capacitor in a rebalance-type bridge circuit. The unbalanced sig-

nal is amplified by the voltage amplifiers that drive a phase discriminating power stage. The output stage supplies power to one phase of a two-phase a.c. motor that mechanically drives a rebalancing potentiometer and indicator pointer. The electronic type system of measuring fuel quantity is more accurate in measuring fuel level, as it measures the fuel by weight instead of in gallons. Fuel volume will vary with temperature (a gallon of gasoline weighs more when it is cold than when it is hot); thus, if it is measured in pounds instead of gallons, the measurement will be more accurate.

In addition to the cockpit fuel quantity indicating system, some aircraft are provided with a means to determine the fuel quantity in each tank when the aircraft is on the ground. This is accomplished in several different ways. Some manufacturers use float-operated, direct-reading fuel gages mounted in the lower surface of the wing. Another means is to use under-wing bayonet gages. There are two types in use, the drip gage and the sight gage.

When using the drip gage it is necessary to proceed slowly, using the trial-and-error method to find the exact fuel level. In large area tanks a proportionately large amount of fuel is represented by a fraction of an inch variation in fuel level. The long, hollow drip tubes require some time to drain once they are filled with fuel, and a substantial error in reading will be made if the diminishing drainage drip is mistaken for the steady drip that signifies that the tube is properly positioned.

When the cap and hollow drip tube are drawn out from the lower wing surface, the fuel enters the open top of the tube when it reaches the level of the fuel. As stated previously steady drip from a drip hole signifies that the tube is properly positioned with a tiny head of fuel above the opening. The drip gage tube may be calibrated in pounds or inches. When calibrated in inches, the reading is compared with a special chart to give a reading of fuel quantity in gallons.

The sight gage is somewhat simpler in construction than the drip gage, and offers unmistakable visual evidence when it is properly positioned for reading. As shown in figure 4–18, the sight gage is basically a long lucite rod, protected by a calibrated tube, which terminates at the top in an exposed quartz tip. When the tip is above the fuel it acts as a reflector. Light rays traveling up the lucite rod are deflected at right angles by

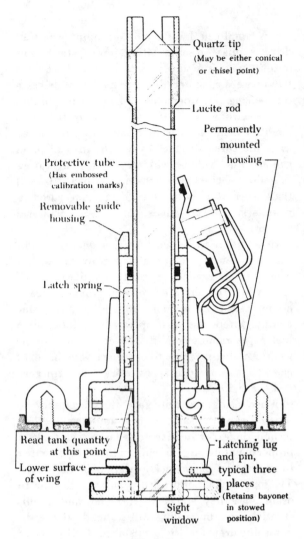

FIGURE 4–18. Under-wing sight gage.

the 45° surface at one side of the tip and deflected 90° again by the 45° surface at the opposite side and returned down the lucite rod.

Any portion of the tip submerged in fuel will not act as a reflector. Consequently, when the fuel level is part way up the taper, a light pattern is created that is visible at the lower end of the lucite rod and that has the dimension and shape described by the intersection of the tip and the fuel. When the reflected light is reduced to the smallest perceptible point in the case of cone-tipped gages, or hairline in the case of chisel-tipped gages, the rod is properly positioned. The fuel tank quantity can be read on the tube where it emerges from the recessed guide housing. Drip gage readings are taken at this location also.

Fuel Flowmeter

The fuel flowmeter is normally used only in multiengine aircraft. The system consists of a transmitter and an indicator. The transmitter is installed in the fuel inlet line to the engine, where it measures the rate of fuel flow. The transmitter is electrically connected to the indicator located in the cockpit. This gage shows the rate of fuel consumption in pounds per hour.

The transmitter signal may be developed by a movable vane mounted in the fuel flow path. The impact of fuel causes the vane to swing and move against the restraining force of a calibrated spring. The final position assumed by the vane represents a measure of the rate at which fuel is passing through the flowmeter and the corresponding signal to be sent to the indicator. A vane-type fuel flowmeter system is illustrated in figure 4–19.

The transmitter used with turbine engines is the mass-flow type having a range of 500 to 2,500 pounds per hour. It consists of two cylinders placed in the fuel stream so that the direction of fuel flow is parallel to the axes of the cylinders. (See figure 4–20.) The cylinders have small vanes in the outer periphery. The upstream cylinder, called the impeller, is driven at a constant angular velocity by the power supply. This velocity imparts an angular momentum to the fuel. The fuel then transmits this angular velocity to the turbine (the downstream cylinder), causing the turbine to rotate until a restraining spring force balances the force due to the angular momentum of the fuel. The deflection of the turbine positions a magnet in the second harmonic transmitter to a position corresponding to the fuel flow. The turbine position is transmitted to the flight station indicator by means of a selsyn system.

Fuel Pressure Gage

The fuel pressure gage indicates the pressure of the fuel entering the carburetor. This gage may be included with the oil pressure gage and the oil temperature gage in one casing, called the engine gage unit. Most aircraft today have separate gages for these functions. An engine gage unit is shown in figure 4–21.

The fuel pressure gage is a differential pressure indicator with two connections on the back of the indicator housing. The air connection (see figure 4–22) is vented to the carburetor air inlet, and the fuel connection is attached to the fuel

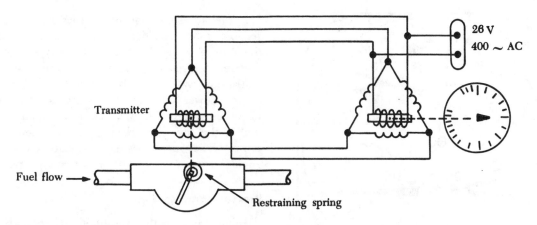

FIGURE 4–19. Vane-type fuel flowmeter system.

inlet chamber of the carburetor. In this way the gage indicates the difference between the fuel pressure entering the carburetor and the air pressure at the carburetor air inlet. In some installations, the air fitting on the gage is left open to the air pressure of the cockpit, which is generally the same as the pressure of the atmosphere. When this venting arrangement is used, the relief valve of the engine-driven fuel pump is also vented to the atmosphere, and the gage indicates the fuel

pressure resulting from the adjusted spring pressure only. In order to dampen pressure pulsations that cause pointer fluctuation, a restrictor fitting (A) is installed at the carburetor end of the fuel gage line. (See the Y connection shown in figure 4–22.) The second restrictor (B) meters fuel to the oil system during oil dilution. The arrangement of these restrictors provides an indicated drop in fuel pressure when the oil dilution system is used. The oil-dilution system will be discussed

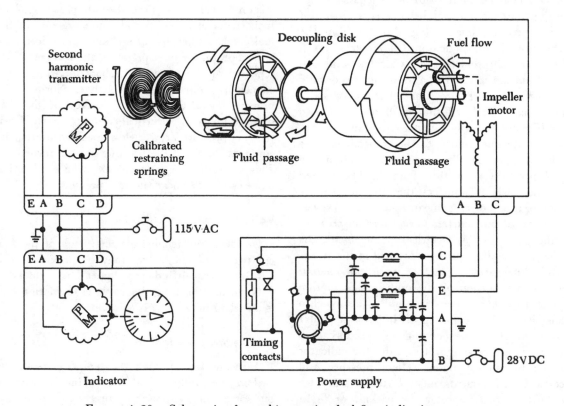

FIGURE 4–20. Schematic of a turbine engine fuel flow indicating system.

91

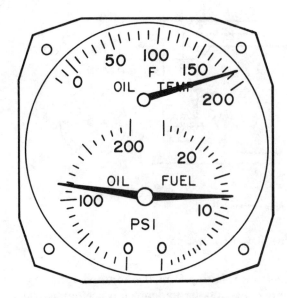

FIGURE 4–21. Engine gage unit.

thoroughly in the Powerplant Handbook, and is mentioned at this time only because the fuel pressure indicator provides a means for a check on the operation of other fuel system units.

In small aircraft the fuel pressure gage may be actuated by a Bourdon tube (an instrument that converts changes in pressure to mechanical motion), or an aneroid and bellows type, installed with a pressure line leading directly from the carburetor to the indicator. On larger aircraft, where the fuel pressure gage is located some distance from the carburetor, a transmitter is usually installed. The pressure transmitter may be a simple cast metal cell that is divided into two chambers by a flexible diaphragm. Pressure applied by the fuel source to the transmitter inlet pushes against the diaphragm and builds up an equal pressure to a thin fluid (highly refined kerosene), which transfers the pressure to the indicator mechanism. Some installations, however, use electrical transmitters to register fuel pressure on the gage. In this electrical arrangement, the pressure-indicating unit is contained in the transmitter. Fuel pressure, acting upon the aneroid and bellows portion of the unit, causes motion of one part of an electrical unit (the synchro transmitter). As the unit turns, it causes a similar movement of a corresponding unit (the synchro motor). This receiving unit actuates the indicator on the instrument panel. These pressure and electrical arrangements make it unnecessary for combustible fuel to enter the cockpit or flight deck, thereby reducing fire risk.

A fuel pressure gage often used with fuel injection systems on light aircraft engines is illustrated in figure 4–23. A gage of this type registers metered fuel pressure at the fuel injection unit distributor valve and is a direct indication of engine power output when installed in a fuel injection system for light aircraft engines. The dial of the gage is marked to indicate percent of power. The gage does not indicate either the engine-driven pump or the boost pump pressure.

Pressure Warning Signal

In an aircraft with several tanks, there is always the possible danger of allowing the fuel supply in one tank to become exhausted before the selector valve is switched to another. To prevent this, pressure-warning signals are installed in some aircraft. The complete installation, shown in figure 4–22, consists of a pressure-sensitive mechanism and a warning light. The warning mechanism has both a fuel and an air connection.

The connection marked "fuel" is connected to the fuel pressure line of the carburetor. The air connection is vented to either atmospheric or carburetor air inlet pressure. This arrangement prevents the warning mechanism from acting in response to changes in the absolute pressure of the fuel. If, for example, the absolute pressure of the fuel decreases because of a change in atmospheric or carburetor air inlet pressure, the change is also reflected at the warning mechanism, which then cancels the effects of the change. Normal fuel pressure against the power surface of the diaphragm holds the electrical contacts apart. When the fuel pressure drops below specified limits, the contacts close and the warning light is turned on. This alerts the operator to take whatever action is necessary to boost the fuel pressure.

Valve-In-Transit Indicator Lights

On large multiengine aircraft, each of the fuel crossfeed and line valves may be provided with a valve-in-transit indicator light. This light is on only during the time the valve is in motion and is off when movement is complete.

Fuel Temperature Indicator

A means for checking the temperature of the fuel in the tanks and at the engine is provided on some turbine-powered aircraft. During extreme cold, especially at altitude, the gage can

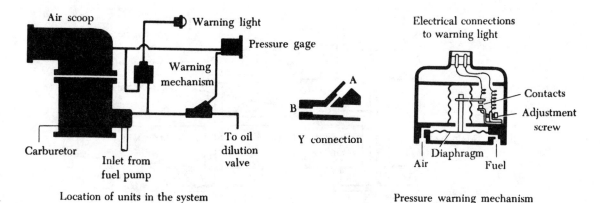

Location of units in the system   **Pressure warning mechanism**

FIGURE 4–22.   Fuel pressure-indicating system.

be checked to determine when fuel temperatures are approaching those at which there may be danger of ice crystals forming in the fuel.

MULTIENGINE FUEL SYSTEMS

The design of the fuel system for an aircraft having two or more engines presents problems not normally encountered in single-engine fuel systems. A large number of tanks are often required to carry the necessary fuel. These tanks may be located in widely separated parts of the aircraft, such as the fuselage and the inboard and outboard sections of the wings. The individual engine fuel systems must be interconnected so that fuel can be fed from the various tanks to any engine. In case of engine failure, the fuel normally supplied to the inoperative engine must be made available to the others.

Crossfeed System

The twin-engine fuel system illustrated in figure 4–24 is the simple crossfeed type. As shown, the tank selector valves are set to supply fuel from the main tanks to the engines. These valves can also be positioned to supply fuel from the auxiliary tanks. The crossfeed valve is shown in the off position. It can also be set to supply fuel from the fuselage tank to either or both engines and to crossfeed. A few of the numerous combinations in which the three valves can be set are also illustrated.

Manifold System

The main feature of the four-engine system shown in figure 4–25 is the fuel manifold. This fuel manifold system is actually a variation of the crossfeed. As shown, fuel is being supplied from the main tanks directly to the engines. The manifold valves can also be set so that all tanks feed into the manifold and each engine receives its fuel supply from this line. The auxiliary fuel supply can be delivered to the engines only through the manifold. The main advantage of this system is its flexibility. Should an engine fail, its fuel is immediately available to the other engines. If a tank is damaged, the corresponding engine can be supplied with fuel from the manifold.

Another advantage of this system is that all fuel tanks can be serviced at the same time through a single line manifold connection. This

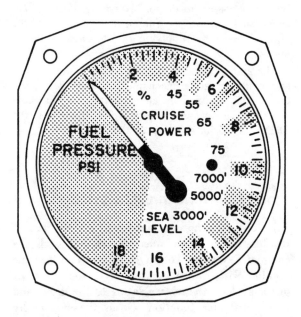

FIGURE 4–23.   Fuel pressure gage for fuel-injection system.

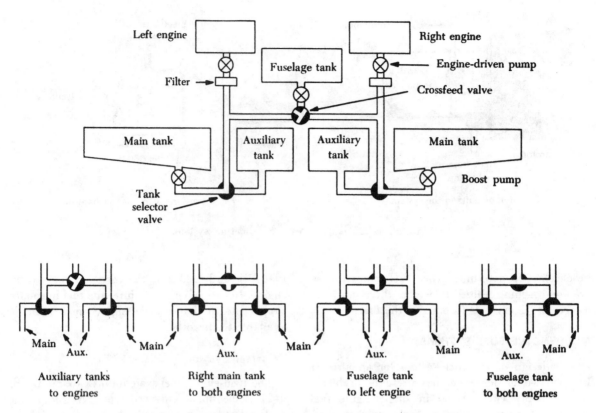

FIGURE 4–24. Twin-engine crossfeed system schematic.

method of fuel servicing has greatly reduced servicing time on large aircraft because fuel can be introduced into the fueling manifold under high pressure.

FUEL JETTISON SYSTEMS

A fuel jettison system is required for transport category and general aviation aircraft if the maximum take-off weight exceeds the maximum landing weight. The maximum take-off and landing weights are design specifications and may be found in the Aircraft Type Certificate data sheets.

A fuel jettison system must be able to jettison enough fuel within 10 minutes for general aviation, or 15 minutes for transport category aircraft, to meet the requirements of the specifications and Federal Air Regulations. It must be operable under the conditions encountered during all operations of the aircraft.

Design requirements are that fuel jettisoning must be stopped with a minimum of fuel for 45 minutes of cruise at maximum continuous power for reciprocating engines. Turbine powered aircraft require enough fuel for take-off and landing and 45 minutes cruising time.

The fuel jettisoning system is usually divided into two separate, independent systems, one for each wing, so that lateral stability can be maintained by jettisoning fuel from the "heavy" wing if it is necessary to do so. Normally, if an unbalanced fuel load exists, fuel will be used from the "heavy" wing by supplying fuel to engines on the opposite wing.

The system consists of lines, valves, dump chutes and chute-operating mechanisms. Each wing contains either a fixed or an extendable dump chute depending upon system design. In either case the fuel must discharge clear of the airplane.

TROUBLESHOOTING THE FUEL SYSTEM

In order to become proficient at the art of troubleshooting, one must be familiar with the complete system. To do this, one can become familiar with the schematics of various portions of the system, the nomenclature of the units, and their particular function within the system by studying aircraft and engine maintenance manuals.

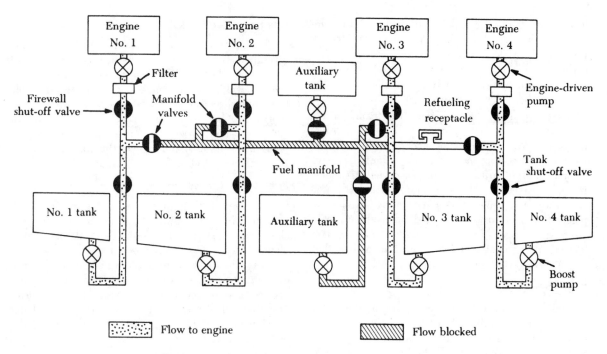

Flow to engine   Flow blocked

FIGURE 4–25. A typical manifold crossfeed system.

Location of Leaks and Defects

The location of leaks and defects within the internal portions of the fuel system is usually a matter of observation of the pressure gage and operation of the selector valves to determine where the trouble lies. Troubleshooting of the internal fuel system can be aided by visualizing the path of flow of the fuel from the fuel tank to the fuel-metering device, noting the location of the pump(s), selector valves, emergency shutoff valves, etc.

The location of leaks or defects in the external portions of the fuel system involves very little time in comparison to locating leaks within the internal system. Usually, fuel leaks are evidenced by stains or wet spots, if they are newly developed, and by the presence of fuel odor. The plumbing, clamps, gaskets, supports, etc., are to be examined carefully at each inspection period. Any defect or leak in the internal or external fuel system is a potential hazard.

Replacement of Gaskets, Seals, and Packings

In order to prevent leakage of fuel, it is of utmost importance that all gaskets, seals, and packings be properly installed. Listed below are some of the general precautions that should always be observed.

When replacing units of the fuel system, it is necessary to check each part for cleanliness, ensure that all of the old gasket material is removed, and ensure that none of the old seal remains in the groove seat. Always replace old gaskets and seals with new ones, check the new gaskets and seals for cleanliness and integrity, and ensure that it is the right part for the job. Mating surfaces should be perfectly flat so that the gasket can do the job for which it is designed. Screws, nuts, and bolts that hold units together should be evenly tightened or torqued to prevent leakage past the gasket or seal.

FUEL TANK REPAIRS

There are three basic type fuel cells used in aircraft. Welded sheet metal integral and fuel cell. No fuel system is airworthy if it will not contain fuel. Inspection of the fuel tank bays or aircraft structure for evidence of fuel leaks is a very important part of the preflight inspection.

Welded Steel Tanks

Welded tanks are most common in the smaller single and twin engine aircraft. If the access plates to the fuel tank compartment are discolored the tank should be inspected for leaks. When leaks are found, the tank must be drained and inerted. Fuel will be drained in accordance with

95

local instructions and the manufacturer's recommendations. Inerting the tank may be accomplished by slowly discharging a CO_2 fire extinguisher (5 lb. minimum size) into the tank. Dry nitrogen may be used if it is available. If the tank is to be welded, removal is necessary.

Before welding, the tank must be steamed for a minimum of 8 hours. This is to remove all traces of fuel. Air pressure not over ½ psi may be used to detect the leaking area. Liquid soap or bubble solution brushed in the suspected area may identify the leak. Aluminum tanks are fabricated from weldable alloys. After riveting patches in place, the rivets may be welded to insure no leaks from that area. Pressure checks should be performed after repairs are completed to assure that all leaks were corrected.

Fuel Cells

Fuel cell leaks will usually appear on the lower skin of the aircraft. A fuel stain in any area should be investigated immediately. Fuel cells suspected of leaking should be drained, removed from the aircraft and pressure checked. When performing a pressure check, ¼ to ½ psi air pressure is adequate. All fuel cell maintenance must be accomplished in accordance with the manufacturer's specifications.

Integral Fuel Tanks

The integral tank is a nonremovable part of the aircraft. Because of the nature of an integral tank, some leaks allow fuel to escape directly to the atmosphere. This makes it completely feasible to disregard certain minute leaks that do not represent a fire hazard or too great a loss of fuel. In order to standardize the procedures for integral tank fuel storage maintenance, the various rates of fuel leakage are classified.

Fuel Leak Classification

The size of the surface area that a fuel leak moistens in a 30-minute period is used as the classification standard. Wipe the leak area completely dry with clean cotton cloths. Compressed air may also be used to dry the leak areas that are difficult to wipe. Wear goggles when using compressed air to dry the leak area. Dust the leak area with dyed red talcum powder. The talcum powder turns red as the fuel wets it, making the wet area easier to see.

At the end of 30 minutes, each leak is classified into one of four classes of leaks: slow seep, seep, heavy seep, or running leak. The four classes of leaks are shown in figure 4–26. *A slow seep* is a leak in which the fuel wets an area around the

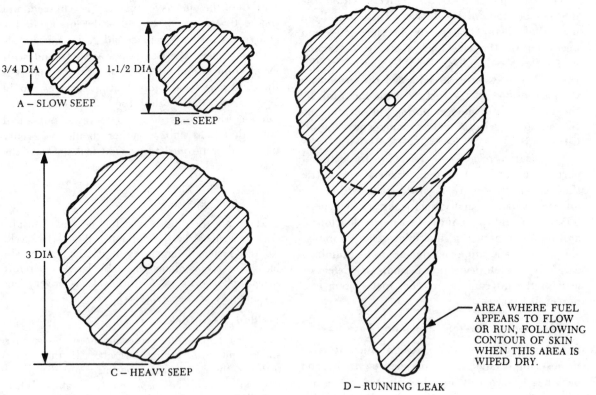

FIGURE 4–26. Fuel leak classification.

96

leak source not over ¾ of an inch in diameter. *A seep* is a leak that wets an area from ¾ inches to 1½ inches in diameter. *A heavy seep* is a fuel leak that wets an area around the leak source from 1½ inches to 3 inches in diameter. In none of these three leak classifications does the fuel run, flow, drip, or resemble any of these conditions at the end of the 30-minute time period.

The last classification, a *running leak*, is the most severe and the most dangerous. It may drip from the aircraft surface, it may run down vertical surfaces, or it may even run down your finger when you touch the wet area. The aircraft is unsafe for flight and must be grounded for repair. When possible, the fuel from the leaking tank should be removed after you mark the leak location. If it is impossible to defuel the tank immediately, the aircraft should be isolated in an approved area. Place appropriate warning signs around the aircraft until qualified personnel can defuel the leaking tank.

Grounding of the aircraft for slow seeps, seeps, and heavy seeps, is determined by the applicable aircraft handbook. This determination may depend on the location of the fuel leak. For example, can the leakage progress to a potential fire source? The number of fuel leaks in a given area is also a contributing factor. There is no rule of thumb for determining if the aircraft is to be grounded. Running leaks ground the aircraft regardless of location.

You may only have to make appropriate entries on the aircraft forms and periodically observe the progress of the fuel leak if it is determined that the aircraft is airworthy and no repair is required. When repair is required, you must find the cause of the fuel leak and make an *effective* repair.

Leak Repairs

Repair of leaks in integral fuel tanks must be accomplished in accordance with the aircraft manufacturer's specifications. No attempt will be made in this handbook to discuss integral tank repairs further.

Fire Safety

The first and most difficult step in the achievement of fire safety is to correct the misconceptions about the "safety" of turbine fuels. At the time these fuels were first introduced many people said, "fire problems in aircraft are over, turbine fuel is completely safe." This is obviously nonsense but it has been persistent nonsense.

Flight line personnel have agreed that aviation gasoline will burn, and therefore they have exercised reasonable care and caution in handling it. However, it has been difficult to convince them that under some circumstances turbine fuels are just as dangerous from the fire standpoint.

The characteristics of turbine fuel do vary from those of gasoline. Kerosene, for example, has a slow flame propagation and burning rate, which makes it less hazardous in the event of spill or a ground accident. However, it does ignite readily when vaporized or when misted, as when sprayed through a small leak in a service hose.

One disadvantage of the low volatility fuels is that they will not evaporate readily and completely if spilled on the ramp, so special treatment of the spill area is required. Small spills of kerosene should be removed with a commercial absorbent cleaning agent. On large spills it is better to apply an approved emulsifier and then flush away the resulting mixture with large volumes of water. This will prevent or appreciably lessen any oily residue.

Just as with gasoline, an electrostatic charge may be built up in pumping turbine fuel through a service hose. In fact, the amount of the charge is higher in kerosene because of the higher specific gravity and wider boiling range. Also, the amount of the charge increases with high linear rate of fuel flow, such as is required for servicing turbine powered aircraft.

In consequence, all of the fire safety precautions observed in the handling of gasoline must be followed with equal care in the handling of turbine fuels. These precautions are well known and have been detailed by the National Fire Protection Association in its bulletin No. 407. It is recommended that this bulletin be made required reading for all personnel handling turbine fuel.

CHAPTER 5

FLUID LINES AND FITTINGS

GENERAL

The term "aircraft plumbing" refers not only to the hose, tubing, fittings, and connectors used in the aircraft, but also to the processes of forming and installing them.

Occasionally it may be necessary to repair or replace damaged aircraft plumbing lines. Very often the repair can be made simply by replacing the tubing. However, if replacements are not available, the needed parts may have to be fabricated. Replacement tubing should be of the same size and material as the original line. All tubing is pressure tested prior to initial installation, and is designed to withstand several times the normal operating pressure to which it will be subjected. If a tube bursts or cracks, it is generally the result of excessive vibration, improper installation, or damage caused by collision with an object. All tubing failures should be carefully studied and the cause of the failure determined.

PLUMBING LINES

Aircraft plumbing lines usually are made of metal tubing and fittings or of flexible hose. Metal tubing is widely used in aircraft for fuel, oil, coolant, oxygen, instrument, and hydraulic lines. Flexible hose is generally used with moving parts or where the hose is subject to considerable vibration.

Generally, aluminum alloy or corrosion-resistant steel tubing have replaced copper tubing. The high fatigue factor of copper tubing is the chief reason for its replacement. It becomes hard and brittle from vibration and finally breaks, however it may be restored to its soft annealed state by heating it red hot and quenching it in cold water. Cooling in air will result in a degree of softness but not equal to that obtained with the cold water quench. This annealing process must be accomplished if copper tubing is removed for any reason. Inspection of copper tubing for cracks, hardness, brittleness and general condition should be accomplished at regular intervals to preclude failure. The workability, resistance to corrosion, and lightweight of aluminum alloy are major factors in its adoption for aircraft plumbing.

In some special high-pressure (3,000 p.s.i.) hydraulic installations, corrosion-resistant steel tubing, either annealed or 1/4-hard, is used. Corrosion-resistant steel tubing does not have to be annealed for flaring or forming; in fact, the flared section is somewhat strengthened by the cold working and strain hardening during the flaring process. Its higher tensile strength permits the use of tubing with thinner walls; consequently the final installation weight is not much greater than that of the thicker-wall aluminum alloy tubing.

IDENTIFICATION OF MATERIALS

Before making repairs to any aircraft plumbing, it is important to make accurate identification of plumbing materials. Aluminum alloy or steel tubing can be identified readily by sight where it is used as the basic plumbing material. However, it is difficult to determine whether a material is carbon steel or stainless steel, or whether it is 1100, 3003, 5052–0, or 2024–T aluminum alloy.

It may be necessary to test samples of the material for hardness by filing or scratching with a scriber. The magnet test is the simplest method for distinguishing between the annealed austenitic and the ferritic stainless steels. The austenitic types are nonmagnetic unless heavily cold worked, whereas the straight chromium carbon and low alloy steels are strongly magnetic. Figure 5–1 gives the methods for identifying five common

Material	Magnet test	Nitric acid test
Carbon steel__	Strongly magnetic.	Slow chemical action, brown.
18–8_____	Nonmagnetic.	No action.
Pure nickel____	Strongly magnetic.	Slow action, pale green.
Monel_____	Slightly magnetic.	Rapid action, greenish blue.
Nickel steel___	Nonmagnetic.	Rapid action, greenish blue.

FIGURE 5–1. Identification of metallic materials.

metallic materials by using the magnet and concentrated nitric acid tests.

By comparing code markings of the replacement tubing with the original markings on the tubing being replaced, it is possible to identify definitely the material used in the original installation.

The alloy designation is stamped on the surface of large aluminum alloy tubing. On small aluminum alloy tubing, the designation may be stamped on the surface, but more often it is shown by a color code. Bands of the color code, not more than 4 inches in width, are painted at the two ends and approximately midway between the ends of some tubing. When the band consists of two colors, one-half the width is used for each color.

Painted color codes used to identify aluminum alloy tubing are:

Aluminum alloy number	Color of band
1100	White
3003	Green
2014	Gray
2024	Red
5052	Purple
6053	Black
6061	Blue and Yellow
7075	Brown and Yellow

Aluminum alloy tubing, 1100 (½-hard) or 3003 (½-hard), is used for general purpose lines of low or negligible fluid pressures, such as instrument lines and ventilating conduits. The 2024–T and 5052–0 aluminum alloy materials are used in general purpose systems of low and medium pressures, such as hydraulic and pneumatic 1,000 to 1,500 p.s.i. systems and fuel and oil lines. Occasionally, these materials are used in high-pressure (3,000 p.s.i.) systems.

Tubing made from 2024–T and 5052–0 materials will withstand a fairly high pressure before bursting. These materials are easily flared and are soft enough to be formed with handtools. They must be handled with care to prevent scratches, dents, and nicks.

Corrosion-resistant steel tubing, either annealed or ¼–hard, is used extensively in high-pressure hydraulic systems for the operation of landing gear, flaps, brakes, and the like. External brake lines should always be made of corrosion-resistant steel to minimize damage from rocks thrown by the tires during takeoff and landing, and from careless ground handling. Although identification markings for steel tubing differ, each usually includes the manufacturer's name or trademark, the SAE number, and the physical condition of the metal.

Metal tubing is sized by outside diameter, which is measured fractionally in sixteenths of an inch. Thus Number 6 tubing is 6/16 (or 3/8 inch) and Number 8 tubing is 8/16 (or ½ inch), etc.

In addition to other classification or means of identification, tubing is manufactured in various wall thicknesses. Thus, it is important when installing tubing to know not only the material and outside diameter, but also the thickness of the wall.

FLEXIBLE HOSE

Flexible hose is used in aircraft plumbing to connect moving parts with stationary parts in locations subject to vibration or where a great amount of flexibility is needed. It can also serve as a connector in metal tubing systems.

Synthetics

Synthetic materials most commonly used in the manufacture of flexible hose are: Buna-N, Neoprene, Butyl and Teflon (trademark of DuPont Corp.). *Buna-N* is a synthetic rubber compound which has excellent resistance to petroleum products. Do not confuse with Buna-S. Do not use for phosphate ester base hydraulic fluid (Skyrol®). *Neoprene* is a synthetic rubber compound which has an acetylene base. Its resistance to petroleum products is not as good as Buna-N but has better abrasive resistance. Do not use for phosphate ester base hydraulic fluid (Skydrol®). *Butyl* is a synthetic rubber compound made from petroleum raw materials. It is an excellent material to use with phosphate ester based hydraulic fluid (Skydrol®). Do not use with petroleum products. *Teflon* is the DuPont trade name for tetrafluoroethylene resin. It has a broad operating temperature range ($-65°$ F. to $+450°$ F.). It is compatible with nearly every substance or agent used. It offers little resistance to flow; sticky viscous materials will not adhere to it. It has less volumetric expansion than rubber and the shelf and service life is practically limitless.

Rubber Hose

Flexible rubber hose consists of a seamless synthetic rubber inner tube covered with layers of cotton braid and wire braid, and an outer layer of rubber-impregnated cotton braid. This type of hose is suitable for use in fuel, oil, coolant, and hydraulic systems. The types of hose are normally classified by the amount of pressure they are designed to withstand under normal operating conditions.

1. Low pressure, any pressure below 250 p.s.i. Fabric braid reinforcement.

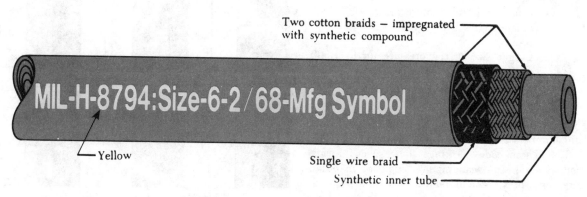

Two cotton braids — impregnated with synthetic compound

MIL-H-8794:Size-6-2/68-Mfg Symbol

Yellow

Single wire braid

Synthetic inner tube

A. Flame- and aromatic-resistant hose

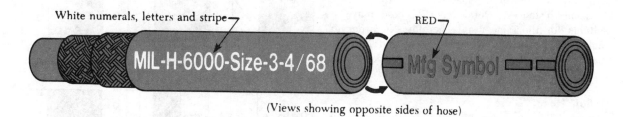

White numerals, letters and stripe

MIL-H-6000-Size-3-4/68

RED

Mfg Symbol

(Views showing opposite sides of hose)

B. Nonself-sealing, Aromatic and Heat-resistant hose

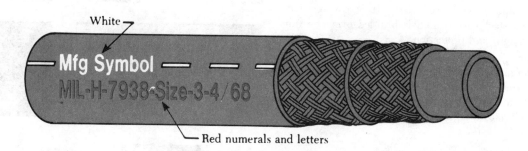

White

Mfg Symbol

MIL-H-7938-Size-3-4/68

Red numerals and letters

C. Flame-, Aromatic-, and Oil-resistant hose

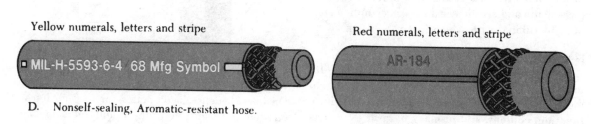

Yellow numerals, letters and stripe

MIL-H-5593-6-4 68 Mfg Symbol

D. Nonself-sealing, Aromatic-resistant hose.

Red numerals, letters and stripe

AR-184

E. Self-sealing, Aromatic-resistant hose

FIGURE 5–2. Hose identification markings.

2. Medium pressure, pressures up to 3,000 p.s.i.

    One wire braid reinforcement.

    Smaller sizes carry pressure up to 3,000 p.s.i.

    Larger sizes carry pressure up to 1,500 p.s.i.

3. High pressure (all sizes up to 3,000 p.s.i. operating pressures).

Identification markings consisting of lines, letters, and numbers are printed on the hose. (See figure 5–2.) These code markings show such information as hose size, manufacturer, date of manufacture, and pressure and temperature limits. Code markings assist in replacing a hose with one of the same specification or a recommended substitute. Hose suitable for use with phosphate ester base hydraulic fluid will be marked "Skydrol ᴿ use". In some instances several types of hose may be suitable for the same use. Therefore, in order to make the correct hose selection, always refer to the maintenance or parts manual for the particular airplane.

Teflon Hose

Teflon hose is a flexible hose designed to meet the requirements of higher operating temperatures and pressures in present aircraft systems. It can generally be used in the same manner as rubber hose. Teflon hose is processed and extruded into tube shape to a desired size. It is covered with stainless steel wire, which is braided over the tube for strength and protection.

Teflon hose is unaffected by any known fuel, petroleum, or synthetic base oils, alcohol, coolants, or solvents commonly used in aircraft. Although it is highly resistant to vibration and fatigue, the principle advantage of this hose is its operating strength.

Size Designation

The size of flexible hose is determined by its inside diameter. Sizes are in one-sixteenth-inch increments and are identical to corresponding sizes of rigid tubing, with which it can be used.

Identification of Fluid Lines

Fluid lines in aircraft are often identified by markers made up of color codes, words, and geometric symbols. These markers identify each line's function, content, and primary hazard, as well as the direction of fluid flow. Figure 5–3 illustrates the various color codes and symbols used to designate the type of system and its contents.

In most instances, fluid lines are marked with 1-inch tape or decals, as shown in figure 5–4 (A).

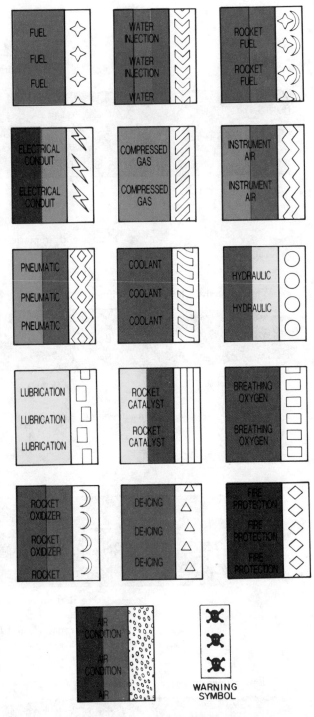

FIGURE 5–3. Identification of aircraft fluid lines. On lines 4 inches in diameter (or larger), lines in oily environment, hot lines, and on some cold lines, steel tags may be used in place of tape or decals, as shown in figure 5–4 (B). Paint is used on lines in engine compartments, where there is the possibility of tapes, decals, or tags being drawn into the engine induction system.

102

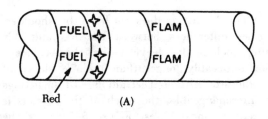

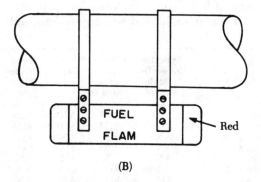

FIGURE 5-4. Fluid line identification using:
(A) tape and decals and (B) metal tags.

In addition to the above-mentioned markings, certain lines may be further identified as to specific function within a system; for example, DRAIN, VENT, PRESSURE, or RETURN.

Lines conveying fuel may be marked FLAM; lines containing toxic materials are marked TOXIC in place of FLAM. Lines containing physically dangerous materials, such as oxygen, nitrogen, or freon, are marked PHDAN.

The aircraft and engine manufacturers are responsible for the original installation of identification markers, but the aviation mechanic is responsible for their replacement when it becomes necessary.

Generally, tapes and decals are placed on both ends of a line and at least once in each compartment through which the line runs. In addition, identification markers are placed immediately adjacent to each valve, regulator, filter, or other accessory within a line. Where paint or tags are used, location requirements are the same as for tapes and decals.

PLUMBING CONNECTORS

Plumbing connectors, or fittings, attach one piece of tubing to another or to system units. There are four types: (1) Flared fitting, (2) flareless fitting, (3) bead and clamp, and (4) swaged. The amount of pressure that the system carries is usually the deciding factor in selecting a connector. The beaded type of joint, which requires a bead and a section of hose and hose clamps, is

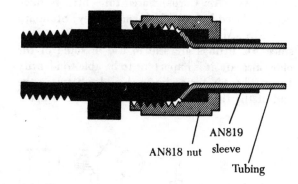

FIGURE 5-5. Flared-tube fitting.

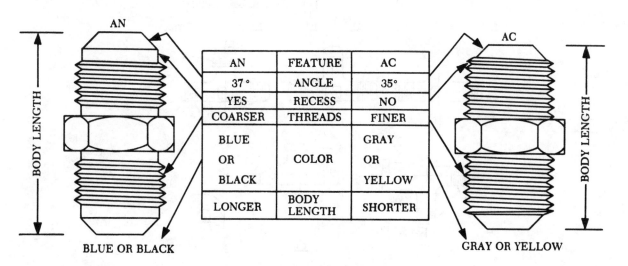

AN	FEATURE	AC
37°	ANGLE	35°
YES	RECESS	NO
COARSER	THREADS	FINER
BLUE OR BLACK	COLOR	GRAY OR YELLOW
LONGER	BODY LENGTH	SHORTER

FIGURE 5-6. AN and AC fitting differences.

used only in low- or medium-pressure systems, such as vacuum and coolant systems. The flared, flareless, and swaged types may be used as connectors in all systems, regardless of the pressure.

Flared-Tube Fittings

A flared-tube fitting consists of a sleeve and a nut, as shown in figure 5–5. The nut fits over the sleeve and, when tightened, draws the sleeve and tubing flare tightly against a male fitting to form a seal. Tubing used with this type of fitting must be flared before installation.

The male fitting has a cone-shaped surface with the same angle as the inside of the flare. The sleeve supports the tube so that vibration does not concentrate at the edge of the flare, and distributes the shearing action over a wider area for added strength. Tube flaring and the installation of flared-tube fittings are discussed in detail later in this chapter.

The AC (Air Corps) flared-tube fittings have been replaced by the AN (Army/Navy) Standard and MS (Military Standard) fittings. However, since AC fittings are still in use in some of the older aircraft, it is important to be able to identify them. The AN fitting has a shoulder between the end of the threads and the flare cone. (See figure 5–6.) The AC fitting does not have this shoulder.

Other differences between the AC and AN fittings include the sleeve design, the AC sleeve being noticeably longer than the AN sleeve of the same size. Although certain flared-tube fittings are interchangeable, the pitch of the threads is different in most cases. Figure 5–7 shows the AN and AC811 fittings that can be safely interchanged. Combinations of end connections, nuts,

Tube Sizes OD	Type End Connection (Male Thread)	Type Nut (Female Thread)	Type Sleeve	Type Tube Flare
All Sizes[1]	AN[1]	AN[1]	AN[1]	AN[1]
All Sizes[2]	811[2]	811[2]	811[2]	811[2]
All Sizes	AN	AN	AN	811
All Sizes	AN	AN	811	811
All Sizes	AN	AN	811	AN
All Sizes	811	811	811	AN
All Sizes	811	811	AN	AN
All Sizes	811	811	AN	811
1/8, 3/16, 1/4, 5/16, 1 3/4, 2	AN	811	AN	811
1/8, 3/16, 1/4, 5/16, 1 3/4, 2	AN	811	AN	AN
1/8, 3/16, 1/4, 5/16, 1 3/4, 2	AN	811	811	AN
1/8, 3/16, 1/4, 5/16, 1 3/4, 2	AN	811	811	AN

[1] This is the normal assembly of AN fittings.
[2] This is the normal assembly of AC811 fittings.

FIGURE 5–7a. Interchangeability of AN and AC811 fittings.

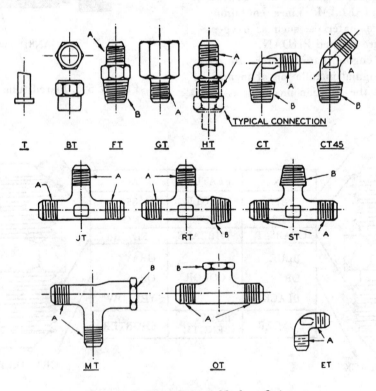

FIGURE 5–7 b. AC811 solderless fittings.

Material:

Aluminum alloy..(code D)
Steel..(code, absence of letter)
Brass..(code B)
Aluminum bronze..(code Z—for AN819 sleeve)

Size:

The dash number following the AN number indicates the size of the tubing (or hose) for which the fitting is made, in 16ths of an inch. This size measures the O. D. of tubing and the I. D. of hose. Fittings having pipe threads are coded by a dash number, indicating the pipe size in 8ths of an inch. The material code letter, as noted above, follows the dash number.

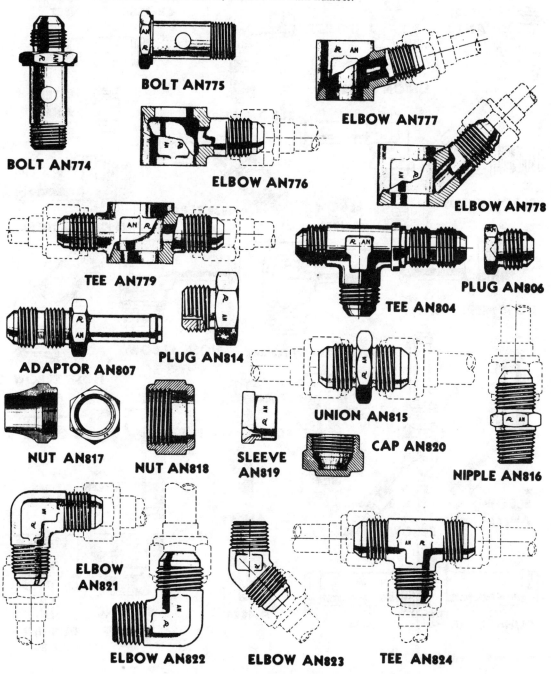

FIGURE 5–8. AN plumbing fittings.

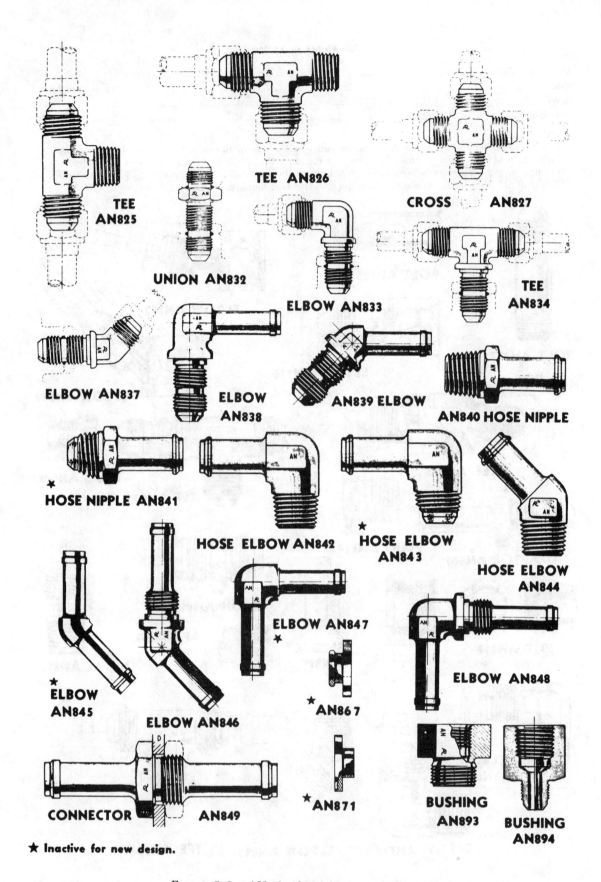

TEE AN826

CROSS AN827

TEE AN825

UNION AN832

ELBOW AN833

TEE AN834

ELBOW AN837

ELBOW AN838

AN839 ELBOW

AN840 HOSE NIPPLE

★ HOSE NIPPLE AN841

HOSE ELBOW AN842

★ HOSE ELBOW AN843

HOSE ELBOW AN844

★ ELBOW AN845

ELBOW AN846

ELBOW AN847

★ AN867

ELBOW AN848

★ AN871

CONNECTOR AN849

BUSHING AN893

BUSHING AN894

★ Inactive for new design.

FIGURE 5–8.   AN plumbing fittings.—Continued

106

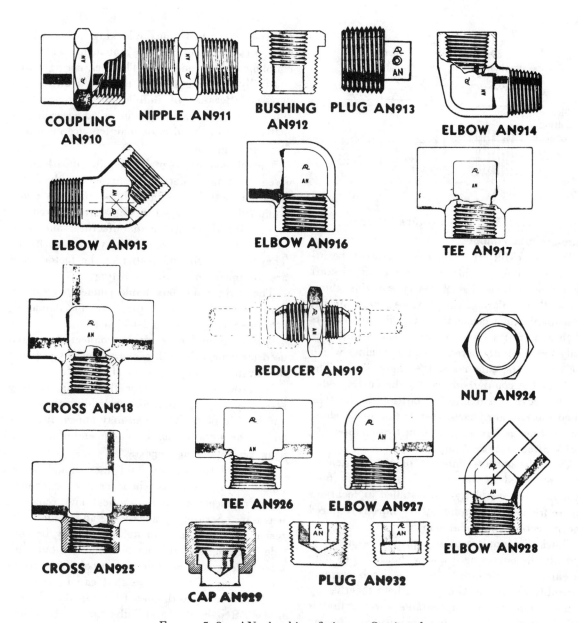

COUPLING AN910   NIPPLE AN911   BUSHING AN912   PLUG AN913   ELBOW AN914

ELBOW AN915   ELBOW AN916   TEE AN917

CROSS AN918   REDUCER AN919   NUT AN924

CROSS AN925   TEE AN926   ELBOW AN927   ELBOW AN928

CAP AN929   PLUG AN932

FIGURE 5–8.   AN plumbing fittings.—Continued

sleeves, and tube flares are allowed to make up a complete fitting assembly. The use of dissimilar metals should be avoided since their contact will cause corrosion.

When combining AC and AN end connections, nuts, sleeves, or tube flares, if the nut will not move more than two threads by hand, stop and investigate for possible trouble.

The AN standard fitting is the most commonly used flared-tubing assembly for attaching the tubing to the various fittings required in aircraft plumbing systems. The AN standard fittings include the AN818 nut and AN819 sleeve. (See figure 5–8.) The AN819 sleeve is used with the AN818 coupling nut. All these fittings have

straight threads, but they have different pitch for the various types.

Flared-tube fittings are made of aluminum alloy, steel, or copper base alloys. For identification purposes, all AN steel fittings are colored black, and all AN aluminum alloy fittings are colored blue. The AN 819 aluminum bronze sleeves are cadmium plated and are not colored. The size of these fittings is given in dash numbers, which equal the nominal tube outside diameter (O.D.) in sixteenths of an inch.

Threaded flared-tube fittings have two types of ends, referred to as male and female. The male end of a fitting is externally threaded, whereas the female end of a fitting is internally threaded.

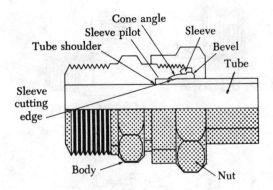

FIGURE 5–9. Flareless-tube fitting.

Flareless-tube Fittings

The MS (Military Standard) flareless-tube fittings are finding wide application in aircraft plumbing systems. Using this type fitting eliminates all tube flaring, yet provides a safe, strong, dependable tube connection. The fitting consists of three parts: a body, a sleeve, and a nut. The body has a counterbored shoulder, against which the end of the tube rests. (See figure 5–9.) The angle of the counterbore causes the cutting edge of the sleeve to cut into the outside of the tube when the two are joined. Installation of flareless-tube fittings is discussed later in this chapter.

Quick-disconnect Couplings

Quick-disconnect couplings of the self-sealing type are used at various points in many fluid systems. The couplings are installed at locations where frequent uncoupling of the lines is required for inspection and maintenance.

Quick-disconnect couplings provide a means of quickly disconnecting a line without loss of fluid or entrance of air into the system. Each coupling assembly consists of two halves, held together by a union nut. Each half contains a valve that is held open when the coupling is connected, allowing fluid to flow through the coupling in either direction. When the coupling is disconnected, a spring in each half closes the valve, preventing the loss of fluid and entrance of air.

The union nut has a quick-lead thread which permits connecting or disconnecting the coupling by turning the nut. The amount the nut must be turned varies with different style couplings. One style requires a quarter turn of the union nut to lock or unlock the coupling while another style requires a full turn.

Some couplings require wrench tightening; others are connected and disconnected by hand. The design of some couplings is such that they must be safetied with safety wire. Others do not require lock wiring, the positive locking being assured by the teeth on the locking spring, which engage ratchet teeth on the union nut when the coupling is fully engaged. The lock spring automatically disengages when the union nut is unscrewed. Because of individual differences, all quick disconnects should be installed according to instructions in the aircraft maintenance manual.

Flexible Connectors

Flexible connectors may be equipped with either swaged fittings or detachable fittings, or they may be used with beads and hose clamps. Those equipped with swaged fittings are ordered by correct length from the manufacturer and ordinarily cannot be assembled by the mechanic. They are swaged and tested at the factory and are equipped with standard fittings.

The fittings on detachable connectors can be detached and reused if they are not damaged; otherwise new fittings must be used.

The bead and hose clamp connector is often used for connecting oil, coolant, and low-pressure fuel system tubing. The bead, a slightly raised ridge around the tubing or the fitting, gives a good gripping edge that aids in holding the clamp and hose in place. The bead may appear near the end of the metal tubing or on one end of a fitting.

TUBE FORMING PROCESSES

Damaged tubing and fluid lines should be replaced with new parts whenever possible. Sometimes replacement is impractical and repair is necessary. Scratches, abrasions, and minor corrosion on the outside of fluid lines may be considered negligible and can be smoothed out with a burnishing tool or aluminum wool. Limitations on the amount of damage that can be repaired in this manner are discussed later in this chapter under "Repair of Metal Tube Lines." If a fluid line assembly is to be replaced, the fittings can often be salvaged; then the repair will involve only tube forming and replacement.

Tube forming consists of four processes: (1) Cutting, (2) bending, (3) flaring, and (4) beading. If the tubing is small and of soft material, the assembly can be formed by hand bending during installation. If the tubing is ¼-inch diameter, or larger, hand bending without the aid of tools is impractical.

Tube Cutting

When cutting tubing, it is important to produce a square end, free of burrs. Tubing may be cut with a tube cutter or a hacksaw. The cutter can be used with any soft metal tubing, such as copper, aluminum, or aluminum alloy. Correct use of the tube cutter is shown in figure 5–10.

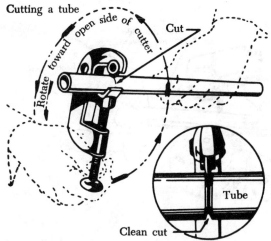

Cutting a tube
Rotate toward open side of cutter
Cut
Tube
Clean cut

FIGURE 5–10. Tube cutting.

A new piece of tubing should be cut approximately 10 percent longer than the tube to be replaced to provide for minor variations in bending. Place the tubing in the cutting tool, with the cutting wheel at the point where the cut is to be made. Rotate the cutter around the tubing, applying a light pressure to the cutting wheel by intermittently twisting the thumbscrew. Too much pressure on the cutting wheel at one time could deform the tubing or cause excessive burring. After cutting the tubing, carefully remove any burrs from inside and outside the tube. Use a knife or the burring edge attached to the tube cutter.

When performing the deburring operation use extreme care that the wall thickness of the end of the tubing is not reduced or fractured. Very slight damage of this type can lead to fractured flares or defective flares which will not seal properly. A fine tooth file can be used to file the end square and smooth.

If a tube cutter is not available, or if tubing of hard material is to be cut, use a fine-tooth hacksaw, preferably one having 32 teeth per inch. The use of a saw will decrease the amount of work hardening of the tubing during the cutting operation. After sawing, file the end of the tube square and smooth, removing all burrs.

An easy way to hold small-diameter tubing, when cutting it, is to place the tube in a combination flaring tool and clamp the tool in a vise. Make the cut about one-half inch from the flaring tool. This procedure keeps sawing vibrations to a minimum and prevents damage to the tubing if it is accidentally hit with the hacksaw frame or file handle while cutting. Be sure all filings and cuttings are removed from the tube.

Tube Bending

The objective in tube bending is to obtain a smooth bend without flattening the tube. Tubing under one-fourth inch in diameter usually can be bent without the use of a bending tool. For larger sizes, a hand tube bender similar to that shown in figure 5–11 is usually used.

To bend tubing with the hand tube bender, insert the tubing by raising the slide bar handle as far as it will go. Adjust the handle so that the full length of the groove in the slide bar is in contact with the tubing. The zero mark on the radius block and the mark on the slide bar must align. Make the bend by rotating the handle until the desired angle of bend is obtained, as indicated on the radius block.

Bend the tubing carefully to avoid excessive flattening, kinking, or wrinkling. A small amount of flattening in bends is acceptable, but the small diameter of the flattened portion must not be less than 75 percent of the original outside diameter. Tubing with flattened, wrinkled, or irregular bends should not be installed. Wrinkled bends usually result from trying to bend thin-wall tubing without using a tube bender. Examples of correct and incorrect tubing bends are shown in figure 5–12.

Tube bending machines for all types of tubing are generally used in repair stations and large maintenance shops. With such equipment, proper bends can be made on large diameter tubing and on tubing made from hard material. The production tube bender is an example of this type of machine.

The ordinary production tube bender will accommodate tubing ranging from ½-inch to 1½-inch outside diameter. Benders for larger sizes are available, and the principle of their operation is similar to that of the hand tube bender. The radius blocks are so constructed that the radius of bend will vary with the tubing diameter. The radius of bend is usually stamped on the block.

When hand or production tube benders are not available or are not suitable for a particular bending operation, a filler of metallic composition or of dry sand may be used to facilitate bending. When using this method, cut the tube slightly longer than is required. The extra length is for inserting a plug (which may be wooden) in each end.

After plugging one end, fill and pack the tube with fine, dry sand and plug tightly. Both plugs must be tight so they will not be forced out when the bend is made. The tube can also be closed by flattening the ends or by soldering metal disks in them. After the ends are closed, bend the tubing

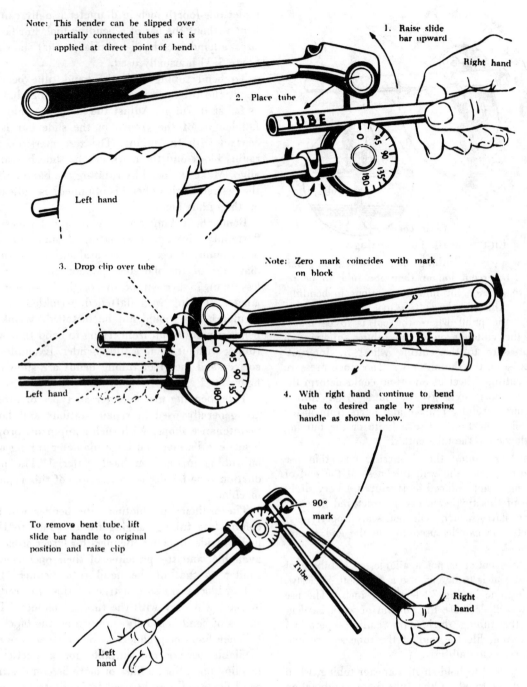

Note: This bender can be slipped over partially connected tubes as it is applied at direct point of bend.

1. Raise slide bar upward

Right hand

2. Place tube

TUBE

0 45 90 135 180

Left hand

3. Drop clip over tube

Note: Zero mark coincides with mark on block

TUBE

0 45 90 135 180

Left hand

4. With right hand continue to bend tube to desired angle by pressing handle as shown below.

To remove bent tube, lift slide bar handle to original position and raise clip

90° mark

Tube

Right hand

Left hand

FIGURE 5–11. Tube bending.

over a forming block shaped to the specified radius.

In a modified version of the filler method, a fusible alloy is used instead of sand. In this method, the tube is filled under hot water with a fusible alloy that melts at 160° F. The alloy-filled tubing is then removed from the water, allowed to cool, and bent slowly by hand around a forming block or with a tube bender. After the bend is made, the alloy is again melted under hot water and removed from the tubing.

When using either filler method, make certain that all particles of the filler are removed so that none will be carried into the system in which the tubing is installed. Store the fusible alloy filler where it will be free from dust or dirt. It can be

110

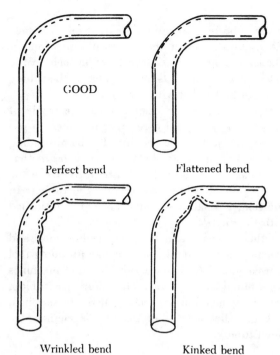

Perfect bend   Flattened bend

Wrinkled bend   Kinked bend

FIGURE 5–12. Correct and incorrect tubing bends.

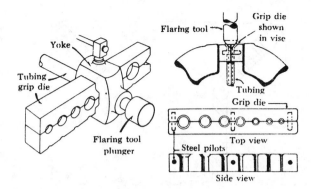

FIGURE 5–13. Hand flaring tool (single flare).

re-melted and re-used as often as desired. Never heat this filler in any other than the prescribed method, as the alloy will stick to the inside of the tubing, making them both unusable.

Tube Flaring

Two kinds of flares are generally used in aircraft plumbing systems, the single flare and the double flare. Flares are frequently subjected to extremely high pressures; therefore, the flare on the tubing must be properly shaped or the connection will leak or fail.

A flare made too small produces a weak joint, which may leak or pull apart; if made too large it interferes with the proper engagement of the screw thread on the fitting and will cause leakage. A crooked flare is the result of the tubing not being cut squarely. If a flare is not made properly, flaws cannot be corrected by applying additional torque when tightening the fitting. The flare and tubing must be free from cracks, dents, nicks, scratches, or any other defects.

The flaring tool used for aircraft tubing has male and female dies ground to produce a flare of 35° to 37°. Under no circumstances is it permissible to use an automotive type flaring tool which produces a flare of 45°.

Single Flare

A hand flaring tool similar to that shown in figure 5–13 is used for flaring tubing. The tool consists of a flaring block or grip die, a yoke, and a flaring pin. The flaring block is a hinged double bar with holes corresponding to various sizes of tubing. These holes are countersunk on one end to form the outside support against which the flare is formed. The yoke is used to center the flaring pin over the end of the tube to be flared.

To prepare a tube for flaring, cut the tube squarely and remove all burrs. Slip the fitting nut and sleeve on the tube and place the tube in the proper size hole in the flaring tool. Center the plunger or flaring pin over the end of the tube. Then project the end of the tubing slightly from the top of the flaring tool, about the thickness of a dime, and tighten the clamp bar securely to prevent slippage.

Make the flare by striking the plunger several light blows with a lightweight hammer or mallet. Turn the plunger a half turn after each blow and be sure it seats properly before removing the tube from the flaring tool. Check the flare by sliding the sleeve into position over the flare. The outside diameter of the flare should extend approximately one-sixteenth inch beyond the end of the sleeve, but should not be larger than the major outside diameter of the sleeve.

Double Flare

A double flare should be used on 5052-O and 6061-T aluminum alloy tubing for all sizes from 1/8- to 3/8-inch outside diameter. This is necessary to prevent cutting off the flare and failure of the tube assembly under operating pressures. Double flaring is not necessary on steel tubing. See figure 5–14 for an illustration of single- and double-flared tubing. The double flare is smoother and more concentric than the single flare and, therefore, seals better. It is also more resistant to the shearing effect of torque.

111

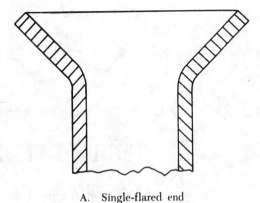

A. Single-flared end

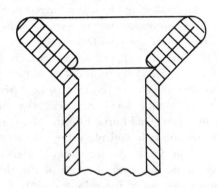

B. Double-flared end

FIGURE 5–14. Cutaway view of single- and double-flared tube ends.

To make the double flare, separate the clamp blocks of the double-flaring tool and insert and clamp the tubing with the burred end flush with the top of the clamp. Insert the starting pin into the flaring pin guide and strike the pin sharply with a hammer until the shoulder of the pin stops against the clamp blocks. Remove the starting pin and insert the finishing pin; hammer it until its shoulder rests on the clamp block.

Beading

Tubing may be beaded with a hand-beading tool, with machine-beading rolls, or with grip dies. The method to be used depends on the diameter and wall thickness of the tube and the material from which it was made.

The hand-beading tool is used with tubing having $\frac{1}{4}$- to 1-inch outside diameter. The bead is formed by using the beader frame with the proper rollers attached. The inside and outside of the tube is lubricated with light oil to reduce the friction between the rollers during beading. The sizes, marked in sixteenths of an inch on the rollers, are for the outside diameter of the tubing that can be beaded with the rollers.

Separate rollers are required for the inside of each tubing size, and care must be taken to use the correct parts when beading. The hand-beading tool works somewhat like the tube cutter in that the roller is screwed down intermittently while rotating the beading tool around the tubing. In addition, a small vise (tube holder) is furnished with the kit.

Other methods and types of beading tools and machines are available, but the hand-beading tool is used most often. As a rule, beading machines are limited to use with large-diameter tubing, over $1\frac{15}{16}$ inch, unless special rollers are supplied. The grip-die method of beading is confined to small tubing.

Flareless-Tube Assemblies

Although the use of flareless-tube fittings eliminates all tube flaring, another operation, referred to as presetting, is necessary prior to installation of a new flareless-tube assembly. Figure 5–15 (steps 1, 2, and 3) illustrates the presetting operation, which is performed as follows:

(a.) Cut the tube to the correct length, with the ends perfectly square. Deburr the inside and outside of the tube. Slip the nut, then the sleeve, over the tube (step 1).

(b.) Lubricate the threads of the fitting and nut with hydraulic fluid. Place the fitting in a vise (step 2), and hold the tubing firmly and squarely on the seat in the fitting. (Tube must bottom firmly in the fitting.) Tighten the nut until the cutting edge of the sleeve grips the tube. This point is determined by slowly turning the tube back and forth while tightening the nut. When the tube no longer turns, the nut is ready for final tightening.

(c.) Final tightening depends upon the tubing. For aluminum alloy tubing up to and including $\frac{1}{2}$-inch outside diameter, tighten the nut from one to one and one-sixth turns. For steel tubing and aluminum alloy tubing over $\frac{1}{2}$-inch outside diameter, tighten from one and one-sixth to one and one-half turns.

After presetting the sleeve, disconnect the tubing from the fitting and check the following points

112

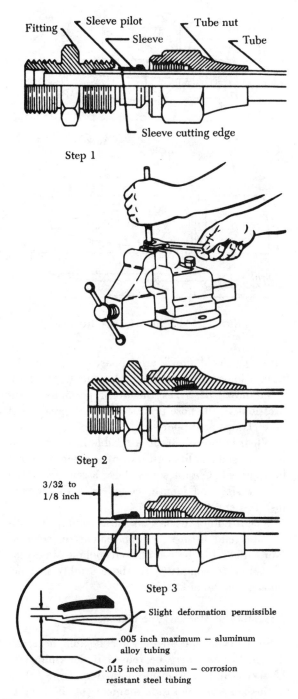

Step 1

Step 2

3/32 to
1/8 inch

Step 3

Slight deformation permissible

.005 inch maximum – aluminum
alloy tubing

.015 inch maximum – corrosion
resistant steel tubing

Fitting
Sleeve pilot
Sleeve
Tube nut
Tube
Sleeve cutting edge

FIGURE 5–15. Presetting flareless-tube assembly.

(illustrated in step 3):

(a.) The tube should extend $\frac{3}{32}$ to $\frac{1}{8}$ inch beyond the sleeve pilot; otherwise blowoff may occur.

(b.) The sleeve pilot should contact the tube or have a maximum clearance of 0.005 inch

for aluminum alloy tubing or 0.015 inch for steel tubing.

(c.) A slight collapse of the tube at the sleeve cut is permissible. No movement of the sleeve pilot, except rotation, is permissible.

REPAIR OF METAL TUBE LINES

Scratches or nicks no deeper than 10 percent of the wall thickness in aluminum alloy tubing may be repaired, if they are not in the heel of a bend. Replace lines with severe die marks, seams, or splits in the tube. Any crack or deformity in a flare is also unacceptable and is cause for rejection. A dent of less than 20 percent of the tube diameter is not objectionable, unless it is in the heel of a bend. Dents can be removed by drawing a bullet of proper size through the tube by means of a length of cable.

A severely damaged line should be replaced. However, the line can be repaired by cutting out the damaged section and inserting a tube section of the same size and material. Flare both ends of the undamaged and replacement tube sections and make the connection by using standard unions, sleeves, and tube nuts. If the damaged portion is short enough, omit the insert tube and repair by using one union and two sets of connecting fittings.

When repairing a damaged line, be very careful to remove all chips and burrs. Any open line that is to be left unattended for some time should be sealed, using metal, wood, rubber, or plastic plugs or caps.

When repairing a low-pressure line using a flexible fluid connection assembly, position the hose clamps carefully in order to prevent overhang of the clamp bands or chafing of the tightening screws on adjacent parts. If chafing can occur, the hose clamps should be repositioned on the hose. Figure 5–16 illustrates the design of a flexible fluid connection assembly and gives the maximum allowable angular and dimensional offset.

Layout of Lines

Remove the damaged or worn assembly, taking care not to further damage or distort it, and use it as a forming template for the new part. If the old length of tubing cannot be used as a pattern, make a wire template, bending the pattern by hand as required for the new assembly. Then bend the tubing to match the wire pattern.

Never select a path that does not require bends

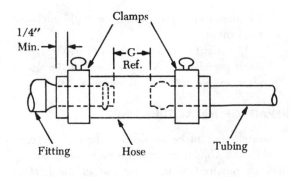

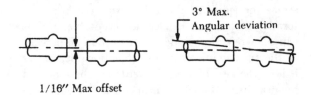

Minimum gap 'G' shall be 1/2'' or Tube OD/4, whichever is greater.

Maximum gap "G" is not limited except on suction lines using other than self-sealing hose. On such suction lines, maximum G shall be 1-1/2 inch or one tube diameter, whichever is greater.

FIGURE 5–16. Flexible fluid connection assembly.

in the tubing. A tube cannot be cut or flared accurately enough so that it can be installed without bending and still be free from mechanical strain. Bends are also necessary to permit the tubing to expand or contract under temperature changes and to absorb vibration. If the tube is small (under one-fourth inch) and can be hand formed, casual bends may be made to allow for this. If the tube must be machine formed, definite bends must be made to avoid a straight assembly.

Start all bends a reasonable distance from the fittings, because the sleeves and nuts must be slipped back during the fabrication of flares and during inspections. In all cases the new tube assembly should be so formed prior to installation that it will not be necessary to pull or deflect the assembly into alignment by means of the coupling nuts.

FABRICATION AND REPLACEMENT OF FLEXIBLE HOSE

Hose and hose assemblies should be checked for deterioration at each inspection period. Leakage, separation of the cover or braid from the inner tube, cracks, hardening, lack of flexibility, and

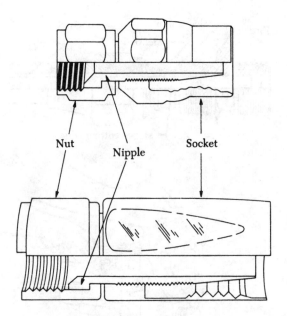

FIGURE 5–17. Sleeve-type fittings.

excessive "cold flow" are apparent signs of deterioration and reason for replacement. The term "cold flow" describes the deep, permanent impressions in the hose produced by the pressure of hose clamps or supports.

When failure occurs in a flexible hose equipped with swaged end fittings, the entire assembly must be replaced. Obtain a new hose assembly of the correct size and length, complete with factory-installed end fittings.

When failure occurs in hose equipped with reusable end fittings, a replacement line can be fabricated with the use of such tooling as may be necessary to comply with the assembly instructions of the manufacturer.

Assembly of Sleeve-Type Fittings

Sleeve-type end fittings for flexible hose are detachable and may be reused if determined to be serviceable. The inside diameter of the fitting is the same as the inside diameter of the hose to which it is attached. Common sleeve-type fittings are shown in figure 5–17.

To make a hose assembly, select the proper size hose and end fittings. Cut the hose to the correct length using a fine-tooth hacksaw. Place the socket in a vise. Screw the hose into the socket counterclockwise until the hose bottoms on the shoulder of the socket (figure 5–18); then back off one-quarter turn. Lubricate inside of hose and nipple threads liberally. Mark the hose position

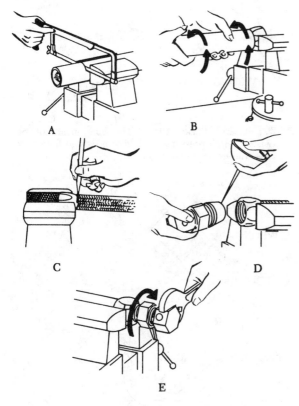

FIGURE 5–18. Assembly of MS fitting to flexible hose.

around the hose at the rear of the socket using a grease pencil or painted line. Insert the nipple into the nut and tighten the nipple and nut on the assembly tool. If an assembly tool is not available, a mating AN815 adapter may be used. Using a wrench on the assembly tool, screw the nipple into the socket and hose. A $\frac{1}{32}$- to $\frac{1}{16}$-inch clearance between the nut and sleeve is required so that the nut will swivel freely when the assembly tool is removed. After assembly, always make sure all foreign matter is removed from inside the hose by blowing out with compressed air.

Proof-test After Assembly

All flexible hose must be proof-tested after assembly by plugging or capping one end of the hose and applying pressure to the inside of the hose assembly. The proof-test medium may be a liquid or a gas. For example, hydraulic, fuel, and oil lines are generally tested using hydraulic oil or water, whereas air or instrument lines are tested with dry, oil-free air or nitrogen. When testing with a liquid, all trapped air is bled from the assembly prior to tightening the cap or plug. Hose tests, using a gas, are conducted underwater. In all cases follow the hose manufacturer's instructions for proof-test pressure and fluid to be used when testing a specific hose assembly.

Place the hose assembly in a horizontal position and observe for leakage while maintaining the test pressure. Proof-test pressures should be maintained for at least 30 seconds.

Installation of Flexible Hose Assemblies

Flexible hose must not be twisted on installation, since this reduces the life of the hose considerably and may also loosen the fittings. Twisting of the hose can be determined from the identification stripe running along its length. This stripe should not spiral around the hose.

Flexible hose should be protected from chafing by wrapping it with tape, but only where necessary.

The minimum bend radius for flexible hose varies according to size and construction of the hose and the pressure under which the hose is to operate. Bends that are too sharp will reduce the bursting pressure of flexible hose considerably below its rated value (figure 5–19).

Flexible hose should be installed so that it will be subject to a minimum of flexing during operation. Although hose must be supported at least every 24 inches, closer supports are desirable. A flexible hose must never be stretched tightly between two fittings. From 5 percent to 8 percent of its total length must be allowed for freedom of movement under pressure. When under pressure, flexible hose contracts in length and expands in diameter.

Protect all flexible hose from excessive temperatures, either by locating the lines so they will not be affected or by installing shrouds around them.

INSTALLATION OF RIGID TUBING

Before installing a line assembly in an aircraft, inspect the line carefully. Remove dents and scratches, and be sure all nuts and sleeves are snugly mated and securely fitted by proper flaring of the tubing. The line assembly should be clean and free of all foreign matter.

Connection and Torque

Never apply compound to the faces of the fitting or the flare, for it will destroy the metal-to-metal contact between the fitting and flare, a contact

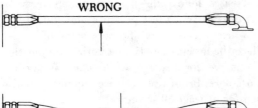

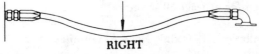

1 . . . provide slack or bend in the hose line to provide for changes in length that will occur when pressure is applied.

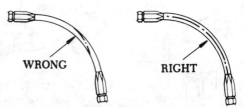

2 . . . observe linear stripe. The hose must not be twisted. High pressures applied to a twisted hose may cause failure or loosen the nut.

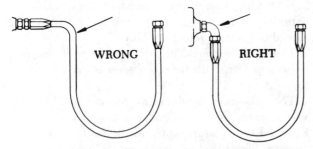

3 . . . relieve sharp bends, avoid strain or hose collapse and make cleaner installations by using Aeroquip elbows or other adapter fittings. Provide as large a bend radius as possible. Never use less than the recommended minimum bend radius specified for the hose.

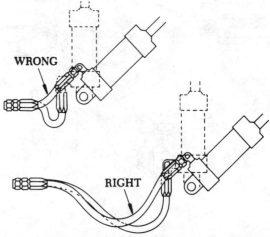

4 . . . provide additional bend radius when lines are subject to flexing and remember that the metal end fittings are not flexible. Place line support clamps so as not to restrict hose flexing.

FIGURE 5–19. Flexible hose installation.

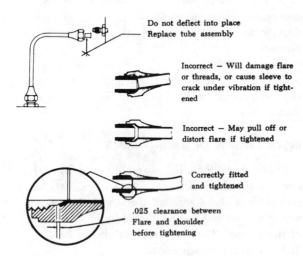

FIGURE 5–20. Correct and incorrect methods of tightening flared fittings.

which is necessary to produce the seal. Be sure that the line assembly is properly aligned before tightening the fittings. Do not pull the installation into place with torque on the nut. Correct and incorrect methods of installing flared-tube assemblies are illustrated in figure 5–20. Proper torque values are given in figure 5–21. It must be remembered that these torque values are for flared-type fittings only. Always tighten fittings to the correct torque value when installing a tube assembly. Overtightening a fitting may badly damage or completely cut off the tube flare, or it may ruin the sleeve or fitting nut. Failure to tighten sufficiently also can be serious, as this condition may allow the line to blow out of the assembly or to leak under system pressure.

The use of torque wrenches and the prescribed torque values prevents overtightening or undertightening. If a tube fitting assembly is tightened properly, it can be removed and retightened many times before re-flaring is necessary.

116

Tubing O.D.	Fitting Bolt or Nut Size	Aluminum Alloy Tubing, Bolt, Fitting or Nut Torque inch–lbs.	Steel Tubing, Bolt Fitting or Nut Torque inch–lbs.	Hose End Fittings and Hose Assemblies MS28740 or Equivalent End Fitting		Minimum bend radii (inches) Alum. alloy 1100-H14 5052-0	Steel
				Minimum	Maximum		
1/8	−2	20 − 30				3/8	
3/16	−3	30 − 40	90 − 100	70	120	7/16	21/32
1/4	−4	40 − 65	135 − 150	100	250	9/16	7/8
5/16	−5	60 − 85	180 − 200	210	420	3/4	1 1/8
3/8	−6	75 − 125	270 − 300	300	480	15/16	1 5/16
1/2	−8	150 − 250	450 − 500	500	850	1 1/4	1 3/4
5/8	−10	200 − 350	650 − 700	700	1150	1 1/2	2 3/16
3/4	−12	300 − 500	900 − 1000			1 3/4	2 5/8
7/8	−14	500 − 600	1000 − 1100				
1	−16	500 − 700	1200 − 1400			3	3 1/2
1−1/4	−20	600 − 900	1200 − 1400			3 3/4	4 3/8
1−1/2	−24	600 − 900	1500 − 1800			5	5 1/4
1−3/4	−28	850 − 1050				7	6 1/8
2	−32	950 − 1150				8	7

Figure 5–21. Flared fitting data.

Flareless Tube Installation

Tighten the nut by hand until an increase in resistance to turning is encountered. Should it be impossible to run the nut down with the fingers, use a wrench, but be alert for the first signs of bottoming. It is important that the final tightening commence at the point where the nut just begins to bottom.

With a wrench, turn the nut 1/6 turn (one flat on a hex nut). Use a wrench on the connector to prevent it from turning while tightening the nut. After the tube assembly is installed, the system should be pressure tested. Should a connection leak, it is permissible to tighten the nut an additional 1/6 turn (making a total of 1/3 turn). If, after tightening the nut a total of 1/3 turn, leakage still exists, the assembly should be removed and the components of the assembly inspected for scores, cracks, presence of foreign material, or damage from overtightening.

NOTE: Overtightening a flareless-tube nut drives the cutting edge of the sleeve deeply into the tube, causing the tube to be weakened to the point where normal in-flight vibration could cause the tube to shear. After inspection (if no discrepancies are found), reassemble the connections and repeat the pressure test procedures.

CAUTION: Do not in any case tighten the nut beyond 1/3 turn (two flats on the hex nut); this is the maximum the fitting may be tightened without the possibility of permanently damaging the sleeve and nut.

Common faults are:

1. Flare distorted into nut threads.
2. Sleeve cracked.
3. Flare cracked or split.
4. Flare out of round.
5. Inside of flare rough or scratched.
6. Fitting cone rough or scratched.
7. Threads of nut or union dirty, damaged or broken.

Some manufacturers service instructions will specify wrench torque values for flareless tubing installations (e.g., see figure 5–22).

PLUMBING ASSEMBLY PRECAUTIONS

Make certain that the material in the fittings used is similar to that of the tubing; for example, use steel fittings with steel tubing and aluminum alloy fittings with aluminum alloy tubing. Brass fittings plated with cadmium may be used with aluminum alloy tubing.

For corrosion prevention, aluminum alloy lines and fittings are usually anodized. Steel lines and fittings, if not stainless steel, are plated to prevent rusting or corroding. Brass and steel fittings are usually cadmium plated, although some may come plated with nickel, chromium, or tin.

To ensure proper sealing of hose connections and to prevent breaking hose clamps or damaging the hose, follow the hose clamp tightening instructions carefully. When available, use the hose clamp torque-limiting wrench. These wrenches are available in calibrations of 15 and 25 inch-pounds. In the absence of torque-limiting wrenches, the finger-tight-plus-turns method should be followed. Be-

117

WRENCH TORQUE FOR 304 1/8 H STEEL TUBES		
Tube Outside Diameter	Wall Thickness	Wrench Torque Inch—Pounds
3/16	0.016	90 – 110
3/16	0.020	90 – 110
1/4	0.016	110 – 140
1/4	0.020	110 – 140
5/16	0.020	100 – 120
3/8	0.020	170 – 230
3/8	0.028	200 – 250
1/2	0.020	300 – 400
1/2	0.028	400 – 500
1/2	0.035	500 – 600
5/8	0.020	300 – 400
5/8	0.035	600 – 700
5/8	0.042	700 – 850
3/4	0.028	650 – 800
3/4	0.049	800 – 960
1	0.020	800 – 950
1	0.065	1600 – 1750
WRENCH TORQUE FOR 304-1A or 3471A STEEL TUBES		
3/8	0.042	145 – 175
1/2	0.028	300 – 400
1/2	0.049	500 – 600
1	0.035	750 – 900
WRENCH TORQUE FOR 6061-T6 OR T4 TUBES		
1/4	0.035	110 – 140
3/8	0.035	145 – 175
1/2	0.035	270 – 330
1/2	0.049	320 – 380
5/8	0.035	360 – 440
5/8	0.049	425 – 525
3/4	0.035	380 – 470
1	0.035	750 – 900
1 1/4	0.035	900 – 1100

FIGURE 5–22. Torque values for flareless fittings.

Hose clamp tightening, finger-tight-plus turns method		
Initial installation only	Worm screw type clamp 10 threads per inch	Clamps—radial and other type—28 threads per inch
Self sealing hose approximately 15 inch-pounds	Finger-tight-plus 2 complete turns	Finger-tight-plus 2-1/2 complete turns
All other aircraft hose approximately 25 inch-pounds	Finger-tight Plus 1¼ complete turns	Finger-tight Plus 2 complete turns

Retightening of Hose Clamps

If Clamps do not seal at specified tightening, examine hose connections and replace parts as necessary

The above is for initial installation and should not be used for loose clamps

For re-tightening loose hose clamps in service proceed as follows:

1. Non-self-sealing hose – If the clamp screw cannot be tightened with the fingers do not disturb unless leakage is evident. If leakage is present tighten 1/4 turn.

2. Self-sealing hose – If looser than finger-tight, tighten to finger tight and add 1/4 turn.

FIGURE 5–23. Hose clamp tightening.

cause of the variations in hose clamp design and hose structure, the values given in figure 5–23 are approximate. Therefore, use good judgment when tightening hose clamps by this method. Since hose connections are subject to "cold flow" or a setting process, a followup tightening check should be made for several days after installation.

SUPPORT CLAMPS

Support clamps are used to secure the various lines to the airframe or powerplant assemblies. Several types of support clamps are used for this purpose. The rubber-cushioned and plain are the most commonly used clamps. The rubber-cushioned clamp is used to secure lines subject to vibration; the cushioning prevents chafing of the tubing. The plain clamp is used to secure lines in areas not subject to vibration.

A Teflon-cushioned clamp is used in areas where the deteriorating effect of Skydrol ® 500, hydraulic fluid (MIL–0–5606), or fuel is expected. However, because it is less resilient, it does not provide as good a vibration-damping effect as other cushion materials.

Use bonded clamps to secure metal hydraulic, fuel, and oil lines in place. Unbonded clamps should be used only for securing wiring. Remove any paint or anodizing from the portion of the tube at the bonding clamp location. Make certain that clamps are of the correct size. Clamps or supporting clips smaller than the outside diameter of the hose may restrict the flow of fluid through the hose.

All plumbing lines must be secured at specified intervals. The maximum distance between supports for rigid fluid tubing is shown in figure 5–24.

Tube OD (in.)	Distance between supports (in.)	
	Aluminum Alloy	Steel
$\frac{1}{8}$	9½	11½
$\frac{3}{16}$	12	14
$\frac{1}{4}$	13½	16
$\frac{5}{16}$	15	18
$\frac{3}{8}$	16½	20
$\frac{1}{2}$	19	23
$\frac{5}{8}$	22	25½
$\frac{3}{4}$	24	27½
1	26½	30

FIGURE 5–24. Maximum distance between supports for fluid tubing.

AIRCRAFT HARDWARE, MATERIALS, AND PROCESSES

AIRCRAFT HARDWARE

Aircraft hardware is the term used to describe the various types of fasteners and miscellaneous small items used in the manufacture and repair of aircraft.

The importance of aircraft hardware is often overlooked because of its small size; however, the safe and efficient operation of any aircraft is greatly dependent upon the correct selection and use of aircraft hardware.

Identification

Most items of aircraft hardware are identified by their specification number or trade name. Threaded fasteners and rivets are usually identified by AN (Air Force–Navy), NAS (National Aircraft Standard), or MS (Military Standard) numbers. Quick-release fasteners are usually identified by factory trade names and size designations.

THREADED FASTENERS

Various types of fastening devices allow quick dismantling or replacement of aircraft parts that must be taken apart and put back together at frequent intervals. Riveting or welding these parts each time they are serviced would soon weaken or ruin the joint. Furthermore, some joints require greater tensile strength and stiffness than rivets can provide. Bolts and screws are two types of fastening devices which give the required security of attachment and rigidity. Generally, bolts are used where great strength is required, and screws are used where strength is not the deciding factor.

Bolts and screws are similar in many ways. They are both used for fastening or holding, and each has a head on one end and screw threads on the other. Regardless of these similarities, there are several distinct differences between the two types of fasteners. The threaded end of a bolt is always blunt while that of a screw may be either blunt or pointed.

The threaded end of a bolt usually has a nut screwed onto it to complete the assembly. The threaded end of a screw may fit into a female receptacle, or it may fit directly into the material being secured. A bolt has a fairly short threaded section and a comparatively long grip length or unthreaded portion, whereas a screw has a longer threaded section and may have no clearly defined grip length. A bolt assembly is generally tightened by turning the nut on the bolt; the head of the bolt may or may not be designed for turning. A screw is always tightened by turning its head.

When it becomes necessary to replace aircraft fasteners, a duplicate of the original fastener should be used if at all possible. If duplicate fasteners are not available, extreme care and caution must be used in selecting substitutes.

Classification of Threads

Aircraft bolts, screws, and nuts are threaded in either the NC (American National Coarse) thread series, the NF (American National Fine) thread series, the UNC (American Standard Unified Coarse) thread series, or the UNF (American Standard Unified Fine) thread series. There is one difference between the American National series and the American Standard Unified series that should be pointed out. In the 1-inch-diameter size, the NF thread specified 14 threads per inch (1–14NF), while the UNF thread specifies 12 threads per inch (1–12UNF). Both type threads are designated by the number of times the incline (threads) rotates around a 1-inch length of a given diameter bolt or screw. For example, a 4–28 thread indicates that a 1/4-inch-diameter bolt has 28 threads in 1 inch of its threaded length.

Threads are also designated by Class of fit. The Class of a thread indicates the tolerance allowed in manufacturing. Class 1 is a loose fit, Class 2 is a free fit, Class 3 is a medium fit, and Class 4 is a close fit. Aircraft bolts are almost always manufactured in the Class 3, medium fit.

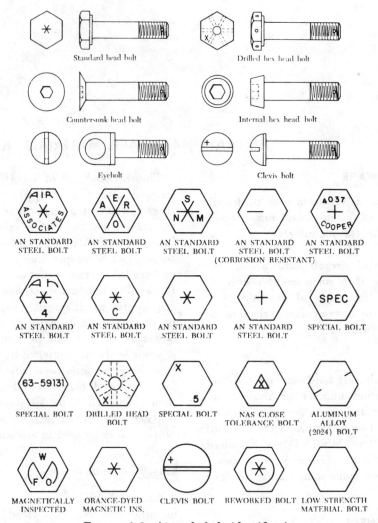

FIGURE 6–1. Aircraft bolt identification.

A Class 4 fit requires a wrench to turn the nut onto a bolt, whereas a Class 1 fit can easily be turned with the fingers. Generally, aircraft screws are manufactured with a Class 2 thread fit for ease of assembly.

Bolts and nuts are also produced with right-hand and left-hand threads. A right-hand thread tightens when turned clockwise; a left-hand thread tightens when turned counterclockwise.

AIRCRAFT BOLTS

Aircraft bolts are fabricated from cadmium- or zinc-plated corrosion-resistant steel, unplated corrosion-resistant steel, and anodized aluminum alloys. Most bolts used in aircraft structures are either general-purpose, AN bolts, or NAS internal-wrenching or close-tolerance bolts, or MS bolts. In certain cases, aircraft manufacturers make bolts of different dimensions or greater strength than the standard types. Such bolts are made for a particular application, and it is of extreme importance to use like bolts in replacement. Special bolts are usually identified by the letter "S" stamped on the head.

AN bolts come in three head styles—hex-head, clevis, and eyebolt (see figure 6–1). NAS bolts are available in hex-head, internal-wrenching, and countersunk head styles. MS bolts come in hex-head and internal-wrenching styles.

General-Purpose Bolts

The hex-head aircraft bolt (AN–3 through AN–20) is an all-purpose structural bolt used for general applications involving tension or shear loads where a light-drive fit is permissible (.006-inch clearance for a $\frac{5}{8}$-inch hole, and other sizes in proportion).

Alloy steel bolts smaller than No. 10–32 and

aluminum alloy bolts smaller than $\frac{1}{4}$-inch diameter are not used in primary structures. Aluminum alloy bolts and nuts are not used where they will be repeatedly removed for purposes of maintenance and inspection. Aluminum alloy nuts may be used with cadmium-plated steel bolts loaded in shear on land airplanes, but are not used on seaplanes due to the increased possibility of dissimilar-metal corrosion.

The AN–73 drilled-head bolt is similar to the standard hex-bolt, but has a deeper head which is drilled to receive wire for safetying. The AN–3 and the AN–73 series bolts are interchangeable, for all practical purposes, from the standpoint of tension and shear strengths.

Close-Tolerance Bolts

This type of bolt is machined more accurately than the general-purpose bolt. Close-tolerance bolts may be hex-headed (AN–173 through AN–186) or have a 100° countersunk head (NAS–80 through NAS–86). They are used in applications where a tight-drive fit is required (the bolt will move into position only when struck with a 12- to 14-ounce hammer).

Internal-Wrenching Bolts

These bolts, (MS–20004 through MS–20024 or NAS–495) are fabricated from high-strength steel and are suitable for use in both tension and shear applications. When they are used in steel parts, the bolthole must be slightly countersunk to seat the large corner radius of the shank at the head. In Dural material, a special heat-treated washer must be used to provide an adequate bearing surface for the head. The head of the internal-wrenching bolt is recessed to allow the insertion of an internal wrench when installing or removing the bolt. Special high-strength nuts are used on these bolts. Replace an internal-wrenching bolt with another internal-wrenching bolt. Standard AN hex-head bolts and washers cannot be substituted for them as they do not have the required strength.

Identification and Coding

Bolts are manufactured in many shapes and varieties. A clear-cut method of classification is difficult. Bolts can be identified by the shape of the head, method of securing, material used in fabrication, or the expected usage.

AN-type aircraft bolts can be identified by the code markings on the boltheads. The markings generally denote the bolt manufacturer, the material of which the bolt is made, and whether the bolt is a standard AN-type or a special-purpose bolt. AN standard steel bolts are marked with either a raised dash or asterisk; corrosion-resistant steel is indicated by a single raised dash; and AN aluminum alloy bolts are marked with two raised dashes. Additional information, such as bolt diameter, bolt length, and grip length may be obtained from the bolt part number.

For example, in the bolt part number AN3DD5A, the "AN" designates that it is an Air Force–Navy Standard bolt, the "3" indicates the diameter in sixteenths of an inch ($\frac{3}{16}$), the "DD" indicates the material is 2024 aluminum alloy. The letter "C" in place of the "DD" would indicate corrosion-resistant steel, and the absence of the letters would indicate cadmium-plated steel. The "5" indicates the length in eighths of an inch ($\frac{5}{8}$), and the "A" indicates that the shank is undrilled. If the letter "H" preceded the "5" in addition to the "A" following it, the head would be drilled for safetying.

Close-tolerance NAS bolts are marked with either a raised or recessed triangle. The material markings for NAS bolts are the same as for AN bolts, except that they may be either raised or recessed. Bolts inspected magnetically (Magnaflux) or by fluorescent means (Zyglo) are identified by means of colored lacquer, or a head marking of a distinctive type.

SPECIAL-PURPOSE BOLTS

Bolts designed for a particular application or use are classified as special-purpose bolts. Clevis bolts, eyebolts, Jo-bolts, and lock bolts are special-purpose bolts.

Clevis Bolts

The head of a clevis bolt is round and is either slotted to receive a common screwdriver or recessed to receive a crosspoint screwdriver. This type of bolt is used only where shear loads occur and never in tension. It is often inserted as a mechanical pin in a control system.

Eyebolt

This type of special-purpose bolt is used where external tension loads are to be applied. The eye is designed for the attachment of such devices as the fork of a turnbuckle, a clevis, or a cable shackle. The threaded end may or may not be drilled for safetying.

Jo-Bolt

Jo-bolt is a trade name for an internally threaded three-piece rivet. The Jo-bolt consists of three parts—a threaded steel alloy bolt, a threaded steel nut, and an expandable stainless steel sleeve. The parts are factory preassembled. As the Jo-bolt is installed, the bolt is turned while the nut is held. This causes the sleeve to expand over the end of the nut, forming the blind head and clamping against the work. When driving is complete, a portion of the bolt breaks off. The high-shear and tensile strength of the Jo-bolt makes it suitable for use in cases of high stresses where some of the other blind fasteners would not be practical. Jo-bolts are often a part of the permanent structure of late-model aircraft. They are used in areas which are not often subjected to replacement or servicing. (Because it is a three-part fastener, it should not be used where any part, in becoming loose, could be drawn into the engine air intake.) Other advantages of using Jo-bolts are their excellent resistance to vibration, weight saving, and fast installation by one person.

Presently, Jo-bolts are available in four diameters: The 200 series, approximately ³⁄₁₆-inch in diameter; the 260 series, approximately ¼-inch in diameter; the 312 series, approximately ⁵⁄₁₆-inch in diameter; and the 375 series, approximately ³⁄₈-inch in diameter. Jo-bolts are available in three head styles which are: F(flush), P(hex-head), and FA(flush millable).

Lockbolts

The lockbolt combines the features of a high-strength bolt and rivet, but it has advantages over both. The lockbolt is generally used in wing-splice fittings, landing-gear fittings, fuel-cell fittings, longerons, beams, skin-splice plates, and other major structural attachments. It is more easily and quickly installed than the conventional rivet or bolt and eliminates the use of lockwashers, cotter pins, and special nuts. Like the rivet, the lockbolt requires a pneumatic hammer or "pull gun" for installation; when installed, it is rigidly and permanently locked in place. Three types of lockbolts are commonly used, the pull type, the stump type, and the blind type. (See figure 6–2.)

Pull type. Pull-type lockbolts are used mainly in aircraft primary and secondary structures. They

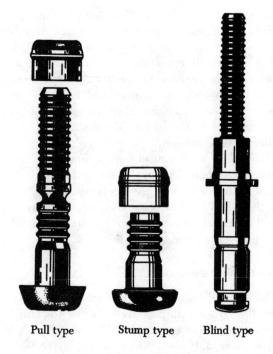

Pull type   Stump type   Blind type

FIGURE 6–2. Lockbolt types.

are installed very rapidly and have approximately one-half the weight of equivalent AN steel bolts and nuts. A special pneumatic "pull gun" is required to install this type of lockbolt. Installation can be accomplished by one person since bucking is not required.

Stump type. Stump-type lockbolts, although they do not have the extended stem with pull grooves, are companion fasteners to pull-type lockbolts. They are used primarily where clearance will not permit installation of the pull-type lockbolt. A standard pneumatic riveting hammer (with a hammer set attached for swaging the collar into the pin-locking grooves) and a bucking bar are tools necessary for the installation of stump-type lockbolts.

Blind type. Blind-type lockbolts come as complete units or assemblies. They have exceptional strength and sheet pull-together characteristics. Blind lockbolts are used where only one side of the work is accessible and, generally, where it is difficult to drive a conventional rivet. This type of lockbolt is installed in the same manner as the pull-type lockbolt.

Common features. Common features of the three types of lockbolts are the annular locking grooves on the pin and the locking collar which is swaged into the pin's lock grooves to lock the pin in tension. The pins of the pull- and blind-type lockbolts are extended for pull installation. The extension is provided with pulling grooves and a tension breakoff groove.

124

Composition. The pins of pull- and stump-type lockbolts are made of heat-treated alloy steel or high-strength aluminum alloy. Companion collars are made of aluminum alloy or mild steel. The blind lockbolt consists of a heat-treated alloy steel pin, blind sleeve and filler sleeve, mild steel collar, and carbon steel washer.

Substitution. Alloy steel lockbolts may be used to replace steel hi-shear rivets, solid steel rivets, or AN bolts of the same diameter and head type. Aluminum alloy lockbolts may be used to replace solid aluminum alloy rivets of the same diameter and head type. Steel and aluminum alloy lockbolts may also be used to replace steel and 2024T aluminum alloy bolts, respectively, of the same diameter. Blind lockbolts may be used to replace solid aluminum alloy rivets, stainless steel rivets, or all blind rivets of the same diameter.

Numbering system. The numbering systems for the various types of lockbolts are explained by the following breakouts (see figure 6–4).

GRIP NO.	GRIP RANGE Min.	Max.	GRIP NO.	GRIP RANGE Min.	Max.
1	.031	.094	17	1.031	1.094
2	.094	.156	18	1.094	1.156
3	.156	.219	19	1.156	1.219
4	.219	.281	20	1.219	1.281
5	.281	.344	21	1.281	1.344
6	.344	.406	22	1.344	1.406
7	.406	.469	23	1.406	1.469
8	.469	.531	24	1.469	1.531
9	.531	.594	25	1.531	1.594
10	.594	.656	26	1.594	1.656
11	.656	.718	27	1.656	1.718
12	.718	.781	28	1.718	1.781
13	.781	.843	29	1.781	1.843
14	.843	.906	30	1.843	1.906
15	.906	.968	31	1.906	1.968
16	.968	1.031	32	1.968	2.031
			33	2.031	2.094

FIGURE 6–3. Pull- and stump-type lockbolt grip ranges.

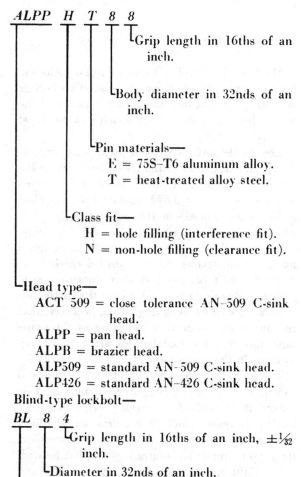

Pull-type lockbolt—

ALPP H T 8 8
              └Grip length in 16ths of an inch.

          └Body diameter in 32nds of an inch.

      └Pin materials—
        E = 75S–T6 aluminum alloy.
        T = heat-treated alloy steel.

   └Class fit—
     H = hole filling (interference fit).
     N = non-hole filling (clearance fit).

└Head type—
  ACT 509 = close tolerance AN–509 C-sink head.
  ALPP = pan head.
  ALPB = brazier head.
  ALP509 = standard AN–509 C-sink head.
  ALP426 = standard AN–426 C-sink head.

Blind-type lockbolt—

BL 8 4
      └Grip length in 16ths of an inch, ±1/32 inch.
    └Diameter in 32nds of an inch.
└Blind lockbolt.

Lockbolt collar—

LC C 8
      └Diameter of pin in 32nds of an inch.
   └*Material—
     C = 24ST aluminum alloy (green color).
     F = 61ST aluminum alloy (plain color).
     R = mild steel (cadmium plated).
└Lockbolt collar.

  * Use 25ST aluminum alloy with heat-treated alloy lockbolts only.
  Use 61ST aluminum alloy with 75ST aluminum alloy lockbolts only.
  Use mild steel with heat-treated alloy steel lockbolts for high temperature applications only.

Stump-type lockbolt—

ALSF E 8 8
              └Grip length in 16ths of an inch.
           └Body diameter in 32nds of an inch.
        └Pin material—
         E = 75S–T6 aluminum alloy.
         T = heat-treated alloy steel.
    └Head type—
      ASCT509 = close tolerance AN–509 C-sink head.
      ALSF = flat head type.
      ALS509 = standard AN–509 C-sink head.
      ALS426 = standard AN–426 C-sink head.

FIGURE 6–4. Lockbolt numbering system.

¼-inch Diameter			⁵⁄₁₆-inch Diameter		
GRIP NO.	GRIP RANGE		GRIP NO.	GRIP RANGE	
	Min.	Max.		Min.	Max.
1	.031	.094	2	.094	.156
2	.094	.156	3	.156	.219
3	.156	.219	4	.219	.281
4	.219	.281	5	.281	.344
5	.281	.344	6	.344	.406
6	.344	.406	7	.406	.469
7	.406	.469	8	.469	.531
8	.469	.531	9	.531	.594
9	.531	.594	10	.594	.656
10	.594	.656	11	.656	.718
11	.656	.718	12	.718	.781
12	.718	.781	13	.781	.843
13	.781	.843	14	.843	.906
14	.843	.906	15	.906	.968
15	.906	.968	16	.968	1.031
16	.968	1.031	17	1.031	1.094
17	1.031	1.094	18	1.094	1.156
18	1.094	1.156	19	1.156	1.219
19	1.156	1.219	20	1.219	1.281
20	1.219	1.281	21	1.281	1.343
21	1.281	1.343	22	1.343	1.406
22	1.343	1.406	23	1.406	1.469
23	1.406	1.469	24	1.460	1.531
24	1.469	1.531			
25	1.531	1.594			

FIGURE 6–5. Blind-type lockbolt grip ranges.

Grip Range. The bolt grip range required for any application should be determined by measuring the thickness of the material with a hook scale inserted through the hole. Once this measurement is determined the correct grip range can be selected by referring to the charts provided by the rivet manufacturer. Examples of grip-range charts are shown in figures 6–3 and 6–5.

When installed, the lockbolt collar should be swaged substantially throughout the complete length of the collar. The tolerance of the broken end of the pin relative to the top of the collar must be within the following dimensions:

Pin diameter	Tolerance		
	Below		Above
³⁄₁₆	.079	to	.032
¼	.079	to	.050
⁵⁄₁₆	.079	to	.050
³⁄₈	.079	to	.060

When removal of a lockbolt becomes necessary, remove the collar by splitting it axially with a sharp, cold chisel. Be careful not to break out or deform the hole. The use of a backup bar on the opposite side of the collar being split is recom-

mended. The pin may then be driven out with a drift punch.

AIRCRAFT NUTS

Aircraft nuts are made in a variety of shapes and sizes. They are made of cadmium-plated carbon steel, stainless steel, or anodized 2024T aluminum alloy, and may be obtained with either right- or left-hand threads. No identifying marking or lettering appears on nuts. They can be identified only by the characteristic metallic luster or color of the aluminum, brass, or the insert when the nut is of the self-locking type. They can be further identified by their construction.

Aircraft nuts can be divided into two general groups: Non-self-locking and self-locking nuts. Non-self-locking nuts are those that must be safetied by external locking devices, such as cotter pins, safety wire, or locknuts. Self-locking nuts contain the locking feature as an integral part.

Non-self-locking Nuts

Most of the familiar types of nuts, including the plain nut, the castle nut, the castellated shear nut, the plain hex nut, the light hex nut, and the plain check nut are the non-self-locking type. (See figure 6–6.)

The castle nut, AN310, is used with drilled-shank AN hex head bolts, clevis bolts, eyebolts, drilled head bolts, or studs. It is fairly rugged and can withstand large tensional loads. Slots (called castellations) in the nut are designed to accommodate a cotter pin or lock wire for safety.

The castellated shear nut, AN320, is designed for use with devices (such as drilled clevis bolts and threaded taper pins) which are normally subjected to shearing stress only. Like the castle nut, it is castellated for safetying. Note, however, that the nut is not as deep or as strong as the castle nut; also that the castellations are not as deep as those in the castle nut.

The plain hex nut, AN315 and AN335 (fine and coarse thread), is of rugged construction. This makes it suitable for carrying large tensional loads. However, since it requires an auxiliary locking device such as a check nut or lockwasher, its use on aircraft structures is somewhat limited.

The light hex nut, AN340 and AN345 (fine and coarse thread), is a much lighter nut than the plain hex nut and must be locked by an auxiliary

126

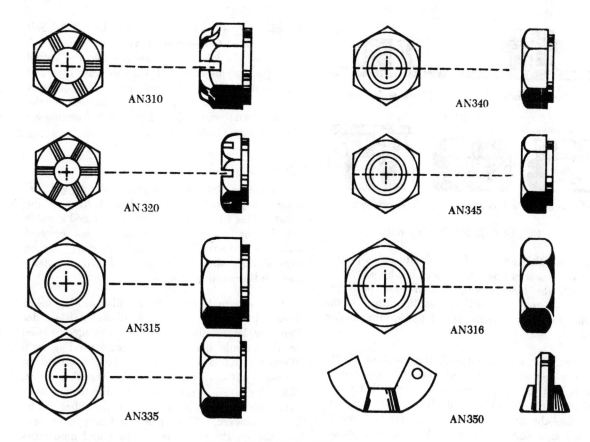

FIGURE 6–6. Non-self-locking nuts.

device. It is used for miscellaneous light-tension requirements.

The plain check nut, AN316, is employed as a locking device for plain nuts, set screws, threaded rod ends, and other devices.

The wing nut, AN350, is intended for use where the desired tightness can be obtained with the fingers and where the assembly is frequently removed.

Self-Locking Nuts NB

As their name implies, self-locking nuts need no auxiliary means of safetying but have a safetying feature included as an integral part of their construction. Many types of self-locking nuts have been designed and their use has become quite widespread. Common applications are: (1) Attachment of antifriction bearings and control pulleys; (2) Attachment of accessories, anchor nuts around inspection holes and small tank installation openings; and (3) Attachment of rocker box covers and exhaust stacks. Self-locking nuts are acceptable for use on certificated aircraft subject to the restrictions of the manufacturer.

Self-locking nuts are used on aircraft to provide tight connections which will not shake loose under severe vibration. Do not use self-locking nuts at joints which subject either the nut or bolt to rotation. They may be used with antifriction bearings and control pulleys, provided the inner race of the bearing is clamped to the supporting structure by the nut and bolt. Plates must be attached to the structure in a positive manner to eliminate rotation or misalignment when tightening the bolts or screws.

The two general types of self-locking nuts currently in use are the all-metal type and the fiber-lock type. For the sake of simplicity, only three typical kinds of self-locking nuts are considered in this handbook: The Boots self-locking and the stainless steel self-locking nuts, representing the all-metal types; and the elastic stop nut, representing the fiber-insert type.

Boots Self-Locking Nut NB

The Boots self-locking nut is of one-piece, all-metal construction, designed to hold tight in spite of severe vibration. Note in figure 6–7 that it has two sections and is essentially two nuts in one, a locking nut and a load-carrying nut. The two sections are connected with a spring which is an integral part of the nut. The spring keeps the locking and load-carrying sections such a distance

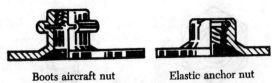

Boots aircraft nut   Elastic anchor nut

Flexloc nut   Fiber locknut   Elastic stop nut

FIGURE 6–7. Self-locking nuts.

apart that the two sets of threads are out-of-phase; that is, so spaced that a bolt which has been screwed through the load-carrying section must push the locking section outward against the force of the spring to engage the threads of the locking section properly.

Thus, the spring, through the medium of the locking section, exerts a constant locking force on the bolt in the same direction as a force that would tighten the nut. In this nut, the load-carrying section has the thread strength of a standard nut of comparable size, while the locking section presses against the threads of the bolt and locks the nut firmly in position. Only a wrench applied to the nut will loosen it. The nut can be removed and reused without impairing its efficiency.

Boots self-locking nuts are made with three different spring styles and in various shapes and sizes. The wing type, which is the most common, ranges in size for No. 6 up to ¼ inch, the Rol-top ranges from ¼ inch to 9/16 inch, and the bellows type ranges in size from No. 8 up to 3/8 inch. Wing-type nuts are made of anodized aluminum alloy, cadmium plated carbon steel, or stainless steel. The Rol-top nut is cadmium-plated steel, and the bellows type is made of aluminum alloy only.

Stainless Steel Self-Locking Nut

The stainless steel self-locking nut may be spun on and off with the fingers, as its locking action takes place only when the nut is seated against a solid surface and tightened. The nut consists of two parts; a case with a beveled locking shoulder and key, and a threaded insert with a locking shoulder and slotted keyway. Until the nut is tightened it spins on the bolt easily, because the threaded insert is the proper size for the bolt. However, when the nut is seated against a solid surface and tightened, the locking shoulder of the insert is pulled downward and wedged against the locking shoulder of the case. This action compresses the

threaded insert and causes it to clench the bolt tightly. The cross-sectional view in figure 6–8 shows how the key of the case fits into the slotted keyway of the insert so that when the case is turned the threaded insert is turned with it. Note that the slot is wider than the key. This permits the slot to be narrowed and the insert to be compressed when the nut is tightened.

Elastic Stop Nut

The elastic stop nut is a standard nut with the height increased to accommodate a fiber-locking collar. This fiber collar is very tough and durable and is unaffected by immersion in hot or cold water or ordinary solvents such as ether, carbon tetrachloride, oils, and gasoline. It will not damage bolt threads or plating.

As shown in figure 6–9, the fiber-locking collar is not threaded and its inside diameter is smaller than the largest diameter of the threaded portion or the outside diameter of a corresponding bolt. When the nut is screwed onto a bolt, it acts as an ordinary nut until the bolt reaches the fiber collar. When the bolt is screwed into the fiber collar, however, friction (or drag) causes the fiber to be pushed upward. This creates a heavy downward pressure on the load-carrying part and automatically throws the load-carrying sides of the nut and bolt threads into positive contact. After the bolt has been forced all the way through the fiber collar, the downward pressure remains constant. This pressure locks and holds the nut securely in place even under severe vibration.

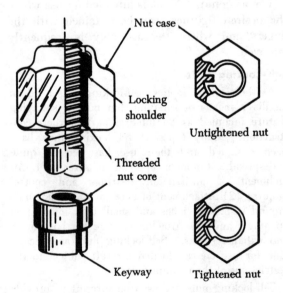

FIGURE 6–8. Stainless steel self-locking nut.

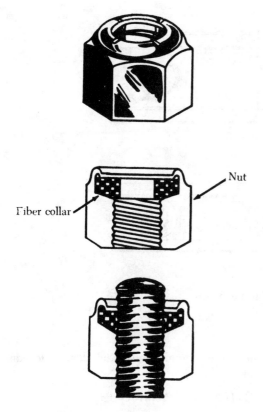

Fiber collar

Nut

FIGURE 6–9. Elastic stop nut.

Nearly all elastic stop nuts are steel or aluminum alloy. However, such nuts are available in practically any kind of metal. Aluminum alloy elastic stop nuts are supplied with an anodized finish. Steel nuts are cadmium plated.

Normally, elastic stop nuts can be used many times with complete safety and without detriment to their locking efficiency. When reusing elastic stop nuts, be sure the fiber has not lost its locking friction or become brittle. If a nut can be turned with the fingers, replace it.

After the nut has been tightened, make sure the rounded or chamfered end of the bolts, studs, or screws extends at least the full round or chamfer through the nut. Flat end bolts, studs, or screws should extend at least $\frac{1}{32}$ inch through the nut. Bolts of $\frac{5}{16}$-inch diameter and over with cotter pin holes may be used with self-locking nuts, but only if free from burrs around the holes. Bolts with damaged threads and rough ends are not acceptable. Do not tap the fiber-locking insert. The self-locking action of the elastic stop nut is the result of having the bolt threads impress themselves into the untapped fiber.

Do not install elastic stop nuts in places where the temperature is higher than 250° F., because the effectiveness of the self-locking action is reduced beyond this point. Self-locking nuts may be used on aircraft engines and accessories when their use is specified by the engine manufacturer.

Self-locking nut bases are made in a number of forms and materials for riveting and welding to aircraft structure or parts. (See figure 6–10.) Certain applications require the installation of self-locking nuts in channels, an arrangement which permits the attachment of many nuts with only a few rivets. These channels are track-like bases with regularly spaced nuts which are either removable or nonremovable. The removable type carries a floating nut, which can be snapped in or out of the channel, thus making possible the easy removal of damaged nuts. Nuts such as the clinch-type and spline-type which depend on friction for their anchorage are not acceptable for use in aircraft structures.

Sheet Spring Nuts

Sheet spring nuts, such as speed nuts, are used with standard and sheet-metal self-tapping screws in nonstructural locations. They find various uses in supporting line clamps, conduit clamps, electrical equipment, access doors, and the like, and are available in several types. Speed nuts are made from spring steel and are arched prior to tightening. This arched spring lock prevents the screw from working loose. These nuts should be used only where originally used in the fabrication of the aircraft.

Internal and External Wrenching Nuts

Two commercial types of high-strength internal or external wrenching nuts are available; they are the internal and external wrenching elastic-stop nut and the Unbrako internal and external wrenching nut. Both are of the self-locking type, are heat-treated, and are capable of carrying high-strength bolt-tension loads.

Identification and Coding

Part numbers designate the type of nut. The common types and their respective part numbers are: Plain, AN315 and AN335; castle AN310;

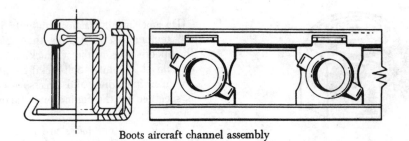

Boots aircraft channel assembly

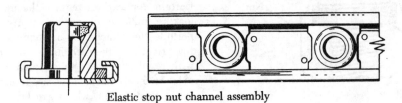

Elastic stop nut channel assembly

FIGURE 6–10. Self-locking nut bases.

plain check, AN316; light hex, AN340 and AN345; and castellated shear, AN320. The patented self-locking types are assigned part numbers ranging from MS20363 through MS20367. The Boots, the Flexloc, the fiber locknut, the elastic stop nut, and the self-locking nut belong to this group. Part number AN350 is assigned to the wing nut.

Letters and digits following the part number indicate such items as material, size, threads per inch, and whether the thread is right or left hand. The letter "B" following the part number indicates the nut material to be brass; a "D" indicates 2017-T aluminum alloy; a "DD" indicates 2024-T aluminum alloy; a "C" indicates stainless steel; and a dash in place of a letter indicates cadmium-plated carbon steel.

The digit (or two digits) following the dash or the material code letter is the dash number of the nut, and it indicates the size of the shank and threads per inch of the bolt on which the nut will fit. The dash number corresponds to the first figure appearing in the part number coding of general-purpose bolts. A dash and the number 3, for example, indicates that the nut will fit an AN3 bolt (10–32); a dash and the number 4 means it will fit an AN4 bolt (¼–28); a dash and the number 5, an AN5 bolt (⁵⁄₁₆–24); and so on.

The code numbers for self-locking nuts end in three- or four-digit numbers. The last two digits refer to threads per inch, and the one or two preceding digits stand for the nut size in 16ths of an inch.

Some other common nuts and their code numbers are:

Code Number AN310D5R:

AN310 = aircraft castle nut.
D = 2024-T aluminum alloy.
5 = ⁵⁄₁₆-inch diameter.
R = right-hand thread (usually 24 threads per inch).

Code Number AN320–10:

AN320 = aircraft castellated shear nut, cadmium-plated carbon steel.
10 = ⅝-inch diameter, 18 threads per inch (this nut is usually right-hand thread).

Code Number AN350B1032:

AN350 = aircraft wingnut.
B = brass.
10 = number 10 bolt.
32 = threads per inch.

AIRCRAFT WASHERS

Aircraft washers used in airframe repair are either plain, lock, or special type washers.

Plain Washers

Plain washers (figure 6–11), both the AN960 and AN970, are used under hex nuts. They provide a smooth bearing surface and act as a shim

130

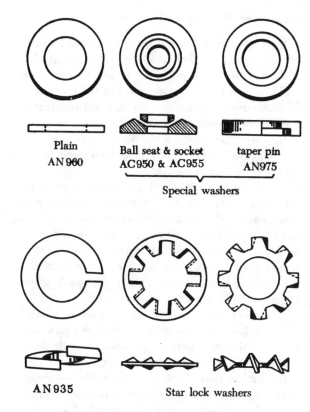

Plain
AN960

Ball seat & socket
AC950 & AC955

taper pin
AN975

Special washers

AN935

Star lock washers

FIGURE 6–11. Various types of washers.

in obtaining correct grip length for a bolt and nut assembly. They are used to adjust the position of castellated nuts in respect to drilled cotterr pin holes in bolts. Plain washers should be used under lockwashers to prevent damage to the surface material.

Aluminum and aluminum alloy washers may be used under boltheads or nuts on aluminum alloy or magnesium structures where corrosion caused by dissimilar metals is a factor. When used in this manner, any electric current flow will be between the washer and the steel bolt. However, it is common practice to use a cadmium-plated steel washer under a nut bearing directly against a structure as this washer will resist the cutting action of a nut better than an aluminum alloy washer.

The AN970 steel washer provides a greater bearing area than the AN960 washer and is used on wooden structures under both the head and the nut of a bolt to prevent crushing the surface.

Lockwashers

Lockwashers, both the AN935 and AN936, are used with machine screws or bolts where the self-locking or castellated type nut is not appropriate. The spring action of the washer (AN935) provides enough friction to prevent loosening of the nut from vibration. (These washers are shown in figure 6–11.)

Lockwashers should never be used under the following conditions:

1. With fasteners to primary or secondary structures.
2. With fasteners on any part of the aircraft where failure might result in damage or danger to the aircraft or personnel.
3. Where failure would permit the opening of a joint to the airflow.
4. Where the screw is subject to frequent removal.
5. Where the washers are exposed to the airflow.
6. Where the washers are subject to corrosive conditions.
7. Where the washer is against soft material without a plain washer underneath to prevent gouging the surface.

Shakeproof Lockwashers

Shakeproof lockwashers are round washers designed with tabs or lips that are bent upward across the sides of a hex nut or bolt to lock the nut in place. There are various methods of securing the lockwasher to prevent it from turning, such as an external tab bent downward 90° into a small hole in the face of the unit, or an internal tab which fits a keyed bolt.

Shakeproof lockwashers can withstand higher heat than other methods of safetying and can be used under high-vibration conditions safely. They should be used only once because the tabs tend to break when bent a second time.

Special Washers

The ball-socket and seat washers, AC950 and AC955, are special washers used where a bolt is installed at an angle to a surface, or where perfect alignment with a surface is required. These washers are used together. They are shown in figure 6–11.

The NAS143 and MS20002 washers are used for internal wrenching bolts of the NAS144 through NAS158 series. This washer is either plain or countersunk. The countersunk washer (designated as NAS143C and MS20002C) is used to seat the bolt head shank radius, and the plain washer is used under the nut.

INSTALLATION OF NUTS AND BOLTS

Bolt and Hole Sizes

Slight clearances in boltholes are permissible wherever bolts are used in tension and are not subject to reversal of load. A few of the applications in which clearance of holes may be permitted are in pulley brackets, conduit boxes, lining trim, and miscellaneous supports and brackets.

Boltholes are to be normal to the surface involved to provide full bearing surface for the bolthead and nut and must not be oversized or elongated. A bolt in such a hole will carry none of its shear load until parts have yielded or deformed enough to allow the bearing surface of the oversized hole to contact the bolt. In this respect, remember that bolts do not become swaged to fill up the holes as do rivets.

In cases of oversized or elongated holes in critical members, obtain advice from the aircraft or engine manufacturer before drilling or reaming the hole to take the next larger bolt. Usually, such factors as edge distance, clearance, or load factor must be considered. Oversized or elongated holes in noncritical members can usually be drilled or reamed to the next larger size.

Many boltholes, particularly those in primary connecting elements, have close tolerances. Generally, it is permissible to use the first lettered drill size larger than the normal bolt diameter, except where the AN hexagon bolts are used in light-drive fit (reamed) applications and where NAS close-tolerance bolts or AN clevis bolts are used.

Light-drive fits for bolts (specified on the repair drawings as .0015-inch maximum clearance between bolt and hole) are required in places where bolts are used in repair, or where they are placed in the original structure.

The fit of holes and bolts cannot be defined in terms of shaft and hole diameters; it is defined in terms of the friction between bolt and hole when sliding the bolt into place. A tight-drive fit, for example, is one in which a sharp blow of a 12- or 14-ounce hammer is required to move the bolt. A bolt that requires a hard blow and sounds tight is considered to fit too tightly. A light-drive fit is one in which a bolt will move when a hammer handle is held against its head and pressed by the weight of the body.

Installation Practices

Examine the markings on the bolthead to determine that each bolt is of the correct material. It is of extreme importance to use like bolts in replacement. In every case, refer to the applicable Maintenance Instructions Manual and Illustrated Parts Breakdown.

Be sure that washers are used under both the heads of bolts and nuts unless their omission is specified. A washer guards against mechanical damage to the material being bolted and prevents corrosion of the structural members. An aluminum alloy washer should be used under the head and nut of a steel bolt securing aluminum alloy or magnesium alloy members. Any corrosion that occurs then attacks the washer rather than the members. Steel washers should be used when joining steel members with steel bolts.

Whenever possible, the bolt should be placed with the head on top or in the forward position. This positioning tends to prevent the bolt from slipping out if the nut is accidently lost.

Be certain that the bolt grip length is correct. Grip length is the length of the unthreaded portion of the bolt shank. Generally speaking, the grip length should equal the thickness of the material being bolted together. However, bolts of slightly greater grip length may be used if washers are placed under the nut or the bolthead. In the case of plate nuts, add shims under the plate.

Safetying of Bolts and Nuts

It is very important that all bolts or nuts, except the self-locking type, be safetied after installation. This prevents them from loosening in flight due to vibration. Methods of safetying are discussed later in this chapter.

TORQUE AND TORQUE WRENCHES

As the speed of an aircraft increases, each structural member becomes more highly stressed. It is therefore extremely important that each member carry no more and no less than the load for which it was designed. In order to distribute the loads safely throughout a structure, it is necessary that proper torque be applied to all nuts, bolts, studs and screws. Using the proper torque allows the structure to develop its designed strength and greatly reduces the possibility of failure due to fatigue.

Torque Wrenches

The three most commonly used torque wrenches are the flexible beam, rigid frame, and the ratchet types (figure 6–12). When using the flexible beam and the rigid frame torque wrenches, the torque value is read visually on a dial or scale mounted on the handle of the wrench.

To use the ratchet type, unlock the grip and adjust the handle to the desired setting on the micrometer type scale, then relock the grip. Install the required socket or adapter to the square drive of the handle. Place the wrench assembly on the nut or bolt and pull the wrench assembly on the nut or bolt and pull in a clockwise direction with a smooth, steady motion. (A fast or jerky motion will result in an improperly torqued unit.) When the applied torque reaches the torque value which indicated on the handle setting, the handle will automatically release or "break" and move

Basic formula $F \times L = T$

F = Applied force

L = Lever length betwen centerline of drive and centerline of applied force (F must be 90 degrees to L)

T = Torque

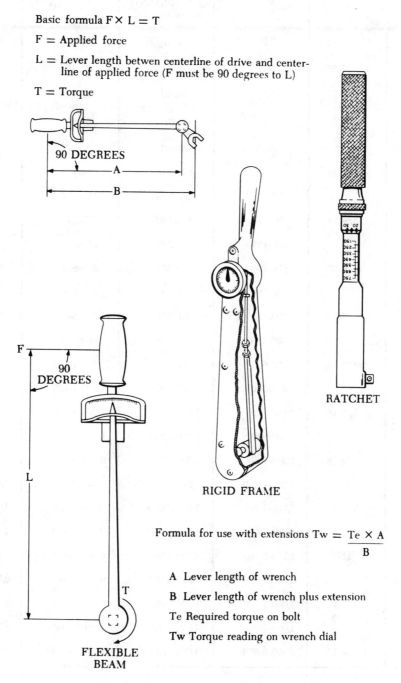

Formula for use with extensions $Tw = \dfrac{Te \times A}{B}$

A Lever length of wrench

B Lever length of wrench plus extension

Te Required torque on bolt

Tw Torque reading on wrench dial

FIGURE 6–12. Common torque wrenches.

133

Bolt, Stud or Screw Size		Torque Values in Inch-Pounds for Tightening Nuts			
		On standard bolts, studs, and screws having a tensile strength of 125,000 to 140,000 p.s.i.		On bolts, studs, and screws having a tensile strength of 140,000 to 160,000 p.s.i.	On high-strength bolts, studs, and screws having a tensile strength 160,000 p.s.i. and over
		Shear type nuts (AN320, AN364 or equivalent)	Tension type nuts and threaded machine parts (AN-310, AN365 or equivalent)	Any nut, except, shear type	Any nut, except shear type
8-32	8-36	7-9	12-15	14-17	15-18
10-24	10-32	12-15	20-25	23-30	25-35
1/4-20		25-30	40-50	45-49	50-68
	1/4-28	30-40	50-70	60-80	70-90
5/16-18		48-55	80-90	85-117	90-144
	5/16-24	60-85	100-140	120-172	140-203
3/8-16		95-110	160-185	173-217	185-248
	3/8-24	95-110	160-190	175-271	190-351
7/16-14		140-155	235-255	245-342	255-428
	7/16-20	270-300	450-500	475-628	500-756
1/2-13		240-290	400-480	440-636	480-792
	1/2-20	290-410	480-690	585-840	690-990
9/16-12		300-420	500-700	600-845	700-990
	9/16-18	480-600	800-1,000	900-1,220	1,000-1,440
5/8-11		420-540	700-900	800-1,125	900-1,350
	5/8-18	660-780	1,100-1,300	1,200-1,730	1,300-2,160
3/4-10		700-950	1,150-1,600	1,380-1,925	1,600-2,250
	3/4-16	1,300-1,500	2,300-2,500	2,400-3,500	2,500-4,500
7/8-9		1,300-1,800	2,200-3,000	2,600-3,570	3,000-4,140
	7/8-14	1,500-1,800	2,500-3,000	2,750-4,650	3,000-6,300
1"-8		2,200-3,000	3,700-5,000	4,350-5,920	5,000-6,840
	1"-14	2,200-3,300	3,700-5,500	4,600-7,250	5,500-9,000
1 1/8-8		3,300-4,000	5,500-6,500	6,000-8,650	6,500-10,800
	1 1/8-12	3,000-4,200	5,000-7,000	6,000-10,250	7,000-13,500
1 1/4-8		4,000-5,000	6,500-8,000	7,250-11,000	8,000-14,000
	1 1/4-12	5,400-6,600	9,000-11,000	10,000-16,750	11,000-22,500

FIGURE 6–13. Standard torque table (inch-pounds).

134

freely for a short distance. The release and free travel is easily felt, so there is no doubt about when the torquing process is completed.

To assure getting the correct amount of torque on the fasteners, all torque wrenches must be tested at least once a month or more often if necessary.

NOTE: It is not advisable to use a handle extension on a flexible beam type torque wrench at any time. A handle extension alone has no effect on the reading of the other types. The use of a drive-end extension on any type of torque wrench makes the use of the formula mandatory. When applying the formula, force must be applied to the handle of the torque wrench at the point from which the measurements were taken. If this is not done, the torque obtained will be in error.

Torque Tables

The standard torque table should be used as a guide in tightening nuts, studs, bolts, and screws whenever specific torque values are not called out in maintenance procedures. The following rules apply for correct use of the torque table (figure 6–13):

1. To obtain values in foot-pounds, divide inch-pounds by 12.
2. Do not lubricate nuts or bolts except for corrosion-resistant steel parts or where specifically instructed to do so.
3. Always tighten by rotating the nut first if possible. When space considerations make it necessary to tighten by rotating the bolt-head, approach the high side of the indicated torque range. Do not exceed the maximum allowable torque value.
4. Maximum torque ranges should be used only when materials and surfaces being joined are of sufficient thickness, area, and strength to resist breaking, warping, or other damage.
5. For corrosion-resisting steel nuts, use torque values given for shear type nuts.
6. The use of any type of drive-end extension on a torque wrench changes the dial reading required to obtain the actual values indicated in the standard torque range tables. When using a drive-end extension, the torque wrench reading must be computed by use of the proper formula, which is included in the handbook accompanying the torque wrench.

Cotter Pin Hole Line-Up

When tightening castellated nuts on bolts, the cotter pin holes may not line up with the slots in the nuts for the range of recommended values. Except in cases of highly stressed engine parts, the nut may be over tightened to permit lining up the

next slot with the cotter pin hole. The torque loads specified may be used for all unlubricated cadmium-plated steel nuts of the fine- or coarse-thread series which have approximately equal number of threads and equal face bearing areas. These values do not apply where special torque requirements are specified in the maintenance manual.

If the head end, rather than the nut, must be turned in the tightening operation, maximum torque values may be increased by an amount equal to shank friction, provided the latter is first measured by a torque wrench.

AIRCRAFT SCREWS

Screws are the most commonly used threaded fastening devices on aircraft. They differ from bolts inasmuch as they are generally made of lower strength materials. They can be installed with a loose-fitting thread, and the head shapes are made to engage a screwdriver or wrench. Some screws have a clearly defined grip or unthreaded portion while others are threaded along their entire length.

Several types of structural screws differ from the standard structural bolts only in head style. The material in them is the same, and a definite grip length is provided. The AN525 washer-head screw and the NAS220 through NAS227 series are such screws.

Commonly used screws are classified in three groups: (1) Structural screws which have the same strength as equal size bolts; (2) machine screws, which include the majority of types used for general repair; and (3) self-tapping screws, which are used for attaching lighter parts. A fourth group, drive screws, are not actually screws but nails. They are driven into metal parts with a mallet or hammer and their heads are not slotted or recessed.

Structural Screws

Structural screws are made of alloy steel, are properly heat treated, and can be used as structural bolts. These screws are found in the NAS204 through NAS235 and AN509 and AN525 series. They have a definite grip and the same shear strength as a bolt of the same size. Shank tolerances are similar to AN hex-head bolts, and the threads are National Fine. Structural screws are available with round, brazier, or countersunk heads. The recessed head screws are driven by either a Phillips or a Reed and Prince screwdriver.

The AN509 (100°) flathead screw is used in

countersunk holes where a flush surface is necessary.

The AN525 washer-head structural screw is used where raised heads are not objectionable. The washer-head screw provides a large contact area.

Machine Screws

Machine screws are usually of the flathead (countersunk), roundhead, or washer-head types. These screws are general-purpose screws and are available in low-carbon steel, brass, corrosion-resistant steel, and aluminum alloy.

Roundhead screws, AN515 and AN520, have either slotted or recessed heads. The AN515 screw has coarse threads and the AN520 has fine threads.

Countersunk machine screws are listed as AN505 and AN510 for 82°, and AN507 for 100°. The AN505 and AN510 correspond to the AN515 and AN520 roundhead in material and usage.

The fillister-head screw, AN500 through AN503, is a general-purpose screw and is used as a capscrew in light mechanisms. This could include attachments of cast aluminum parts such as gearbox cover plates.

The AN500 and AN501 screws are available in low-carbon steel, corrosion-resistant steel, and brass. The AN500 has coarse threads while the AN501 has fine threads. They have no clearly defined grip length. Screws larger than No. 6 have a hole drilled through the head for safetying purposes.

The AN502 and AN503 fillister-head screws are made of heat-treated alloy steel, have a small grip, and are available in fine and coarse threads. These screws are used as capscrews where great strength is required. The coarse-threaded screws are commonly used as capscrews in tapped aluminum alloy and magnesium castings because of the softness of the metal.

Self-tapping Screws

Machine self-tapping screws are listed as AN504 and AN506. The AN504 screw has a roundhead, and the AN506 is 82° countersunk. These screws are used for attaching removable parts, such as nameplates, to castings and parts in which the screw cuts its own threads.

AN530 and AN531 self-tapping sheet-metal screws, such as the Parker-Kalon Z-type sheet-metal screw, are blunt on the end. They are used in the temporary attachment of sheet metal for riveting, and in the permanent assembly of non-structural assemblies. Self-tapping screws should not be used to replace standard screws, nuts, bolts, or rivets.

Drive Screws

Drive screws, AN535, correspond to the Parker-Kalon U-type. They are plain-head self-tapping screws used as capscrews for attaching nameplates in castings and for sealing drain holes in corrosion proofing tubular structures. They are not intended to be removed after installation.

Identification and Coding

The coding system used to identify screws is similar to that used for bolts. There are AN and NAS screws. NAS screws are structural screws. Part numbers 510, 515, 550, and so on, catalog screws into classes such as roundhead, flathead, washerhead, and so forth. Letters and digits indicate their material composition, length, and thickness. Examples of AN and NAS code numbers follow.

AN501B–416–7
    AN = Air Force–Navy standard.
    501 = fillister-head, fine thread.
    B = brass.
    416 = $\frac{4}{16}$-inch diameter.
    7 = $\frac{7}{16}$-inch length.

The letter "D" in place of the "B" would indicate that the material is 2017-T aluminum alloy. The letter "C" would designate corrosion-resistant steel. An "A" placed before the material code letter would indicate that the head is drilled for safetying.

NAS144DH–22
    NAS = National Aircraft Standard.
    144 = head style; diameter and thread—
        $\frac{1}{4}$-28 bolt, internal wrenching.
    DH = drilled head.
    22 = screw length in 16ths of an inch—
        $1\frac{3}{8}$ inches long.

The basic NAS number identifies the part. The suffix letters and dash numbers separate different sizes, plating material, drilling specifications, etc. The dash numbers and suffix letters do not have standard meanings. It is necessary to refer to a specific NAS page in the Standards book for the legend.

REPAIR OF DAMAGED INTERNAL THREADS

Installation or replacement of bolts is simple when compared to the installation or replacement of studs. Bolt heads and nuts are cut in the open, whereas studs are installed into internal threads in a casting or built-up assembly. Damaged threads on bolts or nuts can be seen and only require replacement of the defective part. If internal threads are damaged, two alternatives are apparent: the part may be replaced or the threads repaired or replaced. Correction of the thread problem is usually cheaper and more convenient. Two methods of repairing are by replacement bushings or heli-coils.

Replacement Bushings

Bushings are usually special material (steel or brass spark plug bushings into aluminum cylinder heads). A material that will resist wear is used where removal and replacement is frequent. The external threads on the bushing are usually coarse. The bushing is installed, a thread lock compound may or may not be used, and staked to prevent loosening. Many bushings have left-hand threads external and right-hand threads internal. With this installation, removal of the bolt or stud (right-hand threads) tends to tighten the bushing.

Bushings for common installations such as spark plugs may be up to .040 oversize (in increments of .005). Original installation and overhaul shop replacements are shrunk fit: a heated cylinder head and a frozen bushing.

Heli-coils

Heli-coils are precision formed screw thread coils of 18–8 stainless steel wire having a diamond shaped cross-section (figure 6–14). They form unified coarse or unified fine thread classes 2-band 3B when assembled into (heli-coil) threaded holes. The assembled insert accommodates UNJ (controlled radius root) male threaded members. Each insert has a driving tang with a notch to facilitate removal of the tang after the insert is screwed into a heli-coil tapped hole.

They are used as screw thread bushings. In addition to being used to restore damaged threads, they are used in the original design of missiles, aircraft engines, and all types of mechanical equipment and accessories to protect and strengthen tapped threads in light materials, metals, and plastics, particularly in locations which require frequent assembly and disassembly, and/or where a screw locking action is desired.

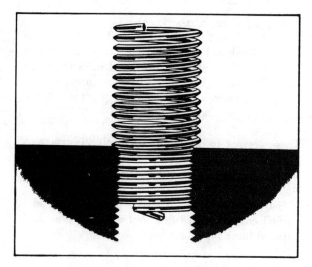

FIGURE 6–14. Heli-coil insert.

Heli-Coil Installation

Heli-coil installation (figure 6–15) is a 5 to 6 step operation, depending upon how the last step is classed. The following steps are for instructional purposes only. The manufacturer's instructions should be followed during installation.

Step 1: Determine what threads are damaged.

Step 2: (a) New installation of heli-coil, drill out damaged threads to minimum depth specified.
(b) Previously installed heli-coil. Using proper size extracting tool, place edge of blade in 90° from the edge of the insert. Tap with hammer to seat tool. Turn to left, applying pressure, until insert backs out. Threads are not damaged if insert is properly removed.

Step 3: Tap. Use the tap of required nominal thread size. The tapping procedure is the same as standard thread tapping. Tap length must be equal to or exceed the requirement.

Step 4: Gage. Threads may be checked with a heli-coil thread gage.

Step 5: Insert Assembly. Using proper tool, install insert to a depth that puts end of top coil $\frac{1}{4}$ to $\frac{1}{2}$ turn below the top surface of the tapped hole.

Step 6: Tang break-off.

Select proper break-off tool. Tangs should be removed from all drilled through holes. In blind holes the tangs may be removed when necessary if enough hole depth is provided below the tang of the installed insert.

These are not to be considered specific instructions on heli-coil installation. The manufacturer's instruction must be followed when making an installation.

Heli-coils are available for the following threads: unified coarse, unified fine, metric, spark plug and national taper pipe threads.

REPAIR OF DAMAGED HOLES WITH ACRES FASTENER SLEEVES

Acres fastener sleeves are thin wall, tubular, elements with a flared end. The sleeves are installed in holes to accept standard bolts and rivet type fasteners. The existing fastener holes are drilled 1/64-inch oversize for installation of the sleeves. The sleeves are manufactured in one inch increments. Along their length grooves provide a place to break or cut off excess length to match fastener grip range. The grooves also provide a place to hold adhesive or sealing agents when bonding sleeve into the hole.

Advantages and Limitations

The sleeves are used in holes which must be drilled 1/64-inch oversize to clean up corrosion or other damage. The oversize hole with the sleeve installed allows the use of the original diameter fastener in the repaired hole. The sleeves can be used in areas of high galvanic corrosion where the corrosion must be confined to a readily replaceable part. Oversizing of holes reduces the net cross sectional area of a part and should not be done unless absolutely required.

The manufacturer of the aircraft, aircraft engine or aircraft component should be consulted prior to repair of damaged holes with acres sleeves.

Identification

The sleeve is identified by a standard code number (figure 6–16A) which represents the type and style of sleeve, a material code, the fastener shank diameter, surface finish code letter and grip tang for the sleeve. The type and material of the sleeve is represented by the basic code number. The first dash number represents the diameter of the sleeve for the fastener installed and the second dash represents the grip length of the sleeve. The required length of the sleeve is determined on installation and the excess is broken off of the sleeve. A JK5512A–05N–10 is a 100° low profile head sleeve of aluminum alloy. The diameter is for a 5/32 inch fastener with no surface finish and is 5/8 inch in length.

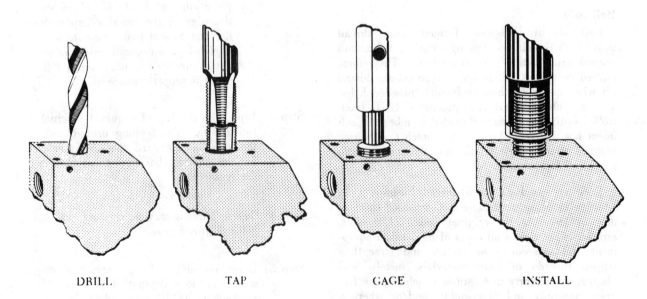

DRILL   TAP   GAGE   INSTALL

FIGURE 6–15. Heli-coil installation.

ACRES SLEEVE	TYPE	Basic Part Number
	100° 509 Tension Head Plus Flange	JK5610
	Protruding Head (Shear)	JK5511
	100° Low Profile Head	JK5512
	100° Standard Profile Head (509 Type)	JK5516
	Protruding Head (Tension)	JK5517
	100° Oversize Tension Head (1/64 Oversize Bolt)	JK5533

SLEEVE PART NO.	BOLT SIZE	[2] SLEEVE LENGTH
JK5511( )04 ( )( ) JK5512( )04 ( )( ) JK5516( )04 ( )( ) JK5517( )04 ( )( )	1/8	8
JK5511( )45 ( )( ) JK5512 JK5516( )45 ( )( ) JK5517( )45 ( )( )	#6	8
JK5511( )05 ( )( ) JK5512( )05 ( )( ) JK5516( )05 ( )( ) JK5517( )05 ( )( )	5/32	10
JK5511( )55 ( )( ) JK5512( )55 ( )( ) JK5516( )55 ( )( ) JK5517( )55 ( )( ) JK5610( )55 ( )( )	#8	10
JK5511( )06 ( )( ) JK5512( )06 ( )( ) JK5516( )06 ( )( ) JK5517( )06 ( )( ) JK5610( )06 ( )( )	#10	12
JK5511( )08 ( )( ) JK5512( )08 ( )( ) JK5516( )08 ( )( ) JK5517( )08 ( )( ) JK5610( )08 ( )( )	1/4	16
JK5511( )10 ( )( ) JK5512( )10 ( )( ) JK5516( )10 ( )( ) JK5517( )10 ( )( ) JK5610( )10 ( )( )	5/16	16
JK5511( )12 ( )( ) JK5512( )12 ( )( ) JK5516( )12 ( )( ) JK5517( )12 ( )( ) JK5610( )12 ( )( )	3/8	16

PART NUMBER BREAKDOWN

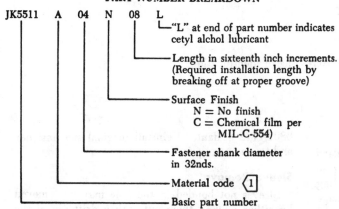

JK5511   A   04   N   08   L

- "L" at end of part number indicates cetyl alchol lubricant
- Length in sixteenth inch increments. (Required installation length by breaking off at proper groove)
- Surface Finish
  N = No finish
  C = Chemical film per MIL-C-554)
- Fastener shank diameter in 32nds.
- Material code [1]
- Basic part number

MATERIAL	MATERIAL CODE
5052 Aluminum alloy (1/2 hard)	A
6061 Aluminum alloy (T6 condition)	B
A286 Stainless steel (passivate)	C

ACRES SLEEVE FOR 1/64 OVERSIZE BOLT

SLEEVE PART NO. [1]	BOLT SIZE	[2] SLEEVE LENGTH
JK5533( )06 ( )( )	13/64	12
JK5533( )08 ( )( )	17/64	16
JK5533( )10 ( )( )	21/64	16
JK5533( )12 ( )( )	25/24	16

NOTES

[1] Acres sleeve, JK5533 1/64 oversize available in A286 steel only.

[2] Acres sleeve length in sixteenth inch increments.

FIGURE 6–16A. Acres sleeve identification.

HOLE PREPARATION FOR 1/64 OVERSIZE BOLT

BOLT SIZE	DRILL NO.	DRILL DIA.
13/64	7/32	0.2187
17/64	9/32	0.2812
21/64	11/32	0.3437
25/64	13/32	0.4062

HOLE PREPARATION

BOLT SIZE	STANDARD FIT		CLOSE FIT	
	DRILL NO.	DRILL DIA.	DRILL NO.	DRILL DIA.
1/8	9/64	0.1406	28	0.1405
#6	23	0.1540	24	0.1520
5/32	11/64	0.1719	18	0.1695
#8	15	0.1800	16	0.1770
#10	5	0.2055	6	0.2040
1/4	14	0.2660	17/64	0.2656
5/16	21/64	0.3281		
3/8	25/64	0.3908		

INSTALLATION PROCEDURE

A. DRILL OUT CORROSION OR DAMAGE TO EXISTING HOLE TO 1/64 OVERSIZE.
B. SELECT PROPER TYPE AND LENGTH ACRES SLEEVE FOR EXISTING FASTENER.
C. BOND SLEEVE IN STRUCTURE HOLE WITH MIL-S-8802 CLASS A 1/2 SEALANT.

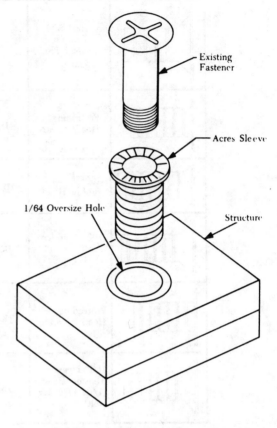

ACRES SLEEVE INSTALLATION

FIGURE 6–16B. Acres sleeve identification.

Hole Preparation

See figure 6–16 for drill number for standard or close fit holes. Inspect hole after drilling to assure all corrosion is removed before installing the sleeve. The hole must also be the correct shape and free from burrs. The countersink must be enlarged to receive the flare of the sleeve so the sleeve is flush with the surrounding surface.

Installation

After the correct type and diameter sleeve have been selected, use the 6501 sleeve breakoff tool for final installation length. See figure 6–16B for the sleeve breakoff procedure. The sleeve may be installed with or without being bonded in the hole. When bonding the sleeve in a hole, use MIL-S- 8802A1/2 sealant. Reinstall original size fastener and torque as required.

Sleeve Removal

Sleeves not bonded in the hole may be removed by either driving them out with a drift pin of the same diameter as the outside diameter of the sleeve or they may be deformed and removed with a pointed tool. Bonded sleeves may be removed by this method, but care should be used not to damage the structure hole. If this method cannot be used, drill the sleeves out with a drill 0.004 to 0.008 smaller than the installation drill size. The remaining portion of the sleeve after drilling can be removed using a pointed tool and applying an adhesive solvent to the sealant.

140

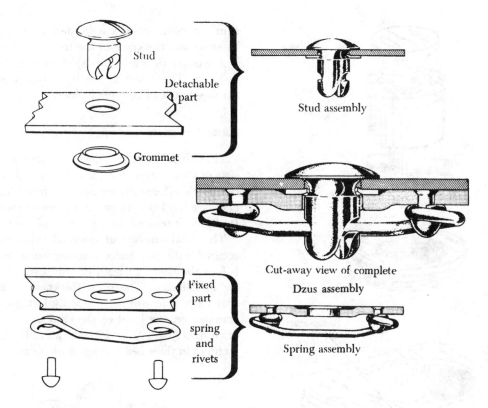

FIGURE 6–17. Dzus fastener.

TURNLOCK FASTENERS

Turnlock fasteners are used to secure inspection plates, doors, and other removable panels on aircraft. Turnlock fasteners are also referred to by such terms as quick-opening, quick-action, and stressed-panel fasteners. The most desirable feature of these fasteners is that they permit quick and easy removal of access panels for inspection and servicing purposes.

Turnlock fasteners are manufactured and supplied by a number of manufacturers under various trade names. Some of the most commonly used are the Dzus, Camloc, and Airloc.

Dzus Fasteners

The Dzus turnlock fastener consists of a stud, grommet, and receptacle. Figure 6–17 illustrates an installed Dzus fastener and the various parts.

The grommet is made of aluminum or aluminum alloy material. It acts as a holding device for the stud. Grommets can be fabricated from 1100 aluminum tubing, if none are available from normal sources.

The spring is made of steel, cadmium plated to prevent corrosion. The spring supplies the force that locks or secures the stud in place when two assemblies are joined.

The studs are fabricated from steel and are cadmium plated. They are available in three head styles; wing, flush, and oval. Body diameter, length, and head type may be identified or determined by the markings found on the head of the stud. (See figure 6–18.) The diameter is always measured in sixteenths of an inch. Stud length is measured in hundredths of an inch and is the distance from the head of the stud to the bottom of the spring hole.

A quarter of a turn of the stud (clockwise) locks the fastener. The fastener may be unlocked only by turning the stud counterclockwise. A

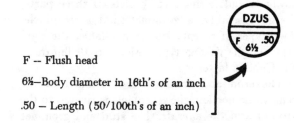

F -- Flush head

6½—Body diameter in 16th's of an inch

.50 — Length (50/100th's of an inch)

FIGURE 6–18. Dzus identification.

141

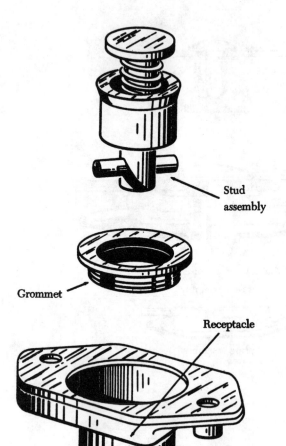

FIGURE 6-19. Camloc fastener.

sunk, or counterbored hole, depending upon the location and thickness of the material involved.

A quarter turn (clockwise) of the stud locks the fastener. The fastener can be unlocked only by turning the stud counterclockwise.

Airloc Fasteners

The Airloc fastener shown in figure 6-20 consists of three parts, a stud, a cross pin, and a stud receptacle. The studs are manufactured from steel and case hardened to prevent excessive wear. The stud hole is reamed for a press fit of the cross pin.

The total amount of material thickness to be secured with the Airloc fastener must be known before the correct length of stud can be selected for installation. The total thickness of material that each stud will satisfactorily lock together is stamped on the head of the stud in thousandths of an inch (.040, .070, .190, etc.). Studs are manufactured in three head styles; flush, oval, and wing.

Installed fastener

Dzus key or a specially ground screwdriver locks or unlocks the fastener.

Camloc Fasteners

Camloc fasteners are made in a variety of styles and designs. Included among the most commonly used are the 2600, 2700, 40S51, and 4002 series in the regular line, and the stressed-panel fastener in the heavy-duty line. The latter is used in stressed panels which carry structural loads.

The Camloc fastener is used to secure aircraft cowlings and fairings. It consists of three parts; a stud assembly, a grommet, and a receptacle. Two types of receptacles are available, the rigid type and the floating type. Figure 6-19 illustrates the Camloc fastener.

The stud and grommet are installed in the removable portion; the receptacle is riveted to the structure of the aircraft. The stud and grommet are installed in either a plain, dimpled, counter-

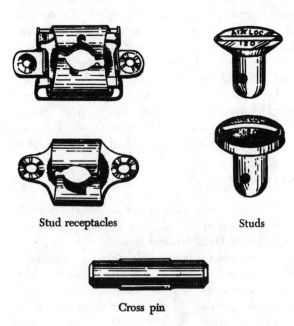

Stud receptacles   Studs

Cross pin

FIGURE 6-20. Airloc fastener.

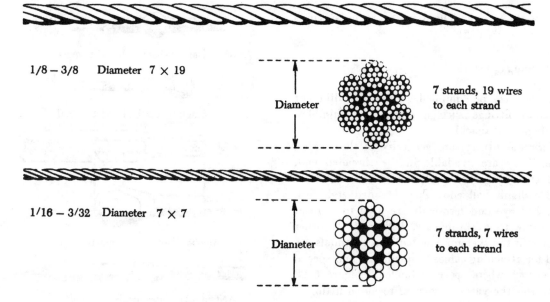

1/8 – 3/8   Diameter 7 × 19

Diameter

7 strands, 19 wires
to each strand

1/16 – 3/32   Diameter 7 × 7

Diameter

7 strands, 7 wires
to each strand

FIGURE 6–21. Cable cross sections.

The cross pin (figure 6–20) is manufactured from chrome-vanadium steel and heat treated to provide maximum strength, wear, and holding power. It should never be used the second time; once removed from the stud, it should be replaced with a new pin.

Receptacles for Airloc fasteners are manufactured in two types, rigid and floating. Sizes are classified by number—No. 2, No. 5, and No. 7. They are also classified by the center-to-center distance between the rivet holes of the receptacle: No. 2, ¾ inch; No. 5, 1 inch; and No. 7, 1⅜ inch. Receptacles are fabricated from high-carbon, heat-treated steel. An upper wing assures ejection of the stud when unlocked and enables the cross pin to be held in a locked position between the upper wing, cam, stop, and wing detent, regardless of the tension to which the receptacle is subjected.

CONTROL CABLES Read

Cables are the most widely used linkage in primary flight control systems. Cable-type linkage is also used in engine controls, emergency extension systems for the landing gear, and various other systems throughout the aircraft.

Cable-type linkage has several advantages over the other types. It is strong and light in weight, and its flexibility makes it easy to route through the aircraft. An aircraft cable has a high mechanical efficiency and can be set up without backlash, which is very important for precise control.

Cable linkage also has some disadvantages. Tension must be adjusted frequently due to stretching and temperature changes.

Aircraft control cables are fabricated from carbon steel or stainless steel.

Cable Construction

The basic component of a cable is a wire. The diameter of the wire determines the total diameter of the cable. A number of wires are preformed into a helical or spiral shape and then formed into a strand. These preformed strands are laid around a straight center strand to form a cable.

Cable designations are based on the number of strands and the number of wires in each strand. The most common aircraft cables are the 7 × 7 and 7 × 19.

The 7 × 7 cable consists of seven strands of seven wires each. Six of these strands are laid around the center strand (see figure 6–21). This is a cable of medium flexibility and is used for trim tab controls, engine controls, and indicator controls.

The 7 × 19 cable is made up of seven strands of 19 wires each. Six of these strands are laid around the center strand (see figure 6–21). This cable is extra flexible and is used in primary control systems and in other places where operation over pulleys is frequent.

Aircraft control cables vary in diameter, ranging

from $\frac{1}{16}$ to $\frac{3}{8}$ inch. The diameter is measured as shown in figure 6–21.

Cable Fittings

Cables may be equipped with several different types of fittings such as terminals, thimbles, bushings, and shackles.

Terminal fittings are generally of the swaged type. They are available in the threaded end, fork end, eye end, single-shank ball end, and double-shank ball end. The threaded end, fork end, and eye end terminals are used to connect the cable to a turnbuckle, bellcrank, or other linkage in the system. The ball-end terminals are used for attaching cables to quadrants and special connections where space is limited. Figure 6–22 illustrates the various types of terminal fittings.

The thimble, bushing, and shackle fittings may be used in place of some types of terminal fittings when facilities and supplies are limited and immediate replacement of the cable is necessary.

Turnbuckles

A turnbuckle assembly is a mechanical screw device consisting of two threaded terminals and a threaded barrel. Figure 6–23 illustrates a typical turnbuckle assembly.

Turnbuckles are fitted in the cable assembly for the purpose of making minor adjustments in cable length and for adjusting cable tension. One of the terminals has right-hand threads and the other has left-hand threads. The barrel has matching right- and left-hand internal threads. The end of the barrel with the left-hand threads can usually be identified by a groove or knurl around that end of the barrel.

When installing a turnbuckle in a control system, it is necessary to screw both of the terminals an equal number of turns into the barrel. It is also essential that all turnbuckle terminals be screwed into the barrel until not more than three threads are exposed on either side of the turnbuckle barrel.

After a turnbuckle is properly adjusted, it must be safetied. The methods of safetying turnbuckles are discussed later in this chapter.

PUSH-PULL TUBE LINKAGE

Push-pull tubes are used as linkage in various types of mechanically operated systems. This

AN663   Double shank ball end terminal

AN664   Single shank ball end terminal

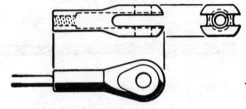
AN665   Rod end terminal

AN666   Threaded cable terminal

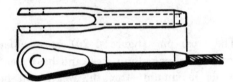
AN667   Fork end cable terminal

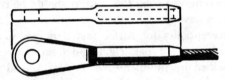
AN668   Eye end cable terminal

FIGURE 6–22. Types of terminal fittings.

type linkage eliminates the problem of varying tension and permits the transfer of either compression or tension stress through a single tube.

A push-pull tube assembly consists of a hollow aluminum alloy or steel tube with an adjustable end fitting and a checknut at either end. (See figure 6–24.) The checknuts secure the end fittings after the tube assembly has been adjusted to its correct length. Push-pull tubes are generally made in short lengths to prevent vibration and bending under compression loads.

PINS

The three main types of pins used in aircraft structures are the taper pin, flathead pin, and cotter pin. Pins are used in shear applications and

144

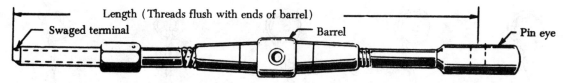

FIGURE 6–23. Typical turnbuckle assembly.

for safetying. Roll pins are finding increasing uses in aircraft construction.

Taper Pins

Plain and threaded taper pins (AN385 and AN386) are used in joints which carry shear loads and where absence of play is essential. The plain taper pin is drilled and usually safetied with wire. The threaded taper pin is used with a taper-pin washer (AN975) and shear nut (safetied with cotter pin) or self-locking nut.

Flathead Pin

Commonly called a clevis pin, the flathead pin (MS20392) is used with tie-rod terminals and in secondary controls which are not subject to continuous operation. The pin is customarily installed with the head up so that if the cotter pin fails or works out, the pin will remain in place.

Cotter Pins

The AN380 cadmium-plated, low-carbon steel cotter pin is used for safetying bolts, screws, nuts, other pins, and in various applications where such safetying is necessary. The AN381 corrosion-resistant steel cotter pin is used in locations where nonmagnetic material is required, or in locations where resistance to corrosion is desired.

Rollpins

The rollpin is a pressed-fit pin with chamfered ends. It is tubular in shape and is slotted the full length of the tube. The pin is inserted with hand tools and is compressed as it is driven into place. Pressure exerted by the roll pin against the hole walls keeps it in place, until deliberately removed with a drift punch or pin punch.

SAFETY METHODS

Safetying is the process of securing all aircraft, bolts, nuts, screws, pins, and other fasteners so that they do not work loose due to vibration. A familiarity with the various methods and means of safetying equipment on an aircraft is necessary in order to perform maintenance and inspection.

There are various methods of safetying aircraft parts. The most widely used methods are safety wire, cotter pins, lockwashers, snap-rings, and special nuts, such as self-locking nuts, pal nuts, and jamnuts. Some of these nuts and washers have been previously described in this chapter.

Safety Wiring   *Read*

Safety wiring is the most positive and satisfactory method of safetying capscrews, studs, nuts, boltheads, and turnbuckle barrels which cannot be safetied by any other practical means. It is a method of wiring together two or more units in

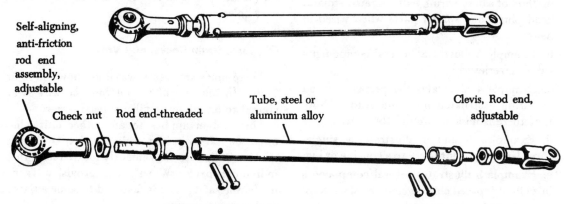

FIGURE 6–24. Push-pull tube assembly.

145

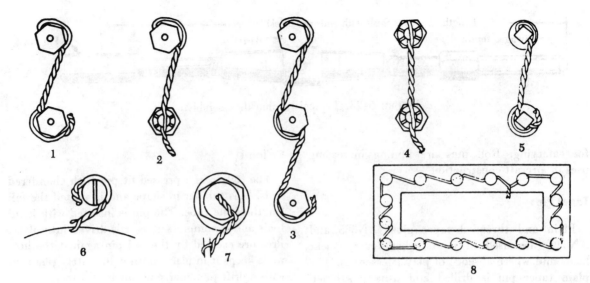

FIGURE 6–25. Safety wiring methods.

such a manner that any tendency of one to loosen is counteracted by the tightening of the wire.

Nuts, Bolts, and Screws

Nuts, bolts, and screws are safety wired by the single-wire or double-twist method. The double-twist method is the most common method of safety wiring. The single-wire method may be used on small screws in a closely spaced closed geometrical pattern, on parts in electrical systems, and in places that are extremely difficult to reach.

Figure 6–25 is an illustration of various methods which are commonly used in safety wiring nuts, bolts, and screws. Careful study of figure 6–25 shows that:

a. Examples 1, 2, and 5 illustrate the proper method of safety wiring bolts, screws, square-head plugs, and similar parts when wired in pairs.

b. Example 3 illustrates several components wired in series.

c. Example 4 illustrates the proper method of wiring castellated nuts and studs. (Note that there is no loop around the nut.)

d. Examples 6 and 7 illustrate a single-threaded component wired to a housing or lug.

e. Example 8 illustrates several components in a closely spaced closed geometrical pattern, using a single-wire method.

When drilled-head bolts, screws, or other parts are grouped together, they are more conveniently safety wired to each other in a series rather than individually. The number of nuts, bolts, or screws that may be safety wired together is dependent on the application. For instance, when safety-wiring widely spaced bolts by the double-twist method, a group of three should be the maximum number in a series.

When safety-wiring closely spaced bolts, the number that can be safety-wired by a 24-inch length of wire is the maximum in a series. The wire is arranged so that if the bolt or screw begins to loosen, the force applied to the wire is in the tightening direction.

Parts being safety-wired should be torqued to recommend values and the holes aligned before attempting the safetying operation. Never over torque or loosen a torqued nut to align safety wire holes.

Oil Caps, Drain Cocks, and Valves

These units are safety wired as shown in figure 6–26. In the case of the oil cap, the wire is anchored to an adjacent fillister head screw.

This system applies to any other unit which must be safety wired individually. Ordinarily, anchorage lips are conveniently located near these individual parts. When such provision is not made, the safety wire is fastened to some adjacent part of the assembly.

146

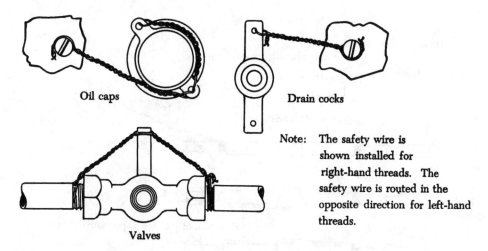

Oil caps

Drain cocks

Valves

Note: The safety wire is shown installed for right-hand threads. The safety wire is routed in the opposite direction for left-hand threads.

FIGURE 6–26. Safety wiring oil caps, drain cocks, and valves.

Electrical Connectors

Under conditions of severe vibration, the coupling nut of a connector may vibrate loose, and with sufficient vibration the connector may come apart. When this occurs, the circuit carried by the cable opens. The proper protective measure to prevent this occurrence is by safety wiring as shown in figure 6–27. The safety wire should be as short as practicable and must be installed in such a manner that the pull on the wire is in the direction which tightens the nut on the plug.

Turnbuckles

After a turnbuckle has been properly adjusted, it must be safetied. There are several methods of safetying turnbuckles; however, only two methods will be discussed in this section. These methods are illustrated in figure 6–28 (A) and 6–28 (B). The clip-locking method is used only on the most modern aircraft. The older type aircraft still use the type turnbuckles that require the wire-wrapping method.

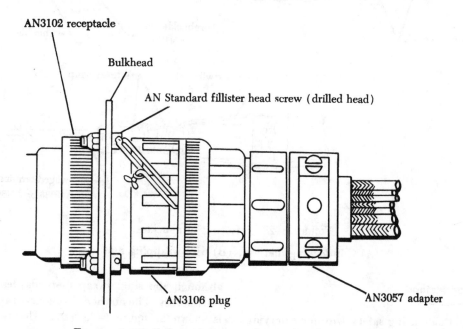

AN3102 receptacle

Bulkhead

AN Standard fillister head screw (drilled head)

AN3106 plug

AN3057 adapter

FIGURE 6–27. Safety wiring attachment for plug connectors.

147

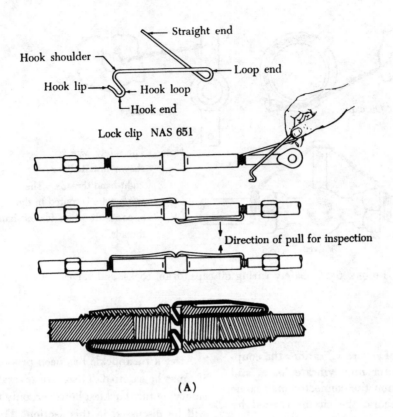

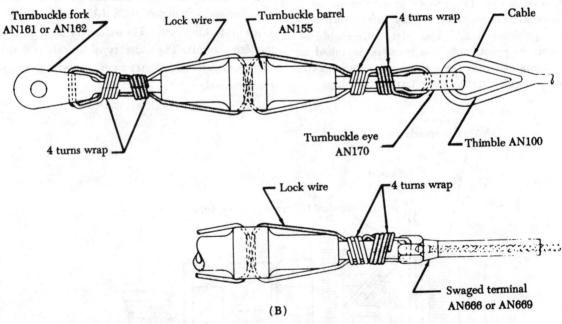

FIGURE 6–28. Safetying turnbuckles;

(A) Clip-locking method; (B) wire-wrapping method.

Of the methods using safety wire for safetying turnbuckles, the double-wrap method is preferred, although the single-wrap methods described are satisfactory. The method of double-wrap safetying is shown in figure 6–28 (B). Use two separate lengths of the proper wire as shown in figure 6–29.

Cable size (in.)	Type of wrap	Diameter of safety wire (in.)	Material (annealed condition)
$\frac{1}{16}$ ---	Single	.020	Stainless steel
$\frac{3}{32}$ ---	Single	.040	Copper, brass[1]
$\frac{1}{8}$ ---	Single	.040	Stainless steel
$\frac{1}{8}$ ---	Double	.040	Copper, brass[1]
$\frac{1}{8}$ ---	Single	.057 min	Copper, brass[1]
$\frac{5}{32}$ and greater_____	Single	.057	Stainless steel

1. Galvanized or tinned steel, or soft iron wires are also acceptable.

FIGURE 6–29. Turnbuckle safetying guide.

Run one end of the wire through the hole in the barrel of the turnbuckle and bend the ends of the wire towards opposite ends of the turnbuckle. Then pass the second length of the wire into the hole in the barrel and bend the ends along the barrel on the side opposite the first. Then pass the wires at the end of the turnbuckle in opposite directions through the holes in the turnbuckle eyes or between the jaws of the turnbuckle fork, as applicable. Bend the laid wires in place before cutting off the wrapped wire. Wrap the remaining length of safety wire at least four turns around the shank and cut it off. Repeat the procedure at the opposite end of the turnbuckle.

When a swaged terminal is being safetied, pass the ends of both wires, if possible, through the hole provided in the terminal for this purpose and wrap both ends around the shank as described above.

If the hole is not large enough to allow passage of both wires, pass the wire through the hole and loop it over the free end of the other wire, and then wrap both ends around the shank as described.

Single-wrap Method

The single-wrap safetying methods described in the following paragraphs are acceptable but are not the equal of the double-wrap methods.

Pass a single length of wire through the cable eye or fork, or through the hole in the swaged terminal at either end of the turnbuckle assembly. Spiral each of the wire ends in opposite directions around the first half of the turnbuckle barrel so that the wires cross each other twice. Thread both wire ends through the hole in the middle of the barrel so that the third crossing of the wire ends is in the hole. Again, spiral the two wire ends in opposite directions around the remaining half of the turnbuckle, crossing them twice. Then, pass one wire end through the cable eye or fork, or through the hole in the swaged terminal. In the manner described above, wrap both wire ends around the shank for at least four turns each, cutting off the excess wire.

An alternate to the above method is to pass one length of wire through the center hole of the turnbuckle and bend the wire ends toward opposite ends of the turnbuckle. Then pass each wire end through the cable eye or fork, or through the hole in the swaged terminal and wrap each wire end around the shank for at least four turns, cutting off the excess wire. After safetying, no more than three threads of the turnbuckle threaded terminal should be exposed.

General Safety Wiring Rules

When using the safety wire method of safetying, the following general rules should be followed:

1. A pigtail of $\frac{1}{4}$ to $\frac{1}{2}$ inch (three to six twists) should be made at the end of the wiring. This pigtail must be bent back or under to prevent it from becoming a snag.
2. The safety wire must be new upon each application.
3. When castellated nuts are to be secured with safety wire, tighten the nut to the low side of the selected torque range, unless otherwise specified, and if necessary, continue tightening until a slot aligns with the hole.

149

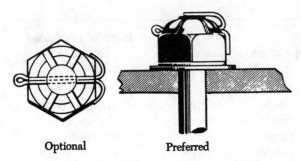

Optional   Preferred

FIGURE 6–30. Cotter pin installations.

4. All safety wires must be tight after installation, but not under such tension that normal handling or vibration will break the wire.

5. The wire must be applied so that all pull exerted by the wire tends to tighten the nut.

6. Twists should be tight and even, and the wire between the nuts as taut as possible without overtwisting.

7. The safety wire should always be installed and twisted so that the loop around the head stays down and does not tend to come up over the bolthead, causing a slack loop.

Cotter Pin Safetying

Cotter pin installation is shown in figure 6–30. Castellated nuts are used with bolts that have been drilled for cotter pins. The cotter pin should fit neatly into the hole, with very little sideplay. The following general rules apply to cotter pin safetying:

1. The prong bent over the bolt end should not extend beyond the bolt diameter. (Cut it off if necessary.)

2. The prong bent down should not rest against the surface of the washer. (Again, cut it off if necessary.)

3. If the optional wraparound method is used, the prongs should not extend outward from the sides of the nut.

4. All prongs should be bent over a reasonable radius. Sharp-angled bends invite breakage. Tapping lightly with a mallet is the best method of bending the prongs.

Snaprings

A snapring is a ring of metal, either round or flat in cross section, which is tempered to have springlike action. This springlike action will hold the snapring firmly seated in a groove. The external types are designed to fit in a groove around the outside of a shaft or cylinder. The internal types fit in a groove inside a cylinder. A special type of pliers is designed to install each type of snapring.

Snaprings can be reused as long as they retain their shape and springlike action.

External-type snaprings may be safety wired, but internal types are never safetied. Safety wiring of an external type snapring is shown in figure 6–31.

RIVETS

An aircraft, even though made of the best materials and strongest parts, would be of doubtful value unless those parts were firmly held together.

Several methods are used to hold metal parts together; they include riveting, bolting, brazing, and welding. The process used must produce a union that will be as strong as the parts that are joined.

Aluminum and its alloys are difficult to solder. To make a good union and a strong joint, aluminum parts can be welded, bolted, or riveted together. Riveting is satisfactory from the standpoint of strength and neatness, and is much easier to do than welding. It is the most common method used to fasten or join aluminum alloys in aircraft construction and repair.

A rivet is a metal pin used to hold two or more metal sheets, plates, or pieces of material together. A head is formed on one end when the rivet is manufactured. The shank of the rivet is placed through matched holes in two pieces of material, and the tip is then upset to form a second head to clamp the two pieces securely together. The second head, formed either by hand or by pneumatic equipment, is called a "shop head." The shop head functions in the

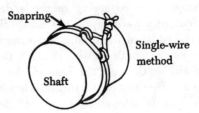

FIGURE 6–31. External type snap ring with safety wire installed.

150

same manner as a nut on a bolt. In addition to their use for joining aircraft skin sections, rivets are also used for joining spar sections, for holding rib sections in place, for securing fittings to various parts of the aircraft, and for fastening innumerable bracing members and other parts together.

Two of the major types of rivets used in the aircraft are the common solid-shank type, which must be driven using a bucking bar, and the special (blind) rivets, which may be installed where it is impossible to use a bucking bar.

Solid-Shank Rivets

Solid-shank rivets are generally used in repair work. They are identified by the kind of material of which they are made, their head type, size of shank, and their temper condition. The designation of the solid-shank rivet head type, such as universal head, roundhead, flathead, countersunk head, and brazier head, depends on the cross sectional shape of the head (see figure 6-33). The temper designation and strength are indicated by special markings on the head of the rivet.

The material used for the majority of aircraft solid-shank rivets is aluminum alloy. The strength and temper conditions of aluminum alloy rivets are identified by digits and letters similar to those adopted for the identification of strength and temper conditions of aluminum and aluminum alloy sheet stock. The 1100, 2017-T, 2024-T, 2117-T, and 5056 rivets are the five grades usually available.

The 1100 rivet, which is composed of 99.45 percent pure aluminum, is very soft. It is for riveting the softer aluminum alloys, such as 1100, 3003, and 5052, which are used for nonstructural parts (all parts where strength is not a factor). The riveting of map cases is a good example of where a rivet of 1100 aluminum alloy may be used.

The 2117-T rivet, known as the field rivet, is used more than any other for riveting aluminum alloy structures. The field rivet is in wide demand because it is ready for use as received and needs no further heat-treating or annealing. It also has a high resistance to corrosion.

The 2017-T and 2024-T rivets are used in aluminum alloy structures where more strength is needed than is obtainable with the same size 2217-T rivet. These rivets are annealed and must be kept refrigerated until they are to be driven. The 2017-T rivet should be driven within approximately 1 hour and the 2024-T rivet within 10 to 20 minutes after removal from refrigeration.

The 5056 rivet is used for riveting magnesium alloy structures because of its corrosion-resistant qualities in combination with magnesium.

Mild steel rivets are used for riveting steel parts. The corrosion-resistant steel rivets are for riveting corrosion-resistant steels in firewalls, exhaust stack brackets, and similar structures.

Monel rivets are used for riveting nickel-steel alloys. They can be substituted for those made of corrosion-resistant steel in some cases.

The use of copper rivets in aircraft repair is limited. Copper rivets can be used only on copper alloys or nonmetallic materials such as leather.

Metal temper is an important factor in the riveting process, especially with aluminum alloy rivets. Aluminum alloy rivets have the same heat-treating characteristics as aluminum alloy sheet stock. They can be hardened and annealed in the same manner as sheet aluminum. The rivet must be soft, or comparatively soft, before a good head can be formed. The 2017-T and 2024-T rivets are annealed before being driven. They harden with age.

The process of heat treating (annealing) rivets is much the same as that for sheet stock. Either an electric air furnace, a salt bath, or a hot oil bath is needed. The heat treating range, depending on the alloy, is 625° F. to 950° F. For convenient handling, rivets are heated in a tray or a wire basket. They are quenched in cold water (70° F.) immediately after heat treating.

The 2017-T and 2024-T rivets, which are heat-treatable rivets, begin to age-harden within a few minutes after being exposed to room temperature. Therefore, they must be used immediately after quenching or else be placed in cold storage. The most commonly used means for holding heat-treatable rivets at low temperature (below 32° F.) is to keep them in an electric refrigerator. They are referred to as "icebox" rivets. Under this storage condition, they will remain soft enough for driving for periods up to 2 weeks. Any rivets not used within that time should be removed for re-heat treating.

Icebox rivets attain about one-half their maximum strength in approximately 1 hour after driving and full strength in about 4 days. When 2017-T rivets are exposed to room temperature for 1 hour or longer, they must be subject to re-heat treatment. This also applies to 2024-T rivets exposed to room temperature for a period exceeding 10 minutes.

Once an icebox rivet has been taken from the refrigerator, it should not be mixed with the rivets still in cold storage. If more rivets are removed from the icebox than can be used in 15 minutes, they should be placed in a separate container and stored for re-heat treatment. Heat treatment of rivets may be repeated a number of times if done properly. Proper heating times and temperatures are:

Heating time—air furnace

Rivet alloy	Time at temperature	Heat treating temperature
2024_____	1 hour	910° F.—930° F.
2017_____	1 hour	925° F.—950° F.

Heating time—salt bath

| 2024_____ | 30 minutes | 910° F.—930° F. |
| 2017_____ | 30 minutes | 925° F.—950° F. |

Most metals, and therefore aircraft rivet stock, are subject to corrosion. Corrosion may be the result of local climatic conditions or the fabrication process used. It is reduced to a minimum by using metals which are highly resistant to corrosion and possess the correct strength-to-weight ratio.

Ferrous metals placed in contact with moist salt air will rust if not properly protected. Nonferrous metals, those without an iron base, do not rust, but a similar process known as corrosion takes place. The salt in moist air (found in the coastal areas) attacks the aluminum alloys. It is a common experience to inspect the rivets of an aircraft which has been operated near salt water and find them badly corroded.

If a copper rivet is inserted into an aluminum

Group A	Group B
1100	2117
3003	2017
5052	2124
6053	7075

FIGURE 6–32. Aluminum groupings.

alloy structure, two dissimilar metals are brought in contact with each other. Remember, all metals possess a small electrical potential. Dissimilar metals in contact with each other in the presence of moisture cause an electrical current to flow between them and chemical by-products to be formed. Principally, this results in the deterioration of one of the metals.

Certain aluminum alloys react to each other and, therefore, must be thought of as dissimilar metals. The commonly used aluminum alloys may be divided into the two groups shown in figure 6–32.

Members within either group A or group B can be considered as similar to each other and will not react to others within the same group. A corroding action will take place, however, if any metal of group A comes in contact with a metal in group B in the presence of moisture.

Avoid the use of dissimilar metals whenever possible. Their incompatibility is a factor which was considered when the AN Standards were adopted. To comply with AN Standards, the manufacturers must put a protective surface coating on the rivets. This may be zinc chromate, metal spray, or an anodized finish.

The protective coating on a rivet is identified by its color. A rivet coated with zinc chromate is yellow, an anodized surface is pearl gray, and the metal-sprayed rivet is identified by a silvery-gray color. If a situation arises in which a protective coating must be applied on the job, paint the rivet with zinc chromate before it is used and again after it is driven.

Identification

Markings on the heads of rivets are used to classify their characteristics. These markings may be either a raised teat, two raised teats, a dimple, a pair of raised dashes, a raised cross, a single triangle, or a raised dash; some other heads have no markings. The different markings indicate the composition of the rivet stock. As explained previously, the rivets have different colors to identify the protective surface coating used by the manufacturers.

Roundhead rivets are used in the interior of the aircraft, except where clearance is required for adjacent members. The roundhead rivet has a deep, rounded top surface. The head is large enough to strengthen the sheet around the hole and, at the same time, offer resistance to tension.

The flathead rivet, like the roundhead rivet, is used on interior structures. It is used where maximum strength is needed and where there isn't sufficient clearance to use a roundhead rivet. It is seldom, if ever, used on external surfaces.

The brazier head rivet has a head of large diameter, which makes it particularly adaptable for riveting thin sheet stock (skin). The brazier head rivet offers only slight resistance to the airflow, and because of this factor, it is frequently used for riveting skin on exterior surfaces, especially on aft sections of the fuselage and empennage. It is used for riveting thin sheets exposed to the slipstream. A modified brazier head rivet is also manufactured; it is simply a brazier head of reduced diameter.

The universal head rivet is a combination of the roundhead, flathead, and brazier head. It is used in aircraft construction and repair in both interior and exterior locations. When replacement is necessary for protruding head rivets—roundhead, flathead, or brazier head—they can be replaced by universal head rivets.

The countersunk head rivet is flat topped and beveled toward the shank so that it fits into a countersunk or dimpled hole and is flush with the material's surface. The angle at which the head slopes may vary from 78° to 120°. The 100° rivet is the most commonly used type. These rivets are used to fasten sheets over which other sheets must fit. They are also used on exterior surfaces of the aircraft because they offer only slight resistance to the slipstream and help to minimize turbulent airflow.

The markings on the heads of rivets, indicate the material of which they are made and, therefore, their strength. Figure 6–33 identifies the rivet head markings and the materials indicated by them. Although there are three materials indicated by a plain head, it is possible to distinguish their difference by color. The 1100 is aluminum color; the mild steel is a typical steel color; and

the copper rivet is a copper color. Any head marking can appear on any head style of the same material.

Each type of rivet is identified by a part number so that the user can select the correct rivet for the job. The type of rivet head is identified by AN or MS standard numbers. The numbers selected are in series and each series represents a particular type of head. (See figure 6–33.) The most common numbers and the types of heads they represent are:

AN426 or MS20426—countersunk head rivets (100°).
AN430 or MS20430—roundhead rivets.
AN441—flathead rivets.
AN456—brazier head rivets.
AN470 or MS20470—universal head rivets.

There are also letters and numbers added to a part number. The letters designate alloy content; the numbers, rivet diameter and length. The letters in common use for alloy designation are:

A—Aluminum alloy, 1100 or 3003 composition.
AD—Aluminum alloy, 2117-T composition.
D—Aluminum alloy, 2017-T composition.
DD—Aluminum alloy, 2024-T composition.
B—Aluminum alloy, 5056 composition.
C—Copper.
M—Monel.

The absence of a letter following the AN standard number indicates a rivet manufactured from mild steel.

The first number following the material composition letters expresses the diameter of the rivet shank in 32nds of an inch. Examples: 3, $\frac{3}{32}$nds; 5, $\frac{5}{32}$nds; etc. (See figure 6–34).

The last number(s), separated by a dash from the preceding number, expresses the length of the rivet shank in 16ths of an inch. Examples: 3, $\frac{3}{16}$ths; 7, $\frac{7}{16}$ths; 11, $\frac{11}{16}$ths; etc. (See figure 6–34.)

An example of identification marking of a rivet is:

AN470AD3–5—complete part number.
AN—Air Force–Navy standard number.
470—universal head rivet.
AD—2117-T aluminum alloy.
3—$\frac{3}{32}$nds in diameter.
5—$\frac{5}{16}$ths in length.

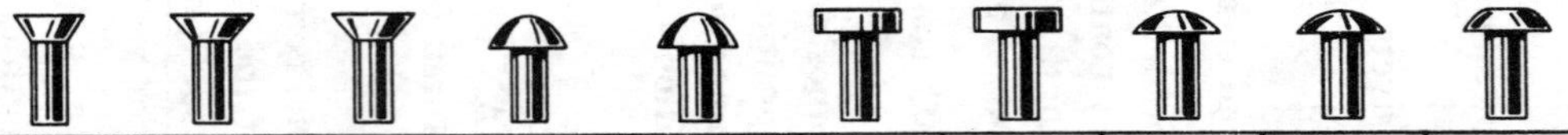

FIGURE 6-33. Rivet identification chart.

Material	Head Marking	AN Material Code	AN425 78° Counter-Sunk Head	AN426 100° Counter-Sunk Head MS20426*	AN427 100° Counter-Sunk Head MS20427*	AN430 Round Head MS20470*	AN435 Round Head MS20613* MS20615*	AN441 Flat Head	AN442 Flat Head MS20470*	AN455 Brazier Head MS20470*	AN456 Brazier Head MS20470*	AN470 Universal Head MS20470*	Heat Treat Before Using*	Shear Strength P.S.I.	Bearing Strength P.S.I.
1100	Plain	A	X	X		X			X	X	X	X	No	10000	25000
2117T	Recessed Dot	AD	X	X		X			X	X	X	X	No	30000	100000
2017T	Raised Dot	D	X	X		X			X	X	X	X	Yes	34000	113000
2017T-HD	Raised Dot	D	X	X		X			X	X	X	X	No	38000	126000
2024T	Raised Double Dash	DD	X	X		X			X	X	X	X	Yes	41000	136000
5056T	Raised Cross	B	X	X		X			X	X	X	X	No	27000	90000
7075-T73	Three Raised Dashes		X	X		X			X	X	X	X	No		
Carbon Steel	Recessed Triangle				X		X MS20613*	X					No	35000	90000
Corrosion Resistant Steel	Recessed Dash	F			X		X MS20613*						No	65000	90000
Copper	Plain	C			X		X	X					No	23000	
Monel	Plain	M			X			X					No	49000	
Monel (Nickel-Copper Alloy)	Recessed Double Dots	C					X MS20615*						No	49000	
Brass	Plain						X MS20615*						No		
Titanium	Recessed Large and Small Dot			MS 20426				X					No	95000	

* New specifications are for Design purposes

154

Special (Blind) Rivets

There are many places on an aircraft where access to both sides of a riveted structure or structural part is impossible, or where limited space will not permit the use of a bucking bar. Also, in the attachment of many nonstructural parts such as aircraft interior furnishings, flooring, deicing boots, and the like, the full strength of solid shank rivets is not necessary.

For use in such places, special rivets have been designed which can be bucked from the front. They are sometimes lighter than solid-shank rivets, yet amply strong for their intended use. These rivets are produced by several manufacturers and have unique characteristics that require special installation tools, special installation procedures, and special removal procedures. That is why they are called special rivets. Because these rivets are often inserted in locations where one head (usually the shop head) cannot be seen, they are also called blind rivets.

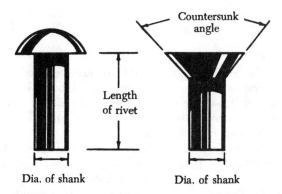

FIGURE 6–34. Methods of measuring rivets.

Mechanically Expanded Rivets

Two classes of mechanically expanded rivets will be discussed here:

(1) Non-structural
  (a) Self-plugging (friction lock) rivets
  (b) Pull-thru rivets
(2) Mechanical lock, flush fracturing, self-plugging rivets.

Self-Plugging

The self-plugging (friction lock) blind rivets are manufactured by several companies: the same general basic information about their fabrication, composition, uses, selection, installation, inspection, and removal procedures apply to all of them.

Self-plugging (friction lock) rivets are fabricated in two parts: A rivet head with a hollow shank or sleeve, and a stem that extends through the hollow

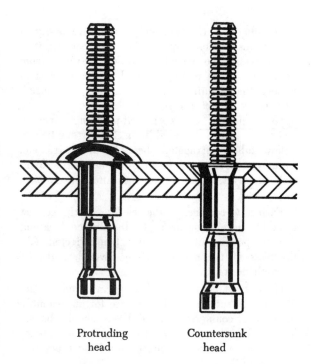

Protruding head   Countersunk head

FIGURE 6–35. Self-plugging (friction lock) rivets.

shank. Figure 6–35 illustrates a protruding head and a countersunk head self-plugging rivet produced by one manufacturer.

Several events, in their proper sequence, occur when a pulling force is applied to the stem of the rivet: (1) The stem is pulled into the rivet shank; (2) the mandrel portion of the stem forces the rivet shank to expand; and (3) when friction (or pulling action pressure) becomes great enough it will cause the stem to snap at a breakoff groove on the stem. The plug portion (bottom end of the stem) is retained in the shank of the rivet giving the rivet much greater shear strength than could be obtained from a hollow rivet.

Self-plugging (friction lock) rivets are fabricated in two common head styles: (1) A protruding head similar to the MS20470 or universal head, and (2) a 100° countersunk head. Other head styles are available from some manufacturers.

The stem of the self-plugging (friction lock) rivet may have a knot or knob on the upper portion, or it may have a serrated portion as shown in figure 6–35.

Self-plugging (friction lock) rivets are fabricated from several materials. Rivets are available in the following material combinations: stem 2017 aluminum alloy and sleeve 2117 aluminum alloy; stem 2017 aluminum alloy and sleeve 5056 aluminum alloy; and stem steel and sleeve steel.

Self-plugging (friction lock) rivets are designed so that installation requires only one person; it is not necessary to have the work accessible from both sides. The pulling strength of the rivet stem is such that a uniform job can always be assured. Because it is not necessary to have access to the opposite side of the work, self-plugging (friction lock) rivets can be used to attach assemblies to hollow tubes, corrugated sheet, hollow boxes, etc. Because a hammering force is not necessary to install the rivet, it can be used to attach assemblies to plywood or plastics.

Factors to consider in the selection of the correct rivet for installation are: (1) Installation location, (2) composition of the material being riveted, (3) thickness of the material being riveted, and (4) strength desired.

If the rivet is to be installed on an aerodynamically smooth surface, or if clearance for an assembly is needed, countersunk head rivets should be selected. In other areas where clearance or smoothness is not a factor, the protruding head type rivet may be utilized.

Material composition of the rivet shank will depend upon the type of material being riveted. Aluminum alloy 2117 shank rivets can be used on most aluminum alloys. Aluminum alloy 5056 shank rivets should be used when the material being riveted is magnesium. Steel rivets should always be selected for riveting assemblies fabricated from steel.

The thickness of the material being riveted determines the overall length of the shank of the rivet. As a general rule, the shank of the rivet should extend beyond the material thickness approximately $\frac{3}{64}$ inch to $\frac{1}{8}$ inch before the stem is pulled (see figure 6–36).

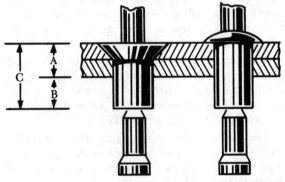

A – Thickness of material (grip range)

B – 3/64 - 1/8 Inch

C – Total rivet shank length

FIGURE 6–36. Determining length of friction lock rivets.

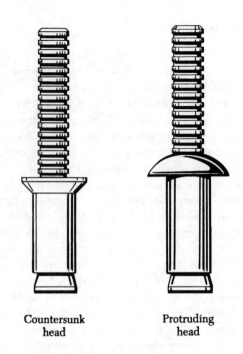

Countersunk head   Protruding head

FIGURE 6–37. Pull-thru rivets.

Pull-Thru Rivets

The pull-thru blind rivets are manufactured by several companies; the same general basic information about their fabrication, composition, uses, selection, installation, inspection, and removal procedures apply to all of them.

Pull-thru rivets are fabricated in two parts: A rivet head with a hollow shank or sleeve and a stem that extends through the hollow shank. Figure 6–37 illustrates a protruding head and a countersunk head pull-thru rivet.

Several events, in their proper sequence, occur when a pulling force is applied to the stem of the rivet: (1) The stem is pulled thru the rivet shank; (2) the mandrel portion of the stem forces the shank to expand forming the blind head and filling the hole.

Pull-thru rivets are fabricated in two common head styles: (1) Protruding head similar to the MS20470 or universal head, and (2) a 100° countersunk head. Other head styles are available from some manufacturers.

Pull-thru rivets are fabricated from several materials. Following are the most commonly used: 2117–T4 aluminum alloy, 5056 aluminum alloy, monel.

Pull-thru rivets are designed so that installation requires only one person; it is not necessary to have the work accessible from both sides.

156

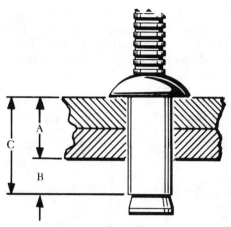

A — Thickness of material (grip range)

B — 3/64 to 1/8 inch

C — Total rivet shank length

FIGURE 6–38. Determining length of
pull-thru rivets.

Factors to consider in the selection of the correct rivet for installation are: (1) Installation location, (2) composition of the material being riveted, (3) thickness of the material being riveted, and (4) strength desired.

The thickness of the material being riveted determines the overall length of the shank of the rivet. As a general rule, the shank of the rivet should extend beyond the material thickness approximately $\frac{3}{64}$ inch to $\frac{1}{8}$ inch before the stem is pulled. See figure 6–38.

Each company that manufactures pull-thru rivets has a code number to help users obtain correct rivet for the grip range of a particular installation. In addition, MS numbers are used for identification purposes. Numbers are similar to those shown on the preceding page.

Self-Plugging Rivets

Self-plugging (mechanical lock) rivets are similar to self-plugging (friction lock) rivets, except for the manner in which the stem is retained in the rivet sleeve. This type of rivet has a positive mechanical locking collar to resist vibrations that cause the friction lock rivets to loosen and possibly fall out. (See figure 6–41.) Also, the mechanical locking type rivet stem breaks off flush with the head and usually does not require further stem trimming when properly installed. Self-plugging (mechanical lock) rivets display all the strength characteristics of solid shank rivets and in most cases can be substituted rivet for rivet.

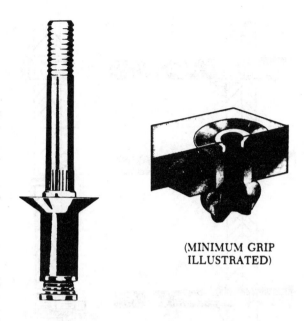

(MINIMUM GRIP
ILLUSTRATED)

FIGURE 6–39. Bulbed cherrylock rivet.

Bulbed Cherrylock Rivets

The large blind head of this fastener introduced the word "bulb" to blind rivet terminology. In conjunction with the unique residual preload developed by the high stem break load, its proven fatigue strength makes it the only blind rivet interchangeable structurally with solid rivets (figure 6–39).

Wiredraw Cherrylock Rivets

A wide range of sizes, materials and strength levels to select from. This fastener is especially suited for sealing applications and joints requiring an excessive amount of sheet take-up (figure 6–40).

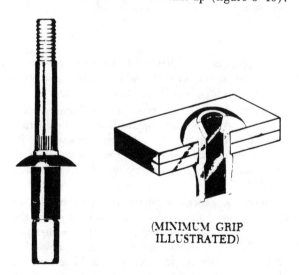

(MINIMUM GRIP
ILLUSTRATED)

FIGURE 6–40. Wiredraw cherrylock rivet.

157

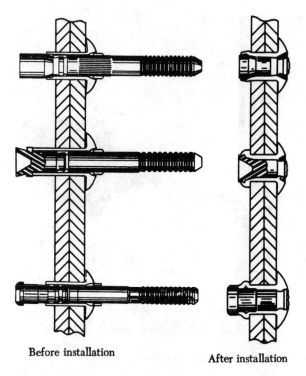

Before installation

After installation

FIGURE 6–41. Self-plugging (mechanical lock) rivets.

Huck Mechanical Locked Rivets

Self-plugging (mechanical lock) rivets are fabricated in two sections—a head and shank (including a conical recess and locking collar in the head), and a serrated stem that extends through the shank. Unlike the friction lock rivet, the mechanical lock rivet has a locking collar that forms a positive lock for retention of the stem in the shank of the rivet. This collar is seated in position during the installation of the rivet.

Material

Self-plugging (mechanical lock) rivets are fabricated with sleeves (rivet shanks) of 2017 and 5056 aluminum alloys, monel, or stainless steel.

The mechanical lock type of self-plugging rivet can be used in the same applications as the friction lock type of rivet. In addition, because of its greater stem retention characteristic, installation in areas subject to considerable vibration is recommended.

The same general requirements must be met in the selection of the mechanical lock rivet as for the friction lock rivet. Composition of the material being joined together determines the composition of the rivet sleeve, for example, 2017 aluminum alloy rivets for most aluminum alloys and 5056 aluminum rivets for magnesium.

Figure 6–42 depicts the sequences of a typical mechanically locked blind rivet. The form and function may vary slightly between blind rivet styles and specifics should be obtained from manufacturers.

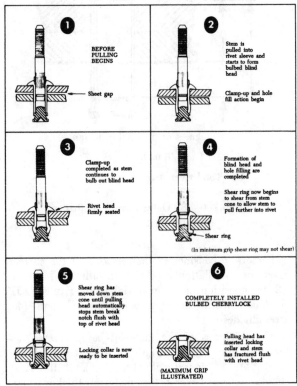

FIGURE 6–42. Cherrylock rivet installation.

Head Styles

Self-plugging mechanical locked blind rivets are available in several head styles (figure 6–43) depending on the installation requirements.

Diameters

Shank diameters are measured in $\frac{1}{32}$ inch increments and are generally identified by the first dash number: $\frac{3}{32}$ diameter = −3; $\frac{1}{8}$ diameter = −4; etc.

Both nominal and $\frac{1}{64}$ inch oversize diameters are available.

Grip Length

Grip length refers to the maximum total sheet thickness to be riveted and is measured in $\frac{1}{16}$ of an inch. This is generally identified by the second dash number. Unless otherwise noted, most blind rivets have their grip lengths (maximum grip)

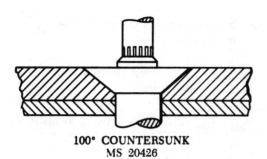

100° COUNTERSUNK
MS 20426

For countersunk applications.

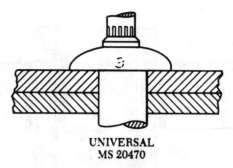

UNIVERSAL
MS 20470

For protruding head applications.

100° COUNTERSUNK
NAS 1097
For thin top sheet machine
countersunk applications

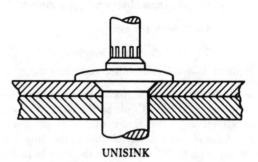

UNISINK

A combination countersunk & protruding head
for use in very thin top sheets. Strength equal to
double-dimpling without the high cost.

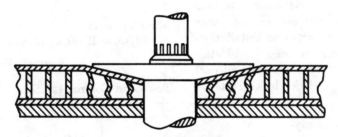

156° COUNTERSUNK

A large diameter, shallow countersunk head
providing wide bearing area for honey-comb
applications.

FIGURE 6–43. Cherrylock rivet heads.

marked on the rivet head and have a total grip range of $\frac{1}{16}$ inch. Figure 6–44 demonstrates a typical grip accommodation.

To determine the proper grip rivet to use, measure the material thickness with a grip selection gage (available from blind rivet manufacturers). The proper use of a grip selector gage is shown in figure 6–45.

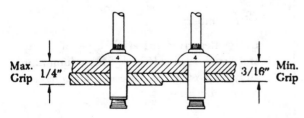

FIGURE 6–44. Typical grip length.

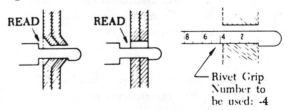

FIGURE 6–45. Grip gage use.

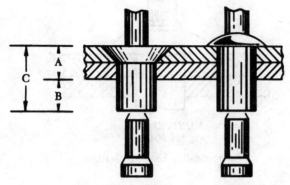

A – Thickness of material (grip range)

B – 3/64 to 1/8 inch

C – Total rivet shank length

FIGURE 6–46. Determining rivet length.

The thickness of the material being riveted determines the overall length of the shank of the rivet. As a general rule, the shank of the rivet should extend beyond the material thickness approximately $\frac{3}{64}$ inch to $\frac{1}{8}$ inch before the stem is pulled (see figure 6–46).

Rivet Identification

Each company that manufactures self-plugging (friction lock) rivets has a code number to help users obtain the correct rivet for the grip range or material thickness of a particular installation. In addition, MS numbers are used for identification purposes. The following examples of part numbers for self-plugging (friction lock) rivets are representative of each.

Huck Manufacturing Company—

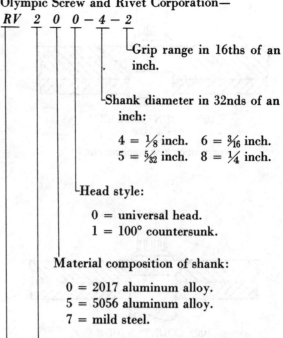

9SP–B — A 6 – 3

Grip range (material thickness) in 16ths of an inch.

Shank diameter in 32nds of an inch:

4 = $\frac{1}{8}$ inch. 6 = $\frac{3}{16}$ inch.
5 = $\frac{5}{32}$ inch. 8 = $\frac{1}{4}$ inch.

Material composition of shank:

A = 2017 aluminum alloy.
B = 5056 aluminum alloy.
R = mild steel.

Head style:

9SP–B = brazier or universal head.
9SP–100 = 100° countersunk head.

Figure 6-47.

Olympic Screw and Rivet Corporation—

RV 2 0 0 – 4 – 2

Grip range in 16ths of an inch.

Shank diameter in 32nds of an inch:

4 = $\frac{1}{8}$ inch. 6 = $\frac{3}{16}$ inch.
5 = $\frac{5}{32}$ inch. 8 = $\frac{1}{4}$ inch.

Head style:

0 = universal head.
1 = 100° countersunk.

Material composition of shank:

0 = 2017 aluminum alloy.
5 = 5056 aluminum alloy.
7 = mild steel.

Rivet type:

2 = self-plugging (friction lock).
5 = hollow pull-thru.

Manufacturer:
Olympic Rivet and Screw Corporation.

Figure 6-48.

Townsend Company, Cherry Rivet Division—

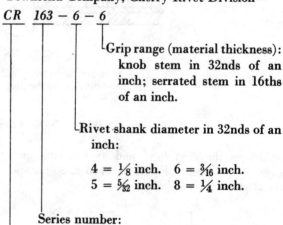

CR 163 – 6 – 6

Grip range (material thickness): knob stem in 32nds of an inch; serrated stem in 16ths of an inch.

Rivet shank diameter in 32nds of an inch:

4 = $\frac{1}{8}$ inch. 6 = $\frac{3}{16}$ inch.
5 = $\frac{5}{32}$ inch. 8 = $\frac{1}{4}$ inch.

Series number:

Designates rivet material, type of rivet, and head style (163 = 2117 aluminum alloy, self-plugging (friction lock) rivet, protruding head).

Cherry Rivet.

Figure 6-49.

Military Standard Number—

MS 20600 B 4 K 2

Grip range (material thickness) in ⅙ths of an inch.

Type of stem:
  K = knot head stem.
  W = serrated stem.

Shank diameter in 32nds of an inch:
  4 = ⅛ inch. 6 = ³⁄₁₆ inch.
  5 = ⁵⁄₃₂ inch. 8 = ¼ inch.

Material composition of sleeve:
  AD = 2117 aluminum alloy.
  B = 5056 aluminum alloy.

Type of rivet and head style:
  20600 = self-plugging (friction lock) protruding head.
  20601 = self-plugging (friction lock) 100° countersunk head.

Military Standard.

Figure 6-50.

Rivnuts

This is the trade name of a hollow, blind rivet made of 6053 aluminum alloy, counterbored and threaded on the inside. Rivnuts can be installed by one person using a special tool which heads the rivet on the blind side of the material. The Rivnut is threaded on the mandrel of the heading tool and inserted in the rivet hole. The heading tool is held at right angles to the material, the handle is squeezed, and the mandrel crank is turned clockwise after each stroke. Continue squeezing the handle and turning the mandrel crank of the heading tool until a solid resistance is felt, which indicates that the rivet is set.

The Rivnut is used primarily as a nut plate and in the attachment of deicer boots to the leading edges of wings. It may be used as a rivet in secondary structures or for the attachment of accessories such as brackets, instruments, or soundproofing materials.

Rivnuts are manufactured in two head types, each with two ends; the flat head with open or closed end, and the countersunk head with open or closed end. All Rivnuts, except the thin-head countersunk type, are available with or without small projections (keys) attached to the head to

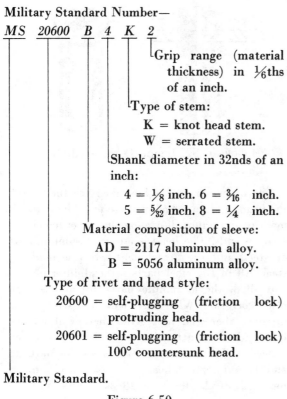

Flat—0.32 Head Thickness		
6-45	6-75	6-100
8-45	8-75	8-100
10-45	10-75	10-100
6B45	6B75	6B100
8B45	8B75	8B100
10B45	10B75	10B100
6K45	6K75	6K100
8K45	8K75	8K100
10K45	10K75	10K100
6KB45	6KB75	6KB100
8KB45	8KB75	8KB100
10KB45	10KB75	10KB100
100°—0.48 Head Thickness		
6-91	6-121	6-146
8-91	8-121	8-146
10-91	10-121	10-146
6B91	6B121	6B146
8B91	8B121	8B146
10B91	10B121	10B146
100°—0.63 Head Thickness		
6-106	6-136	6-161
8-106	8-136	8-161
10-106	10-136	10-161
6B106	6B136	6B161
8B106	8B136	8B161
10B106	10B136	10B161
6K106	6K136	6K161
8K106	8K136	8K161
10K106	10K136	10K161
6KB106	6KB136	6KB161
8KB106	8KB136	8KB161
10KB106	10KB136	10KB161

FIGURE 6–51. Rivnut data chart.

keep the Rivnut from turning. Keyed Rivnuts are used as a nut plate, while those without keys are used for straight blind riveting repairs where no torque loads are imposed. A keyway cutter is needed when installing Rivnuts which have keys.

The countersunk style Rivnut is made with two different head angles; the 100° with .048- and .063-inch head thickness, and the 115° with .063-inch head thickness. Each of these head styles is made in three sizes, 6–32, 8–32, and 10–32. These numbers represent the machine screw size of the threads on the inside of the Rivnut. The actual outside diameters of the shanks are ³⁄₁₆ inch for the 6–32 size, ⁷⁄₃₂ inch for the 8–32 size, and ¼ inch for the 10–32 size.

Open-end Rivnuts are the most widely used and are recommended in preference to the closed-end type wherever possible. However, closed-end Rivnuts must be used in pressurized compartments.

Rivnuts are manufactured in six grip ranges. The minimum grip length is indicated by a plain head, and the next higher grip length by one radial dash mark on the head. Each succeeding grip range is indicated by an additional radial dash mark until five marks indicate the maximum range.

Notice in figure 6–51 that some part number codes consist of a "6", an "8", or a "10", a "dash", and two or three more numbers. In some, the dash is replaced by the letters "K" or "KB". The first number indicates the machine screw size of the thread, and the last two or three numbers indicate the maximum grip length in thousandths of an inch. A dash between the figures indicates that the Rivnut has an open end and is keyless; a "B" in place of the dash means it has a closed end and is keyless; a "K" means it is an open end and has a key; and a "KB" indicates that it has a closed end and a key. If the last two or three numbers are divisible by five, the Rivnut has a flathead; if they are not divisible by five, the Rivnut has a countersunk head.

An example of a part number code is:

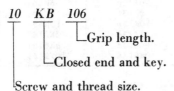

10   KB   106
└ Grip length.
└ Closed end and key.
└ Screw and thread size.

Dill Lok-Skrus and Dill Lok-Rivets

Dill "Lok-Skru" and "Lok-Rivet" (see figure 6–52) are trade names for internally threaded rivets. They are used for blind attachment of such accessories as fairings, fillets, access door covers, door and window frames, floor panels, and the like. Lok-Skrus and Lok-Rivets are similar to the Rivnut in appearance and application; however, they come in two parts and require more clearance on the blind side than the Rivnut to accommodate the barrel.

The Lok-Rivet and the Lok-Skru are alike in construction, except the Lok-Skru is tapped internally for fastening an accessory by using an attaching screw, whereas the Lok-Rivet is not tapped and can be used only as a rivet. Since both Lok-Skrus and Lok-Rivets are installed in the same manner, the following discussion for the Lok-Skru also applies to the Lok-Rivet.

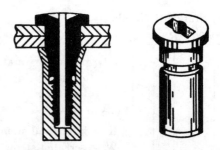

FIGURE 6–52. Internally threaded rivet

The main parts of a Lok-Skru are the barrel, the head, and an attachment screw. The barrel is made of aluminum alloy and comes in either closed or open ends. The head is either aluminum alloy or steel, and the attachment screw is made of steel. All of the steel parts are cadmium plated, and all of the aluminum parts are anodized to resist corrosion. When installed, the barrel screws up over the head and grips the metal on the blind side. The attaching screw is then inserted if needed. There are two head types, the flathead and the countersunk head. The Lok-Skru is tapped for 7–32, 8–32, 10–32, or 10–24 screws, and the diameters vary from .230 inch for 6–32 screws, to .292 inch for 10–32 screws. Grip ranges vary from .010 inch to .225 inch.

Deutsch Rivets

This rivet is a high-strength blind rivet used on late model aircraft. It has a minimum shear strength of 75,000 p.s.i., and can be installed by one man.

The Deutsch rivet consists of two parts, the stainless steel sleeve and the hardened steel drive pin (see figure 6–53). The pin and sleeve are coated with a lubricant and a corrosion inhibitor.

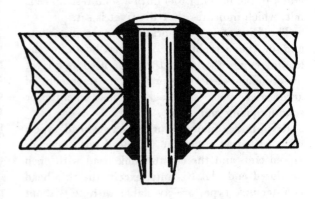

FIGURE 6–53. Deutsch rivet.

The Deutsch rivet is available in diameters of $\frac{3}{16}$, $\frac{1}{4}$, or $\frac{3}{8}$ inch. Grip lengths for this rivet range from $\frac{3}{16}$ to 1 inch. Some variation is allowed in grip length when installing the rivet; for example, a rivet with a grip length of $\frac{3}{16}$ inch can be used where the total thickness of materials is between 0.198 and 0.228 inch.

When driving a Deutsch rivet, an ordinary hammer or a pneumatic rivet gun and a flathead set are used. The rivet is seated in the previously drilled hole and then the pin is driven into the sleeve. The driving action causes the pin to exert pressure against the sleeve and forces the sides of the sleeve out. This stretching forms a shop head on the end of the rivet and provides positive fastening. The ridge on the top of the rivet head locks the pin into the rivet as the last few blows are struck.

Pin Rivets

Pin (Hi-shear) rivets are classified as special rivets but are not of the blind type. Access to both sides of the material is required to install this type of rivet. Pin rivets have the same shear strength as bolts of equal diameters, are about 40 percent of the weight of a bolt, and require only about one-fifth as much time for installation as a bolt, nut, and washer combination. They are approximately three times as strong as solid-shank rivets.

Pin rivets are essentially threadless bolts. The pin is headed at one end and is grooved about the circumference at the other. A metal collar is swaged onto the grooved end effecting a firm, tight fit (see figure 6–54).

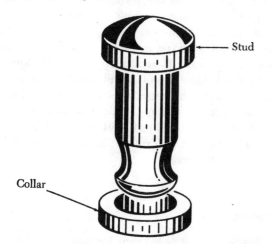

FIGURE 6–54. Pin (Hi-shear) rivet.

Pin rivets are fabricated in a variety of materials but should be used only in shear applications. They should never be used where the grip length is less than the shank diameter.

Part numbers for pin rivets can be interpreted to give the diameter and grip length of the individual rivets. A typical part number breakdown would be:

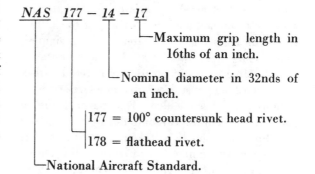

PLASTICS

Plastics are used in many applications throughout modern aircraft. These applications range from structural components of thermosetting plastics reinforced with fiber glass to decorative trim of thermoplastic materials.

Transparent Plastics

Transparent plastic materials used in aircraft canopies, windshields, and other similar transparent enclosures may be divided into two major classes or groups. These plastics are classified according to their reaction to heat. The two classes are *Thermoplastic* and *Thermosetting*.

Thermoplastic materials will soften when heated and harden when cooled. These materials can be heated until soft, and then formed into the desired shape. When cooled, they will retain this shape. The same piece of plastic can be reheated and reshaped any number of times without changing the chemical composition of the material.

Thermosetting plastics harden upon heating, and reheating has no softening effect. These plastics cannot be reshaped after once being fully cured by the application of heat.

In addition to the above classes, transparent plastics are manufactured in two forms, monolithic (solid) and laminated. Laminated transparent plastics are made from transparent plastic face sheets bonded by an inner-layer material, usually polyvinyl butyral. Because of its shatter-resistant qualities, laminated plastic is superior

163

to solid plastics and is used in many pressurized aircraft. Most of the transparent sheet used in aviation is manufactured in accordance with various military specifications.

A new development in transparent plastics is stretched acrylic. Stretched acrylic is a type of plastic which, before being shaped, is pulled in both directions to rearrange its molecular structure. Stretched acrylic panels have a greater resistance to impact and are less subject to shatter; its chemical resistance is greater, edging is simpler, and crazing and scratches are less detrimental.

Individual sheets of plastic are covered with a heavy masking paper to which a pressure-sensitive adhesive has been added. This paper helps to prevent accidental scratching during storage and handling. Care should be taken to avoid scratches and gouges which may be caused by sliding sheets against one another or across rough or dirty tables.

Sheets should be stored in bins which are tilted at approximately 10° from vertical, if possible. If they must be stored horizontally, piles should not be over 18 inches high, and small sheets should be stacked on the larger ones to avoid unsupported overhang. Storage should be in a cool, dry place away from solvent fumes, heating coils, radiators, and steampipes. The temperature in the storage room should not exceed 120° F.

While direct sunlight does not harm acrylic plastic, it will cause drying and hardening of the masking adhesive, making removal of the paper difficult. If the paper will not roll off easily, place the sheet in an oven at 250° F. for 1 minute, maximum. The heat will soften the masking adhesive for easy removal of the paper.

If an oven is not available, hardened masking paper may be removed by softening the adhesive with aliphatic naphtha. Rub the masking paper with a cloth saturated with naphtha. This will soften the adhesive and free the paper from the plastic. Sheets so treated must be washed immediately with clean water, taking care not to scratch the surfaces.

NOTE: Aliphatic naphtha is not to be confused with aromatic naphtha and other dry-cleaning solvents which are definitely harmful in their effects on plastic. However, aliphatic naphtha is flammable and all precautions regarding the use of flammable liquids must be observed.

Reinforced Plastic

Reinforced plastic is a thermosetting material used in the manufacture of radomes, antenna covers, and wingtips, and as insulation for various pieces of electrical equipment and fuel cells. It has excellent dielectric characteristics which make it ideal for radomes; however, its high strength-weight ratio, resistance to mildew, rust, and rot, and ease of fabrication make it equally suited for other parts of the aircraft.

Reinforced plastic components of aircraft are formed of either solid laminates or sandwich-type laminates. Resins used to impregnate glass cloths are of the contact-pressure type (requiring little or no pressure during cure). These resins are supplied as a liquid which can vary in viscosity from a waterlike consistency to a thick sirup. Cure or polymerization is effected by the use of a catalyst, usually benzoyl peroxide.

Solid laminates are constructed of three or more layers of resin-impregnated cloths "wet laminated" together to form a solid sheet facing or molded shape.

Sandwich-type laminates are constructed of two or more solid sheet facings or a molded shape enclosing a fiberglass honeycomb- or foam-type core. Honeycomb cores are made of glass cloths impregnated with a polyester or a combination of nylon and phenolic resins. The specific density and cell size of honeycomb cores varies over a considerable latitude. Honeycomb cores are normally fabricated in blocks that are later cut to the desired thickness on a bandsaw.

Foam-type cores are formulated from combinations of alkyd resins and metatoluene di-isocyanate. Sandwich-type fiberglass components filled with foam-type cores are manufactured to exceedingly close tolerances on overall thickness of the molded facing and core material. To achieve this accuracy, the resin is poured into a close-tolerance, molded shape. The resin formulation immediately foams up to fill the void in the molded shape and forms a bond between the facing and the core.

RUBBER

Rubber is used to prevent the entrance of dirt, water, or air, and to prevent the loss of fluids, gases, or air. It is also used to absorb vibration, reduce noise, and cushion impact loads.

The term "rubber" is as all-inclusive as the term "metal." It is used to include not only natural rubber, but all synthetic and silicone rubbers.

Natural Rubber

Natural rubber has better processing and physical properties than synthetic or silicone rubber. These properties include: Flexibility, elasticity, tensile strength, tear strength, and low heat buildup due to flexing (hysteresis). Natural rubber is a general-purpose product; however, its suitability for aircraft use is somewhat limited because of its inferior resistance to most influences that cause deterioration. Although it provides an excellent seal for many applications, it swells and often softens in all aircraft fuels and in many solvents (naphthas, etc.). Natural rubber deteriorates more rapidly than synthetic rubber. It is used as a sealing material for water/methanol systems.

Synthetic Rubber

Synthetic rubber is available in several types, each of which is compounded of different materials to give the desired properties. The most widely used are the butyls, Bunas, and neoprene.

Butyl is a hydrocarbon rubber with superior resistance to gas permeation. It is also resistant to deterioration; however, its comparative physical properties are significantly less than those of natural rubber. Butyl will resist oxygen, vegetable oils, animal fats, alkalies, ozone, and weathering.

Like natural rubber, butyl will swell in petroleum or coal tar solvents. It has a low water-absorption rate and good resistance to heat and low temperature. Depending on the grade, it is suitable for use in temperatures ranging from −65° F. to 300° F. Butyl is used with phosphate ester hydraulic fluids (Skydrol), silicone fluids, gases, ketones, and acetones.

Buna-S rubber resembles natural rubber both in processing and performance characteristics. Buna-S is as water-resistant as natural rubber, but has somewhat better aging characteristics.

It has good resistance to heat, but only in the absence of severe flexing. Generally, Buna-S has poor resistance to gasoline, oil, concentrated acids, and solvents. Buna-S is normally used for tires and tubes as a substitute for natural rubber.

Buna-N is outstanding in its resistance to hydrocarbons and other solvents; however, it has poor resilience in solvents at low temperature. Buna-N compounds have good resistance to temperatures up to 300° F., and may be procured for low temperature applications down to −75° F. Buna-N has fair tear, sunlight, and ozone resistance. It has good abrasion resistance and good breakaway properties when used in contact with metal. When used as a seal on a hydraulic piston, it will not stick to the cylinder wall. Buna-N is used for oil and gasoline hose, tank linings, gaskets, and seals.

Neoprene can take more punishment than natural rubber and has better low-temperature characteristics. It possesses exceptional resistance to ozone, sunlight, heat, and aging. Neoprene looks and feels like rubber. Neoprene, however, is less like rubber in some of its characteristics than butyl or Buna. The physical characteristics of neoprene, such as tensile strength and elongation, are not equal to natural rubber but do have a definite similarity. Its tear resistance as well as its abrasion resistance is slightly less than that of natural rubber. Although its distortion recovery is complete, it is not as rapid as natural rubber.

Neoprene has superior resistance to oil. Although it is good material for use in nonaromatic gasoline systems, it has poor resistance to aromatic gasolines. Neoprene is used primarily for weather seals, window channels, bumper pads, oil-resistant hose, and carburetor diaphragms. It is also recommended for use with Freons and silicate ester lubricants.

Thiokol, known also as polysulfide rubber, has the highest resistance to deterioration but ranks the lowest in physical properties. Thiokol, in general, is not seriously affected by petroleum, hydrocarbons, esters, alcohols, gasoline, or water. Thiokols are ranked low in such physical properties as compression set, tensile strength, elasticity, and tear abrasion resistance. Thiokol is used for oil hose, tank linings for aromatic aviation gasolines, gaskets, and seals.

Silicone rubbers are a group of plastic rubber materials made from silicon, oxygen, hydrogen, and carbon. The silicons have excellent heat stability and very low temperature flexibility. They are suitable for gaskets, seals, or other applications where elevated temperatures up to 600° F. are prevalent. Silicone rubbers are also resistant to temperatures down to −150° F. Throughout this temperature range, silicone rubber remains extremely flexible and useful with no hardness or gumminess. Although this material has good resistance to oils, it reacts unfavorably to both aromatic and nonaromatic gasolines.

Silastic, one of the best known silicones, is used to insulate electrical and electronic equipment. Because of its dielectric properties over a wide range of temperatures, it remains flexible and free from crazing and cracking. Silastic is also used for gaskets and seals in certain oil systems.

SHOCK ABSORBER CORD

Shock absorber cord is made from natural rubber strands encased in a braided cover of woven cotton cords treated to resist oxidation and wear. Great tension and elongation are obtained by weaving the jacket upon the bundle of rubber strands while they are stretched about three times their original length.

There are two types of elastic shock-absorbing cord. Type I is a straight cord, and type II is a continuous ring, known as a "bungee." The advantages of the type II cord are that they are easily and quickly replaced and do not have to be secured by stretching and whipping. Shock cord is available in standard diameters from ¼ inch to $^{13}\!/_{16}$ inch.

Three colored threads are braided into the outer cover for the entire length of the cord. Two of these threads are of the same color and represent the year of manufacture; the third thread, a different color, represents the quarter of the year in which the cord was made. The code covers a 5-year period and then repeats itself. This makes it easy to figure forward or backward from the years shown in figure 6–55.

Year marking

Year	Threads	Color
1968	2	blue
1969	2	yellow
1970	2	black
1971	2	green
1972	2	red

Quarter marking

Quarter	Threads	Color
Jan., Feb., Mar.	1	red
Apr., May, June	1	blue
July, Aug., Sept.	1	green
Oct., Nov., Dec.	1	yellow

FIGURE 6–55. Shock absorber cord color coding.

SEALS

Seals are used to prevent fluid from passing a certain point, as well as to keep air and dirt out of the system in which they are used. The increased use of hydraulics and pneumatics in aircraft systems has created a need for packings and gaskets of varying characteristics and design to meet the many variations of operating speeds and temperatures to which they are subjected. No one style or type of seal is satisfactory for all installations. Some of the reasons for this are: (1) Pressure at which the system operates, (2) the type fluid used in the system, (3) the metal finish and the clearance between adjacent parts, and (4) the type motion (rotary or reciprocating), if any. Seals are divided into three main classes: (1) Packings, (2) gaskets, and (3) wipers.

Packings

Packings are made of synthetic or natural rubber. They are generally used as "running seals," that is, in units that contain moving parts, such as actuating cylinders, pumps, selector valves, etc. Packings are made in the form of O-rings, V-rings, and U-rings, each designed for a specific purpose. (See figure 6–56.)

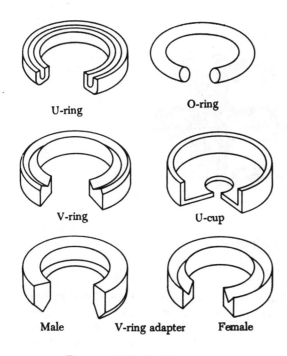

U-ring   O-ring

V-ring   U-cup

Male   V-ring adapter   Female

FIGURE 6–56. Packing rings.

O-Ring Packings

O-ring packings are used to prevent both internal and external leakage. This type of packing ring seals effectively in both directions and is the type most commonly used. In installations subject to pressures above 1,500 p.s.i., backup rings are used with O-rings to prevent extrusion.

When an O-ring packing is to be subjected to pressure from both sides, as in actuating cylinders, two backup rings must be used (one on either side of the O-ring). When an O-ring is subject to pressure on only one side, a single backup ring is generally used. In this case the backup ring is always placed on the side of the O-ring away from the pressure.

The materials from which O-rings are manufactured have been compounded for various operating conditions, temperatures, and fluids. An O-ring designed specifically as a static (stationary) seal will probably not do the job when installed on a moving part such as a hydraulic piston. Most O-rings are similar in appearance and texture, but their characteristics may differ widely. An O-ring will be useless if it is not compatible with the system fluid and operating temperature.

Advances in aircraft design have necessitated new O-ring compositions to meet changed operating conditions. Hydraulic O-rings were originally established under AN specification numbers (6227, 6230, and 6290) for use in MIL–H–5606 fluid at temperatures ranging from −65° F. to +160° F. When new designs raised operating temperatures to a possible 275° F., more compounds were developed and perfected.

Recently a compound was developed that offered improved low-temperature performance without sacrificing high-temperature performance, rendering the other series obsolete. This superior material was adopted in the MS28775 series. This series is now the standard for MIL–H–5606 systems where the temperature may vary from −65° F. to +275° F.

Manufacturers provide color coding on some O-rings, but this is not a reliable or complete means of identification. The color coding system does not identify sizes, but only system fluid or vapor compatibility and in some cases the manufacturer. Color codes on O-rings that are compatible with MIL–H–5606 fluid will always contain blue, but may also contain red or other colors. Packings and gaskets suitable for use with Skydrol fluid will always be coded with a green stripe, but may also have a blue, grey, red, green, or yellow dot as a part of the color code. Color codes on O-rings that are compatible with hydrocarbon fluid will always contain red, and will never contain blue. A colored stripe around the circumference indicates that the O-ring is a boss gasket seal. The color of the stripe indicates fluid compatibility: red for fuel, blue for hydraulic fluid.

The coding on some rings is not permanent. On others it may be omitted due to manufacturing difficulties or interference with operation. Furthermore, the color coding system provides no means to establish the age of the O-ring or its temperature limitations.

Because of the difficulties with color coding, O-rings are available in individual hermetically sealed envelopes, labeled with all pertinent data. When selecting an O-ring for installation, the basic part number on the sealed envelope provides the most reliable compound identification.

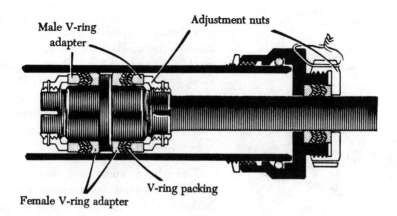

FIGURE 6–57. V-ring installation.

Although an O-ring may appear perfect at first glance, slight surface flaws may exist. These flaws are often capable of preventing satisfactory O-ring performance under the variable operating pressures of aircraft systems; therefore, O-rings should be rejected for flaws that will affect their performance. Such flaws are difficult to detect, and one aircraft manufacturer recommends using a 4-power magnifying glass with adequate lighting to inspect each ring before it is installed.

By rolling the ring on an inspection cone or dowel, the inner diameter surface can also be checked for small cracks, particles of foreign material, or other irregularities that will cause leakage or shorten the life of the O-ring. The slight stretching of the ring when it is rolled inside out will help to reveal some defects not otherwise visible.

Backup Rings

Backup rings (MS28782) made of Teflon do not deteriorate with age, are unaffected by any system fluid or vapor, and can tolerate temperature extremes in excess of those encountered in high-pressure hydraulic systems. Their dash numbers indicate not only their size but also relate directly to the dash number of the O-ring for which they are dimensionally suited. They are procurable under a number of basic part numbers, but they are interchangeable; that is, any Teflon backup ring may be used to replace any other Teflon backup ring if it is of proper overall dimension to support the applicable O-ring. Backup rings are not color coded or otherwise marked and must be identified from package labels.

The inspection of backup rings should include a check to ensure that surfaces are free from irregularities, that the edges are clean-cut and sharp, and that scarf cuts are parallel. When checking Teflon spiral backup rings, make sure that the coils do not separate more than $\frac{1}{4}$ inch when unrestrained.

V-Ring Packings

V-ring packings (AN6225) are one-way seals and are always installed with the open end of the "V" facing the pressure. V-ring packings must have a male and female adapter to hold them in the proper position after installation. It is also necessary to torque the seal retainer to the value specified by the manufacturer of the component being serviced, or the seal may not give satisfactory service. An installation using V-rings is shown in figure 6–57.

U-Ring Packings

U-ring packings (AN6226) and U-cup packings are used in brake assemblies and brake master cylinders. The U-ring and U-cup will seal pressure in only one direction; therefore, the lip of the packings must face toward the pressure. U-ring packings are primarily low-pressure packings to be used with pressures of less than 1,000 p.s.i.

GASKETS

Gaskets are used as static (stationary) seals between two flat surfaces. Some of the more

168

common gasket materials are asbestos, copper, cork, and rubber. Asbestos sheeting is used wherever a heat-resistant gasket is needed. It is used extensively for exhaust system gaskets. Most asbestos exhaust gaskets have a thin sheet of copper edging to prolong their life.

A solid copper washer is used for spark plug gaskets where it is essential to have a noncompressible yet semisoft gasket.

Cork gaskets can be used as an oil seal between the engine crankcase and accessories, and where a gasket is required that is capable of occupying an uneven or varying space caused by a rough surface or expansion and contraction.

Rubber sheeting can be used where there is a need for a compressible gasket. It should not be used in any place where it may come in contact with gasoline or oil because the rubber will deteriorate very rapidly when exposed to these substances.

Gaskets are used in fluid systems around the end caps of actuating cylinders, valves, and other units. The gasket generally used for this purpose is in the shape of an O-ring, similar to O-ring packings.

WIPERS

Wipers are used to clean and lubricate the exposed portions of piston shafts. They prevent dirt from entering the system and help protect the piston shaft against scoring.

Wipers may be either the metallic or the felt type. They are sometimes used together, with the felt wiper installed behind the metallic wiper.

SEALING COMPOUNDS

Certain areas of all aircraft are sealed to withstand pressurization by air, to prevent leakage of fuel, to prevent passage of fumes, or to prevent corrosion by sealing against the weather. Most sealants consist of two or more ingredients properly proportioned and compounded to obtain the best results. Some materials are ready for use as packaged, but others will require mixing before application.

One-Part Sealants

One-part sealants are prepared by the manufacturer and are ready for application as packaged. However, the consistency of some of these compounds may be altered to satisfy a particular method of application. If thinning is desired, the thinner recommended by the sealant manufacturer should be used.

Two-Part Sealants

Two-part sealants are compounds requiring separate packaging to prevent cure prior to application and are identified as the base sealing compound and the accelerator. Any alteration of the prescribed ratios will reduce the quality of the material. Generally two-part sealants are mixed by combining equal portions (by weight) of base compound and accelerator.

All sealant material should be carefully weighed in accordance with the sealant manufacturer's recommendations. Sealant material is usually weighed with a balance scale equipped with weights specially prepared for various quantities of sealant and accelerator.

Before weighing the sealant materials, both the base sealant compound and the accelerator should be thoroughly stirred. Accelerator which is dried out, lumpy, or flaky should not be used. Preweighed sealant kits do not require weighing of the sealant and accelerator before mixing when the entire quantity is to be mixed.

After the proper amount of base sealant compound and accelerator has been determined, add the accelerator to the base sealant compound. Immediately after adding the accelerator, thoroughly mix the two parts by stirring or folding, depending on the consistency of the material. The material should be mixed carefully to prevent entrapment of air in the mixture. Too rapid or prolonged stirring must be avoided as it will build up heat in the mixture and will shorten the normal application time (working life) of the mixed sealant.

To ensure a well-mixed compound, it may be tested by smearing a small portion on a clean, flat metal or glass surface. If flecks or lumps are found, continue mixing. If the flecks or lumps cannot be eliminated, the batch should be rejected.

The working life of mixed sealant is from one-half hour to 4 hours (depending upon the class of sealant); therefore, mixed sealant should be applied as soon as possible or placed in refrigerated storage. Figure 6–58 presents general information concerning various sealants.

The curing rate of mixed sealants varies with changes in temperature and humidity. Curing of sealants will be extremely slow if the temperature

Sealant Base	Accelerator (catalyst)	Mixing ratio by weight	Application life (work)	Storage (shelf) life after mixing	Storage (shelf) life unmixed	Temperature range	Application and limitations
EC-801 (black) MIL-S-7502A Class B-2.	EC-807.	12 parts of EC-807 to 100 parts of EC-801.	2-4 hours.	5 days at −20°F. after flash freeze at −65°F.	6 months.	−65°F. to 200°F.	Faying surfaces, fillet seals, and packing gaps.
EC-800 (red)	None.	Use as is.	8-12 hours.	Not applicable.	6-9 months.	−65°F. to 200°F.	Coating rivets.
EC-612 P (pink) MIL-P-20628.	None.	Use as is.	Indefinite non-drying.	Not applicable.	6-9 months.	−40°F. to 200°F.	Packing voids up to 1/4 inch.
PR-1302HT (red) MIL-S-8784.	PR-1302HT-A.	10 parts of PR-1302HT-A to 100 parts of PR-1302HT.	2-4 hours.	5 days at −20°F. after flash freeze at −65°F.	6 months.	−65°F. to 200°F.	Sealing access. door gaskets.
PR-727 potting compound MIL-S-8516B.	PR-727A.	12 parts of PR-727A to 100 parts of PR-727.	1½ hours minimum.	5 days at −20°F. after flash freeze at −65°F.	6 months.	−65°F. to 200°F.	Potting electrical connections and bulkhead seals.
HT-3 (greygreen)	None.	Use as is.	Solvent release, sets up in 2 to 4 hours.	Not applicable.	6 to 9 months.	−60°F. to 850°F.	Sealing hot air ducts passing through bulkheads.
EC-776 (clear amber) MIL-S-4383B.	None.	Use as is.	8-12 hours.	Not applicable.	Indefinite in airtight containers.	−65°F. to 250°F.	Top coating.

FIGURE 6–58. General sealant information.

is below 60° F. A temperature of 77° F. with 50 percent relative humidity is the ideal condition for curing most sealants.

Curing may be accelerated by increasing the temperature, but the temperature should never be allowed to exceed 120° F. at any time in the curing cycle. Heat may be applied by using infra-red lamps or heated air. If heated air is used, it must be properly filtered to remove moisture and dirt.

Heat should not be applied to any faying surface sealant installation until all work is completed. All faying surface applications must have all attachments, permanent or temporary, completed within the application limitations of the sealant.

Sealant must be cured to a tack-free condition before applying brush top coatings. (Tack-free consistency is the point at which a sheet of cellophane pressed onto the sealant will no longer adhere.)

CORROSION CONTROL

Metal corrosion is the deterioration of the metal by chemical or electrochemical attack and can take place internally as well as on the surface. As in the rotting of wood, this deterioration may change the smooth surface, weaken the interior, or damage or loosen adjacent parts.

Water or water vapor containing salt combine with oxygen in the atmosphere to produce the main source of corrosion in aircraft. Aircraft operating in a marine environment or in areas where the atmosphere contains industrial fumes which are corrosive are particularly susceptible to corrosive attacks.

Corrosion can cause eventual structural failure if left unchecked. The appearance of the corrosion varies with the metal. On aluminum alloys and magnesium it appears as surface pitting and etching, often combined with a grey or white powdery deposit. On copper and copper alloys the corrosion forms a greenish film; on steel a reddish rust. When the grey, white, green, or reddish deposits are removed, each of the surfaces may appear etched and pitted, depending upon the length of exposure and severity of attack. If these surface pits are not too deep, they may not significantly alter the strength of the metal; however, the pits may become sites for crack development. Some types of corrosion can travel beneath surface coatings and can spread until the part fails.

Types of Corrosion

There are two general classifications of corrosion which cover most of the specific forms. These are direct chemical attack and electrochemical attack. In both types of corrosion the metal is converted into a metallic compound such as an oxide, hydroxide, or sulfate. The corrosion process always involves two simultaneous changes: The metal that is attacked or oxidized suffers what may be called anodic change, and the corrosive agent is reduced and may be considered as undergoing cathodic change.

Direct Chemical Attack *Read*

Direct chemical attack, or pure chemical corrosion, is an attack resulting from a direct exposure of a bare surface to caustic liquid or gaseous agents. Unlike electrochemical attack where the anodic and cathodic changes may be taking place a measurable distance apart, the changes in direct chemical attack are occurring simultaneously at the same point. The most common agents causing direct chemical attack on aircraft are: (1) Spilled battery acid or fumes from batteries; (2) residual flux deposits resulting from inadequately cleaned, welded, brazed, or soldered joints; and (3) entrapped caustic cleaning solutions. Spilled battery acid is becoming less of a problem with the advent of aircraft using nickel-cadmium batteries which are usually closed units. The use of these closed units lessens the hazards of acid spillage and battery fumes.

Many types of fluxes used in brazing, soldering, and welding are corrosive and they chemically attack the metals or alloys with which they are used. Therefore, it is important that residual flux be removed from the metal surface immediately after the joining operation. Flux residues are hygroscopic in nature; that is, they are capable of absorbing moisture, and unless carefully removed, tend to cause severe pitting.

Caustic cleaning solutions in concentrated form should be kept tightly capped and as far from aircraft as possible. Some cleaning solutions used in corrosion removal are, in themselves, potentially corrosive agents, and particular attention should be directed toward their complete removal after use on aircraft. Where entrapment of the cleaning solution is likely to occur, a noncorrosive cleaning agent should be used even though it is less efficient.

Electrochemical Attack

An electrochemical attack may be likened chemically to the electrolytic reaction which takes place in electroplating, anodizing, or in a dry-cell battery. The reaction in this corrosive attack requires a medium, usually water, which is capable of conducting a tiny current of electricity. When a metal comes in contact with a corrosive agent and is also connected by a liquid or gaseous path through which electrons may flow, corrosion begins as the metal decays by oxidation. During the attack, the quantity of corrosive agent is reduced and, if not renewed or removed, may completely react with the metal (become neutralized). Different areas of the same metal surface have varying levels of electrical potential and if connected by a conductor, such as salt water, will set up a series of corrosion cells and corrosion will commence.

All metals and alloys are electrically active and have a specific electrical potential in a given chemical environment. The constituents in an alloy also have specific electrical potentials which are generally different from each other. Exposure of the alloy surface to a conductive, corrosive medium causes the more active metal to become anodic and the less active metal to become cathodic, thereby establishing conditions for corrosion. These are called local cells. The greater the difference in electrical potential between the two metals, the greater will be the severity of a corrosive attack, if the proper conditions are allowed to develop.

As can be seen, the conditions for these corrosion reactions are a conductive fluid and metals having a difference in potential. If, by regular cleaning and surface refinishing, the medium is removed and the minute electrical circuit eliminated, corrosion cannot occur; this is the basis for effective corrosion control.

The electrochemical attack is responsible for most forms of corrosion on aircraft structure and component parts.

FORMS OF CORROSION

There are many forms of corrosion. The form of corrosion depends on the metal involved, its size and shape, its specific function, atmospheric conditions, and the corrosion-producing agents present. Those described in this section are the more common forms found on airframe structures.

 ### Surface Corrosion

Surface corrosion appears as a general roughening, etching, or pitting of the surface of a metal, frequently accompanied by a powdery deposit of corrosion products. Surface corrosion may be caused by either direct chemical or electrochemical attack. Sometimes corrosion will spread under the surface coating and cannot be recognized by either the roughening of the surface or the powdery deposit. Instead, the paint or plating will be lifted off the surface in small blisters which result from the pressure of the underlying accumulation of corrosion products.

Dissimilar Metal Corrosion

Extensive pitting damage may result from contact between dissimilar metal parts in the presence of a conductor. While surface corrosion may or may not be taking place, a galvanic action, not unlike electroplating, occurs at the points or areas of contact where the insulation has broken down or been omitted. This electrochemical attack can be very serious because the action is, in many instances, taking place out of sight, and the only way to detect it prior to structural failure is by disassembly and inspection.

Intergranular Corrosion

This type of corrosion is an attack along the grain boundaries of an alloy and commonly results from a lack of uniformity in the alloy structure. Aluminum alloys and some stainless steels are particularly susceptible to this form of electrochemical attack. The lack of uniformity is caused by changes that occur in the alloy during heating and cooling. Intergranular corrosion may exist without visible surface evidence. Very severe intergranular corrosion may sometimes cause the surface of a metal to "exfoliate." This is a lifting or flaking of the metal at the surface due to delamination of the grain boundaries caused by the pressure of corrosion residual product buildup. This type of corrosion is difficult to detect in its original stage. Ultrasonic and eddy current inspection methods are being used with a great deal of success.

Stress Corrosion

Stress corrosion occurs as the result of the combined effect of sustained tensile stresses and a corrosive environment. Stress corrosion cracking is found in most metal systems; however, it is particularly characteristic of aluminum, copper, certain stainless steels, and high-strength alloy steels (over 240,000 p.s.i.). It usually occurs along lines of cold working and may be transgranular or intergranular in nature. Aluminum alloy bell-cranks with pressed-in bushings, landing gear shock struts with pipe-thread type grease fittings, clevis pin joints, shrink fits, and overstressed tubing B-nuts are examples of parts which are susceptible to stress corrosion cracking.

Fretting Corrosion

Fretting corrosion is a particularly damaging form of corrosive attack which occurs when two mating surfaces, normally at rest with respect to one another, are subject to slight relative motion. It is characterized by pitting of the surfaces, and the generation of considerable quantities of finely divided debris. Since the restricted movements of the two surfaces prevent the debris from escaping very easily, an extremely localized abrasion occurs. The presence of water vapor greatly increases this type of deterioration. If the contact areas are small and sharp, deep grooves resembling brinell markings or pressure indentations may be worn in the rubbing surface. As a result, this type of corrosion (on bearing surfaces) has also been called false brinelling.

FACTORS AFFECTING CORROSION

Many factors affect the type, speed, cause, and seriousness of metal corrosion. Some of these factors can be controlled and some cannot.

Climate

The environmental conditions under which an aircraft is maintained and operated greatly affect corrosion characteristics. In a predominately marine environment (with exposure to sea water and salt air), moisture-laden air is considerably more detrimental to an aircraft than it would be if all operations were conducted in a dry climate. Temperature considerations are important because the speed of electrochemical attack is increased in a hot, moist climate.

Size and Type of Metal

It is a well known fact that some metals will corrode faster than others. It is a less known fact that variations in size and shape of a metal can indirectly affect its corrosion resistance.

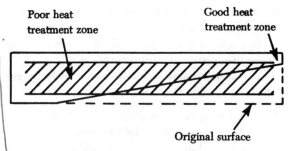

Tapering exposes zone of poor heat treatment to corrosive environment

FIGURE 6–59. The effect of machining thick heat-treated wrought aluminum alloys.

Thick structural sections are more susceptible to corrosive attack than thin sections because variations in physical characteristics are greater. When large pieces are machined or chemically milled after heat treatment, the thinner areas will have different physical characteristics than the thicker areas. (See figure 6–59.)

From a corrosion control standpoint, the best approach is to recognize the critical nature of the integrity and strength of major structural parts and to maintain permanent protection over such areas at all times to prevent the onset of deterioration.

Foreign Material

Among the controllable factors which affect the onset and spread of corrosive attack is foreign material which adheres to the metal surfaces. Such foreign material includes:

(1) Soil and atmospheric dust.
(2) Oil, grease, and engine exhaust residues.
(3) Salt water and salt moisture condensation.
(4) Spilled battery acids and caustic cleaning solutions.
(5) Welding and brazing flux residues.

It is important that aircraft be kept clean. How often and to what extent an aircraft should be cleaned depends on several factors, such as location, model of aircraft, and type of operation.

PREVENTIVE MAINTENANCE

Much has been done to improve the corrosion resistance of aircraft: improvement in materials, surface treatments, insulation, and protective finishes. All of these have been aimed at reducing maintenance effort as well as improving reliability. In spite of these improvements, corrosion and its control is a very real problem that requires continuous preventive maintenance.

Corrosion-preventive maintenance includes the following specific functions:

(1) An adequate cleaning.
(2) Thorough periodic lubrication.
(3) Detailed inspection for corrosion and failure of protective systems.
(4) Prompt treatment of corrosion and touchup of damaged paint areas.
(5) Keeping drainholes free of obstruction.
(6) Daily draining of fuel cell sumps.
(7) Daily wipe-down of exposed critical areas.
(8) Sealing of aircraft against water during foul weather and proper ventilation on warm, sunny days.
(9) Making maximum use of protective covers on parked aircraft.

After any period during which regular corrosion-preventive maintenance is interrupted, the amount of maintenance required to repair accumulated corrosion damage and bring the aircraft back up to standard will usually be quite high.

INSPECTION

Inspection for corrosion is a continuing problem and should be handled on a daily basis. Over-emphasizing a particular corrosion problem when it is discovered and then forgetting about corrosion until the next crisis is an unsafe, costly, and troublesome practice.

Most scheduled maintenance checklists are complete enough to cover all parts of the aircraft or engine, and no part of the aircraft should go unchecked. Use these checklists as a general guide when an area is to be inspected for corrosion. Through experience it will be learned that most aircraft have trouble areas where corrosion will set in despite routine inspection and maintenance.

In addition to routine maintenance inspections, amphibians or seaplanes should be checked daily and critical areas cleaned or treated, as necessary.

CORROSION-PRONE AREAS

Discussed briefly in this section are most of the trouble areas common to all aircraft. However, this coverage is not necessarily complete and may be amplified and expanded to cover the special characteristics of the particular aircraft model involved by referring to the applicable maintenance manual.

Exhaust Trail Areas

Both jet and reciprocating engine exhaust deposits are very corrosive and give particular trouble where gaps, seams, hinges, and fairings are located down the exhaust path and where deposits may be trapped and not reached by normal cleaning methods. Special attention should be paid to areas around rivet heads and in skin crevices. Fairings and access plates in the exhaust areas should be removed for inspection. Exhaust deposit buildup in remote areas such as the empennage surfaces should not be overlooked. Buildup in these areas will be slower and sometimes completely absent, but it has become a problem on some currently operating aircraft.

Battery Compartments and Battery Vent Openings

Despite improvements in protective paint finishes and in methods of sealing and venting, battery compartments continue to be corrosion problem areas. Fumes from overheated electrolyte are difficult to contain and will spread to adjacent cavities and cause a rapid, corrosive attack on all unprotected metal surfaces. Battery vent openings on the aircraft skin should be included in the battery compartment inspection and maintenance procedure. Regular cleaning and neutralization of acid deposits will minimize corrosion from this cause.

Bilge Areas

These are natural sumps for waste hydraulic fluids, water, dirt, and odds and ends of debris. Residual oil quite often masks small quantities of water which settle to the bottom and set up a hidden chemical cell. Seaplane and amphibian aircraft bilge areas are protected by small bags of potassium dichromate inhibitor suspended near the low point in each bilge compartment. These crystals dissolve in any waste water and tend to inhibit the attack on exposed metal surfaces.

Inspection procedures should include replacement of these bags when most of the chemical has been dissolved. Particular attention must be paid to areas located under galleys and lavatories and to human waste disposal openings on the aircraft exteriors. Human waste products and the chemicals used in lavatories are very corrosive to the common aircraft metals. Clean these areas frequently and keep the paint touched up.

Wheel Well and Landing Gear

This area probably receives more punishment due to mud, water, salt, gravel, and other flying debris than any other area on the aircraft.

Because of the many complicated shapes, assemblies, and fittings, complete area paint film coverage is difficult to attain. A partially applied preservative tends to mask corrosion rather than prevent it. Due to heat generated by braking action, preservatives cannot be used on some main landing gear wheels. During inspection of this area, pay particular attention to the following trouble spots:

1. Magnesium wheels, especially around boltheads, lugs, and wheel web areas, particularly for the presence of entrapped water or its effects.
2. Exposed rigid tubing, especially at B-nuts and ferrules, under clamps and tubing identification tapes.
3. Exposed position indicator switches and other electrical equipment.
4. Crevices between stiffeners, ribs, and lower skin surfaces, which are typical water and debris traps.

Water Entrapment Areas

Design specifications require that aircraft have drains installed in all areas where water may collect. Daily inspection of low-point drains should be a standard requirement. If this inspection is neglected, the drains may become ineffective because of accumulated debris, grease, or sealants.

Engine Frontal Areas and Cooling Air Vents

These areas are being constantly abraded with airborne dirt and dust, bits of gravel from runways, and rain erosion which tend to remove the protective finish. Inspection of these areas should include all sections in the cooling air path, with special attention to places where salt deposits may be built up during marine operations. It is imperative that incipient corrosion be inhibited and that paint touchup and hard film preservative coatings be maintained intact on seaplane and amphibian engine surfaces at all times.

Wing Flap and Spoiler Recesses

Dirt and water may collect in flap and spoiler recesses and go unnoticed because they are normally retracted. For this reason these recesses are potential corrosion problem areas.

External Skin Areas

External aircraft surfaces are readily visible and accessible for inspection and maintenance. Even here, certain types of configurations or combinations of materials become troublesome under certain operating conditions and require special attention.

Relatively little corrosion trouble is experienced with magnesium skins if the original surface finish and insulation are adequately maintained. Trimming, drilling, and riveting destroy some of the original surface treatment which is never completely restored by touchup procedures. Any inspection for corrosion should include all magnesium skin surfaces with special attention to edges, areas around fasteners, and cracked, chipped, or missing paint.

Piano-type hinges are prime spots for corrosion due to the dissimilar metal contact between the steel pin and aluminum hinge. They are also natural traps for dirt, salt, and moisture. Inspection of hinges should include lubrication and actuation through several cycles to ensure complete lubricant penetration.

Corrosion of metal skin joined by spot welding is the result of the entrance and entrapment of corrosive agents between the layers of metal. This type of corrosion is evidenced by corrosion products appearing at the crevices through which the corrosive agents enter. More advanced corrosive attack causes skin buckling and eventual spot weld fracture. Skin buckling in its early stages may be detected by sighting along spot-welded seams or by using a straightedge. The only technique for preventing this condition is to keep potential moisture entry points, including seams and holes created by broken spot welds, filled with a sealant or a suitable preservative compound.

Miscellaneous Trouble Areas

Helicopter rotor heads and gearboxes, in addition to being constantly exposed to the elements, contain bare steel surfaces, many external working parts, and dissimilar metal contacts. These areas should be inspected frequently for evidence of corrosion. The proper maintenance, lubrication, and the use of preservative coatings can prevent corrosion in these areas.

All control cables, whether plain carbon steel or corrosion-resistant steel, should be inspected to determine their condition at each inspection period. Cables should be inspected for corrosion by random cleaning of short sections with solvent-soaked cloths. If external corrosion is evident, tension should be relieved and the cable checked for internal corrosion. Cables with internal corrosion should be replaced. Light external corrosion should be removed with a steel-wire brush. When corrosion products have been removed, re-coat the cable with preservative.

CORROSION REMOVAL

In general, any complete corrosion treatment involves the following: (1) Cleaning and stripping of the corroded area, (2) removing as much of the corrosion products as practicable, (3) neutralizing any residual materials remaining in pits and crevices, (4) restoring protective surface films, and (5) applying temporary or permanent coatings or paint finishes.

The following paragraphs deal with the correction of corrosive attack on aircraft surfaces and components where deterioration has not progressed to the point requiring rework or structural repair of the part involved.

Surface Cleaning and Paint Removal

The removal of corrosion necessarily includes removal of surface finishes covering the attacked or suspected area. In order to assure maximum efficiency of the stripping compound, the area must be cleaned of grease, oil, dirt, or preservatives. This preliminary cleaning operation is also an aid in determining the extent of corrosion spread, since the stripping operation will be held to the minimum consistent with full exposure of the corrosion damage. Extensive corrosion spread on any panel should be corrected by fully treating the entire section.

The selection of the type of materials to be used in cleaning will depend on the nature of the matter to be removed. Drycleaning solvent may be used for removing oil, grease, or soft preservative compounds. For heavy-duty removal of thick or dried preservatives, other compounds of the solvent-emulsion type are available.

The use of a general-purpose, water-rinsable stripper is recommended for most applications. Wherever practicable, paint removal from any large area should be accomplished outside (in open air) and preferably in shaded areas. If inside removal is necessary, adequate ventilation must be assured. Synthetic rubber surfaces, including aircraft tires, fabric, and acrylics, must be thoroughly protected against possible contact with paint remover. Care must also be exercised in using paint remover around gas or watertight seam sealants, since this material will tend to soften and destroy the integrity of these sealants.

Mask off any opening that would permit the stripping compound to get into aircraft interiors or critical cavities. Paint stripper is toxic and contains ingredients harmful to both skin and eyes. Rubber gloves, aprons of acid-repellent material, and goggle-type eyeglasses should be worn if any extensive paint removal is to be accomplished. The following is a general stripping procedure:

1. Brush the entire area to be stripped with a cover of stripper to a depth of $\frac{1}{32}$ to $\frac{1}{16}$ inch. Any paint brush makes a satisfactory applicator, except that the bristles will be loosened by the effect of paint remover on the binder, and the brush should not be used for other purposes after being exposed to paint remover.

2. Allow the stripper to remain on the surface for a sufficient length of time to wrinkle and lift the paint. This may be from 10 minutes to several hours, depending on both the temperature and humidity, and the condition of the paint coat being removed. Scrub the surface with a bristle brush saturated with paint remover to further loosen finish that may still be adhering to the metal.

3. Reapply the stripper as necessary in areas that remain tight or where the material has dried, and repeat the above process. Only nonmetallic scrapers may be used to assist in removing persistant paint finishes.

4. Remove the loosened paint and residual stripper by washing and scrubbing the surface with water and a broom or brush. If water spray is available, use a low-to-medium pressure stream of water directly on the scrubbing broom or brush. If steam cleaning equipment is available and the area is sufficiently large, cleaning may be accomplished using this equipment together with a solution

176

of steam cleaning compound. On small areas, any method may be used that will assure complete rinsing of the cleaned area.

CORROSION OF FERROUS METALS *Read*

One of the most familiar types of corrosion is ferrous oxide (rust), generally resulting from atmospheric oxidation of steel surfaces. Some metal oxides protect the underlying base metal, but rust is not a protective coating in any sense of the word. Its presence actually promotes additional attack by attracting moisture from the air and acting as a catalyst in causing additional corrosion to take place. As a result, all rust must be removed from steel surfaces, if complete control of the corrosive attack is to be realized.

Rust first shows on boltheads, holddown nuts, or other unprotected aircraft hardware. Its presence in these areas is generally not dangerous and has no immediate effect on the structural strength of any major components. However, it is indicative of a need for maintenance and of possible corrosive attack in more critical areas. It is also a factor in the general appearance of the equipment. When paint failures occur or mechanical damage exposes highly stressed steel surfaces to the atmosphere, even the smallest amount of rusting is potentially dangerous in these areas and must be removed and controlled.

Mechanical Removal of Iron Rust

The most practicable means of controlling the corrosion of steel is the complete removal of corrosion products by mechanical means and restoring corrosion-preventive coatings. Except on highly stressed steel surfaces, the use of abrasive papers and compounds, small power buffers and buffing compounds, hand wire brushing, or steel wool are all acceptable cleanup procedures. However, it should be recognized that in any such use of abrasives, residual rust usually remains in the bottom of small pits and other crevices. It is practically impossible to remove all corrosion products by abrasive or polishing methods alone. As a result, once a part has rusted it usually corrodes again more easily than it did the first time.

Chemical Surface Treatment of Steel

There are approved methods for converting active rust to phosphates and other protective coatings. Parco Lubrizing and the use of other phosphoric acid proprietary chemicals are examples of such treatments. However, these processes require shop-installed equipment and are impracticable for field use. Other commercial preparations are effective rust converters where tolerances are not critical and where thorough rinsing and neutralizing of residual acid is possible. These situations are generally not applicable to assembled aircraft, and the use of chemical inhibitors on installed steel parts is not only undesirable but very dangerous. The danger of entrapment of corrosive solutions and the resulting uncontrolled attack which could occur when such materials are used under field conditions outweigh any advantages to be gained from their use.

Removal of Corrosion From Highly Stressed Steel Parts

Any corrosion on the surface of a highly stressed steel part is potentially dangerous, and the careful removal of corrosion products is required. Surface scratches or change in surface structure from overheating can also cause sudden failure of these parts. Corrosion products must be removed by careful processing, using mild abrasive papers such as rouge or fine grit aluminum oxide, or fine buffing compounds on cloth buffing wheels. It is essential that steel surfaces not be overheated during buffing. After careful removal of surface corrosion, protective paint finishes should be re-applied immediately.

CORROSION OF ALUMINUM AND ALUMINUM ALLOYS

Read

Corrosion attack on aluminum surfaces is usually quite obvious, since the products of corrosion are white and generally more voluminous than the original base metal. Even in its early stages, aluminum corrosion is evident as general etching, pitting, or roughness of the aluminum surfaces. NOTE: Aluminum alloys commonly form a smooth surface oxidation which is from .001 in. to .0025 in. thick. This is not considered detrimental as such a coating provides a hard shell barrier to the introduction of corrosive elements. Such oxidation is not to be confused with the severe corrosion discussed in this paragraph.

General surface attack of aluminum penetrates relatively slowly, but is speeded up in the presence of dissolved salts. Considerable attack can usually take place before serious loss of structural strength

177

develops. However, at least three forms of attack on aluminum alloys are particularly serious: (1) The penetrating pit-type corrosion through the walls of aluminum tubing, (2) stress-corrosion cracking of materials under sustained stress, and (3) the intergranular attack which is characteristic of certain improperly heat-treated aluminum alloys.

In general, corrosion of aluminum can be more effectively treated in place than corrosion occurring on other structural materials used in aircraft. Treatment includes the mechanical removal of as much of the corrosion products as practicable, and the inhibition of residual materials by chemical means, followed by the restoration of permanent surface coatings.

Treatment of Unpainted Alumium Surfaces

Relatively pure aluminum has considerably more corrosion resistance compared with the stronger aluminum alloys. Advantage is taken of this by laminating a thin sheet of relatively pure aluminum over the base aluminum alloy. The protection obtained is good, and the alclad surface can be maintained in a polished condition. In cleaning such surfaces, however, care must be taken to prevent staining and marring of the exposed aluminum and, more important from a protection standpoint, to avoid unnecessary mechanical removal of the protective alclad layer and the exposure of the more susceptible aluminum alloy base material. A typical aluminum corrosion treatment sequence follows:

1. Remove oil and surface dirt with any suitable mild cleaner prior to abrasive cleaning of aluminum surfaces.
2. Hand polish the corroded areas with fine abrasives or with metal polish. Metal polish intended for use on clad aluminum aircraft surfaces must not be used on anodized aluminum since it is abrasive enough to actually remove the protective anodized film. It effectively removes stains and produces a high, lasting polish on unpainted alclad. If a surface is particularly difficult to clean, a cleaner and brightener compound for aluminum, can be used before polishing to shorten the time and lessen the effort necessary to get a clean surface.
3. Treat any superficial corrosion present, using an inhibitive wipe-down material. An alternate treatment is processing with a solution of sodium dichromate and chromium trioxide. Allow these solutions to remain on the corroded area for 5 to 20 minutes, and then remove the excess by rinsing and wiping the surface dry with a clean cloth.
4. Overcoat the polished surfaces with waterproof wax.

Aluminum surfaces that are to be subsequently painted can be exposed to more severe cleaning procedures and can also be given more thorough corrective treatment prior to painting. The following sequence is generally used:

1. Thoroughly clean the affected surfaces of all soil and grease residues prior to processing. Any general aircraft cleaning procedure may be used.
2. If residual paint films remain, strip the area to be treated. Procedures for the use of paint removers, and the precautions to observe, were previously mentioned in this chapter under "Surface Cleaning and Paint Removal."
3. Treat superficially corroded areas with a 10 percent solution of chromic acid and sulphuric acid. Apply the solution by swab or brush. Scrub the corroded area with the brush while it is still damp. While chromic acid is a good inhibitor for aluminum alloys, even when corrosion products have not been completely removed, it is important that the solution penetrate to the bottom of all pits and underneath any corrosion that may be present. Thorough brushing with a stiff fiber brush should loosen or remove most existing corrosion and assure complete penetration of the inhibitor into crevices and pits. Allow the chromic acid to remain in place for at least 5 minutes, then remove the excess by flushing with water or wiping with a wet cloth. There are several commercial chemical surface treatment compounds, similar to the type described above, which may also be used.
4. Dry the treated surface and restore recommended permanent protective coatings as required in accordance with the aircraft manufacturer's procedures. Restoration of paint coatings should immediately follow any surface treatment performed. In any case, make sure that corrosion treatment is accomplished or is re-applied on the same day that paint refinishing is scheduled.

Treatment of Anodized Surfaces

As previously stated, anodizing is a common surface treatment of aluminum alloys. When this coating is damaged in service, it can be only partially restored by chemical surface treatment. Therefore, any corrosion correction of anodized surfaces should avoid destruction of the oxide film in the unaffected area. Avoid the use of steel wool, steel wire brushes, or severe abrasive materials.

Aluminum wool, aluminum wire brushes, or fiber bristle brushes are the approved tools for cleaning corroded anodized surfaces. Care must be exercised in any cleaning process to avoid unnecessary breaking of the adjacent protective film.

Take every precaution to maintain as much of the protective coating as practicable. Otherwise, treat anodized surfaces in the same manner as other aluminum finishes. Chromic acid and other inhibitive treatments tend to restore the oxide film.

Treatment of Intergranular Corrosion in Heat-Treated Aluminum Alloy Surfaces

As previously described, intergranular corrosion is an attack along grain boundaries of improperly or inadequately heat-treated alloys, resulting from precipitation of dissimilar constituents following heat treatment. In its most severe form, actual lifting of metal layers (exfoliation) occurs. More severe cleaning is a must when intergranular corrosion is present. The mechanical removal of all corrosion products and visible delaminated metal layers must be accomplished to determine the extent of the destruction and to evaluate the remaining structural strength of the component.

Corrosion depth and removal limits have been established for some aircraft. Any loss of structural strength should be evaluated prior to repair or replacement of the part.

CORROSION OF MAGNESIUM ALLOYS

Magnesium is the most chemically active of the metals used in aircraft construction and is, therefore, the most difficult to protect. When a failure in the protective coating does occur, the prompt and complete correction of the coating failure is imperative if serious structural damage is to be avoided. Magnesium attack is probably the easiest type of corrosion to detect in its early stages, since magnesium corrosion products occupy several

times the volume of the original magnesium metal destroyed. The beginning of attack shows as a lifting of the paint films and white spots on the magnesium surface. These rapidly develop into snowlike mounds or even "white whiskers." Re-protection involves the removal of corrosion products, the partial restoration of surface coatings by chemical treatment, and a re-application of protective coatings.

Treatment of Wrought Magnesium Sheet and Forgings

Magnesium skin attack will usually occur around edges of skin panels, underneath holddown washers, or in areas physically damaged by shearing, drilling, abrasion, or impact. If the skin section can be removed easily, this should be done to assure complete inhibition and treatment. If insulating washers are involved, screws should be loosened, at least sufficiently to permit brush treatment of the magnesium under the insulating washer. Complete mechanical removal of corrosion products should be practiced insofar as practicable. Such mechanical cleaning should be limited to the use of stiff, hog-bristle brushes and similar nonmetallic cleaning tools, particularly if treatment is to be performed under field conditions. Any entrapment of steel particles from steel-wire brushes or steel tools, or contamination of treated surfaces by dirty abrasives, can cause more trouble than the initial corrosive attack. Corroded magnesium may generally be treated as follows:

1. Clean and strip the paint from the area to be treated. (Paint stripping procedures were discussed earlier in this chapter.)
2. Using a stiff, hog-bristle brush, break loose and remove as much of the corrosion products as practicable. Steel-wire brushes, carborundum abrasives, or steel cutting tools should not be used.
3. Treat the corroded area liberally with a chromic acid solution, to which has been added sulphuric acid, and work into pits and crevices by brushing the area while still wet with chromic acid, again using a nonmetallic brush.
4. Allow the chromic acid to remain in place for 5 to 20 minutes before wiping up the excess with a clean, damp cloth. Do not allow the excess solution to dry and remain on the surface, as paint lifting will be caused by such deposits.

5. As soon as the surfaces are dry, restore the original protective paint.

Treatment of Installed Magnesium Castings

Magnesium castings, in general, are more porous and more prone to penetrating attack than wrought magnesium skins. However, treatment is, for all practical purposes, the same for all magnesium areas. Engine cases, bellcranks, fittings, numerous covers, plates, and handles are the most common magnesium castings.

When attack occurs on a casting, the earliest practicable treatment is required if dangerous corrosive penetration is to be avoided. In fact, engine cases submerged in salt water overnight can be completely penetrated. If it is at all practicable, parting surfaces should be separated to effectively treat the existing attack and prevent its further progress. The same general treatment sequence in the preceding paragraph for magnesium skin should be followed.

If extensive removal of corrosion products from a structural casting is involved, a decision from the manufacturer may be necessary to evaluate the adequacy of structural strength remaining. Specific structural repair manuals usually include dimensional tolerance limits for critical structural members and should be referred to, if any question of safety is involved.

TREATMENT OF TITANIUM AND TITANIUM ALLOYS

Attack on titanium surfaces is generally difficult to detect. Titanium is, by nature, highly corrosion resistant, but it may show deterioration from the presence of salt deposits and metal impurities, particularly at high temperatures. Therefore, the use of steel wool, iron scrapers, or steel brushes for cleaning or for the removal of corrosion from titanium parts is prohibited.

If titanium surfaces require cleaning, hand polishing with aluminum polish or a mild abrasive is permissable, if fiber brushes only are used and if the surface is treated following cleaning with a suitable solution of sodium dichromate. Wipe the treated surface with dry cloths to remove excess solution, but do not use a water rinse.

PROTECTION OF DISSIMILAR METAL CONTACTS

Certain metals are subject to corrosion when placed in contact with other metals. This is commonly referred to as electrolytic or dissimilar metals corrosion. Contact of different bare metals creates an electrolytic action when moisture is present. If this moisture is salt water, the electrolytic action is accelerated. The result of dissimilar-metal contact is oxidation (decomposition) of one or both metals. The chart shown in figure 6–60 lists the metal combinations requiring a protective separator. The separating materials may be metal primer, aluminum tape, washers, grease, or sealant, depending on the metals involved.

Contacts Not Involving Magnesium

All dissimilar joints not involving magnesium are protected by the application of a minimum of two coats of zinc chromate primer in addition to normal primer requirements. Primer is applied by brush or spray and allowed to air-dry 6 hours between coats.

Contacts Involving Magnesium

To prevent corrosion between dissimilar-metal joints in which magnesium alloy is involved, each surface is insulated as follows:

At least two coats of zinc chromate are applied to each surface. Next, a layer of pressure-sensitive vinyl tape 0.003-inch thick is applied smoothly and firmly enough to prevent air bubbles and wrinkles. To avoid creep-back, the tape is not stretched during application. When the thickness of the tape interferes with the assembly of parts, where relative motion exists between parts, or when service temperatures above 250° F. are anticipated, the use of tape is eliminated and extra coats (minimum of three) of primer are applied.

CORROSION LIMITS

Corrosion, however slight, is damage. Therefore, corrosion damage is classified under the four standard types, as is any other damage. These types are: (1) Negligible damage, (2) damage repairable by patching, (3) damage repairable by insertion, and (4) damage necessitating replacement of parts.

The term "negligible," as used here, does not imply that little or nothing should be done. The corroded surface should be cleaned, treated, and painted as appropriate. Negligible damage, generally, is corrosion which has scarred or eaten away the surface protective coats and begun to etch the metal.

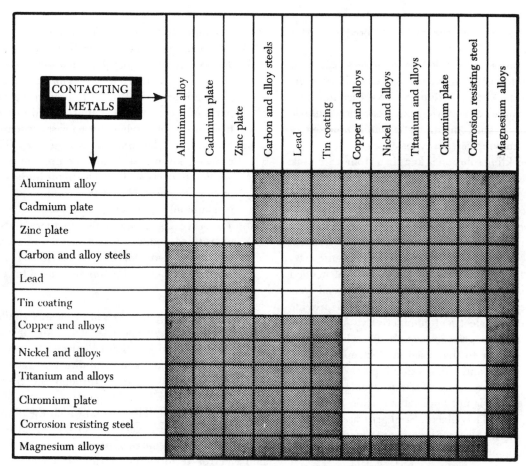

Shaded areas indicate dissimiliar metal contacts

FIGURE 6–60. Dissimilar metal contacts that will result in electrolytic corrosion.

Corrosion damage extending to classifications of "repairable by patching" and "repairable by insertion" should be rapaired in accordance with the applicable structural repair manual.

When corrosion damage exceeds the damage limits to the extent that repair is not possible, the component or structure should be replaced.

PROCESSES AND MATERIALS USED IN CORROSION CONTROL

Metal Finishing

Aircraft parts are almost always given some type of surface finish by the manufacturer. The main purpose is to provide corrosion resistance; however, surface finishes may also be applied to increase wear resistance or to provide a suitable base for paint.

In most instances the original finishes cannot be restored in the field due to nonavailability of equipment or other limitations. However, an understanding of the various types of metal finishes is necessary if they are to be properly maintained in the field and if the partial restoration techniques used in corrosion control are to be effective.

Surface Preparation

Original surface treatments for steel parts usually include a cleaning treatment to remove all traces of dirt, oil, grease, oxides, and moisture. This is necessary to provide an effective bond between the metal surface and the final finish. The cleaning process may be either mechanical or chemical. In mechanical cleaning the following methods are employed: wire brush, steel wool, emery cloth, sandblasting, or vapor blasting.

Chemical cleaning is preferred over mechanical since none of the base metal is removed by cleaning. There are various chemical processes now in use, and the type used will depend on the material being cleaned and the type of foreign matter being removed.

Steel parts are pickled to remove scale, rust, or other foreign matter, particularly before plating. The pickling solution can be either muriatic (hydrochloric) or sulfuric acid. Cost-wise, sulfuric acid is preferable, but muriatic acid is more effective in removing certain types of scale.

The pickling solution is kept in a stoneware tank and is usually heated by means of a steam coil. Parts not to be electroplated after pickling are immersed in a lime bath to neutralize the acid from the pickling solution.

Electrocleaning is another type of chemical cleaning used to remove grease, oil, or organic matter. In this cleaning process, the metal is suspended in a hot alkaline solution containing special wetting agents, inhibitors, and materials to provide the necessary electrical conductivity. An electric current is then passed through the solution in a manner similar to that used in electroplating.

Aluminum and magnesium parts are also cleaned by using some of the foregoing methods. Blast cleaning is not applicable to thin aluminum sheets, particularly alclad. Steel grits are not used on aluminum or corrosion-resistant metals.

Polishing, buffing, and coloring of metal surfaces play a very important part in the finishing of metal surfaces. Polishing and buffing operations are sometimes used when preparing a metal surface for electroplating, and all three operations are used when the metal surface requires a high-luster finish.

Electroplating   *Read*

Electroplating is the process of transferring metal from one object to another by chemical and electrical means. Several reasons for applying plated coatings are:

1. To protect the base metal (metal being plated) against corrosion. Tin, zinc, nickel, and cadmium are some of the metals used to form a protective coating on another metal by electrolytic action.
2. To protect the base metal against wear, caused by abrasion or fretting corrosion. Chromium plating is extensively used for wear resistance on gages, dies, oleo pistons, and cylinder barrels. Nickel plating can also be used for this purpose.
3. To produce and retain a desired appearance (color and luster), as well as improve resistance to tarnish. Gold, nickel, or chromium plating can be used in this application.
4. To protect a base metal against some special chemical reaction; for example, copper plating is sometimes used to prevent certain parts of a component manufactured of steel from absorbing carbon during casehardening.
5. To increase the dimensions of a part. This process, known as "building up," may be applied to parts accidentally made undersize, or to worn parts. Nickel or chromium plating is commonly used for this purpose.
6. To serve as a base for further plating operations, reduce buffing costs, and ensure bright deposits of nickel or nickel and chromium. Copper is commonly used for this purpose.

All electroplating processes are basically similar. The equipment used consists of a tank or bath containing a liquid solution called an electrolyte, a control panel, and a source of direct current.

When a current is passed through the circuit, the plating material is the positive electrode or anode of the circuit. The part on which the plating is deposited is the negative electrode or cathode of the circuit. The source of power anode, cathode, and electrolyte form the plating electrical circuit and cause tiny particles of the plating material to be deposited on the surface of the part being plated. The process is continued until a plating of the required thickness is obtained. The electrolyte, anode, cathode, and current setting will vary with the type of plating material being used.

Some plating operations do not use anodes of the metal being deposited but obtain the metal from the electrolyte alone. Chromium plating is an example of this type plating. Lead anodes, instead of chromium anodes, which are unsatisfactory, are employed to complete the electrical circuit. The chromium for the plating comes from the chromic acid in the electrolyte.

Metal Spraying   *Read*

Metal spraying, or metallizing, is the surface application of molten metal on any solid base material. It is possible to spray aluminum, cadmium, copper, nickel, steel, or any of several metals using this process. In aircraft work the process is used primarily to spray a coat of pure aluminum on steel parts to improve their corrosion resistance.

The base material must be roughened (usually by sandblasting) and perfectly clean in order for the sprayed metal to adhere to the surface of the base material.

Metal-spraying equipment consists of a supply of oxygen and acetylene piped to the spray gun, which ends in a nozzle. At this point they can be ignited as in a welding torch. A supply of compressed air is also piped to the spray gun. This compressed air operates a feeding mechanism that draws the wire through the spray gun. The wire is melted by the hot oxyacetylene flame and is thrown against the surface being metallized by the compressed air.

CHEMICAL TREATMENTS

Parco Lubrizing

Parco Lubrizing is a chemical treatment for iron and steel parts which converts the surface to a nonmetallic oil-absorptive phosphate coating. It is designed primarily to reduce wear on moving parts.

The process is a modification of Parkerizing, and consists of a precleaning treatment in which vapor degreasing, acid pickle, or spray emulsion is used, followed by a 15-minute dip in a solution of water and 10 percent by volume of Parco Lubrite. This is followed by a water rinse and a dip in water-soluble oil. The phosphate surface soaks up oil and retains it.

Anodizing

Anodizing is the most common surface treatment of nonclad aluminum alloy surfaces. The aluminum alloy sheet or casting is the positive pole in an electrolytic bath in which chromic acid or other oxidizing agent produces an aluminum oxide film on the metal surface. Aluminum oxide is naturally protective, and anodizing merely increases the thickness and density of the natural oxide film. When this coating is damaged in service, it can only be partially restored by chemical surface treatments. Therefore, any processing of anodized surfaces, including corrosion removal, should avoid unnecessary destruction of the oxide film.

The anodized coating provides excellent resistance to corrosion. The coating is soft and easily scratched, making it necessary to use extreme caution when handling it prior to coating it with primer.

Aluminum wool, nylon webbing impregnated with aluminum oxide abrasive or fiber bristle brushes are the approved tools for cleaning anodized surfaces. The use of steel wool, steel wire brushes, or harsh abrasive materials on any aluminum surfaces is prohibited. Producing a buffed or wire brush finish by any means is also prohibited. Otherwise, anodized surfaces are treated in much the same manner as other aluminum finishes.

In addition to its corrosion-resistant qualities, the anodic coating is also an excellent bond for paint. In most cases parts are primed and painted as soon as possible after anodizing. The anodic coating is a poor conductor of electricity; therefore, if parts require bonding, the coating is removed where the bonding wire is to be attached.

Alclad surfaces that are to be left unpainted require no anodic treatment; however, if the alclad surface is to be painted, it is usually anodized to provide a bond for the paint.

Alodizing

Alodizing is a simple chemical treatment for all aluminum alloys to increase their corrosion resistance and to improve their paint-bonding qualities. Because of its simplicity, it is rapidly replacing anodizing in aircraft work.

The process consists of precleaning with an acidic or alkaline metal cleaner that is applied by either dipping or spraying. The parts are then rinsed with fresh water under pressure for 10 to 15 seconds. After thorough rinsing, alodine is applied by dipping, spraying, or brushing. A thin, hard coating results which ranges in color from light, bluish-green with a slight iridescence on copper-free alloys to an olive green on copper-bearing alloys. The alodine is first rinsed with clear, cold or warm water for a period of 15 to 30 seconds. An additional 10- to 15-second rinse is then given in a Deoxylyte bath. This bath is to counteract alkaline material and to make the alodyzed aluminum surface slightly acid on drying.

Chemical Surface Treatment and Inhibitors

As previously described, aluminum and magnesium alloys in particular are protected originally by a variety of surface treatments. Steels may have been Parco Lubrized or otherwise oxidized on the surface during manufacture. Most of these coatings can only be restored by processes which are completely impractical in the field. But, corroded areas where such protective films have been destroyed require some type of treatment prior to refinishing. The following inhibiting materials are particularly effective in the field treatment of aluminum, are beneficial to bare magnesium, and are of some value even on bare steel parts.

The labels on the containers of surface treatment chemicals will provide warnings if a material is toxic or flammable. However, the label might not be large enough to accommodate a list of all the possible hazards which may ensue if the materials are mixed with incompatible substances. For example, some chemicals used in surface treatments will react violently if inadvertently mixed with paint thinners. Chemical surface treatment materials must be handled with extreme care and mixed exactly according to directions.

Chromic Acid Inhibitor

A 10-percent solution by weight of chromic acid, activated by a small amount of sulfuric acid, is particularly effective in treating exposed or corroded aluminum surfaces. It may also be used to treat corroded magnesium.

This treatment tends to restore the protective oxide coating on the metal surface. Such treatment must be followed by regular paint finishes as soon as practicable, and never later than the same day as the latest chromic acid treatment. Chromium trioxide flake is a powerful oxidizing agent and a fairly strong acid. It must be stored away from organic solvents and other combustibles. Wiping cloths used in chromic-acid pickup should either be rinsed thoroughly after use or disposed of.

Sodium Dichromate Solution

A less active chemical mixture for surface treatment of aluminum is a solution of sodium dichromate and chromic acid. Entrapped solutions of this mixture are less likely to corrode metal surfaces than chromic acid inhibitor solutions.

Chemical Surface Treatments

Several commercial, activated chromate acid mixtures are available under Specification MIL-C-5541 for field treatment of damaged or corroded aluminum surfaces. Precautions should be taken to make sure that sponges or cloths used are thoroughly rinsed to avoid a possible fire hazard after drying. (See figure 6–61)

TYPE OF CORROSION	STEP 1 CLEANING TO REMOVE FOREIGN MATTER	STEP 2 PAINT STRIPPING (WHEN APPLICABLE)	STEP 3 CORROSION REMOVAL	STEP 4 SURFACE TREATMENT (WHEN APPLICABLE)
Light or heavy pitting or etching of aluminum (clad)	Remove foreign matter with cleaner, Spec MIL-C-25769	Readily accessible areas: Strip with stripper, Spec MIL-R-25134 Confined areas: Strip with solvent	Remove corrosion with brightener, Spec MIL-C-25378	Chromate conversion coating Spec MIL-C-5541
Light or heavy pitting or etching of aluminum (clad)	As above	As above	Remove corrosion by mechanical method — or — Remove corrosion with brightener, Spec MIL-C-25378	As above
Intergranular or exfoliation corrosion of aluminum	As above	As above	Remove corrosion by mechanical method	As above
Light or heavy corrosion on small aluminum parts which can be removed for treatment	**Painted Parts** Clean and strip in solution of paint and varnish remover, Spec MIL-R-7751 **Unpainted Parts** Clean with compound, Spec P-C-426, MIL-C-5543 or vapor degrease	**Not Required** If cleaning accomplished with paint and varnish remover Spec MIL-R-7751	Remove corrosion and oxide film by immersion of parts in phosphoric-chromate acid solution	Immersion chromate conversion coating, Spec MIL-C-5541
Stress corrosion cracking of aluminum	**Not Applicable**	See Step 1	See Step 1	See Step 1

FIGURE 6-61. Typical corrosion removal and treatment procedures for aluminum alloys.

PROTECTIVE PAINT FINISHES

A good, intact paint finish is the most effective barrier between metal surfaces and corrosive media. The three most common finishes are a nitrocellulose finish, an acrylic nitrocellulose finish, and an epoxy finish. In addition, high-visibility fluorescent materials may also be used, along with a variety of miscellaneous combinations of special materials. There may also be rain-erosion-resistant coatings on metal leading edges, and several different baked enamel finishes on engine cases and wheels.

AIRCRAFT CLEANING

Cleaning an aircraft and keeping it clean are extremely important. A cracked landing gear fitting covered with mud and grease may be easily overlooked. Dirt can hide cracks in the skin. Dust and grit cause hinge fittings to wear excessively. A film of dirt if left on the aircraft's outer surface, reduces flying speed and adds extra weight. Dirt or trash blowing or bouncing around the inside of the aircraft is annoying and dangerous. Small pieces of dirt blown into the eyes of the pilot at a critical moment can cause an accident. A coating of dirt and grease on moving parts makes a sort of grinding compound that can cause excessive wear. Salt water has a serious corroding effect on exposed metal parts of the aircraft, and should be washed off immediately.

There are many different kinds of cleaning agents approved for use in cleaning aircraft. It is impractical to cover each of the various types of cleaning agents since their use varies under different conditions, such as the type of material to be removed, the aircraft finish, and whether the cleaning is internal or external.

In general, the types of cleaning agents used on aircraft are solvents, emulsion cleaners, soaps, and synthetic detergents. Their use must be in accordance with the applicable maintenance manual. The types of cleaning agents named above are also classed as light- or heavy-duty cleaners. The soap and synthetic detergent type cleaners are used for light-duty cleaning, while the solvent and emulsion type cleaners are used for heavy-duty cleaning. The light-duty cleaners, which are nontoxic and nonflammable, should be used whenever possible.

Exterior Cleaning

There are three methods of cleaning the aircraft exterior: (1) Wet wash, (2) dry wash, and (3) polishing. Polishing can be further broken down into hand polishing and mechanical polishing. The type and extent of soiling and the final desired appearance determine the cleaning method to be used.

Wet wash removes oil, grease, or carbon deposits and most soils, with the exception of corrosion and oxide films. The cleaning compounds used are usually applied by spray or mop, after which high-pressure running water is used as a rinse. Either alkaline or emulsion cleaners can be used in the wet-wash method.

Dry wash is used to remove airport film, dust, and small accumulations of dirt and soil when the use of liquids is neither desirable nor practical. This method is not suitable for removing heavy deposits of carbon, grease, or oil, especially in the engine exhaust areas. Dry-wash materials are applied with spray, mops, or cloths, and removed by dry mopping or wiping with clean, dry cloths.

Polishing restores the luster to painted and unpainted surfaces of the airplane, and is usually performed after the surfaces have been cleaned. Polishing is also used to remove oxidation and corrosion. Polishing materials are available in various forms and degrees of abrasiveness. It is important that the aircraft manufacturer's instructions be used in specific applications.

The washing of aircraft should be performed in the shade whenever possible as cleaning compounds tend to streak the surface if applied to hot metal, or permitted to dry on the area. Install covers over all openings where water or cleaners might enter and cause damage.

Various areas of aircraft, such as the sections housing radar and the area forward of the cockpit that are finished with a dull paint, should not be cleaned more than necessary and should never be scrubbed with stiff brushes or coarse rags. A soft sponge or cheesecloth with a minimum of manual rubbing is advisable. Any oil or exhaust stains on the surface should first be removed with a solvent such as kerosene or other petroleum-base solvent. The surfaces should be rinsed immediately after cleaning to prevent the compound from drying on the surface.

Before applying soap and water to plastic surfaces, flush the plastic surfaces with fresh water to dissolve salt deposits and wash away dust particles. Plastic surfaces should be washed with soap and water, preferably by hand. Rinse with fresh water and dry with chamois or absorbent cotton. In view of the soft surface, do not rub plastic with a dry cloth since this is not only likely to cause scratches, but it also builds up an electrostatic charge which attracts dust particles to the surface. The charge as well as the dust may be removed by patting or gently blotting with a clean, damp chamois. Do not use scouring powder or other material which can mar the finish. Remove oil and grease by rubbing gently with a cloth wet with soap and water. Do not use acetone, benzene, carbon tetrachloride, lacquer thinners, window cleaning sprays, gasoline, fire extinguisher or deicer fluid on plastics because they soften the plastic and cause crazing.

Surface oil, hydraulic fluid, grease, or fuel can be removed from aircraft tires by washing with a mild soap solution.

After cleaning, lubricate all grease fittings, hinges, etc., where removal, contamination, or dilution of the grease is suspected during washing of the aircraft.

INTERIOR CLEANING

Keeping the interior of the aircraft clean is just as important as maintaining a clean exterior surface. Corrosion can establish itself on the inside structure to a greater degree because it is difficult to reach some areas for cleaning. Nuts, bolts, bits of wire, or other metal objects carelessly dropped and neglected, combined with moisture and dis-similar-metal contact, can cause electrolytic corrosion.

When performing structural work inside the aircraft, all metal particles and other debris should be cleaned up as soon as possible. To make cleaning easier and prevent the metal particles and debris from getting into inaccessible areas, a drop-cloth can be used in the work area to catch this debris.

A vacuum cleaner can be used to pick up dust and dirt from the interior of the cockpit and cabin.

Aircraft interior present certain problems during cleaning operations. The following is taken from The National Fire Protection Association (NFPA) Bulletin #410F "Aircraft Cabin Cleaning Operation".

Basic to an understanding of the problem is the fact that aircraft cabin compartments constitute relatively small enclosures as measured by their cubic footage. This presents the possibility of restricted ventilation and the quick build-up of flammable vapor-air mixtures where there is any indiscriminate use of flammable cleaning agents or solvents. Within the same volume there may also exist the possibility of an ignition source in the form of an electrical fault, a friction or static spark, an open flame device, or some other potential introduced by concurrent maintenance work.

Wherever possible, nonflammable agents should be used in these operations to reduce to the minimum the fire and explosion hazards.

Types of Cleaning Operations

The principal areas of aircraft cabins which may need periodic cleaning are:

(1) Aircraft passenger cabin areas (seats, carpets, side panels, headliners, overhead racks, curtains, ash trays, windows, doors, decorative panels of plastic, wood or similar materials).

(2) Aircraft flight station areas (similar materials to those found in passenger cabin areas plus instrument panels, control pedestals, glare shields, flooring materials, metallic surfaces of instruments and flight control equipment, electrical cables and contacts, etc.).

(3) Lavatories and buffets (similar materials to those found in passenger cabin areas plus toilet facilities, metal fixtures and trim, trash containers, cabinets, wash and sink basins, mirrors, ovens, etc.).

Nonflammable Aircraft Cabin Cleaning Agents and Solvents

(1) *Detergents and Soaps.* These have widespread application for most aircraft cleaning operations involving fabrics, headliners, rugs, windows and similar surfaces that are not damageable by water solutions since they are colorfast and nonshrinkable. Care is frequently needed to prevent leaching of water soluble fire-retardant salts which may have been used to treat such materials in order to reduce their flame spread characteristics.

(2) *Alkaline Cleaners.* Most of these agents are water soluble and thus have no fire hazard properties. They can be used on fabrics, headliners, rugs and similar surfaces in the same manner as detergent and soap solutions with only minor added limitations resulting from their inherent caustic character which may increase their efficiency as cleaning agents but result in somewhat greater deteriorating effects on certain fabrics and plastics.

(3) *Acid Solutions.* A number of proprietary acid solutions are available for use as cleaning agents. They are normally mild solutions designed primarily to remove carbon smut or corrosive stains. As water based solutions, they have no flash point but may require more careful and judicious use not only to prevent damage to fabrics, plastics, or other surfaces but also to protect the skin and clothing of those using the materials.

(4) *Deodorizing or Disinfecting Agents.* A number of proprietary agents useful for aircraft cabin deodorizing or disinfecting are nonflammable. Most of these are designed for spray application (aerosol type) and have a nonflammable pressurizing agent but it is well to check this carefully as some may contain a flammable compressed gas for pressurization.

(5) *Abrasives.* Some proprietary nonflammable mild abrasive materials are available for rejuvenating painted or polished surfaces. They present no fire hazard.

(6) *Dry Cleaning Agents.* Perchlorethylene and trichlorethylene as used at ambient temperatures are examples of nonflammable dry cleaning agents. These materials do have a toxicity hazard requiring care in their use. Fire retardant treated materials may be adversely affected by the application of these agents as is true of the water-soluble agents.

Flammable and Combustible Agents

(1) *High Flash Point Solvents.* Specially refined petroleum products, first developed as "Stoddard Solvent" but now sold under a variety of trade names by different companies, have solvent properties approximating gasoline but have fire hazard properties similar to those of kerosene as commonly used (not heated). Most of these are stable products having a flash point from 100° F. to 140° F. with a comparatively low degree of toxicity.

(2) *Low Flash Point Solvents.* Class I (flash point at below 100° F.) flammable liquids should not be used for aircraft cleaning or refurbishing. Common materials falling into this "Class" are acetone, aviation gasoline, methyl ethyl ketone, naphtha and toluol.

In cases where it is absolutely necessary to use a flammable liquid, high flash point liquids (those having a flash point of 100° F. or more) should be used.

(3) *Mixed Liquids.* Some commercial solvents are mixtures of liquids with differing rates of evaporation such as a mixture of one of the various naphthas and a chlorinated material. The different rates of evaporation may present problems from both the toxicity and fire hazard viewpoints and such mixtures should not be used unless they are stored and handled with full knowledge of these hazards and appropriate precautions taken.

Container Controls

Flammable liquids should be handled only in approved containers or safety cans appropriately labeled.

Fire Prevention Precautions

During aircraft cleaning or refurbishing operations where flammable or combustible liquids are used, the following general safeguards are recommended:

(1) Aircraft cabins should be provided with ventilation sufficient at all times to prevent the accumulation of flammable vapors. To accomplish this, doors to cabins shall be open to secure maximum advantage of natural ventilation. Where such natural ventilation is insufficient under all conditions to prevent the accumulation of flammable vapors, approved mechanical ventilation equipment shall be provided and used. The accumulation of flammable vapors above 25 percent of the lower flammability limit of the particular vapor being used, measured at a point five feet from the location of use, shall result in emergency revisions of operations in progress.

(2) All open flame and spark producing equipment or devices that might be brought within the vapor hazard area should be shut down and not operated during the period when flammable vapors may exist.

(3) Electrical equipment of a hand portable nature used within an aircraft cabin shall be of the type approved for use in Class I, Group D, Hazardous Locations as defined by the National Electrical Code.

(4) Switches to aircraft cabin lighting and to the aircraft electrical system components within the cabin area should not be worked on or switched on or off during cleaning operations.

(5) Suitable warning signs should be placed in conspicuous locations at aircraft doors to indicate that flammable liquids are being or have been used in the cleaning or refurbishing operation in progress.

Fire Protection Recommendations

During aircraft cleaning or refurbishing operations where flammable liquids are used the following *general* fire protection safeguards are recommended:

(1) Aircraft undergoing such cleaning or refurbishing should preferably be located outside of the hangar buildings when weather conditions permit. This provides for added natural ventilation and normally assures easier access to the aircraft in the event of fire.

(2) It is recommended that during such cleaning or refurbishing operations in an aircraft outside of the hangar that portable fire extinguishers be provided at cabin entrances having a minimum rating of 20–B and, at minimum, a booster hoseline with an adjustable water spray nozzle be available capable of reaching the cabin area for use pending the arrival of airport fire equipment. As an alternate to the previous recommendations a Class A fire extinguisher having a minimum rating of 4–A plus or a Class B fire extinguisher having a minimum rating of 20–B should be placed at aircraft cabin doors for immediate use if required.

NOTE 1: All-purpose (dry chemical) type extinguishers should not be used in situations where aluminum corrosion is a problem.

NOTE 2: Portable and semi-portable fire detection and extinguishing equipment has been developed, tested and installed to provide protection to aircraft during construction and maintenance operations. Operators are urged to investigate the feasibility of utilizing such equipment during aircraft cabin cleaning and refurbishing operations.

(3) Aircraft undergoing such cleaning or refurbishing where the work must be done under cover should be in hangars equipped with automatic fire protection equipment.

POWERPLANT CLEANING

Cleaning the powerplant is an important job and should be done thoroughly. Grease and dirt accumulations on an air-cooled engine provide an effective insulation against the cooling effect of air flowing over it. Such an accumulation can also cover up cracks or other defects.

When cleaning an engine, open or remove the cowling. Beginning with the top, the engine and accessories are washed down with a fine spray of kerosene or solvent. A bristle brush may be used to help clean some of the surfaces.

Fresh water and soap, and approved cleaning solvents may be used for cleaning propeller and rotor blades. Except in the process of etching, caustic material should not be used on a propeller. Scrapers, power buffers, steel brushes, or any tool or substances that will mar or scratch the surface should not be used on propeller blades, except as recommended for etching and repair.

Water spray, rain, or other airborne abrasive material strikes a whirling propeller blade with such force that small pits are formed in the blade's leading edge. If preventive measures are not taken, corrosion causes these pits to rapidly grow larger. The pits may become so large that it is necessary to file the blade's leading edge until it is smooth.

Steel propeller blades have more resistance to abrasion and corrosion than aluminum alloy blades. Steel blades, if rubbed down with oil after each flight, retain a smooth surface for a long time.

Propellers should be examined regularly because cracks in steel or aluminum alloy blades can become filled with oil which tends to oxidize. This can readily be seen when the blade is inspected. Keeping the surface wiped with oil serves as a safety feature by helping to make cracks more obvious.

Propeller hubs must be inspected regularly for cracks and other defects. Unless the hubs are kept clean, defects may not be found. Steel hubs should be cleaned with soap and fresh water, or with an approved cleaning solvent. These cleaning solvents may be applied by cloths or brushes. Tools and abrasives that scratch or otherwise damage the plating should be avoided.

In special cases in which a high polish is desired, the use of a good grade of metal polish is recommended. Upon completion of the polishing, all traces of polish must be removed immediately, the blades cleaned, and then coated with clean engine oil.

All cleaning substances must be removed immediately after completion of the cleaning of any propeller part. Soap in any form can be removed by rinsing repeatedly with fresh water. After rinsing, all surfaces should be dried and coated with clean engine oil.

After cleaning the powerplant, all control arms, bellcranks, and moving parts should be lubricated according to instructions in the applicable maintenance manual.

SOLVENT CLEANERS

In general, solvent cleaners used in aircraft cleaning should have a flashpoint of not less than 105° F., if explosion proofing of equipment and other special precautions are to be avoided. Chlorinated solvents of all types meet the non-flammable requirements but are toxic, and safety precautions must be observed in their use. Use of carbon tetrachloride should be avoided.

Dry-cleaning Solvent

Stoddard solvent is the most common petroleum-base solvent used in aircraft cleaning. Its flashpoint is slightly above 105° F. and can be used to remove grease, oils, or light soils. Drycleaning solvent is preferable to kerosene for all cleaning purposes, but like kerosene it leaves a slight residue upon evaporation which may interfere with the application of some final paint films.

Aliphatic and Aromatic Naphtha

Aliphatic naphtha is recommended for wipe-down of cleaned surfaces just before painting. This material can also be used for cleaning acrylics and rubber. It flashes at approximately 80° F. and must be used with care.

Aromatic naphtha should not be confused with the aliphatic material. It is toxic and attacks acrylics and rubber products, and must be used with adequate controls.

Safety Solvent

Safety solvent, trichloroethane (methyl chloroform), is used for general cleaning and grease removal. It is nonflammable under ordinary circumstances, and is used as a replacement for carbon tetrachloride. The use and safety precautions necessary when using chlorinated solvents must be observed. Prolonged use can cause dermatitis on some persons.

Methyl Ethyl Ketone (MEK)

MEK is also available as a solvent cleaner for metal surfaces and paint stripper for small areas. This is a very active solvent and metal cleaner, with a flashpoint of about 24° F. It is toxic when inhaled, and safety precautions must be observed during its use.

Kerosene

Kerosene is mixed with solvent-emulsion type cleaners for softening heavy preservative coatings. It is also used for general solvent cleaning, but its use should be followed by a coating or rinse with some othes type of protective agent. Kerosene does not evaporate as rapidly as dry cleaning solvent and generally leaves an appreciable film on cleaned surfaces, which may actually be corrosive. Kerosene films may be removed with safety solvent, water emulsion cleaners, or detergent mixtures.

Cleaning Compound For Oxygen Systems

Cleaning compounds for use in the oxygen system are anhydrous (waterless) ethyl alcohol, isopropyl (anti-icing fluid) alcohol, or a mixture of freon and isopropyl alcohol. These may be used to clean accessible components of the oxygen system such as crew masks and lines. Fluids should not be put into tanks or regulators.

Do not use any cleaning compounds which may leave an oily film when cleaning oxygen equipment. Avoid prolonged skin contact with the freon-alcohol mixture or breathing of the vapors. Instructions of the manufacturer of the oxygen equipment and cleaning compounds must be followed at all times.

EMULSION CLEANERS

Solvent- and water-emulsion compounds are used in general aircraft cleaning. Solvent emulsions are particularly useful in the removal of heavy deposits, such as carbon, grease, oil, or tar. When used in accordance with instructions, these solvent emulsions do not affect good paint coatings or organic finishes.

Water-Emulsion Cleaner

Material available under Specification MIL-C-22543A is a water-emulsion cleaning compound intended for use on both painted and unpainted aircraft surfaces. This material is also acceptable for cleaning fluorescent painted surfaces and is safe for use on acrylics. However, these properties will vary with the material available, and a sample application should be checked carefully before general uncontrolled use.

Solvent-Emulsion Cleaners

One type of solvent-emulsion cleaner is non-phenolic and can be safely used on painted surfaces without softening the base paint. Repeated use may soften acrylic nitrocellulose lacquers. It is effective, however, in softening and lifting heavy preservative coatings. Persistent materials should be given a second or third treatment as necessary.

Another type of solvent-emulsion cleaner has a phenolic base which is more effective for heavy-duty application, but it also tends to soften paint coatings. It must be used with care around rubber, plastics, or other nonmetallic materials. Rubber gloves and goggles should be worn for protection when working with phenolic-base cleaners.

SOAPS AND DETERGENT CLEANERS

A number of materials are available for mild cleaning use. In this section, some of the more common materials are discussed.

Cleaning Compound, Aircraft Surfaces

Specification MIL-C-5410 Type I and II materials are used in general cleaning of painted and unpainted aircraft surfaces for the removal of light-to-medium soils, operational films, oils, or greases. They are safe to use on all surfaces, including fabrics, leather, and transparent plastics. Nonglare finishes should not be cleaned more than necessary and should never be scrubbed with stiff brushes.

Nonionic Detergent Cleaners

These materials may be either water-soluble or oil-soluble. The oil-soluble detergent cleaner is effective in a 3- to 5-percent solution in dry-cleaning solvent for softening and removing heavy preservative coatings. This mixture's performance is similar to the emulsion cleaners mentioned previously.

MECHANICAL CLEANING MATERIALS

Mechanical cleaning materials must be used with care and in accordance with directions given, if damage to finishes and surfaces is to be avoided.

Mild Abrasive Materials

No attempt is made in this section to furnish detailed instructions for using various materials listed. Some do's and don'ts are included as an aid in selecting materials for specific cleaning jobs.

Powdered pumice is used for cleaning corroded aluminum surfaces. Similar mild abrasives may also be used.

Impregnated cotton wadding material is used for removal of exhaust-gas stains and polishing corroded aluminum surfaces. It may also be used on other metal surfaces to produce a high reflectance.

Aluminum metal polish is used to produce a high-luster, long-lasting polish on unpainted aluminum clad surfaces. It should not be used on anodized surfaces because it will remove the oxide coat.

Three grades of aluminum wool, coarse, medium, and fine, are used for general cleaning of aluminum surfaces. Impregnated nylon webbing material is preferred over aluminum wool for the removal of corrosion products and stubborn paint films and for the scuffing of existing paint finishes prior to touchup.

Lacquer rubbing compound material can be used to remove engine exhaust residues and minor oxidation. Heavy rubbing over rivet heads or edges where protective coatings may be worn thin should be avoided.

Abrasive Papers

Abrasive papers used on aircraft surfaces should not contain sharp or needlelike abrasives which can imbed themselves in the base metal being cleaned or in the protective coating being maintained. The abrasives used should not corrode the material being cleaned. Aluminum oxide paper, 300 grit or finer, is available in several forms and is safe to use on most surfaces. Type I, Class 2 material under Federal Specification P-C-451 is available in 1½- and 2-inch widths. The use of carborundum (silicon carbide) papers should be avoided, particularly on aluminum or magnesium. The grain structure of carborundum is sharp, and the material is so hard that individual grains will penetrate and bury themselves even in steel surfaces. The use of emery paper or crocus cloth on aluminum or magnesium can cause serious corrosion of the metal by imbedded iron oxide.

CHEMICAL CLEANERS

Chemical cleaners must be used with great care in cleaning assembled aircraft. The danger of entrapping corrosive materials in faying surfaces and crevices counteracts any advantages in their speed and effectiveness. Any materials used must be relatively neutral and easy to remove. It is emphasized that all residue must be removed. Soluble salts from chemical surface treatments such as chromic acid or dichromate treatment will liquefy and promote blistering in the paint coatings.

Phosphoric-Citric Acid

A phosphoric-citric acid mixture (Type I) for cleaning aluminum surfaces is available and is ready to use as packaged. Type II is a concentrate which must be diluted with mineral spirits and water. Skin contact should be avoided by wearing rubber gloves and goggles. Any acid burns may be neutralized by copious water washing, followed by treatment with a diluted solution of baking soda (sodium bicarbonate).

Baking Soda

Baking soda may be used to neutralize acid deposits in lead-acid battery compartments and to treat acid burns from chemical cleaners and inhibitors.

STRUCTURAL METALS

Knowledge and understanding of the uses, strengths, limitations, and other characteristics of structural metals is vital to properly construct and maintain any equipment, especially airframes. In aircraft maintenance and repair, even a slight deviation from design specification, or the substitution of inferior materials, may result in the loss of both lives and equipment. The use of unsuitable materials can readily erase the finest craftsmanship. The selection of the correct material for a specific repair job demands familiarity with the most common physical properties of various metals.

Properties of Metals

Of primary concern in aircraft maintenance are such general properties of metals and their alloys as hardness malleability, ductility, elasticity, toughness, density, brittleness, fusibility, conductivity contraction and expansion, and so forth. These terms are explained to establish a basis for further discussion of structural metals.

Explanation of Terms

Hardness refers to the ability of a metal to resist abrasion, penetration, cutting action, or permanent distortion. Hardness may be increased by cold-working the metal and, in the case of steel and certain aluminum alloys, by heat treatment. Structural parts are often formed from metals in their soft state and are then heat treated to harden them so that the finished shape will be retained. Hardness and strength are closely associated properties of metals.

Brittleness is the property of a metal which allows little bending or deformation without shattering. A brittle metal is apt to break or crack without change of shape. Because structural metals are often subjected to shock loads, brittleness is not a very desirable property. Cast iron, cast aluminum, and very hard steel are examples of brittle metals.

A metal which can be hammered, rolled, or pressed into various shapes without cracking, breaking, or having some other detrimental effect, is said to be malleable. This property is necessary in sheet metal that is worked into curved shapes-such as cowlings, fairings, or wingtips. Copper is an example of a malleable metal.

Ductility is the property of a metal which permits it to be permanently drawn, bent, or twisted into various shapes without breaking. This property is essential for metals used in making wire and tubing. Ductile metals are greatly preferred for aircraft use because of their ease of forming and resistance to failure under shock loads. For this reason, aluminum alloys are used for cowl rings, fuselage and wing skin, and formed or extruded parts, such as ribs, spars, and bulkheads. Chrome molybdenum steel is also easily formed into desired shapes. Ductility is similar to malleability.

Elasticity is that property which enables a metal to return to its original shape when the force which causes the change of shape is removed. This property is extremely valuable because it would be highly undesirable to have a part permanently distorted after an applied load was removed. Each metal has a point known as the elastic limit beyond which it cannot be loaded without causing permanent distortion. In aircraft construction, members and parts are so designed that the maximum loads to which they are subjected will not stress them beyond their elastic limits. This desirable property is present in spring steel.

A material which possesses toughness will withstand tearing or shearing and may be stretched or otherwise deformed without breaking. Toughness is a desirable property in aircraft metals.

Density is the weight of a unit volume of a material. In aircraft work, the specified weight of a material per cubic inch is preferred since this figure can be used in determining the weight of a part before actual manufacture. Density is an important consideration when choosing a material to be used in the design of a part in order to maintain the proper weight and balance of the aircraft.

Fusibility is the ability of a metal to become liquid by the application of heat. Metals are fused in welding. Steels fuse around 2,600° F. and aluminum alloys at approximately 1,100° F.

Conductivity is the property which enables a metal to carry heat or electricity. The heat conductivity of a metal is especially important in welding because it governs the amount of heat that will be required for proper fusion. Conductivity of the metal, to a certain extent, determines the type of jig to be used to control expansion and contraction. In aircraft, electrical conductivity must also be considered in conjunction with bonding, to eliminate radio interference.

Contraction and expansion are reactions produced in metals as the result of heating or cooling. Heat applied to a metal will cause it to expand or become larger. Cooling and heating affect the design of welding jigs, castings, and tolerances necessary for hot-rolled material.

Selection Factors

Strength, weight, and reliability are three factors which determine the requirements to be met by any material used in airframe construction and repair. Airframes must be strong and yet as light in weight as possible. There are very definite limits to which increases in strength can be accompanied by increases in weight. An airframe so heavy that it could not support a few hundred pounds of additional weight would be of little use.

All metals, in addition to having a good strength/weight ratio, must be thoroughly reliable, thus minimizing the possibility of dangerous and unexpected failures. In addition to these general properties, the material selected for a definite application must possess specific qualities suitable for the purpose.

The material must possess the strength required by the dimensions, weight, and use. There are five basic stresses which metals may be required to withstand. These are tension, compression, shear, bending, and torsion.

The tensile strength of a material is its resistance to a force which tends to pull it apart. Tensile strength is measured in p.s.i. (pounds per square inch) and is calculated by dividing the load, in pounds, required to pull the material apart by its cross-sectional area, in square inches.

The compression strength of a material is its resistance to a crushing force which is the opposite of tensile strength. Compression strength is also measured in p.s.i.

When a piece of metal is cut, the material is subjected, as it comes in contact with the cutting edge, to a force known as shear. Shear is the tendency on the part of parallel members to slide in opposite directions. It is like placing a cord or thread between the blades of a pair of scissors. The shear strength is the shear force in p.s.i. at which a material fails. It is the load divided by the shear area.

Bending can be described as the deflection or curving of a member due to forces acting upon it. The bending strength of material is the resistance it offers to deflecting forces.

Torsion is a twisting force. Such action would occur in a member fixed at one end and twisted at the other. The torsional strength of material is its resistance to twisting.

The relationship between the strength of a material and its weight per cubic inch, expressed as a ratio, is known as the strength/weight ratio. This ratio forms the basis for comparing the desirability of various materials for use in airframe construction and repair. Neither strength nor weight alone can be used as a means of true comparison. In some applications, such as the skin of monocoque structures, thickness is more important than strength, and, in this instance, the material with the lightest weight for a given thickness or gage is best. Thickness or bulk is necessary to prevent buckling or damage caused by careless handling.

Corrosion is the eating away or pitting of the surface or the internal structure of metals. Because of the thin sections and the safety factors used in aircraft design and construction, it would be dangerous to select a material possessing poor corrosion-resistant characteristics.

Another significant factor to consider in maintenance and repair is the ability of a material to be formed, bent, or machined to required shapes. The hardening of metals by cold-working or forming is termed work-hardening. If a piece of metal is formed (shaped or bent) while cold, it is said to be cold-worked. Practically all the work an aviation mechanic does on metal is cold-work. While this is convenient, it causes the metal to become harder and more brittle.

If the metal is cold-worked too much, that is, if it is bent back and forth or hammered at the same place too often, it will crack or break. Usually, the more malleable and ductile a metal is, the more cold-working it can stand. Any process which involves controlled heating and cooling of metals to develop certain desirable characteristics (such as hardness, softness, ductility, tensile strength, or refined grain structure) is called heat treatment or heat treating. With steels the term "heat treating" has a broad meaning and includes such processes as annealing, normalizing, hardening, and tempering.

In the heat treatment of aluminum alloys, only two processes are included: (1) The hardening and toughening process, and (2) the softening process. The hardening and toughening process is called heat treating, and the softening process is called annealing.

Aircraft metals are subjected to both shock and

fatigue (vibrational) stresses. Fatigue occurs in materials which are exposed to frequent reversals of loading or repeatedly applied loads, if the fatigue limit is reached or exceeded. Repeated vibration or bending will ultimately cause a minute crack to occur at the weakest point. As vibration or bending continues, the crack lengthens until the part completely fails. This is termed shock and fatigue failure. Resistance to this condition is known as shock and fatigue resistance. It is essential that materials used for critical parts be resistant to these stresses.

METALWORKING PROCESSES

There are three methods of metalworking: (1) Hot-working, (2) cold-working, and (3) extruding. The method used will depend on the metal involved and the part required, although in some instances both hot- and cold-working methods may be used to make a single part.

Hot-working

Almost all steel is hot-worked from the ingot into some form from which it is either hot- or cold-worked to the finished shape. When an ingot is stripped from its mold, its surface is solid, but the interior is still molten. The ingot is then placed in a soaking pit which retards loss of heat, and the molten interior gradually solidifies. After soaking, the temperature is equalized throughout the ingot, then it is reduced to intermediate size by rolling, making it more readily handled.

The rolled shape is called a bloom when its section dimensions are 6 x 6 inches or larger and approximately square. The section is called a billet when it is approximately square and less than 6 x 6 inches. Rectangular sections which have a width greater than twice their thickness are called slabs. The slab is the intermediate shape from which sheets are rolled.

Blooms, billets, or slabs are heated above the critical range and rolled into a variety of shapes of uniform cross section. The more common of these rolled shapes are sheet, bar, channels, angles, I-beams, and the like. As will be discussed later in this chapter, hot-rolled material is frequently finished by cold-rolling or drawing to obtain accurate finish dimensions and a bright, smooth surface.

Complicated sections which cannot be rolled, or sections of which only a small quantity is required, are usually forged. Forging of steel is a mechanical working at temperatures above the critical range to shape the metal as desired. Forging is done either by pressing or hammering the heated steel until the desired shape is obtained,

Pressing is used when the parts to be forged are large and heavy; this process also replaces hammering where high-grade steel is required. Since a press is slow acting, its force is uniformly transmitted to the center of the section, thus affecting the interior grain structure as well as the exterior to give the best possible structure throughout.

Hammering can be used only on relatively small pieces. Since hammering transmits its force almost instantly, its effect is limited to a small depth. Thus, it is necessary to use a very heavy hammer or to subject the part to repeated blows to ensure complete working of the section. If the force applied is too weak to reach the center, the finished forged surface will be concave. If the center was properly worked, the surface will be convex or bulged. The advantage of hammering is that the operator has control over both the amount of pressure applied and the finishing temperature, and is able to produce small parts of the highest grade. This type of forging is usually referred to as smith forging. It is used extensively where only a small number of parts are needed. Considerable machining time and material are saved when a part is smith forged to approximately the finished shape.

Steel is often harder than necessary and too brittle for most practical uses when put under severe internal strain. To relieve such strain and reduce brittleness, it is tempered after being hardened. This consists of heating the steel in a furnace to a specified temperature and then cooling it in air, oil, water, or a special solution. Temper condition refers to the condition of metal or metal alloys with respect to hardness or toughness. Rolling, hammering, or bending these alloys, or heat treating and aging them, causes them to become tougher and harder. At times these alloys become too hard for forming and have to be re-heat treated or annealed.

Metals are annealed to relieve internal stresses, soften the metal, make it more ductile, and refine the grain structure. Annealing consists of heating the metal to a prescribed temperature, holding it there for a specified length of time, and then cooling the metal back to room temperature. To produce maximum softness, the metal must be cooled very slowly. Some metals must be furnace cooled; others may be cooled in air.

Normalizing applies to iron-base metals only. Normalizing consists of heating the part to the proper temperature, holding it at that temperature until it is uniformaly heated, and then cooling it in still air. Normalizing is used to relieve stresses in metals.

Cold-Working

Cold-working applies to mechanical working performed at temperatures below the critical range. It results in a strain hardening of the metal. In fact, the metal often becomes so hard that it is difficult to continue the forming process without softening the metal by annealing.

Since the errors attending shrinkage are eliminated in cold-working, a much more compact and better metal is obtained. The strength and hardness, as well as the elastic limit, are increased; but the ductility decreases. Since this makes the metal more brittle, it must be heated from time to time during certain operations to remove the undesirable effects of the working.

While there are several cold-working processes, the two with which the aviation mechanic will be principally concerned are cold-rolling and cold-drawing. These processes give the metals desirable qualities which cannot be obtained by hot-working.

Cold-rolling usually refers to the working of metal at room temperature. In this operation, the materials that have been rolled to approximate sizes are pickled to remove the scale, after which they are passed through chilled finishing rolls. This gives a smooth surface and also brings the pieces to accurate dimensions. The principal forms of cold-rolled stocks are sheets, bars, and rods.

Cold-drawing is used in making seamless tubing, wire, streamlined tie rods, and other forms of stock. Wire is made from hot-rolled rods of various diameters. These rods are pickled in acid to remove scale, dipped in lime water, and then dried in a steam room where they remain until ready for drawing. The lime coating adhering to the metal serves as a lubricant during the drawing operation.

The size of the rod used for drawing depends upon the diameter wanted in the finished wire. To reduce the rod to the desired size, it is drawn cold through a die. One end of the rod is filed or hammered to a point and slipped through the die opening. Here it is gripped by the jaws of the drawing block and pulled through the die. This series of operations is done by a mechanism known as a drawbench.

In order to reduce the rod gradually to the desired size, it is necessary to draw the wire through successively smaller dies. Because each of these drawings reduces the ductility of the wire, it must be annealed from time to time before further drawings can be accomplished. Although cold-working reduces the ductility, it increases the tensile strength of the wire.

In making seamless steel aircraft tubing, the tubing is cold-drawn through a ring-shaped die with a mandrel or metal bar inside the tubing to support it while the drawing operations are being performed. This forces the metal to flow between the die and the mandrel and affords a means of controlling the wall thickness and the inside and outside diameters.

Extruding

The extrusion process involves the forcing of metal through an opening in a die, thus causing the metal to take the shape of the die opening. Some metals such as lead, tin, and aluminum may be extruded cold; but generally metals are heated before the operation is begun.

The principal advantage of the extrusion process is its flexibility. Aluminum, because of its workability and other favorable properties, can be economically extruded to more intricate shapes and larger sizes than is practicable with many other metals.

Extruded shapes are produced in very simple as well as extremely complex sections. In this process a cylinder of aluminum, for instance, is heated to 750° F. to 850° F. and is then forced through the opening of a die by a hydraulic ram. The opening is the shape desired for the cross section of the finished extrusion.

Many structural parts, such as channels, angles, T-sections, and Z-sections are formed by the extrusion process.

FERROUS AIRCRAFT METALS

Many different metals are required in the repair of aircraft. This is a result of the varying needs with respect to strength, weight, durability, and resistance to deterioration of specific structures of parts. In addition, the particular shape or form of the material plays an important role. In selecting materials for aircraft repair, these factors plus many others are considered in relation to the mechanical and physical properties. Among the common materials used are ferrous metals. The term "ferrous" applies to the group of metals having iron as their principal constituent.

Identification

If carbon is added to iron, in percentages

ranging up to approximately 1 percent, the product is vastly superior to iron alone and is classified as carbon steel. Carbon steel forms the base of those alloy steels produced by combining carbon steel with other elements known to improve the properties of steel. A base metal (such as iron) to which small quantities of other metals have been added is called an alloy. The addition of other metals changes or improves the chemical or physical properties of the base metal for a particular use.

Nomenclature and Chemical Compositions of Steels

In order to facilitate the discussion of steels, some familiarity with their nomenclature is desirable. A numerical index, sponsored by the Society of Automotive Engineers (SAE) and the American Iron and Steel Institute (AISI), is used to identify the chemical compositions of the structural steels. In this system, a four-numeral series is used to designate the plain carbon and alloy steels; five numerals are used to designate certain types of alloy steels. The first two digits indicate the type of steel, the second digit also generally (but not always) gives the approximate amount of the major alloying element and the last two (or three) digits are intended to indicate the approximate middle of the carbon range. However, a deviation from the rule of indicating the carbon range is sometimes necessary.

Small quantities of certain elements are present in alloy steels that are not specified as required. These elements are considered as incidental and may be present to the maximum amounts as follows: copper, 0.35 percent; nickel, 0.25 percent; chromium, 0.20 percent; molybdenum, 0.06 percent.

The list of standard steels is altered from time to time to accommodate steels of proven merit and to provide for changes in the metallurgical and engineering requirements of industry. Refer to the numerical index table in figure 6–62.

Metal stock is manufactured in several forms and shapes, including sheets, bars, rods, tubings, extrusions, forgings, and castings. Sheet metal is made in a number of sizes and thicknesses. Specifications designate thicknesses in thousandths of an inch. Bars and rods are supplied in a variety of shapes, such as round, square, rectangular, hexagonal, and octagonal. Tubing can be obtained in round, oval, rectangular, or streamlined shapes. The size of tubing is generally specified by outside diameter and wall thickness.

The sheet metal is usually formed cold in such machines as presses, bending brakes, drawbenches,

Series designation	Types
100xx –	Nonsulphurized carbon steels
11xx –	Resulphurized carbon steels (free machining)
12xx –	Rephosphorized and resulphurized carbon steels (free machining)
13xx –	Manganese 1.75%
•23xx –	Nickel 3.50%
•25xx –	Nickel 5.00%
31xx –	Nickel 1,25%, chromium 0.65%
33xx –	Nickel 3.50%, chromium 1.55%
40xx –	Molybdenum 0.20 or 0.25%
41xx –	Chromium 0.50 or 0.95%, molybdenum 0.12 or 0.20%
43xx –	Nickel 1.80%, chromium 0.50 or 0.80%, molybdenum 0.25%
44xx –	Molybdenum 0.40%
45xx –	Molybdenum 0.52%
46xx –	Nickel 1.80%, molybdenum 0.25%
47xx –	Nickel 1.05%, chromium 0.45%, molybdenum 0.20 or 0.35%
48xx –	Nickel 3.50%, molybdenum 0.25%
50xx –	Chromium 0.25, or 0.40 or 0.50%
50xxx –	Carbon 1.00%, chromium 0.50%
51xx –	Chromium 0.80, 0.90, 0.95, or 1.00%
51xxx –	Carbon 1.00%, chromium 1.05%
52xxx –	Carbon 1.00%, chromium 1.45%
61xx –	Chromium 0.60, 0.80, or 0.95%, vanadium 0.12%, 0.10% min., or 0.15% min.
81xx –	Nickel 0.30%, chromium 0.40%, molybdenum 0.12%
86xx –	Nickel 0.55%, chromium 0.50%, molybdenum 0.20%
87xx –	Nickel 0.55%, chromium 0.05%, molybdenum 0.25%
88xx –	Nickel 0.55%, chromium 0.05%, molybdenum 0.35%
92xx –	Manganese 0.85%, silicon 2.00%, chromium 0 or 0.35%
93xx –	Nickel 3.25%, chromium 1.20%, molybdenum 0.12%
94xx –	Nickel 0.45%, chromium 0.40%, molybdenum 0.12%
98xx –	Nickel 1.00%, chromium 0.80%, molybdenum 0.25%

•Not included in the current list of standard steels.

FIGURE 6–62. SAE numerical index.

or rolls. Forgings are shaped or formed by pressing or hammering heated metal in dies. Castings are produced by pouring molten metal into molds. The casting is finished by machining.

Spark testing is a common means of identifying various ferrous metals. In this test the piece of iron or steel is held against a revolving grinding stone and the metal is identified by the sparks thrown off. Each ferrous metal has its own peculiar spark characteristics. The spark streams vary from a few tiny shafts to a shower of sparks several feet in length. (Few nonferrous metals give off sparks when touched to a grinding stone. Therefore, these metals cannot be successfully identified by the spark test.)

Identification by spark testing is often inexact unless performed by an experienced person, or the test pieces differ greatly in their carbon content and alloying constituents.

Wrought iron produces long shafts that are straw colored as they leave the stone and white at the end. Cast iron sparks are red as they leave the stone and turn to a straw color. Low-carbon steels give off long, straight shafts having a few white sprigs. As the carbon content of the steel increases, the number of sprigs along each shaft increases and the stream becomes whiter in color. Nickel steel causes the spark stream to contain small white blocks of light within the main burst.

Types, Characteristics, and Uses of Alloyed Steels

Steel containing carbon in percentages ranging from 0.10 to 0.30 percent is classed as low-carbon steel. The equivalent SAE numbers range from 1010 to 1030. Steels of this grade are used for making such items as safety wire, certain nuts, cable bushings, or threaded rod ends. This steel in sheet form is used for secondary structural parts and clamps, and in tubular form for moderately stressed structural parts.

Steel containing carbon in percentages ranging from 0.30 to 0.50 percent is classed as medium-carbon steel. This steel is especially adaptable for machining or forging, and where surface hardness is desirable. Certain rod ends and light forgings are made from SAE 1035 steel.

Steel containing carbon in percentages ranging from 0.50 to 1.05 percent is classed as high-carbon steel. The addition of other elements in varying quantities adds to the hardness of this steel. In the fully heat-treated condition it is very hard, will withstand high shear and wear, and will have little deformation. It has limited use in aircraft. SAE 1095 in sheet form is used for making flat springs and in wire form for making coil springs.

The various nickel steels are produced by combining nickel with carbon steel. Steels containing from 3 to 3.75 percent nickel are commonly used. Nickel increases the hardness, tensile strength, and elastic limit of steel without appreciably decreasing the ductility. It also intensifies the hardening effect of heat treatment. SAE 2330 steel is used extensively for aircraft parts, such as bolts, terminals, keys, clevises, and pins.

Chromium steel is high in hardness, strength, and corrosion-resistant properties, and is particularly adaptable for heat-treated forgings which require greater toughness and strength than may be obtained in plain carbon steel. It can be used for such articles as the balls and rollers of anti-friction bearings.

Chrome-nickel or stainless steels are the corrosion-resistant metals. The anticorrosive degree of this steel is determined by the surface condition of the metal as well as by the composition, temperature, and concentration of the corrosive agent.

The principal alloy of stainless steel is chromium. The corrosion-resistant steel most often used in aircraft construction is known as 18-8 steel because of its content of 18 percent chromium and 8 percent nickel. One of the distinctive features of 18-8 steel is that its strength may be increased by cold-working.

Stainless steel may be rolled, drawn, bent, or formed to any shape. Because these steels expand about 50 percent more than mild steel and conduct heat only about 40 percent as rapidly, they are more difficult to weld. Stainless steel can be used for almost any part of an aircraft. Some of its common applications are in the fabrication of exhaust collectors, stacks and manifolds, structural and machined parts, springs, castings, tie rods, and control cables.

The chrome-vanadium steels are made of approximately 18 percent vanadium and about 1 percent chromium. When heat treated, they have strength, toughness, and resistance to wear and fatigue. A special grade of this steel in sheet form can be cold-formed into intricate shapes. It can be folded and flattened without signs of breaking or failure. SAE 6150 is used for making springs; and chrome-vanadium with high-carbon content, SAE 6195, is used for ball and roller bearings.

Molybdenum in small percentages is used in combination with chromium to form chrome-molybdenum steel, which has various uses in aircraft. Molybdenum is a strong alloying element. It raises the ultimate strength of steel without affecting ductility or workability. Molybdenum steels are tough and wear resistant, and they harden throughout when heat treated. They are especially adaptable for welding and, for this reason, are used principally for welded structural parts and assemblies. This type steel has practically replaced carbon steel in the fabrication of fuselage tubing, engine mounts, landing gears, and other structural parts. For example, a heat-treated SAE X4130 tube is approximately four times as strong as an SAE 1025 tube of the same weight and size.

A series of chrome-molybdenum steel most used in aircraft construction is that series containing 0.25 to 0.55 percent carbon, 0.15 to 0.25 percent molybdenum, and 0.50 to 1.10 percent chromium. These steels, when suitably heat treated, are deep hardening, easily machined, readily welded by either gas or electric methods, and are especially adapted to high-temperature service.

Inconel is a nickel-chromium-iron alloy closely resembling stainless steel in appearance. Because these two metals look very much alike, a distinguishing test is often necessary. One method of identification is to use a solution of 10 grams of cupric chloride in 100 cubic centimeters of hydrochloric acid. With a medicine dropper, place 1 drop of the solution on a sample of each metal to be tested and allow it to remain for 2 minutes. At the end of this period, slowly add 3 or 4 drops of water to the solution on the metal samples, 1 drop at a time; then wash the samples in clear water and dry them. If the metal is stainless steel, the copper in the cupric chloride solution will be deposited on the metal leaving a copper-colored spot. If the sample is inconel, a new-looking spot will be present.

The tensile strength of inconel is 100,000 p.s.i. annealed, and 125,000 p.s.i., when hard rolled. It is highly resistant to salt water and is able to withstand temperatures as high as 1,600° F. Inconel welds readily and has working qualities quite similar to those of corrosion-resistant steels.

NONFERROUS AIRCRAFT METALS

The term "nonferrous" refers to all metals which have elements other than iron as their base or principal constituent. This group includes such metals as aluminum, titanium, copper, and magnesium, as well as such alloyed metals as Monel and babbit.

Aluminum and Aluminum Alloys

Commercially pure aluminum is a white lustrous metal which stands second in the scale of malleability, sixth in ductility, and ranks high in its resistance to corrosion. Aluminum combined with various percentages of other metals forms alloys which are used in aircraft construction.

Aluminum alloys in which the principal alloying ingredients are either manganese, chromium, or magnesium and silicon show little attack in corrosive environments. Alloys in which substantial percentages of copper are used are more susceptible to corrosive action. The total percentage of alloying elements is seldom more than 6 or 7 percent in the wrought alloys.

Aluminum is one of the most widely used metals in modern aircraft construction. It is vital to the aviation industry because of its high strength-to-weight ratio and its comparative ease of fabrication. The outstanding characteristic of aluminum is its light weight. Aluminum melts at the comparatively low temperature of 1,250° F. It is nonmagnetic and is an excellent conductor.

Commercially pure aluminum has a tensile strength of about 13,000 p.s.i., but by rolling or other cold-working processes its strength may be approximately doubled. By alloying with other metals, or by using heat-treating processes, the tensile strength may be raised to as high as 65,000 p.s.i. or to within the strength range of structural steel.

Aluminum alloys, although strong, are easily worked because they are malleable and ductile. They may be rolled into sheets as thin as .0017 inch or drawn into wire .004 inch in diameter. Most aluminum alloy sheet stock used in aircraft construction ranges from .016 to .096 inch in thickness; however, some of the larger aircraft use sheet stock which may be as thick as .356 inch.

The various types of aluminum may be divided into two general classes: (1) The casting alloys (those suitable for casting in sand, permanent mold, or die castings), and (2) the wrought alloys (those which may be shaped by rolling, drawing, or forging). Of these two, the wrought alloys are the most widely used in aircraft construction, being used for stringers, bulkheads, skin, rivets, and extruded sections.

Aluminum casting alloys are divided into two basic groups. In one, the physical properties of the alloys are determined by the alloying elements and cannot be changed after the metal is cast. In the other, the alloying elements make it possible to heat treat the casting to produce the desired physical properties.

The casting alloys are identified by a letter preceding the alloy number. When a letter precedes a number, it indicates a slight variation in the composition of the original alloy. This variation in composition is simply to impart some desirable quality. In casting alloy 214, for example, the addition of zinc to improve its pouring qualities is indicated by the letter A in front of the number, thus creating the designation A214.

When castings have been heat treated, the heat treatment and the composition of the casting is indicated by the letter T, followed by an alloying number. An example of this is the sand casting alloy 355, which has several different compositions and tempers and is designated by 355-T6, 355-T51, or C355-T51.

Aluminum alloy castings are produced by one of three basic methods: (1) Sand mold, (2) permanent mold, or (3) die cast. In casting aluminum, it must be remembered that in most cases different types of alloys must be used for different types of castings. Sand castings and die castings require different types of alloys than those used in permanent molds.

Sand and permanent mold castings are parts produced by pouring molten metal into a previously prepared mold, allowing the metal to solidify or freeze, and then removing the part. If the mold is made of sand, the part is a sand casting: if it is a metallic mold (usually cast iron) the part is a permanent mold casting. Sand and permanent castings are produced by pouring liquid metal into the mold, the metal flowing under the force of gravity alone.

The two principal types of sand casting alloys are 112 and 212. Little difference exists between the two metals from a mechanical properties standpoint, since both are adaptable to a wide range of products.

The permanent mold process is a later development of the sand casting process, the major difference being in the material from which the molds are made. The advantage of this process is that there are fewer openings (called porosity) than in sand castings. The sand and the binder, which is mixed with the sand to hold it together, give off a certain amount of gas which causes porosity in a sand casting.

Permanent mold castings are used to obtain higher mechanical properties, better surfaces, or more accurate dimensions. There are two specific types of permanent mold castings: (1) The permanent metal mold with metal cores, and (2) the semipermanent types containing sand cores. Because finer grain structure is produced in alloys subjected to the rapid cooling of metal molds, they are far superior to the sand type castings. Alloys 122, A132, and 142 are commonly used in permanent mold castings, the principal uses of which are in internal combustion engines.

Die castings used in aircraft are usually aluminum or magnesium alloy. If weight is of primary importance, magnesium alloy is used because it is lighter than aluminum alloy. Aluminum alloy is frequently used since it is stronger than most magnesium alloys.

A die casting is produced by forcing molten metal under pressure into a metallic die and allowing it to solidify; then the die is opened and the part removed. The basic difference between permanent mold casting and die casting is that in the permanent mold process the metal flows into the die under gravity. In the die casting operation, the metal is forced under great pressure.

Die castings are used where relatively large production of a given part is involved. Remember, any shape which can be forged can be cast.

Wrought aluminum and wrought aluminum alloys are divided into two general classes, nonheat-treatable alloys and heat-treatable alloys.

Nonheat-treatable alloys are those in which the mechanical properties are determined by the amount of cold-work introduced after the final annealing operation. The mechanical properties obtained by cold working are destroyed by any subsequent heating and cannot be restored except by additional cold working, which is not always possible. The "full hard" temper is produced by the maximum amount of cold-work that is commercially practicable. Metal in the "as fabricated" condition is produced from the ingot without any subsequent controlled amount of cold working or thermal treatment. There is, consequently, a variable amount of strain hardening, depending upon the thickness of the section.

For heat-treatable aluminum alloys the mechanical properties are obtained by heat treating to a suitable temperature, holding at that temperature long enough to allow the alloying constituent to enter into solid solution, and then quenching to hold the constituent in solution. The metal is left in a supersaturated, unstable state and is then age hardened either by natural aging at room temperature or by artificial aging at some elevated temperature.

Aluminum Alloy Designations

Wrought aluminum and wrought aluminum alloys are designated by a four-digit index system. The system is broken into three distinct groups: 1xxx group, 2xxx through 8xxx group, and 9xxx group (which is at present unused).

The first digit of a designation identifies the alloy type. The second digit indicates specific alloy modifications. Should the second number be zero, it would indicate no special control over individual impurities. Digits 1 through 9, however, when assigned consecutively as needed for the second number in this group, indicate the number of controls over individual impurities in the metal.

The last two digits of the 1xxx group are used to indicate the hundredths of 1 percent above the original 99 percent designated by the first digit. Thus, if the last two digits were 30, the alloy would contain 99 percent plus 0.30 percent of pure aluminum, or a total of 99.30 percent pure aluminum. Examples of alloys in this group are:

1100—99.00 percent pure aluminum with one control over individual impurities.

1130—99.30 percent pure aluminum with one control over individual impurities.

1275—99.75 percent pure aluminum with two controls over individual impurities.

In the 2xxx through 8xxx groups, the first digit indicates the major alloying element used in the formation of the alloy as follows:

2xxx—copper.
3xxx—manganese.
4xxx—silicon.
5xxx—magnesium.
6xxx—magnesium and silicon.
7xxx—zinc.
8xxx—other elements.

In the 2xxx through 8xxx alloy groups, the second digit in the alloy designation indicates alloy modifications. If the second digit is zero, it indicates the original alloy, while digits 1 through 9 indicate alloy modifications.

The last two of the four digits in the designation identify the different alloys in the group (figure 6–63).

Effect of Alloying Element

1000 series. 99% or higher, excellent corrosion resistance, high thermal and electrical conductivity, low mechanical properties, excellent workability. Iron and silicon are major impurities.

2000 series. Copper is the principle alloying element. Solution heat treatment, optimum properties equal to mild steel, poor corrosion resistance unclad. It is usually clad with 6000 or high purity alloy. Its best known alloy is 2024.

3000 series. Manganese is the principle alloying element of this group which is generally non-heat-treatable. The percentage of manganese which will be alloy effective is 1.5%. The most popular is 3003 which is of moderate strength, and has good working characteristics.

4000 series. Silicon is the principle alloying element. This lowers the melting temperature. Its primary use is in welding and brazing. When used in welding heat-treatable alloys, this group will respond to a limited amount of heat treatment.

5000 series. Magnesium is the principle alloying element. It has good welding and corrosion resistant characteristics. High temperatures (over 150° F.) or excessive cold working will increase susceptibility to corrosion.

6000 series. Silicon and magnesium form magnesium silicide which makes alloys heat-treatable. It is of medium strength, good forming and has corrosion resistant characteristics.

Alloy	Per cent of alloying elements—aluminum and normal impurities constitute remainder								
	Copper	Silicon	Manganese	Magnesium	Zinc	Nickel	Chromium	Lead	Bismuth
1100	......	......	......	......	......	......	......	......	......
3003	......	......	1.2	......	......	......	......	......	......
2011	5.5	......	......	......	......	......	......	0.5	0.5
2014	4.4	0.8	0.8	0.4	......	......	......	......	......
2017	4.0	......	0.5	0.5	......	......	......	......	......
2117	2.5	......	......	0.3	......	......	......	......	......
2018	4.0	......	......	0.5	......	2.0	......	......	......
2024	4.5	......	0.6	1.5	......	......	......	......	......
2025	4.5	0.8	0.8	......	......	......	......	......	......
4032	0.9	12.5	......	1.0	......	0.9	......	......	......
6151	......	1.0	......	0.6	......	......	0.25	......	......
5052	......	......	......	2.5	......	......	0.25	......	......
6053	......	0.7	......	1.3	......	......	0.25	......	......
6061	0.25	0.6	......	1.0	......	......	0.25	......	......
7075	1.6	......	......	2.5	5.6	......	0.3	......	......

FIGURE 6-63. Nominal composition of wrought aluminum alloys.

7000 series. Zinc is the principle alloying element. The most popular alloy of the series is 6061. When coupled with magnesium, it results in heat-treatable alloys of very high strength. It usually has copper and chromium added. The principle alloy of this is 7075.

Hardness Identification

Where used, the temper designation follows the alloy designation and is separated from it by a dash: i.e., 7075–T6, 2024–T4, etc. The temper designation consists of a letter indicating the basic temper which may be more specifically defined by the addition of one or more digits. These designations are as follows:

—F As fabricated.

—O Annealed, recrystallized (wrought products only).

—H Strain hardened.

   —H1 (plus one or more digits) strain hardened only.

   —H2 (plus one or more digits) strain hardened and partially annealed.

   —H3 (plus one or more digits) strain hardened and stabilized.

The digit following the designations H1, H2, and H3 indicate the degree of strain hardening, number 8 representing the ultimate tensile strength equal to that achieved by a cold reduction of approximately 75% following a full anneal, 0 representing the annealed state.

Heat Treatment Identification

In the wrought form, commercially pure aluminum is known as 1100. It has a high degree of resistance to corrosion and is easily formed into intricate shapes. It is relatively low in strength and does not have the properties required for structural aircraft parts. High strengths are generally obtained by the process of alloying. The resulting alloys are less easily formed and, with some exceptions, have lower resistance to corrosion than 1100 aluminum.

Alloying is not the only method of increasing the strength of aluminum. Like other materials, aluminum becomes stronger and harder as it is rolled, formed, or otherwise cold-worked. Since the hardness depends on the amount of cold working done, 1100 and some wrought aluminum alloys are available in several strain-hardened tempers. The soft or annealed condition is designated O. If the material is strain hardened, it is said to be in the H condition.

The most widely used alloys in aircraft construction are hardened by heat treatment rather than by cold-work. These alloys are designated by a somewhat different set of symbols: —T4 and W indicate solution heat treated and quenched but not aged, and T6 indicates an alloy in the heat treated hardened condition.

—W Solution heat treated, unstable temper.

—T Treated to produce stable tempers other than —F, —O, or —H.

   —T2 Annealed (cast products only).

   —T3 Solution heat treated and then cold worked.

   —T4 Solution heat treated.

   —T5 Artificially aged only.

   —T6 Solution heat treated and then artificially aged.

   —T7 Solution heat treated and then stabilized.

   —T8 Solution heat treated, cold worked, and then artificially aged.

   —T9 Solution heat treated, artificially aged, and then cold worked.

   —T10 Artificially aged and then cold worked.

Additional digits may be added to T1 through T10 to indicate a variation in treatment which significantly alters the characteristics of the product.

In the wrought form, commercially pure aluminum is known as 1100. It has a high degree of resistance to corrosion and is easily formed into intricate shapes. It is relatively low in strength, however, and does not have the strength required for structural aircraft parts. Higher strengths are generally obtained by the process of alloying. The

resulting alloys are less easily formed and, with some exceptions, have lower resistance to corrosion than 1100 aluminum.

Alloying is not the only method of increasing the strength of aluminum. Like other materials, aluminum becomes stronger and harder as it is rolled, formed, or otherwise cold-worked. Since the hardness depends on the amount of cold working done, 1100 and some wrought aluminum alloys are available in several strain-hardened tempers. The soft or annealed condition is designated O. If the material is strain hardened, it is said to be in the H condition.

The most widely used alloys in aircraft construction are hardened by heat treatment rather than by cold-work. These alloys are designated by a somewhat different set of symbols: —T4 and W indicate solution heat treated and quenched but not aged, and T6 indicates an alloy in the heat treated hardened condition.

Aluminum alloy sheets are marked with the specification number on approximately every square foot of material. If for any reason this identification is not on the material, it is possible to separate the heat-treatable alloys from the nonheat-treatable alloys by immersing a sample of the material in a 10-percent solution of caustic soda (sodium hydroxide). The heat-treatable alloys will turn black due to the copper content, whereas the others will remain bright. In the case of clad material, the surface will remain bright, but there will be a dark area in the middle when viewed from the edge.

Alclad Aluminum

The terms "Alclad and Pureclad" are used to designate sheets that consist of an aluminum alloy core coated with a layer of pure aluminum to a depth of approximately 5½ percent on each side. The pure aluminum coating affords a dual protection for the core, preventing contact with any corrosive agents, and protecting the core electrolytically by preventing any attack caused by scratching or from other abrasions.

Titanium and Titanium Alloys

Titanium was discovered by an English priest named Gregot. A crude separation of titanium ore was accomplished in 1825. In 1906 a sufficient amount of pure titanium was isolated in metallic form to permit a study. Following this study, in 1932, an extraction process was developed which became the first commercial method for producing titanium. The United States Bureau of Mines began making titanium sponge in 1946, and 4 years later the melting process began.

The use of titanium is widespread. It is used in many commercial enterprises and is in constant demand for such items as pumps, screens, and other tools and fixtures where corrosion attack is prevalent. In aircraft construction and repair, titanium is used for fuselage skins, engine shrouds, firewalls, longerons, frames, fittings, air ducts, and fasteners,

Titanium is used for making compressor disks, spacer rings, compressor blades and vanes, through bolts, turbine housings and liners, and miscellaneous hardware for turbine engines.

Titanium, in appearance, is similar to stainless steel. One quick method used to identify titanium is the spark test. Titanium gives off a brilliant white trace ending in a brilliant white burst. Also, identification can be accomplished by moistening the titanium and using it to draw a line on a piece of glass. This will leave a dark line similar in appearance to a pencil mark.

Titanium falls between aluminum and stainless steel in terms of elasticity, density, and elevated temperature strength. It has a melting point of from 2,730° F. to 3,155° F., low thermal conductivity, and a low coefficient of expansion. It is light, strong, and resistant to stress-corrosion cracking. Titanium is approximately 60 percent heavier than aluminum and about 50 percent lighter than stainless steel.

Because of the high melting point of titanium, high-temperature properties are disappointing. The ultimate yield strength of titanium drops rapidly above 800° F. The absorption of oxygen and nitrogen from the air at temperatures above 1,000° F. makes the metal so brittle on long exposure that it soon becomes worthless. However, titanium does have some merit for short-time exposure up to 3,000° F. where strength is not important. Aircraft firewalls demand this requirement.

Titanium is nonmagnetic and has an electrical resistance comparable to that of stainless steel. Some of the base alloys of titanium are quite hard. Heat treating and alloying do not develop the hardness of titanium to the high levels of some of the heat-treated alloys of steel. It was only recently that a heat-treatable titanium alloy was developed. Prior to the development of this alloy, heating and rolling was the only method of forming that could be accomplished. However, it is possible to form the new alloy in the soft condition and heat treat it for hardness.

Iron, molybdenum, and chromium are used to stabilize titanium and produce alloys that will quench harden and age harden. The addition of these metals also adds ductility. The fatigue resistance of titanium is greater than that of aluminum or steel.

Titanium becomes softer as the degree of purity is increased. It is not practical to distinguish between the various grades of commercially pure or unalloyed titanium by chemical analysis; therefore, the grades are determined by mechanical properties.

Titanium Designations

The A-B-C classification of titanium alloys was established to provide a convenient and simple means of describing all titanium alloys. Titanium and titanium alloys possess three basic types of crystals: A (alpha), B (beta), and C (combined alpha and beta). Their characteristics are:

A (alpha)—All-around performance; good weldability; tough and strong both cold and hot, and resistant to oxidation.

B (beta)—Bendability; excellent bend ductility; strong both cold and hot, but vulnerable to contamination.

C (combined alpha and beta for compromise performances)—Strong when cold and warm, but weak when hot; good bendability; moderate contamination resistance; excellent forgeability.

Titanium is manufactured for commercial use in two basic compositions; commercially pure titanium and alloyed titanium. A-55 is an example of a commercially pure titanium. It has a yield strength of 55,000 to 80,000 p.s.i. and is a general-purpose grade for moderate to severe forming. It is sometimes used for nonstructural aircraft parts and for all types of corrosion-resistant applications, such as tubing.

Type A-70 titanium is closely related to type A-55 but has a yield strength of 70,000 to 95,000 p.s.i. It is used where higher strength is required, and it is specified for many moderately stressed aircraft parts. For many corrosion applications, it is used interchangeably with type A-55. Both type A-55 and type A-70 are weldable.

One of the widely used titanium-base alloys is designated as C-110M. It is used for primary structural members and aircraft skin, has 110,000 p.s.i. minimum yield strength, and contains 8 percent manganese.

Type A-110AT is a titanium alloy which contains 5 percent aluminum and 2.5 percent tin. It also has a high minimum yield strength at elevated temperatures with the excellent welding characteristics inherent in alpha-type titanium alloys.

Corrosion Characteristics

The corrosion resistance of titanium deserves special mention. The resistance of the metal to corrosion is caused by the formation of a protective surface film of stable oxide or chemi-absorbed oxygen. Film is often produced by the presence of oxygen and oxidizing agents.

Corrosion of titanium is uniform. There is little evidence of pitting or other serious forms of localized attack. Normally, it is not subject to stress corrosion, corrosion fatigue, intergranular corrosion, or galvanic corrosion. Its corrosion resistance is equal or superior to 18-8 stainless steel.

Laboratory tests with acid and saline solutions show titanium polarizes readily. The net effect, in general, is to decrease current flow in galvanic and corrosion cells. Corrosion currents on the surface of titanium and metallic couples are naturally restricted. This partly accounts for good resistance to many chemicals; also, the material may be used with some dissimilar metals with no harmful galvanic effect on either.

Copper and Copper Alloys

Copper is one of the most widely distributed metals. It is the only reddish-colored metal and is second only to silver in electrical conductivity. Its use as a structural material is limited because of its great weight. However, some of its outstanding characteristics, such as its high electrical and heat conductivity, in many cases overbalance the weight factor.

Because it is very malleable and ductile, copper is ideal for making wire. It is corroded by salt water but is not affected by fresh water. The ultimate tensile strength of copper varies greatly. For cast copper, the tensile strength is about 25,000 p.s.i., and when cold rolled or cold drawn its tensile strength increases to a range of 40,000 to 67,000 p.s.i.

In aircraft, copper is used primarily in the

electrical system for bus bars, bonding, and as lockwire.

Beryllium copper is one of the most successful of all the copper base alloys. It is a recently developed alloy containing about 97 percent copper, 2 percent beryllium, and sufficient nickel to increase the percentage of elongation. The most valuable feature of this metal is that the physical properties can be greatly stepped up by heat treatment, the tensile strength rising from 70,000 p.s.i. in the annealed state to 200,000 p.s.i. in the heat-treated state. The resistance of beryllium copper to fatigue and wear makes it suitable for diaphragms, precision bearings and bushings, ball cages, and spring washers.

Brass is a copper alloy containing zinc and small amounts of aluminum, iron, lead, manganese, magnesium, nickel, phosphorous, and tin. Brass with a zinc content of 30 to 35 percent is very ductile, but that containing 45 percent has relatively high strength.

Muntz metal is a brass composed of 60 percent copper and 40 percent zinc. It has excellent corrosion-resistant qualities in salt water. Its strength can be increased by heat treatment. As cast, this metal has an ultimate tensile strength of 50,000 p.s.i., and it can be elongated 18 percent. It is used in making bolts and nuts, as well as parts that come in contact with salt water.

Red brass, sometimes termed bronze because of its tin content, is used in fuel and oil line fittings. This metal has good casting and finishing properties and machines freely.

Bronzes are copper alloys containing tin. The true bronzes have up to 25 percent tin, but those with less than 11 percent are most useful, especially for such items as tube fittings in aircraft.

Among the copper alloys are the copper aluminum alloys, of which the aluminum bronzes rank very high in aircraft usage. They would find greater usefulness in structures if it were not for their strength-to-weight ratio as compared with alloy steels. Wrought aluminum bronzes are almost as strong and ductile as medium-carbon steel, and they possess a high degree of resistance to corrosion by air, salt water, and chemicals. They are readily forged, hot- or cold-rolled, and many react to heat treatment.

These copper-base alloys contain up to 16 percent of aluminum (usually 5 to 11 percent), to which other metals such as iron, nickel, or manganese may be added. Aluminum bronzes have good tearing qualities, great strength, hardness,

and resistance to both shock and fatigue. Because of these properties, they are used for diaphragms, gears, and pumps. Aluminum bronzes are available in rods, bars, plates, sheets, strips, and forgings.

Cast aluminum bronzes, using about 89 percent copper, 9 percent aluminum, and 2 percent of other elements, have high strength combined with ductility, and are resistant to corrosion, shock, and fatigue. Because of these properties, cast aluminum bronze is used in bearings and pump parts. These alloys are useful in areas exposed to salt water and corrosive gases.

Manganese bronze is an exceptionally high strength, tough, corrosion-resistant copper zinc alloy containing aluminum, manganese, iron and, occasionally, nickel or tin. This metal can be formed, extruded, drawn, or rolled to any desired shape. In rod form, it is generally used for machined parts, for aircraft landing gears and brackets.

Silicon bronze is a more recent development composed of about 95 percent copper, 3 percent silicon, and 2 percent manganese, zinc, iron, tin, and aluminum. Although not a bronze in the true sense because of its small tin content, silicon bronze has high strength and great corrosion resistance.

Monel

Monel, the leading high-nickel alloy, combines the properties of high strength and excellent corrosion resistance. This metal consists of 68 percent nickel, 29 percent copper, 0.2 percent iron, 1 percent manganese, and 1.8 percent of other elements. It cannot be hardened by heat treatment.

Monel, adaptable to casting and hot- or cold-working, can be successfully welded. It has working properties similar to those of steel. When forged and annealed, it has a tensile strength of 80,000 p.s.i. This can be increased by cold-working to 125,000 p.s.i., sufficient for classification among the tough alloys.

Monel has been successfully used for gears and chains to operate retractable landing gears, and for structural parts subject to corrosion. In aircraft, Monel is used for parts demanding both strength and high resistance to corrosion (such as exhaust manifolds and carburetor needle valves and sleeves).

K-Monel

K-Monel is a nonferrous alloy containing mainly nickel, copper, and aluminum. It is produced by adding a small amount of aluminum to the Monel formula. It is corrosion resistant and capable of being hardened by heat treatment.

K-Monel has been successfully used for gears, and structural members in aircraft which are subjected to corrosive attacks. This alloy is nonmagnetic at all temperatures. K-Monel sheet has been successfully welded by both oxyacetylene and electric-arc welding.

Magnesium and Magnesium Alloys

Magnesium, the world's lightest structural metal, is a silvery-white material weighing only two-thirds as much as aluminum. Magnesium does not possess sufficient strength in its pure state for structural uses, but when alloyed with zinc, aluminum, and manganese it produces an alloy having the highest strength-to-weight ratio of any of the commonly used metals.

Magnesium is probably more widely distributed in nature than any other metal. It can be obtained from such ores as dolomite and magnesite, and from sea water, underground brines, and waste solutions of potash. With about 10 million pounds of magnesium in 1 cubic mile of sea water, there is no danger of a dwindling supply,

Some of today's aircraft require in excess of one-half ton of this metal for use in hundreds of vital spots. Some wing panels are fabricated entirely from magnesium alloys, weigh 18 percent less than standard aluminum panels, and have flown hundreds of satisfactory hours. Among the aircraft parts that have been made from magnesium with a substantial savings in weight are nosewheel doors, flap cover skin, aileron cover skin, oil tanks, floorings, fuselage parts, wingtips, engine nacelles, instrument panels, radio masts, hydraulic fluid tanks, oxygen bottle cases, ducts, and seats.

Magnesium alloys possess good casting characteristics. Their properties compare favorably with those of cast aluminum. In forging, hydraulic presses are ordinarily used, although, under certain conditions, forging can be accomplished in mechanical presses or with drop hammers.

Magnesium alloys are subject to such treatments as annealing, quenching, solution heat treatment, aging, and stabilizing. Sheet and plate magnesium are annealed at the rolling mill. The solution heat treatment is used to put as much of the alloying ingredients as possible into solid solution, which results in high tensile strength and maximum ductility. Aging is applied to castings following heat treatment where maximum hardness and yield strength are desired.

Magnesium embodies fire hazards of an unpredictable nature. When in large sections, its high thermal conductivity makes it difficult to ignite and prevents it from burning. It will not burn until the melting point is reached, which is 1,204° F. However, magnesium dust and fine chips are ignited easily. Precautions must be taken to avoid this if possible. Should a fire occur, it can be extinguished with an extinguishing powder, such as powdered soapstone, or graphite powder. Water or any standard liquid or foam fire extinguishers cause magnesium to burn more rapidly and can cause explosions.

Magnesium alloys produced in the United States consist of magnesium alloyed with varying proportions of aluminum, manganese, and zinc. These alloys are designated by a letter of the alphabet, with the number 1 indicating high purity and maximum corrosion resistance.

Many of the magnesium alloys manufactured in this country are produced by the Dow Chemical Company and have been given the trade name of Dowmetal alloys. To distinguish between these alloys, each is assigned a letter. Thus, we have Dowmetal J, Dowmetal M, and so forth.

Another manufacturer of magnesium alloys is the American Magnesium Corporation, a subsidiary of the Aluminum Company of America. This company uses an identification system similar to that used for aluminum alloys, with the exception that magnesium alloy numbers are preceded with the letters AM. Thus, AM240C is a cast alloy, and AM240C4 is the same alloy in the heat-treated state. AM3S0 is an annealed wrought alloy, and AM3SRT is the same alloy rolled after heat treatment.

SUBSTITUTION OF AIRCRAFT METALS

In selecting substitute metals for the repair and maintenance of aircraft, it is very important to check the appropriate structural repair manual. Aircraft manufacturers design structural members to meet a specific load requirement for a particular aircraft. The methods of repairing these members, apparently similar in construction, will thus vary with different aircraft.

Four requirements must be kept in mind when selecting substitute metals. The first and most important of these is maintaining the original strength of the structure. The other three are: (1) Maintaining contour or aerodynamic smoothness, (2) maintaining original weight, if possible, or keeping added weight to a minimum, and (3) maintaining the original corrosion-resistant properties of the metal.

PRINCIPLES OF HEAT TREATMENT

Heat treatment is a series of operations involving the heating and cooling of metals in the solid state. Its purpose is to change a mechanical property or combination of mechanical properties so that the metal will be more useful, serviceable, and safe for a definite purpose. By heat treating, a metal can be made harder, stronger, and more resistant to impact, Heat treating can also make a metal softer and more ductile. No one heat-treating operation can produce all of these characteristics. In fact, some properties are often improved at the expense of others. In being hardened, for example, a metal may become brittle.

The various heat-treating processes are similar in that they all involve the heating and cooling of metals. They differ, however, in the temperatures to which the metal is heated, the rate at which it is cooled, and, of course, in the final result.

The most common forms of heat treatment for ferrous metals are hardening, tempering, normalizing, annealing, and casehardening. Most nonferrous metals can be annealed and many of them can be hardened by heat treatment. However, there is only one nonferrous metal, titanium, that can be casehardened, and none can be tempered or normalized.

Internal Structure of Metals

The results obtained by heat treatment depend to a great extent on the structure of the metal and on the manner in which the structure changes when the metal is heated and cooled. A pure metal cannot be hardened by heat treatment because there is little change in its structure when heated. On the other hand, most alloys respond to heat treatment since their structures change with heating and cooling.

An alloy may be in the form of a solid solution, a mechanical mixture, or a combination of a solid solution and a mechanical mixture. When an alloy is in the form of a solid solution, the elements and compounds which form the alloy are absorbed, one into the other, in much the same way that salt is dissolved in a glass of water, and the constituents cannot be identified even under a microscope.

When two or more elements or compounds are mixed but can be identified by microscopic examination, a mechanical mixture is formed. A mechanical mixture can be compared to the mixture of sand and gravel in concrete. The sand and gravel are both visible. Just as the sand and gravel are held together and kept in place by the matrix of cement, the other constituents of an alloy are embedded in the matrix formed by the base metal.

An alloy in the form of a mechanical mixture at ordinary temperatures may change to a solid solution when heated. When cooled back to normal temperature, the alloy may return to its original structure. On the other hand, it may remain a solid solution or form a combination of a solid solution and mechanical mixture. An alloy which consists of a combination of solid solution and mechanical mixture at normal temperatures may change to a solid solution when heated. When cooled, the alloy may remain a solid solution, return to its original structure, or form a complex solution.

HEAT-TREATING EQUIPMENT

Successful heat treating requires close control over all factors affecting the heating and cooling of metals. Such control is possible only when the proper equipment is available and the equipment is selected to fit the particular job. Thus, the furnace must be of the proper size and type and must be so controlled that temperatures are kept within the limits prescribed for each operation. Even the atmosphere within the furnace affects the condition of the part being heat treated. Further, the quenching equipment and the quenching medium must be selected to fit the metal and the heat-treating operation. Finally, there must be equipment for handling parts and materials, for cleaning metals, and for straightening parts.

Furnaces and Salt Baths

There are many different types and sizes of furnaces used in heat treatment. As a general rule, furnaces are designed to operate in certain specific temperature ranges and attempted use in other ranges frequently results in work of inferior quality. In addition, using a furnace beyond its rated maximum temperature shortens its life and may necessitate costly and time-consuming repairs.

Fuel-fired furnaces (gas or oil) require air for proper combustion and an air compressor or blower is therefore necessary. These furnaces are usually of the muffler type: that is, the combustion of the fuel takes place outside of and around the chamber in which the work is placed. If an open muffler is used, the furnace should be designed so as to prevent the direct impingement of flame on the work.

In furnaces heated by electricity the heating elements are generally in the form of wire or ribbon. Good design requires incorporation of additional heating elements at locations where maximum heat loss may be expected. Such furnaces commonly operate up to a maximum temperature of about 2,000° F. Furnaces operating at temperatures up to about 2,500° F. usually employ resistor bars of sintered carbides.

Temperature Measurement and Control

Temperature in the heat-treating furnace is measured by a thermoelectric instrument known as a pyrometer. This instrument measures the electrical effect of a thermocouple and, hence, the temperature of the metal being treated. A complete pyrometer consists of three parts—a thermocouple, extension leads, and meter.

Furnaces intended primarily for tempering may be heated by gas or electricity and are frequently equipped with a fan for circulating the hot air.

Salt baths are available for operating at either tempering or hardening temperatures. Depending on the composition of the salt bath, heating can be conducted at temperatures as low as 325° F. to as high as 2,450° F. Lead baths can be used in the temperature range of 650° F. to 1,700° F. The rate of heating in lead or salt baths is much faster in furnaces.

Heat-treating furnaces differ in size, shape, capacity, construction, operation, and control. They may be circular or rectangular and may rest on pedestals or directly on the floor. There are also pit-type furnaces, which are below the surface of the floor. When metal is to be heated in a bath of molten salt or lead, the furnace must contain a pot or crucible for the molten bath.

The size and capacity of a heat-treating furnace depends on the intended use. A furnace must be capable of heating rapidly and uniformly, regardless of the desired maximum temperature or the mass of the charge. An oven-type furnace should have a working space (hearth) about twice as long and three times as wide as any part that will be heated in the furnace.

Accurate temperature measurement is essential to good heat treating. The usual method is by means of thermocouples: the most common base-metal couples are copper-constantan (up to about 700° F.), iron-constantan (up to about 1,400° F.), and chromel-alumel (up to about 2,200° F.). The most common noble-metal couples (which can be used up to about 2,800° F.) are platinum coupled with either the alloy 87 percent platinum—13 percent rhodium or the alloy 90 percent platinum—10 percent rhodium. The temperatures quoted are for continuous operation.

The life of thermocouples is affected by the maximum temperature (which may frequently exceed those given above) and by the furnace atmosphere. Iron-constantan is more suited for use in reducing and chromel-alumel in oxidizing atmospheres. Thermocouples are usually encased in metallic or ceramic tubes closed at the hot end to protect them from the furnace gases. A necessary attachment is an instrument, such as a millivoltmeter or potentiometer, for measuring the electromotive force generated by the thermocouple. In the interest of accurate control, the hot junction of the thermocouple should be placed as close to the work as possible. The use of an automatic controller is valuable in controlling the temperature at the desired value.

Pyrometers may have meters either of the indicating type or recording type. Indicating pyrometers give direct reading of the furnace temperature. The recording type produces a permanent record of the temperature range throughout the heating operation by means of an inked stylus attached to an arm which traces a line on a sheet of calibrated paper or temperature chart.

Pyrometer installations on all modern furnaces provide automatic regulation of the temperature at any desired setting. Instruments of this type are called controlling potentiometer pyrometers. They include a current regulator and an operating mechanism such as a relay.

Heating

The object in heating is to transform pearlite (a mechanical mixture of iron carbide that exists in a finely mixed condition) to austenite as the steel is heated through the critical range. Since this transition takes time, a relatively slow rate of heating must be used. Ordinarily, the cold steel is inserted when the temperature in the furnace is from 300° F. to 500° F. below the hardening temperature. In this way, too rapid heating through the critical range is prevented.

If temperature-measuring equipment is not available, it becomes necessary to estimate temperatures by some other means. An inexpensive, yet fairly accurate method involves the use of commercial crayons, pellets, or paints that melt at various temperatures within the range of 125° F. to 1,600° F. The least accurate method of temperature estimation is by observation of the color of the hot hearth of the furnace or of the work. The heat colors observed are affected by many factors, such as the conditions of artificial or natural light, the character of the scale on the work, etc.

Steel begins to appear dull red at about 1,000° F., and as the temperature increases the color changes gradually through various shades of red to orange, to yellow, and finally to white. A rough approximation of the correspondence between color and temperature is indicated in figure 6–64.

It is also possible to secure some idea of the temperature of a piece of carbon or low-alloy steel, in the low temperature range used for tempering, from the color of the thin oxide film that forms on the cleaned surface of the steel when heated in this range. The approximate temperature-color relationship for a time at temperature of about one-half is indicated on the lower portion of the scale in figure 6–64.

Protective Atmospheres

It is often necessary or desirable to protect steel or cast iron from surface oxidation (scaling) and loss of carbon from the surface layers (decarburization). Commercial furnaces, therefore, are generally equipped with some means of atmosphere control. This usually is in the form of a burner for burning controlled amounts of gas and air and directing the products of combustion into the furnace muffle. Water vapor, a product of this combustion, is detrimental and many furnaces are equipped with a means for eliminating it. For furnaces not equipped with atmosphere control, a variety of external atmosphere generators are available. The gas so generated is piped into the furnace and one generator may supply several furnaces. If no method of atmosphere control is available, some degree of protection may be secured by covering the work with cast iron borings or chips.

Since the work in salt or lead baths is surrounded by the liquid heating medium, the problem of preventing scaling or decarburization is simplified.

Vacuum furnaces also are used for annealing steels, especially when a bright non-oxidized surface is a prime consideration.

Soaking

The temperature of the furnace must be held constant during the soaking period, since it is during this period that rearrangement of the internal structure of the steel takes place. Soaking

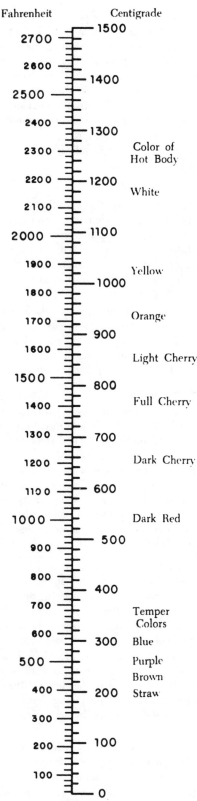

FIGURE 6–64. Temperature chart indicating conversion of Centigrade to Fahrenheit or visa versa, color temperatures scale for hardening-temperature range, and tempering-temperature range.

temperatures for various types of steel are specified in ranges varying as much as 100° F. (See figure 6–65.) Small parts are soaked in the lower part of the specified range and heavy parts in the upper part of the specified range. The length of the soaking period depends upon the type of steel and the size of the part. Naturally, heavier parts require longer soaking to ensure equal heating throughout. As a general rule, a soaking period of 30 minutes to 1 hour is sufficient for the average heat-treating operation.

Cooling

The rate of cooling through the critical range determines the form that the steel will retain. Various rates of cooling are used to produce the desired results. Still air is a slow cooling medium, but is much faster than furnace cooling. Liquids are the fastest cooling media and are therefore used in hardening steels.

There are three commonly used quenching liquids—brine, water, and oil. Brine is the most severe medium, water is next, and oil is the least severe. Generally an oil quench is used for alloy steels, and brine or water for carbon steels.

Quenching Media

Quenching solutions act only through their ability to cool the steel. They have no beneficial chemical action on the quenched steel and in themselves impart no unusual properties. Most requirements for quenching media are met satisfactorily by water or aqueous solutions of inorganic salts such as table salt or caustic soda, or by some type of oil. The rate of cooling is relatively rapid during quenching in brine, somewhat less rapid in water, and slow in oil.

Brine usually is made of a 5- to 10-percent solution of salt (sodium chloride) in water. In addition to its greater cooling speed, brine has the ability to "throw" the scale from steel during quenching. The cooling ability of both water and brine, particularly water, is considerably affected by their temperature. Both should be kept cold—well below 60° F. If the volume of steel being quenched tends to raise the temperature of the bath appreciably, the quenching bath should be cooled by adding ice or by some means of refrigeration.

There are many specially prepared quenching oils on the market; their cooling rates do not vary widely. A straight mineral oil with a Saybolt viscosity of about 100 at 100° F. is generally used. Unlike brine and water, the oils have the greatest cooling velocity at a slightly elevated temperature—about 100 to 140° F.—because of their decreased viscosity at these temperatures.

When steel is quenched, the liquid in immediate contact with the hot surface vaporizes; this vapor reduces the rate of heat abstraction markedly. Vigorous agitation of the steel or the use of a pressure spray quench is necessary to dislodge these vapor films and thus permit the desired rate of cooling.

The tendency of steel to warp and crack during the quenching process is difficult to overcome because certain parts of the article cool more rapidly than others. The following recommendations will greatly reduce the warping tendency.

1. A part should never be thrown into the quenching bath. By permitting it to lie on the bottom of the bath, it is apt to cool faster on the top side than on the bottom side, thus causing it to warp or crack.
2. The part should be agitated slightly to destroy the coating of vapor which might prevent it from cooling rapidly. This allows the bath to convey its heat to the atmosphere.
3. Irregular-shaped parts should be immersed in such a way that the heavy end enters the bath first.

Quenching Equipment

The quenching tank should be of the proper size to handle the material being quenched. Circulating pumps and coolers may be used to maintain approximately constant temperatures when a large amount of quenching is to be done. To avoid building up a high concentration of salt in the quenching tank, provision must be made to add fresh water to the quench tank used for molten salt baths.

Tank location in reference to the heat-treating furnace is very important. The tank should be situated to permit rapid transfer of the part from the furance to the quenching medium. A delay of more than a few seconds will, in many instances, prove detrimental to the effectiveness of the heat treatment. When material of thin section is being heat treated, guard sheets should be emploped to retard the loss of heat during transfer to the quench tank. A rinse tank must be provided to remove all salt from the material after quenching if the salt has not been adequately removed in the quenching tank.

HEAT TREATMENT OF FERROUS METALS

The first important consideration in the heat treatment of a steel part is to know its chemical

Steel No.	Temperatures			Quenching medium (n)	Tempering (drawing) temperature for tensile strength (p.s.i.)				
	Normalizing air cool	Annealing	Hardening		100,000	125,000	150,000	180,000	200,000
	°F	°F	°F		°F	°F	°F	°F	°F
1020	1,650–1,750	1,600–1,700	1,575–1,675	Water	—	—	—	—	—
1022(x1020)	1,650–1,750	1,600–1,700	1,575–1,675	Water	—	—	—	—	—
1025	1,600–1,700	1,575–1,650	1,575–1,675	Water	(a)	—	—	—	—
1035	1,575–1,650	1,575–1,625	1,525–1,600	Water	875	—	—	—	—
1045	1,550–1,600	1,550–1,600	1,475–1,550	Oil or water	1,150	—	—	(n)	—
1095	1,475–1,550	1,450–1,500	1,425–1,500	Oil	(b)	—	1,100	850	750
2330	1,475–1,525	1,425–1,475	1,450–1,500	Oil or water	1,100	950	800	—	—
3135	1,600–1,650	1,500–1,550	1,475–1,525	Oil	1,250	1,050	900	750	650
3140	1,600–1,650	1,500–1,550	1,475–1,525	Oil	1,325	1,075	925	775	700
4037	1,600	1,525–1,575	1,525–1,575	Oil or water	1,225	1,100	975	—	—
4130(x4130)	1,600–1,700	1,525–1,575	1,575–1,625	Oil (c)	(d)	1,050	900	700	575
4140	1,600–1,650	1,525–1,575	1,525–1,575	Oil	1,350	1,100	1,025	825	675
4150	1,550–1,600	1,475–1,525	1,500–1,550	Oil	—	1,275	1,175	1,050	950
4340(x4340)	1,550–1,625	1,525–1,575	1,475–1,525	Oil	—	1,200	1,050	950	850
4640	1,675–1,700	1,525–1,575	1,500–1,550	Oil	—	1,200	1,050	750	625
6135	1,600–1,700	1,550–1,600	1,575–1,625	Oil	1,300	1,075	950	800	750
6150	1,600–1,650	1,525–1,575	1,550–1,625	Oil	(d)(e)	1,200	1,000	900	800
6195	1,600–1,650	1,525–1,575	1,500–1,550	Oil	(f)	—	—	—	—
NE8620	—	—	1,525–1,575	Oil	—	1,000	—	—	—
NE8630	1,650	1,525–1,575	1,525–1,575	Oil	—	1,125	975	775	675
NE8735	1,650	1,525–1,575	1,525–1,575	Oil	—	1,175	1,025	875	775
NE8740	1,625	1,500–1,550	1,500–1,550	Oil	—	1,200	1,075	925	850
30905	—	(g)(h)	(i)	—	—	—	—	—	—
51210	1,525–1,575	1,525–1,575	1,775–1,825 (j)	Oil	1,200	1,100	(k)	750	—
51335	—	1,525–1,575	1,775–1,850	Oil	—	—	—	—	—
52100	1,625–1,700	1,400–1,450	1,525–1,550	Oil	(f)	—	—	—	—
Corrosion resisting (16–2) (1)	—	—	—	—	(m)	—	—	—	—
Silicon chromium (for springs)	—	—	1,700–1,725	Oil	—	—	—	—	—

NOTES

(a) Draw at 1150° F. for tensile strength of 70,000 p.s.i.

(b) For spring temper draw at 800° to 900° F. Rockwell Hardness C-40-45.

(c) Bars or forgings may be quenched in water from 1,500°–1,600° F.

(d) Air-cooling from the normalizing temperature will produce a tensile strength of approximately 90,000 p.s.i.

(e) For spring temper draw at 850° to 950° F. Rockwell Hardness C-40-45.

(f) Draw at 350° to 450° F. to remove quenching strains. Rockwell Hardness C-60-65.

(g) Anneal at 1,600° to 1,700° F. to remove residual stresses due to welding or cold work. May be applied only to steel containing titanium or columbium.

(h) Anneal at 1,900° to 2,100° F. to produce maximum softness and corrosion resistance. Cool in air or quench in water.

(i) Harden by cold work only.

(j) Lower side of range for sheet 0.06 inch and under. Middle of range for sheet and wire 0.125 inch. Upper side of range for forgings.

(k) Not recommended for intermediate tensile strengths because of low impact.

(l) AN-QQ-S-770.—It is recommended that, prior to tempering, corrosion-resisting (16 Cr-2 Ni) steel be quenched in oil from a temperature of 1,875° to 1,900° F., after a soaking period of 1/2 hour at this temperature. To obtain a tensile strength at 115,000 p.s.i., the tempering temperature should be approximately 525° F. A holding time at these temperatures of about 2 hours is recommended. Tempering temperatures between 700° and 1,100° F. will not be approved.

(m) Draw at approximately 800° F. and cool in air for Rockwell Hardness of C-50.

(n) Water used for quenching shall not exceed 65° F. Oil used for quenching shall be within the temperature range of 80°–150° F.

FIGURE 6–65. Heat treatment procedures for steels.

composition. This, in turn, determines its upper critical point. When the upper critical point is known, the next consideration is the rate of heating and cooling to be used. Carrying out these operations involves the use of uniform heating furnaces, proper temperature controls, and suitable quenching mediums.

Behavior of Steel During Heating and Cooling

Changing the internal structure of a ferrous metal is accomplished by heating to a temperature above its upper critical point, holding it at that temperature for a time sufficient to permit certain internal changes to occur, and then cooling to atmospheric temperature under predetermined, controlled conditions.

At ordinary temperatures, the carbon in steel exists in the form of particles of iron carbide scattered throughout an iron matrix known as "ferrite." The number, size, and distribution of these particles determine the hardness of the steel. At elevated temperatures, the carbon is dissolved in the iron matrix in the form of a solid solution called "austenite," and the carbide particles appear only after the steel has been cooled. If the cooling is slow, the carbide particles are relatively coarse and few. In this condition, the steel is soft. If the cooling is rapid, as by quenching in oil or water, the carbon precipitates as a cloud of very fine carbide particles, and the steel is hard. The fact that the carbide particles can be dissolved in austenite is the basis of the heat treatment of steel. The temperatures at which this transformation takes place are called the critical points and vary with the composition of the steel. The element normally having the greatest influence is carbon.

Hardening

Pure iron, wrought iron, and extremely low-carbon steels cannot be appreciably hardened by heat treatment, since they contain no hardening element. Cast iron can be hardened, but its heat treatment is limited. When cast iron is cooled rapidly, it forms white iron, which is hard and brittle. When cooled slowly, it forms gray iron, which is soft but brittle under impact.

In plain carbon steel, the maximum hardness depends almost entirely on the carbon content of the steel. As the carbon content increases, the ability of the steel to be hardened increases. However, this increase in hardenability with an increase in carbon content continues only to a certain point. In practice, that point is 0.85 percent carbon content. When the carbon content is increased beyond 0.85 percent, there is no increase in wear resistance.

For most steels, the hardening treatment consists of heating the steel to a temperature just above the upper critical point, soaking or holding for the required length of time, and then cooling it rapidly by plunging the hot steel into oil, water, or brine. Although most steels must be cooled rapidly for hardening, a few may be cooled in still air. Hardening increases the hardness and strength of the steel but makes it less ductile.

When hardening carbon steel, it must be cooled to below 1,000° F. in less than 1 second. Should the time required for the temperature to drop to 1,000° F. exceed 1 second, the austenite begins to transform into fine pearlite. This pearlite varies in hardness, but is much harder than the pearlite formed by annealing and much softer than the martensite desired. After the 1,000° F. temperature is reached, the rapid cooling must continue if the final structure is to be all martensite.

When alloys are added to steel, the time limit for the temperature drop to 1,000° F. increases above the 1-second limit for carbon steels. Therefore, a slower quenching medium will produce hardness in alloy steels.

Because of the high internal stresses in the "as quenched" condition, steel must be tempered just before it becomes cold. The part should be removed from the quenching bath at a temperature of approximately 200° F., since the temperature range from 200° F. down to room temperature is the cracking range.

Hardening temperatures and quenching mediums for the various types of steel are listed in figure 6–65.

Hardening Precautions

A variety of different shapes and sizes of tongs for handling hot steels is necessary. It should be remembered that cooling of the area contacted by the tongs is retarded and that such areas may not harden, particularly if the steel being treated is very shallow hardening. Small parts may be wired together or quenched in baskets made of wire mesh.

Special quenching jigs and fixtures are frequently used to hold steels during quenching in a manner to restrain distortion.

When selective hardening is desired, portions of the steel may be protected by covering with alundum cement or some other insulating material. Selective hardening may be accomplished also by the use of water or oil jets designed to direct quenching medium on the areas to be hardened. This also is accomplished by the induction and flame-hardening procedures previously described, particularly on large production jobs.

Shallow hardening steels, such as plain carbon and certain varieties of alloy steels, have such a high critical cooling rate that they must be quenched in brine or water to effect hardening. In general, intricately shaped sections should not be made of shallow hardening steels because of the tendency of these steels to warp and crack during hardening. Such items should be made of deeper hardening steels capable of being hardened by quenching in oil or air.

Tempering

Tempering reduces the brittleness imparted by hardening and produces definite physical properties within the steel. Tempering always follows, never precedes, the hardening operation. In addition to reducing brittleness, tempering softens the steel.

Tempering is always conducted at temperatures below the low critical point of the steel. In this respect, tempering differs from annealing, normalizing, or hardening, all of which require temperatures above the upper critical point. When hardened steel is re-heated, tempering begins at 212° F. and continues as the temperature increases toward the low critical point. By selecting a definite tempering temperature, the resulting hardness and strength can be predetermined. Approximate temperatures for various tensile strengths are listed in figure 6–65. The minimum time at the tempering temperature should be 1 hour. If the part is over 1 inch in thickness, the time should be increased by 1 hour for each additional inch of thickness. Tempered steels used in aircraft work have from 125,000 to 200,000 p.s.i. ultimate tensile strength.

Generally, the rate of cooling from the tempering temperature has no effect on the resulting structure; therefore, the steel is usually cooled in still air after being removed from the furnace.

Annealing

Annealing of steel produces a fine-grained, soft, ductile metal without internal stresses or strains. In the annealed state, steel has its lowest strength. In general, annealing is the opposite of hardening.

Annealing of steel is accomplished by heating the metal to just above the upper critical point, soaking at that temperature, and cooling very slowly in the furnace. (See figure 6–65 for recommended temperatures.) Soaking time is approximately 1 hour per inch of thickness of the material. To produce maximum softness in steel, the metal must be cooled very slowly. Slow cooling is obtained by shutting off the heat and allowing the furnace and metal to cool together to 900° F. or lower, then removing the metal from the furnace and cooling in still air. Another method is to bury the heated steel in ashes, sand, or other substance that does not conduct heat readily.

Normalizing

Normalizing of steel removes the internal stresses set up by heat treating, welding, casting, forming, or machining. Stress, if not controlled, will lead to failure. Because of the better physical properties, aircraft steels are often used in the normalized state, but seldom, if ever, in the annealed state.

One of the most important uses of normalizing in aircraft work is in welded parts. Welding causes strains to be set up in the adjacent material. In addition, the weld itself is a cast structure as opposed to the wrought structure of the rest of the material. These two types of structures have different grain sizes, and to refine the grain as well as to relieve the internal stresses, all welded parts should be normalized after fabrication.

Normalizing is accomplished by heating the steel above the upper critical point and cooling in still air. The more rapid quenching obtained by air cooling, as compared to furnace cooling, results in a harder and stronger material than that obtained by annealing. Recommended normalizing temperatures for the various types of aircraft steels are listed in figure 6–65.

CASEHARDENING

Casehardening produces a hard wear-resistant surface or case over a strong, tough core. Casehardening is ideal for parts which require a wear-resistant surface and, at the same time, must be tough enough internally to withstand the applied loads. The steels best suited to casehardening are the low-carbon and low-alloy steels. If high-carbon steel is casehardened, the hardness penetrates the core and causes brittleness.

In casehardening, the surface of the metal is changed chemically by introducing a high carbide or nitride content. The core is unaffected chemically. When heat treated, the surface responds to hardening while the core toughens. The common forms of casehardening are carburizing, cyaniding, and nitriding. Since cyaniding is not used in aircraft work, only carburizing and nitriding are discussed in this section.

Carburizing

Carburizing is a casehardening process in which carbon is added to the surface of low-carbon steel. Thus, a carburized steel has a high-carbon surface and a low-carbon interior. When the carburized steel is heat treated, the case is hardened while the core remains soft and tough.

A common method of carburizing is called "pack carburizing." When carburizing is to be done by this method, the steel parts are packed in a container with charcoal or some other material rich in carbon. The container is then sealed with fire clay, placed in a furnace, heated to approximately 1,700° F., and soaked at that temperature for several hours. As the temperature increases, carbon monoxide gas forms inside the container and, being unable to escape, combines with the gamma iron in the surface of the steel. The depth to which the carbon penetrates depends on the length of the soaking period. For example, when carbon steel is soaked for 8 hours, the carbon penetrates to a depth of about 0.062 inch.

In another method of carburizing, called "gas carburizing," a material rich in carbon is introduced into the furnace atmosphere. The carburizing atmosphere is produced by the use of various gases or by the burning of oil, wood, or other materials. When the steel parts are heated in this atmosphere, carbon monoxide combines with the gamma iron to produce practically the same results as those described under the pack-carburizing process.

A third method of carburizing is that of "liquid carburizing." In this method the steel is placed in a molten salt bath that contains the chemicals required to produce a case comparable with one resulting from pack or gas carburizing.

Alloy steels with low-carbon content as well as low-carbon steels may be carburized by either of the three processes. However, some alloys, such as nickel, tend to retard the absorption of carbon. As a result, the time required to produce a given thickness of case varies with the composition of the metal.

Nitriding

Nitriding is unlike other casehardening processes in that, before nitriding, the part is heat treated to produce definite physical properties. Thus, parts are hardened and tempered before being nitrided. Most steels can be nitrided, but special alloys are required for best results. These special alloys contain aluminum as one of the alloying elements and are called "nitralloys."

In nitriding, the part is placed in a special nitriding furnace and heated to a temperature of approximately 1,000° F. With the part at this temperature, ammonia gas is circulated within the specially constructed furnace chamber. The high temperature cracks the ammonia gas into nitrogen and hydrogen. The ammonia which does not break down is caught in a water trap below the regions of the other two gases. The nitrogen reacts with the iron to form nitride. The iron nitride is dispersed in minute particles at the surface and works inward. The depth of penetration depends on the length of the treament. In nitriding, soaking periods as long as 72 hours are frequently required to produce the desired thickness of case.

Nitriding can be accomplished with a minimum of distortion, because of the low temperature at which parts are casehardened and because no quenching is required after exposure to the ammonia gas.

HEAT TREATMENT OF NONFERROUS METALS

Aluminum Alloys

There are two types of heat treatments applicable to aluminum alloys. One is called solution heat treatment, and the other is known as precipitation heat treatment. Some alloys, such as 2017 and 2024, develop their full properties as a result of solution heat treatment followed by about 4 days of aging at room temperature. Other alloys, such as 2014 and 7075, require both heat treatments.

The alloys that require precipitation heat treatment (artificial aging) to develop their full strength also age to a limited extent at room temperature; the rate and amount of strengthening depends upon the alloy. Some reach their maximum natural or room-temperature aging strength in a few days, and are designated as —T4 or —T3 temper. Others continue to age appreciably over a long period of time. Because of this natural aging, the −W designation is specified only when the period of aging is indicated, for example, 7075-W (½ hour). Thus, there is considerable difference in the mechanical and physical properties of freshly quenched (−W) material and material that is in the −T3 or −T4 temper.

The hardening of an aluminum alloy by heat treatment consists of four distinct steps:

1. Heating to a predetermined temperature.
2. Soaking at temperature for a specified length of time.
3. Rapidly quenching to a relatively low temperature.
4. Aging or precipitation hardening either spontaneously at room temperature, or as a result of a low-temperature thermal treatment.

The first three steps above are known as solution heat treatment, although it has become common practice to use the shorter term, "heat treatment". Room-temperature hardening is known as natural aging, while hardening done at moderate temperatures is called artificial aging, or precipitation heat treatment.

SOLUTION HEAT TREATMENT

Temperature

The temperatures used for solution heat treating vary with different alloys and range from 825° F. to 980° F. As a rule, they must be controlled within a very narrow range (plus or minus 10°) to obtain specified properties.

If the temperature is too low, maximum strength will not be obtained. When excessive temperatures are used, there is danger of melting the low-melting constituents of some alloys with consequent lowering of the physical properties of the alloy. Even if melting does not occur, the use of higher-than-recommended temperatures promotes discoloration and increases quenching strains.

Time at Temperature

The time at temperature, referred to as soaking time, is measured from the time the coldest metal reaches the minimum limit of the desired temperature range. The soaking time varies, depending upon the alloy and thickness, from 10 minutes for thin sheets to approximately 12 hours for heavy forgings. For the heavy sections, the nominal soaking time is approximately 1 hour for each inch of cross-sectional thickness (see figure 6–66).

The soaking time is chosen so that it will be the minimum necessary to develop the required physical properties. The effect of an abbreviated soaking time is obvious. An excessive soaking period aggravates high-temperature oxidation. With clad material, prolonged heating results in excessive diffusion of copper and other soluble constituents into the protective cladding and may defeat the purpose of cladding.

Quenching

After the soluble constituents are in solid solution, the material is quenched to prevent or retard immediate re-precipitation. Three distinct quenching methods are employed. The one to be used in any particular instance depends upon the part, the alloy, and the properties desired.

Cold Water Quenching

Parts produced from sheet, extrusions, tubing, small forgings, and similar type material are generally quenched in a cold water bath. The temperature of the water before quenching should not exceed 85° F. A sufficient quantity of water

Thickness, in.	Time, Minutes
Up to .032	30
.032 to 1/8	30
1/8 to 1/4	40
Over 1/4	60

NOTES: Soaking time starts when the metal (or the molten bath) reaches a temperature within the range specified above.

FIGURE 6–66. Typical soaking times for heat treatment.

213

should be used to keep the temperature rise under 20° F. Such a drastic quench ensures maximum resistance to corrosion. This is particularly important when working with such alloys as 2017, 2024, and 7075. This is the reason a drastic quench is preferred, even though a slower quench may produce the required mechanical properties.

Hot Water Quenching

Large forgings and heavy sections can be quenched in hot or boiling water. This type of quench minimizes distortion and alleviates cracking which may be produced by the unequal temperatures obtained during the quench. The use of a hot water quench is permitted with these parts because the temperature of the quench water does not critically affect the resistance to corrosion of the forging alloys. In addition, the resistance to corrosion of heavy sections is not as critical a factor as for thin sections.

Spray Quenching

High-velocity water sprays are useful for parts formed from clad sheet and for large sections of almost all alloys. This type of quench also minimizes distortion and alleviates quench cracking. However, many specifications forbid the use of spray quenching for bare 2017 and 2024 sheet materials because of the effect on their resistance to corrosion.

Lag Between Soaking and Quenching

The time interval between the removal of the material from the furnace and quenching is critical for some alloys and should be held to a minimum. When solution heat treating 2017 or 2024 sheet material, the elapsed time must not exceed 10 seconds. The allowable time for heavy sections may be slightly greater.

Allowing the metal to cool slightly before quenching promotes re-precipitation from the solid solution. The precipitation occurs along grain boundaries and in certain slip planes causing poorer formability. In the case of 2017, 2024, and 7075 alloys, their resistance to intergranular corrosion is adversely affected.

Re-heat Treatment

The treatment of material which has been previously heat treated is considered a re-heat treatment. The unclad heat-treatable alloys can be solution heat treated repeatedly without harmful effects.

The number of solution heat treatments allowed for clad sheet is limited due to increased diffusion of core and cladding with each re-heating. Existing specifications allow one to three re-heat treatments of clad sheet depending upon cladding thickness.

Straightening After Solution Heat Treatment

Some warping occurs during solution heat treatment, producing kinks, buckles, waves, and twists. These imperfections are generally removed by straightening and flattening operations.

Where the straightening operations produce an appreciable increase in the tensile and yield strengths and a slight decrease in the percent of elongation, the material is designated −T3 temper. When the above values are not materially affected, the material is designated −T4 temper.

PRECIPITATION HEAT TREATING

As previously stated, the aluminum alloys are in a comparatively soft state immediately after quenching from a solution heat-treating temperature. To obtain their maximum strengths, they must be either naturally aged or precipitation hardened.

During this hardening and strengthening operation, precipitation of the soluble constituents from the supersaturated solid solution takes place. As precipitation progresses, the strength of the material increases, often by a series of peaks, until a maximum is reached. Further aging (overaging) causes the strength to steadily decline until a somewhat stable condition is obtained. The submicroscopic particles that are precipitated provide the keys or locks within the grain structure and between the grains to resist internal slippage and distortion when a load of any type is applied. In this manner, the strength and hardness of the alloy are increased.

Precipitation hardening produces a great increase in the strength and hardness of the material with corresponding decreases in the ductile properties. The process used to obtain the desired increase in strength is therefore known as aging, or precipitation hardening.

The strengthening of the heat-treatable alloys by aging is not due merely to the presence of a precipitate. The strength is due to both the uniform distribution of a finely dispersed submicro-

Alloy	Solution heat-treatment			Precipitation heat-treatment		
	Temp., °F	Quench	Temper desig.	Temp., °F	Time of aging	Temper desig.
2017	930-950	Cold water	T4			T
2117	930-950	Cold water	T4			T
2024	910-930	Cold water	T4			T
6053	960-980	Water	T4	445-455	1-2 hr	T5
				or		
				345-355	8 hr	T6
6061	960-980	Water	T4	315-325	18 hr	T6
				or		
				345-355	8 hr	T6
7075	870	Water		250	24 hr	T6

FIGURE 6–67. Conditions for heat treatment of aluminum alloys.

scopic precipitate and its effects upon the crystal structure of the alloy.

The aging practices used depend upon many properties other than strength. As a rule, the artificially aged alloys are slightly overaged to increase their resistance to corrosion. This is especially true with the artificially aged high-copper-content alloys that are susceptible to intergranular corrosion when inadequately aged.

The heat-treatable aluminum alloys are subdivided into two classes, those that obtain their full strength at room temperature and those that require artificial aging.

The alloys that obtain their full strength after 4 or 5 days at room temperature are known as natural aging alloys. Precipitation from the supersaturated solid solution starts soon after quenching, with 90 percent of the maximum strength generally being obtained in 24 hours. Alloys 2017 and 2024 are natural aging alloys.

The alloys that require precipitation thermal treatment to develop their full strength are artificially aged alloys. However, these alloys also age a limited amount at room temperature, the rate and extent of the strengthening depending upon the alloys.

Many of the artificially aged alloys reach their maximum natural or room temperature aging strengths after a few days. These can be stocked for fabrication in the −T4 or −T3 temper. High-zinc-content alloys such as 7075 continue to age appreciably over a long period of time, their mechanical property changes being sufficient to

reduce their formability.

The advantage of −W temper formability can be utilized, however, in the same manner as with natural aging alloys; that is, by fabricating shortly after solution heat treatment, or retaining formability by the use of refrigeration.

Refrigeration retards the rate of natural aging. At 32° F., the beginning of the aging process is delayed for several hours, while dry ice (−50° F. to −100° F.) retards aging for an extended period of time.

Precipitation Practices

The temperatures used for precipitation hardening depend upon the alloy and the properties desired, ranging from 250° F. to 375° F. They should be controlled within a very narrow range (plus or minus 5°) to obtain best results. (See figure 6–67.)

The time at temperature is dependent upon the temperature used, the properties desired, and the alloy. It ranges from 8 to 96 hours. Increasing the aging temperature decreases the soaking period necessary for proper aging. However, a closer control of both time and temperature is necessary when using the higher temperatures.

After receiving the thermal precipitation treatment, the material should be air cooled to room temperature. Water quenching, while not necessary, produces no ill effects. Furnace cooling has a tendency to produce overaging.

ANNEALING OF ALUMINUM ALLOYS

The annealing procedure for aluminum alloys consists of heating the alloys to an elevated temperature, holding or soaking them at this temperature for a length of time depending upon the mass of the metal, and then cooling in still air. Annealing leaves the metal in the best condition for cold-working. However, when prolonged forming operations are involved, the metal will take on a condition known as "mechanical hardness" and will resist further working. It may be necessary to anneal a part several times during the forming process to avoid cracking. Aluminum alloys should not be used in the annealed state for parts or fittings.

Clad parts should be heated as quickly and carefully as possible, since long exposure to heat tends to cause some of the constituents of the core to diffuse into the cladding. This reduces the corrosion resistance of the cladding.

HEAT TREATMENT OF ALUMINUM ALLOY RIVETS

Aluminum alloy rivets are furnished in the following compositions: Alloys 1100, 5056, 2117, 2017, and 2024.

Alloy 1100 rivets are used in the "as fabricated" condition for riveting aluminum alloy sheets where a low-strength rivet is suitable. Alloy 5056 rivets are used in the "as fabricated" condition for riveting magnesium alloy sheets.

Alloy 2117 rivets have moderately high strength and are suitable for riveting aluminum alloy sheets. These rivets receive only one heat treatment, which is performed by the manufacturer, and are anodized after being heat treated. They require no further heat treatment before they are used. Alloy 2117 rivets retain their characteristics indefinitely after heat treatment and can be driven anytime. Rivets made of this alloy are the most widely used in aircraft construction.

Alloy 2017 and 2024 rivets are high-strength rivets suitable for use with aluminum alloy structures. They are purchased from the manufacturer in the heat-treated condition. Since the aging characteristics of these alloys at room temperatures are such that the rivets are unfit for driving, they must be re-heat treated just before they are to be used. Alloy 2017 rivets become too hard for driving in approximately 1 hour after quenching. Alloy 2024 rivets become hardened in 10 minutes after quenching. Both of these alloys may be re-heat treated as often as required; however, they must be anodized before the first re-heat treatment to prevent intergranular oxidation of the material. If these rivets are stored in a refrigerator at a temperature lower than 32° F. immediately after quenching, they will remain soft enough to be usable for several days.

Rivets requiring heat treatment are heated either in tubular containers in a salt bath, or in small screen-wire baskets in an air furnace. The heat treatment of alloy 2017 rivets consists of subjecting the rivets to a temperature between 930° F. to 950° F. for approximately 30 minutes, and immediately quenching in cold water. These rivets reach maximum strength in about 9 days after being driven. Alloy 2024 rivets should be heated to a temperature of 910° F. to 930° F. and immediately quenched in cold water. These rivets develop a greater shear strength than 2017 rivets and are used in locations where extra strength is required. Alloy 2024 rivets develop their maximum shear strength in 1 day after being driven.

The 2017 rivet should be driven within approximately 1 hour and the 2024 rivet within 10 to 20 minutes after heat treating or removal from refrigeration. If not used within these times, the rivets should be re-heat treated before being refrigerated.

HEAT TREATMENT OF MAGNESIUM ALLOYS

Magnesium alloy castings respond readily to heat treatment, and about 95 percent of the magnesium used in aircraft construction is in the cast form.

The heat treatment of magnesium alloy castings is similar to the heat treatment of aluminum alloys in that there are two types of heat treatment: (1) Solution heat treatment and (2) precipitation (aging) heat treatment. Magnesium, however, develops a negligible change in its properties when allowed to age naturally at room temperatures.

Solution Heat Treatment

Magnesium alloy castings are solution heat treated to improve tensile strength, ductility, and shock resistance. This heat-treatment condition is indicated by using the symbol —T4 following the alloy designation. Solution heat treatment plus artificial aging is designated —T6. Artificial aging is necessary to develop the full properties of the metal.

Solution heat-treatment temperatures for magnesium alloy castings range from 730° F. to 780° F., the exact range depending upon the type of alloy. The temperature range for each type of alloy is listed in Specification MIL-H-6857. The upper limit of each range listed in the specification is the maximum temperature to which the alloy may be heated without danger of melting the metal.

The soaking time ranges from 10 to 18 hours, the exact time depending upon the type of alloy as well as the thickness of the part. Soaking periods longer than 18 hours may be necessary for castings over 2 inches in thickness. Magnesium alloys must *never* be heated in a salt bath as this may result in an explosion.

A serious potential fire hazard exists in the heat treatment of magnesium alloys. If through oversight or malfunctioning of equipment, the maximum temperatures are exceeded, the casting may ignite and burn freely. For this reason, the furnace used should be equipped with a safety cutoff that will turn off the power to the heating elements and blowers if the regular control equipment malfunctions or fails.

Some magnesium alloys require a protective atmosphere of sulfur dioxide gas during solution heat treatment. This aids in preventing the start of a fire even if the temperature limits are slightly exceeded.

Air-quenching is used after solution heat treatment of magnesium alloys since there appears to be no advantage in liquid cooling.

Precipitation Heat Treatment

After solution treatment, magnesium alloys may be given an aging treatment to increase hardness and yield strength. Generally, the aging treatments are used merely to relieve stress and stabilize the alloys in order to prevent dimensional changes later, especially during or after machining. Both yield strength and hardness are improved somewhat by this treatment at the expense of a slight amount of ductility. The corrosion resistance is also improved, making it closer to the "as cast" alloy.

Precipitation heat-treatment temperatures are considerably lower than solution heat-treatment temperatures and range from 325° F. to 500° F. Soaking time ranges from 4 to 18 hours.

HEAT TREATMENT OF TITANIUM

Titanium is heat treated for the following purposes:

1. Relief of stresses set up during cold forming or machining.
2. Annealing after hot working or cold working, or to provide maximum ductility for subsequent cold working.
3. Thermal hardening to improve strength.

Stress Relieving

Stress relieving is generally used to remove stress concentrations resulting from forming of titanium sheet. It is performed at temperatures ranging from 650° F. to 1,000° F. The time at temperature varies from a few minutes for a very thin sheet to an hour or more for heavier sections. A typical stress-relieving treatment is 900° F. for 30 minutes, followed by an air cool.

The discoloration or scale which forms on the surface of the metal during stress relieving is easily removed by pickling in acid solutions. The recommended solution contains 10 to 20 percent nitric acid and 1 to 3 percent hydrofluoric acid. The solution should be at room temperature or slightly above.

Full Annealing

The annealing of titanium and titanium alloys provides toughness, ductility at room temperature, dimensional and structural stability at elevated temperatures, and improved machinability.

The full anneal is usually called for as preparation for further working. It is performed at 1,200° F. to 1,650° F. The time at temperature varies from 16 minutes to several hours, depending on the thickness of the material and the amount of cold work to be performed. The usual treatment for the commonly used alloys is 1,300° F. for 1 hour, followed by an air cool. A full anneal generally results in sufficient scale formation to require the use of caustic descaling, such as sodium hydride salt bath.

Thermal Hardening

Unalloyed titanium cannot be heat treated, but the alloys commonly used in aircraft construction can be strengthened by thermal treatment, usually at some sacrifice in ductility. For best results, a water quench from 1,450° F., followed by re-heating to 900° F. for 8 hours is recommended.

Casehardening

The chemical activity of titanium and its rapid absorption of oxygen, nitrogen, and carbon at relatively low temperatures make casehardening advantageous for special applications. Nitriding, carburizing, or carbonitriding can be used to produce a wear-resistant case of 0.0001 to 0.0002 inch in depth.

HARDNESS TESTING

Hardness testing is a method of determining the results of heat treatment as well as the state of a metal prior to heat treatment. Since hardness values can be tied in with tensile strength values and, in part, with wear resistance, hardness tests are a valuable check of heat-treat control and of material properties.

Practically all hardness-testing equipment now uses the resistance to penetration as a measure of hardness. Included among the better known hardness testers are the Brinell and Rockwell, both of which are described and illustrated in this section. Also included is a popular portable-type hardness tester currently being used.

Brinell Tester

The Brinell tester (figure 6–68) uses a hardened spherical ball, which is forced into the surface of the metal. This ball is 10 millimeters (0.3937 inch) in diameter. A pressure of 3,000 kilograms is used for ferrous metals and 500 kilograms for nonferrous metals. The pressure must be maintained at least 10 seconds for ferrous metals and at least 30 seconds for nonferrous metals. The load is applied by hydraulic pressure. The hydraulic pressure is built up by a hand pump or an electric motor, depending on the model of tester. A pressure gage indicates the amount of pressure. There is a release mechanism for relieving the pressure after the test has been made, and a calibrated microscope is provided for measuring the diameter of the impression in millimeters. The machine has various shaped anvils for supporting the specimen and an elevating screw for bringing the specimen in contact with the ball penetrator. These are attachments for special tests.

In order to determine the Brinell hardness number for a metal, the diameter of the impression is first measured, using the calibrated microscope furnished with the tester. After measuring the diameter of the impression, the measurement is

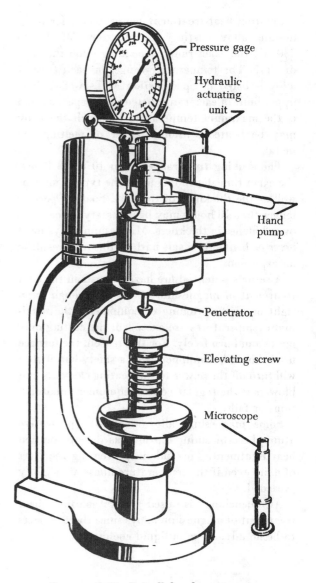

FIGURE 6–68. Brinell hardness tester.

converted into the Brinell hardness number on the conversion table furnished with the tester.

Rockwell Tester

The Rockwell hardness tester (figure 6–69) measures the resistance to penetration, as does the Brinell tester. Instead of measuring the diameter of the impression, the Rockwell tester measures the depth, and the hardness is indicated directly on a dial attached to the machine. The dial numbers in the outer circle are black, and the inner numbers are red. Rockwell hardness numbers are based on the difference between the depth of penetration at major and minor loads. The greater

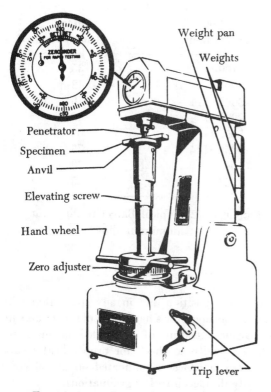

Weight pan

Weights

Penetrator

Specimen

Anvil

Elevating screw

Hand wheel

Zero adjuster

Trip lever

FIGURE 6–69. Rockwell hardness tester.

Scale symbol	Penetrator	Major load (kg.)	Dial number
A	Diamond	60	Black
B	1/16-inch ball	100	Red
C	Diamond	150	Black
D	Diamond	100	Black
E	1/8-inch ball	100	Red
F	1/16-inch ball	60	Red
G	1/16-inch ball	150	Red
H	1/8-inch ball	60	Red
K	1/8-inch ball	150	Red

FIGURE 6–70. Standard Rockwell hardness scales.

this difference, the less the hardness number and the softer the material.

Two types of penetrators are used with the Rockwell tester, a diamond cone and a hardened steel ball. The load which forces the penetrator into the metal is called the major load and is measured in kilograms. The results of each penetrator and load combination are reported on separate scales, designated by letters. The penetrator, the major load, and the scale vary with the kind of metal being tested

For hardened steels, the diamond penetrator is used; the major load is 150 kilograms; and the hardness is read on the "C" scale. When this reading is recorded, the letter "C" must precede the number indicated by the pointer. The C-scale setup is used for testing metals ranging in hardness from C-20 to the hardest steel (usually about C-70). If the metal is softer than C-20, the B-scale setup is used. With this setup, the 1/16-inch ball is used as a penetrator; the major load is 100 kilograms; and the hardness is read on the B-scale.

In addition to the "C" and "B" scales, there are other setups for special testing. The scales, penetrators, major loads, and dial numbers to be read are listed in figure 6-70.

The Rockwell tester is equipped with a weight pan, and two weights are supplied with the machine. One weight is marked in red. The other weight is marked in black. With no weight in the weight pan, the machine applies a major load of 60 kilograms. If the scale setup calls for a 100-kilogram load, the red weight is placed in the pan. For a 150-kilogram load, the black weight is added to the red weight. The black weight is always used with the red weight; it is never used alone.

Practically all testing is done with either the B-scale setup or the C-scale setup. For these scales, the colors may be used as a guide in selecting the weight (or weights) and in reading the dial. For the B-scale test, use the red weight and read the red numbers. For a C-scale test, add the black weight to the red weight and read the black numbers.

In setting up the Rockwell machine, use the diamond penetrator for testing materials known to be hard. If the hardness is unknown, try the diamond, since the steel ball may be deformed if used for testing hard materials. If the metal tests below C-22, then change to the steel ball.

Use the steel ball for all soft materials, those testing less than B-100. Should an overlap occur at the top of the B-scale and the bottom of the C-scale, use the C-scale setup.

Before the major load is applied, the test specimen must be securely locked in place to prevent slipping and to seat the anvil and penetrator properly. To do this, a load of 10 kilograms is applied before the lever is tripped. This preliminary load is called the minor load. The minor load is 10 kilograms regardless of the scale setup.

The metal to be tested in the Rockwell tester must be ground smooth on two opposite sides and be free of scratches and foreign matter. The surface should be perpendicular to the axis of penetration, and the two opposite ground surfaces should be parallel. If the specimen is tapered, the amount of error will depend on the taper. A curved surface will also cause a slight error in the hardness test. The amount of error depends on the curvature; i.e., the smaller the radius of curvature, the greater the error. To eliminate such error, a small flat should be ground on the curved surface if possible.

Clad aluminum-alloy sheets cannot be tested directly with any accuracy with a Rockwell hardness tester. If the hardness value of the base metal is desired, the pure aluminum coating must be removed from the area to be checked prior to testing.

Barcol Tester

The Barcol tester (figure 6-71) is a portable unit designed for testing aluminum alloys, copper, brass, or other relatively soft materials. It should not be used on aircraft steels. Approximate range of the tester is 25 to 100 Brinell. The unit can be

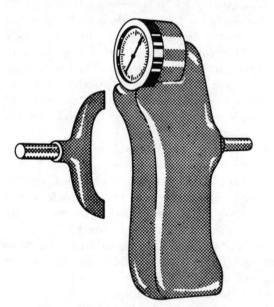

FIGURE 6–71. Barcol portable hardness tester.

Alloy and temper	Barcol number
1100-O	35
3003-O	42
3003-H14	56
2024-O	60
5052-O	62
5052-H34	75
6061-T	78
2024-T	85

FIGURE 6–72. Typical Barcol readings for aluminum alloy.

used in any position and in any space that will allow for the operator's hand. It is of great value in the hardness testing of assembled or installed parts, especially to check for proper heat treatment. The hardness is indicated on a dial conveniently divided into 100 graduations.

The design of the Barcol tester is such that operating experience is not necessary. It is only necessary to exert a light pressue against the instrument to drive the spring-loaded indenter into the material to be tested. The hardness reading is instantly indicated on the dial.

Several typical readings for aluminum alloys are listed in figure 6-72. Note that the harder the material is, the higher the Barcol number will be.

To prevent damage to the point, avoid sliding or scraping when it is in contact with the material being tested. If the point should become damaged, it must be replaced with a new one. No attempt should be made to grind the point.

Each tester is supplied with a test disk for checking the condition of the point. To check the point, press the instrument down on the test disk. When the downward pressure brings the end of the lower plunger guide against the surface of the disk, the indicator reading should be within the range shown on the test disk.

GENERAL

Physics is the term applied to that area of knowledge regarding the basic and fundamental nature of matter and energy. It does not attempt to determine why matter and energy behave as they do in their relation to physical phenomena, but rather how they behave.

The persons who maintain and repair aircraft should have a knowledge of basic physics, which is sometimes called the science of matter and energy.

MATTER

Although matter is the most basic of all things related to the field of physics and the material world, it is the hardest to define. Since it cannot be rigidly defined, this chapter will point out those characteristics which are easily recognizable.

Matter itself cannot be destroyed, but it can be changed from one state into another state by chemical or physical means. It is usually considered in terms of the energy it contains, absorbs, or gives off. Under certain controlled conditions, it can be made to aid man in his everyday life.

Matter is any substance that occupies space and has weight. There are three states of matter: (1) Solids, (2) liquids, and (3) gases. Solids have a definite volume and a definite shape; liquids have a definite volume, but they take the shape of the containing vessel; gases have neither a definite volume nor a definite shape. Gases not only take the shape of the containing vessel, but they expand and fill the vessel, no matter what its volume.

Water is a good example of matter changing from one state to another. At high temperature it is in the gaseous state known as steam. At moderate temperatures it is a liquid, and at low temperatures it becomes ice, a solid state. In this example, the temperature is the dominant factor in determining the state that the substance assumes. Pressure is another important factor that will effect changes in the state of matter. At pressures lower than atmospheric, water will boil and thus change into steam at temperatures lower than 212° F. Pressure is a critical factor in changing some gases to liquids or solids. Normally, when pressure and chilling are both applied to a gas, it assumes a liquid state. Liquid air, which is a mixture of oxygen and nitrogen, is produced in this manner.

Characteristics of Matter

All matter has certain characteristics or general properties. These properties are defined elementally and broadly at this point, and more specifically in applications throughout the text. Among these properties and relationships are:

a. Volume—meaning to occupy space; having some measurements such as length, width, and height. It may be measured in cubic inches, cubic centimeters, or the like.

b. Mass—the measurement of quantity or the measure of the quantity of matter in a body. Mass does not vary even though the state changes.

c. Attraction—a force acting mutually between particles of matter, tending to draw them together. Sir Issac Newton called this the "Law of Universal Gravitation." He showed how each particle of matter attracts every other particle, how people are bound to the earth, and how the planets are attracted in the solar system.

d. Weight—the measure of universal gravitation. The pull of gravity on a body is called the weight of the body and indicates how heavy the body is.

e. Density—the mass (weight) of a substance per unit volume. Density can be used to distinguish various types of matter. If a substance is very dense, a large quantity of this matter would occupy a small volume.

f. Inertia—the opposition which a body offers to any change of motion. The property of inertia is common to all matter. It is best expressed in Newton's first law: "A body at rest remains at rest, and a body in motion continues to move at constant speed along a straight line, unless the body is acted upon in either case by an external force."

g. Porosity—having pores or spaces where smaller particles may fit when a mixture takes place. This is sometimes referred to as granular; consisting or appearing to consist of small grains or granules.

h. Impenetrability—simply stated means that no two objects can occupy the same place at the same time. Thus, two portions of matter cannot at the same time occupy the same space.

Matter may be classified as either an element or a compound, depending upon the complexity of its structure. An element is matter that cannot be reduced chemically into a simpler substance. A compound is matter formed by some combination of elements.

Two basic particles, the atom and the molecule, make up all matter. The molecule is the smallest particle of a substance which still has all the properties of the original substance. In *physics* the molecule is the unit of matter. The atom is the smallest particle of an element that can combine with other atoms to form molecules. In *chemistry*, the atom is the unit of matter.

While the subject of matter may seem complex, it is difficult to think of anything simpler than matter. It can be referred to as "anything that occupies space."

Systems of Measurement

The two most commonly used systems of measurement are the English system, which is still in general use in the United States, and the metric system, used in most European countries and now adopted by the Armed Forces of the United States. The metric system is normally used in all scientific applications.

The three basic quantities which require units of measurement are mass (weight), length (distance), and time.

The metric system is sometimes called the CGS system because it uses as basic measuring units, the centimeter (C) to measure length, the gram (G) to measure mass, and the second (S) to measure time.

The English system uses different units for the measurement of mass and length. The pound is the unit of weight; the foot is used to measure

length. The second is used to measure time as in the metric system.

The units of one system can be converted to units in the other system by using a conversion factor or by referring to a chart similar to that shown in figure 7–1. In this figure the English and the metric systems are compared; in addition, a column of equivalents is included which can be used to convert units from one system to the other.

FLUIDS

General

Because both liquids and gases flow freely, they are called fluids, from the Latin word "fluidus," meaning to flow. A fluid is defined as a substance which changes its shape easily and takes the shape of its container. This applies to both liquids and gases. The characteristics of liquids and gases may be grouped under similarities and differences.

Similar characteristics are as follows:

1. Each has no definite shape but conforms to the shape of the container.
2. Both readily transmit pressures.

Differential characteristics are as follows:

1. Gases fill their containers completely, but liquids may not.
2. Gases are lighter than equal volumes of liquids.
3. Gases are highly compressible, but liquids are only slightly so.

These differences are described in the appropriate areas of the following discussion concerning the properties and characteristics of fluids at rest. Also included are some of the factors which affect fluids in different situations.

Density and Specific Gravity

The density of a substance is its weight per unit volume. The unit volume selected for use in the English system of measurement is 1 cubic foot. In the metric system it is 1 cubic centimeter. Therefore, density is expressed in lbs./cu. ft. (pounds per cubic foot) or in g./cu. cm. (grams per cubic centimeter).

To find the density of a substance, its weight and volume must be known. Its weight is then divided by its volume to find the weight per unit volume.

	Metric System	English System	Equivalents
Length (distance)	CENTIMETER 1 centimeter = 10 millimeters 1 decimeter = 10 centimeters 1 meter = 100 centimeters 1 kilometer = 1000 meters	FOOT 1 foot = 12 inches 1 yard = 3 feet 1 mile = 5,280 feet	1 in. = 2.54 cm. 1 ft. = 30.5 cm. 1 meter = 39.37 in. 1 km. = 0.62 mile
Weight (mass)	GRAM 1 gram = 1000 milligrams 1 kilogram = 1000 grams	POUND 1 pound = 16 ounces 1 ton = 2,000 pounds	1 lb. = 453.6 gr. 1 kg. = 2.2 lb.
Time	SECOND Same as for English system	SECOND 1 second = $\dfrac{1}{86,400}$ of average solar day.	Time same for both systems

FIGURE 7–1. Comparison of metric and English systems of measurement.

For example, the liquid which fills a certain container weighs 1,497.6 pounds. The container is 4 feet long, 3 feet wide, and 2 feet deep. Its volume is 24 cubic feet (4 ft. × 3 ft. × 2 ft.). If 24 cubic feet of liquid weights 1,497.6 pounds, then 1 cubic foot weighs 1,497.6/24, or 62.4 pounds. Therefore, the density of the liquid is 62.4 lbs./cu. ft.

This is the density of water at 4° C. (centigrade) and is usually used as the standard for comparing densities of other substances. (In the metric system the density of water is 1 g./cu. cm.). The standard temperature of 4° C. is used when measuring the density of liquids and solids. Changes in temperature will not change the weight of a substance, but will change the volume of the substance by expansion or contraction, thus changing its weight per unit volume.

The procedure for finding density applies to all substances; however, it is necessary to consider the pressure when finding the density of gases. Temperature is more critical when measuring the density of gases than it is for other substances. The density of a gas increases in direct proportion to the pressure exerted on it. Standard conditions for the measurement of the densities of gases have been established at 0° C. for temperature and a pressure of 76 cm. of mercury. (This is the average pressure of the atmosphere at sea level.) Density is computed based on these conditions for all gases.

It is often necessary to compare the density of one substance with that of another. For this purpose, a standard is needed. Water is the standard that physicists have chosen to use when comparing the densities of all liquids and solids. For gases, air is most commonly used. However, hydrogen is sometimes used as a standard for gases. In physics, the word specific implies a ratio. Thus, specific gravity is calculated by comparing the weight of a definite volume of the given substance with the weight of an equal volume of water. The terms "specific weight" or "specific density" are sometimes used to express this ratio.

The following formulas are used to find the sp. gr. (specific gravity) of liquids and solids:

$$\text{sp. gr.} = \frac{\text{Weight of the substance}}{\text{Weight of an equal volume of water}}$$

or,

$$\text{sp. gr.} = \frac{\text{Density of the substance}}{\text{Density of water}}$$

The same formulas are used to find the density of gases by substituting air or hydrogen for water.

Specific gravity is not expressed in units, but as pure numbers. For example, if a certain hydraulic liquid has a sp. gr. of 0.8, 1 cu. ft. of the liquid weighs 0.8 times as much as 1 cu. ft. of water: 62.4 times 0.8 or 49.92 pounds. In the metric system, 1 cu. cm. of a substance with a

Solids	Sp. gr.	Liquids (Room temperatures)	Sp. gr.	Gases (Air standard at 0°C, and 76.0 centimeters of mercury)	Sp. gr.
Aluminum	2.7	Alcohol, ethyl	0.789	Air	1.000
Bronze	8.8	Gasoline	0.68 0.72	Hydrogen	0.0695
Copper	8.9	Oil (paraffin)	0.8	Nitrogen	0.967
Ice	0.917	Water	1.00	Oxygen	1.105

FIGURE 7–2. Typical values of specific gravity.

specific gravity of 0.8 weighs 1 times 0.8 or 0.8 gr. (Note that in the metric system the specific gravity of a liquid or solid has the same numerical value as its density. Since air weighs 1.293 gr./l. (grams per liter), the specific gravity of gases does not equal the metric densities.)

Specific gravity and density are independent of the size of the sample under consideration and depend only upon the substance of which it is made. See figure 7–2 for typical values of sp. gr. for various substances.

A device called a hydrometer is used for measuring specific gravity of liquids. This device consists of a tubular-shaped glass float contained in a larger glass tube. (See figure 7–3.) The larger glass tube provides the container for the liquid. A rubber suction bulb draws the liquid up into the container. There must be enough liquid to raise the float and prevent it from touching the bottom. The float is weighted and has a vertically graduated scale. To determine specific gravity, the scale is read at the surface of the liquid in which the float is immersed. An indication of 1000 is read when the float is immersed in pure water. When immersed in a liquid of greater density, the float rises, indicating a greater specific gravity. For liquids of lesser density the float sinks, indicating a lower specific gravity.

An example of the use of the hydrometer is its use in determining the specific gravity of the electrolyte (battery liquid) in an aircraft battery. When a battery is discharged, the calibrated float immersed in the electrolyte will indicate approximately 1150. The indication of a charged battery is between 1275 and 1310.

Buoyancy

A solid body submerged in a liquid or a gas weighs less than when weighed in free space. This is because of the upward force, called buoyant force, which any fluid exerts on a body submerged in it. An object will float if this upward force of the fluid is greater than the weight of the object. Objects denser than the fluid, even though they sink readily, appear to lose a part of their weight when submerged. A person can lift a larger weight under water than he can possibly lift in the air.

The following experiment is illustrated in figure 7–4. The overflow can is filled up to the spout with water. The heavy metal cylinder is first weighed in still air and then is weighed while completely submerged in the water. The difference between the two weights is the buoyant force of the water. As the cylinder is lowered into the overflow can, the water is caught in the catch bucket. The volume of water which overflows equals the volume of the cylinder. (The volume of irregular-shaped objects can be measured by this method.) If this experiment is performed carefully, the weight of the water displaced by the metal cylinder exactly equals the buoyant force of the water.

Similar experiments were performed by Archimedes (287–212 B.C.). As a result of his experiments, he discovered that the buoyant force which a fluid exerts upon a submerged body is equal to the weight of the fluid the body displaces. This statement is referred to as Archimedes' principle. This principle applies to all fluids, gases as well as liquids. Just as water exerts a buoyant

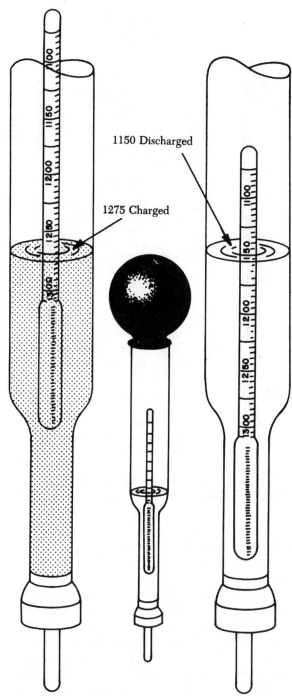

1150 Discharged

1275 Charged

FIGURE 7–3.   A hydrometer.

force on submerged objects, air exerts a buoyant force on objects submerged in it.

TEMPERATURE

Temperature is a dominant factor affecting the physical properties of fluids. It is of particular

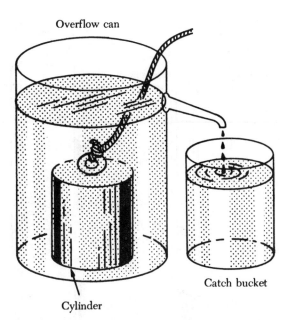

Overflow can

Catch bucket

Cylinder

FIGURE 7–4.   Measurement of buoyant force.

concern when calculating changes in the state of gases.

The three temperature scales used extensively are the centigrade, the Fahrenheit, and the absolute or Kelvin scales. The centigrade scale is constructed by using the freezing and boiling points of water, under standard conditions, as fixed points of zero and 100, respectively, with 100 equal divisions between. The Fahrenheit scale uses 32° as the freezing point of water and 212° as the boiling point, and has 180 equal divisions between. The absolute or Kelvin scale is constructed with its zero point established as −273° C., or −459.4° F. below the freezing point of water. The relationships of the other fixed points of the scales are shown in B of figure 7–5.

Absolute zero, one of the fundamental constants of physics, is commonly used in the study of gases. It is usually expressed in terms of the centigrade scale. If the heat energy of a given gas sample could be progressively reduced, some temperature would be reached at which the motion of the molecules would cease entirely. If accurately determined, this temperature could then be taken as a natural reference, or as a true "absolute zero" value.

Experiments with hydrogen indicated that if a gas were cooled to −273.16° C. (used as −273° for most calculations), all molecular motion would cease, and no additional heat could be extracted from the substance.

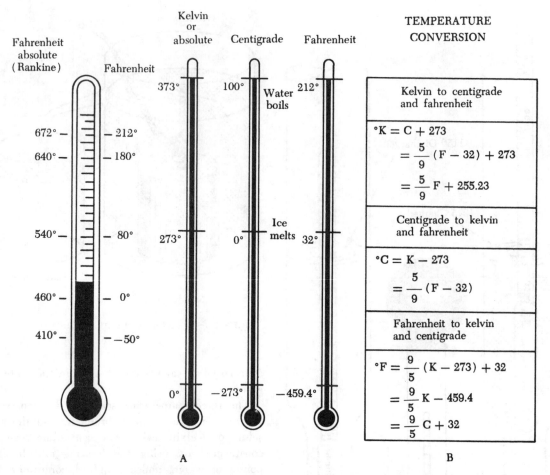

FIGURE 7–5. (A) Rankine scale used to convert Farenheit to absolute. (B) Comparison of Fahrenheit, centigrade, and Kelvin temperature.

When temperatures are measured with respect to the absolute zero reference, they are expressed as zero in the absolute or Kelvin scale. Thus, absolute zero may be expressed as 0° K., as −273° C., or as −459.4° F. (used as −460° for most calculations).

When working with temperatures, always make sure which system of measurement is being used and know how to convert from one to another. The conversion formulas are shown in B of figure 7–5. For purposes of calculations, the Rankine scale illustrated in A of figure 7–5 is commonly used to convert Fahrenheit to absolute. For Fahrenheit readings above zero, 460° is added. Thus, 72° F. equals 460° plus 72°, or 532° absolute. If the Fahrenheit reading is below zero, it is subtracted from 460°. Thus −40° F. equals 460° minus 40°, or 420° absolute. It should be stressed that the Rankine scale does not indicate absolute temperature readings in accordance with the

Kelvin scale, but these conversions may be used for the calculations of changes in the state of gases.

The Kelvin and centigrade scales are used more extensively in scientific work; therefore, some technical manuals may use these scales in giving directions and operating instructions. The Fahrenheit scale is commonly used in the United States, and most people are familar with it. Therefore, the Fahrenheit scale is used in most areas of this text.

PRESSURE

The term "pressure" as used throughout this chapter is defined as a force per unit area. Pressure is usually measured in p.s.i. (pounds per square inch). Sometimes pressure is measured in inches of mercury or, for very low pressure, inches of water.

226

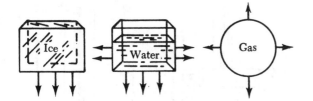

FIGURE 7–6.   Exertion of pressure.

Pressure may be in one direction, several directions, or in all directions. (See figure 7–6.) Ice (a solid) exerts pressure downward only. Water (a fluid) exerts pressure on all surfaces with which it comes in contact. Gas (a fluid) exerts pressure in all directions because it completely fills the container.

Atmospheric Pressure

The atmosphere is the whole mass of air surrounding the earth. Although it extends upward for about 500 miles, the section which is of primary interest is that portion of the air which rests on the earth's surface and extends upward for about 7½ miles. This layer is called the troposphere, and the higher above the earth, the lower its pressure.

This is because air has weight. If a column of air 1-inch square extending all the way to the top of the atmosphere could be weighed, it would weigh approximately 14.7 pounds at sea level. Thus, atmospheric pressure at sea level is approximately 14.7 p.s.i. As altitude increases, the atmospheric pressure decreases approximately 1.0 p.s.i. for every 2,343 feet. However, below sea level, atmospheric pressure increases. Pressures under water differ from those under air only because the weight of the water must be added to the weight of the air.

Atmospheric pressure, its temperature effects, and the means used to measure it are discussed in greater detail in another section of this chapter.

Absolute Pressure

As stated previously, absolute temperature is used in the calculation of changes in the state of gas. It is also necessary to use absolute pressure for these calculations.

Absolute pressure is measured from absolute zero pressure rather than from normal or atmospheric pressure (approximately 14.7 p.s.i.). Gage

pressure is used on all ordinary gages, and indicates pressure in excess of atmospheric. Therefore, absolute pressure is equal to atmospheric pressure plus gage pressure. For example, 100 p.s.i.g. (pounds per square inch gage) equals 100 p.s.i. plus 14.7 p.s.i. or 114.7 p.s.i.a. (pounds per square inch absolute).

Incompressibility and Expansion of Liquids

Liquids can be compressed only slightly; that is, the reduction of the volume which they occupy, even under extreme pressure, is very small. If a pressure of 100 p.s.i. is applied to a body of water, the volume will decrease only 3/10,000 of its original volume. It would take a force of 64,000 p.s.i. to reduce its volume 10 percent. Since other liquids behave in about the same manner, liquids are usually considered incompressible.

In some applications of hydraulics where extremely close tolerances are required, the compressibility of liquids must be considered in the design of the system. In this study, however, liquids are considered to be incompressible.

Liquids usually expand when heated. This action is normally referred to as thermal expansion. All liquids do not expand the same amount for a certain increase in temperature. If two flasks are placed in a heated vessel, and if one of these flasks is filled with water and the other with alcohol, it will be found that the alcohol expands much more than the water for the same rise in temperature. Most oils expand more than water. Aircraft hydraulic systems contain provisions for compensating for this increase of volume in order to prevent breakage of equipment.

Compressibility and Expansion of Gases

The two major differences between gases and liquids are their compressibility and expansion characteristics. Although liquids are practically incompressible, gases are highly compressible. Gases completely fill any closed vessel in which they are contained, but liquids fill a container only to the extent of their normal volume.

KINETIC THEORY OF GASES

The simple structure of gases makes them readily adaptable to mathematical analysis from which has evolved a detailed theory of the behavior of gases. This is called the kinetic theory of gases. The theory assumes that a body of gas is composed of identical molecules which behave like minute elastic spheres, spaced relatively far apart and continuously in motion.

The degree of molecular motion is dependent upon the temperature of the gas. Since the molecules are continuously striking against each other and against the walls of the container, an increase in temperature with the resulting increase in molecular motion causes a corresponding increase in the number of collisions between the molecules. The increased number of collisions results in an increase in pressure because a greater number of molecules strike against the walls of the container in a given unit of time.

If the container were an open vessel, the gas would expand and overflow from the container. However, if the container is sealed and possesses elasticity (such as a rubber balloon), the increased pressure causes the container to expand.

For instance, when making a long drive on a hot day, the pressure in the tires of an automobile increases, and a tire which appeared to be somewhat "soft" in cool morning temperature may appear normal at a higher midday temperature.

Such phenomena as these have been explained and set forth in the form of laws pertaining to gases and tend to support the kinetic theory.

At any given instant, some molecules of a gas are moving in one direction, some in another direction; some are traveling fast while some are traveling slowly; some may even be in a state of rest. The combined effect of these varying velocities corresponds to the temperature of the gas. In any considerable amount of gas, there are so many molecules present that in accordance with the "laws of probability" some average velocity can be found. If this average velocity were possessed by every molecule in the gas, it would produce the same effect at a given temperature as the total of the many varying velocities.

Boyle's Law

As previously stated, compressibility is an outstanding characteristic of gases. The English scientist Robert Boyle was among the first to study this characteristic which he called the "springiness of air." By direct measurement he discovered that when the temperature of a combined sample of gas was kept constant and the pressure doubled, the volume was reduced to half the former value;

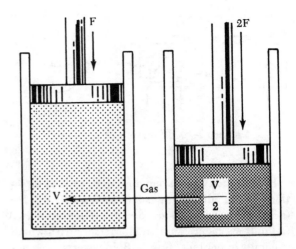

FIGURE 7–7. Gas compressed to half its original volume by a double force.

as the applied pressure was decreased, the resulting volume increased. From these observations, he concluded that for a constant temperature the product of the volume and pressure of an enclosed gas remains constant. Boyle's law is normally stated: "The volume of an enclosed dry gas varies inversely with its pressure, provided the temperature remains constant."

This law can be demonstrated by confining a quantity of gas in a cylinder which has a tightly fitted piston. A force is then applied to the piston so as to compress the gas in the cylinder to some specific volume. When the force applied to the piston is doubled, the gas is compressed to one-half its original volume, as indicated in figure 7–7.

In equation form, this relationship may be expressed either

$$V_1 P_1 = V_2 P_2$$

or

$$\frac{V_1}{V_2} = \frac{P_2}{P_1}$$

where V_1 and P_1 are the original volume and pressure, and V_2 and P_2 are the revised volume and pressure.

Example of Boyle's law: 4 cu. ft. of nitrogen are under a pressure of 100 p.s.i.g. The nitrogen is allowed to expand to a volume of 6 cu. ft. What is the new gage pressure?

Formula or equation:

$$V_1 P_1 = V_2 P_2$$

Substituting:

$$4 \times (100) = 6 \times P_2$$

$$P_2 = \frac{4 \times 100}{6}$$

$$P_2 = 66.6 \text{ p.s.i.g.}$$

A gas which conforms to Boyle's law is termed an ideal gas. When pressure is increased upon such a gas, its volume decreases proportionally and its density is increased. Thus, the density of a gas varies directly with the pressure, if the temperature remains constant as in the case of an ideal gas. Density also varies with temperature, since gases expand when heated and contract when cooled.

The useful applications of Boyle's law are many and varied. Some applications more common to aviation are: (1) The carbon dioxide (CO_2) bottle used to inflate life rafts and life vests; (2) the compressed oxygen and the acetylene tanks used in welding; (3) the compressed air brakes and shock absorbers; and (4) the use of oxygen tanks for high-altitude flying and emergency use.

Charles' Law

The French scientist Jacques Charles provided much of the foundation for the modern kinetic theory of gases. He found that all gases expand and contract in direct proportion to the change in the absolute temperature, provided the pressure is held constant. In equation form, this part of the law may be expressed.

$$V_1 T_2 = V_2 T_1$$

or

$$\frac{V_1}{V_2} = \frac{T_1}{T_2}.$$

This equation means that with a constant volume, the absolute pressure of a gas varies directly with the absolute temperature.

Examples of Charles' law: A cylinder of gas under a pressure of 1,800 p.s.i.g. at 70° F. is left out in the sun in the tropics and heats up to a temperature of 130° F. What is the new pressure within the cylinder? The pressure and temperature must be converted to absolute pressure and temperature.

Formula or equation:

$$\frac{P_1}{P_2} = \frac{T_1}{T_2}$$

Using the Rankine system:

70° F. = 530° absolute

130° F. = 590° absolute

Substituting:

$$\frac{1,800 + 14.7}{P_2} = \frac{530}{590}$$

Then:

$$P_2 = \frac{(590)(1,814.7)}{530}$$

$$P_2 = 2,020 \text{ p.s.i.a.}$$

Converting absolute pressure to gage pressure:

$$\begin{array}{r} 2,020.0 \\ -14.7 \\ \hline 2,005.3 \text{ p.s.i.g.} \end{array}$$

Free balloon flights into the stratosphere, the expanding gases of jet-propelled aircraft, and the effects of clouds and weather on instrument recordings may be explained by the use of Charles' law. Here are practical applications of a law of physics that aid the pilot, air controller, and aerographer in their work. Flying is made safer when humans are able to apply this law in handling weather data so vital to aviation.

General Gas Law

The facts concerning gases discussed in the preceding sections are summed up and illustrated in figure 7–8. Boyle's law is expressed in (A) of the figure, and the effects of temperature changes on pressure and volume (Charles' law) are illustrated in (B) and (C), respectively.

By combining Boyle's and Charles' laws, a single expression can be derived which states all the information contained in both. This expression is called the general gas law, a very useful form of which is given in the following equation. (NOTE: The capital P and T signify absolute pressure and temperature, respectively.)

$$\frac{P_1 V_1}{T_1} = \frac{P_2 V_2}{T_2}$$

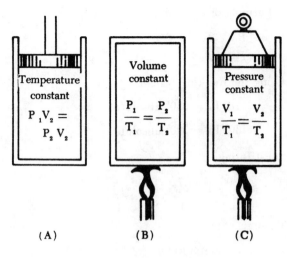

FIGURE 7-8. The general gas law.

An examination of figure 7-8 reveals that the three equations are special cases of the general equation. Thus, if the temperature remains constant, T_1 equals T_2, and both can be eliminated from the general formula, which then reduces to the form shown in (A). When the volume remains constant, V_1 equals V_2, reducing the general equation to the form given in (B). Similarly P_1 is equated to P_2 for constant pressure, and the equation then takes the form given in (C).

The general gas law applies with exactness only to "ideal" gases in which the molecules are assumed to be perfectly elastic. However, it describes the behavior of actual gases with sufficient accuracy for most practical purposes.

Two examples of the general equation follow:

1. Two cu. ft. of a gas at 75 p.s.i.g. and 80° F. are compressed to a volume of 1 cu. ft. and then heated to a temperature of 300° F. What is the new gage pressure?

Formula or equation:

$$\frac{P_1 V_1}{T_1} = \frac{P_2 V_2}{T_2}$$

Using the Rankine system:

$$80° \text{ F.} = 540° \text{ absolute}$$

$$300° \text{ F.} = 760° \text{ absolute}$$

Substituting:

$$\frac{(75 + 14.7)(2)}{540} = \frac{P_2(1)}{760}$$

Then:

$$\frac{179.4}{540} = \frac{P_2}{760}$$

$$P_2 = \frac{(179.4)(760)}{540}$$

$$P_2 = 252.5 \text{ p.s.i.a.}$$

Converting absolute pressure to gage pressure:

$$\begin{array}{r} 252.5 \\ -14.7 \\ \hline 237.8 \text{ p.s.i.g.} \end{array}$$

2. Four cubic feet of a gas at 75 p.s.i.g. and 80° F. are compressed to 237.8 p.s.i.g. and heated to a temperature of 300° F. What is the volume of the gas resulting from these changes?

Formula or equation:

$$\frac{P_1 V_1}{T_1} = \frac{P_2 V_2}{T_2}$$

Using the Rankine system:

$$80° \text{ F.} = 540° \text{ absolute}$$

$$300° \text{ F.} = 760° \text{ absolute}$$

Substituting:

$$\frac{(75 + 14.7)(4)}{540} = \frac{(237.8 + 14.7) V_2}{760}$$

Then:

$$\frac{(89.7)(4)}{540} = \frac{(252.5) V_2}{760}$$

$$V_2 = \frac{358.8 \times 760}{540 \times 252.5}$$

$$V_2 = 2 \text{ cu. ft.}$$

Avogadro's Law

An Italian physicist, Avogadro, conceived the theory that "at the same temperature and pressure, equal volumes of different gases contain equal numbers of molecules." This theory was proven by experiment and found to agree with the kinetic theory, so it has come to be known as Avogadro's law.

Dalton's Law

If a mixture of two or more gases which do not combine chemically is placed in a container, each

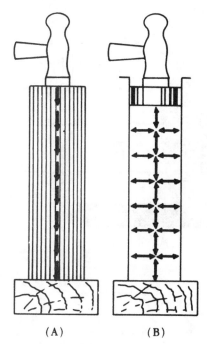

FIGURE 7-9. Transmission of force:
(A) solid; (B) fluid.

gas expands throughout the total space and the absolute pressure of each gas is reduced to a lower value, called its partial pressure. This reduction is in accordance with Boyle's law. The pressure of the mixed gases is equal to the sum of the partial pressures. This fact was discovered by Dalton, an English physicist, and is set forth in Dalton's law: "A mixture of several gases which do not react chemically exerts a pressure equal to the sum of the pressures which the several gases would exert separately if each were allowed to occupy the entire space alone at the given temperature."

Transmission of Forces Through Fluids

When the end of a bar is struck, the main force of the blow is carried straight through the bar to the other end (see A of figure 7–9). This happens because the bar is rigid. The direction of the blow almost entirely determines the direction of the transmitted force. The more rigid the bar, the less force is lost inside the bar or transmitted outward at right angles to the direction of the blow.

When a force is applied to the end of a column of confined liquid (B of figure 7–9), it is transmitted straight through to the other end and also

equally and undiminished in every direction throughout the column—forward, backward, and sideways—so that the containing vessel is literally filled with pressure.

If a gas is used instead of a liquid, the force is transmitted in the same manner. The one difference is that gas, being compressible, provides a much less rigid force than the liquid, which is incompressible. (This is the main difference in the action of liquids and gases in fluid power systems.)

Pascal's Law

The foundations of modern hydraulics and pneumatics were established in 1653 when Pascal discovered that pressure set up in a fluid acts equally in all directions. This pressure acts at right angles to containing surfaces. Thus, in figure 7–10, if the liquid standing on a square inch (A) at the bottom of the tank weighs 8 pounds, a pressure of 8 p.s.i. is exerted in every direction at (A). The liquid resting on (A) pushes equally downward and outward. The liquid on every square inch of the bottom surface is pushing downward and outward in the same way, so that the pressures on different areas are in balance. At the edge of the tank bottom, the pressures act against the wall of the tank, which must be strong enough to resist them with a force exactly equal to the push. Every square inch of the bottom of the tank must also be strong enough to resist the downward pressure of the liquid resting on it. The same balance of pressures exists at every other level in the tank, though of lesser pressures as one approaches the surface. There-

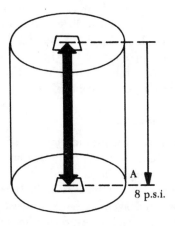

FIGURE 7–10.   Pressure acting on a container.

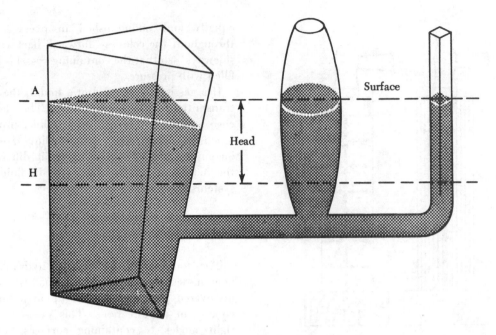

FIGURE 7–11. Pressure relationship with shape.

fore, the liquid remains at rest; it does not leak out and the tank does not collapse.

One of the consequences of Pascal's law is that the shape of the container in no way alters pressure relations. Thus, in figure 7–11, if the pressure due to the weight of the liquid at one point on the horizontal line (H) is 8 p.s.i., the pressure is 8 p.s.i. everywhere at level (H) in the system.

Pressure due to the weight of a fluid depends, at any level, on the height of the fluid from the level to the surface of the fluid. The vertical distance between two horizontal levels in a fluid is known as the head of the fluid. In figure 7–11, the liquid head of all points on level (H) with respect to the surface is indicated.

Pressure due to fluid head also depends on the density of the fluid. Water, for example, weighs 62.4 lbs./cu. ft. or 0.036 lb./cu. in., but a certain oil might weigh 55 lbs./cu. ft., or 0.032 lb./cu. in. To produce a pressure of 8 p.s.i., it would take 222 inches of head using water, and 252 inches of head using the oil (see figure 7–12).

Force and Pressure

In order to understand how Pascal's law is applied to fluid power, a distinction must be made between the terms "force" and "pressure." Force may be defined as a push or pull. It is the push or pull exerted against the total area of a particular surface and is expressed in pounds. As previously stated, pressure is the amount of force on a unit area of the surface acted upon. In hydraulics and pneumatics, pressure is expressed in pounds per square inch. Thus, pressure is the amount of force acting upon 1 square inch of area.

Computing Force, Pressure, and Area

A formula, similar to those used with the gas laws, is used in computing force, pressure, and area in fluid power systems. Although there appears to be three formulas, it is only one formula written in three variations, where P refers to pressure, F indicates force, and A represents area.

Force equals pressure times area. Thus, the

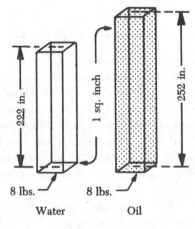

FIGURE 7–12. Pressure and density relationship.

232

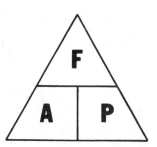

FIGURE 7–13. Device for determining the arrangement of the force, pressure, and area formulas.

formula is written:

$$F = P \times A.$$

Pressure equals force divided by the area. By rearranging the formula, this statement is condensed into:

$$P = \frac{F}{A}.$$

Since area equals force divided by pressure, the formula is written:

$$A = \frac{F}{P}.$$

Figure 7–13 illustrates a device for recalling these formulas. Any letter in the triangle may be expressed as the product or quotient of the other two, depending upon its position within the triangle.

For example, to find area, consider the letter "A" as being set off by itself, followed by an equal sign. Now look at the other two letters. The letter "F" is above the letter "P"; therefore, $A = F/P$.

In order to find pressure, consider the letter "P" as being set off by itself, and look at the other two letters. The letter "F" is above the letter "A"; therefore, $P = F/A$.

In a similar manner, to find force, consider the letter "F" as being set off by itself. The letters "P" and "A" are side by side; therefore, $F = P \times A$.

Sometimes the area may not be expressed in square inches. If it is a rectangular surface, the area may be found by multiplying the length (in inches) by the width (in inches). The majority of areas to be considered in these calculations are

circular. Either the diameter or the radius (one half the diameter) may be given. The radius in inches must be known to find the area. Then, the formula for finding the area of a circle is used. This is written $A = \pi r^2$, where A is the area, π is 3.1416 (3.14 or $3\frac{1}{7}$ for most calculations), and r^2 indicates radius squared.

Pressure and Force in Fluid Power Systems

In accordance with Pascal's law, any force applied to a confined fluid is transmitted equally in all directions throughout the fluid regardless of the shape of the container. Consider the effect of this in the system shown in figure 7–14, which is a modification of B in figure 7–9. The column of fluid is curved upward to its original level, with a second piston at this point. It is clear that when the input piston (1) is pushed downward, a pressure is created through the fluid, which acts equally at right angles to surfaces in all parts of the container.

Referring to figure 7–14, if the force (1) is 100 lbs. and the area of the piston is 10 sq. in., then the pressure in the fluid is 10 p.s.i. ($^{100}\!/_{10}$). This pressure acts on piston (2), so that for each square inch of its area it is pushed upward with a force of 10 pounds. In this case, a fluid column of uniform cross section is considered so that the area of the output piston (2) is the same as the input piston (1), or 10 square inches. Therefore, the upward force on the output piston (2) is 100 pounds, the same as applied to the input piston (1). All that has been accomplished in this system was to transmit the 100-pound force around a

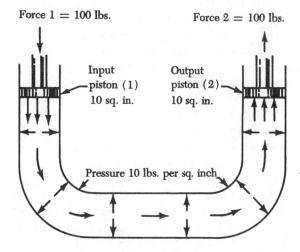

FIGURE 7–14. Force transmitted through fluid.

233

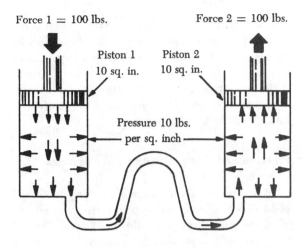

Force 1 = 100 lbs.　　　Force 2 = 100 lbs.

Piston 1
10 sq. in.

Piston 2
10 sq. in.

Pressure 10 lbs.
per sq. inch

FIGURE 7–15.　Transmitting force through small
tube.

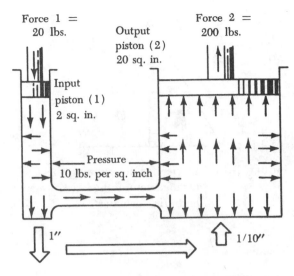

Force 1 =
20 lbs.

Output
piston (2)
20 sq. in.

Force 2 =
200 lbs.

Input
piston (1)
2 sq. in.

Pressure
10 lbs. per sq. inch

1″　　　　　　　　　　　1/10″

FIGURE 7–16.　Multiplication of forces.

bend. However, this principle underlies practically all mechanical applications of fluid power.

At this point it should be noted that since Pascal's law is independent of the shape of the container, it is not necessary that the tube connecting the two pistons be the full area of the pistons. A connection of any size, shape, or length will do if an unobstructed passage is provided. Therefore, the system shown in figure 7–15, in which a relatively small, bent tube connects two cylinders, will act exactly the same as that shown in figure 7–14.

Multiplication of Forces

In figures 7–14 and 7–15 the systems contain pistons of equal area in which the output force is equal to the input force. Consider the situation in figure 7–16, where the input piston is much smaller than the output piston. Assume that the area of the input piston (1) is 2 sq. in. Pushing down on the input piston (1) with a force of 20 pounds creates 10 p.s.i. ($20/2$) in the fluid. Although this force is much smaller than the applied force in figures 7–14 and 7–15, the pressure is the same. This is because the force is concentrated on a relatively small area.

This pressure of 10 p.s.i. acts on all parts of the fluid container, including the bottom of the output piston (2). The upward force on the output piston (2) is therefore 10 pounds for each of its 20 square inches of area, or 200 pounds (10×20). In this case, the original force has been multiplied tenfold while using the same pressure in the fluid as before. Obviously, the system would work just the same for any other forces and pressures, so

that the ratio of output force to input force is always the same.

The system works the same in reverse. Consider piston (2) in figure 7–16 as the input and piston (1) as the output. Then the output force will always be one-tenth the input force. Sometimes such results are desired.

Therefore, if two pistons are used in a fluid power system, the force acting on each is directly proportional to its area, and the magnitude of each force is the product of the pressure and its area.

Differential Areas

Consider the special situation shown in figure 7–17. Here, a single piston in a cylinder has a piston rod attached to one side of the piston which extends out of the cylinder at one end. Fluid under pressure is admitted to both ends of the cylinder equally through tubes. The opposed faces of the piston behave like two pistons acting against each other. The area of one face is the full area of the cylinder, for example, 6 sq. in. The area of the other face is the area of the cylinder minus the area of the piston rod, which is 2 sq. in., leaving an effective area of 4 sq. in. on the right face of the piston. The pressure on both faces is the same, in this case, 20 p.s.i. Applying the rule just stated, the force pushing the piston to the right is its area times the pressure, or 120 pounds (20×6). Similarly, the force pushing it to the left is its area times the pressure, or 80 pounds. Therefore, there is a net

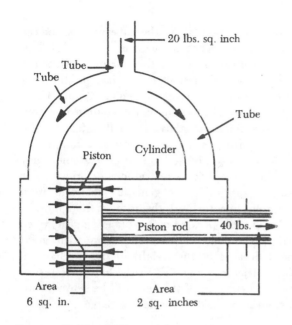

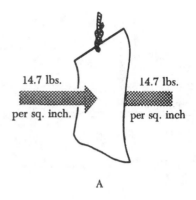

A

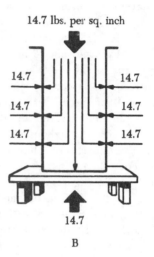

B

FIGURE 7-17. Differential areas on a piston.

unbalanced force of 40 pounds acting to the right, and the piston will move in that direction. The net effect is the same as if the piston and cylinder were just the size of the piston rod, since all other forces are in balance.

Volume and Distance Factors

In the systems illustrated in figures 7–14 and 7–15, the pistons have areas of 10 sq. in. each. Therefore, if one of these pistons is pushed down 1 inch, 10 cu. in. of fluid is displaced. Since liquid is practically incompressible, this volume must go somewhere. In the case of a gas, it will compress momentarily, but will eventually expand to its original volume. Thus, this volume moves the other piston. Since the area of this piston is also 10 sq. in., it will move 1 inch in order to accommodate the 10 cu. in. of fluid. The pistons are of equal areas, and will therefore move equal distances, though in opposite directions.

Applying this reasoning to the system in figure 7–16, it is obvious that if the input piston (1) is pushed down 1 inch, only 2 cu. in. of fluid is displaced. In order to accommodate these 2 cu. in. of fluid, the output piston (2) will have to move only one-tenth of an inch, because its area is 10 times that of the input piston (1). This leads to the second basic rule for two pistons in the same fluid power system, which is, that the distances moved are inversely proportional to their areas.

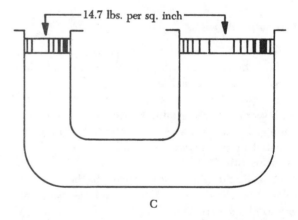

C

FIGURE 7-18. Effects of atmospheric pressure.

Effects of Atmospheric Pressure

Atmospheric pressure, described previously, obeys Pascal's law the same as pressure set up in fluids. As illustrated in figure 7–14, pressures due to a liquid head are distributed equally in all directions. This is also true of atmospheric pres-

235

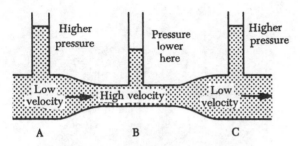

FIGURE 7–19. Pressures and velocities in a venturi tube.

sures. The situation is the same if these pressures act on opposite sides of any surface, or through fluids. In A of figure 7–18 the suspended sheet of paper is not torn by atmospheric pressure, as it would be by an unbalanced force, because atmospheric pressure acts equally on both sides of the paper. In B of figure 7–18, atmospheric pressure acting on the surface of the liquid is transmitted equally throughout the liquid to the walls of the container, but is balanced by the same pressure acting directly on the outer walls of the container. In C of figure 7–18, atmospheric pressure acting on the surface of one piston is balanced by the same pressure acting on the surface of the other. The different areas of the two surfaces make no difference, since for a unit of area, the pressures are in balance.

Bernoulli's Principle

Bernoulli's principle was originally stated to explain the action of a liquid flowing through the varying cross-sectional areas of tubes.

In figure 7–19 a tube is shown in which the cross-sectional area gradually decreases to a minimum diameter in its center section. A tube constructed in this manner is called a "venturi," or "venturi tube."

As a liquid (fluid) flows through the venturi tube, the three vertical tubes act as pressure gages, filling with liquid until the pressure of the liquid in each tube equals the pressure of the moving liquid in the venturi.

The venturi in figure 7–19 can be used to illustrate Bernoulli's principle, which states that: The pressure of a fluid (liquid or gas) decreases at points where the velocity of the fluid increases.

In the wide section of the venturi (points A and C of figure 7–19), the liquid moves at low velocity, producing a high pressure, as indicated by the height of the liquid in the vertical tubes

at these two points. As the tube narrows in the center, it must contain the same volume of fluid as the two end areas. In this narrow section, the liquid moves at a higher velocity, producing a lower pressure than that at points A and C, as indicated by the height of the column of liquid in the vertical tube above point B of figure 7–19.

The venturi principle, in any of a number of shapes and sizes, is used in aircraft systems. They may be referred to as restrictions or orifices. For example, an orifice is generally installed in a hydraulic line to limit the rate of fluid flow. A hydraulically operated aircraft landing gear, when being extended, will tend to drop with great speed because of the weight of the mechanism. If a restrictor is installed in the hydraulic return line the extension of the gear will be slowed, thus preventing possible structural damage.

ATMOSPHERE

General

Aviation is so dependent upon that category of fluids called gases and the effect of forces and pressures acting upon gases, that a discussion of the subject of the atmosphere is important to the persons maintaining and repairing aircraft.

Data available about the atmosphere may determine whether a flight will succeed, or whether it will even become airborne. The various components of the air around the earth, the changes in temperatures and pressures at different levels above the earth, the properties of weather encountered by aircraft in flight, and many other detailed data are considered in the preparation of flight plans.

Pascan and Torricelli have been credited with developing the barometer, and instrument for measuring atmospheric pressure. The results of their experiments are still used today with very little improvement in design or knowledge. They determined that air has weight which changes as altitude is changed with respect to sea level. Today scientists are also interested in how the atmosphere affects the performance of the aircraft and its equipment.

Composition of the Atmosphere

The atmosphere is a complex and ever changing mixture. Its ingredients vary from place to place and from day to day. In addition to a number of gases, it contains quantities of foreign matter such as pollen, dust, bacteria, soot, volcanic ash, spores, and dust from outer space.

The composition of the air remains almost constant from sea level up to its highest level, but its density diminishes rapidly with altitude. Six miles up, for example, it is too thin to support respiration, and 12 miles up there is not enough oxygen to support combustion. At a point several hundred miles above the earth, some gas particles spray out into space; some dragged by gravity fall back into the ocean of air below; others never return, but travel like satellites around the earth; and still others like hydrogen and helium escape forever from the earth's gravitational field. Physicists disagree as to the boundaries of the outer fringes of the atmosphere. Some think it begins 240 miles above the earth and extends to 400 miles; others place its lower edge at 600 miles and its upper boundary at 6,000 miles.

There are also certain nonconformities at various levels. Between 12 and 30 miles, high solar ultraviolet radiation reacts with oxygen molecules to produce a thin curtain of ozone, a very poisonous gas without which life on earth could not exist. This ozone filters out a portion of the sun's lethal ultraviolet rays, allowing only enough to come through to give man sunburn, kill bacteria, and prevent rickets. At 50 or 65 miles up, most of the oxygen molecules begin to break down under solar radiation into free atoms, and to form the incomplete molecule, hydroxyl (OH) from water vapor. Also in this region all the atoms become ionized.

Studies of the atmosphere have revealed that the temperature does not decrease uniformly with increasing altitude; instead it gets steadily colder up to a height of about 7 miles, where the rate of temperature change slows down abruptly and remains almost constant at $-55°$ C. (218° K.) up to about 20 miles. Then the temperature begins to rise to a peak value of 77° C. (350° K.) at the 55-mile level. Thereafter it climbs steadily, reaching 2,270° C. (2,543° K.) at a height of 250 to 400 miles. From the 50-mile level upward, a man or any other living creature, without the protective cover of the atmosphere, would be broiled on the sunny side and frozen on the other.

The atmosphere is divided into concentric layers or levels. Transition through these layers is gradual and without sharply defined boundaries. However, one boundary, the tropopause, exists between the first and second layer. The tropopause is defined as the point in the atmosphere at which the decrease in temperature (with increasing altitude) abruptly ceases, between the troposphere and the stratosphere. The four atmosphere layers are the troposphere, stratosphere, ionosphere, and the exosphere. The upper portion of the stratosphere is often called the chemosphere or ozonosphere, and the exosphere is also known as the mesosphere.

The troposphere extends from the earth's surface to about 35,000 feet at middle latitudes; but varies from 28,000 feet at the poles to about 54,000 feet at the equator. The troposphere is characterized by large changes in temperature and humidity and by generally turbulent conditions. Nearly all cloud formations are within the troposphere. Approximately three-fourths of the total weight of the atmosphere is within the troposphere. The temperature and absolute pressure in the troposphere steadily decrease with increasing altitude to a point where the temperature is approximately $-55°$ C. (or 218° K.), and the pressure is about 6.9 Hg on a standard day.

The stratosphere extends from the upper limits of the troposphere (and the tropopause) to an average altitude of 60 miles. In the stratosphere the temperature decline virtually stops; however, at 18 or 20 miles up, it often descends to $-63°$ C. (210° K.).

The ionosphere ranges from the 50-mile level to a level of 300 to 600 miles. Little is known about the characteristics of the ionosphere, but it is thought that many electrical phenomena occur there. Basically, this layer is characterized by the presence of ions and free electrons, and the ionization seems to increase with altitude and in successive layers. The temperature increases from about 200° K. at the lower limit to about 2,500° K. at the upper limit. These extremely high temperatures in the upper altitudes do not have the same significance as would corresponding temperatures at sea level. A thermometer reading in this region would be determined more by solar radiation than by the temperature, because of the energy of the particles.

The exosphere (or mesosphere) is the outer layer of the atmosphere. It begins at an altitude of 600 miles and extends to the limits of the atmosphere. In this layer the temperature is fairly constant at 2,500° K., and propagation of sound is thought to be impossible due to lack of molecular substance.

Atmospheric Pressure

The human body is under pressure, since it exists at the bottom of a sea of air. This pressure is due to the weight of the atmosphere. The pressure which the atmosphere applies to a square inch of area is equal to the weight of a column of air one square inch in cross section which extends from that area to the "top" of the atmosphere.

Since atmospheric pressure at any altitude is due to the weight of air above it, pressure decreases with increased altitude, Obviously, the total weight of air above an area at 15,000 feet would be less than the total weight of the air above an area at 10,000 feet.

Atmospheric pressure is often measured by a mercury barometer. A glass tube somewhat over 30 inches in length is sealed at one end and filled with mercury (Hg). It is then inverted and the open end placed in a dish of mercury. Immediately, the mercury level in the inverted tube will drop a short distance, leaving a small volume of mercury vapor at nearly zero absolute pressure in the tube just above the top of the liquid mercury column. The pressure acting upward at the lower end of the tube above the level of mercury in the dish is atmospheric pressure. The pressure acting downward at the same point is the weight of the column of mercury. Thus, the height of the column of mercury indicates the pressure exerted by the atmosphere.

This means of measuring atmospheric pressure gives rise to the practice of expressing atmospheric pressure in inches of mercury (in. Hg) rather than in pounds per square inch (p.s.i.). It may be seen, however, that a simple relationship exists between pressure measurements in p.s.i. and in inches Hg. One cu. in. of mercury weighs 0.491 pound. Therefore, a pressure of 30 inches of mercury would be the equivalent of:

$$0.491 \times 30 = 14.73 \text{ p.s.i.}$$

A second means of measuring atmospheric pressure is with an aneroid barometer. This mechanical instrument lends itself to use on airplanes much more adequately than does the mercury barometer. Aneroid barometers (altimeters) are used to indicate altitude in flight. The calibrations are made in thousands of feet rather than in p.s.i. For example, the standard pressure at sea level is 29.92 in. Hg, or 14.69 p.s.i. At 10,000 feet above sea level, standard pressure is 20.58 in. Hg, or 10.10 p.s.i. Altimeters are calibrated so that if the pressure exerted by the atmosphere were 20.58 in. Hg, the altimeter would point to 10,000 feet. In other words, the altimeter is calibrated so that it indicates the altitude at which the prevailing atmospheric pressure would be considered standard pressure. Thus, the altitude read from the altimeter, being dependent upon atmospheric pressure, is called pressure altitude (H_p). Actually, an altimeter will read pressure altitude only when the altimeter adjustment is set at 29.92 inches Hg.

A third expression is occasionally used to indicate atmospheric pressure. Atmospheric pressure may be expressed in atmospheres. For example, a test may be conducted in a pressurized chamber under a pressure of six atmospheres. This merely means that the pressure is six times as great as standard sea level pressure.

Atmospheric Density

Since both temperature and pressure decrease with altitude, it might appear that the density of the atmosphere would remain fairly constant with increased altitude. This is not true, however, for pressure drops more rapidly with increased altitude than does the temperature. The result is that density decreases with increased altitude.

By use of the general gas law, studied earlier, it can be shown that for a particular gas, pressure and temperature determine the density. Since standard pressures and temperatures have been associated with each altitude, the density of the air at these standard temperatures and pressures must also be considered standard. Thus, a particular atmospheric density is associated with each altitude. This gives rise to the expression "density altitude," symbolized H_d. A density altitude of 15,000 feet is the altitude at which the density is the same as that considered standard for 15,000 feet. Remember, however, that density altitude is not necessarily true altitude. For example, on a day when the atmospheric pressure is higher than standard and the temperature is lower than standard, the density which is standard at 10,000 feet might occur at 12,000 feet. In this case, at an actual altitude of 12,000 feet, we have air which has the same density as standard air at 10,000 feet. Density altitude is a calculated altitude obtained by correcting pressure altitude for temperature.

The water content of the air has a slight effect on the density of the air. It should be remembered that humid air at a given temperature and pressure is lighter than dry air at the same temperature and pressure.

Water Content of the Atmosphere

In the troposphere the air is seldom completely dry. It contains water vapor in either of two forms: (1) Fog or (2) water vapor. Fog consists of minute droplets of water held in suspension by the air. Clouds are composed of fog. The height to which some clouds extend is a good indication of the presence of water in the atmosphere almost up to the stratosphere.

As a result of evaporation, the atmosphere always contains some moisture in the form of water vapor. The moisture in the air is called the humidity of the air. Moisture does not consist of tiny particles of liquid held in suspension in the air as in the case of fog, but is an invisible vapor truly as gaseous as the air with which it mixes.

Fog and humidity both affect the performance of an aircraft. In flight, at cruising power, the effects are small and receive no consideration. During takeoff, however, humidity has important effects. Two things are done to compensate for the effects of humidity on takeoff performance. Since humid air is less dense than dry air, the allowable takeoff gross weight of an aircraft is generally reduced for operation in areas that are consistently humid. Secondly, because the power output of reciprocating engines is decreased by humidity, the manifold pressure may have to be increased above that recommended for takeoff in dry air in order to obtain the same power output.

Engine power output is calculated on dry air. Since water vapor is incombustible, its pressure in the atmosphere is a total loss as far as contributing to power output. The mixture of water vapor and air is drawn through the carburetor and fuel is metered into it as though it were all air. This mixture of water vapor, air, and fuel enters the combustion chamber where it is ignited. Since the water vapor will not burn, the effective fuel/air ratio is enriched and the engine operates as though it were on an excessively rich mixture. The resulting horsepower loss under humid conditions can therefore be attributed to the loss in volumetric efficiency due to displaced air, and the incomplete combustion due to excessively rich fuel/air mixture.

The reduction in power that can be expected from humidity is usually given in charts in the flight manual. There are several types of charts in use. Some merely show the expected reduction in power due to humidity; others show the boost in manifold pressure necessary to restore full takeoff power.

The effect of fog on the performance of an engine is very noticeable, particularly on engines with high compression ratios. Normally, some detonation will occur during acceleration, due to the high BMEP (Brake Mean Effective Pressures) developed. However, on a foggy day it is difficult to cause detonation to occur. The explanation of this lies in the fact that fog consists of unvaporized particles of water. When these particles enter the cylinders, they absorb a tremendous amount of heat energy in the process of vaporizing. The temperature is thus lowered, and the decrease is sufficient to prevent detonation.

Fog will generally cause a decrease in horsepower output. However with a supercharged engine, it will be possible to use higher manifold pressures without danger of detonation.

Absolute Humidity

Absolute humidity is the actual amount of the water vapor in a mixture of air and water. It is sometimes expressed in g./cu.m. (grams per cubic meter), sometimes in lbs./cu. ft. The amount of water vapor that can be present in the air is dependent upon the temperature and pressure. The higher the temperatures, the more water vapor the air is capable of holding, assuming constant pressure. When air has all the water vapor it can hold at the prevailing temperature and pressure, it is said to be saturated.

Relative Humidity

Relative humidity is the ratio of the amount of water vapor actually present in the atmosphere to the amount that would be present if the air were saturated at the prevailing temperature and pressure. This ratio is usually multiplied by 100 and expressed as a percentage. Suppose, for example, that a weather report includes the information that the temperature is 75° F. and the relative humidity is 56 percent. This indicates that the air holds 56 percent of the water vapor required to saturate it at 75° F. If the temperature drops and the absolute humidity remains constant, the relative humidity will increase. This is because less water vapor is required to saturate the air at the lower temperature.

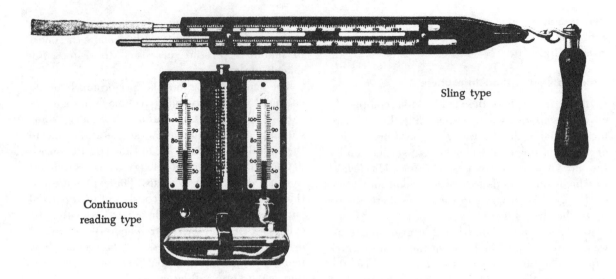

Sling type

Continuous
reading type

FIGURE 7-20. Wet-bulb hygrometers.

Dew Point

The dew point is the temperature to which humid air must be cooled at constant pressure to become saturated. If the temperature drops below the dew point, condensation occurs. People who wear glasses have had the experience of going from cold outside air into a warm room and having moisture collect quickly on their glasses. This happened because the glasses were below the dew point temperature of the air in the room. The air immediately in contact with the glasses was cooled below its dew point temperature, and some of the water vapor was condensed out. This principle is applied in determining the dew point. A vessel is cooled until water vapor begins to condense on its surface. The temperature at which this occurs is the dew point.

Vapor Pressure

Vapor pressure is the portion of atmospheric pressure that is exerted by the moisture in the air (expressed in tenths of an inch Hg). The dew point for a given condition depends on the amount of water pressure present; thus a direct relationship exists between the vapor pressure and the dew point.

Wet- and Dry-Bulb Temperatures

Vapor pressure and humidity may be determined from charts based on the wet- and dry-bulb temperatures (figure 7-20). The dry-bulb temperature is obtained from an ordinary thermometer.

The wet-bulb temperature is obtained from a thermometer which has its bulb covered with a thin piece of wet cloth.

Because of moisture evaporation from the wet cloth, the wet bulb will read lower than the dry bulb. The more rapid the evaporation, the greater will be the difference in readings. The rate of evaporation is dependent upon the degree of saturation of the air. In using the wet-bulb thermometer, it must be moved through the air at a rate of about 1,200 f.p.m. to give a worthwhile reading. This is accomplished by mounting both the wet- and dry-bulb thermometers on a frame which can be hand rotated around a pivot and the desirable rate of 1,200 f.p.m. attained.

If the air is saturated, no evaporation will take place and the wet- and dry-bulb temperatures will be the same. Thus, these two temperatures coincide at the dew point.

Physical Laws Related to the Atmosphere

Although air is composed of various gases and must be treated as a mixture for certain purposes, it is treated as a uniform gas in aerodynamic calculations. Air is a fluid since it has the fluid property to flow, and it is also a gas, since its density is readily varied.

As is usual in engineering work, certain simplifying assumptions are made. One standard assumption is that in dry air there is no water vapor present. Ordinary flight-takeoff charts may be corrected for vapor pressure, but subsonic flight does not consider vapor pressure as an appreciable factor. Another standard assumption is that friction or "viscosity effect" may be neglected when dealing with airflow. The air is then considered to be a perfect fluid. However, some exceptions must be made, particularly in the case of thin boundary layers of slow moving air directly adjacent to a moving body.

The Kinetic Theory of Gases Applied to Air

The kinetic theory states that a gas is composed of small, distinct particles called molecules. The size of the molecules is small compared to the average distance between them. Further, the molecules are moving about at a high rate of speed in random directions so that they are constantly colliding with one another and with the walls of any container that may surround them. The pressure produced by a gas is the result of these continuous impacts against a surface, and since the impacts are essentially infinite in number, a steady pressure is effected.

Just as pressure is produced by molecular impact against a surface, it is also transmitted by molecular impact. Assuming that molecules are perfectly elastic (that no friction exists between them), a pressure wave once started will continue indefinitely. For most purposes this assumption is adequate; however, it is not completely correct. For instance, sound represents a series of weak pressure waves to which the ear is sensitive. If the energy that the sound represents were not lost, the sound would continue indefinitely. It follows then that this imperfect elasticity must in some way be associated with fluid friction or viscosity, since the presence of viscosity is also a source of energy loss.

On the basis of the kinetic theory, pressure may be increased in two ways: First, by increasing the number of molecules in a given space, which is the same as increasing the density; and secondly, by increasing the speed of the molecules, which can be done by increasing the temperature, since the temperature increase produces an increase in the molecular speed.

Analysis of the kinetic theory leads to one definite relationship between the temperature, pressure, and density of a gas when the gas is subjected to a given set of conditions. This relationship is known as the equation of state.

Equation of State

Provided that the temperature and pressure of a gas are not excessively different from those normally experienced on the earth's surface, the following equation holds true:

$$PV = RT$$

where: P = pressure in lbs./sq. ft.
V = specific volume.
R = a constant for a given gas (for air $R = 53.345$).
T = absolute temperature (Rankine = °F. + 459.4).

If the temperature and pressure are such that the gas becomes a liquid, or if the pressure falls to such a value that uniform pressure no longer exists, the equation will be invalid. In practical aeronautical work, these extremes are only encountered in a supersonic wind tunnel or in the outer portions of the atmosphere. This formula must be further clarified for practical engineering, by the introduction of air density.

Standard Atmosphere

If the performance of an aircraft is computed, either through flight tests or wind tunnel tests, some standard reference condition must be determined first in order to compare results with those of similar tests. The conditions in the atmosphere vary continuously, and it is generally not possible to obtain exactly the same set of conditions on two different days or even on two successive flights. Accordingly, there must be set up a group of standard conditions that may be used arbitrarily for reference. The set of standard conditions presently used in the United States is known as the U. S. Standard Atmosphere.

The standard atmosphere approximates the average conditions existing at 40° latitude, and is determined on the basis of the following assumptions. The standard sea level conditions are:

Pressure at 0 altitude (P_0) = 29.92 inches of mercury.
Temperature at 0 altitude (T_0) = 15° C. = 59° F.
Gravity at 0 altitude (g_0) = 32.174 ft./sec.^{2}

The U.S. Standard Atmosphere is in agreement with the International Civil Aviation Organization (ICAO) Standard Atmosphere over their common altitude range. The ICAO Standard Atmosphere has been adopted as standard by most of the principal nations of the world.

Variations from Standard Days

As may be expected, the temperature, pressure, density, and water vapor content of the air varies considerably in the troposphere. The temperature at 40° latitude may range from 50° C. at low altitudes during the summer to −70° C. at high altitudes during the winter. As previously stated, temperature usually decreases with an increase in altitude. Exceptions to this rule occur when cooler air is trapped near the earth by a warmer layer. This is called a temperature inversion, commonly associated with frontal movement of air masses.

Pressure likewise varies at any given point in the atmosphere. On a standard day, at sea level, pressure will be 29.92 in Hg. On nonstandard days, pressure at sea level will vary considerably above or below this figure.

Density of the air is determined by the pressure and temperature acting upon it. Since the atmosphere can never be assumed to be "standard," a convenient method of calculating density has been devised. Since air pressure is measured in inconvenient terms, it is expedient to utilize the aneroid altimeter as a pressure gage and refer to the term "pressure altitude" instead of atmospheric pressure.

Pressure Altitude

Pressure altitude is the altitude in the standard atmosphere corresponding to a particular value of air pressure. The aircraft altimeter is essentially a sensitive barometer calibrated to indicate altitude in the standard atmosphere.

With the altimeter of an aircraft set at 29.92 in. Hg, the dial will indicate the number of feet above or below a level where 29.92 in. Hg exists, not necessarily above or below sea level, unless standard day conditions exist. In general, the altimeter will indicate the altitude at which the existing pressure would be considered standard pressure. The symbol H_p is used to indicate pressure altitude.

BERNOULLI'S PRINCIPLE

General

In the earlier discussion of fluids, Bernoulli's principle was introduced to explain the relationship between velocity and pressure of a liquid flowing through a venturi. Since Bernoulli's principle applies to fluids, which by definition include both gases and liquids, its application to gases (air) is included at this point to explain the relationship between air velocity and pressure on the surfaces of an airfoil.

How an Aircraft Wing Reacts with the Atmosphere

An airfoil is any surface designed to obtain a reaction from the air through which it moves. Wings, ailerons, elevators, stabilizers, propeller blades, and helicopter rotors are all airfoils.

The reaction for which wings are designed is called lift. A wing produces lift because of a pressure difference; and the greater this difference, the more lift developed. If the air pressure above a wing is the same as that below it, there is no lift. But if the pressure above a wing is reduced and the pressure below increased, then lift is produced. The strong air pressure below the wing moves the wing upward against the weaker pressure above the wing. But what causes these unequal pressures?

An examination of the shape of an aircraft wing discloses that it has been designed to create a pressure difference. If a wing is cut from leading edge to trailing edge, the end view of the cut is a profile section similar to the one shown in figure 7–21. The forward part of the airfoil profile is rounded and is called the leading edge. The aft part is narrow and tapered and is called the trailing edge. A reference line often used in discussing airfoils is the chord, an imaginary straight line joining the extremities of the leading and trailing edges. The curved upper surface of the airfoil is called the camber. The lower surface is normally straight, or only slightly curved.

An airfoil is very similar in shape to half a venturi section. In A of figure 7–22, the throat, or restricted portion of a venturi is illustrated. The airflow through the venturi is indicated by flow lines. In B of figure 7–22, one-half of a

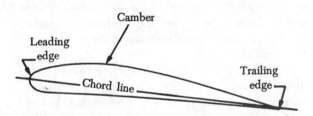

FIGURE 7–21.   Cross-sectional view of an airfoil.

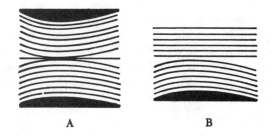

FIGURE 7-22. Airflow in venturi sections.

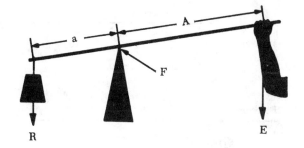

FIGURE 7-23. A simple lever.

venturi restriction is shown, together with the airflow over its curved surface. Note that this portion of a venturi has the same profile as that of an airfoil.

To understand how lift is produced by an aircraft's wings, Bernoulli's principle is applied to an airfoil. This principle reveals that the pressure of fluid (liquid or gas) decreases at points where the speed of the fluid increases. In other words, high speed is associated with low pressure, and low speed with high pressure. The wing, or airfoil, of an aircraft is designed to increase the velocity of the airflow above its surface, thereby decreasing pressure above the airfoil. Simultaneously, the impact of the air on the lower surface of the airfoil increases the pressure below. This combination of pressure decrease above the airfoil and increase below the airfoil produces lift.

MACHINES

General

Ordinarily, a machine is thought of as a complex device, such as an internal-combustion engine or a typewriter. These are machines, but so is a hammer, a screwdriver, or a wheel. A machine is any device with which work may be accomplished. Machines are used to transform energy, as in the case of a generator transforming mechanical energy into electrical energy. Machines are used to transfer energy from one place to another, as in the examples of the connecting rods, crankshaft, and reduction gears transferring energy from an aircraft's engine to its propeller.

Another use of machines is to multiply force; for example, a system of pulleys may be used to lift a heavy load. The pulley system enables the load to be raised by exerting a force which is smaller than the weight of the load.

Machines are also used to multiply speed. A good example is the bicycle, by which speed can be gained by exerting a greater force.

Finally, machines can be used to change the direction of a force. An example of this use is the flag hoist. A downward force on one side of the rope exerts an upward force on the other side, raising the flag toward the top of the pole.

There are only six simple machines. They are the lever, the pulley, the wheel and axle, the inclined plane, the screw, and the gear. However, physicists recognize only two basic principles in machines; namely, the lever and the inclined plane. The wheel and axle, the block and tackle, and gears may be considered levers. The wedge and the screw use the principle of the inclined plane.

An understanding of the principles of simple machines provides a necessary foundation for the study of compound machines, which are combinations of two or more simple machines.

The Lever

The simplest machine, and perhaps the most familiar one, is the lever. A seasaw is a familiar example of a lever in which one weight balances the other.

There are three basic parts in all levers; namely, the fulcrum "F," a force or effort "E," and a resistance "R." Shown in figure 7-23 are the pivotal point "F" (fulcrum); the effort "E," which is applied at a distance "A" from the fulcrum; and a resistance "R," which acts at a distance "a" from the fulcrum. Distances "A" and "a" are the lever arms.

Classes of Levers

The three classes of levers are illustrated in figure 7-24. The location of the fulcrum (the fixed or pivot point) with relation to the resistance (or weight) and the effort determines the lever class.

243

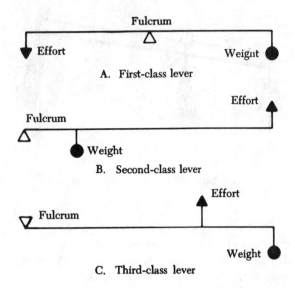

FIGURE 7–24. Three classes of levers.

First-Class Levers

In the first-class lever (A of figure 7–24), the fulcrum is located between the effort and the resistance. As mentioned earlier, the seesaw is a good example of the first-class lever. The amount of weight and the distance from the fulcrum can be varied to suit the need. Another good example is the oars of a rowboat. Notice that the fisherman in figure 7–25 applies his effort on the handles of the oars. The oarlock acts as the fulcrum, and the water acts as the resistance to be overcome. In this case, as in A of figure 7–24, the force is applied on one side of the fulcrum, and the resistance to be overcome is applied to the opposite side; hence, this is a first-class lever. Crowbars, shears, and pliers are common examples of this class of lever.

Second-Class Levers

The second-class lever (B of figure 7–24) has the fulcrum at one end; the effort is applied at the other end. The resistance is somewhere between these points. The wheelbarrow in figure 7–26 is a good example of a second-class lever.

Both first- and second-class levers are commonly used to help in overcoming big resistances with a relatively small effort.

Third-Class Levers

There are occasions when it is desirable to speed up the movement of the resistance even though a large amount of effort must be used. Levers that help accomplish this are third-class levers. As shown in C of figure 7–24, the fulcrum is at one end of the lever and the weight or resistance to be overcome is at the other end, with the effort applied at some point between. Third-class levers are easily recognized because the effort is applied between the fulcrum and the resistance. This is illustrated by the diagram in figure 7–27. While point "*E*" is moving the short

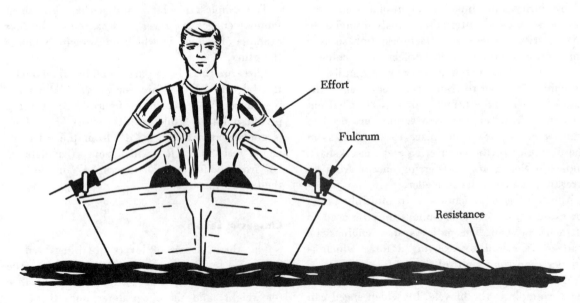

FIGURE 7–25. Oars are levers.

244

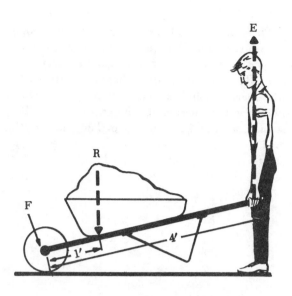

FIGURE 7–26. A second-class lever.

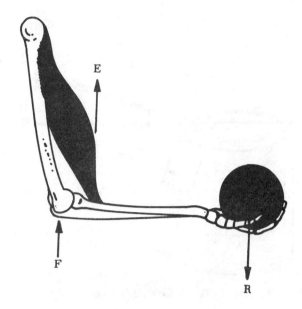

FIGURE 7–28. The arm is a third-class lever.

distance "*e*," the resistance "*R*" moves a greater distance "*r*." The speed of "*R*" must be greater than that of "*E*," since "*R*" covers a greater distance in the same length of time.

The human arm (figure 7–28) is a third-class lever. It is this lever action that makes possible the quick flexing of the arms. Note that the elbow is the fulcrum. The biceps muscle, which is tied onto the forearm below the elbow, applies the effort; and the hand, is the resistance. Third-class levers should be used to gain speed, rather than to move heavy loads.

The forces required to operate machines, as well as the forces they will exert, can be easily determined. Consider the iron bar used as a first-class lever in figure 7–29. The bar is 9 feet long and is used to raise a 300-pound weight. Assume that a maximum of 100 pounds is available to lift the weight. If a fulcrum "*F*" is placed 2 feet from the center of the weight, a 6-foot length of the bar becomes the effort arm. This 6-foot length

is three times as long as the distance from the fulcrum to the center of the weight. With a 100-pound effort at "*E*", the 300-pound weight can be lifted, since the length of the effort arm has multiplied the effort three times. This is an example of the direct relationship between lengths of lever arms and the forces acting on the arms.

This relationship can be stated in general terms: The length of the effort arm is the same number of times greater than the length of the resistance arm as the resistance to be overcome is greater than the effort that must be applied.

The mathematical equation for this relation-

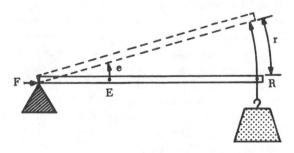

FIGURE 7–27. A third-class lever.

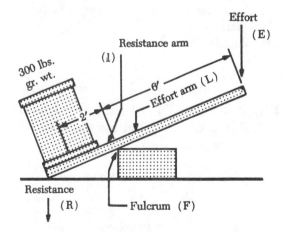

FIGURE 7–29. Computing the forces in a first-class lever.

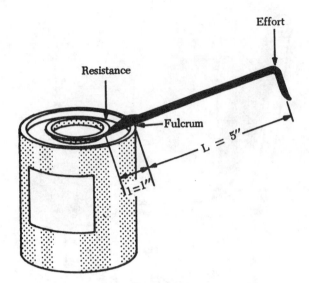

FIGURE 7–30. A first-class lever problem.

ship is:

$$\frac{L}{1} = \frac{R}{E}$$

where:
- L = length of effort arm.
- 1 = length of resistance arm.
- R = resistance weight or force.
- E = effort force.

Remember that all distances must be in the same units, and all forces must also be in the same units.

In figure 7–30 another first-class lever problem is illustrated: To pry up the lid of the paint can with a 6-inch bar when the average force holding the lid is assumed to be 50 pounds. If the distance from the edge of the can to the edge of the cover is 1 inch, what force must be applied to the end of the bar?

According to the formula:

$$\frac{L}{1} = \frac{R}{E}$$

Here, L = 5 inches; 1 = 1 inch; R = 50 pounds, and E is unknown. Substitute the numbers in their proper places; then

$$\frac{5}{1} = \frac{50}{E}$$

and $\quad E = \dfrac{50 \times 1}{5} = 10$ pounds.

A force of 10 pounds is required.

The same general formula applies for second-class levers; but it is important to measure the proper lengths of the effort arm and the resistance arm. Referring to figure 7–26, the length of the wheelbarrow handles from the axle of the wheel (which is the fulcrum) to the grip is 4 feet. This is an effort arm 4 feet in length. The center of the load of sand is 1 foot from the axle; thus, the length of the resistance arm is 1 foot.

By substituting in the formula,

$$\frac{L}{1} = \frac{R}{E}$$

$$\frac{4}{1} = \frac{200}{E}$$

$$E = 50 \text{ lb.}$$

A third-class lever problem is illustrated in figure 7–28. With one hand, a weight of 10 pounds is to be lifted. If the biceps muscle is attached to the forearm 1 inch below the elbow, and the distance from the elbow to the palm of the hand is 18 inches, what pull must the muscle exert in order to hold the weight and flex the arm at the elbow? By substituting in the formula,

$$\frac{L}{1} = \frac{R}{E} \text{ it becomes } \frac{1}{18} = \frac{10}{E}$$

and $\quad E = 18 \times 10 = 180$ lb.

The muscle must exert a 180-pound pull to hold up the 10-pound weight. This illustrates that the biceps muscle is poorly arranged for lifting or pulling. It also illustrates that third-class levers should be used primarily to speed up motion of a resistance.

Mechanical Advantage of Levers

Levers may provide mechanical advantages, since they can be applied in such manner that they can magnify an applied force. This is true of first- and second-class levers. The third-class lever provides what is called a fractional disadvantage, i.e., one in which a greater force is required than the force of the load lifted.

In the problem involving the wheelbarrow (figure 7–26), a 50-pound pull overcomes the 200-pound weight of the sand. In this case, the effort was magnified four times. Thus the mechanical advantage gained by using the wheelbarrow is 4.

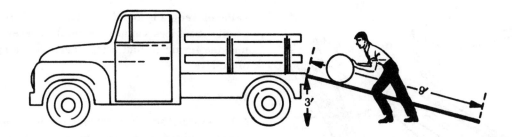

FIGURE 7–31. An inclined plane.

Expressing the same idea in mathematical terms,

$$\text{Mechanical Advantage} = \frac{\text{Resistance}}{\text{Effort}}$$

or

$$MA = \frac{R}{E}$$

Thus, in the case of the wheelbarrow,

$$MA = \frac{200}{50} = 4.$$

This rule applies to all machines.

Mechanical advantage of levers may also be found by dividing the length of the effort arm "A" by the length of the resistance arm "a." Stated as a formula, this reads:

$$\text{Mechanical Advantage} = \frac{\text{Effort Arm}}{\text{Resistance Arm}}$$

or $\quad MA = \dfrac{A}{a}$

How does this apply to third-class levers? If a muscle pulls with a force of 1,800 pounds in order to lift a 100-pound projectile, a mechanical advantage of $^{100}/_{1,800}$ or $\frac{1}{18}$ is obtained. This is a fractional disadvantage, since it is less than 1.

The Inclined Plane

The inclined plane is a simple machine that facilitates the raising or lowering of heavy objects by application of a small force over a relatively long distance. Some familiar examples of the inclined plane are mountain highways and cattle loading ramps.

The inclined plane permits a large resistance to be overcome by application of a small force through a longer distance than the load is to be raised. In figure 7–31, a 300-pound barrel is being rolled up a ramp to the bed of a truck, 3 feet above the sidewalk. The ramp is 9 feet long.

Without the ramp, a force of 300 pounds, applied straight up through the 3-foot distance, would be required to load the barrel. With the ramp, a force can be applied over the entire 9 feet of the ramp as the barrel is rolled slowly up to a height of 3 feet. It can be determined by observation that a force of only three-ninths of 300, or 100 pounds, will be required to raise the barrel by using an inclined plane. This can also be determined mathematically, using the formula,

$$\frac{L}{1} = \frac{R}{E}$$

where:

L = length of the ramp, measured along the slope.

1 = height of the ramp.

R = weight of object to be raised, or lowered.

E = force required to raise or lower object.

In this case, $L = 9$ ft.; $1 = 3$ ft.; and $R = 300$ lb. Substituting these values in the formula,

$$\frac{9}{3} = \frac{300}{E}$$

$$9E = 900$$

$$E = 100 \text{ pounds.}$$

Since the ramp is three times as long as its height, the mechanical advantage is three. The theoretical mechanical advantage is found by dividing the total distance through which the effort is exerted by the vertical distance through which the load is raised or lowered.

The Wedge

The wedge is a special application of the inclined plane. The blades of knives, axes, hatchets, and

247

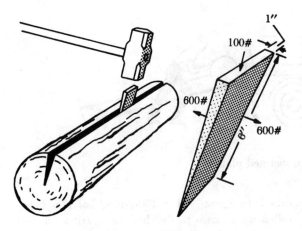

FIGURE 7–32.   A wedge.

chisels act as wedges when they are forced into a piece of wood. The wedge is two inclined planes, set base-to-base. By driving the wedge full-length into the material to be cut or split, the material is forced apart a distance equal to the width of the broad end of the wedge (see figure 7–32).

Long, slim wedges have high mechanical advantages. For example, the wedge in figure 7–32 has a mechanical advantage of 6. The greatest

value of wedges is found in situations where other simple machines cannot be used. For example, imagine trying to pull a log apart with a system of pulleys.

The Pulley

Pulleys are simple machines in the form of a wheel mounted on a fixed axis and supported by a frame. The wheel, or disk, is normally grooved to accommodate a rope. The wheel is sometimes referred to as a "sheave" (sometimes "sheaf"). The frame that supports the wheel is called a block. A block and tackle consists of a pair of blocks. Each block contains one or more pulleys and a rope connecting the pulley(s) of each block.

Single Fixed Pulley

A single fixed pulley is really a first-class lever with equal arms. The arms "EF" and "FR" in figure 7–33 are equal; hence the mechanical advantage is one. Thus, the force of the pull on the rope must be equal to the weight of the object being lifted. The only advantage of a single fixed pulley is to change the direction of the force, or pull on the rope.

A single pulley can be used to magnify the force exerted. In figure 7–34 the pulley is not

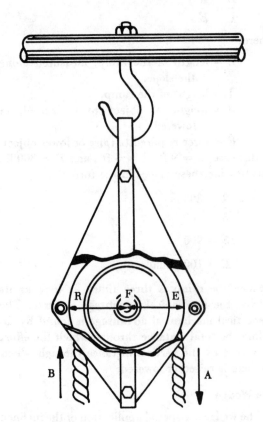

FIGURE 7–33.   A single fixed pulley.

FIGURE 7–34.   A single movable pulley.

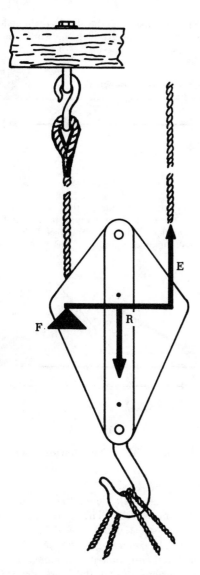

FIGURE 7–35. A single movable pulley as a second-class lever.

fixed, and the rope is doubled because it supports a 200-pound weight. Used in this manner, a single block and tackle can lift the 200-pound weight with a 100-pound pull, since each half of the rope (tackle) carries one-half the total load. The mechanical advantage is 2, which can be verified by using the formula:

$$MA = \frac{R}{E} = \frac{200}{100} = 2.$$

The single movable pulley used in the manner shown in figure 7-34 is a second-class lever. To see this refer to figure 7–35. The effort "E" acts upward on the arm "EF," which is the diameter of the pulley. The resistance "R" acts downward on the arm "FR," which is the radius of the pulley. Since the diameter is twice the radius, the mechanical advantage is 2.

However, when the effort at "E" moves up 2 feet, the load at "R" is raised only 1 foot. This is true of all systems of block and tackle, for if a mechanical advantage is obtained, the length of rope passed through the hands is greater than the distance that the load is raised.

The mechanical advantage of a pulley system is found by measuring the resistance and the effort and dividing the amount of resistance by the effort. A shorthand method often used is simply to count the number of rope strands that move or support the movable block.

WORK, POWER, AND ENERGY

Work

The study of machines, both simple and complex, is in one sense a study of the energy of mechanical work. This is true because all machines transfer input energy, or the work done on the machine to output energy, or the work done by the machine.

Work, in the mechanical sense of the term, is done when a resistance is overcome by a force acting through a measurable distance. Two factors are involved: (1) Force and (2) movement through a distance. As an example, suppose a small aircraft is stuck in the snow. Two men push against it for a period of time, but the aircraft does not move. According to the technical definition, no work was done in pushing against the aircraft. By definition, work is accomplished only when an object is displaced some distance against a resistive force.

In equation form, this relationship is,

Work = Force (F) x distance (d).

The physicist defines work as "work is force times displacement. Work done by a force acting as a body is equal to the magnitude of the force multiplied by the distance through which the force acts."

In the metric system, the unit of work is the *joule*, where one joule is the amount of work done by a force of one newton when it acts through a distance of one meter. That is,

1 joule = 1 newton-m

Hence we can write the definition in the form

W (joules) = F (newtons) x d (meters)

If we push a box for 8 m across a floor with a force of 100 newtons, the work we perform is

$W = Fd = 100$ newtons x 8 m = 800 joules

How much work is done in raising a 500-kg (kilogram) elevator cab from the ground floor of a building to its tenth floor, 30 m (meters) higher? We note that the force needed is equal to the weight of the cab, which is *mg*.

In the metric system, mass rather than weight is normally specified. To find the weight in newtons (the metric unit of force) of something whose mass in kilograms is known, we simply turn to F=mg and set G=9.8 m/SEC²

F (newtons) = M (kilograms) x G (9.8 m/sec²)

W (joules) = M (kilograms) x G (9.8 m/sec²) x D (meters)

$W = Fd = mgd = 500$ kg x 9.8 m/Sec² x 30m

= 147,000 joules

= 1.47 x 10⁵ joules

Force Parallel To Displacement

If force is expressed in pounds and distances in feet, work will be expressed in ft. lbs. (foot-pounds). Example: How much work is accomplished in lifting a 40-pound weight to a vertical height of 25 feet?

$W = Fd$

= 40 x 25

= 1,000 ft.-lb.

Example: How much work is accomplished in pushing a small aircraft into a hangar a distance of 115 feet if a force of 75 pounds is required to keep it moving?

$W = Fd$

= 75 x 115

= 8,625 ft.-lb.

Force Not Parallel To Displacement

In this equation, F is assumed to be in the same direction as *d*. If it is not, for example the case of a body pulling a wagon with a rope not parallel to the ground, we must use *F* for the component of the applied force that acts in the direction of the motion, figure 7-37(A).

The component of a force in the direction of a displacement *d* is:

$F \cos \theta$

where θ is the angle between *F* and *d*. Hence the most general equation for work is

$W = Fd \cos \theta$

When *F* and *d* are parallel, $\theta = 0$ and $\cos \theta = 1$, so that $Fd \cos \theta$ reduces to just Fd. When *F* and *d* are perpendicular, $\theta = 90°$ and $\cos \theta = 0$, so that no work is done. A force that is perpendicular to the motion of an object can do no work upon it. Thus gravity, which results in a downward force on everything near the earth, does no work on objects moving horizontally along the earth's surface. However, if we drop an object, as it falls to the ground work is definitely done upon it.

When a force and the distance through which it acts are parallel, the work done is equal to the product of F and d.

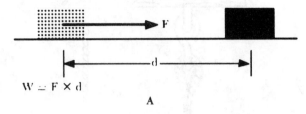

W = F × d

A

When they are not in the same direction, the work done is equal to the product of d and the component of F in the direction of d, namely (F cos θ) × d.

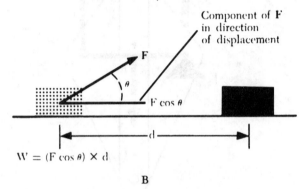

W = (F cos θ) × d

B

FIGURE 7-36. Direction of work.

Friction

In calculating work done, the actual resistance overcome is measured. This is not necessarily the weight of the object being moved. This point can be illustrated by referring to figure 7-37. A 900-pound load is being pulled a distance of 200 feet. This does not mean that the work done (force x distance) is 180,000 foot-pounds (900 pounds x 200 feet). This is because the man pulling the load is not working against the total weight of the load, but rather against the rolling friction of the cart, which may be no more than 90 pounds.

Friction is one of the most important aspects of life. Without friction it would be impossible to walk. One would have to shove oneself from place to place, and would have to bump against some obstacle to stop at a destination. Yet friction is a liability as well as an asset, and requires consideration when dealing with any moving mechanism.

In experiments relating to friction, measurement of the applied forces reveals that there are three kinds of friction. One force is required to start a body moving, while another is required to keep the body moving at constant speed. Also, after a body is once in motion, a definitely larger force is required to keep it sliding than to keep it rolling.

250

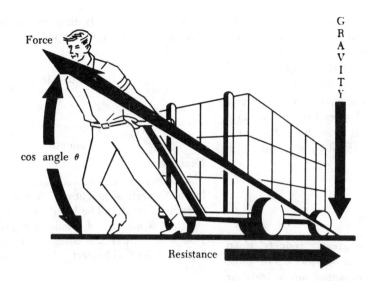

FIGURE 7–37. Working against friction.

Thus, the three kinds of friction may be classified as: (1) Starting (static) friction, (2) sliding friction, and (3) rolling friction.

Static Friction

When an attempt is made to slide a heavy object along a surface, the object must first be broken loose or started. Once in motion, it slides more easily. The "breaking loose" force is, of course, proportional to the weight of the body. The force necessary to start the body moving slowly is designated "F," and "F'" is the normal force pressing the body against the surface (usually its weight). Since the nature of the surfaces rubbing against each other is important, they must be considered. The nature of the surfaces is indicated by the coefficient of starting friction which is designated by the letter "k." This coefficient can be established for various materials and is often published in tabular form. Thus, when the load (weight of the object) is known, starting friction can be calculated by using the equation,

$$F = kF'.$$

For example, if the coefficient of sliding friction of a smooth iron block on a smooth, horizontal surface is 0.3, the force required to start a 10-pound block would be 3 pounds; a 40-pound block, 12 pounds.

Starting friction for objects equipped with wheels and roller bearings is much smaller than that for sliding objects. Nevertheless, a locomotive would have difficulty getting a long train of cars in motion all at one time. Therefore, the couples between the cars are purposely made to have a few inches of play. When the engineer is about to start the train, he backs the engine until all the cars are pushed together. Then, with a quick start forward the first car is set in motion. This technique is employed to overcome the static friction of each wheel (as well as the inertia of each car). It would be impossible for the engine to start all of the cars at the same instant, for static friction, which is the resistance of being set in motion, would be greater than the force exerted by the engine. Once the cars are in motion, however, static friction is greatly reduced and a smaller force is required to keep the train in motion than was required to start it.

Sliding Friction

Sliding friction is the resistance to motion offered by an object sliding over a surface. It pertains to friction produced after the object has once been set into motion, and is always less than starting friction. The amount of sliding resistance is dependent on the nature of the surface of the object, the surface over which it slides, and the normal force between the object and the surface. This resistive force may be computed by the formula,

$$F = \mu N$$

where: "F" is the resistive force due to friction expressed in pounds; "N" is the force exerted on or by the object perpendicular (normal) to the

251

surface over which it slides; and "μ" (mu) is the coefficient of sliding friction. (On a horizontal surface, N is equal to the weight of the object in pounds.) The area of the sliding object exposed to the sliding surface has no effect on the results. A block of wood, for example, will not slide any easier on one of the broad sides than it will on a narrow side, (assuming all sides have the same smoothness). Therefore, area does not enter into the equation above.

Rolling Friction

Resistance to motion is greatly reduced if an object is mounted on wheels or rollers. The force of friction for objects mounted on wheels or rollers is called rolling friction. This force may be computed by the same equation used in computing sliding friction, but the values of μ will be much smaller. For example, μ for rubber tires on concrete or macadam is about .02. The value of μ for roller bearings is very small, usually ranging from .001 to .003 and is often disregarded.

Example:

An aircraft with a gross weight of 79,600 lb. is towed over a concrete ramp. What force must be exerted by the towing vehicle to keep the airplane rolling after once set in motion?

$$F = \mu N$$

$$= .02 \times 79,600 = 1,592 \text{ lb.}$$

Power

Power is a badly abused term. In speaking of power-driven equipment, people often confuse the term "power" with the ability to move heavy loads. This is not the meaning of power. A sewing machine motor is powerful enough to rotate an aircraft engine propeller providing it is connected to the crankshaft through a suitable mechanism. It could not rotate the propeller at 2,000 r.p.m., however, for it is not powerful enough to move a large load at a high speed. Power, thus, means rate of doing work. It is measured in terms of work accomplished per unit of time. In equation form, it reads:

$$\text{Power} = \frac{\text{Force x Distance}}{\text{time}}$$

$$\text{or, } P = \frac{FD}{t}$$

If force is expressed in pounds, distance in feet, and time in seconds, then power is given in ft.-lbs./sec. (foot-pounds per second). Time may also be given in minutes. If time in minutes is used in this equation, then power will be expressed in ft.-lbs./min.

$$\text{Power} = \frac{\text{pounds x feet}}{\text{seconds}} = \text{ft.-lbs./sec.}$$

or,

$$\text{Power} = \frac{\text{pounds x feet}}{\text{minutes}} = \text{ft.-lbs./min.}$$

Example:

An aircraft engine weighing 3,500 pounds was hoisted a vertical height of 7 feet in order to install it on an aircraft. The hoist was hand-powered and required 3 minutes of cranking to raise the engine. How much power was developed by the man cranking the hoist? (Neglect friction in the hoist.)

$$\text{Power} = \frac{Fd}{t}$$

$$= \frac{3,500 \text{ pounds x 7 feet}}{3 \text{ minutes}}$$

$$= 8,167 \text{ ft.-lbs./min.}$$

Power is often expressed in units of horsepower. One horsepower is equal to 550 ft.-lbs./sec. or 33,000 ft.-lbs./min.

Example:

In the hoist example above, calculate the horsepower developed by the man.

$$\text{Horsepower} = \frac{\text{Power in ft.-lbs./min.}}{33,000}$$

$$\text{hp.} = \frac{\frac{Fd}{t}}{33,000}$$

$$= \frac{8167}{33,000} = 0.247, \text{ or about } \frac{1}{4} \text{ hp}$$

Power is rate of doing work:

$$P = \frac{W}{t}$$

In the metric system the unit of power is the *watt*, where

1 watt = 1 joule/sec.

The watt is the metric unit of power, thus a motor with a power output of 5,000 watts is capable of doing 5,000 joules of work per second.

A *kilowatt* (kw) is equal to 1,000 watts. Hence the above motor has a power output of 5 kw.

How much time does the elevator cab of the previous example need to ascend 30 meters if it is being lifted by a 5-kw motor? We rewrite P=W/t in the form

$$t = \frac{W}{P}$$

and then substitute w=1.47 x 10^5 joules and p=5.10^3 watts to find that

$$t = \frac{W}{P} = \frac{1.47 \times 10^5 \text{ joules}}{5 \times 10^3 \text{ watts}} = 29.4 \text{ sec.}$$

Energy

In many cases when work is done on an object, something is given to the object which it retains and which later enables it to do work. When a weight is lifted to a certain height such as in the case of a trip-hammer, or when a clock spring is wound, the object acquires, through having work done on it, the ability to do work itself. In storage batteries and gasoline, energy is stored which can be used later to do work. Energy stored in coal or food can be used to do work. This storage gives such objects the ability to do work; thus, energy is defined as the ability to do work

In general, a change in energy is equal to the work done; the loss in energy of a body may be measured by the work it does, or the gain in energy of a body may be measured by the amount of work done on it. For convenience, energy which bodies possess is classified into two categories: (1) Potential and (2) kinetic.

Potential energy may be classified into three groups: (1) That due to position, (2) that due to distortion of an elastic body, and (3) that which produces work through chemical action. Water in an elevated reservoir, and the lifted weight of a pile-driver are examples of the first group; a stretched rubber band or compressed spring are examples of the second group; and energy in coal, food, and storage batteries are examples of the third group.

Bodies in motion required work to put them in motion. Thus, they possess energy of motion. Energy due to motion is known as kinetic energy. A moving vehicle, a rotating flywheel, and a hammer in motion are examples of kinetic energy.

Energy is expressed in the same units as those used to express work. The quantity of potential energy possessed by an elevated weight may be computed by the equation,

Potential Energy = Weight × Height.

If weight is given in pounds and height in feet, the final unit of energy will be ft.-lbs. (foot-pounds).

Example: An aircraft with a gross weight of 110,000 pounds is flying at an altitude of 15,000 feet above the surface of the earth. How much potential energy does the airplane possess with respect to the earth?

Potential Energy = Weight × Height
$$PE = 110,000 \times 15,000$$
$$= 1,650,000,000 \text{ ft.-lbs.}$$

Forms of Energy

The most common forms of energy are heat, mechanical, electrical, and chemical. The various forms of energy can be changed, or transformed, into another form in many different ways. For example, in the case of mechanical energy, the energy of work done against friction is always converted into heat energy, and the mechanical energy that turns an electric generator develops electrical energy at the output of the generator.

MOTION OF BODIES

General

The study of the relationship between the motion of bodies or objects and the forces acting on them is often called the study of "force and motion." In a more specific sense, the relationship between velocity, acceleration, and distance is known as kinematics.

Uniform Motion

Motion may be defined as a continuing change of position or place, or as the process in which a body undergoes displacement. When an object is at different points in space at different times, that object is said to be in motion, and if the distance the object moves remains the same for a given period of time, the motion may be described as uniform. Thus, an object in uniform motion always has a constant speed.

Speed and Velocity

In everyday usage, speed and velocity often mean the same thing. In physics they have definite and distinct meanings. Speed refers to how fast an object is moving, or how far the object will travel in a specific time. The speed of an object tells nothing about the direction an object is moving. For example, if the information is supplied that an airplane leaves New York City and travels 8 hours at a speed of 150 m.p.h., this information tells nothing about the direction in which the airplane is moving. At the end of 8 hours, it might be in Kansas City, or if it traveled in a circular route, it could be back in New York City.

Velocity is that quantity in physics which denotes both the speed of an object and the direction in which the object moves. Velocity can be defined as the rate of motion in a particular direction.

The average velocity of an object can be calculated using the formula,

$$V_a = \frac{s}{t}$$

where:

V_a = the average velocity.
s = the rate of motion or average speed.
t = the elapsed time.

Acceleration

Acceleration is defined by the physicist as the rate of change of velocity. If the velocity of an object is increased from 20 m.p.h. to 30 m.p.h., the object has been accelerated. If the increase in velocity is 10 m.p.h. in 5 seconds, the rate of change in velocity is 10 m.p.h. in 5 seconds, or

$\frac{2 \text{ m.p.h.}}{\text{sec.}}$. Expressed as an equation,

$$A = \frac{V_f - V_i}{t}$$

where:

A = acceleration.
V_f = the final velocity (30 m.p.h.).
V_i = the initial velocity (20 m.p.h.).
t = the elapsed time.

The example used can be expressed as follows:

$$A = \frac{30 \text{ m.p.h.} - 20 \text{ m.p.h.}}{5 \text{ sec.}}$$

$$A = \frac{2 \text{ m.p.h.}}{\text{sec.}}$$

If the object accelerated to 22 m.p.h. in the first second, 24 m.p.h. in the next second, and 26 m.p.h. in the third second, the change in velocity each second is 2 m.p.h. The acceleration is said to be constant, and the motion is described as uniformly accelerated motion.

If a body has a velocity of 3 m.p.h. at the end of the first second of its motion, 5 m.p.h. at the end of the next second, and 8 m.p.h. at the end of the third second, its motion is described as acceleration, but it is variable accelerated motion.

Newton's Law of Motion

When a magician snatches a tablecloth from a table and leaves a full setting of dishes undisturbed, he is not displaying a mystic art; he is demonstrating the principle of inertia.

Inertia is responsible for the discomfort felt when an airplane is brought to a sudden halt in the parking area and the passengers are thrown forward in their seats. Inertia is a property of matter. This property of matter is described by Newton's first law of motion, which states:

Objects at rest tend to remain at rest; objects in motion tend to remain in motion at the same speed and in the same direction.

Bodies in motion have the property called momentum. A body that has great momentum has a strong tendency to remain in motion and is therefore hard to stop. For example, a train moving at even low velocity is difficult to stop because of its large mass. Newton's second law applies to this property. It states:

When a force acts upon a body, the momentum of that body is changed. The rate of change of momentum is proportional to the applied force.

The momentum of a body is defined as the product of its mass and its velocity. Thus,

Momentum = mass x velocity or,
$M = mV$

Now if a force is applied, the momentum changes at a rate equal to the force or:

F = rate of change of momentum

$$= \frac{M_f - M_i}{t}$$

Substituting mV for M:

$$F = \frac{m_f V_f - m_i V_i}{t}$$

Since the mass does not usually change, $m_f = m_i = m$. Then

$$F = \frac{mV_f - mV_i}{t}$$

$$= m\frac{(V_f - V_i)}{t}$$

From the previous section the second term is recognized as acceleration. Then the second law becomes:

$$F = ma$$

On earth, gravity exerts a force on each body causing an acceleration of 32 ft./sec.^{2} which is usually designated as "g". The force is commonly called weight, W. Using the formula above:

$$W = mg$$

and;

$$m = \frac{W}{g}$$

Then on earth the second law becomes:

$$F = ma$$

$$= \frac{W}{g}(a)$$

The following examples illustrate the use of this formula.

Example:
A train weighs 32,000 lbs. and is traveling at 10 ft./sec. What force is required to bring it to rest in 10 seconds?

$$F = \frac{W}{g}(a)$$

$$= \frac{W}{g}\frac{(V_f - V_i)}{t}$$

$$= \frac{32,000}{32}\frac{(0-10)}{10}$$

$$= \frac{32,000 \times (-10)}{32 \times 10}$$

$$= -1,000 \text{ lbs.}$$

The negative sign means that the force must be applied against the train's motion.

Example:
An aircraft weighs 6,400 pounds. How much force is needed to give it an acceleration of 6 ft./sec.^{2}?

$$F = \frac{W}{g}(a)$$

$$= \frac{6400 \times 6}{32} = 1,200 \text{ lb.}$$

Newton's third law of motion is often called the law of action and reaction. It states that for every action there is an equal and opposite reaction. This means that if a force is applied to an object, the object will supply a resistive force exactly equally to and in the opposite direction of the force applied. It is easy to see how this might apply to objects at rest. For example, as a man stands on the floor, the floor exerts a force against his feet exactly equal to his weight. But this law is also applicable when a force is applied to an object in motion.

When a force applied to an object is more than sufficient to produce and sustain uniform motion, inertia of the object will cause such a resistive force that the force opposing the motion of the object equals the force producing the motion. This resistance to change in velocity due to inertia is usually referred to as internal force. When several forces act upon an object to produce accelerated motion, the sums of the external forces are in a state of unbalance; however, the sums of the external and the internal forces are always in a state of balance, whether motion is being either sustained or produced.

Forces always occur in pairs. The term "acting force" means the force one body exerts on a second body, and reacting force means the force the second body exerts on the first.

When an aircraft propeller pushes a stream of air backward with a force of 500 pounds, the air pushes the blades forward with a force of 500 pounds. This forward force causes the aircraft to move forward. In like manner, the discharge of exhaust gases from the tailpipe of a turbine engine is the action which causes the aircraft to move forward.

The three laws of motion which have been discussed here are closely related. In many cases, all three laws may be operating on a body at the same time.

Circular Motion

Circular motion is the motion of an object along a curved path that has a constant radius. For example, if one end of a string is tied to an object and the other end is held in the hand, the object can be swung in a circle. The object is constantly deflected from a straight (linear) path by the pull exerted on the string, as shown in figure 7–38.

As an object in figure 7–38 travels along the circumference from X to Y, the pull or force on the string deflects it from Y toward Z. This pull is called centripetal force, which deflects an object from a straight path and forces it to travel in a curved path. Thus, the string exerts a centripetal

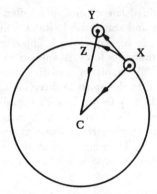

FIGURE 7–38. Circular motion.

force on the object, and the object exerts an equal but opposite force on the string, obeying Newton's third law of motion.

The force that is equal to centripetal force, but acting in an opposite direction, is called centrifugal force. In the example of figure 7–38, it is the force exerted by the object on the string. Without a centripetal force, there is no centrifugal force.

Centripetal force is always directly proportional to the mass of the object in circular motion. Thus, if the mass of the object in figure 7–38 is doubled, the pull on the string must be doubled to keep the object in its circular path, provided the speed of the object remains constant.

Centripetal force is inversely proportional to the radius of the circle in which an object travels. If the string in figure 7–38 is shortened and the speed remains constant, the pull on the string must be increased since the radius is decreased, and the string must pull the object from its linear path more rapidly.

Using the same reasoning, the pull on the string must be increased if the object is swung more rapidly in its orbit. Centripetal force is thus directly proportional to the square of the velocity of the object. The formula for centripetal force is:

$$C.P. = \frac{MV^2}{R}$$

where:

M = the mass of the object.
V = velocity.
R = radius of the object's path.

Rotary Motion

The motion of a body turning about an axis is called rotary motion. This is the familiar motion that occurs as the crankshaft of an engine turns.

The difference between rotary and circular motion is that, in the case of rotary motion, the body or object spins, while in circular motion the whole object moves along a curved path.

When an object spins at a constant speed about a fixed axis, it has uniform rotary motion. When its direction or rate of spin changes, it has variable rotary motion.

Momentum

Momentum is defined as the product of an object's mass and its velocity. The force required to accelerate an object is proportional to an object's mass and the acceleration given it. Acceleration has been defined as the rate of change of an object's velocity. This is expressed as a formula:

$$A = \frac{V_f - V_i}{t}$$

where:

A = acceleration.
V_f = final velocity.
V_i = initial velocity.
t = elapsed time.

Newton's second law of motion, $F = MA$, involves acceleration. If the original expression for acceleration is substituted in Newton's second law, it becomes:

$$F = \frac{MV_f - MV_i}{t}.$$

This formula can be further resolved to illustrate momentum by multiplying both sides by t:

$$Ft = MV_f - MV_i.$$

This formula illustrates that an object's momentum is a product of its mass and its velocity.

HEAT

Heat is a form of energy. It is produced only by the conversion of one of the other forms of energy. Heat may also be defined as the total kinetic energy of the molecules of any substance.

Some forms of energy which can be converted into heat energy are as follows:

(1) *Mechanical Energy.* This includes all methods of producing increased motion of molecules such as friction, impact of bodies, or compression of gases.

256

(2) *Electrical Energy.* Electrical energy is converted to heat energy when an electric current flows through any form of resistance. This might be an electric iron, electric light, or an electric blanket.

(3) *Chemical Energy.* Most forms of chemical reaction convert stored potential energy into heat. Some examples are the explosive effects of gunpowder, the burning of oil or wood, and the combining of oxygen and grease.

(4) *Radiant Energy.* Electromagnetic waves of certain frequencies produce heat when they are absorbed by the bodies they strike. Included are X-rays, light rays, and infrared rays.

(5) *Nuclear Energy.* Energy stored in the nucleus of atoms is released during the process of nuclear fission in a nuclear reactor or atomic explosion.

(6) *The Sun.* All heat energy can be directly or indirectly traced to the nuclear reactions occurring in the sun.

Mechanical Equivalent of Heat

When a gas is compressed, work is done and the gas becomes warm or hot. Conversely, when a gas under high pressure is allowed to expand, the expanding gas becomes cool. In the first case, work was converted into energy in the form of heat; in the second case heat energy was expended. Since heat is given off or absorbed, there must be a relationship between heat energy and work. Also, when two surfaces are rubbed together, the friction develops heat. However, work was required to cause the heat, and by experimentation, it has been shown that the work required and the amount of heat produced by friction are proportional. Thus, heat can be regarded as a form of energy.

According to this theory of heat as a form of energy, the molecules, atoms, and electrons in all bodies are in a continual state of motion. In a hot body, these small particles possess relatively large amounts of kinetic energy, but in cooler bodies they have less. Because the small particles are given motion, and hence kinetic energy, work must be done to slide one body over the other. Mechanical energy apparently is transformed, and what we know as heat is really kinetic energy of the small molecular subdivisions of matter.

Two different units are used to express quantities of heat energy. They are the calorie and the British thermal unit. One calorie is equal to the amount of heat required to change the temperature of 1 gram of water 1 degree centigrade.

This term "calorie" (spelled with a small c) is $\frac{1}{1,000}$ of the Calorie (spelled with a capital C) used in the measurement of heat-producing or energy-producing value in foods. One B.t.u. (British thermal unit) is defined as the amount of heat required to change the temperature of 1 pound of water 1 degree Fahrenheit. The calorie and the gram are seldom used in discussing aviation maintenance. The B.t.u., however, is commonly referred to in discussions of engine thermal efficiencies and the heat content of aviation fuel.

A device known as the calorimeter is used to measure quantities of heat energy. For example, it may be used to determine the quantity of heat energy available in 1 pound of aviation gasoline. A given weight of the fuel is burned in the calorimeter, and the heat energy is absorbed by a large quantity of water. From the weight of the water and the increase in its temperature, it is possible to compute the heat yield of the fuel.

A definite relationship exists between heat and mechanical energy. This relationship has been established and verified by many experiments which show that:

One B.t.u. = 778 ft.-lbs.

Thus, if the 1-pound sample of the fuel mentioned above were found to yield 20,000 B.t.u., it would be the equivalent of 20,000 B.t.u. × 778 ft.-lbs./B.t.u. or 15,560,000 ft.-lbs. of mechanical energy.

Unfortunately no heat engine is capable of transforming all of the available heat energy in the fuel it burns into mechanical energy. A large portion of this energy is wasted through heat losses and operational friction.

Methods of Heat Transfer

There are three methods by which heat is transferred from one location to another or from one substance to another. These three methods are conduction, convection, and radiation.

Conduction

Everyone knows from experience that the metal handle of a heated pan can burn the hand. A

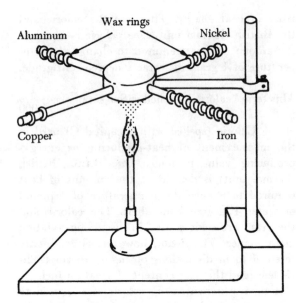

FIGURE 7–39. Various metals conduct heat at
different rates.

plastic or wood handle, however, remains relatively cool even though it is in direct contact with the pan. The metal transmits the heat more easily than the wood because it is a better conductor of heat. Different materials conduct heat at different rates. Some metals are much better conductors of heat than others. Aluminum and copper are used in pots and pans because they conduct heat very rapidly. Woods and plastics are used for handles because they conduct heat very slowly.

Figure 7–39 illustrates the different rates of conduction of various metals. Four rods of different metals have several wax rings handing on them. One flame is used to heat one end of each rod simultaneously. The rings melt and drop off the copper rod first, then from the aluminum rod, then from the nickel rod, and last from the iron rod. This example shows that among the four metals used, copper is the best conductor of heat and iron is the poorest.

Liquids are poorer conductors of heat than metals. Notice that the ice in the test tube shown in figure 7–40 is not melting rapidly even though the water at the top is boiling. The water conducts heat so poorly that not enough heat reaches the ice to melt it.

Gases are even poorer conductors of heat than liquids. It is possible to stand quite close to a stove without being burned because air is such a poor conductor. Since conduction is a process whereby the increase in molecular energy is passed

along by actual contact, gases are poor conductors.

At the point of application of the heat source the molecules become violently agitated. These molecules strike adjacent molecules causing them to become agitated. This process continues until the heat energy is distributed evenly throughout the substance. Because molecules are farther apart in gases than in solids, the gases are much poorer conductors of heat.

Materials that are poor conductors are used to prevent the transfer of heat and are called heat insulators. A wooden handle on a pot or a soldering iron serves as a heat insulator. Certain materials such as finely spun glass or asbestos are particularly poor heat conductors. These materials are therefore used for many types of insulation.

Convection

Convection is the process by which heat is transferred by movement of a heated fluid (gas or liquid). For example, an electronic tube will, when heated, become increasingly hotter until the air surrounding it begins to move. The motion of the air is upward. This upward motion of the heated air carries the heat away from the hot tube by convection. Transfer of heat by convection may be hastened by using a ventilating fan to move the air surrounding a hot object. The rate of cooling of a hot vacuum tube can be increased if it is provided with copper fins that conduct heat

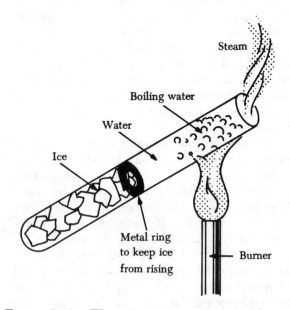

FIGURE 7–40. Water is a poor conductor of heat.

258

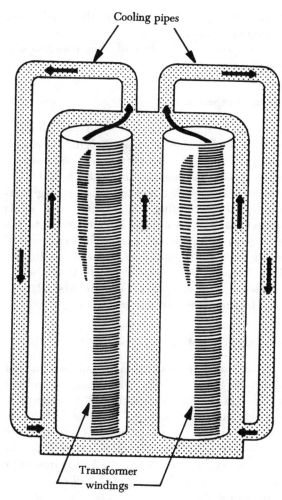

Cooling pipes

Transformer windings

FIGURE 7–41.   Oil convection currents cool a transformer.

away from the hot tube. The fins provide large surfaces against which cool air can be blown.

A convection process may take place in a liquid as well as in a gas. Figure 7–41 shows a transformer in an oil bath. The hot oil is less dense (has less weight per unit volume) and rises, while the cool oil falls, is heated, and rises in turn.

When the circulation of gas or liquid is not rapid enough to remove sufficient heat, fans or pumps are used to accelerate the motion of the cooling material. In some installations, pumps are used to circulate water or oil to help cool large equipment. In airborne installations electric fans and blowers are used to aid convection.

Radiation

Conduction and convection cannot wholly account for some of the phenomena associated with heat transfer. For example, the heat one feels when sitting in front of an open fire cannot be transferred by convection because the air currents are moving toward the fire. It cannot be transferred through conduction because the conductivity of the air is very small, and the cooler currents of air moving toward the fire would more than overcome the transfer of heat outward. Therefore, there must be some way for heat to travel across space other than by conduction and convection.

The existence of another process of heat transfer is still more evident when the heat from the sun is considered. Since conduction and convection take place only through some medium, such as a gas or a liquid, heat from the sun must reach the earth by another method, since space is an almost perfect vacuum. Radiation is the name given to this third method of heat transference.

The term "radiation" refers to the continual emission of energy from the surface of all bodies. This energy is known as radiant energy. It is in the form of electromagnetic waves, radio waves, or X-rays, which are all alike except for a difference in wave lengths. These waves travel at the velocity of light and are transmitted through a vacuum more easily than through air because air absorbs some of them. Most forms of energy can be traced back to the energy of sunlight. Sunlight is a form of radiant heat energy which travels through space to reach the earth. These electromagnetic heat waves are absorbed when they come in contact with nontransparent bodies. The result is that the motion of the molecules in the body is increased as indicated by an increase in the temperature of the body.

The differences between conduction, convection, and radiation may now be considered. First, although conduction and convection are extremely slow, radiation takes place with the speed of light. This fact is evident at the time of an eclipse of the sun when the shutting off of the heat from the sun takes place at the same time as the shutting off of the light. Second, radiant heat may pass through a medium without heating it. For example, the air inside a greenhouse may be much warmer than the glass through which the sun's rays pass. Third, although conducted or convected heat may travel in roundabout routes, radiant heat always travels in a straight line. For example, radiation can be cut off with a screen placed between the source of heat and the body to be protected.

Material	Specific heat
Mercury	0.033
Copper	0.095
Iron and steel	0.113
Glass	0.200
Alcohol	0.500
Water	1.000

FIGURE 7–42.   Specific heat values for some common materials.

The sun, a fire, and an electric light bulb all radiate energy, but a body need not glow to give off heat. A kettle of hot water or a hot soldering iron radiates heat. If the surface is polished or light in color, less heat is radiated. Bodies which do not reflect are good radiators and good absorbers, and bodies that reflect are poor radiators and poor absorbers. For this reason white clothing is worn in the summer season.

A practical example of the control of loss of heat is the thermos bottle. The flask itself is made of two walls of glass separated by a vacuum. The vacuum prevents the loss of heat by conduction and convection, and a silver coating on the walls prevents the loss of heat by radiation.

Specific Heat

One important way in which substances differ is in the requirement of different quantities of heat to produce the same temperature change in a given mass of the substance. Each substance requires a quantity of heat, called its specific heat capacity, to increase the temperature of a unit of its mass 1° C. The specific heat of a substance is the ratio of its specific heat capacity to the specific heat capacity of water. Specific heat is expressed as a number which, because it is a ratio, has no units and applies to both the English and the metric systems.

It is fortunate that water has a high specific heat capacity. The larger bodies of water on the earth keep the air and solid matter on or near the surface of the earth at a fairly constant temperature. A great quantity of heat is required to change the temperature of a large lake or river. Therefore, when the temperature falls below that of such bodies of water, they give off large quantities of heat. This process keeps the atmospheric temperature at the surface of the earth from changing rapidly.

The specific heat values of some common materials are listed in figure 7–42.

Thermal Expansion

Thermal expansion takes place in solids, liquids, and gases when they are heated. With few exceptions, solids will expand when heated and contract when cooled. Because the molecules of solids are much closer together and are more strongly attracted to each other, the expansion of solids when heated is very slight in comparison to the expansion in liquids and gases. The expansion of fluids has been discussed in the study of Boyle's law. Thermal expansion in solids must be explained in some detail because of its close relationship to aircraft metals and materials.

Expansion in Solids

Solid materials expand in length, width, and thickness when they are heated. An example of the expansion and contraction of substances is the ball and ring, illustrated in figure 7–43. The ball and ring are made of iron. When both are at the same temperature, the ball will barely slip through the ring. When the ball is heated or the ring is cooled, however, the ball cannot slip through the ring.

Experiments show that for a given change in temperature, the change in length or volume is different for each substance. For example, a given change in temperature causes a piece of copper

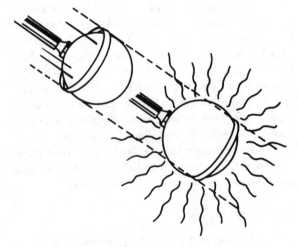

FIGURE 7–43.   Ball and ring.

260

to expand nearly twice as much as a piece of glass of the same size and shape. For this reason, the lead wires into an electronic tube cannot be made of copper but must be made of a metal that expands at the same rate as glass. If the metal does not expand at the same rate as the glass, the vacuum in the tube is broken by air leaking past the wires in the glass stem.

Because some substances expand more than others, it is necessary to measure experimentally the exact rate of expansion of each one. The amount that a unit length of any substance expands for a one-degree rise in temperature is known as the coefficient of linear expansion for that substance.

Coefficients of Expansion

To estimate the expansion of any object, such as a steel rail, it is necessary to know three things about it; namely, its length, the rise in temperature to which it is subjected, and its coefficient of expansion. This relationship is expressed by the equation:

$$\text{Expansion} = (\text{coefficient}) \times (\text{length})$$
$$\times (\text{rise in temperature})$$

$$e = kL(t_2 - t_1).$$

In this equation, the letter "k" represents the coefficient of expansion for the particular substance. In some instances, the Greek letter "α" (alpha) is used to indicate the coefficient of linear expansion.

If a steel rod measures exactly 9 feet at 21° C., what is its length at 55° C.? The value of "k" for steel is 10×10^{-6}. If the equation $e = kL(t_2 - t_1)$ is used,

then:
$$e = (10 \times 10^{-6}) \times 9 \times (55 - 21)$$
$$e = 0.000010 \times 9 \times 34$$
$$e = 0.00306.$$

This amount, when added to the original length of the rod, makes the rod 9.00306 feet long.

The increase in the length of the rod is relatively small; but if the rod were placed where it could not expand freely, there would be a tremendous force exerted due to thermal expansion. Thus, thermal expansion must be taken into consideration when designing airframes, powerplants, or related equipment.

Figure 7–44 contains a list of the coefficients of linear expansion for some common substances.

Substance	Coefficient of linear expansion (per degree C.)
Aluminum	24×10^{-6}
Brass	19×10^{-6}
Copper	17×10^{-6}
Glass	4 to 9×10^{-6}
Quartz	0.4×10^{-6}
Steel	11×10^{-6}
Zinc	26×10^{-6}

FIGURE 7–44. Expansion coefficients of some common materials.

A practical application which uses the difference in the coefficients of linear expansion of metals is the thermostat. This instrument consists of an arrangement of two bars of dissimilar metal fastened together. When the temperature changes, a bending takes place because of the unequal expansion of the metals. Figure 7–45 shows such an instrument, made with a wooden handle for laboratory demonstrations. Thermostats are used in overload relays in motors, in temperature-sensitive switches, and in heating systems.

SOUND

Sound has been defined as a series of disturbances in matter that the human ear can detect. This definition can also be applied to disturbances which are beyond the range of human hearing.

There are three elements which are necessary for the transmission and reception of sound. These are the source, a medium for carrying the sound,

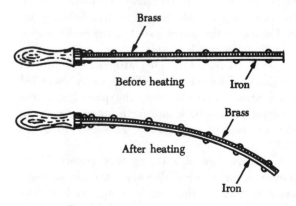

FIGURE 7–45. Compound bar.

261

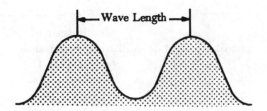

FIGURE 7-46. A transverse wave.

and the detector. Anything which moves back and forth (vibrates) and disturbs the medium around it may be considered a sound source.

An example of the production and transmission of sound is the ring of a bell. When the bell is struck and begins to vibrate, the particles of the medium (the surrounding air) in contact with the bell also vibrate. The vibrational disturbance is transmitted from one particle of the medium to the next, and the vibrations travel in a "wave" through the medium until they reach the ear. The eardrum, acting as detector, is set in motion by the vibrating particles of air, and the brain interprets the eardrum's vibrations as the characteristic sound associated with a bell.

Wave Motion

Since sound is a wave motion in matter, it can best be understood by first considering water waves. When a stone is thrown into a pool, a series of circular waves travel away from the disturbance. In figure 7-46 such waves are diagramed as though seen in cross section, from the side. Notice that water waves are a succession of crests and troughs. The wavelength is the distance from the crest of one wave to the crest of the next. Water waves are known as transverse waves because the motion of the water molecules is up and down, or at right angles to the direction in which the waves are traveling. This can be seen by observing a cork on the water, bobbing up and down as the waves pass by; the corks moves very little from side to side.

Sound travels through matter in the form of longitudinal wave motions. These waves are called longitudinal waves because the particles of the medium vibrate back and forth longitudinally in the direction of propagation, as shown in figure 7-47.

When the tine of a tuning fork (figure 7-47) moves in an outward direction, the air immediately in front of the tine is compressed so that its momentary pressure is raised above that at

other points in the sorrounding medium. Because air is elastic, this disturbance is transmitted progressively in an outward direction from the tine in the form of a compression wave.

When the tine returns and moves in an inward direction, the air in front of the tine is rarefied so that its momentary pressure is reduced below that at other points in the surrounding medium. This disturbance is transmitted in the form of a rarefaction (expansion) wave and follows the compression wave through the medium.

The progress of any wave involves two distinct motions: (1) The wave itself moves forward with constant speed, and (2) simultaneously, the particles of the medium that convey the wave vibrate harmonically. (Examples of harmonic motion are the motion of a clock pendulum, the balance wheel in a watch, and the piston in a reciprocating engine.)

The period of a vibrating particle is the time "t" (in seconds) required for the particle to complete one vibration.

The frequency "f" is the number of vibrations completed per second and may be expressed in c.p.s. When expressed in this unit, the word "cycles" means vibrations. The period is the reciprocal of the frequency:

$$t = 1/f.$$

The velocity of a wave is equal to the wavelength λ (lambda) divided by the period. Since the period is the reciprocal of the frequency, the velocity is,

$$v = f\lambda$$

where:

v = velocity in ft./sec.
f = frequency in c.p.s.
λ = wavelength in ft.

The amplitude of vibration is the maximum displacement of the particle from its equilibrium position.

Two particles are in phase when they are vibrating with the same frequency, and continually pass through corresponding points of their paths at the same time. For any other condition the particles are out of phase. The two particles are in phase opposition when they reach their maximum displacement in opposite directions at the same time.

The wavelength is the distance measured along the direction of propagation between two corre-

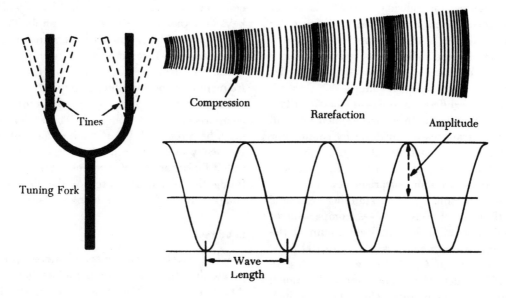

FIGURE 7–47.   Sound propagation by a tuning fork.

sponding points of equal intensity that are in phase on adjacent waves. This length can be represented by the distance between the adjacent maximum rarefaction points in the traveling sound wave (figure 7–47). When referring to figure 7–47, keep in mind that the transverse wave drawn below the compressional wave is merely a device for simplifying the concept and relating it to the type of wave illustration commonly used in discussions of electromagnetic waves.

When an advancing wave encounters a medium of different character, some of its energy is reflected back into the initial medium, and some is transmitted into the second medium.

Reflection of Sound Waves

To understand wave reflection, it is helpful to think of the wave as a ray. A ray is a line which indicates the direction the wave is traveling. In a uniform medium, a ray will travel in a straight line. Only at the boundary of two media or in an area where the medium is changing do the rays change their direction.

If a line, called a "normal," is drawn perpendicular to a boundary, the angle between an incoming ray and this normal is called the angle of incidence, "i" as shown in figure 7–48. The angle which the reflected ray makes with the normal is called the angle of reflection "r." Any wave being reflected is reflected in such a way that the angle of incidence equals the angle of reflection.

Light is often thought of first when reflection is discussed; however, reflection is equally common in other types of waves. As an example, echoes are caused by reflection of sound waves.

When a hard surface is situated so that a sound reflection from it is outstanding, it appears as a distinct echo, and is heard an appreciable interval later than the direct sound. If the surface is concave, it may have a focusing effect and concentrate the reflected sound energy at one locality. Such a reflection may be several levels higher in intensity than the direct sound, and its arrival at a later time may have particular significance in such applications as sonar.

Speed of Sound

In any uniform medium, under given physical conditions, sound travels at a definite speed. In

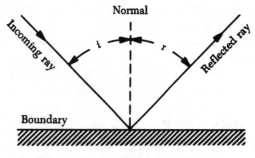

FIGURE 7–48.   Reflection of a ray.

263

some substances, the velocity of sound is higher than in others. Even in the same medium under different conditions of temperature, pressure, etc., the velocity of sound varies. Density and elasticity of a medium are the two basic physical properties which govern the velocity of sound.

In general, a difference in density between two substances is sufficient to indicate which one will be the faster transmission medium for sound. For example, sound travels faster through water than it does through air at the same temperature. However, there are some surprising exceptions to this rule-of-thumb. An outstanding example among these exceptions involves comparison of the speed of sound in lead and aluminum at the same temperature. Sound travels at 16,700 f.p.s. in aluminum at 20° C., and only 4,030 f.p.s. in lead at 20° C., despite the fact that lead is much more dense than aluminum. The reason for such exceptions is found in the fact, mentioned above, that sound velocity depends on elasticity as well as density.

Using density as a rough indication of the speed of sound in a given substance, it can be stated as a general rule that sound travels fastest in solid materials, slower in liquids, and slowest in gases.

For a fixed temperature, the velocity of sound is constant for any medium and is independent of the period, frequency, or amplitude of the disturbance. Thus, the velocity of sound in air at 0° C. (32° F.) is 1,087 f.p.s. and increases by 2 f.p.s. for each centrigrade degree of temperature rise (1.1 f.p.s. for each degree Fahrenheit). For practical purposes, the speed of sound in air may be considered 1,100 f.p.s.

Mach Number

In the study of aircraft that fly at supersonic speeds, it is customary to discuss aircraft speed in relation to the velocity of sound (approximately 750 miles per hour). The term "Mach number" has been given to the ratio of the speed of an aircraft to the speed of sound, in honor of Ernst Mach, an Austrian scientist.

Thus, if the speed of sound at sea level is 750 miles per hour, an aircraft flying at a Mach number of 2.2 would be traveling at a speed of 750 m.p.h. $\times$ 2.2 = 1,650 miles per hour.

Frequency of Sound

The term "pitch" is used to describe the frequency of a sound. The outstanding recognizable differ-

ence between the tones produced by two different keys on a piano is a difference in pitch. The pitch of a tone is proportional to the number of compressions and rarefactions received per second, which in turn, is determined by the vibration frequency of the sounding source.

Frequency, or pitch, is usually measured by comparison with a standard. The standard tone may be produced by a tuning fork of known frequency or by a siren whose frequency is computed for a particular speed of rotation. By regulating the speed, the pitch of the siren is made equal to that of the tone being measured.

Loudness

When a bell rings, the sound waves spread out in all directions and the sound is heard in all directions. When a bell is struck lightly, the vibrations are of small amplitude and the sound is weak. A stronger blow produces vibrations of greater amplitude in the bell, and the sound is louder. It is evident that the amplitude of the air vibrations is greater when the amplitude of the vibrations of the source is increased. Hence, the loudness of the sound depends on the amplitude of the vibrations of the sound waves. As the distance from the source increases, the energy in each wave spreads out, and the sound becomes weaker.

The intensity of sound is the energy per unit area per second. In a sound wave of simple harmonic motion, the energy is half kinetic and half potential; half is due to the speed of the particles, and half is due to the compression and rarefaction of the medium. These two energies are 90 degrees out of phase at any instant. That is, when the speed of particle motion is at a maximum, the pressure is normal, and when the pressure is at a maximum or a minimum, the speed of the particles is zero.

The loudness of sound depends upon both intensity and frequency. The intensity of a sound wave in a given medium is proportional to the following quantities;

(1) Square of the frequency of vibration.
(2) Square of the amplitude.
(3) Density of the medium.
(4) Velocity of propagation.

At any distance from a source of sound (point), the intensity of the wave varies inversely as the square of the distance from the source.

As the sound wave advances, variations in pressure occur at all points in the transmitting medium. The greater the pressure variations, the more intense the sound wave will be. It can be shown that the intensity is proportional to the square of the pressure variation regardless of the frequency. Thus, by measuring pressure changes, the intensities of sounds having different frequencies can be compared directly.

Measurement of Sound Intensity

The loudness (intensity) of sound is not measured by the same type of scale used to measure length. The human ear has a nonlinear response pattern, and units of sound measurement are used that vary logarithmically with the amplitude of the sound variations. These units are the "bel" and "decibel," which refer to the difference between sounds of unequal intensity or sound levels. The decibel, which is one-tenth of a bel, is the minimum change of sound level perceptible to the human ear. Hence, the decibel merely describes the ratio of two sound levels. For example, 5 decibels may represent almost any volume of sound, depending on the intensity of the reference level or the sound level on which the ratio is based.

GENERAL

Anyone concerned with aircraft maintenance is aware of the increasing use of electricity in modern systems and recognizes the importance to the mechanic of a thorough understanding of electrical principles. While the use of electricity today is so common as to be taken for granted, its widespread use in aircraft electrical systems emphasizes the importance of a sound electrical background for the airframe and powerplant technician.

In the study of physics, the electron theory of the structure of matter was introduced to explain the fundamental nature of matter. A more detailed examination of this theory is necessary to explain the behavior of the electron as it applies to the study of basic electricity.

MATTER

Matter can be defined as anything that has mass (weight) and occupies space. Thus, matter is everything that exists. It may exist in the form of solids, liquids, or gases. The smallest particle of matter in any state or form, that still possesses its identity, is called a molecule.

Substances composed of only one type of atom are called elements. But most substances occur in nature as compounds, that is, combinations of two or more types of atoms. Water, for example is a compound of two atoms of hydrogen and one atom of oxygen. A molecule of water is illustrated in figure 8–1. It would no longer retain the characteristics of water if it was compounded of one atom of hydrogen and two atoms of oxygen.

The Atom

The atom is considered the basic building block of all matter. It is the smallest possible particle that an element can be divided into and still retain its chemical properties. In its simplest form, it consists of one or more electrons orbiting at a high rate of speed around a center, or nucleus, made up of one or more protons, and, in most atoms, one or more neutrons as well. Since an atom is so small that some 200,000 could be placed side by side in a line 1 inch long, it cannot be seen, of course. Nevertheless, a great deal is known about its behavior from various tests and experiments.

The simplest atom is that of hydrogen, which is one electron orbiting around one proton, as shown in figure 8–2. A more complex atom is that of oxygen (see figure 8–3), which consists of eight electrons rotating in two different orbits around a nucleus made up of eight protons and eight neutrons.

An electron is the basic negative charge of electricity and cannot be divided further. Some electrons are more tightly bound to the nucleus of their atom than others and rotate in an imaginary shell or sphere closer to the nucleus, while others are more loosely bound and orbit at a greater distance from the nucleus. These latter electrons are called "free" electrons because they can be freed easily from the positive attraction of the protons in the nucleus to make up the flow of electrons in a practical electrical circuit.

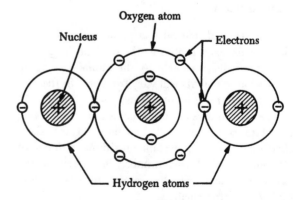

FIGURE 8–1. A water molecule.

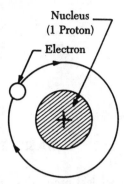

FIGURE 8–2. Hydrogen atom.

The neutrons in a nucleus have no electrical charge. They are neither positive nor negative but are equal in size and weight to the proton. Since a proton weighs approximately 1,845 times as much as an electron, the overall weight of an atom is determined by the number of protons and neutrons in its nucleus. The weight of an electron is not considered in determining the weight of an atom. Indeed, the nature of electricity cannot be defined clearly because it is not certain whether the electron is a negative charge with no mass (weight) or a particle of matter with a negative charge.

Electricity is best understood in terms of its behavior, which is based in part on the charge an atom carries. When the total positive charge of the protons in the nucleus equals the total negative charge of the electrons in orbit around the nucleus, the atom is said to have a neutral charge. If an atom has a shortage of electrons, or negative charges, it is positively charged and is called a positive ion. If it possesses an excess of electrons, it is said to be negatively charged and is called a negative ion.

Electron Movement

In a state of neutral charge, an atom has one electron for each proton in the nucleus. Thus, the number of electrons held by the atoms making up the various elements will vary from one, in the case of hydrogen, to 92 for uranium.

The electrons revolving around a nucleus travel in orbits, sometimes called shells or layers. Each shell can contain a certain maximum number of electrons, and if this number is exceeded, the extra electrons will be forced into the next higher, or outer, shell.

The shell nearest the nucleus can contain no

more than two electrons. In an atom containing more than two electrons, the excess electrons will be located in the outer shells. The second shell can have a maximum of eight electrons. The third shell can hold up to 18 electrons, the fourth 32, etc. It should be noted, however, that in some large complex atoms electrons may be arranged in outer shells before some inner shells are filled.

STATIC ELECTRICITY

Electricity is often described as being either static or dynamic. Since all electrons are alike, these words do not actually describe two different types of electricity; rather, they distinguish between electrons at rest and those in motion. The word static means "stationary" or "at rest," and refers to the deficiency or to the excess of electrons. Originally it was thought that static electricity was electricity at rest because electrical energy produced by friction did not move. A simple experiment, such as running a dry comb through hair, will produce cracking or popping sounds, indicating static discharges are taking place. The charges thus built up consist of electrons transferred to the comb as the result of friction. The discharge is caused by the rapid movement of electrons in the opposite direction from the comb to the hair as the charges neutralize each other. In the dark it is possible to see these discharges as tiny sparks.

Static electricity has little practical value, and often causes problems. It is difficult to control and discharges quickly. Conversely, dynamic, or current electricity, is generated and controlled easily and provides energy for useful work.

A summary of that part of the electron theory

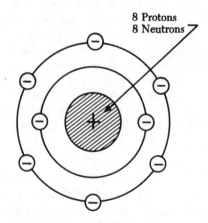

FIGURE 8–3. Oxygen atom.

dealing with charges will help explain static electricity. All electrons are alike and repel each other. Similarly, all protons are alike and repel each other. Electrons and protons are not alike, but attract each other. Hence, the fundamental law of electricity is that like charges repel and unlike charges attract.

Generation of Static Electricity

Static electricity can be produced by contact, friction, or induction. As an example of the friction method, a glass rod rubbed with fur becomes negatively charged, but if rubbed with silk, becomes positively charged. Some materials that build up static electricity easily are flannel, silk, rayon, amber, hard rubber, and glass.

When two materials are rubbed together, some electron orbits of atoms in one material may cross the orbits or shells of the other, and one material may give up electrons to the other. The transferred electrons are those in the outer shells or orbits and are called free electrons.

When a glass rod is rubbed with silk, the glass rod gives up electrons and becomes positively charged. The silk becomes negatively charged since it now has excess electrons. The source of these electric charges is friction. This charged glass rod may be used to charge other substances. For example, if two pith balls are suspended, as shown in figure 8–4, and each ball is touched with the charged glass rod, some of the charge from the rod is transferred to the balls. The balls now have similar charges and, consequently, repel each other as shown in part B of figure 8–4. If a plastic rod is rubbed with fur, it becomes negatively charged and the fur is positively charged. By touching each ball with these differently charged sources, the balls obtain opposite charges and attract each other as shown in part C of figure 8–4.

Although most objects become charged with static electricity by means of friction, a charged substance can also influence objects near it by contact. This is illustrated in figure 8–5. If a positively charged rod touches an uncharged metal bar, it will draw electrons from the uncharged bar to the point of contact. Some electrons will enter the rod, leaving the metal bar with a deficiency of electrons (positively charged) and making the rod less positive than it was or, perhaps, even neutralizing its charge completely.

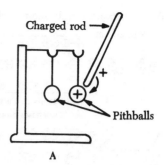

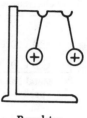

Repulsion
B

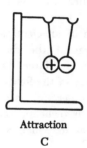

Attraction
C

FIGURE 8–4.   Reaction of like and unlike charges.

A method of charging a metal bar by induction is demonstrated in figure 8–6. A positively charged rod is brought near, but does not touch, an uncharged metal bar. Electrons in the metal bar are attracted to the end of the bar nearest the positively charged rod, leaving a deficiency of electrons at the opposite end of the bar. If this positively charged end is touched by a neutral object, electrons will flow into the metal bar and neutralize the charge. The metal bar is left with an overall excess of electrons.

Electrostatic Field

A field of force exists around a charged body. This field is an electrostatic field (sometimes called a dielectric field) and is represented by lines extending in all directions from the charged

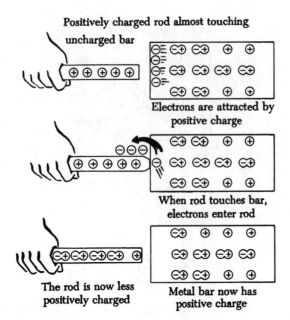

Positively charged rod almost touching uncharged bar

Electrons are attracted by positive charge

When rod touches bar, electrons enter rod

The rod is now less positively charged

Metal bar now has positive charge

FIGURE 8–5. Charging by contact.

body and terminating where there is an equal and opposite charge.

To explain the action of an electrostatic field, lines are used to represent the direction and intensity of the electric field of force. As illustrated in figure 8–7, the intensity of the field is indicated by the number of lines per unit area, and the direction is shown by arrowheads on the lines pointing in the direction in which a small test

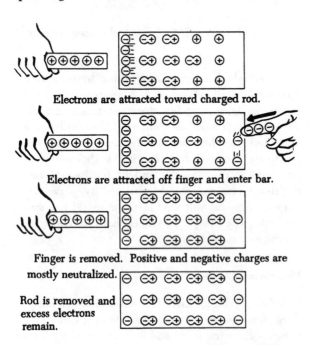

Electrons are attracted toward charged rod.

Electrons are attracted off finger and enter bar.

Finger is removed. Positive and negative charges are mostly neutralized.

Rod is removed and excess electrons remain.

FIGURE 8–6. Charging a bar by induction.

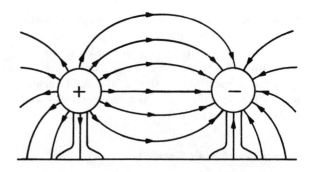

FIGURE 8–7. Direction of electric field around positive and negative charges.

charge would move or tend to move if acted upon by the field of force.

Either a positive or negative test charge can be used, but it has been arbitrarily agreed that a small positive charge will always be used in determining the direction of the field. Thus, the direction of the field around a positive charge is always away from the charge, as shown in figure 8–7, because a positive test charge would be repelled. On the other hand, the direction of the lines about a negative charge is toward the charge, since a positive test charge is attracted toward it.

Figure 8–8 illustrates the field around bodies having like charges. Positive charges are shown, but regardless of the type of charge, the lines of force would repel each other if the charges were alike. The lines terminate on material objects and always extend from a positive charge to a negative charge. These lines are imaginary lines used to show the direction a real force takes.

It is important to know how a charge is distributed on an object. Figure 8–9 shows a small metal disk on which a concentrated negative charge has been placed. By using an electrostatic

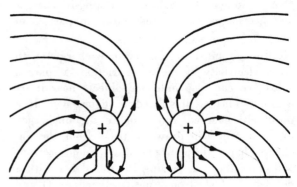

FIGURE 8–8. Field around two positively charged bodies.

FIGURE 8–9. Even distribution of charge on metal disk.

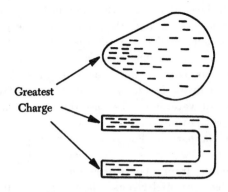

FIGURE 8–11. Charge on irregularly shaped objects.

detector, it can be shown that the charge is spread evenly over the entire surface of the disk. Since the metal disk provides uniform resistance everywhere on its surface, the mutual repulsion of electrons will result in an even distribution over the entire surface.

Another example, shown in figure 8–10, is the charge on a hollow sphere. Although the sphere is made of conducting material, the charge is evenly distributed over the outside surface. The inner surface is completely neutral. This phenomenon is used to safeguard operating personnel of the large Van de Graaff static generators used for atom-smashing. The safest area for the operators is inside the large sphere, where millions of volts are being generated.

The distribution of the charge on an irregularly shaped object differs from that on a regularly shaped object. Figure 8–11 shows that the charge on such objects is not evenly distributed. The greatest charge is at the points, or areas of sharpest curvature, of the objects.

The effects of static electricity must be considered in the operation and maintenance of aircraft. Static interference in the aircraft communication systems and the static charge created by the aircraft's movement through the air are examples of problems created by static electricity. Parts of the aircraft must be "bonded" or joined together to provide a low-resistance (or easy) path for static discharge, and radio parts must

be shielded. Static charges must be considered in the refueling of the aircraft to prevent possible igniting of the fuel, and provision must be made to ground the aircraft structure, either by static-conducting tires or by a grounding wire.

ELECTROMOTIVE FORCE

The flow of electrons from a negative point to a positive point is called an electric current; this current flows because of a difference in electric pressure between the two points.

If an excess of electrons with a negative charge exists at one end of a conductor and a deficiency of electrons with a positive charge at the other, an electrostatic field exists between the two charges. Electrons are repelled from the negatively charged point and are attracted by the positively charged point.

The flow of electrons of electric current can be compared to the flow of water between two interconnected water tanks when a difference of pressure exists between two tanks. Figure 8–12 shows the level of water in tank A to be at a higher level than the water level in tank B. If the valve in the interconnecting line between the tanks is opened, water will flow from tank A into tank B

FIGURE 8–10. Charge on a hollow sphere.

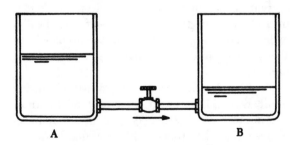

FIGURE 8–12. Difference of pressure.

271

until the level of water is the same in both tanks. It is important to note that it was not the pressure in tank A that caused the water to flow; rather, it was the difference in pressure between tank A and tank B that caused the flow. When the water in the two tanks are at the same level, the flow of water ceases because there is no longer a difference of pressure.

This comparison illustrates the principle that causes the electrons to move, when a proper path is available, from a point of excess electrons to a point deficient in electrons. The force that causes this movement is the potential difference in electrical energy between the two points. This force is called the electrical pressure or the potential difference or the electromotive force (electron-moving force) which can all be considered the same thing. Electromotive force, abbreviated e.m.f., causes current (electrons) to move in an electric path or circuit. The practical unit of measurement of e.m.f., or potential difference, is the volt. The symbol for e.m.f. is the capital letter "E."

If the water pressure in tank A of figure 8–12 is 10 p.s.i. and the pressure in tank B is 2 p.s.i., there is a difference in pressure of 8 p.s.i. Similarly, it can be said that an electromotive force of 8 volts exists between two electrical points. Since potential difference is measured in volts, the word "voltage" can also be used to describe amounts of potential difference. Thus, it is correct to say that the voltage of a certain aircraft battery is 24 volts, another means of indicating that a potential difference of 24 volts exists between two points connected by a conductor.

CURRENT FLOW

Electrons in motion make up an electric current. This electric current is usually refered to as "current" or "current flow," no matter how many electrons are moving. When the current flow is in one direction only, it is called direct current. Later in the study of electrical fundamentals, current that reverses itself periodically, called alternating current, will be discussed. In the present study all references are to direct current.

Since an electric current may consist of varying numbers of electrons, it is important to know the number of electrons flowing in a circuit in a given time. Electrons can be counted by measuring the basic electrical charge on each electron.

FIGURE 8–13.   Electron movement.

Since this charge is very small, a practical unit, the coulomb, is used to measure an amount, or quantity, of electrical charge. The accumulated charge on 6.28 billion billion electrons is called one coulomb. When this quantity of electrons flows past a given point in an electrical circuit, one ampere of current is said to be flowing in the circuit. Current flow is measured in amperes or parts of amperes by an electrical instrument called an ammeter. The symbol used to indicate current in formulas or on schematics is the capital letter "I," which stands for the intensity of current flow.

The drift of free electrons must not be confused with the concept of current flow that approaches the speed of light. When a voltage is applied to a circuit, the free electrons travel but a short distance before colliding with atoms. These collisions usually knock other electrons free from their atoms, and these electrons travel on toward the positive terminal of the wire, colliding with other atoms as they drift at a comparatively slow rate of speed. To understand the almost instantaneous speed of the effect of electric current, it is helpful to visualize a long tube filled with steel balls as shown in figure 8–13.

It can be seen that a ball introduced in one end of the tube, which represents a conductor, will immediately cause a ball to be emitted at the opposite end of the tube. Even if the tube were long enough to reach clear across the country, this effect could still be visualized as being instantaneous. Thus, electric current flow can be viewed as occurring instantaneously, even though it is a result of a comparatively slow drift of electrons.

RESISTANCE

The property of a conductor of electricity that limits or restricts the flow of electric current is called its resistance. Electrical pressure is required to overcome this resistance, which is the attractive force holding the electrons in their orbits. The materials from which electrical conductors are manufactured, usually in the form of extruded wire, are materials that offer very little resistance to current flow. While wire of any size or resistance value may be used, the word "conductor" usually refers to materials which offer low resistance to current flow, and the word "insulator" describes materials that offer high resistance to current. There is no distinct dividing line between conductors and insulators; under the proper conditions, all types of material conduct some current. Materials offering a resistance to current flow midway between the best conductors and the poorest conductors (insulators) are sometimes referred to as "semiconductors," and find their greatest application in the field of transistors.

The best conductors are materials, chiefly metals, which possess a large number of free electrons; conversely, insulators are materials having few free electrons. The best conductors are silver, copper, gold, and aluminum, but some non-metals, such as carbon and water, can be used as conductors. Materials such as rubber, glass, ceramics, and plastics are such poor conductors that they are usually used as insulators. The current flow in some of these materials is so low that it is usually considered zero.

The unit used to measure resistance is called the ohm. The symbol for the ohm is the Greek letter omega(Ω). In mathematical formulas, the capital letter "R" refers to resistance. The resistance of a conductor and the voltage applied to it determine the number of amperes of current flowing through the conductor. Thus, 1 ohm of resistance will limit the current flow to 1 ampere in a conductor to which a voltage of 1 volt is applied.

Factors Affecting Resistance

Among the four major factors affecting the resistance of a conductor, one of the most important is the type of conductor material. It has been pointed out that certain metals are commonly used as conductors because of the large number of free electrons in their outer orbits. Copper is usually considered the best available conductor material, since a copper wire of a particular diameter offers a lower resistance to current flow than an aluminum wire of the same diameter. However, aluminum is much lighter than copper, and for this reason as well as cost considerations, aluminum is often used when the weight factor is important.

A second resistance factor is the length of the conductor. The longer the length of a given

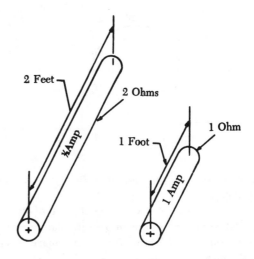

FIGURE 8–14.   Resistance varies with length of conductor.

size of wire, the greater the resistance. Figure 8–14 pictures two wire conductors of different lengths. If 1 volt of electrical pressure is applied across the two ends of the conductor that is 1 foot in length and the resistance to the movement of free electrons is assumed to be 1 ohm, the current flow is limited to 1 ampere. If the same size conductor is doubled in length, the same electrons set in motion by the 1 volt applied now find twice the resistance; consequently, the current flow will be reduced by one-half.

A third factor affecting the resistance of a conductor is cross-sectional area, or the end surface of a conductor. This area may be triangular or even square, but is usually circular. If the cross-sectional area of a conductor is doubled, the resistance to current flow will be reduced in half. This is true because of the increased area in which an electron can move without collision or capture by an atom. Thus, the resistance varies inversely with the cross-sectional area of a conductor.

To compare the resistance of one conductor with that of another having greater cross-sectional area, a standard, or unit, size of conductor must be established. The most convenient unit of measurement of wire diameter is the mil (0.001 of an inch). The most convenient unit of wire length is the foot. Using these standards, the unit of size will be the mil-foot. Thus, a wire will have unit size if it has a diameter of 1 mil and the length of 1 foot. The resistance specified in ohms of a unit conductor of a certain material is called the

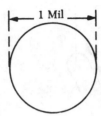

FIGURE 8–15. Circular mil.

specific resistance, or specific resistivity, of the substance.

The square mil is a convenient unit of cross-sectional area for square or rectangular conductors. A square mil is the area of a square, each side of which measures 1 mil.

To compute the cross-sectional area of a conductor in square mils, the length in mils of one side is squared. In the case of a rectangular conductor, the length of one side is multiplied by the length of the other. For example, a common rectangular bus bar (large, special conductor) is ⅜ inch thick and 4 inches wide. The ⅜ inch thickness may be expressed as 0.375 inch. Since 1,000 mils equals 1 inch, the width in inches can be converted to 4,000 mils. The cross-sectional area of the rectangular conductor is .375 × 4,000 or 1,500 square mils.

More common than the square or rectangular shape is the circular conductor. Because the diameters of round conductors may be only a fraction of an inch, it is convenient to express these diameters in mils to avoid the use of decimals. The circular mil is the standard unit of wire cross-sectional area used in American and English wire tables. Thus, the diameter of a wire that is 0.025 inch may be more conveniently expressed as 25 mils.

Figure 8–15 illustrates a circle having a diameter of 1 mil. The area in circular mils is obtained by squaring the diameter measured in mils. Thus, a wire with a diameter of 25 mils has an area of 25 squared, or 25 × 25, or 625 circular mils.

In comparing square and round conductors, it should be noted that the circular mil is a smaller unit of area than the square mil. To determine the circular-mil area when the square-mil area is known, the area in square mil is divided by 0.7854. Conversely, to find the square-mil area when the circular-mil area is known, the area in circular mils is multiplied by 0.7854.

Wires are manufactured in sizes numbered according to a table known as the American wire gage (AWG). Wire diameters become smaller as the gage numbers become larger. This table is available to aviation technicians for reference, not only on wire size but also resistance and cross-sectional area.

The last major factor influencing the resistance of a conductor is temperature. Although some substances, such as carbon, show a decrease in resistance as the ambient (surrounding) temperature increases, most materials used as conductors increase in resistance as temperature increases. The resistance of a few alloys, such as constantan and maganin, change very little as the temperature changes. The amount of increase in the resistance of a 1-ohm sample of a conductor per degree rise in temperature above 0° Centigrade (C.), the assumed standard, is called the temperature coefficient of resistance. For each metal this is a different value; for example, for copper the value is approximately 0.00427 ohm. Thus, a copper wire having a resistance of 50 ohms at a temperature of 0° C. will have an increase in resistance of 50 × 0.00427, or 0.214 ohm, for each degree rise in temperature above 0° C. The temperature coefficient of resistance must be considered where there is an appreciable change in temperature of a conductor during operation. Charts listing the temperature coefficient of resistance for different materials are available.

BASIC CIRCUIT COMPONENTS AND SYMBOLS

An electrical circuit consists of: (1) A source of electrical pressure or e.m.f.; (2) resistance in the form of an energy-consuming electrical device; and (3) conductors, usually in the form of copper or aluminum wires, to provide a path for electron flow from the negative side of the power source through the resistance and back to the positive side of the power source. Figure 8–16 is a pictorial representation of a practical circuit.

This circuit contains a source of e.m.f. (storage battery), a conductor to provide a path for the flow of electrons from the negative to the positive terminal of the battery, and a power-dissipating device (lamp) to limit the current flow. Without some resistance in the circuit the potential difference between the two terminals would be neutralized very quickly or the flow of electrons would become so heavy that the conductor would become overheated and burn.

At the same time that the lamp acts as a

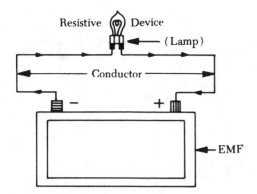

FIGURE 8–16.   A practical circuit.

current-limiting resistance in the circuit, it is also accomplishing the desired funtion of creating light.

Figure 8–17 is a schematic representation of figure 8–16, in which symbols rather than pictures are used to represent the circuit components.

All components used in electrical circuits are represented in drawings, blueprints, and illustrations in schematic form by symbols. The components commonly used in basic circuits, together with their schematic symbols, are discussed to provide the necessary background for interpretation of circuit diagrams.

Source of Power

The source of power, or applied voltage, for a circuit may be any one of the common sources of e.m.f , such as a mechanical source (generator), a chemical source (battery), a photoelectric source (light), or a thermal source (heat). Figure 8–18 illustrates two schematic symbols for a generator. Most electrical components have only one symbol; however, in the case of the generator and a few others, more than one symbol has been developed to represent a single electrical component. These symbols are normally very similar

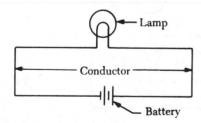

FIGURE 8–17.   Circuit components represented by symbols.

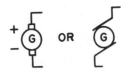

FIGURE 8–18.   Electrical symbols for a d.c. generator.

in design. Figure 8–18 illustrates that the two symbols for a generator are so nearly alike there is little chance for confusion.

Another common source for the voltage applied to a circuit is the battery, a chemical source of power. Figure 8–19 shows symbols for a single-cell battery and a three-cell battery.

The following statements are true of battery symbols used in schematic diagrams (refer to figure 8–19):

(1) The shorter vertical line represents the negative terminal.
(2) The longer vertical line is the positive terminal.
(3) The horizontal lines represent the conductors connected to the terminals.
(4) Each cell of a battery has one negative and one positive terminal.

Dry cell batteries, such as those used to operate flashlights, are called primary cells. The larger storage batteries containing several primary cells are called secondary cells. The schematic symbol for the primary cell is shown in figure 8–20. The center rod is the positive terminal of the cell, and the case of the cell is the negative terminal. When more than 1.5 volts are required, cells are connected in series. To connect the cells in series, the negative terminal of each cell is connected to the positive terminal of the succeeding cell as shown in A of figure 8–21. The voltage is then equal to the sum of the voltages of the individual cells. Since the same current must flow through each cell in succession, the current that the battery can supply is equal to the current rating of a single cell. Thus, a battery composed of cells in series provides a higher voltage, but not a greater current capacity.

FIGURE 8–19.   One-cell and three-cell battery symbols.

FIGURE 8–20.   Schematic symbol for a dry cell battery.

To obtain a greater current flow than one cell is able to supply, the cells are connected in parallel. The total current available is equal to the sum of the individual currents from each cell, but the voltage is equal to the voltage of a single cell. To connect cells in parallel, all positive terminals are connected together and all negative terminals are connected together. In A of figure 8–22, a schematic diagram of cells connected in parallel is shown. B of figure 8–22 illustrates the symbol used to represent this group of cells connected in parallel. Each cell must have the same voltage; otherwise, a cell with higher voltage will force current through the lower voltage cells.

Another method of arranging cells is to connect them in series-parallel. In this method, shown in figure 8–23, two groups of cells are connected in series, and then these two groups are connected in parallel. This arrangement provides both a greater voltage and a greater current output.

Conductor

Another basic requirement of a circuit is the conductor or wire connecting the various electrical components. This is always represented in schematic diagrams as a line. Figure 8–24 illustrates

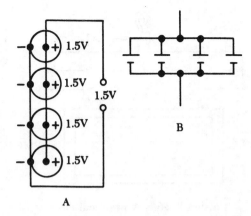

FIGURE 8–22.   Cells connected in parallel.

two different symbols used to indicate wires (conductors) that cross but are not connected. While either of these symbols may be used, the symbol shown in B of figure 8–24 is now found more often, since it is less likely to be misinterpreted.

Figure 8–25 illustrates the two different symbols used to represent connected wires. Either of these two symbols may be used, but it is important that no conflict exists with the symbol selected to represent unconnected wires. For example, if the symbol for unconnected wires shown in A of figure 8–24 is selected, the symbol for connected wires must be that shown in A of figure 8–25.

A circuit component found in all practical circuits is the fuse. This is a safety or protective device used to prevent damage to the conductors and circuit components by excessive current flow.

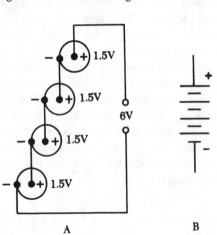

FIGURE 8–21.   Schematic diagram and symbol of cells connected in series.

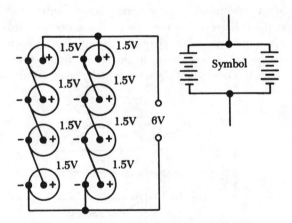

FIGURE 8–23.   Cells in series-parallel arrangement.

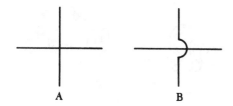

FIGURE 8–24. Unconnected crossed-over wires.

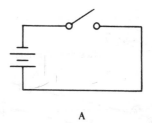

A

B

FIGURE 8–27. Open and closed switch symbols.

The schematic symbol for a fuse is shown in figure 8–26.

Another symbol found in basic circuit schematics is the symbol for the switch, shown in figure 8–27. The open switch symbol is shown in A of figure 8–27, and in B of figure 8–27 the closed switch symbol is shown connected in a circuit. There are many different types of switches, but these symbols can represent all but the most complex.

Figure 8–28 illustrates the symbol for "ground" or the common reference point in a circuit. This is the reference point from which most circuit

connected across (in parallel with) a circuit component, never in a series arrangement.

Resistors

The last of the basic component requirements of a complete circuit can be grouped under the

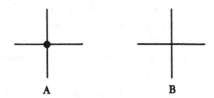

A

B

FIGURE 8–25. Connected wires.

FIGURE 8–28. Ground or common reference point symbol.

voltages are measured. This point is normally considered to be at zero potential.

Sometimes meters for measuring current flow or voltage are temporarily connected to the circuit, and in some circuits these meters are permanent components. In figure 8–29, the symbols for an ammeter and a voltmeter are used in a simple circuit. It is important that these components be connected properly. The ammeter, which measures current flow, is always connected in series with the power source and circuit resistances. The voltmeter, which measures the voltage across a circuit component, is always

single heading of resistance. Resistance in a practical circuit may take the form of any electrical device, such as a motor or a lamp, which uses electrical power and produces some useful function. On the other hand, the resistance of a circuit may be in the form of resistors inserted in the circuit to limit current flow.

FIGURE 8–26. Schematic symbol for a fuse.

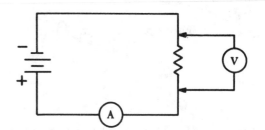

FIGURE 8–29. Ammeter and voltmeter symbols.

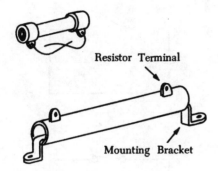

FIGURE 8–30.   Fixed wire-wound resistors.

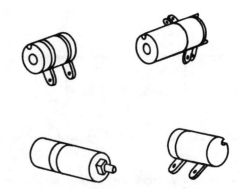

FIGURE 8–32.   Precision wire-wound resistors.

A wide variety of resistors are available. Some have a fixed ohmic value and others are variable. They are manufactured from special resistance wire, graphite (carbon), or metal film. Wire-wound resistors control large currents, while carbon resistors control relatively small currents. Wire-wound resistors are constructed by winding resistance wire on a porcelain base, attaching the wire ends to metal terminals, and coating the wire for protection and heat conduction. (See figure 8–30.)

Wire-wound resistors are available with fixed taps which can be used to change the resistance value in increments or steps. They may also be provided with sliders which can be adjusted to change the resistance to any fraction of the total resistance. (See figure 8–31.) Still another type is the precision wire-wound resistors (figure 8–32) made of manganin wire. They are used where the resistance value must be very accurate.

Carbon resistors are manufactured from a rod of compressed graphite and binding material, with wire leads, called "pigtail" leads, attached to each end of the resistor. (See figure 8–33.)

Variable resistors are used to vary the resistance while the equipment is in operation. Wire-wound variable resistors control large currents, and carbon variable resistors control small currents. Wire-wound variable resistors are constructed by winding resistance wire on a porcelain or bakelite circular form. A contact arm which can be adjusted to any position on the circular form by means of a rotating shaft is used to select resistance settings. (See figure 8–34.)

Carbon variable resistors (see figure 8–35), used to control small currents, are constructed of a carbon compound deposited on a fiber disk. A contact on a movable arm varies the resistance as the arm shaft is turned.

The two symbols used on a schematic or circuit diagram to represent variable resistors are shown in figure 8–36.

The schematic symbol for a fixed resistor is shown in A of figure 8–37. A variation of this

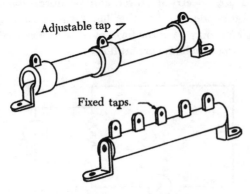

FIGURE 8–31.   Wire-wound resistors with fixed and adjustable taps.

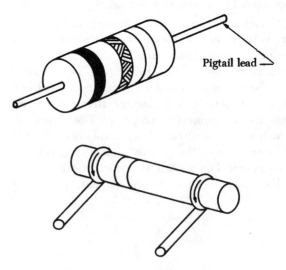

FIGURE 8–33.   Carbon resistors.

278

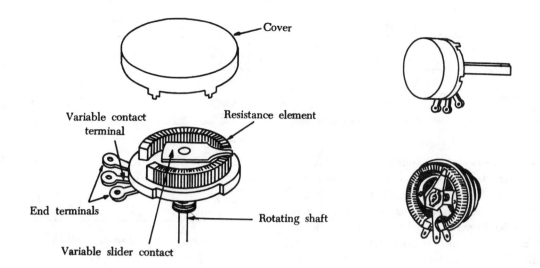

FIGURE 8–34. Wire-wound variable resistor.

symbol represents the tapped resistor, which has a fixed value but is provided with taps from which selected amounts of resistance can be obtained. (See B of figure 8—37.)

Resistor Color Code

The resistance value of any resistor can be measured by using an ohmmeter. But this is seldom necessary. Most wire-wound resistors have their resistance value in ohms printed on the body of the resistor. Many carbon resistors are similarly marked, but are often mounted in such a manner that it is difficult or impossible to read the resistance value. Additionally, heat often discolors the resistor body, making the printed marking illegible, and many carbon resistors are so small that a printed marking cannot be used. Thus, a color code marking is used to identify the resistance value of carbon resistors.

There is only one color code for carbon resistors, but there are two systems or methods used to paint this color code on resistors. One is the body-end-dot system, and the other is the end-to-center band system.

In each color code system, three colors are used to indicate the resistance value in ohms, and a fourth color is sometimes used to indicate the tolerance of the resistor. By reading the colors in the correct order and by substituting numbers from the color code, the resistance value of a resistor can be determined.

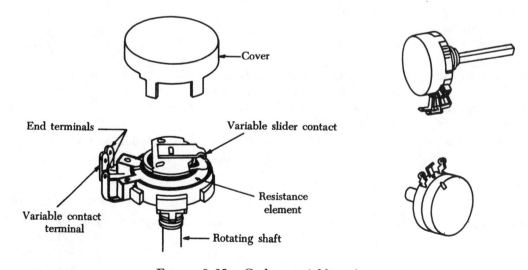

FIGURE 8–35. Carbon variable resistor.

279

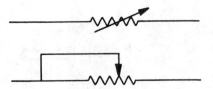

FIGURE 8–36. Symbols for variable resistors.

It is very difficult to manufacture a resistor to an exact standard of ohmic values. Fortunately, most circuit requirements are not extremely critical. For many uses the actual resistance in ohms can be 20 percent higher or lower than the value marked on the resistor without causing difficulty. The percentage variation between the marked value and the actual value of a resistor is known as the "tolerance" of a resistor. A resistor coded for a 5-percent tolerance will not be more than 5 percent higher or lower than the value indicated by the color code.

The resistor color code (see figure 8–38) is made up of a group of colors, numbers, and tolerance values. Each color is represented by a number and in most cases by a tolerance value.

When the color code is used with the end-to-center band marking system, the resistor is normally marked with bands of color at one end of the resistor. The body or base color of the resistor has nothing to do with the color code, and in no way indicates a resistance value. To prevent confusion, this body will never be the same color as any of the bands indicating resistance value.

When the end-to-center band marking system is used, the resistor will be marked by either three or four bands. The first color band (nearest the end of the resistor) will indicate the first digit in the numerical resistance value. This band will never be gold or silver in color.

The second color band (refer to figure 8–39) will always indicate the second digit of ohmic value. It will never be gold or silver in color. The third color band indicates the number of zeros to be added to the two digits derived from the first and

Resistor color code		
Color	Number	Tolerance
Black	0	....
Brown	1	1%
Red	2	2%
Orange	3	3%
Yellow	4	4%
Green	5	5%
Blue	6	6%
Violet	7	7%
Gray	8	8%
White	9	9%
Gold	....	5%
Silver	....	10%
No color	....	20%

FIGURE 8–38.   Resistor color code.

second bands, except in the following two cases:

(1)   If the third band is gold in color, the first two digits must be multiplied by 10 percent.

(2)   If the third band is silver in color, the first two digits must be multiplied by 1 percent.

If there is a fourth color band, it is used as a multiplier for percentage of tolerance, as indicated in the color code chart in figure 8-38. If there is no fourth band, the tolerance is understood to be 20 percent.

Figure 8–39 illustrates the rules for reading the resistance value of a resistor marked with the end-to-center band system. This resistor is marked with three bands of color, which must be read from the end toward the center.

These are the values that should be obtained:

Color	Numerical Value	Significance
1st band—Red	2	1st digit
2nd band—Green	5	2nd digit
3rd band—Yellow	4	No. of zeros to add

There is no fourth color band, so the tolerance is understood to be 20 percent. 20 percent of 250,000 = 50,000.

Since the 20 percent tolerance is plus or minus,

Maximum resistance = 250,000 + 50,000
= 300,000 ohms
Minimum resistance = 250,000 − 50,000
= 200,000 ohms.

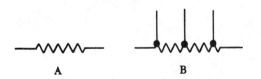

FIGURE 8–37.   Symbols for fixed resistors.

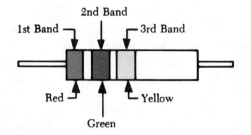

FIGURE 8–39. End-to-center band marking.

Figure 8–40 contains a resistor with another set of colors. This resistor code should be read as follows:

The resistance of this resistor is 86,000 ±10 percent ohms. The maximum resistance is 94,600 ohms and the minimum resistance is 77,400 ohms.

As another example, the resistance of the resistor in figure 8–41 is 960 ± 5 percent ohms. The maximum resistance is 1,008 ohms, and the minimum resistance is 912 ohms.

Sometimes circuit considerations dictate that the tolerance must be smaller than 20 percent. Figure 8–42 shows an example of a resistor with a 2 percent tolerance. The resistance value of this resistor is 2,500 ± 2 percent ohms. The maximum resistance is 2,550 ohms, and the minimum resistance is 2,450 ohms.

Figure 8–43 contains an example of a resistor with a black third color band. The color code value of black is zero, and the third band indicates the number of zeros to be added to the first two digits.

In this case, a zero number of zeros must be added to the first two digits; therefore, no zeros are added. Thus, the resistance value is 10 ± 1 percent ohms. The maximum resistance is 10.1 ohms, and the minimum resistance is 9.9 ohms.

There are two exceptions to the rule stating the third color band indicates the number of zeros. The first of these exceptions is illustrated in figure 8–44. When the third band is gold in color,

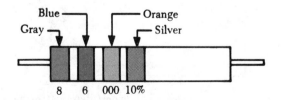

FIGURE 8-40. Resistor color code example.

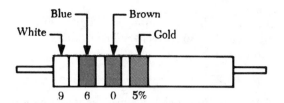

FIGURE 8-41. Resistor color code example.

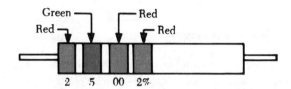

FIGURE 8-42. Resistor with 2 percent tolerance.

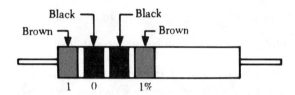

FIGURE 8-43. Resistor with black third color band.

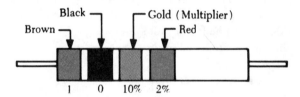

FIGURE 8-44. Resistor with a gold third band.

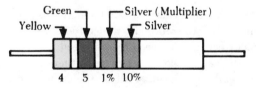

FIGURE 8-45. Resistor with a silver third band.

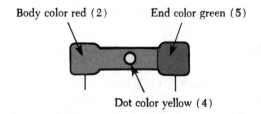

FIGURE 8-46. Resistor coded with body-end-dot system.

it indicates that the first two digits must be multiplied by 10 percent. The value of this resistor is

$$10 \times .10 \pm 2\% = 1 \pm .02 \text{ ohms.}$$

When the third band is silver, as is the case in figure 8–45, the first two digits must be multiplied by 1 percent. The value of the resistor is .45 ± 10 percent ohms.

Body-End-Dot System

The body-end-dot system of marking is rarely used today. A few examples will explain it. The location of the colors has the following significance:

Body color . . . . 1st digit of ohmic value

End color . . . . 2nd digit of ohmic value

Dot color . . . . Number of zeros to be added

If only one end of the resistor is painted, it indicates the second figure of the resistor value, and the tolerance will be 20 percent. The other two tolerance values are gold (5 percent) and silver (10 percent). The opposite end of the resistor will be painted to indicate a tolerance other than 20 percent. Figure 8–46 shows a resistor coded by the body-end-dot system.
The values are as follows:

Body—1st digit—2.

End—2nd digit—5.

Dot—No. of zeros—0000 (4).

The resistor value is 250,000 ± 20 percent ohms. The tolerance is understood to be 20 percent because no second dot is used.

If the same color is used more than once, the body, end, and dot may all be the same color, or any two may be the same; but the color code is used in exactly the same way. For example, a 33,000-ohm resistor will be entirely orange.

OHM'S LAW

The most important law applicable to the study of electricity is Ohm's law. This law, which outlines the relationship between voltage, current, and resistance in an electrical circuit, was first stated by the German physicist, George Simon Ohm (1787–1854). This law applies to all direct-current circuits. In a modified form it may be applied to the alternating circuits to be studied later in this text. Ohm's experiments showed that current flow in an electrical circuit is directly proportional to the amount of voltage applied to the circuit. Stated in different words, this law says that as the voltage increases, the current increases; and when the voltage decreases, the current flow decreases. It should be added that this relationship is true only if the resistance in the circuit remains constant. For it can be readily seen that if the resistance changes, current also changes.

Ohm's law may be expressed as an equation, as follows:

$$I = \frac{E}{R}.$$

Where I is current in amperes, E is the potential difference measured in volts, and R is the resistance measured in ohms (designated by the Greek letter omega, whose symbol is Ω).

If any two of these circuit quantities are known, the third may be found by simple algebraic transposition.

The circuit shown in figure 8–47 contains a voltage source of 24 volts and a resistance of 3 ohms.

If an ammeter is inserted in the circuit, as shown in figure 8–47, the intensity of current flowing in the circuit can be read directly. Assuming that no ammeter is available, the intensity of current flow can be determined by using Ohm's law as follows:

$$I = \frac{E}{R} \qquad I = \frac{24 \text{ V}}{3 \Omega} \qquad I = 8 \text{ amperes.}$$

Some features of figure 8–47 that are typical of all electrical circuits drawn in schematic form should be reviewed. The electrical pressure or potential difference appiled to the circuit is rep-

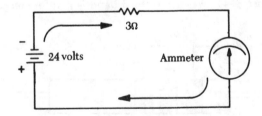

FIGURE 8–47.   Electrical circuit demonstrating Ohm's law.

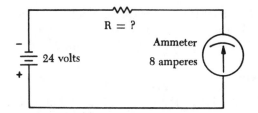

FIGURE 8–48.   A circuit with unknown resistance.

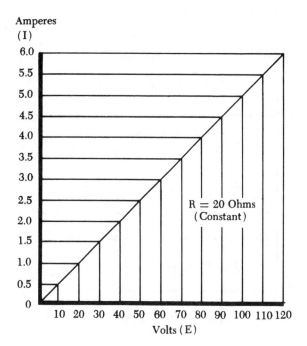

FIGURE 8–50.   Voltage vs. current in a constant-resistance circuit.

resented in schematic form by the symbol for a battery. The negative sign is located near one side to indicate the negative terminal of the source, or battery. The opposite side is marked positive with a + symbol. Arrows are sometimes used to indicate the direction of current flow from the negative terminal, through the conducting wires and other circuit devices, to the positive terminal of the source.

Figure 8–48 shows that the values of voltage and current are known. To find the quantity of resistance in the circuit, Ohm's law can be transposed to solve for R.

Transposing the basic formula $I = \dfrac{E}{R}$ to $R = \dfrac{E}{I}$,

and substituting the known circuit values in the

equation, $R = \dfrac{24 \text{ volts}}{8 \text{ amperes}} = 3$ ohms, or 3 Ω.

Ohm's law can also be transposed to determine the voltage applied to a circuit when current flow and resistance are known, as shown in figure 8–49.

In this circuit the unknown circuit quantity, the voltage, is represented by the symbol E. The value of resistance is 3 ohms, and the current flow is 8 amperes. (The word amperes is often shortened to "amps.")

Transposing Ohm's law from its basic formula, the equation to solve for E becomes $E = I \times R$.

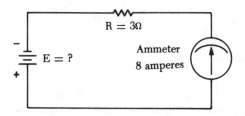

FIGURE 8–49.   Circuit with unknown voltage.

Substituting the known values in the equation,

$$E = 8 \times 3$$

$$E = 24 \text{ volts or 24 V.}$$

The relationship between the various circuit quantities can be further demonstrated if the resistance in a circuit is held constant. In such a case, the current will increase or decrease in direct proportion to the increase or decrease of voltage applied to the circuit. For example, if the voltage applied to a circuit is 120 volts and the resistance of the circuit is 20 ohms, the current flow will be $\dfrac{120}{20}$, or 6 amperes. If this resistance remains constant at 20 ohms, a graph of voltage-current relationship, as shown in figure 8–50, can be ploted.

The relationship between voltage and current in this example shows voltage plotted horizontally along the X axis in values from 0 to 120 volts, and the corresponding values of current are plotted vertically in values from 0 to 6.0 amperes along the Y axis. A straight line drawn through all the points where the voltage and current lines meet represents the equation $I = \dfrac{E}{20}$

and is called a linear relationship. The constant,

283

$$\text{Current} = \frac{\text{Electromotive force}}{\text{Resistance}}$$

$$I = \frac{E}{R} \qquad \text{Amperes} = \frac{\text{Volts}}{\text{Ohms}}$$

$$\text{Resistance} = \frac{\text{Electromotive force}}{\text{Current}}$$

$$R = \frac{E}{I} \qquad \text{Ohms} = \frac{\text{Volts}}{\text{Amperes}}$$

Electromotive force = current × resistance

$$E = IR \qquad \text{Volts} = \text{amperes} \times \text{ohms}$$

FIGURE 8–51.   Ohm's law.

20, represents the resistance, which is assumed not to change in this example. This graph represents an important characteristic of the basic law, that the current varies directly with the applied voltage if the resistance remains constant.

The basic equations derived from Ohm's law are summarized, together with the units of measurements of circuit quantities, in figure 8–51.

The various equations which may be derived by transposing the basic law can be easily obtained by using the triangles in figure 8–52.

The triangles containing E, I, and R are divided into two parts, with E above the line and $I \times R$ below it. To determine an unknown circuit quantity when the other two are known, cover the unknown quantity with a thumb. The location of the remaining uncovered letters in the triangle will indicate the mathematical operation to be performed. For example, to find I, refer to (a) of figure 8–52, and cover I with the thumb. The uncovered letters indicate that E is to be divided by R, or $I = \frac{E}{R}$. To find R, refer to (b) of figure 8–52, and cover R with the thumb. The result indicates that E is to be divided by I, or $R = \frac{E}{I}$. To find E, refer to (c) of figure 8–52, and cover E with the thumb. The result indicates I is to be multiplied by R, or $E = I \times R$.

This chart is useful when learning to use Ohm's law. It should be used to supplement the beginner's knowledge of the algebraic method.

Power

In addition to the volt, ampere, and ohm, there is one other unit frequently used in electrical circuit calculations. This is the unit of power.

The unit used to measure power in d.c. electrical circuits is the watt. Power is defined as the rate of doing work and is equal to the product of the voltage and current in a d.c. circuit. When the current in amperes (I) is multiplied by e.m.f. in volts (E), the result is power measured in watts (P). This indicates that the electrical power delivered to a circuit varies directly with the applied voltage and current flowing in the circuit. Expressed as an equation, this becomes

$$P = IE.$$

This equation may be transposed to determine any one of the three circuit quantities as long as the other two are known. Thus, if the power is read directly from a wattmeter and the voltage is measured with a voltmeter, the intensity of the current (I) flowing in the circuit can be determined by transposing the basic equation to $I = \frac{P}{E}$.

Similarly, the voltage (E) can be found by transposing the basic power formula to $E = \frac{P}{I}$.

Since some of the values used to determine the power delivered to a circuit are the same as those used in Ohm's law, it is possible to substitute Ohm's law values for equivalents in the power formula.

In Ohm's law, $I = \frac{E}{R}$. If this value $\frac{E}{R}$ is substituted for I in the power formula, it becomes

$$P = I \times E; \quad P = E \times \frac{E}{R}; \quad \text{or } P = \frac{E^2}{R}.$$

This equation, $P = \frac{E^2}{R}$, illustrates that the power in watts delivered to a circuit varies directly with the square of the applied voltage and inversely with the circuit resistance.

284

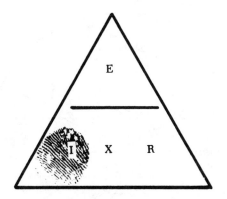

To find I (amperes) place thumb over I and divide E by R as indicated.

(a)

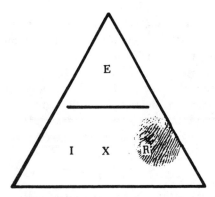

To find R (ohms) place thumb over R and divide as indicated.

(b)

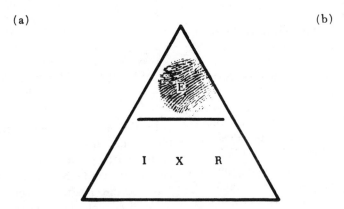

To find E (volts) place thumb over X and multiply as indicated.

(c)

E = volts   I = amperes   R = ohms

FIGURE 8–52.   Ohm's law chart.

The watt is named for James Watt, the inventor of the steam engine. Watt devised an experiment to measure the power of a horse in order to find a means of measuring the mechanical power of his steam engine. One horsepower is required to move 33,000 pounds 1 foot in 1 minute. Since power is the rate of doing work, it is equivalent to the work divided by time. Stated as a formula, this is

$$\text{Power} = \frac{33{,}000 \text{ ft.-lb.}}{60 \text{ sec. (1 min.)}}, \text{ or}$$

$$P = 550 \text{ ft.-lb./sec.}$$

Electrical power can be rated in a similar manner. For example, an electric motor rated as a 1-horsepower motor requires 746 watts of electrical energy. But the watt is a relatively small unit of power. Much more common is the kilowatt or 1,000 watts. (The prefix kilo means 1,000.) In measuring amounts of electrical energy consumed, the kilowatt hour is used. For example, if a 100-watt bulb consumes electrical energy for 20 hours,

it has used 2,000 watt hours or 2 kilowatt hours of electrical energy.

Electrical power that is lost in the form of heat when current flows through an electrical device is often referred to as power loss. This heat is usually dissipated into the surrounding air and serves no useful purpose, except when used for heating. Since all conductors possess some resistance, circuits are designed to reduce these losses. Referring again to the basic power formula, $P = I \times E$, it is possible to substitute the Ohm's law values for E in the power formula to obtain a power formula that directly reflects the power losses in a resistance.

$$P = I \times E; E = I \times R.$$

Substituting the Ohm's law value for E ($I \times R$) in the power formula,

$$P = I \times I \times R.$$

Collecting terms, this gives,

$$P = I^2 R.$$

From this equation, it can be seen that the power in watts in a circuit varies as the square of the circuit current in amperes and varies directly with the circuit resistance in ohms.

Finally, the power delivered to a circuit can be expressed as a function of current and resistance by transposing the power equation $P = I^2 R$. Transposing to solve for current gives

$$I^2 = \frac{P}{R}$$

and by extracting the square root of both sides of the equation, $I = \sqrt{\frac{P}{R}}$.

Thus, the current through a 500-watt, 100-ohm load (resistance) is as follows:

$$I = \sqrt{\frac{P}{R}} = \frac{500}{100} = 2.24 \text{ amperes.}$$

The electrical equations derived from Ohm's law and the basic power formula do not reveal all about the behavior of circuits. They do indicate the numerical relation between the volt, ampere, ohm, and watt. Figure 8–53 provides a summary of all the possible transpositions of these formulas in a 12-segment circle.

SERIES D. C. CIRCUITS

The series circuit is the most basic of electrical circuits. All other types of circuits are elaborations or combinations of series circuits. Figure 8–54 is an example of a simple series circuit. It is a circuit because it provides a complete path for current to flow from the negative to the positive terminal of the battery. It is a series circuit because there is only one possible path in which current can flow, as indicated by the arrows showing the direction of electron movement. It is also called a series circuit because current must pass through the circuit components, the battery and the resistor, one after the other, or "in series."

The circuit shown in figure 8–55 contains the basic components required for any circuit: a source of power (battery), a load or current-limiting resistance (resistor), and a conductor (wire). Most practical circuits contain at least two other items: a control device (switch) and a safety device (fuse). With all five components in the circuit it would appear as shown in figure 8–55, which is a d.c. series circuit.

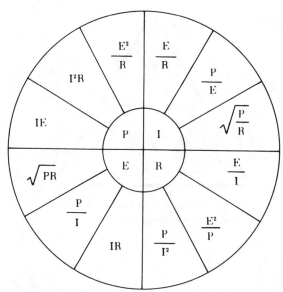

FIGURE 8–53. Summary of basic equations using the volt, ampere, ohm, and watt.

In the d.c. or direct-current circuit, current flows in one direction from the negative terminal of the battery through the switch (which must be closed) through the load resistance and the fuse to the positive terminal of the battery.

To discuss the behavior of electric current in a d.c. series circuit, figure 8–56 is redrawn in figure 8–57 to include three ammeters and two resistors. Since an ammeter measures the intensity of current flow, three have been located in the circuit to measure the current flowing at various points in the circuit.

With the switch closed to complete the circuit, all three ammeters will indicate the same amount of current. This is an important characteristic of all series circuits: No matter how many components are included in a series circuit, the current is the same intensity throughout the circuit. While it is true that an increase in the number of circuit components will increase the resistance to current flow in the circuit, whatever the value of current flowing in the circuit, it will be the same value at all points in the circuit.

In figure 8–56, the current through resistor R_1 is labeled I_1 and the current through resistor R_2 is labeled I_2. If the total current in the circuit is I_T, the formula describing the current flow is,

$$I_T = I_1 = I_2.$$

If the number of resistors is increased to five, the formula will be

$$I_T = I_1 = I_2 = I_3 = I_4 = I_5.$$

286

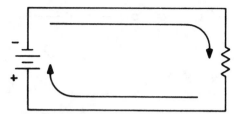

FIGURE 8–54. A series circuit.

Without indicating how much current is flowing, it will always be true that the current through any resistor in a series circuit will be the same as that through any other resistor.

Figure 8–57 is a series circuit containing two resistances. In order to determine the amount of current flow in this circuit, it is necessary to know how much resistance or opposition the current flow will encounter. Thus, the second characteristic of series circuits is: Total resistance in a series circuit is the sum of the separate resistances in the circuit. Stated as a formula, this becomes

$$R_T = R_1 + R_2.$$

In figure 8–57, this is

$$R_T = R_1 \ (5 \ \Omega) + R_2 \ (10 \ \Omega) \ \text{or}$$

$$R_T = 5 + 10 = 15 \ \Omega.$$

The total resistance of the circuit in figure 8–57 is 15 ohms. It is important to remeber that, if the circuit were altered to include 10, 20, or even 100 resistors, the total resistance would still be the sum of all the separate resistances. It is also true that there is a certain negligible resistance in the battery, as well as in the fuse and the switch. These small values of resistance will not be considered in determining the value of current flow in this circuit.

The Ohm's law formula for finding current is $I = E/R$. Since the battery voltage is 30 volts and the total circuit resistance is 15 ohms, the equation becomes

$$I = \frac{30 \ V}{15 \ \Omega} = 2 \ \text{amperes}.$$

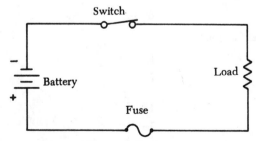

FIGURE 8–55. A d.c. series circuit.

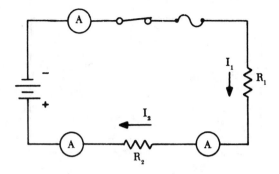

FIGURE 8–56. Current flow in a series circuit.

The current flow is 2 amperes (sometimes the word amperes is shortened to amps), and this value of current is everywhere in the circuit.

To consider what effect a change in resistance will have on current flow when the voltage remains constant, the total resistance is doubled to 30 ohms. Using Ohm's law

$$I = \frac{E}{R}, \ I = \frac{30 \ V}{30 \ \Omega} = 1 \ \text{ampere}.$$

It can be seen that current will be reduced to half its former value when resistance is doubled. On the other hand, if voltage remains constant, and resistance is reduced to half its former value the current will double its original value.

$$I = \frac{E}{R} = I = \frac{30 \ V}{7.5 \ \Omega} = 4 \ \text{amperes}.$$

Thus, if voltage remains constant and resistance increases, current must decrease. Conversely, if resistance decreases, current must increase.

However, if resistance is held constant and voltage is doubled, the current flow will double its original value. If the voltage applied to the circuit in figure 8–58 is doubled to 60 volts and the original value of resistance is maintained at

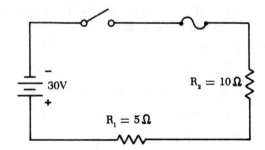

FIGURE 8–57. A series circuit with two resistors.

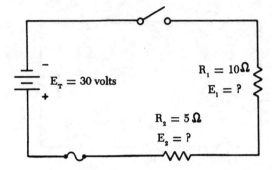

FIGURE 8–58. Voltage drops in a circuit.

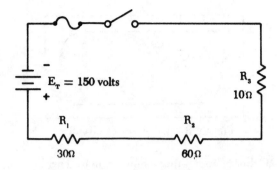

FIGURE 8–59. Applying Ohm's law.

15 ohms,

$$I = \frac{E}{R} = \frac{60\ V}{15\ \Omega} = 4\ \text{amperes},$$

and if voltage is reduced to half its original value, with resistance constant, current will decrease to half its original value.

$$I = \frac{E}{R} = \frac{15\ V}{15\ \Omega} = 1\ \text{ampere}.$$

Thus, if resistance remains constant, and voltage increases, current must also increase. If voltage decreases, current decreases also.

It is important to distinguish between the terms "voltage" and "voltage drop" in discussing series circuits. Voltage drop refers to the loss in electrical pressure caused by forcing electrons through a resistance. In figure 8–58, the applied voltage (the battery) is 30 volts and is labeled E_T.

Since there are two resistances in the circuit, there will be two separate voltage drops. These two voltage drops will be the loss in electrical pressure used to force electrons through the resistances. The amount of electrical pressure required to force a given number of electrons through a resistance is proportional to the size of the resistance. Thus, the voltage drop across R_1 will be twice that across R_2 since R_1 has two times the resistance value of R_2. The drop across R_1 is labeled E_1, and that across R_2 is E_2. The current, I, is the same throughout the circuit.

Using:

$$E = IR \qquad\qquad E_2 = IR_2$$
$$E_1 = IR_1 \qquad\quad E_2 = 2a \times 5$$
$$E_1 = 2a \times 10 \qquad E_2 = 10\ V.$$
$$E_1 = 20\ V$$

If the voltage drops (used) across the two resistors are added (10 V + 20 V), a value equal to the applied voltage, 30 volts, is obtained. This confirms the basic formula for series circuits:

$$E_T = E_1 + E_2.$$

In any d.c. series circuit, a missing quantity such as voltage, resistance, or current can be calculated by using Ohm's law if any two of the quantities are known.

Figure 8–59 is a series circuit containing three known values of resistance and an applied voltage of 150 volts. Using these values, the unknown circuit quantities can be determined by applying Ohm's law as follows:

$$R_1 = 30\ \Omega$$
$$R_2 = 60\ \Omega$$
$$R_3 = 10\ \Omega$$
$$R_T = \underline{\hspace{2cm}}$$
$$I_T = \underline{\hspace{2cm}}$$
$$E_{R_1} = \underline{\hspace{2cm}}$$
$$E_{R_2} = \underline{\hspace{2cm}}$$
$$E_{R_3} = \underline{\hspace{2cm}}$$

Total resistances:

$$R_T = R_1 + R_2 + R_3$$
$$= 30 + 60 + 10$$
$$= 100\ \Omega.$$

Total Current:

$$I_T = \frac{E_T}{R_T}$$
$$= \frac{150\ V}{100\ \Omega}$$
$$= 1.5\ \text{amperes}.$$

288

Voltage Drops:

$$E = IR$$

$$E_{R_1} = I_T \times R_1$$
$$= 1.5 \text{ amps} \times 30$$
$$= 45 \text{ V.}$$

$$E_{R_2} = I_T \times R_2$$
$$= 1.5 \text{ amps} \times 60$$
$$= 90 \text{ V.}$$

$$E_{R_3} = I_T \times R_3$$
$$= 1.5 \text{ amps} \times 10$$
$$= 15 \text{ V.}$$

Do these values for voltage drops equal the applied voltage?

$$E_T = E_{R_1} + E_{R_2} + E_{R_3}$$

$$E_T = 150 \text{ volts}$$

$$150 \text{ V} = 45 \text{ V} + 90 \text{ V} + 15 \text{ V.}$$

The sum of the voltage drops equals the applied voltage.

Kirchhoff Laws

In 1847, a German physicist, G. R. Kirchhoff, elaborated on Ohm's law and developed two statements that are known as Kirchhoff's laws for current and voltage. An understanding of these laws enables the aircraft technician to gain a better understanding of the behavior of electricity. Using Kirchhoff's laws, it is possible to find: (1) The current in each branch of a network circuit when both the resistance and the electromotive force in each branch are known, or (2) the electromotive force in each branch when both the resistance of, and the current in, each branch are known. These laws are stated as follows:

Current Law—The algebraic sum of the currents at any junction of conductors in a circuit is zero. This means that the amount of current flowing away from a point in a circuit is equal to the amount flowing to that point.

Voltage Law—The algebraic sum of the applied voltage and the voltage drop around any closed circuit is zero, which means that the voltage drop around any closed circuit is equal to the applied voltage.

When applying Kirchhoff's laws, use the follow-

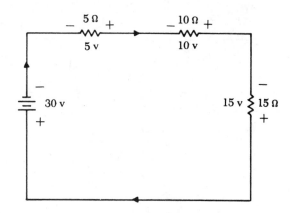

FIGURE 8–60. Polarity of voltage drops.

ing procedures to simplify the work:

1. When the direction of current is not apparent, assume a direction of flow. If the assumption is wrong, the answer will be numerically correct but preceded by a negative sign.
2. Place polarity markings (plus and minus signs) on all resistors and batteries in the circuit being solved. The assumed direction of current flow will not affect the polarities of the batteries, but it will affect the polarity of the voltage drop on resistors. Therefore, the voltage drop should be marked so that the end of a resistor into which the current is assumed to flow is negative, and the end from which it leaves is positive.

In the statements of Kirchhoff's laws, the term algebraic sum was used. An algebraic sum differs from an arithmetic sum in that both the magnitude and the sign of each number must be considered. In electrical circuits a voltage drop occurs when current flows through a resistor. The magnitude of the voltage is determined by the size of the resistor and the amount of current flow. The polarity (sign) of the voltage drop is determined by the direction of the current flow. For example, observe the polarities of the applied electromotive force (e.m.f.) and the voltage drop as shown in figure 8–60. The applied e.m.f. causes electrons to flow through the opposition offered by the resistances. The voltage drop across each resistance is therefore opposite in polarity to that of the applied e.m.f. Note that the side of each resistor where the current enters is labeled the negative side.

289

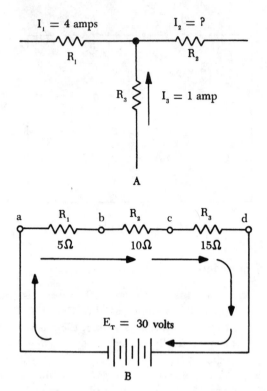

FIGURE 8–61. Circuit demonstrating Kirchhoff's laws, (A) current law and (B) voltage law.

A portion of a circuit which illustrates Kirchhoff's current law is shown in figure 8–61.

The current flowing through resistor R_1 has an intensity of four amperes. The current flowing through resistor R_3 has a magnitude of one ampere and is flowing into the same junction as the current through R_1. Using Kirchhoff's current law, it is possible to determine how much current is flowing through R_2 and whether it is flowing toward or away from the common junction. This is expressed in equation form as:

$$I_1 + I_2 + I_3 = 0.$$

Substituting the current values in the equation gives

$$4 + I_2 + (-1) = 0$$

$$I_2 = 1 + 4$$

$$I_2 = 5$$

$$-4 + (-1) + 5 = 0.$$

Kirchhoff's current law finds a wider application in more complex parallel or series-parallel circuits.

Figure 8–61(B) is a series d.c. circuit which is used to demonstrate Kirchhoff's voltage law.

The total resistance is the sum of R_1, R_2, and R_3 which is 30 ohms. Since the applied voltage is 30 volts, the current flowing in the circuit is 1 ampere. Therefore, the voltage drops across R_1, R_2, and R_3 are 5 volts, 10 volts, and 15 volts, respectively. The sum of the voltage drops is equal to the applied voltage of 30 volts.

This circuit may also be solved by using the polarities of the voltages and showing that the algebraic sum of the voltages is zero. Consider voltages positive if the $(+)$ sign is met first and negative if the $(-)$ sign is met first when tracing the current flow. By starting at the battery and going in the direction of current flow (as indicated by the arrows) the following equation may be set up:

$$\text{Total voltage } (E_t) = +30 - 5 - 10 - 15$$

$$E_t = 0.$$

The point to start around the circuit and the polarity to use are arbitrary and are a matter of choice for each circuit.

PARALLEL D. C. CIRCUITS

A circuit in which two or more electrical resistances, or loads, are connected across the same voltage source is a parallel circuit. The parallel circuit differs from the series circuit in that more than one path is provided for current flow—the more paths added in parallel, the less opposition to flow of electrons from the source. In a series circuit the addition of resistance increases the opposition to current flow. The minimum requirements for a parallel circuit are the following:

(1) a power source.
(2) conductors.
(3) a resistance or load for each current path.
(4) two or more paths for current flow.

Figure 8–62 shows a parallel circuit with three paths for current flow. Points A, B, C, and D are connected to the same conductor and are at the same electrical potential. In a similar manner, points E, F, G, and H are at the same potential. Since the applied voltage appears between points A and E, the same voltage is applied between points B and F, points C and G, and between points D and H. Thus, when resistors are connected in parallel across a voltage source, each resistor has the same applied voltage, although the currents through the resistors may differ de-

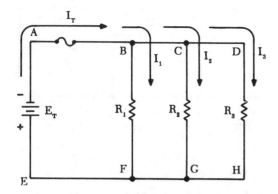

FIGURE 8–62. A parallel circuit.

pending on the values of resistance. The voltage in a parallel circuit may be expressed as follows:

$$E_T = E_1 = E_2 = E_3.$$

Where E_T is the applied voltage, E_1 is the voltage across R_1, E_2 is the voltage across R_2, and E_3 is the voltage across R_3 (figure 8–62).

The current in a parallel circuit divides among the various branches in a manner depending on the resistance of each branch (see figure 8–63). A branch containing a small value of resistance will have a greater current flow than a branch containing a high resistance. Kirchhoff's current law states that the current flowing toward a point is equal to the current flowing away from that point. Thus, the current flow in a circuit may be expressed mathematically as follows:

$$I_T = I_1 + I_2 + I_3$$

where I_T is the total current and I_1, I_2, and I_3 are the currents through R_1, R_2, and R_3, respectively.

Kirchhoff's and Ohm's law can be applied to find the total current flow in the circuit shown in figure 8–63.

The current flow through the branch containing resistance R_1 is

$$I_1 = \frac{E}{R_1} = \frac{6}{15} = .4 \text{ amps}.$$

The current through R_2 is

$$I_2 = \frac{E}{R_2} = \frac{6}{25} = .24 \text{ amps}.$$

The current through R_3 is

$$I_3 = \frac{E}{R_3} = \frac{6}{12} = .5 \text{ amps}.$$

The total current, I_T, is

$$I_T = I_1 + I_2 + I_3$$

$$I_T = .4 \text{ amps} + .24 \text{ amps} + .5 \text{ amps}$$

$$I_T = 1.14 \text{ amps}.$$

In a parallel circuit, $I_T = I_1 + I_2 + I_3$. By Ohm's law the following relationships can be obtained:

$$I_T = \frac{E_T}{R_T}, \ I_1 = \frac{E_1}{R_1}, \ I_2 = \frac{E_2}{R_2}, \text{ and } I_3 = \frac{E_3}{R_3}.$$

Substituting these values in the equation for total current,

$$\frac{E_T}{R_T} = \frac{E_1}{R_1} + \frac{E_2}{R_2} + \frac{E_3}{R_3}.$$

In a parallel circuit $E_T = E_1 = E_2 = E_3$. Therefore,

$$\frac{E}{R_T} = \frac{E}{R_1} + \frac{E}{R_2} + \frac{E}{R_3}.$$

Dividing through by E gives,

$$\frac{I}{R_T} = \frac{I}{R_1} + \frac{I}{R_2} + \frac{I}{R_3}.$$

This equation is the reciprocal formula for finding the total or equivalent resistance of a parallel circuit. Another form of the equation may be derived by solving for R_T.

$$R_T = \frac{1}{\dfrac{I}{R_1} + \dfrac{I}{R_2} + \dfrac{I}{R_3}}.$$

An analysis of the equation for total resistance in a parallel circuit shows that R_T is always less

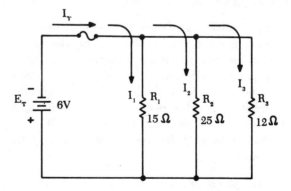

FIGURE 8–63. Current flow in a parallel circuit.

291

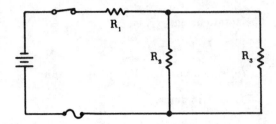

FIGURE 8–64.   A series-parallel circuit.

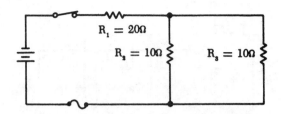

FIGURE 8–65.   A series-parallel circuit.

than the smallest resistance in a parallel circuit. Thus a 10-ohm, a 20-ohm, and a 40-ohm resistor connected in parallel have a total resistance of less than 10 ohms.

If there are only two resistors in a parallel circuit, the reciprocal formula is

$$\frac{I}{R_T} = \frac{I}{R_1} + \frac{I}{R_2}.$$

Simplified, this becomes:

$$R_T = \frac{R_1 R_2}{R_1 + R_2}.$$

This simplified, shorter formula can be used when two resistances are in parallel. Another method can be used for any number of resistors in parallel if they are of equal resistance. The resistance value of one resistor is divided by the number of resistors in parallel to determine the total resistance. Expressed mathematically this becomes:

$$R_T = \frac{R}{N}.$$

Where R_T is the total resistance, R is the resistance of one resistor, and N is the number of resistors.

SERIES-PARALLEL D. C. CIRCUITS

Most circuits in electrical equipment are not series or parallel circuits. They are usually series-parallel circuits, which are combinations of series and parallel circuits. A series-parallel circuit consists of groups of parallel resistors connected in series with other resistors. An example of a series-parallel circuit is shown in figure 8–64.

The requirements for a series-parallel circuit are as follows:

(1) power source (battery).
(2) conductors (wires).
(3) load (resistances).
(4) more than one path for current flow.
(5) a control (switch).
(6) safety device (fuse).

While series-parallel circuits may appear extremely complex, the same rule used for series and parallel circuits can be applied to simplify and solve them.

The easiest method of handling series-parallel circuits is to break them apart and redraw them as equivalent circuits. The circuit in figure 8–65 is an example of a simple series-parallel circuit that can be redrawn to illustrate this procedure.

In this circuit the same voltage is applied to R_2 and R_3; thus they are in parallel. The equivalent resistance of these two resistors is equal to the value of one resistor divided by the number of resistors in parallel. This is true only when the parallel resistors have the same ohmic value. If this rule is applied, the circuit can be redrawn as shown in figure 8–66.

This has converted the original series-parallel circuit into a simple series circuit containing two resistances. To further simplify the circuit, the two series resistances can be added, and the circuit can be redrawn as shown in figure 8–67.

Although the last redrawing of the circuit could have been omitted and the calculations done mentally, this circuit illustrates clearly that one 25-ohm resistor is the resistive equiv-

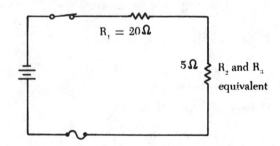

FIGURE 8–66.   A redrawn series-parallel circuit.

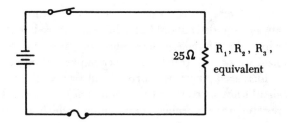

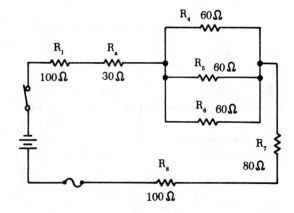

FIGURE 8–67. An equivalent series-parallel circuit

FIGURE 8–69. Series-parallel circuit with one equivalent resistance.

alent of the three resistors of the original circuit. Figure 8–68 contains a more complex series-parallel circuit.

The first step in simplifying this circuit is to reduce each group of parallel resistors to a single equivalent resistor. The first group is the parallel combination of R_2 and R_3. Since these resistors have unequal values of resistance, the formula for two parallel resistances is used:

$$R_a = \frac{R_2\,R_3}{R_2 + R_3} = \frac{120 \times 40}{120 + 40} = \frac{4800}{160} = 30 \ \Omega.$$

Then the parallel combination of R_2 and R_3 can be replaced with a single 30 Ω resistor, as shown in figure 8–69.

Next, the equivalent resistance of the parallel combination of R_4, R_5, and R_6 can be determined using the formula $R_b = R/N$: where, R_b is the equivalent resistance of R_4, R_5, and R_6, R is the value of one of the resistors, and N is the number of resistors in parallel,

$$R_b = \frac{R}{N} = \frac{60}{3} = 20 \ \Omega.$$

The parallel combination of R_4, R_5, and R_6 can

now be redrawn as a single 20 Ω resistor, as shown in figure 8–70.

The original series-parallel circuit has now been replaced with its equivalent series circuit. This circuit could be redrawn again to replace the five resistors in series with one 330-ohm resistor.

This can be proved by using the total resistance formula for series circuits:

$$
\begin{aligned}
R_T &= R_1 + R_a + R_b + R_7 + R_8 \\
&= 100 + 30 + 20 + 80 + 100 \\
&= 330 \text{ ohms.}
\end{aligned}
$$

The first series-parallel circuit used is redrawn to discuss the behavior of current flow (figure 8–71).

Unlike the parallel circuit, the branch currents, I_1 and I_2, cannot be established using the applied voltage. Since R_1 is in series with the parallel combination of R_2 and R_3, a portion of the applied voltage is dropped across R_1. In order to find the branch currents, total resistance and total current must be found first. Since R_2 and R_3 are

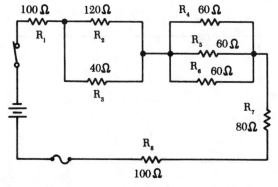

FIGURE 8–68. A more complex series-parallel circuit.

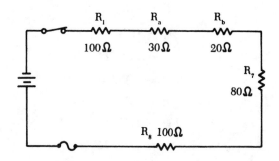

FIGURE 8–70. Series-parallel equivalent circuit.

293

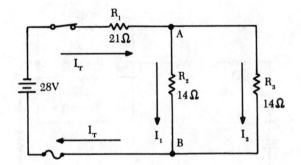

FIGURE 8–71. Current flow in a series-parallel circuit.

equal resistance,

$$R_{equiv.} = \frac{R}{N} = \frac{14}{2} = 7\ \Omega.$$

Total resistance is

$$R_T = R_1 + R_{equiv.}$$
$$= 21\ \Omega + 7\ \Omega$$
$$= 28\ \Omega.$$

Using Ohm's law, total current is

$$I_T = \frac{E_T}{R_T} = \frac{28\ V}{28\ \Omega} = 1\ ampere.$$

The total current, 1 ampere, flows through R_1 and divides at point A, with part of the current flowing through R_2, and the other part through R_3. Since R_2 and R_3 are of equal size, it is obvious that half of the total current, or .5 amps, will flow through each branch.

The voltage drops in the circuit are determined by Ohm's law:

$$E = IR.$$
$$E_{R_1} = I_T R_1$$
$$= 1 \times 21$$
$$= 21\ Volts.$$
$$E = IR.$$
$$E_{R_2} = I_1 R_2$$
$$= .5 \times 14$$
$$= 7\ Volts.$$
$$E = IR.$$
$$E_{R_3} = I_2 R_3$$
$$= .5 \times 14$$
$$= 7\ Volts.$$

The voltage drops across parallel resistors are always equal. It should also be remembered that, when the voltage is held constant and the resistance of any resistor in a series-parallel circuit is increased, the total current will decrease. This should not be confused as adding another parallel resistor to a parallel combination, which could reduce total resistance and increase total current flow.

VOLTAGE DIVIDERS

Voltage dividers are devices which make it possible to obtain more than one voltage from a single power source.

A voltage divider usually consists of a resistor, or resistors connected in series, with fixed or movable contacts and two fixed terminal contacts. As current flows through the resistor, different voltages can be obtained between the contacts. A typical voltage divider is shown in figure 8–72.

A load is any device which draws current. A heavy load means a heavy current drain. In addition to the current drawn by the various loads, there is a certain amount drawn by the voltage divider itself. This is known as bleeder current.

To understand how a voltage divider works, examine the illustration in figure 8–73 carefully and observe the following:

Each load draws a given amount of current: I_1, I_2, I_3. In addition to the load currents, some bleeder current (I_B) flows. The current I_t is drawn from the power source and is equal to the sum of all currents.

The voltage at each point is measured with respect to a common point. Note that the common

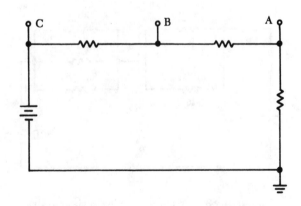

FIGURE 8–72. A voltage divider circuit.

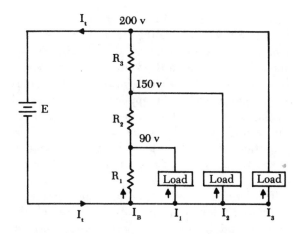

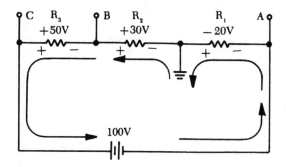

FIGURE 8-75. Current flow through a voltage divider.

FIGURE 8-73. A typical voltage divider.

point is the point at which the total current (I_t) divides into separate currents (I_1, I_2, I_3).

Each part of the voltage divider has a different current flowing in it. The current distribution is as follows:

Through R_1—bleeder current (I_B)
Through R_2—I_B plus I_1
Through R_3—I_B plus I_1, plus I_2.

The voltage across each resistor of the voltage divider is:

90 volts across R_1
60 volts across R_2
50 volts across R_3.

The voltage divider circuit discussed up to this point has had one side of the power supply (battery) at ground potential. In figure 8-74 the common reference point (ground symbol) has been moved to a different point on the voltage divider.

The voltage drop across R_1 is 20 volts; however, since tap A is connected to a point in the circuit that is at the same potential as the negative

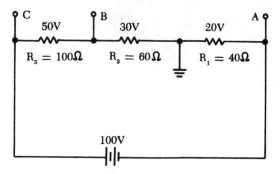

FIGURE 8-74. Positive and negative voltage on a voltage divider.

side of the battery, the voltage between tap A and the reference point is a negative (−) 20 volts. Since resistors R_2 and R_3 are connected to the positive side of the battery, the voltages between the reference point and tap B or C are positive.

A simple method of determining negative and positive voltages is provided by the following rules: (1) If current enters a resistance flowing away from the reference point, the voltage drop across that resistance is positive in respect to the reference point; (2) if current flows out of a resistance toward the reference point, the voltage drop across that resistance is negative in respect to the reference point. It is the location of the reference point that determines whether a voltage is negative or positive.

Tracing the current flow provides a means for determining the voltage polarity. Figure 8-75 shows the same circuit with the polarities of the voltage drops and the direction of current flow indicated.

The current flows from the negative side of the battery to R_1. Tap A is at the same potential as the negative terminal of the battery since the slight voltage drop caused by the resistance of the conductor is disregarded; however, 20 volts of the source voltage are required to force the current through R_1 and this 20-volt drop has the polarity indicated. Stated another way, there are only 80 volts of electrical pressure left in the circuit on the ground side of R_1.

When the current reaches tap B, 30 more volts have been used to move the electrons through R_2, and in a similar manner the remaining 50 volts are used for R_3. But the voltages across R_2 and R_3 are positive voltages, since they are above ground potential.

Figure 8-76 shows the voltage divider used

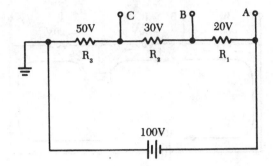

FIGURE 8–76. Voltage divider with changed ground.

previously. The voltage drops across the resistances are the same; however, the reference point (ground) has been changed. The voltage between ground and tap A is now a negative 100 volts, or the applied voltage. The voltage between ground and tap B is a negative 80 volts, and the voltage between ground and tap C is a negative 50 volts.

RHEOSTATS AND POTENTIOMETERS

The voltage dividers discussed thus far have consisted of resistors of various sizes across which a variety of voltage drops were developed. Rheostats and potentiometers are variable resistors which are sometimes used in connection with voltage dividers.

A rheostat is a variable resistor used to vary the amount of current flowing in a circuit. The rheostat is represented schematically as a two-terminal resistance with a sliding arm contact. Figure 8–77 shows a rheostat connected in series with an ordinary resistance in a series circuit. As the slider arm moves from point A to B, the amount of rheostat resistance (AB) is increased. Since the rheostat resistance and the fixed resistance are in series, the total resistance in the circuit also increases, and the current in the circuit decreases. On the other hand, if the slider arm is moved toward point A, the total resistance decreases and the current in the circuit increases.

The potentiometer is a variable resistor which has three terminals. Two ends and a slider arm are connected in a circuit. A potentiometer is used to vary the amount of voltage in a circuit and is one of the most common controls used in electrical and electronic equipment. Some examples are the volume control in radio receivers and the brightness control in television receivers.

In A of figure 8–78 a potentiometer is used to obtain a variable voltage from a fixed voltage source to apply to an electrical load. The voltage applied to the load is the voltage between points B and C. When the slider arm is moved to point A, the entire voltage is applied to the electrical device (load); when the arm is moved to point C, the voltage applied to the load is zero. The potentiometer makes possible the application of any voltage between zero and full voltage to the load.

The current flowing through the circuit of figure 8–78 leaves the negative terminal of the battery and divides, one part flowing through the lower portion of the potentiometer (points C to B) and the other part through the load. Both parts combine at point B and flow through the upper portion of the potentiometer (points B to A) back to the positive terminal of the battery. In B of figure 8–78, a potentiometer and its schematic symbol are shown.

In choosing a potentiometer resistance, consideration should be given to the amount of current drawn by the load as well as the current flow through the potentiometer at all settings of the slider arm. The energy of the current through the potentiometer is dissipated in the form of

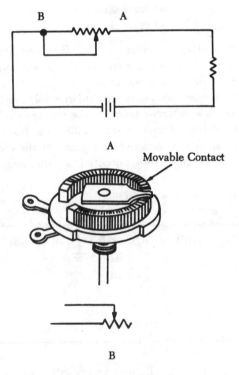

FIGURE 8–77. Rheostat.

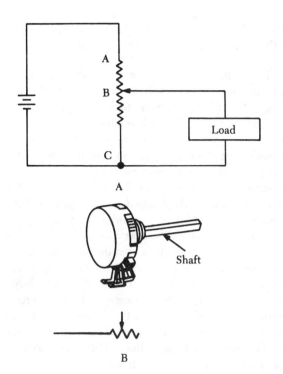

FIGURER 8–78.   Potentiometer.

heat. It is important to keep this wasted current as small as possible by making the resistance of the potentiometer as large as practicable. In most cases, the resistance of the potentiometer can be several times the resistance of the load.

Rheostats and potentiometers are constructed of a circular resistance material over which a sliding contact moves. The resistance may be distributed in many ways, and the method used determines the classification as either linear or tapered. The linear type provides a resistance evenly distributed over its entire length, while the tapered has more resistance per unit length at one end than at the other. As an example, a one-half turn of a linear rheostat places one half of the total resistance between either end and the slider, while a one-half turn of a tapered rheostat places one-tenth (or any desired fraction) of the total resistance between one end and the slider.

Prefixes

In any system of measurements, a single set of units is usually not sufficient for all the computations involved in electrical repair and main-

tenance. Small distances, for example, can usually be measured in inches, but larger distances are more meaningfully expressed in feet, yards, or miles. Since electrical values often vary from numbers that are a millionth part of a basic unit of measurement to very large values, it is often necessary to use a wide range of numbers to represent the values of such units as volts, amperes, or ohms. A series of prefixes which appear with the name of the unit have been devised for the various multiples or submultiples of the basic units. There are 12 of these prefixes, which are also known as conversion factors. Six of the most commonly used prefixes with a short definition of each are as follows:

Mega means one million (1,000,000).

Kilo means one thousand (1,000).

Centi means one-hundredth (1/100).

Milli means one-thousandth (1/1000).

Micro means one-millionth (1/1,000,000).

Micro micro means one-millionth-millionth (1/1,000,000,000,000).

One of the most extensively used conversion factors, kilo, can be used to explain the use of prefixes with basic units of measurement. Kilo means 1,000, and when used with volts is expressed as kilovolt, meaning 1,000 volts. The symbol for kilo is the letter "K". Thus, 1,000 volts is one kilovolt or 1KV. Conversely, one volt would equal one-thousandth of a KV, or 1/1000 KV. This could also be written 0.001 KV.

Similarly, the word "milli" means one-thousandth, and thus, 1 millivolt equals one-thousandth (1/1000) of a volt.

These prefixes may be used with all electrical units. They provide a convenient method for writing extremely large or small values. Most electrical formulas require the use of values expressed in basic units; therefore, all values must usually be converted before computation can be made. Figure 8–79 contains a conversion table which lists a number of the most commonly used electrical values.

```
         1 ampere = 1,000,000 microamperes.
         1 ampere = 1,000 milliamperes.
          1 farad = 1,000,000,000,000 micromicrofarads.
          1 farad = 1,000,000 microfarads.
          1 farad = 1,000 millifarads.
          1 henry = 1,000,000 microhenrys.
          1 henry = 1,000 millihenrys.
       1 kilovolt = 1,000 volts.
      1 kilowatt = 1,000 watts.
       1 megohm = 1,000,000 ohms.
  1 microampere = .000001 ampere.
     1 microfarad = .000001 farad.
       1 microhm = .000001 ohm.
      1 microvolt = .000001 volt.
     1 microwatt = .000001 watt.
1 micromicrofarad = .000000000001 farad.
    1 milliampere = .001 ampere.
     1 millihenry = .001 henry.
      1 millimho = .001 mho.
       1 milliohm = .001 ohm.
       1 millivolt = .001 volt.
      1 milliwatt = .001 watt.
           1 volt = 1,000,000 microvolts.
           1 volt = 1,000 millivolts.
          1 watt = 1,000 milliwatts.
          1 watt = .001 kilowatt.
```

FIGURE 8–79.   Conversion table.

Figure 8–80 contains a complete list of the multiples used to express electrical quantities, together with the prefixes and symbols used to represent each number.

MAGNETISM

Magnetism is so closely allied with electricity in the modern industrial world it can be safely stated that without magnetism the electrical world would not be possible. Knowledge of magnetism has existed for many centuries, but it was not until the eighteenth century that this stream of knowledge was joined with that of electricity by the discoveries of science.

The earliest known magnetism was the lodestone, a natural mineral found in Asia Minor. Today this substance is called magnetite or magnetic oxide of iron. When a piece of this ore is suspended horizontally by a thread or floated on wood in undisturbed water, it will align itself in a north-south direction. This characteristic led to its use as a compass and the name lodestone, meaning leading stone. Other than the earth itself,

the lodestone is the only natural magnet. All other magnets are produced artifically.

From the earliest times a great deal was known about the elementary behavior of magnets. For example, it was known that the property of magnetism could be induced in an iron bar by stroking it with a lodestone. In addition, it was known that if the north-seeking end of a suspended magnet was brought near the north-seeking end of another, the magnets would repel each other. On the other hand, they found that a north-seeking and a south-seeking end would attract each other.

Magnetism is defined as the property of an object to attract certain metallic substances. In general, these substances are ferrous materials; that is, materials composed of iron or iron alloys, such as soft iron, steel, and alnico. These materials, sometimes called magnetic materials, today include at least three nonferrous materials: nickel, cobalt and gadolinium, which are magnetic to a limited degree. All other substances are considered nonmagnetic, and a few of these nonmagnetic substances can be classified as diamagnetic since they are repelled by both poles of a magnet.

Magnetism is an invisible force, the ultimate nature of which has not been fully determined.

Number	Prefix	Symbol
1,000,000,000,000	tera	t
1,000,000,000	giga	g
1,000,000	mega	m
1,000	kilo	k
100	hecto	h
10	deka	dk
0.1	deci	d
0.01	centi	c
0.001	milli	m
0.000,001	micro	u
0.000,000,001	nano	n
0.000,000,000,001	pico	p

FIGURE 8–80.   Prefixes and symbols for multiples of basic quantities.

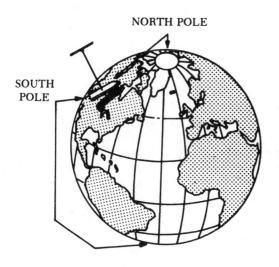

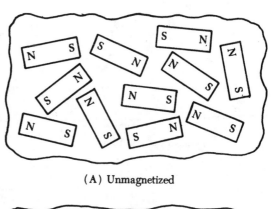

(A) Unmagnetized

FIGURE 8-81. One end of magnetized strip points to the magnetic north pole.

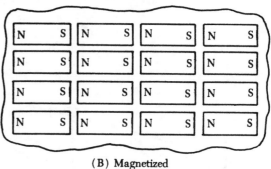

(B) Magnetized

FIGURE 8-83. Arrangement of molecules in a piece of magnetic material.

It can best be described by the effects it produces. Examination of a simple bar magnet similar to that illustrated in figure 8-81 discloses some basic characteristics of all magnets. If the magnet is suspended to swing freely, it will align itself with the earth's magnetic poles. One end is labelled "N," meaning the north-seeking end or pole of the magnet. If the "N" end of a compass or magnet is referred to as north-seeking rather than north, there will be no conflict in referring to the pole it seeks, which is the north magnetic pole. The opposite end of the magnet, marked "S," is the south-seeking end and points to the south magnetic pole. Since the earth is a giant magnet, its poles attract the ends of the magnet. These poles are not located at the geographic poles.

The somewhat mysterious and completely invisible force of a magnet depends on a magnetic field that surrounds the magnet as illustrated in figure 8-82. This field always exists between the poles of a magnet, and will arrange itself to conform to the shape of any magnet.

The theory that explains the action of a magnet holds that each molecule making up the iron bar is itself a tiny magnet, with both north and south poles as illustrated in A of figure 8-83. These molecular magnets each possess a magnetic field, but in an unmagnetized state the molecules are arranged at random throughout the iron bar. If a magnetizing force, such as stroking with a lodestone, is applied to the unmagnetized bar, the molecular magnets rearrange themselves in line with the magnetic field of the lodestone, with all north ends of the magnets pointing in one direction and all south ends in the opposite direction. This is illustrated in B of figure 8-83. In such a configuration, the

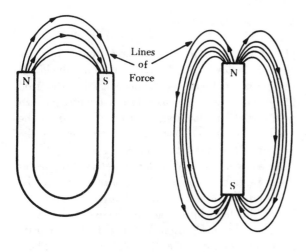

FIGURE 8-82. Magnetic field around magnets.

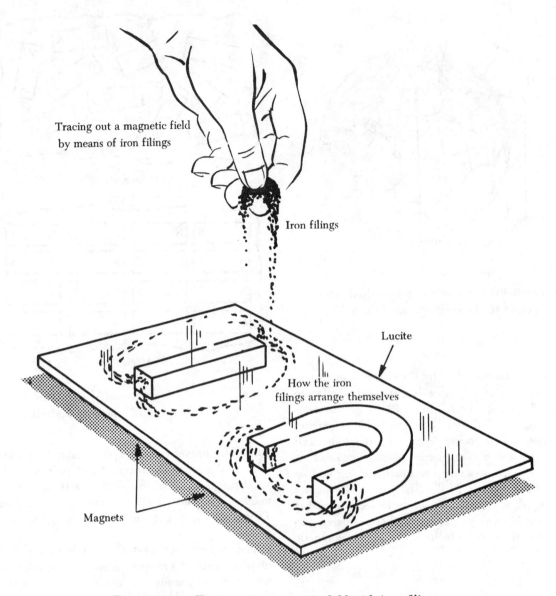

Tracing out a magnetic field
by means of iron filings

Iron filings

Lucite

How the iron
filings arrange themselves

Magnets

FIGURE 8–84.   Tracing out a magnetic field with iron filings.

magnetic fields of the magnets combined to produce the total field of the magnetized bar.

When handling a magnet, avoid applying direct heat, or hammering or dropping it. Heating or sudden shock will cause misalignement of the molecules, causing the strength of a magnet to decrease. When a magnet is to be stored, devices known as "keeper bars" are installed to provide an easy path for flux lines from one pole to the other. This promotes the retention of the molecules in their north-south alignement.

The presence of the magnetic force or field around a magnet can best be demonstrated by the experiment illustrated in figure 8–84. A sheet of transparent material such as glass or lucite is

placed over a bar magnet and iron filings are sprinkled slowly on this transparent shield. If the glass or lucite is tapped lightly, the iron filings will arrange themselves in a definite pattern around the bar, forming a series of lines from the north to south end of the bar to indicate the pattern of the magnetic field.

As shown, the field of a magnet is made up of many individual forces that appear as lines in the iron-filing demonstration. Although they are not "lines" in the ordinary sense, this word is used to describe the individual nature of the separate forces making up the entire magnetic field. These lines of force are also referred to as magnetic flux. They are separate and individual forces,

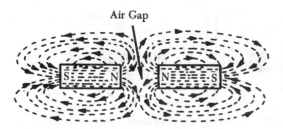

FIGURE 8–85. Like poles repel.

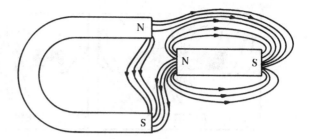

FIGURE 8–87. Bypassing flux lines.

since one line will never cross another; indeed, they actually repel one another. They remain parallel to one another and resemble stretched rubber bands, since they are held in place around the bar by the internal magnetizing force of the magnet.

The demonstration with iron filings further shows that the magnetic field of a magnet is concentrated at the ends of the magnet. These areas of concentrated flux are called the north and south poles of the magnet. There is a limit to the number of lines of force that can be crowded into a magnet of a given size. When a magnetizing force is applied to a piece of magnetic material, a point is reached where no more lines of force can be induced or introduced. The material is then said to be saturated.

The characteristics of the magnetic flux can be demonstrated by tracing the flux patterns of two bar magnets with like poles together, as shown in figure 8–85. The two like poles repel one another because the lines of force will not cross each other. As the arrows on the individual lines indicate, the lines turn aside as the two like poles are brought near each other and travel in a path parallel to each other. Lines moving in this manner repel each other, causing the magnets as a whole to repel each other.

By reversing the position of one of the magnets, the attraction of unlike poles can be demonstrated, as shown in figure 8–86.

As the unlike poles are brought near each other, the lines of force rearrange their paths and most of the flux leaving the north pole of one magnet enters the south pole of the other. The tendency of lines of force to repel each other is indicated by the bulging of the flux in the air gap between the two magnets.

To further demonstrate that lines of force will not cross one another, a bar magnet and a horseshoe magnet can be positioned to display a magnetic field similar to that of figure 8–87. The magnetic fields of the two magnets do not combine, but are re-arranged into a distorted flux pattern.

The two bar magnets may be held in the hands and the north poles brought near each other to demonstrate the force of repulsion between like poles. In a similar manner the two south poles can demonstrate this force. The force of attraction between unlike poles can be felt by bringing a south and a north end together, These experiments are illustrated in figure 8–88.

Figure 8–89 illustrates another characteristic of magnets. If the bar magnet is cut or broken into pieces, each piece immediately becomes a magnet itself, with a north and south pole. This feature supports the theory that each molecule is a magnet, since each successive division of the magnet produces still more magnets.

Since the magnetic lines of force form a continuous loop, they form a magnetic circuit. It is impossible to say where in the magnet they originate or start. Arbitrarily, it is assumed that all lines of force leave the north pole of any magnet and enter at the south pole.

There is no known insulator for magnetic flux, or lines of force, since they will pass through all materials. However, it has been found that they will pass through some materials more easily than others. Thus, it is possible to shield certain areas, such as instruments, from the effects

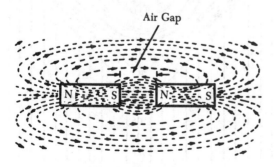

FIGURE 8–86. Unlike poles attract.

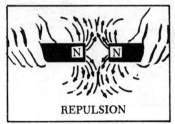 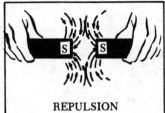 

REPULSION   REPULSION   ATTRACTION

FIGURE 8–88. Repulsion and attraction of magnet poles.

of the flux by surrounding them with a material that offers an easier path for the lines of force. Figure 8–90 shows an instrument surrounded by a path of soft iron, which offers very little opposition to magnetic flux. The lines of force take the easier path, the path of greater permeability, and are guided away from the instrument.

Materials, such as soft iron and other ferrous metals, are said to have a high permeability, the measure of the ease with which magnetic flux can penetrate a material. The permeability scale is based on a perfect vacuum with a rating of one. Air and other nonmagnetic materials are so close to this that they are also considered to have a rating of one. The nonferrous metals having a permeability greater than one, such as nickel and cobalt, are called paramagnetic, while the term ferromagnetic is applied to iron and its alloys, which have by far the greatest permeability. Any substance, such as bismuth, having a permeability of less than one, is considered diamagnetic.

Reluctance, the measure of opposition to the lines of force through a material, can be compared to the resistance of an electrical circuit. The reluctance of soft iron, for instance, is much lower than that of air. Figure 8–91 demonstrates that a piece of soft iron placed near the field of a magnet can distort the lines of force, which follow the path of lowest reluctance through the soft iron.

The magnetic circuit can be compared in many respects to an electrical circuit. The

magnetomotive force (m.m.f.), causing lines of force in the magnetic circuit, can be compared to the electromotive force or electrical pressure of an electrical circuit. The m.m.f. is measured in gilberts, symbolized by the capital letter "F." The symbol for the intensity of the lines of force, or flux, is the Greek letter phi (ϕ), and the unit of field intensity is the gauss. An individual line of force, called a maxwell, in an area of one square centimeter produces a field intensity of one gauss. Using reluctance rather than permeability, the law for magnetic circuits can be stated: A magnetomotive force of one gilbert will cause one maxwell, or line of force, to be set up in a material when the reluctance of the material is one.

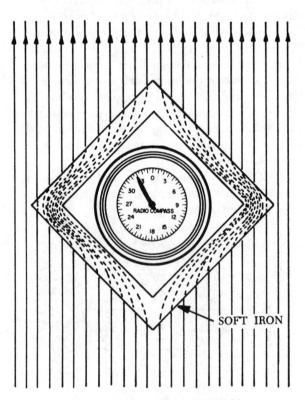

SOFT IRON

FIGURE 8–90. Magnetic shield.

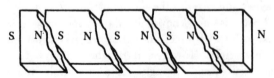

S   N   S   N   S   N   S   N   S   N

FIGURE 8–89. Magnetic poles in a broken magnet.

302

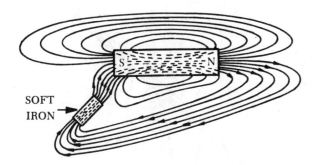

FIGURE 8–91. Effect of a magnetic substance in a magnetic field.

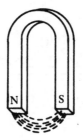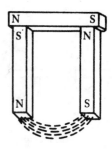

FIGURE 8–92. Two forms of horseshoe magnets.

Types of Magnets

Magnets are either natural or artifical. Since naturally occurring magnets or lodestones have no practical use, all magnets considered in this study are artifical or man-made. Artifical magnets can be further classified as permanent magnets, which retain their magnetism long after the magnetizing force has been removed, and temporary magnets, which quickly lose most of their magnetism when the external magnetizing force is removed.

Hard steel has long been used to make permanent magnets, but magnets of even better quality are now available from various alloys. Alnico, an alloy of iron, alluminum, nickel and cobalt, is considered one of the very best. Others with excellent magnetic qualities are alloys such as Remalloy and Permendur.

The old method of producing a magnet by stroking a piece of steel or iron with a natural magnet has been replaced by other means. A piece of metal placed in contact with, or even near, a magnet will become magnetized by induction and the process can be accelerated by heating the metal and then placing it in a magnetic field to cool. Magnets can also be produced by placing the metal to be magnetized in a strong magnetic field and striking it several times with a hammer, This process can be used to produce permanent magnets from metals such as hard steel.

The ability of a magnet to hold its magnetism varies greatly with the type of metal and is known as retentivity. Magnets made of soft iron are very eaily magnetized but quickly lose most of their magnetism when the external magnetizing force is removed. The small amount of magnetism remaining, called residual magnetism, is of great importance in such electrical applications as generator operation.

Horseshoe magnets are commonly manufactured in two forms, as shown in figure 8–92. The most common type is made from a long bar curved into a horseshoe shape, while a variation of this type consists of two bars connected by a third bar, or yoke.

Magnets can be made in many different shapes, such as balls, cylinders, or disks. One special type of magnet is the ring magnet, or Gramme ring, often used in instruments. This is a closed-loop magnet, similar to the type used in transformer cores, and is the only type that has no poles.

Sometimes special applications require that the field of force lie through the thickness rather than the length of a piece of metal. Such magnets are called flat magnets and are used as pole pieces in generators and motors.

Electromagnetism

In 1819, the Danish physicist, Hans Christian Oersted, discovered that the needle of a compass brought near a current-carrying conductor would be deflected. When the current flow stopped, the compass needle returned to its original position. This important discovery demonstrated a relationship between electricity and magnetism that led to the electromagnet and to many of the inventions on which modern industry is based.

Oersted discovered that the magnetic field had no connection with the conductor in which the electrons were flowing, because the conductor was made of nonmagnetic copper. The magnetic field around the conductor was created by the electrons moving through the wire. Since a magnetic field accompanies a charged particle, the greater the current flow the greater the magnetic field. Figure 8–93 illustrates the magnetic field around a current-carrying wire. A series of concentric circles around the conductor represent the field, which,

303

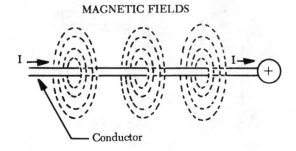

FIGURE 8–93. Magnetic field formed around a conductor in which current is flowing.

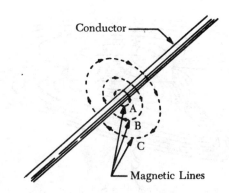

FIGURE 8–94. Expansion of magnetic field as current increases.

if all the lines were shown, would appear more as a continuous cylinder of such circles around the conductor.

As long as current flows in the conductor, the lines of force remain around it, as shown in figure 8–94. If a small current flows through the conductor, there will be a line of force extending out to circle A. If the current flow is increased, the line of force will increase in size to circle B, and a further increase in current will expand it to circle C. As the original line (circle) of force expands from circle A to B, a new line of force will appear at circle A. As the current flow increases, the number of circles of force increases, expanding the outer circles farther from the surface of the current-carrying conductor.

If the current flow is a steady nonvarying direct current, the magnetic field remains stationary. When the current stops, the magnetic field collapses and the magnetism around the conductor disappears.

A compass needle is used to demonstrate the direction of the magnetic field around a current-carrying conductor. A of figure 8–95 shows a compass needle positioned at right angles to, and approximately one inch from, a current-carrying conductor. If no current were flowing, the north-seeking end of the compass needle would point toward the earth's magnetic pole. When current flows, the needle lines itself up at right angles to a radius drawn from the conductor. Since the compass needle is a small magnet, with lines of force extending from south to north inside the metal, it will turn until the direction of these lines agrees with the direction of the lines of force around the conductor. As the compass needle is moved around the conductor, it will maintain itself in a position at right angles to the conductor, indicating that the magnetic field around a

current-carrying conductor is circular. As shown in B of figure 8–95, when the direction of current flow through the conductor is reversed, the compass needle will point in the opposite direction, indicating the magnetic field has reversed its direction.

A method used to determine the direction of the lines of force when the direction of the current flow is known, is shown in figure 8–96. If the conductor is grasped in the left hand, with the thumb pointing in the direction of current flow, the fingers will be wrapped around the conductor in the same direction as the lines of the magnetic field. This is called the left-hand rule.

Although it has been stated that the lines of force have direction, this should not be construed to mean that the lines have motion in a circular direction around the conductor. Although the lines of force tend to act in a clockwise or counterclockwise direction they are not revolving around the conductor.

Since current flows from negative to positive, many illustrations indicate current direction with a dot symbol on the end of the conductor when the electrons are flowing toward and a plus sign when the current is flowing away from the observer. This is illustrated in figure 8–97.

When a wire is bent into a loop and an electric current flows through it, the left-hand rule remains valid, as shown in figure 8–98.

If the wire is coiled into two loops, many of the lines of force become large enough to include both loops. Lines of force go through the loops in the same direction, circle around the outside of the two coils, and come in at the opposite end. (See figure 8–99.)

When a wire contains many such loops, it is called a coil. The lines of force form a pattern

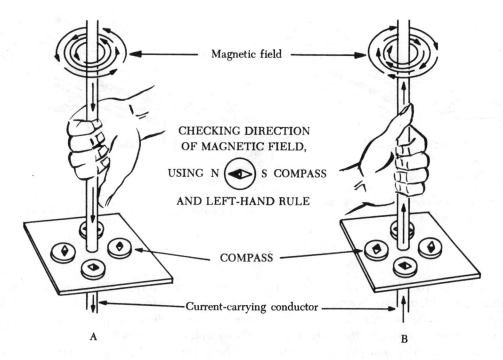

CHECKING DIRECTION
OF MAGNETIC FIELD,

USING N ⬦ S COMPASS

AND LEFT-HAND RULE

Magnetic field

COMPASS

Current-carrying conductor

A   B

FIGURE 8-95.   Magnetic field around a current-carrying conductor.

through all the loops, causing a high concentration of flux lines through the center of the coil. (See figure 8-100.)

In a coil made from loops of a conductor, many of the lines of force are dissipated between the loops of the coil. By placing a soft iron bar inside the coil, the lines of force will be concentrated in the center of the coil, since soft iron has a greater permeability than air. (See figure 8-101.) This combination of an iron core in a coil of wire loops, or turns, is called an electromagnet, since the poles (ends) of the coil possess the characteristics of a bar magnet.

The addition of the soft iron core does two things for the current-carrying coil. First, the magnetic flux is increased, and second, the flux lines are more highly concentrated.

When direct current flows through the coil, the core will become magnetized with the same polarity (location of north and south poles) as the coil would have without the core. If the current is reversed, the polarity will also be reversed.

The polarity of the electromagnet is determined by the left-hand rule in the same manner as the polarity of the coil without the core was determined. If the coil is grasped in the left hand in such a manner that the fingers curve around the coil in the direction of electron flow (minus to

plus), the thumb will point in the direction of the north pole. (See figure 8-102.)

The strength of the magnetic field of the electromagnet can be increased by either increasing the flow of current or the number of loops in the wire. Doubling the current flow approximately doubles the strength of the field, and in a similar manner, doubling the number of loops approximately doubles magnetic field strength. Finally, the type metal in the core is a factor in the field strength of the electromagnet.

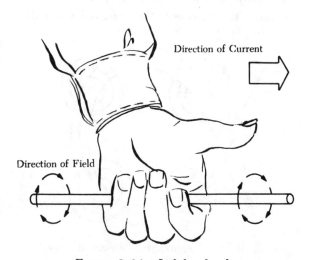

Direction of Current

Direction of Field

FIGURE 8-96.   Left-hand rule.

305

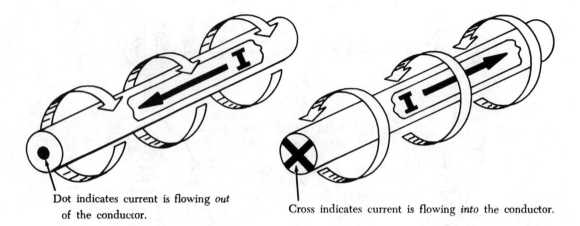

Dot indicates current is flowing *out* of the conductor.

Cross indicates current is flowing *into* the conductor.

FIGURE 8–97.   Direction of current flow in a conductor.

A soft-iron bar is attracted to either pole of a permanent magnet and, likewise, is attracted by a current-carrying coil. As shown in figure 8–103, the lines of force extend through the soft iron, magnetizing it by induction and pulling the iron bar toward the coil. If the bar is free to move, it will be drawn into the coil to a position near the center where the field is strongest.

Electromagnets are used in electrical instruments, motors, generators, relays, and other devices. Some electromagnetic devices operate on the principle that an iron core held away from the center of a coil will be rapidly pulled into a center position when the coil is energized. This principle is used in the solenoid, also called solenoid switch or relay, in which the iron core is spring-loaded off center and moves to complete a circuit when the coil is energized.

The application of the solenoid is shown in figure 8–104, where it is a solenoid relay. When the cockpit switch is closed, the energized coil pulls the core switch down, which completes the circuit to the motor. Since this solenoid relay operates on low current, it eliminates high-amperage wiring in the cockpit of the aircraft.

The solenoid-and-plunger type of magnet in various forms is used extensively to open circuit breakers automatically, when the load current becomes excessive, and to operate valves, magnetic brakes, and many other devices. The armature-type of electromagnet also has extensive applications. For this type of magnet, the coil is wound on and insulated from the iron core; the core is not movable. When current flows through the coil, the iron core becomes magnetized and causes a pivoted soft-iron armature located near the electromagnet to be attracted to it. These magnets are used in doorbells, relays, circuit breakers, telephone receivers, and many other devices.

STORAGE BATTERIES

There are two sources of electrical energy in an aircraft: (1) The generator, which converts mechanical energy into electrical energy, and (2) the battery, which converts chemical energy into electrical energy. During normal engine operation, electrical energy is taken from the engine-driven generator. The storage battery is used as an auxiliary source of power when the generator is not operating.

When the generators are operating at a speed too low to supply electrical energy for the airplane, electrical power is taken from the battery and the battery discharges, losing some of the chemical energy stored in it. During flight, the airplane

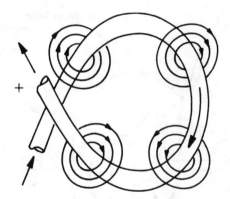

FIGURE 8–98.   Magnetic field around a looped conductor.

306

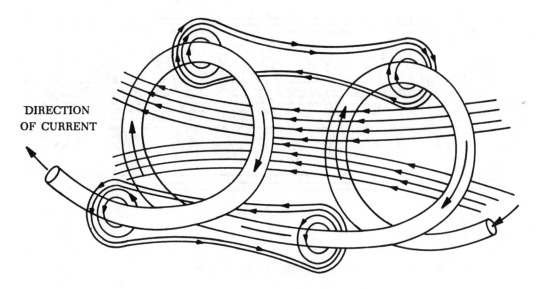

FIGURE 8–99.   Magnetic field around a conductor with two loops.

generator charges the battery over a long period of time and restores the chemical energy. Lead-acid and nickel-cadmium batteries are the types of storage batteries in general use.

LEAD-ACID BATTERIES

Lead-acid batteries used in aircraft are similar to automobile batteries. The cells of a battery are connected in series. Each cell contains positive plates of lead peroxide, negative plates of spongy lead, and electrolyte (sulphuric acid and water). In discharging, the chemical energy stored in the battery is changed to electrical energy; in charging, the electrical energy supplied to the battery is changed to chemical energy and stored. It is possible to charge a storage battery many times before it deteriorates permanently.

Lead-acid Cell Construction

The components of a typical lead-acid cell are shown in figure 8–105. Each plate consists of a framework called a grid, made of lead and antimony, to which the active material (spongy lead or lead peroxide) is attached. The positive and negative plates, (1) of figure 8–105, are so assembled that each positive plate is between two negative plates. Thus, the end plate in each cell is a negative plate. Between the plates are

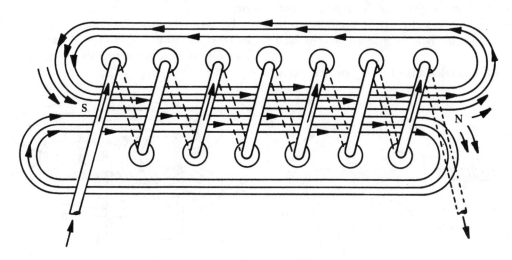

FIGURE 8–100.   Magnetic field of a coil.

307

FIGURE 8–101.   Electromagnet.

porous separators (7) which keep the positive and negative plates from touching each other and and shorting out the cell. The separators have vertical ribs on the side facing the positive plate. This construction permits the electrolyte to circulate freely around the plates. In addition, it provides a path for sediment to settle to the bottom of the cell.

Each cell is sealed in a hard rubber casing through the top of which are terminal posts and a hole into which is screwed a nonspill vent cap (4). The hole provides access for testing the strength of the electrolyte and adding water. The vent plug permits gases to escape from the cell with a minimum of leakage of electrolyte, regardless of the position the airplane might assume. In figure 8–106, the construction of the vent plug is shown. In level flight, the lead weight permits venting of gases through a small hole. In inverted flight, this hole is covered by the lead weight.

The individual cells of the battery are connected in series by means of cell straps, as illustrated in figure 8–107. The complete assembly is enclosed in an acid-resisting metal container (battery box), which serves as electrical shielding and mechanical protection. The battery box has a removable top. It also has a vent-tube nipple at each end. When the battery is installed in an airplane, a vent tube is attached to each nipple. One tube is the intake tube and is exposed to the slipstream. The other is the exhaust vent tube and is attached to the battery drain sump, which is a glass jar containing a felt pad moistened with a concentrated solution of sodium bicarbonate (baking soda). With this arrangement, the airstream is directed through the battery case where battery gases are picked up, neutralized in the sump, and then expelled overboard without damage to the airplane.

To facilitate installation and removal of the battery in some aircraft, a quick-disconnect assembly is used to connect the power leads to the

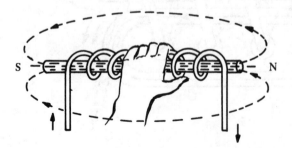

FIGURE 8–102.   Left-hand rule applied to a coil.

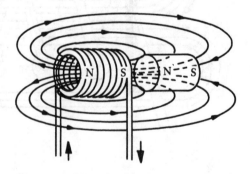

FIGURE 8–103.   Solenoid with iron core.

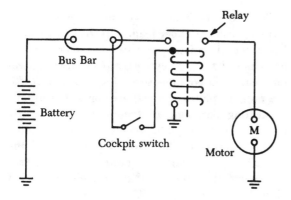

FIGURE 8–104.   Use of a solenoid in a circuit.

battery. This assembly, which is shown in figure 8–108, attaches the battery leads in the aircraft to a receptacle mounted on the side of the battery. The receptacle covers the battery terminal posts and prevents accidental shorting during the installation and removal of the battery. The plug consists of a socket and a handwheel with a course-pitch thread. It can be readily connected to the receptacle by the handwheel. Another advantage of this assembly is that the plug can be installed in only one position, eliminating the possibility of reversing the battery leads.

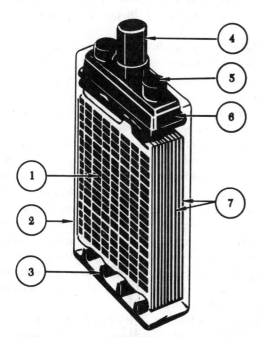

1.	Plates	3.	Supporting ribs	6.	Cell cover
2.	Cell container	4.	Vent cap	7.	Separators
		5.	Terminal post		

FIGURE 8–105.   Lead-acid cell construction.

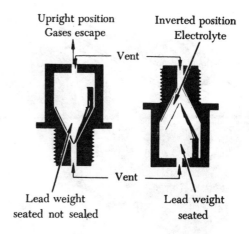

FIGURE 8–106.   Nonspill battery vent plug.

Operation of Lead-acid Cells

A lead-acid cell contains positive plates coated with lead peroxide (PbO_2); negative plates made of lead (Pb); and a liquid electrolyte, consisting of sulphuric acid (H_2SO_4) and water (H_2O). During discharge, lead sulfate ($PbSO_4$) is formed on both the positive and negative plates, the acid content of the electrolyte is decreased, and its water content is increased. As discharge continues, the amount of lead sulfate on the plates increases until the sulfate coatings become so thick that the weakened electrolyte cannot effectively reach the active materials (lead and lead peroxide). When this happens, chemical reaction is retarded and the output of the cell is reduced. In practice, the cell is not permitted to be discharged to this extent because thick coatings of lead sulfate are difficult to remove in charging. Additionally, a cell ap-

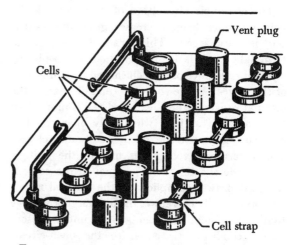

FIGURE 8–107.   Connection of storage battery.

FIGURE 8–108.   A battery quick-disconnect assembly.

proaching a state of total discharge is of little use because the high internal resistance (IR) caused by the sulfate coatings on its plates reduces the current to a value too low for practical use.

When a cell is being charged, lead sulfate is removed from both the positive and negative plates, and sulphuric acid is again formed. In the process, the water content of the electrolyte is decreased and the density of the electrolyte is increased.

The open-circuit voltage of a lead-acid cell, that is, its voltage when there is no load drawing current, is approximately 2.2 volts. This voltage is the same for every lead-acid cell regardless of its plate size and remains at this value until the cell is practically dead, regardless of its state of discharge. When the cell approaches total discharge, its voltage begins to drop rapidly.

The closed-circuit voltage of a cell, that is, its voltage under load, decreases gradually as the cell is discharged. This gradual decrease in terminal voltage is due to a gradual increase in the internal resistance of the cell caused by sulphation of the plates. At the end of normal discharge, the internal resistance of a lead-acid cell is more than twice as high as it is when fully charged. The difference between the open-circuit and closed-circuit terminal voltages is due to the voltage drop inside the cell. This is equal to the current the load draws multiplied by the internal resistance in the cell. Therefore, the discharging voltage that a lead-acid cell can supply under closed-circuit conditions is equal to the open-circuit voltage of the cell minus the IR drop in the cell.

To give a high discharge current and a high terminal voltage under load, a battery must have low internal resistance. This characteristic can be achieved through extensive plate area. Therefore, each cell contains several sets of plates. All the positive plates of a cell are connected by one connecting bar, and all the negative plates by another. Thus, the plates are connected in parallel, further decreasing the internal resistance of the cell. The open circuit cell voltage is not affected; it remains the same as that of a single pair of plates.

Lead-acid Battery Ratings

The voltage of a battery is determined by the number of cells connected in series to form the battery. Although the voltage of one lead-acid cell just removed from a charger is approximately 2.2 volts, a lead-acid cell is normally rated at only 2 volts, because it soon drops to that value. A battery rated at 12 volts consists of 6 lead-acid cells connected in series, and a battery rated at 24 volts is composed of 12 cells.

The capacity of a storage battery is rated in ampere-hours (amperes furnished by the battery times the amount of time current can be drawn). This rating indicates how long the battery may be used at a given rate before it becomes completely discharged.

Theoretically, a 100 ampere-hour battery will furnish 100 amperes for 1 hour, 50 amperes for 2 hours, or 20 amperes for 5 hours. Actually, the ampere-hour output of a particular battery depends on the rate at which it is discharged. Heavy discharge current heats the battery and decreases its efficiency and total ampere-hour output. For airplane batteries, a period of 5 hours has been established as the discharge time in rating battery capacity, However, this time of 5 hours is only a basis for rating and does not necessarily mean the length of time during which the battery is expected to furnish current. Under actual service conditions, the battery can be completely discharged within a few minutes, or it may never be discharged if the generator provides sufficient charge.

The ampere-hour capacity of a battery depends upon its total effective plate area. Connecting batteries in parallel increases ampere-hour capacity. Connecting batteries in series increases the total voltage but not the ampere-hour capacity. In multiengine airplanes, where more than one battery is used, the batteries are usually connected in parallel. The voltage is equal to that of one battery, but the ampere-hour capacity is increased. The total capacity is the sum of the ampere-hour ratings for the individual batteries.

Factors Affecting Lead-acid Battery Life

Various factors cause deterioration of a battery and shorten its service life. These include over-discharging, which causes excess sulphation and too rapid charging or discharging, resulting in over-heating of the plates and shedding of active material. The accumulation of shedded material, in turn, causes shorting of the plates and results in internal discharge. A battery that remains in a low or discharged condition for a long period of time may be permanently damaged. In addition to causing deterioration of the battery, these factors also decrease battery capacity.

Lead-acid Battery Testing Methods

The state of charge of a storage battery depends upon the condition of its active materials, primarily the plates. However, the state of charge of a battery is indicated by the density of the electrolyte and is checked by a hydrometer, an instrument which measures the specific gravity (weight as compared with water) of liquids.

The hydrometer commonly used consists of a small sealed glass tube weighted at its lower end so it will float upright, as shown in figure 8–109. Within the narrow stem of the tube is a paper scale with a range of 1.100 to 1.300. When a hydrometer is used, a quantity of electrolyte sufficient to float the hydrometer is drawn up into the syringe. The depth to which the hydrometer sinks into the electrolyte is determined by the density of the electrolyte, and the scale value indicated at the level of the electrolyte is its specific gravity. The more dense the electrolyte, the higher the hydrometer will float; therefore, the highest number on the scale (1.300) is at the lower end of the hydrometer scale.

In a new, fully charged aircraft storage battery, the electrolyte is approximately 30 percent acid and 70 percent water (by volume) and is 1.300 times as heavy as pure water. During discharge, the solution (electrolyte) become less dense and its specific gravity drops below 1.300. A specific gravity reading between 1.300 and 1.275 indicates a high state of charge; between 1.275 and 1.240, a medium state of charge; and between 1.240 and 1.200, a low state of charge. Aircraft batteries are generally of small capacity but are subject to heavy loads. The values specified for state of charge are therefore rather high. Hydrometer tests are made periodically on all storage batteries installed in aircraft. An aircraft battery in a low state of charge may have perhaps 50 percent charge remaining, but is nevertheless considered low in the face of heavy demands which would soon exhaust it. A battery in such a state of charge is considered in need of immediate recharging.

When a battery is tested using a hydrometer, the temperature of the electrolyte must be taken into consideration. The specific gravity readings on the hydrometer will vary from the actual specific gravity as the temperature changes. No correction is necessary when the temperature is between 70° F. and 90° F., since the variation is not great enough to be considered. When temperatures are greater than 90° F. or less than 70° F., it is necessary to apply a correction factor. Some hydrometers are equipped with a correction scale inside the tube. With other hydrometers it is necessary to refer to a chart provided by the manufacturer.

In both cases, the corrections should be added to, or subtracted from, the reading shown on the hydrometer.

The specific gravity of a cell is reliable only if nothing has been added to the electrolyte except occasional small amounts of distilled water to replace that lost as a result of normal evaporation. Hydrometer readings should always be taken before adding distilled water, never after. This is necessary to allow time for the water to mix thoroughly with the electrolyte and to avoid drawing up into the hydrometer syringe a sample which does not represent the true strength of the solution.

Extreme care should be exercised when making the hydrometer test of a lead-acid cell. The electrolyte should be handled carefully, for sulphuric acid will burn clothing and skin. If the acid does contact the skin the area should be washed thoroughly with water and then bi-carbonate of soda applied.

Lead-acid Battery Charging Methods

A storage battery may be charged by passing direct current through the battery in a direction opposite to that of the discharge current. Because of the internal resistance (IR) in the battery, the

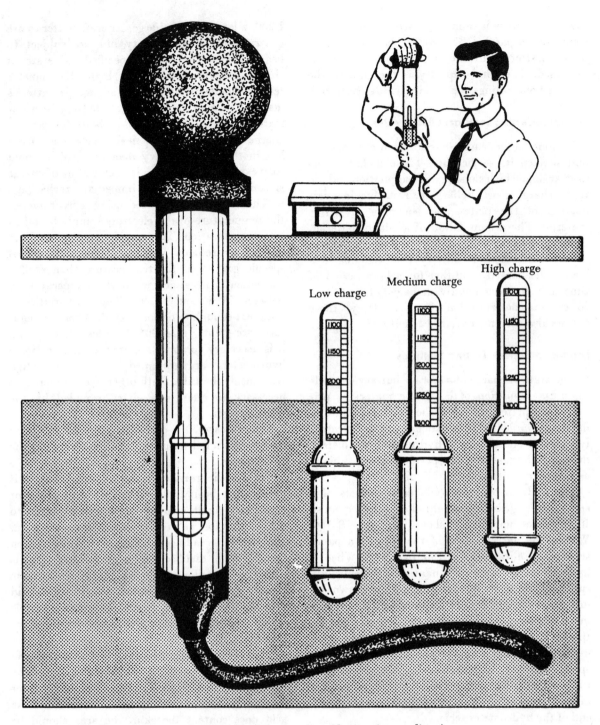

Low charge   Medium charge   High charge

FIGURE 8–109. Hydrometer (specific gravity readings).

voltage of the external charging source must be greater than the open-circuit voltage. For example, the open-circuit voltage of a fully charged 12-cell, lead-acid battery is approximately 26.4 volts (12 × 2.2 volts), but approximately 28 volts are required to charge it. This larger voltage is needed for charging because of the voltage drop in the battery caused by the internal resistance. Hence, the charging voltage of a lead-acid battery must equal the open-circuit voltage plus the *IR* drop within the battery (product of the charging current and the internal resistance).

312

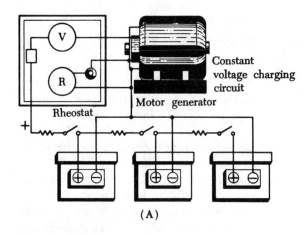

Constant voltage charging circuit

Motor generator

Rheostat

(A)

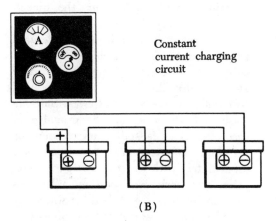

Constant current charging circuit

(B)

FIGURE 8–110. Battery charging methods.

Batteries are charged by either the constant-voltage or constant-current method. In the constant-voltage method (A of figure 8–110), a motor-generator set with a constant, regulated voltage forces the current through the battery. In this method, the current at the start of the process is high but automatically tapers off, reaching a value of approximately 1 ampere when the battery is fully charged. The constant-voltage method requires less time and supervision than does the constant-current method.

In the constant-current method (B of figure 8–110), the current remains almost constant during the entire charging process.

This method requires a longer time to charge a battery fully and, toward the end of the process, presents the danger of overcharging, if care is not exercised.

In the aircraft, the storage battery is charged by direct current from the aircraft generator system. This method of charging is the constant-voltage method, since the generator voltage is held constant by use of a voltage regulator.

When a storage battery is being charged, it generates a certain amount of hydrogen and oxygen. Since this is an explosive mixture, it is important that steps be taken to prevent ignition of the gas mixture. The vent caps should be loosened and left in place. No open flames, sparks, or other source of ignition should be permitted in the vicinity. Before disconnecting or connecting a battery to the charge, always turn off the power by means of a remote switch.

NICKEL-CADMIUM BATTERIES

Nickel-cadmium batteries have been available for some time, but they did not come into extensive use in aviation until the increase in the number of commercial and executive jet aircraft made them economically practicable. The many advantages of the nickel-cadmium battery were well known, but its initial cost was several times that of the lead-acid battery. The increasing use of the nickel-cadmium battery (often referred to as "ni-cad") stems largely from the low maintenance cost derived from the long service life of the battery. Additionally, the nickel-cadmium battery has a short recharge time, excellent reliability, and good starting capability.

Nickel-Cadmium Cell Construction

As in the lead-acid type, the cell is the basic unit of the nickel-cadmium battery. It consists of positive and negative plates, separators, electrolyte, cell vent, and cell container. The positive plates are made from a porous plaque on which nickel-hydroxide has been deposited. The negative plates are made from similar plaques on which cadmium-hydroxide is deposited. In both cases the porous plaque is obtained by sintering nickel powder to a fine-mesh wire screen. Sintering is a process which fuses together extremely small granules of powder at a high temperature. After the active positive and negative materials are deposited on the plaque, it is formed and cut into the proper plate size. A nickel tab is then welded to a corner of each plate and the plates are assembled with the tabs welded to the proper terminals. The plates are separated from each other by a continuous strip of porous plastic.

The electrolyte used in the nickel-cadmium battery is a 30 percent solution (by weight) of potassium hydroxide (KOH) in distilled water. The specific gravity of the electrolyte remains between 1.240 and 1.300 at room temperature. No

313

appreciable changes occur in the electrolyte during charge or discharge. As a result, the battery charge cannot be determined by a specific gravity check of the electrolyte. The electrolyte level should be maintained just above the tops of the plates.

Operation of Nickel-Cadmium Cells

When a charging current is applied to a nickel-cadmium battery, the negative plates lose oxygen and begin forming metallic cadmium. The active material of the positive plates, nickel-hydroxide, becomes more highly oxidized. This process continues while the charging current is applied or until all the oxygen is removed from the negative plates and only cadmium remains.

Toward the end of the charging cycle the cells emit gas. This will also occur if the cells are over-charged. This gas is caused by decomposition of the water in the electrolyte into hydrogen at the negative plates and oxygen at the positive plates. The voltage used during charging, as well as the temperature, determines when gassing will occur. To completely charge a nickel-cadmium battery, some gassing, however slight, must take place; thus, some water will be used.

The chemical action is reversed during discharge. The positive plates slowly give up oxygen, which is regained by the negative plates. This process results in the conversion of the chemical energy into electrical energy. During discharge the plates absorb a quantity of the electrolyte. On recharge, the level of the electrolyte rises and, at full charge, the electrolyte will be at its highest level. Therefore, water should be added only when the battery is fully charged.

The nickel-cadmium battery is usually interchangeable with the lead-acid type. When replacing a lead-acid battery with a nickel-cadmium battery, the battery compartment must be clean, dry, and free of all traces of acid from the old battery. The compartment must be washed out and neutralized with ammonia or boric acid solution, allowed to dry thoroughly, and then painted with an alkali-resisting varnish.

The pad in the battery sump jar should be saturated with a three percent (by weight) solution of boric acid and water before connecting the battery vent system.

Servicing Nickel-Cadmium Batteries

There are significant differences in the servicing methods required for the nickel-cadmium batteries and those of the lead-acid batteries. The most important points to be observed are as follows:

(1) A separate storage and maintenance area should be provided for nickel-cadmium batteries. The electrolyte is chemically opposite to the sulphuric acid used in a lead-acid battery. Fumes from a lead-acid battery can contaminate the electrolyte in a nickel-cadmium battery. This precaution should include equipment, such as hand tools and syringes, used with lead-acid batteries. Indeed, every possible precaution must be taken to keep anything containing acid away from the nickel-cadmium battery shop.

(2) The potassium hydroxide electrolyte used in nickel-cadmium batteries is extremely corrosive. Protective goggles, rubber gloves, and rubber aprons should be used to handle and service batteries. Suitable washing facilities should be provided in case electrolyte is spilled on clothing or the skin. Such exposures should be rinsed immediately with water or vinegar, lemon juice, or a boric acid solution. When potassium hydroxide and distilled water are mixed to make electrolyte, the potassium hydroxide should be added slowly to the water, not vice versa.

(3) Severe arcing may result if a wire brush is used to clean a battery. The vent plugs should be closed during the cleaning process and the battery should never be cleaned with acids, solvents, or any chemical solution. Spilled electrolyte can react with carbon dioxide to form crystals of potassium carbonate. These, which are nontoxic and noncorrosive, can be loosened with a fiber brush and wiped off with a damp cloth. When potassium carbonate forms on a properly serviced battery, it may indicate the battery is overcharging because the voltage regulator is out of adjustment.

(4) Additional water should never be added to the battery earlier than three or four hours after it has been fully charged. Should it be necessary to add water, use only distilled or demineralized water.

(5) Since the electrolyte does not react chemically with the cell plates, the specific gravity of the electrolyte does not change appreci-

ably. Thus, it is not possible to determine the state of charge of the battery with a hydrometer; nor can the charge be determined by a voltage test because the voltage of a nickel-cadmium battery remains constant during 90 percent of the discharge cycle.

(6) Nickel-cadmium batteries should be serviced at regular intervals based on experience since water consumption varies with ambient temperature and operating methods. At greater intervals the battery should be removed from the aircraft and given a bench check in the shop. If a battery is completely discharged, some cells may reach zero potential and charge in the reverse direction, affecting the battery in such a manner that it will not retain a full capacity charge. In such cases, the battery should be discharged and each cell short-circuited to obtain a zero potential cell balance before recharging the battery. This process is called "equalization."

(7) Charging can be accomplished by either the constant-voltage or the constant-current method. For the constant potential charging, maintain the charging voltage constant until the charging current decays to 3 amperes or less assuring that the battery cell temperature does not exceed 100° F. For constant current charging start the charge and continue until the voltage reaches the desired potential, then reduce the current level to 4 amperes continuing the charging until its desired voltage or until the battery temperature exceeds 100° F. and the voltage begins to decline.

The troubleshooting chart outlined in figure 8–111 can be used as a guide in troubleshooting battery malfunctions.

CIRCUIT PROTECTIVE AND CONTROL DEVICES

Electricity, when properly controlled, is of vital importance to the operation of aircraft. When it is not properly controlled, it can become dangerous and destructive. It can destroy aircraft components or complete aircraft; it can injure personnel and even cause their death.

It is of the greatest importance, then, that all necessary precautions be taken to protect the electrical circuits and units in the aircraft and to keep this force under proper control at all times.

Protective Devices

When an aircraft is built, the greatest care is taken to ensure that each electrical circuit is fully insulated from all others so that the current in a circuit will follow its intended individual path. Once the aircraft is put into service, however, there are many things that can happen to alter the original circuitry. Some of these changes can cause serious trouble if not detected and corrected in time.

Perhaps the most serious trouble in a circuit is a direct short. The term, "direct short," describes a situation in which some point in the circuit, where full system voltage is present, comes in direct contact with the ground or return side of the circuit. This establishes a path for current flow that contains no resistance other than that present in the wires carrying the current, and these wires have very little resistance.

According to Ohm's law, if the resistance in a circuit is small, the current will be great. When a direct short occurs, there will be an extremely heavy current flowing through the wires. Suppose, for instance, that the two leads from a battery to a motor came in contact with each other. Not only would the motor stop running because of the current going through the short, but the battery would become discharged quickly (perhaps destroyed); there would also be danger of fire.

The battery cables in this example would be very large wires, capable of carrying very heavy currents. Most wires used in aircraft electrical circuits are considerably smaller and their current-carrying capacity is quite limited. The size of the wires used in any given circuit is determined by the amount of current the wires are expected to carry under normal operating condidions. Any current flow greatly in excess of normal, such as the case of a direct short, would cause a rapid generation of heat.

If the excessive current flow caused by the short is left unchecked, the heat in the wire will continue to increase until something gives way. Perhaps a portion of the wire will melt and open the circuit so that nothing is damaged other than the wires involved. The probability exists, however, that much greater damage would result. The heat in the wires could char and burn their insulation and that of other wires bundled with them, which could cause more shorts. If a fuel or oil leak is

OBSERVATION	PROBABLE CAUSE	CORRECTIVE ACTION
High trickle charge—When charging at constant voltage of 28.5 ($\pm$0.1) volts, current does not drop below 1 amp after a 30-minute charge.	Defective cells.	While still charging, check individual cells. Those below .5 volts are defective and should be replaced. Those between .5 and 1.5 volts may be defective or may be unbalanced, those above 1.5 volts are all right.
High trickle charge after replacing defective cells, or battery fails to meet amp-hour capacity check.	Cell imbalance.	Discharge battery and short out individual cells for eight hours. Charge battery using constant current method. Check capacity and if O.K., recharge using constant current method.
Battery fails to deliver rated capacity.	Cell imbalance or faulty cells.	Repeat capacity check, discharge and constant current charge a maximum of three times. If capacity does not develop, replace faulty cells.
No potential available.	Complete battery failure.	Check terminals and all electrical connections. Check for dry cell. Check for high trickle charge.
Excessive white crystal deposits on cells. (There will always be some potassium carbonate present due to normal gassing.)	Excessive spewage.	Battery subject to high charge current, high temperature or high liquid level. Clean battery, constant current charge and check liquid level. Check charger operation.
Distortion of cell case.	Overcharge or high heat.	Replace cell.
Foreign material in cells—black or gray particles.	Impure water, high heat, high concentration of KOH or improper water level.	Adjust specific gravity and electrolyte level. Check battery for cell imbalance or replace defective cell.
Excessive corrosion of hardware.	Defective or damaged plating.	Replace parts.
Heat or blue marks on hardware.	Loose connections causing overheating of inter-cell connector or hardware.	Clean hardware and properly torque connectors.
Excessive water consumption. Dry cell.	Cell imbalance.	Proceed as above for cell imbalance.

FIGURE 8–111. Nickel-cadmium troubleshooting chart.

near any of the hot wires, a disastrous fire might be started.

To protect aircraft electrical systems from damage and failure caused by excessive current, several kinds of protective devices are installed in the systems. Fuses, circuit breakers, and thermal protectors are used for this purpose.

Circuit protective devices, as the name implies, all have a common purpose—to protect the units and the wires in the circuit. Some are designed primarily to protect the wiring and to open the circuit in such a way as to stop the current flow when the current becomes greater than the wires can safely carry. Other devices are designed to protect a unit in the circuit by stopping the current flow to it when the unit becomes excessively warm.

Fuses

A fuse is a strip of metal that will melt when current in excess of its carefully determined capacity flows through it. The fuse is installed in the circuit so that all the current in the circuit passes through it. In most fuses, the strip of metal is made of an alloy of tin and bismuth. Other fuses are made of copper and are called current limiters; these are used primarily to sectionalize an aircraft circuit.

A fuse melts and breaks the circuit when the current exceeds the rated capacity of the fuse, but a current limiter will stand a considerable overload for a short period of time. Since the fuse is intended to protect the circuit, it is quite important that its capacity match the needs of the circuit in which it is used. When a fuse is replaced, the applicable manufacturer's instructions should be consulted to be sure a fuse of the correct type and capacity is installed. Fuses are installed in two type fuse holders in aircraft. "Plug-in holders" are used for small type and low capacity fuses. "Clip" type holders are used for heavy high capacity fuses and current limiters.

Circuit Breakers

A circuit breaker is designed to break the circuit and stop the current flow when the current exceeds a predetermined value. It is commonly used in place of a fuse and may sometimes eliminate the need for a switch. A circuit breaker differs from a fuse in that it "trips" to break the circuit and it may be reset, while a fuse melts and must be replaced.

There are several types of circuit breakers in general use in aircraft systems. One is a magnetic type. When excessive current flows in the circuit, it makes an electromagnet strong enough to move a small armature which trips the breaker. Another type is the thermal overload switch or breaker. This consists of a bimetallic strip which, when it becomes overheated from excessive current, bends away from a catch on the switch lever and permits the switch to trip open.

Most circuit breakers must be reset by hand. When the circuit breaker is reset, if the overload condition still exists, the circuit breaker will trip again to prevent damage to the circuit.

Thermal Protectors

A thermal protector, or switch, is used to protect a motor. It is designed to open the circuit automatically whenever the temperature of the motor becomes excessively high. It has two positions, open and closed. The most common use for a thermal switch is to keep a motor from overheating. If a malfunction in the motor causes it to overheat, the thermal switch will break the circuit intermittently.

The thermal switch contains a bimetallic disk, or strip, which bends and breaks the circuit when it is heated. This occurs because one of the metals expands more than the other when they are subjected to the same temperature. When the strip or disk cools, the metals contract and the strip returns to its original position and closes the circuit.

Control Devices

The units in the electrical circuits in an aircraft are not all intended to operate continuously or automatically. Most of them are meant to operate at certain times, under certain conditions, to perform very definite functions. There must be some means of controlling their operation. Either a switch or a relay, or both, may be included in the circuit for this purpose.

SWITCHES

Switches control the current flow in most aircraft electrical circuits. A switch is used to start, to stop, or to change the direction of the current flow in the circuit. The switch in each circuit must be able to carry the normal current of the circuit and must be insulated heavily enough for the voltage of the circuit.

Knife switches are seldom used on aircraft. They

 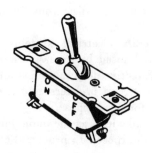

FIGURE 8–112. Single-pole single-throw knife and toggle switches.

are included here to simplify the operation of the toggle switch. Toggle switches operate much the same as knife switches, but their moving parts are enclosed. They are used in aircraft circuits more than any other kind of switch.

Toggle switches, as well as some other type of switches, are designated by the number of poles, throws, and positions they have. A pole of a switch is its movable blade or contactor. The number of poles is equal to the number of circuits, or paths for current flow, that can be completed through the switch at any one time. The throw of a switch indicates the number of circuits, or paths for current, that it is possible to complete through the switch with each pole or contactor. The number of positions a switch has is the number of places at which the operating device (toggle, plunger, etc.) will come to rest and at the same time open or close one or more circuits.

As shown in figure 8–112, when it is possible to complete only one circuit through a switch, the switch is a single-pole single-throw (spst) switch. A single-pole switch through which two circuits can be completed (not at the same time) is a single-pole double-throw (spdt) switch. (See figure 8–113.)

A switch with two contactors, or poles, each of which completes only one circuit, is a double-pole single-throw (dpst) switch. Double-pole single-

throw knife and toggle switches are illustrated in figure 8–114.

A double-pole switch that can complete two circuits, one circuit at a time through each pole, is a double-pole double-throw (dpdt) switch. Both a knife and a toggle switch illustrating this type of switch are shown in figure 8–115.

The schematic representations for the most commonly used switches are shown in figure 8–116.

A toggle switch that is spring-loaded to the OFF position and must be held in the ON position to complete the circuit is a momentary contact two-position switch. One that will come to rest at either of two positions, opening the circuit in one position and closing it in another, is a two-position switch. A toggle switch that will come to rest at any one of three positions is a three-position switch.

A switch that stays open, except when it is held in the closed position, is a normally open switch (usually identified as NO). One that stays closed, except when it is held in the open position, is a normally closed switch (NC). Both kinds are spring-loaded to their normal position and will return to that position as soon as they are released.

Push-Button Switches

Push-button switches have one stationary contact and one movable contact. The movable

FIGURE 8–113. Single-pole double-throw knife and toggle switches.

318

FIGURE 8–114. Double-pole single-throw knife and toggle switches.

contact is attached to the push button. The push button is either an insulator itself or is insulated from the contact. This switch is spring-loaded and designed for momentary contact.

Microswitches

A microswitch will open or close a circuit with a very small movement of the tripping device (1/16 inch or less). This is what gives the switch its name, since micro means small.

Microswitches are usually push-button switches. They are used primarily as limit switches to provide automatic control of landing gears, actuator motors, and the like. The diagram in figure 8–117 shows a normally closed microswitch in cross section and illustrates how these switches operate. When the operating plunger is pressed in, the spring and the movable contact are pushed, opening the contacts and the circuit.

Rotary-Selector Switches

A rotary-selector switch takes the place of several switches. As shown in figure 8–118, when the knob of the switch is rotated, the switch opens one circuit and closes another. Ignition switches and voltmeter selector switches are typical examples of this kind of switch.

Relays

Relays, or relay switches, are used for remote control of circuits carrying heavy currents, A relay is connected in the circuit between the unit controlled and the nearest source of power (or power bus bar) so that the cables carrying heavy current will be as short as possible.

A relay switch consists of a coil, or solenoid, an iron core, and both fixed and movable contacts. A small wire connects one of the coil terminals (which is insulated from the housing) to the source of power through a control switch usually located in the cockpit. The other coil terminal is usually grounded to the housing. When the control switch is closed, an electromagnetic field is set up around the coil.

In one type of relay switch, an iron core is fixed firmly in place inside the coil. When the control switch is closed, the core is magnetized and pulls a soft iron armature toward it, closing the main contacts. The contacts are spring-loaded to the open position as shown in figure 8–119. When the control switch is turned off, the magnetic field collapses and the spring opens the contacts.

In another type of relay switch, part of the core is movable. A spring holds the movable part a short distance away from the fixed part, as illus-

FIGURE 8–115. Double-pole double-throw knife and toggle switches.

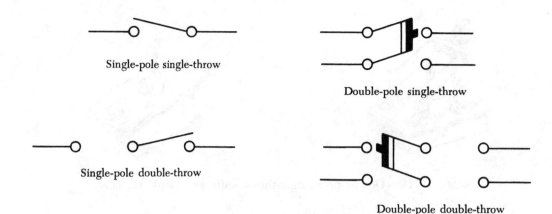

Single-pole single-throw

Double-pole single-throw

Single-pole double-throw

Double-pole double-throw

FIGURE 8–116. Schematic representation for typical switches.

trated in figure 8–120. When the coil is energized, the magnetic field tries to pull the movable part of the core into the coil. This pull overcomes the spring tension. As the core moves inward, it brings the movable contacts, which are attached to but insulated from it, down against the stationary contacts. This completes the main circuit. When the control switch is turned off, the magnetic field collapses and the spring returns the movable core to its original position, opening the main contacts.

Relays vary in construction details according to their intended use. When selecting a relay to be installed in a circuit, make sure it is designed for the job it is intended to do.

Some relay switches are made to operate continuously, while others are designed to operate only intermittently. The starter-relay switch is

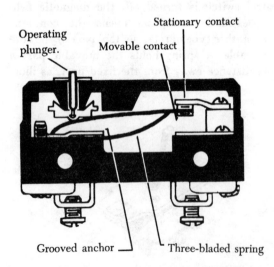

FIGURE 8–117. Cross section of a microswitch.

made to operate intermittently and would overheat if used continuously. The battery-relay switch can be operated continuously because its coil has a fairly high resistance which prevents overheating.

In a circuit carrying a large current, the more quickly the circuit is opened the less it will arc at the relay, and the less the switch contacts will be burned. Relays used in circuits with large motors have strong return springs to open the circuit quickly.

Most of the relays use in the a.c. circuitry of an aircraft are energized by d.c. current. These devices will be discussed, as necessary, in the appropriate areas covering alternating current devices.

D. C. MEASURING INSTRUMENTS

Understanding the functional design and operation of electrical measuring instruments is very important, since they are used in repairing, maintaining, and troubleshooting electrical circuits. While some meters can be used for both d.c. and a.c. circuit measurement, only those used as d.c. instruments are discussed in this section. The meters used for a.c., or for both a.c. and d.c., are discussed in the study of a.c. theory and circuitry.

Effects of Current

The effect of current may be classified as follows: chemical, physiological, photoelectric, piezoelectric, thermal, or electromagnetic.

Chemical

When an electric current is passed through certain solutions, a chemical reaction takes place and

320

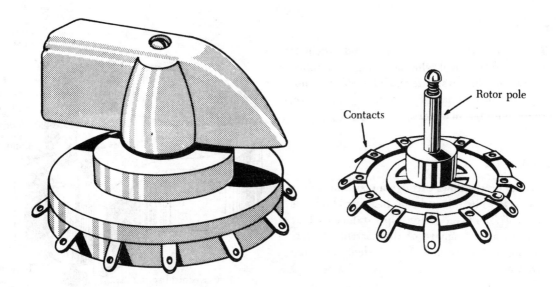

FIGURE 8–118. Rotary-selector switch.

a deposit forms on one electrode. The amount of this deposit is proportional to the amount of current. Industrially, this process is useful in electroplating and electrolysis. Although the chemical effect is useful in defining the standard ampere (the amount of current which causes .001118 grams of silver to be deposited in one second from a 15 percent solution of silver nitrate), it is of no practical use in meters.

Physiological

The physiological effect of current refers to the reaction of the human body to an electric current.

An electric shock, although painful at times, is too difficult to evaluate quantitatively and is, therefore, not practical for use in meters.

Photoelectric

When electrons strike certain materials, a glow appears at the point of contact. The picture tube of a television set and the scope of a radar set illustrate this effect. Using the intensity of the light produced as a means of measuring the amount of current is neither accurate nor practical.

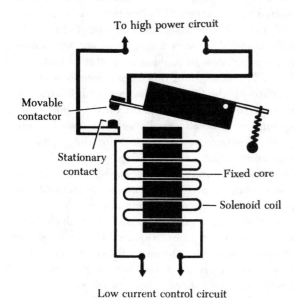

FIGURE 8–119. Fixed-core relay.

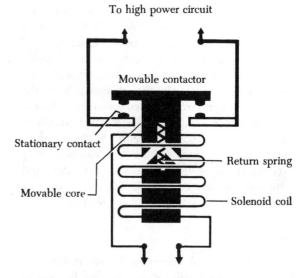

FIGURE 8–120. Movable-core relay.

321

Piezoelectric

Certain crystals such as quartz and Rochelle salts become deformed when a voltage is applied across two of the crystal faces. This effect is not visible to the human eye and is, therefore, impractical for use in meters.

Thermal

When a current flows through a resistance, heat is produced. The amount of heat produced is equal to I^2R. This relationship establishes that heat varies as the square of the current. Meters which employ the thermal effect in their operation are common.

Electromagnetic

Whenever electrons flow through a conductor, a magnetic field proportional to the current is created. This effect is useful for measuring current and is employed in many practical meters.

The first four effects discussed are of no practical importance as electrical measuring devices. The last two effects, thermal and magnetic, are of practical use in meters. Since most of the meters in use have D'Arsonval movements, which operate because of the magnetic effect, only this type will be discussed in detail.

D'Arsonval Meter

The basic d.c. meter movement is known as the D'Arsonval meter movement because it was first employed by the French scientist, D'Arsonval, in making electrical measurement. This type of meter movement is a current-measuring device which is used in the ammeter, voltmeter, and ohmmeter. Basically, both the ammeter and the voltmeter are current-measuring instruments, the principal difference being the method in which they are connected in a circuit. While an ohmmeter is also basically a current-measuring instrument, it differs from the ammeter and voltmeter in that it provides its own source of power and contains other auxiliary circuits.

Ammeter

The D'Arsonval ammeter is an instrument designed for measuring direct current flowing in an electrical circuit and consists of the following parts: a permanent magnet, a moving element

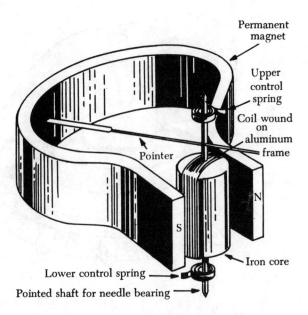

FIGURE 8–121.   Moving-coil element with pointer and springs.

mounting, bearings, and a case which includes terminals, a dial, and screws. Each part and its function are described in the discussion which follows.

The permanent magnet furnishes a magnetic field which will react with the magnetic field set up by the moving element.

The moving element is mounted so that it is free to rotate when energized by the current to be measured. A pointer which moves across a calibrated scale is attached to this element. A moving-coil mechanism is shown in figure 8–121. The controlling element is a spring, or springs, whose main function is to provide a counter or restoring force. The strength of this force increases with the turning of the moving element and brings the pointer to rest at some point on the scale. Two springs are generally used; they are wound in opposite drections to compensate for the expansion and contraction of the spring material due to temperature variation. The springs are made of nonmagnetic material and conduct current to and from the moving coil in some meters.

The moving element consists of a shaft with very hard pivot points to carry the moving coil or other movable element (figure 8–121). The pivot points are so fitted into highly polished jewels or very hard glass bearings that the moving element can rotate with very little friction. Another type of mounting has been

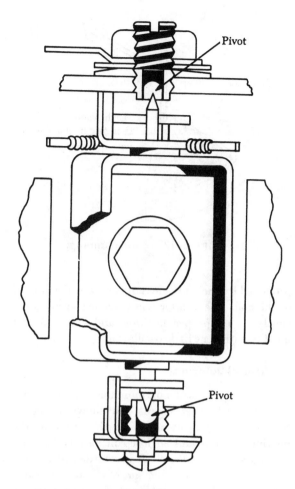

FIGURE 8–122. Method of mounting moving elements.

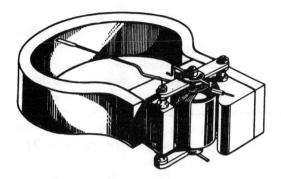

FIGURE 8–123. D'Arsonval meter movement.

scale, units of measurement, and meter uses. The terminals are made of materials having very low electrical resistance. Their function is to conduct the required current into and away from the meter.

Operation of the Meter Movement

The major units are mounted in their relationship to one another (figure 8–123). Note that the coil portion of the moving element is in the magnetic field of the permanent magnet.

In order to understand how the meter works, assume that the coil of the moving element is placed in a magnetic field as shown in figure 8–124.

The coil is pivoted so that it is able to rotate back and forth within the magnetic field set up by the magnet. When the coil is connected in a circuit, current flows through the coil in the direction indicated by the arrows and sets up a magnetic field within the coil. This field has the same polarity as the adjacent poles of the magnet. The interaction of the two fields causes the coil to rotate to a position so that the two magnetic fields are aligned. This force of rotation (torque) is proportional to the interaction between the like poles of the coil and the magnet and, therefore, to

designed in which the pivot points are reversed and the bearings are inside the moving-coil assembly. A method of mounting moving elements is shown in figure 8–122.

The bearings are highly polished jewels such as sapphires, synthetic jewels, or very hard glass. These are usually round and have a conical depression in which the pivots rotate. They are set in threaded nuts which allow adjustment. The radius of the depression in the jewel is greater than the radius of the pivot point. This limits the area of contact surfaces and provides a bearing which, when operated dry, probably has the lowest constant friction value of any known type of bearing.

The case houses the instrument movement and protects it from mechanical injury and exposure. It also has a window for viewing the movement of the pointer across a calibrated scale. The dial has printed on it pertinent information such as the

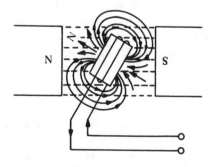

FIGURE 8–124. Effect of a coil in a magnetic field.

the amount of current flow in the coil. As a result, a pointer attached to the coil will indicate the amount of current flowing in the circuit as it moves across a graduated scale.

In the arrangement just discussed, note that any torque sufficient to overcome the inertia and friction of moving parts causes the coil to rotate until the fields align. This uncontrolled movement would cause inaccruate current readings. Therefore, the turning motion of the coil is opposed by two springs. The value of the current flowing through the coil determines the turning force of the coil. When the turning force is equal to the opposition of the springs, the coil stops moving and the pointer indicates the current reading on a calibrated scale. In some meters the springs are made of conducting material and conduct current to and from the coil. The pole pieces of the magnet form a circular air gap within which the coil is pivoted.

To obtain a clockwise rotation, the north pole of the permanent magnet and that of the coil must be adjacent. The current flowing through the coil must, therefore, always be in the same direction. The D'Arsonval movement can be used only for d.c. measurements and the correct polarity must be observed. If the current is allowed to flow in the wrong direction through the coil, the coil will rotate counterclockwise and the pointer will be damaged. Since the movement of the coil is directly proportional to the current through the coil, the scale is normally a linear scale.

Damping

In order that meter readings can be made quickly and accurately, it is desirable that the moving pointer overshoot its proper position only a small amount and come to rest after not more than one or two small oscillations. The term "damping" is applied to methods used to bring the pointer of an electrical meter to rest after it has been set in motion. Damping may be accomplished by electrical means, by mechanical means, or by a combination of both.

Electrical Damping

A common method of damping by electrical means is to wind the moving coil on an aluminum frame. As the coil moves in the field of the permanent magnet, eddy currents are set up in the aluminum frame. The magnetic field

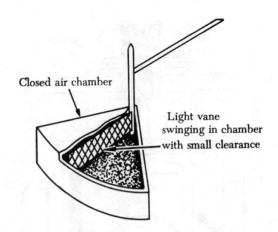

FIGURE 8–125.   Air damping.

produced by the eddy currents opposes the motion of the coil. The pointer will therefore swing more slowly to its proper position and come to rest quickly with very little oscillation.

Mechanical Damping

Air damping is a common method of damping by mechanical means. As shown in figure 8–125, a vane is attached to the shaft of the moving element and enclosed in an air chamber. The movement of the shaft is retarded because of the resistance which the air offers to the vane. Effective damping is achieved if the vane nearly touches the walls of the chamber.

Meter Sensitivity

The sensitivity of a meter movement is usually expressed as the amount of current required to give full-scale deflection. In addition, the sensitivity may be expressed as the number of millivolts across the meter when full-scale current flows through it. This voltage drop is obtained by multiplying the full-scale current by the resistance of the meter movement. A meter movement, whose resistance is 50 ohms and which requires 1 milliampere (ma.) for full-scale reading, may be described as a 50-millivolt 0–1 milliammeter.

Extending the Range of an Ammeter

A 0–1 milliammeter movement may be used to measure currents greater than 1 ma. by connecting a resistor in parallel with the movement. The parallel resistor is called a shunt because it bypasses a portion of the current around the movement, extending the range of the ammeter.

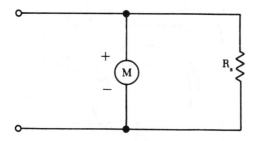

FIGURE 8–126. Meter movement with shunt.

A schematic drawing of a meter movement with a shunt connected across it to extend its range is shown in figure 8–126.

Determining the Value of a Shunt

The value of a shunt resistor can be computed by applying the basic rules for parallel circuits. If a 50 millivolt 0–1 milliammeter is to be used to measure values of current up to 10 ma., the following procedure can be used: The first step involves drawing a schematic of the meter shunted by a resistor labeled R_s (shunt resistor), as shown in figure 8–127.

Since the sensitivity of the meter is known, the meter resistance can be computed. The circuit is then redrawn as shown in figure 8–128, and the branch currents can be computed, since a maximum of 1 ma. can flow through the meter. The voltage drop across R_s is the same as that across the meter, R_m:

$$E = IR$$
$$= 0.001 \times 50$$
$$= 0.050 \text{ volt.}$$

R_s can be found by applying Ohm's law:

$$R_s = \frac{E_{rs}}{I_{rs}}$$
$$= \frac{0.050}{0.009}$$
$$= 5.55 \text{ ohms.}$$

The value of the shunt resistor (5.55 Ω) is very small, but this value is critical. Resistors used as shunts musts must have close tolerances, usually 1 percent.

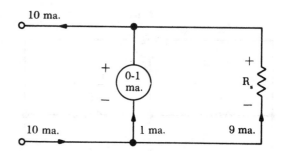

FIGURE 8–127. Circuit schematic for shunt resistor.

Universal Ammeter Shunt

The schematic drawing in figure 8–129, the universal shunt, shows an arrangement whereby two or more ranges are provided by tapping the shunt resistor at the proper points. In this arrangement, a 0–5 ma. movement with a resistance of 20 ohms is shunted to provide a 0–25 ma. range and a 0–50 ma. range.

Ammeters having a number of internal shunts are called multirange ammeters. A scale for each range is provided on the meter face (figure 8–130). Some multimeters avoid internal switching through the use of external shunts. Changing ammeter ranges involves the selection and installation on the meter case of the proper size shunt.

MULTIMETERS

Ammeters are commonly incorporated in multiple-purpose instruments such as multimeter or volt-ohm-milliammeters. These instruments vary somewhat according to the design used by different manufacturers, but most incorporate the functions of an ammeter, a voltmeter, and an ohmmeter in one unit. A typical multimeter is shown in figure 8–131. This multimeter has two

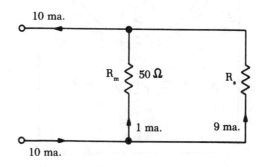

FIGURE 8–128. Equivalent meter circuit.

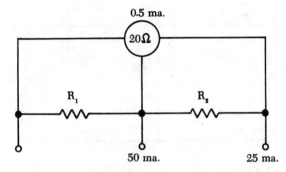

FIGURE 8–129. Universal ammeter shunt.

selector switches: a function switch and a range switch. Since a multimeter is actually three meters in one case, the function switch must be placed in proper position for the type of measurement to be made. In figure 8–131, the function switch is shown in the ammeter position to measure d.c. milliamperes and the range switch is set at 1000. Set in this manner, the ammeter can measure up to 1,000 milliamperes or 1 ampere.

Multimeters have several scales, and the one used should correspond properly to the position of the range switch. If current of unknown value is to be measured, always select the highest possible range to avoid damage to the meter. The test leads should always be connected to the meter in the manner prescribed by the manufacturer. Usually the red lead is positive and the black lead is negative, or common. Many multimeters employ color coded jacks as an aid

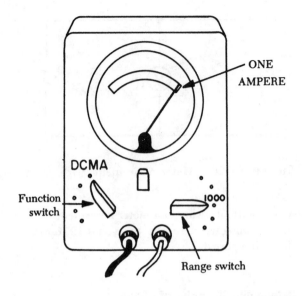

FIGURE 8–131. A multimeter set to measure one ampere.

in connecting the meter into the circuit to be tested. In figure 8–132, a multimeter properly set to measure current flow is connected into a circuit.

The precautions to be observed when using an ammeter are summarized as follows:

1. Always connect an ammeter in series with the element through which the current flow is to be measured.
2. Never connect an ammeter across a source of voltage, such as a battery or generator. Remember that the resistance of an ammeter, particularly on the higher ranges, is extremely low and that any voltage, even a volt or so, can cause very high current to flow through the meter, causing damage to it.
3. Use a range large enough to keep the deflection less than full scale. Before measuring a current, form some idea of its magnitude. Then switch to a large enough scale or start with the highest range and work down until the appropriate scale is reached. The most accurate readings are obtained at approximately half-scale deflection. Many milliammeters have been ruined by attempts to measure amperes. Therefore, be sure to read the lettering either on the dial or on the switch positions and choose proper scale before connecting the meter in the circuit.
4. Observe proper polarity in connecting the meter in the circuit. Current must flow

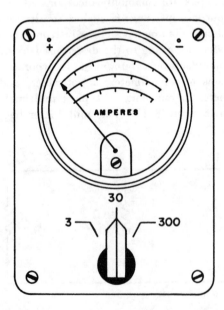

FIGURE 8–130. A multirange ammeter.

326

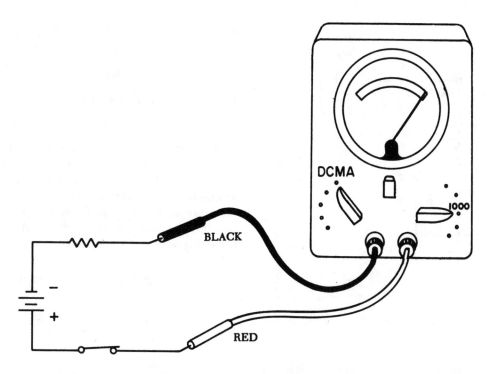

FIGURE 8–132.   A multimeter set to measure current flow.

through the coil in a definite direction in order to move the indicator needle up-scale. Current reversal because of incorrect connection in the circuit results in a reversed meter deflection and frequently causes bending of the meter needle. Avoid improper meter connections by observing the polarity markings on the meter.

VOLTMETER

The D'Arsonval meter movement can be used either as an ammeter or a voltmeter (figure 8–133). Thus, an ammeter can be converted to a voltmeter by placing a resistance in series with the meter coil and measuring the current flowing through it. In other words, a voltmeter is a current-measuring instrument, designed to indicate voltage by measuring the current flow through a resistance of known value. Various voltage ranges can be obtained by adding resistors in series with the meter coil. For low-range instruments, this resistance is mounted inside the case with the D'Arsonval movement and usually consists of resistance wire having a low temperature coefficient which is wound either on spools or card frames. For higher voltage ranges, the series resistance may be connected externally. When

this is done, the unit containing the resistance is commonly called a multiplier.

Extending the Voltmeter Range

The value of the necessary series resistance is determined by the current required for full-scale deflection of the meter and by the range of voltage

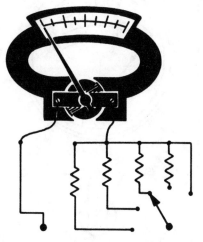

FIGURE 8–133.   Simplified diagram of a voltmeter.

327

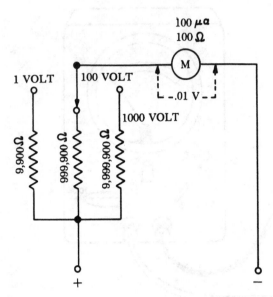

FIGURE 8–134. Multirange voltmeter schematic.

meter coil and the series resistance is

$$R = \frac{E}{I} = \frac{1}{0.0001} = 10,000 \text{ ohms},$$

and the series resistance alone is

$$R_s = 10,000 - 100 = 9,900 \text{ ohms}.$$

Multirange voltmeters utilize one meter movement with the required resistances connected in series with the meter by a convenient switching arrangement. A multirange voltmeter circuit with three ranges is shown in figure 8–134. The total circuit resistance for each of the three ranges beginning with the 1-volt range is:

$$R = \frac{E}{I} = \frac{1}{100} = 0.01 \text{ megohm}$$

$$\frac{100}{100} = 1 \text{ megohm}$$

$$\frac{1,000}{100} = 10 \text{ megohms}.$$

to be measured. Because the current through the meter circuit is directly proportional to the applied voltage, the meter scale can be calibrated directly in volts for a fixed series resistance.

For example, assume that the basic meter (microammeter) is to be made into a voltmeter with a full-scale reading of 1 volt. The coil resistance of the basic meter is 100 ohms, and 0.0001 ampere (100 microamperes) causes a full-scale deflection. The total resistance, R, of the

Multirange voltmeters, like multirange ammeters, are used frequently. They are physically very similar to ammeters, and their multipliers are usually located inside the meter with suitable switches or sets of terminals on the outside of the meter for selecting ranges (see figure 8–135).

Voltage-measuring instruments are connected across (in parallel with) a circuit. If the approximate value of the voltage to be measured is not known, it is best, as in using the ammeter, to start with the highest range of the voltmeter and progressively lower the range until a suitable reading is obtained.

In many cases, the voltmeter is not a central-zero indicating instrument. Thus, it is necessary to observe the proper polarity when connecting the instrument to the circuit, as is the case when connecting the d.c. ammeter. The positive terminal of the voltmeter is always connected to the positive terminal of the source, and the negative terminal to the negative terminal of the source, when the source voltage is being measured. In any case, the voltmeter is connected so that electrons will flow into the negative terminal and out of the positive terminal of the meter. In figure 8–136 a multimeter is properly connected to a circuit to measure the voltage drop across a resistor. The function switch is set at the d.c. volts position and the range switch is placed in the 50-volt position.

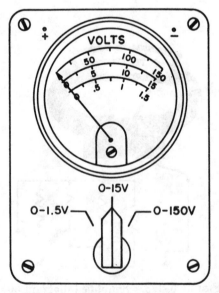

FIGURE 8–135. Typical multirange voltmeter.

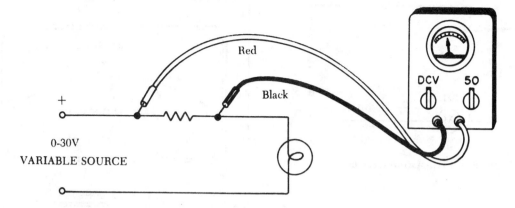

FIGURE 8–136.   A multimeter connected to measure a circuit voltage drop.

The function of a voltmeter is to indicate the potential difference between two points in a circuit. When the voltmeter is connected across a circuit, it shunts the circuit. If the voltmeter has low resistance, it will draw an appreciable amount of current. The effective resistance of the circuit will be lowered, and the voltage reading will consequently be lowered.

When voltage measurements are made in high-resistance circuits, it is necessary to use a high-resistance voltmeter to prevent the shunting action of the meter. The effect is less noticeable in low-resistance circuits because the shunting effect is less.

Voltmeter Sensitivity

The sensitivity of a voltmeter is given in ohms per volt (Ω/E) and is determined by dividing the resistance (R_m) of the meter plus the series resistance (R_s) by the full-scale reading in volts. Thus,

$$\text{sensitivity} = \frac{R_m + R_s}{E}.$$

This is the same as saying that the sensitivity is equal to the reciprocal of the current (in amperes); that is,

$$\text{sensitivity} = \frac{\text{ohms}}{\text{volts}} = \frac{1}{\dfrac{\text{volts}}{\text{ohms}}} = \frac{1}{\text{amperes}}$$

Thus, the sensitivity of a 100-microampere movement is the reciprocal of 0.0001 ampere, or 10,000 ohms per volt.

The sensitivity of a voltmeter can be increased by increasing the strength of the permanent magnet, by using lighter weight materials for the moving element (consistent with increased number of turns on the coil), and by using sapphire jewel bearings to support the moving coil.

Voltmeter Accuracy

The accuracy of a meter is generally expressed in percent. For example, a meter with an accuracy of 1 percent will indicate a value within 1 percent of the correct value. The statement means that, if the correct value is 100 units, the meter indication may be anywhere within the range of 99 to 101 units.

OHMMETERS

Two instruments are commonly used to check the continuity or to measure the resistance of a circuit or circuit element. These instruments are the ohmmeter and the megger, or megohmmeter. The ohmmeter is widely used to measure resistance and to check the continuity of electrical circuits and devices. Its range usually extends to a few megohms. The megger is widely used for measuring insulation resistance, such as the resistance between the windings and the frame of electric machinery, and for measuring the insulation resistance of cables, insulators, and bushings. Its range may extend to more than 1,000 megohms. When measuring very high resistances of this nature, it is not necessary to find the exact value of resistance, but rather to know that the insulation is either above or below a certain standard. When precision measurements are required, some type of bridge circuit is used. Ohmmeters may be of the series or shunt type.

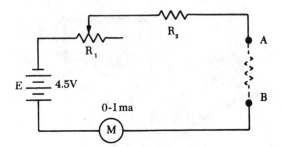

FIGURE 8–137. Ohmmeter circuit.

Series-type Ohmmeters

A simplified schematic of an ohmmeter is shown in figure 8–137. E is a source of EMF; R_1 is a variable resistor used to zero the meter; R_2 is a fixed resistor used to limit the current in the meter movement; and A and B are test terminals across which the resistance to be measured is placed.

If A and B are connected together (short-circuited), the meter, the battery, and resistors R_1 and R_2 form a simple series circuit. With R_1 adjusted so that the total resistance in the circuit is 4,500 ohms, the current through the meter is 1 ma. and the needle deflects full scale. Since there is no resistance between A and B, this position of the needle is labeled zero (figure 8–138). If a resistance equal to 4,500 ohms is placed between terminals A and B, the total resistance is 9,000 ohms and the current is .5 ma.

This causes the needle to deflect half scale. This half-scale reading, labeled 4.5 K ohms, is equal to the internal resistance of the meter, in this instance 4,500 ohms. If a resistance of 9,000 ohms is placed between terminals A and B, the needle deflects one-third scale. Resistances of 13.5 K and 1.5 K placed between terminals A and B will cause a deflection of one-fourth and three-fourths scale, respectively.

If terminals A and B are not connected (open-circuited), no current flows and the needle does not move. The left side of the scale is, therefore, labeled infinity to indicate an infinite resistance.

A typical ohmmeter scale is shown in figure 8–138. Note that the scale is not linear and is crowded at the high resistance end. For this reason, it is good practice to use an ohmmeter range in which the readings are not too far from mid-scale. A good rule is to use a range in which the reading obtained does not exceed ten times, or is not less than one-tenth, the mid-scale reading.

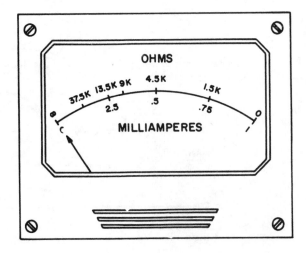

FIGURE 8–138. A typical ohmmeter scale.

The useful range of the scale shown is, by this rule, from 450 ohms to 45,000 ohms.

Most ohmmeters have more than one scale. Additional scales are made possible by using various values of limiting resistors and battery voltages. Some ohmmeters have a special scale called a low-ohm scale for reading low resistances. A shunt-type ohmmeter circuit is used for this scale.

Shunt-Type Ohmmeter

Shunt-type ohmmeters are used to measure small values of resistance. In the circuit shown in figure 8–139, E (voltage) is applied across a limiting resistor R and a meter movement in series. Resistance and battery values are chosen so that the meter movement deflects full scale when terminals A and B are open. When the terminals are short-circuited, the meter reads zero; the short circuit conducts all the current around the meter. The unknown resistance R_x is placed between terminals A and B in parallel with the meter movement. The smaller the resistance value being measured, the less current flows through the meter movement.

The value of the limiting resistor R is usually made large compared to the resistance of the meter movement. This keeps the current drawn from the battery practically constant. Thus, the value of R_x determines how much of this constant current flows through the meter and how much through R_x.

Note that in a shunt-type ohmmeter, current is always flowing from the battery through the meter

330

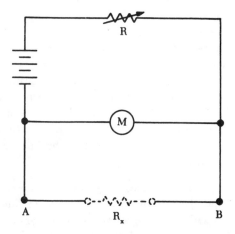

FIGURE 8–139. Shunt-type ohmmeter circuit.

movement and the limiting resistor. Therefore, when using an ohmmeter with a low-ohm scale, do not leave the switch in low-ohm position.

Use of the Ohmmeter

The ohmmeter is not as accurate a measuring device as the ammeter or the voltmeter because of the associated circuitry. Thus, resistance values cannot be read with greater than 5 to 10 percent accuracy. While there are instruments which read the resistance of an element with very great accuracy, they usually are more complicated to use.

In addition to measuring the resistance, the ohmmeter is a very useful instrument for checking continuity in a circuit. Often, when troubleshooting electronic circuits or wiring a circuit, visual inspections of all parts of the current path cannot be readily accomplished. Therefore, it is not always apparent whether a circuit is complete or whether current might be flowing in the wrong part of the circuit because of contact with adjacent circuits. The best method of checking a circuit under these conditions is to send a current through the circuit. The ohmmeter is the ideal instrument for checking circuits in this manner. It provides the power and the meter to indicate whether the current is flowing.

Observe the following precautions when using an ohmmeter:

(1) Choose a scale which will contain the resistance of the element to be measured. In general, use a scale in which the reading will fall in the upper half of the scale (near full-scale deflection).

(2) Short the leads together and set the meter to read zero ohms by setting the zero adjustment. If the scale is changed, readjust to zero ohms.

(3) Connect the unknown resistance between the test leads and read its resistance from the scale. Never attempt to measure resistance in a circuit while it is connected to a source of voltage. Disconnect at least one end of the element being measured to avoid reading the resistance of parallel paths.

Megger (Megohmmeter)

The megger, or megohmmeter, is a high-range ohmmeter containing a hand-operated generator. It is used to measure insulation resistance and other high resistance values. It is also used for ground, continuity, and short-circuit testing of electrical power systems. The chief advantage of the megger over an ohmmeter is its capacity to measure resistance with a high potential, or "breakdown" voltage. This type of testing ensures that insulation or a dielectric material will not short or leak under potential electrical stress.

The megger (figure 8–140) consists of two primary elements, both of which are provided with individual magnetic fields from a common permanent magnet: (1) A hand-driven d.c. generator, G, which supplies the necessary current for making the measurement and (2) the instrument portion, which indicates the value of the resistance being measured. The instrument portion is of the opposed-coil type. Coils A and B are mounted on the movable member with a fixed angular relationship to each other and are free to turn as a unit in a magnetic field. Coil B tends to move the pointer counterclockwise and coil A, clockwise. The coils are mounted on a light, movable frame that is pivoted in jewel bearings and free to move about axis 0.

Coil A is connected in series with R3 and the

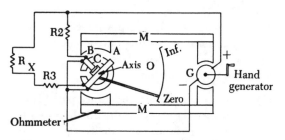

FIGURE 8–140. Simplified megger circuit.

331

unknown resistance, R_x, to be measured. The series combination of coil A, R3, and R_x is connected between the $+$ and $-$ brushes of the d.c. generator. Coil B is connected in series with R2 and this combination is also connected across the generator. There are no restraining springs on the movable member of the instrument portion of the megger. When the generator is not in operation, the pointer floats freely and may come to rest at any position on the scale.

If the terminals are open-circuited, no current flows in coil A, and the current in coil B alone controls the movement of the moving element. Coil B takes a position opposite the gap in the core (since the core cannot move and coil B can), and the pointer indicates infinity on the scale. When a resistance is connected between the terminals, current flows in coil A, tending to move the pointer clockwise. At the same time, coil B tends to move the pointer counterclockwise. Therefore, the moving element, composed of both coils and the pointer, comes to rest at a position at which the two forces are balanced. This position depends upon the value of the external resistance, which controls the relative magnitude of current of coil A. Because changes in voltage affect both coil A and B in the same proportion, the position of the moving element is independent of the voltage. If the terminals are short-circuited, the pointer rests at zero because the current in A is relatively large. The instrument is not damaged under these circumstances because the current is limited by R3.

There are two types of hand-driven meggers: the variable type and the constant-pressure type. The speed of the variable-pressure megger is dependent on how fast the hand crank is turned. The constant-pressure megger utilizes a centrifugal governor, or slip clutch. The governor becomes effective only when the megger is operated at a speed above its slip speed, at which speed its voltage remains constant.

BASIC CIRCUIT ANALYSIS AND TROUBLE-SHOOTING

Troubleshooting is the process of locating causes for malfunctions or trouble in a circuit. The following definitions serve as a guide in the troubleshooting discussion:

(1) Short circuit—a low resistance path. It can be across the power source or between the sides of a circuit. It usually creates high current flow which will burn out or cause

damage to the circuit conductor or components.

(2) Open circuit—a circuit that is not complete or continuous.

(3) Continuity—the state of being continuous, or connected together; said of a circuit that is not broken or does not have an open.

(4) Discontinuity—the opposite of continuity, indicating that a circuit is broken or not continuous.

Figure 8–141 includes some of the most common sources of open circuits (commonly called "opens" or "an open"). A loose connection or no connection is a frequent cause of an open circuit. In A of figure 8–141, the end of a conductor has separated from the battery terminal. This type of malfunction opens a circuit and stops the flow of current. Another type of malfunction that will cause an open circuit is a burned-out resistor, shown in B of figure 8–141. When a resistor overheats, its resistance value changes; and, if the current flow through it is great enough, it can burn and open the circuit. In C, D, and E of figure 8–141, three more likely causes of open circuits are shown.

The opens shown can often be located by visual inspection; however, many circuit opens cannot be seen. In such cases, a meter must be used.

The circuit shown in figure 8–142 is designed to cause current to flow through a lamp, but because of the open resistor, the lamp will not light. To locate this open, a voltmeter or an ohmmeter can be used.

If a voltmeter is connected across the lamp, as shown in figure 8–143, the voltmeter will read zero. Since no current can flow in the circuit because of the open resistor, there is no voltage drop across the lamp. This illustrates a troubleshooting rule that should be remembered: When a voltmeter is connected across a good (not defective) component in an open circuit, the voltmeter will read zero.

Next, the voltmeter is connected across the open resistor, as shown in figure 8–144. The voltmeter has closed the circuit by shunting (paralleling) the burned-out resistor, allowing current to flow. Current will flow from the negative terminal of the battery, through the switch, through the voltmeter and the lamp, back to the positive terminal of the battery. However, the resistance of the voltmeter is so high that only a very small current flows in the circuit. The current is too small to light the lamp, but the voltmeter will read the battery voltage. Another troubleshooting point worth

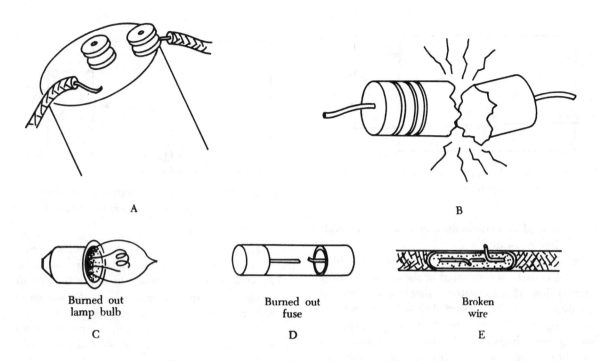

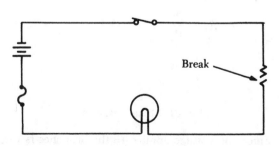

Burned out
lamp bulb

C

Burned out
fuse

D

Broken
wire

E

FIGURE 8–141.   Common causes of open circuits.

remembering is: When a voltmeter is placed across an open component in a series circuit, it will read the battery, or applied voltage.

This type of open circuit malfunction can also be traced by using an ohmmeter. When an ohmmeter is used, the circuit component to be tested must be isolated and the power source removed from the circuit. In this case, as shown in figure 8–145, these requirements can be met by opening the circuit switch. The ohmmeter is zeroed and placed across (in parallel with) the lamp. In this circuit, some value of resistance is read. This illustrates another important troubleshooting point: when an ohmmeter is properly connected across a circuit component and a resistance reading is obtained, the component has continuity and is not open.

When the ohmmeter is connected across the open resistor, as shown in figure 8–146, it indicates infinite resistance, or a discontinuity. Thus, the circuit open has been located with both a voltmeter and an ohmmeter.

An open in a series circuit will cause the current flow to stop. A short circuit, or "short," will cause the opposite effect. A short across a series circuit produces a greater than normal current flow. Some examples of shorts, as shown in figure 8–147, are two bare wires in a circuit that are touching each other, two terminals of a resistor connected together, etc. Thus, a short can be described as a

FIGURE 8–142.   An open circuit.

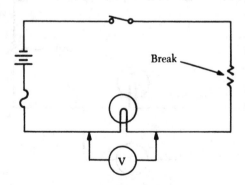

FIGURE 8–143.   Voltmeter across a lamp in an open circuit.

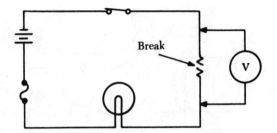

FIGURE 8–144. Voltmeter across a resistor in an open circuit.

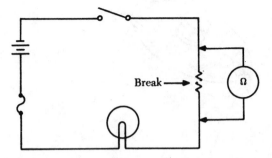

FIGURE 8–146. Using an ohmmeter to locate an open in a circuit component.

connection of two conductors of a circuit through a very low resistance.

In figure 8–148, a circuit is designed to light a lamp. A resistor is connected in the circuit to limit current flow. If the resistor is shorted, as shown in the illustration, the current flow will increase and the lamp will become brighter. If the applied voltage were high enough, the lamp would burn out, but in this case the fuse would protect the lamp by opening first.

Usually a short circuit will produce an open circuit by either blowing (opening) the fuse or burning out a circuit component. But in some circuits, such as that illustrated in figure 8–149, there may be additional resistors which will not allow one shorted resistor to increase the current flow enough to blow the fuse or burn out a component. Thus, with one resistor shorted out, the circuit will still function since the power dissipated by the other resistors does not exceed the rating of the fuse.

To locate the shorted resistor while the circuit is functioning, a voltmeter could be used. When it is connected across any of the unshorted resistors, a portion of the applied voltage will be indicated on

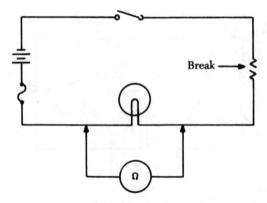

FIGURE 8–145. Using an ohmmeter to check a circuit component.

the voltmeter scale. When it is connected across the shorted resistor, the voltmeter will read zero.

The shorted resistor shown in figure 8–150 can be located with an ohmmeter. First the switch is opened to isolate the circuit components. In figure 8–150, this circuit is shown with an ohmmeter connected across each of the resistors. Only the ohmmeter connected across the shorted resistor shows a zero reading, indicating that this resistor is shorted.

The procedures used in troubleshooting a parallel circuit are sometimes different from those used in a series circuit. Unlike a series circuit, a parallel circuit has more than one path in which current flows. A voltmeter cannot be used, since, when it is placed across an open resistor, it will read the voltage drop in a parallel branch. But an ammeter or the modified use of an ohmmeter can be employed to detect an open branch in a parallel circuit.

If the open resistor shown in figure 8–151 was not visually apparent, the circuit would appear to be functioning properly, since current would continue to flow in the other two branches of the circuit. To determine that the circuit is not operating properly, the total resistance, total current, and the branch currents of the circuit should be calculated as if there were no open in the circuit:

$$R_t = \frac{N}{R}$$

$$= \frac{30}{3}$$

$$= 10 \; \Omega \text{ total resistance.}$$

Since the voltage applied to the branches is the same and the value of each branch resistance is

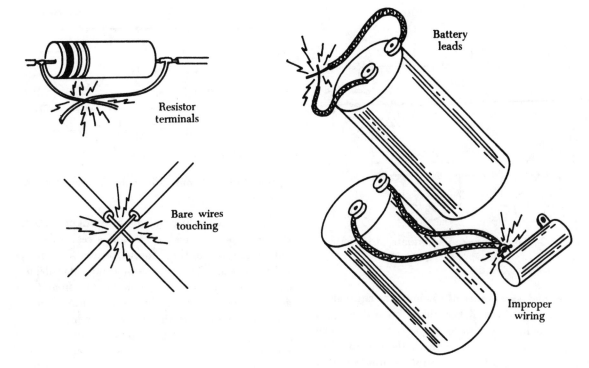

FIGURE 8–147. Common causes of short circuits.

known,

$$I_1 = \frac{E_1}{R_1} \qquad I_2 = \frac{E_2}{R_2}$$

$$= \frac{30V}{30\ \Omega} \qquad = \frac{30V}{30\ \Omega}$$

$$= 1 \text{ ampere.} \qquad = 1 \text{ ampere.}$$

$$I_3 = \frac{E_3}{R_3} \qquad I_T = \frac{E_T}{R_T}$$

$$= \frac{30V}{30\ \Omega} \qquad = \frac{30V}{10\ \Omega}$$

$$= 1 \text{ ampere.} \qquad = 3 \text{ amperes (total current).}$$

An ammeter placed in the circuit to read total current would show 2 amperes instead of the calculated 3 amperes. Since 1 ampere of current should be flowing through each branch, it is obvious that one branch is open. If the ammeter is connected into the branches, one after another, the open branch will be located by a zero ammeter reading.

A modified use of the ohmmeter can also locate this type of open. If the ohmmeter is connected across the open resistor, as shown in figure 8–152, an erroneous reading of continuity would be obtained. Even though the circuit switch is open, the open resistor is still in parallel with R_1 and R_2, and the ohmmeter would indicate the open

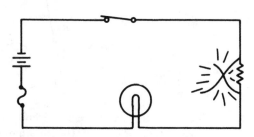

FIGURE 8–148. A shorted resistor.

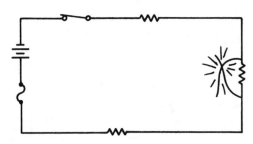

FIGURE 8–149. A short that does not open the circuit.

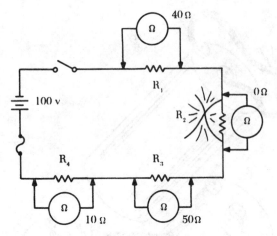

FIGURE 8–150. Using an ohmmeter to locate a shorted resistor.

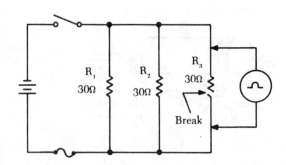

FIGURE 8–152. A misleading ohmmeter indication.

resistor had a resistance of 15 ohms, the equivalent resistance of the parallel combination of R_1 and R_2. Thus, it is necessary to open the circuit as shown in figure 8–153 in order to check the resistance of R_3. In this way the resistor is not shunted (paralleled) and the reading on the ohmmeter will indicate infinite resistance. On the other hand, if an open should occur in this circuit (figure 8–153) between the battery and point A, or between the battery and point B, current would not flow in the circuit.

As in a series circuit, a short in a parallel circuit will usually cause an open circuit by blowing the fuse. But, unlike a series circuit, one shorted component in a parallel circuit will stop current flow by causing the fuse to open. This can be seen by referring to the circuit in figure 8–154. If resistor R_3 is shorted, a path of almost zero resistance will be offered the current, and all the circuit current will flow through the branch containing the shorted resistor. Since this is practically the same as connecting a wire between the terminals of the battery, the current will rise

to an excessive value, and the fuse will open. Since the fuse opens almost as soon as a resistor shorts out, there is no time to perform a current or voltage check. Thus, troubleshooting a parallel d.c. circuit for a shorted component should be accomplished with an ohmmeter. But, as in the case of checking for an open resistor in a parallel circuit, a shorted resistor can be detected with an ohmmeter only if one end of the shorted resistor is disconnected.

Troubleshooting a series-parallel resistive circuit involves locating malfunctions similar to those found in a series or a parallel circuit.

In the circuit shown in figure 8–155, an open has occurred in the series portion of the circuit. When an open occurs anywhere in the series portion of a series-parallel circuit, current flow in the entire circuit will stop. In this case, the circuit will not function, and the lamp, L_1, will not be lit.

If an open occurs in the parallel portion of a series-parallel circuit, as shown in figure 8–156, part of the circuit will continue to function. In this case, the lamp will continue to burn, but its brightness will diminish, since the total resistance

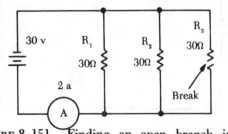

FIGURE 8–151. Finding an open branch in a parallel circuit.

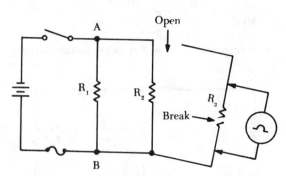

FIGURE 8–153. Opening a branch circuit to obtain an accurate ohmmeter reading.

336

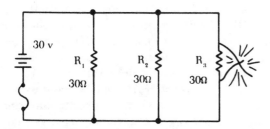

FIGURE 8–154. A shorted component causes the fuse to open.

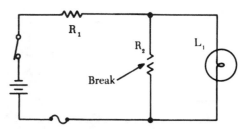

FIGURE 8–156. An open in the parallel portion of a series-parallel circuit.

of the circuit has increased and the total current has decreased.

If a break occurs in the branch containing the lamp, as shown in figure 8–157, the circuit will continue to function with increased resistance and decreased current, but the lamp will not burn.

To explain how the voltmeter and ohmmeter can be used to troubleshoot series-parallel circuits, the circuit shown in figure 8–158 has been labeled at various points. By connecting a voltmeter between points A and D, the battery and switch can be checked for opens. By connecting the voltmeter between points A and B, the voltage drop across R_1 can be checked. This voltage drop is a portion of the applied voltage. Also, if R_1 is open, the reading between B and D will be zero. The conductor between the positive terminal of the battery and point E, as well as the fuse, can be checked for continuity by connecting the voltmeter between points A and E. If the conductor or fuse is open, the voltmeter will read zero.

If the lamp is burning, it is obvious that no open exists in the branch containing the lamp, and the voltmeter could be used to detect an open in the branch containing R_2 by removing lamp, L_1, from the circuit.

Troubleshooting the series portion of a series-parallel circuit presents no difficulties, but in the

parallel portion of the circuit misleading readings can be obtained.

An ohmmeter can be used to troubleshoot this same circuit. With the switch open, the series portion of the circuit can be checked by placing the ohmmeter leads between points A and B. If R_1 or the conductor is open, the ohmmeter will read infinity; if not, the value of the resistor will be indicated on the ohmmeter. Between points D and E the fuse and conductor can be checked for continuity, but in the parallel portion of the circuit, care must be exercised, since misleading ohmmeter indications can be obtained. To check between points B and E, the branch must be disconnected at one of these points, and while one of these points and the switch are open, the branch containing the lamp can be checked with the ohmmeter.

A short in the series part of a series-parallel circuit will cause a decrease in total resistance, which will cause total current to increase. In the circuit shown in figure 8–159, the total resistance is 100 ohms and the total current is 2 amperes. If R_1 became shorted, total resistance would become 50 ohms, and the total current would double to 4 amperes. In the circuit shown, this would cause the 3-amp fuse to blow, but with a 5-amp fuse the circuit would continue to function. The result would be the same if R_2 or R_3 were to become shorted. The total resistance in either case would

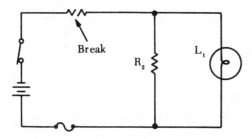

FIGURE 8–155. An open in the series portion of a series-parallel circuit.

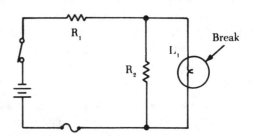

FIGURE 8–157. An open lamp in a series-parallel circuit.

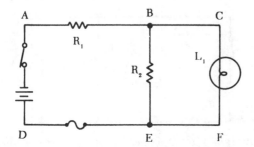

FIGURE 8–158. Using the voltmeter to trouble-shoot a series-parallel circuit.

drop to 50 ohms. From this, it can be stated that when a short occurs in a series-parallel circuit, the total resistance will decrease and the total current will increase. A short will normally cause an open circuit by either blowing the fuse or burning out a circuit component. And, as in the case of an open, a short in a series-parallel circuit can be detected with either an ohmmeter or a voltmeter.

ALTERNATING CURRENT AND VOLTAGE

Alternating current has largely replaced direct current in commercial power systems for a number of reasons. It can be transmitted over long distances more readily and more economically than direct current, since a.c. voltages can be increased or decreased by means of transformers.

Because more and more units are being operated electrically in airplanes, the power requirements are such that a number of advantages can be realized by using a.c. Space and weight can be saved, since a.c. devices, especially motors, are smaller and simpler than d.c. devices. In most a.c. motors no brushes are required, and commutation trouble at high altitude is eliminated. Circuit breakers will operate satisfactorily under load at high altitudes in an a.c. system, whereas arcing is so excessive on d.c. systems that circuit breakers must be replaced frequently. Finally, most airplanes using a 24-volt d.c. system have special equipment which requires a certain amount of 400-cycle a.c. current.

A. C. and D. C. Compared

Many of the principles, characteristics, and effects of alternating current are similar to those of direct current. Similarly, there are a number of differences which are explained later. Direct current flows constantly in only one direction with a constant polarity. It changes magnitude only when the circuit is opened or closed, as shown in the d.c. wave form in figure 8–160. Alternating current changes direction at regular intervals, increases in value at a definite rate from zero to a maximum positive strength, and decreases back to zero; then it flows in the opposite direction, similarly increasing to a maximum negative value, and again decreasing to zero. D.C. and a.c. wave forms are compared in figure 8–160.

Since alternating current constantly changes direction and intensity, two effects take place in a.c. circuits that do not occur in d.c. circuits. They are inductive reactance and capacitive reactance. Both are discussed later in this chapter.

Generator Principles

After the discovery that an electric current flowing through a conductor creates a magnetic field around the conductor, there was considerable scientific speculation about whether a magnetic field could create a current flow in a conductor. In 1831, the English scientist, Michael Faraday, demonstrated this could be accomplished. This discovery is the basis for the operation of the generator, which signalled the beginning of the electrical age.

To show how an electric current can be created by a magnetic field, a demonstration similar to that illustrated in figure 8–161 can be used. Several turns of a conductor are wrapped around a cylindrical form, and the ends of the conductor are connected together to form a complete circuit which includes a galvanometer. If a simple bar magnet is plunged into the cylinder, the galvanometer can be observed to deflect in one direction from its zero (center) position (A of figure 8–161). When the magnet is at rest inside the cylinder, the

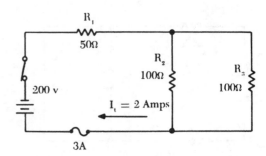

FIGURE 8–159. Finding a short in a series-parallel circuit.

338

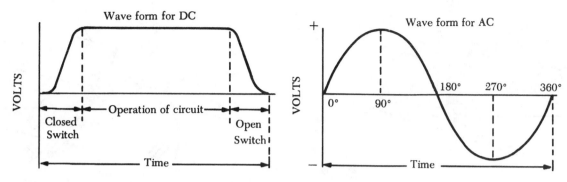

FIGURE 8–160.   D.C. and a.c. voltage curves.

galvanometer shows a reading of zero, indicating that no current is flowing (*B* of figure 8–161).

In *C* of figure 8–161, the galvanometer indicates a current flow in the opposite direction when the magnet is pulled from the cylinder.

The same results may be obtained by holding the magnet stationary and moving the cylinder over the magnet, indicating that a current flows when there is relative motion between the wire coil and the magnetic field. These results obey a law first stated by the German scientist, Heinrich Lenz. Lenz's law states that the induced current caused by the relative motion of a conductor and a magnetic field always flows in such a direction that its magnetic field opposes the motion.

When a conductor is moved through a magnetic field, as shown in figure 8–162, an electromotive force (e.m.f.) is induced in the conductor. The direction (polarity) of the induced e.m.f. is determined by the magnetic lines of force and the direction the conductor is moved through the magnetic field. The generator left-hand rule (not to be confused with the left-hand rules used with a coil) can be used to determine the direction of the induced e.m.f., as shown in figure 8–163. The first finger of the left hand is pointed in the direction of the magnetic lines of force (north to south), the thumb is pointed in the direction of movement of the conductor through the magnetic field, and the second finger points in the direction of the induced

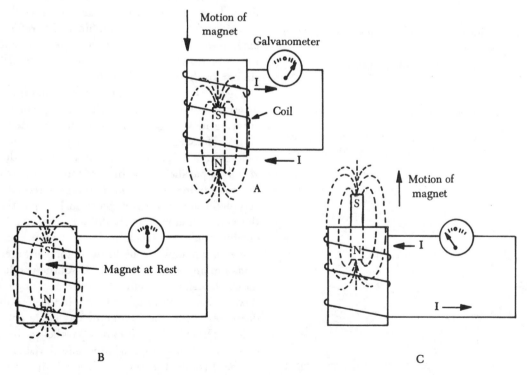

FIGURE 8–161.   Inducing a current flow.

339

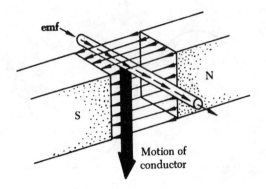

FIGURE 8–162. Inducing an e.m.f. in a conductor.

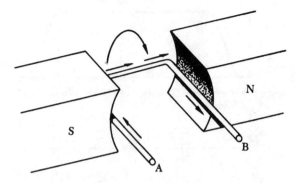

FIGURE 8–164. Voltage induced in a loop.

e.m.f. When two of these three factors are known, the third may be determined by the use of this rule.

When a loop conductor is rotated in a magnetic field (see figure 8–164), a voltage is induced in each side of the loop. The two sides cut the magnetic field in opposite directions, and although the current flow is continuous, it moves in opposite directions with respect to the two sides of the loop. If sides A and B and the loop are rotated half a turn and the sides of the conductor have exchanged positions, the induced e.m.f. in each wire reverses its direction, since the wire formerly cutting the lines of force in an upward direction is now moving downward.

The value of an induced e.m.f. depends on three factors:

(1) The number of wires moving through the magnetic field.
(2) The strength of the magnetic field.
(3) The speed of rotation.

Generators of Alternating Current

Generators used to produce an alternating current are called a.c. generators or alternators.

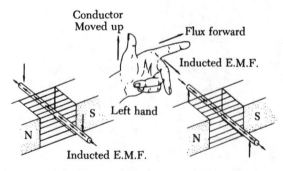

FIGURE 8–163. An application of the generator left-hand rule.

The simple generator shown in figure 8–165 constitutes one method of generating an alternating voltage. It consists of a rotating loop, marked A and B, placed between two magnetic poles, N and S. The ends of the loop are connected to two metal slip rings (collector rings), C_1 and C_2. Current is taken from the collector rings by brushes. If the loop is considered as separate wires A and B, and the left-hand rule for generators (not to be confused with the left-hand rule for coils) is applied, then it can be observed that as wire A moves up across the field, a voltage is induced which causes the current to flow inward. As wire B moves down across the field, a voltage is induced which causes the current to flow outward. When the wires are formed into a loop, the voltages induced in the two sides of the loop are combined. Therefore, for explanatory purposes, the action of either conductor, A or B, while rotating in the magnetic field is similar to the action of the loop.

Figure 8–166 illustrates the generation of alternating current with a simple loop conductor rotating in a magnetic field. As it is rotated in a counterclockwise direction, varying values of voltages are induced in it. At position 1, conductor A moves parallel to the lines of force. Since it cuts no lines of force, the induced voltage is zero. As the conductor advances from position 1 to position 2, the voltage induced gradually increases. At 2, the conductor moves perpendicular to the flux and cuts a maximum number of lines of force; therefore, a maximum voltage is induced. As the conductor moves beyond 2, it cuts a decreasing amount of flux at each instant, and the induced voltage decreases. At 3, the conductor has made one half of a revoltion and again moves parallel to the lines of force, and no voltage is induced in the conductor. As the A conductor passes position 3, the direction of induced voltage reverses since the A conductor

340

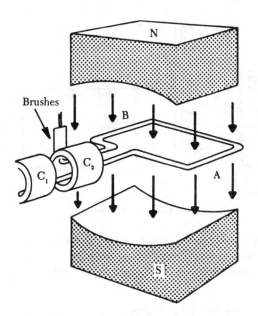
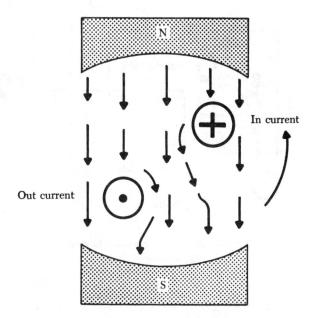

FIGURE 8–165. Simple generator.

now moves downward, cutting flux in the opposite direction. As the *A* conductor moves across the south pole, the induced voltage gradually increases in a negative direction, until at position 4 the conductor again moves perpendicular to the flux and generates a maximum negative voltage. From position 4 to 5, the induced voltage gradually decreases until the voltage is zero, and the conductor and wave are ready to start another cycle.

The curve shown at position 5 is called a sine wave. It represents the polarity and the magnitude of the instantaneous values of the voltages generated. The horizontal base line is divided into degrees, or time, and the vertical distance above or below the base line represents the value of voltage at each particular point in the rotation of the loop.

Cycle and Frequency

Whenever a voltage or current passes through a series of changes, returns to the starting point, and then again starts the same series of changes, the series is called a cycle. The cycle is represented by the symbol $\sim$. In the cycle of voltage shown in figure 8–167, the voltage increases from zero to a maximum positive value, decreases to zero; then increases to a maximum negative value, and again decreases to zero. At this point it is ready to go through the same series of changes. There are two

alternations in a complete cycle, the positive alternation and the negative. Each is half a cycle.

The number of times each cycle occurs in a period of time is called the frequency. The frequency of an electric current or voltage indicates the number of times a cycle recurs in 1 second.

In a generator, the voltage and current pass through a complete cycle of values each time a coil or conductor passes under a north and south pole of the magnet. The number of cycles for each revolution of the coil or conductor is equal to the number of pairs of poles. The frequency, then, is equal to the number of cycles in one revolution multiplied by the number of revolutions per second. Expressed in equation form,

$$F = \frac{\text{Number of poles}}{2} \times \frac{\text{r.p.m.}}{60}$$

where $\frac{P}{2}$ is the number of pairs of poles, and $\frac{\text{r.p.m.}}{60}$

the number of revolutions per second. If in a 2-pole generator, the conductor is turning at 3,600 r.p.m., the revolutions per second are

$$\text{r.p.s.} = \frac{3600}{60} = 60 \text{ revolutions per second.}$$

Since there are 2 poles, $\frac{P}{2}$ is 1, and the frequency

is 60 c.p.s. In a 4-pole generator with an armature

341

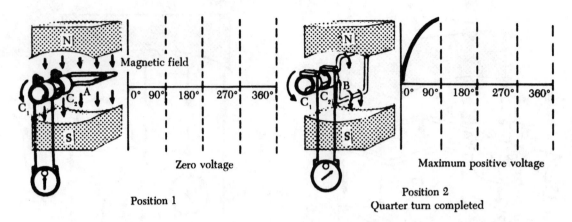

Position 1

Rotating conductors moving parallel to magnetic field, cutting minimum lines of force.

Position 2
Quarter turn completed

Conductors cutting directly across the magnetic field as conductor A passes across the North magnetic pole and B passes across the S pole.

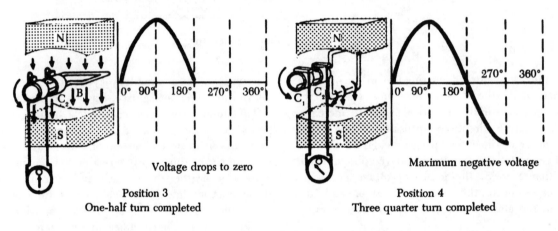

Position 3
One-half turn completed

Conductors again moving parallel to magnetic field, cutting minimum lines of force.

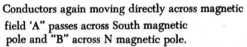

Position 4
Three quarter turn completed

Conductors again moving directly across magnetic field 'A" passes across South magnetic pole and "B" across N magnetic pole.

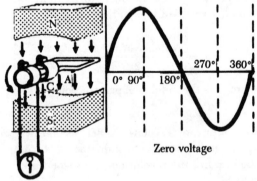

Conductor A has made one complete cycle and is in same position as in position A. The generator has generated one complete cycle of alternating voltage or current.

Position 5
Full turn completed

FIGURE 8–166.   Generation of a sine wave.

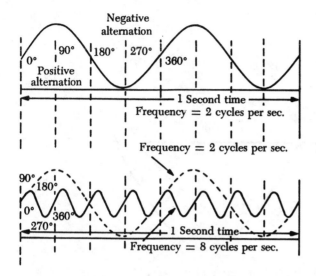

FIGURE 8–167. Frequency in cycles per second.

speed of 1,800 r.p.m., substitute in the equation,

$$F = \frac{P}{2} \times \frac{r.p.m.}{60} \text{, as follows:}$$

$$F = \frac{4}{2} \times \frac{1800}{60}$$

$$F = 2 \times 30$$

$$F = 60 \text{ c.p.s.}$$

In addition to frequency and cycle characteristics, alternating voltage and current also have a relationship called "phase." In a circuit that is fed (supplied) by one alternator, there must be a certain phase relationship between voltage and current if the circuit is to function efficiently. In a system fed by two or more alternators, not only must there be a certain phase relationship between voltage and current of one alternator, but there must be a phase relationship between the individual voltages and the individual currents. Also, two separate circuits can be compared by comparing the phase characteristics of one to the phase characteristics of the other.

When two or more sine waves pass through 0° and 180° at the same time and reach their peaks at the same time, an in-phase condition exists, as shown in figure 8–168. The peak values (magnitudes) do not have to be the same for the in-phase condition to exist. When the sine waves pass through 0° and 180° at different times and reach their peaks at different times, an out-of-phase condition exists, as shown in figure 8–169. The amount that the two sine waves are out of phase is indicated by the number of electrical degrees between corresponding peaks on the sine waves. In figure 8–169, the current and voltage are 30° out of phase.

Values of Alternating Current

There are three values of alternating current which should be considered. They are instantaneous, maximum, and effective.

An instantaneous value of voltage or current is the induced voltage or current flowing at any instant. The sine wave is a series of these values. The instantaneous value of the voltage varies from zero at 0° to maximum at 90°, back to zero at 180°, to maximum in the opposite direction at 270°, and to zero again at 360°. Any point on the sine wave is considered the instantaneous value of voltage.

The maximum value is the largest instantaneous value. The largest single positive value occurs when the sine wave of voltage is at 90°, and the largest single negative value occurs when it is at 270°. These are called maximum values. Maximum value is 1.41 times the effective value. (See figure 8–170.)

The effective value of alternating current is the same as the value of a direct current which can produce an equal heating effect. The effective value is less than the maximum value, being equal to .707 times the maximum value. Thus, the 110-volt value given for alternating current supplied to homes is only .707 of the maximum voltage of this supply. The maximum voltage is approximately 155 volts (110 × 1.41 = 155 volts maximum).

In the study of alternating current, any values given for current or voltage are assumed to be effective values unless otherwise specified, and in

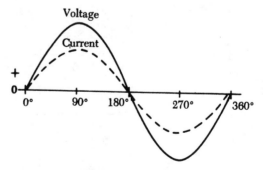

FIGURE 8–168. In-phase condition of current and voltage.

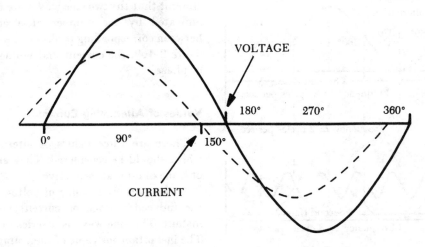

FIGURE 8–169. Out-of-phase condition of current and voltage.

practice, only the effective values of voltage and current are used. Similarly, alternating current voltmeters and ammeters measure the effective value.

INDUCTANCE

When an alternating current flows through a coil of wire, the rise and fall of the current flow, first in one direction, and then in another, sets up an expanding and collapsing magnetic field about the coil. A voltage is induced in the coil which is opposite in direction to the applied voltage and which opposes any change in the alternating current (see figure 8–171). The induced voltage is called the counter-electromotive force(abbreviated c.e.m.f.), since it opposes the applied voltage. This property of a coil to oppose any change in the current flowing through it is called inductance.

The inductance of a coil is measured in henrys. In any coil, the inductance depends on several factors, principally the number of turns, the cross-sectional area of the coil, and the material in the center of the coil or core. A core of magnetic material greatly increases the inductance of the coil.

It must be remembered, however, that even a straight wire has inductance, small though it may be when compared to that of a coil. A.C. motors, relays, and transformers contribute inductance to a circuit. Practically all a.c. circuits contain inductive elements.

The symbol for inductance in formulas is the capital letter "L." Inductance is measured in henrys (abbreviated h). An inductor (coil) has an inductance of 1 henry if an e.m.f. of 1 volt is induced in the inductor when the current through the inductor is changing at the rate of 1 ampere per second. However, the henry is a large unit of inductance and is used with relatively large inductors having iron cores. The unit used for small air-core inductors is the millihenry (mh). For still smaller air-core inductors the unit of

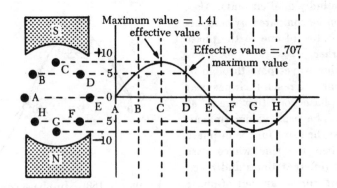

FIGURE 8–170. Effective and maximum values of voltage.

344

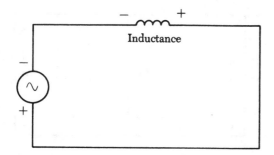

FIGURE 8–171. A.C. circuit containing inductance.

inductance is the microhenry (μh). Figure 8–172 shows a few of the various types of inductors, together with their symbols.

Inductors may be connected in a circuit in the same manner as resistors. When connected in series, the total inductance is the sum of the inductances of the inductors, or

$$L_T = L_1 + L_2 + L_3 \text{ , etc.}$$

When two or more inductors are connected in parallel, the total inductance is, like resistances in parallel, less than that of the smallest inductor, or

$$L_T = \frac{1}{\frac{1}{L_1} + \frac{1}{L_2} + \frac{1}{L_3}}.$$

The total inductance of inductors connected in series-parallel can be computed by combining the parallel inductances and then adding the series values. In all cases, these formulas are valid, providing the magnetic fields of the inductors do not interact.

Inductive Reactance

The opposition to the flow of current which inductances put in a circuit is called inductive reactance. The symbol for inductive reactance is X_L, and is measured in ohms, just as resistance is.

In any circuit in which there is only resistance, the expression for the relationship of voltage and current is Ohm's law: $I = \dfrac{E}{R}$. Similarly, when there is inductance in an a.c. circuit, the relationship between voltage and current can be expressed as:

$$\text{Current} = \frac{\text{Voltage}}{\text{Reactance}} \text{, or } I = \frac{E}{X_L} .$$

Where:

> X_L = inductive reactance of the circuit in ohms.

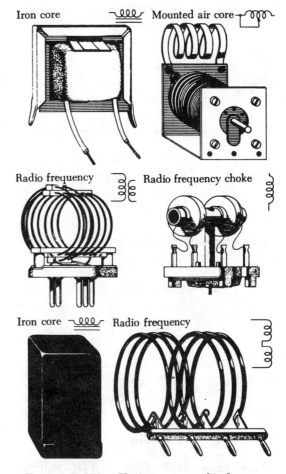

FIGURE 8–172.   Various types of inductors.

If all other circuit values remain constant, the greater the inductance in a coil, the greater the effect of self-induction, or opposition to the change in the value of current. As the frequency increases, the inductive reactance increases, since the greater the rate of current change the more the opposition to change by the coil increases. Therefore, inductive reactance is proportional to inductance and frequency or,

$$X_L = 2\pi fL.$$

Where:

> X_L = inductive reactance in ohms.
> f = frequency in cycles per second.
> π = 3.1416.

In figure 8–173, an a.c. series circuit is assumed in which the inductance is 0.146 henry and the voltage is 110 volts at a frequency of 60 cycles per second. What is the inductive reactance and the current flow? (The symbol $\bigodot$ represents an a.c. generator.)

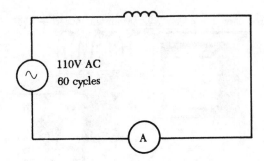

FIGURE 8–173.   A.C. circuit containing inductance.

Solution:

To find the inductive reactance:

$$X_L = 2\pi \times f \times L$$

$$X_L = 6.28 \times 60 \times 0.146.$$

To find current:

$$I = \frac{E}{X_L}$$

$$I = \frac{110}{55}$$

$$I = 2 \text{ amperes.}$$

In a.c. series circuits (figure 8–174), inductive reactances are added like resistances in series in a d.c. circuit. Thus, the total reactance in the circuit illustrated in figure 8–174 equals the sum of the individual reactances.

The total reactance of inductors connected in parallel (figure 8–175) is found the same way as the total resistance in a parallel circuit. Thus, the total reactance of inductances connected in parallel, as shown, is expressed as,

$$(X_L)_T = \cfrac{1}{\cfrac{1}{(X_L)_1} + \cfrac{1}{(X_L)_2} + \cfrac{1}{(X_L)_3}}$$

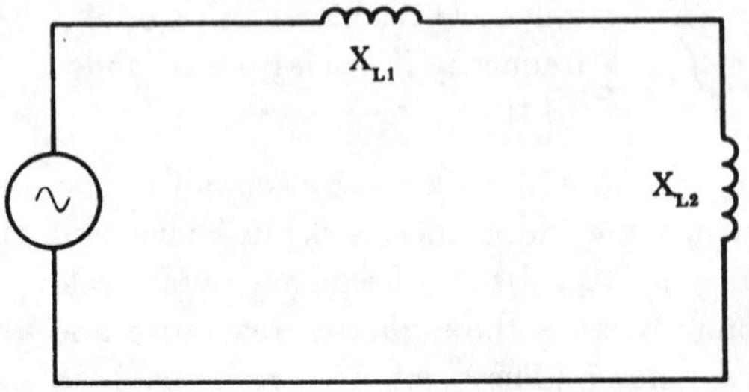

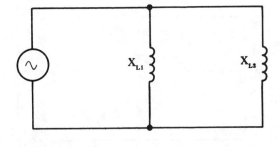

FIGURE 8–175.   Inductances in parallel.

CAPACITANCE

Another important property in a.c. circuits, besides resistance and inductance, is capacitance. While inductance is represented in a circuit by a coil, capacitance is represented by a capacitor.

Any two conductors separated by a nonconductor, called a dielectric, constitute a capacitor. In an electrical circuit, a capacitor serves as a reservoir or storehouse for electricity.

When a capacitor is connected across a source of direct current, such as a storage battery in the circuit shown in figure 8–176, and the switch is then closed, the plate marked B becomes positively charged, and the A plate negatively charged. Current flows in the external circuit during the time the electrons are moving from B to A. The current flow in the circuit is maximum the instant the switch is closed, but continually decreases thereafter until it reaches zero. The current becomes zero as soon as the difference in voltage of A and B becomes the same as the voltage of the battery. If the switch is opened, the plates remain charged. However, the capacitor quickly discharges when it is short circuited.

The amount of electricity a capacitor can store depends on several factors, including the type of material of the dielectric. It is directly proportional to the plate area and inversely proportional to the distance between the plates.

FIGURE 8–174.   Inductances in series.

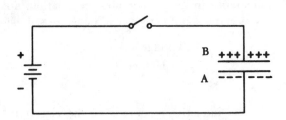

FIGURE 8–176.   Capacitor in a d.c. circuit.

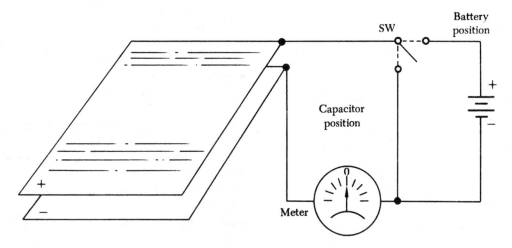

FIGURE 8-177. A basic capacitor (condenser) circuit.

In figure 8-177, two flat metal plates are placed close to each other (but not touching). Usually the plates are electrically neutral; that is, no electrical charge will be evident on either plate. At the instant the switch is closed to the battery position, the meter will show a definite current surge in one direction, but almost instantly will return to zero.

If the battery is then taken out of the circuit and the switch closed in the capacitor position, the meter again shows a momentary current surge, but this time in an opposite direction. From this experiment it is apparent that the two plates store energy when connected to a voltage source, and release the energy when short-circuited. The two plates make up a simple electrical capacitor, or condenser, and possess the property of storing electricity. The energy is actually stored in the electric, or dielectric, field between the plates.

Also, it should be clear that during the time the capacitor is being charged or discharged there is current in the circuit, even though the circuit is broken by the gap between the capacitor plates. However, there is current only during the time of charge and discharge, and this period of time is very short. There can be no continuous movement of direct current through a capacitor. A good capacitor will block direct current (not pulsating d.c.) and will pass the effects of alternating current.

The charge of electricity that can be placed on a capacitor is proportional to the applied voltage and to the capacitance of the capacitor (condenser). Capacitance depends upon the total area of the plates, the thickness of the dielectric and the composition of the dielectric.

If a thin sheet of bakelite (mica-filled) is substituted for air between the plates of a capacitor, for example, the capacitance will be increased about five times.

Any electric charge produced by applied voltage and kept in bounds by an insulator (dielectric) creates a dielectric field. Once the field is created, it tends to oppose any voltage change which would affect its original position. All circuits contain some capacitance, but unless they contain a unit called a capacitor, the capacitance, for all practical purposes, is disregarded. Two conductors, called electrodes or plates, separated by a nonconductor (dielectric) make up a simple capacitor. The plates may be made of copper, tin, or aluminum. Frequently, they are made of foil (metals compressed into thin sheets and capable of being rolled). The dielectric may be air, glass, mica, or an electrolyte made by an oxide film, but the type used will determine the amount of voltage that may be applied and the quantity of energy that will be stored. The dielectric materials have different atomic structures and present different quantities of atoms to the electrostatic field. All dielectric materials are compared to a vacuum and are given a numerical value according to the capacity ratio between them. The number given to a material is based on the same area and thickness as used in the vacuum. The numbers used to express this ratio are called dielectric constants and are expressed as the letter "K." The chart in figure 8-178 gives the K-value of some materials used.

If a source of alternating current is substituted for the battery, the capacitor acts quite differently than it does with direct current. When an

Material	K (Dielectric constant)
Air	1.0
Resin	2.5
Asbestos paper	2.7
Hard rubber	2.8
Dry paper	3.5
Isolantite	3.5
Common glass	4.2
Quartz	4.5
Mica	4.5–7.5
Porcelain	5.5
Flint glass	7.0
Crown glass	7.9

FIGURE 8–178.   Dielectric constants.

alternating current is impressed on the circuit (figure 8–179), the charge on the plates constantly changes. This means that electricity must flow first from Y clockwise around to X, then from X counterclockwise around to Y, then from Y clockwise around to X, and so on. Although no current flows through the insulator between the plates of the capacitor, it constantly flows in the remainder of the circuit between X and Y. In a circuit in which there is only capacitance, current leads the impressed voltage as contrasted with a circuit in which there is inductance, where the current lags the voltage.

The unit of measurement of capacitance is the farad, for which the symbol is the letter "f." The farad is too large for practical use, and the units generally used are the microfarad (μf.), one millionth of a farad, and the micromicrofarad ($\mu\mu$f.), one millionth of a microfarad.

Types of Capacitors

Capacitors may be divided into two groups: fixed and variable. The fixed capacitors, which

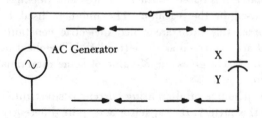

FIGURE 8–179.   Capacitor in an a.c. circuit.

have approximately constant capacitance, may then be further divided, according to the type of dielectric used, into the following classes: paper, oil, mica, and electrolytic capacitors. Ceramic capacitors are also used in some circuits.

When connecting electrolytic capacitors in a circuit, the proper polarity *must* be observed. Paper capacitors may have one terminal marked "ground," which means that this terminal connects to the outside foil. Polarity does not ordinarily have to be observed in connecting paper, oil, mica, or ceramic capacitors.

Paper Capacitors

The plates of paper capacitors are strips of metal foil separated by waxed paper (figure 8–180). The capacitance of paper capacitors ranges from about 200 $\mu\mu$f. to several μf. The strips of foil and paper are rolled together to form a cylindrical cartridge, which is then sealed in wax to keep out moisture and to prevent corrosion and leakage. Two metal leads are soldered to the plates, one extending from each end of the cylinder. The assembly is enclosed either in a cardboard cover or in a hard, molded plastic covering.

Bathtub-type capacitors consist of paper-capacitor cartridges hermetically sealed in metal containers. The container often serves as a common terminal for several enclosed capacitors, but when not a terminal, the cover serves as a shield against electrical interference (figure 8–181).

Oil Capacitors

In radio and radar transmitters, voltages high enough to cause arcing, or breakdown, of paper dielectrics are often employed. Consequently, in these applications capacitors that use oil or oil-impregnated paper for the dielectric material are preferred. Capacitors of this type are considerably more expensive than ordinary paper capacitors, and their use is generally restricted to radio and radar transmitting equipment (figure 8–182).

Mica Capacitors

The fixed mica capacitor is made of metal foil plates that are separated by sheets of mica, which form the dielectric. The whole assembly is covered in molded plastic, which keeps out moisture. Mica is an excellent dielectric and will withstand higher voltages than paper without allowing arcing between the plates. Common values of mica

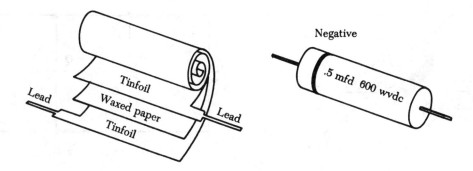

FIGURE 8–180.   Paper capacitors.

capacitors range from approximately 50 $\mu\mu f$, to about 0.02 μf. Mica capacitors are shown in figure 8–183.

Electrolytic Capacitors

For capacitances greater than a few microfarads, the plate areas of paper or mica capacitors must become very large; thus, electrolytic capacitors are usually employed instead. These units provide large capacitance in small physical sizes. Their values range from 1 to about 1,500 microfarads. Unlike the other types, electrolytic capacitors are generally polarized, and should be subjected to direct voltage, or pulsating direct voltage only; however, a special type of electrolytic capacitor is made for use in motors.

The electrolytic capacitor is widely used in electronic circuits and consists of two metal plates separated by an electrolyte. The electrolyte in contact with the negative terminal, either in paste or liquid form, comprises the negative electrode. The dielectric is an exceedingly thin film of oxide deposited on the positive electrode of the capacitor. The positive electrode, which is an aluminum sheet, is folded to achieve maximum area. The capacitor is subjected to a forming process during manufacture, in which current is passed through it. The flow of current results in the deposit of the thin coating of oxide on the aluminum plate.

The close spacing of the negative and positive electrodes gives rise to the comparatively high capacitance value, but allows greater possibility of voltage breakdown and leakage of electrons from one electrode to the other.

Two kinds of electrolytic capacitors are in use: (1) Wet-electrolytic and (2) dry-electrolytic capacitors. In the former, the electrolyte is a liquid and the container must be leakproof. This type should always be mounted in a vertical position.

The electrolyte of the dry-electrolytic unit is a paste contained in a separator made of an absorbent material such as gauze or paper. The separator not only holds the electrolyte in place but also prevents short-circuiting the plates. Dry-electrolytic capacitors are made in both cylindrical and rectangular-block form and may be contained either within cardboard or metal covers. Since the electrolyte cannot spill, the dry capacitor may be mounted in any convenient position. Electrolytic capacitors are shown in figure 8–184.

Capacitors in Parallel and in Series

Capacitors may be combined in parallel or series to give equivalent values, which may be either the

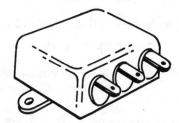

FIGURE 8–181.   Bathtub-case paper capacitor.

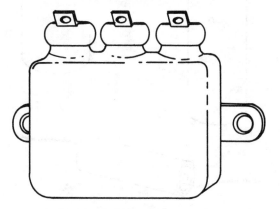

FIGURE 8–182.   Oil capacitor.

349

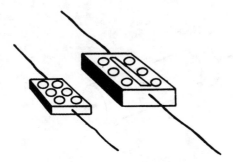

FIGURE 8–183. Mica capacitors.

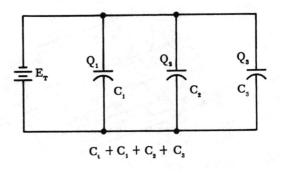

$$C_t + C_1 + C_2 + C_3$$

A Parallel

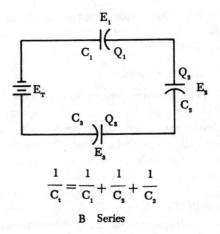

$$\frac{1}{C_t} = \frac{1}{C_1} + \frac{1}{C_2} + \frac{1}{C_3}$$

B Series

FIGURE 8–185. Capacitors in parallel and in series.

sum of the individual values (in parallel) or a value less than that of the smallest capacitance (in series). Figure 8–185 shows the parallel and series connections.

Two units used in the measurement of capacitance are the farad and the coulomb. As previously defined, the farad is the amount of capacitance present in a capacitor when one coulomb of electrical energy is stored on the plates and one volt is applied across the capacitor. One coulomb is the electrical charge of 6.28 billion billion electrons. From this it can be seen that

$$C \text{ (in farads)} = \frac{Q \text{ (in coulombs)}}{E \text{ (in volts)}}.$$

In A of figure 8–185 the voltage, E, is the same for all the capacitors. The total charge, Q_t, is the sum of all the individual charges, Q_1, Q_2, and Q_3.

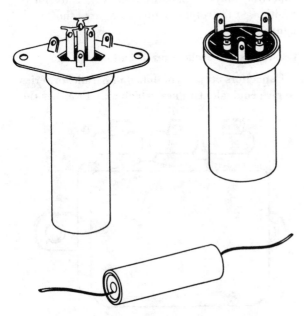

FIGURE 8–184. Electrolytic capacitors.

Using the basic equation for the capacitor,

$$C = \frac{Q}{E}.$$

The total charge is $Q_t = C_t E$, where C_t is the total capacitance. Since the total charge on capacitors in parallel is the sum of the individual capacitor charges,

$$Q_t = Q_1 + Q_2 + Q_3.$$

Using both equations for total charge develops the equation

$$C_t E = C_1 E + C_2 E + C_3 E.$$

Dividing both sides of this equation by E gives

$$C_t = C_1 + C_2 + C_3.$$

This formula is used to determine the total capacitance of any number of capacitors in parallel.

In the series arrangement, (B of figure 8–185), the current is the same in all parts of the circuit.

Each capacitor develops a voltage during charge, and the sum of the voltages of all the capacitors must equal the applied voltage, E. By the capacitor equation, the applied voltage, E, is equal to the total charge divided by the total capacitance, or

$$E = \frac{Q_t}{C_t}.$$

The total charge, Q_t, is equal to the charge on any one of the capacitors because the same current flows in all for the same length of time, and because the charge equals current multiplied by time in seconds $(Q_t = I \times T)$. Therefore,

$$Q_t = Q_1 = Q_2 = Q_3,$$

and, since in a circuit with capacitors in series

$$E_t = E_1 + E_2 + E_3,$$

where E_1, E_2, and E_3 are the voltages of the three capacitors. Then

$$\frac{Q_t}{C_t} = \frac{Q_t}{C_1} + \frac{Q_t}{C_2} + \frac{Q_t}{C_3}.$$

Dividing both sides of the equation by Q_t gives

$$\frac{1}{C_t} = \frac{1}{C_1} + \frac{1}{C_2} + \frac{1}{C_3}.$$

The reciprocal of the total capacitance of any number of capacitors in series is equal to the sum of the reciprocals of the individual values.

Parallel capacitors combine by a rule similar to that used to combine resistors in series. Series capacitors combine by a rule similar to that for combining parallel resistors.

In the series arrangement of two capacitors, C_1 and C_2, the total capacitance is given by the equation:

$$C_t = \frac{C_1 \times C_2}{C_1 + C_2}.$$

Voltage Rating of Capacitors

In selecting or substituting a capacitor for use in a particular circuit, the following must be considered: (1) The value of capacitance desired and (2) the amount of voltage to which the capacitor is to be subjected. If the voltage applied across the plates is too great, the dielectric will break down and arcing will occur between the plates. The capacitor is then short-circuited, and

Dielectric	K	Dielectric Strength (volts per .001 inch)
Air	1.0	80
Paper		
(1) Paraffined	2.2	1,200
(2) Beeswaxed	3.1	1,800
Glass	4.2	200
Castor oil	4.7	380
Bakelite	6.0	500
Mica	6.0	2,000
Fiber	6.5	50

FIGURE 8–186. Strength of some dielectric materials.

the possible flow of direct current through it can cause damage to other parts of the equipment. Capacitors have a voltage rating that should not be exceeded.

The working voltage of the capacitor is the maximum voltage that can be steadily applied without danger of arc-over. The working voltage depends on (1) the type of material used as the dielectric and (2) the thickness of the dielectric.

The voltage rating of the capacitor is a factor in determining the capacitance because capacitance decreases as the thickness of the dielectric increases. A high-voltage capacitor that has a thick dielectric must have a larger plate area in order to have the same capacitance as a similar low-voltage capacitor having a thin dielectric. The strength of some commonly used dielectric materials is listed in figure 8–186. The voltage rating also depends on frequency because the losses, and the resultant heating effect, increase as the frequency increases.

A capacitor that can be safely charged to 500 volts d.c. cannot be safely subjected to a.c. or pulsating d.c. whose effective values are 500 volts. An alternating voltage of 500 volts (r.m.s.) has a peak voltage of 707 volts, and a capacitor to which it is applied should have a working voltage of at least 750 volts. The capacitor should be selected so that its working voltage is at least 50 percent greater than the highest voltage to be applied to it.

Capacitance Reactance

Capacitance, like inductance, offers opposition to the flow of current. This opposition is called capacitive reactance and is measured in ohms. The symbol for capacitive reactance is X_c. The

351

equation,

$$\text{Current} = \frac{\text{Voltage}}{\text{Capacitive reactance}}, \text{ or}$$

$$I = \frac{E}{X_c},$$

is similar to Ohm's law and the equation for current in an inductive circuit. The greater the frequency, the less the reactance. Hence, the capacitive reactance,

$$X = \frac{1}{2\pi \times f \times C}$$

where: f = frequency in c.p.s.
C = capacity in farads.
2π = 6.28.

Problem:

A series circuit is assumed in which the impressed voltage is 110 volts at 60 c.p.s., and the capacitance of a condenser is 80 μf. Find the capacitive reactance and the current flow.

Solution:

To find capacitive reactance, the equation $X_c = \frac{1}{2\pi fC}$ is used. First, the capacitance, 80 μf., is changed to farads by dividing 80 by 1,000,000, since 1 million microfarads is equal to 1 farad. This quotient equals .000080 farad. This is substituted in the equation and

$$X_c = \frac{1}{6.28 \times 60 \times .000080}$$

$$X_c = 33.2 \text{ ohms reactance.}$$

Find the current flow:

$$I = \frac{E}{X_c}$$

$$I = \frac{110}{33.2}$$

$$I = 3.31 \text{ amperes.}$$

Capacitive Reactances in Series and in Parallel

When capacitors are connected in series, the total reactance is equal to the sum of the individual reactances. Thus,

$$X_{ct} = (X_c)_1 + (X_c)_2.$$

The total reactance of capacitors connected in parallel is found in the same way total resistance is computed in a parallel circuit:

$$(X_c)_t = \frac{1}{\dfrac{1}{(X_c)_1} + \dfrac{1}{(X_c)_2} + \dfrac{1}{(X_c)_3}}.$$

Phase of Current and Voltage in Reactive Circuits

When current and voltage pass through zero and reach maximum value at the same time, the current and voltage are said to be in phase (A of figure 8–187). If the current and voltage pass through zero and reach the maximum values at different times, the current and voltage are said to be out of phase. In a circuit containing only inductance, the current reaches a maximum value later than the voltage, lagging the voltage by 90°, or one-fourth cycle (B of figure 8–187). In a circuit containing only capacitance, the current reaches its maximum value ahead of the voltage and the current leads the voltage by 90°, or one-fourth cycle (C of figure 8–187). The amount the current lags or leads the voltage in a circuit depends on the relative amounts of resistance, inductance, and capacitance in the circuit.

OHM'S LAW FOR A. C. CIRCUITS

The rules and equations for d.c. circuits apply to a.c. circuits only when the circuits contain resistance alone, as in the case of lamps and heating elements. In order to use effective values of voltage and current in a.c. circuits, the effect of inductance and capacitance with resistance must be considered.

The combined effect of resistance, inductive reactance, and capacitive reactance makes up the total opposition to current flow in an a.c. circuit. This total opposition is called impedance and is represented by the letter "Z." The unit for the measurement of impedance is the ohm.

Series A. C. Circuits

If an a.c. circuit consists of resistance only, the value of the impedance is the same as the

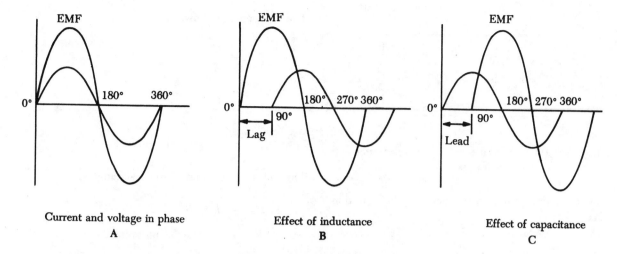

Current and voltage in phase A	Effect of inductance B	Effect of capacitance C

FIGURE 8–187. Phase of current and voltage.

resistance, and Ohm's law for an a.c. circuit, $I = \dfrac{E}{Z}$, is exactly the same as for a d.c. circuit. In figure 8–188 a series circuit containing a lamp with 11 ohms resistance connected across a source is illustrated. To find how much current will flow if 110 volts d.c. are applied and how much current will flow if 110 volts a.c. are applied, the following examples are solved:

$$I = \frac{E}{R} \qquad\qquad I = \frac{E}{Z} \text{ (where } Z = R)$$

$$= \frac{110\text{V}}{11\Omega} \qquad\qquad = \frac{110\text{V}}{11\Omega}$$

$$= 10 \text{ amperes d.c.} \qquad = 10 \text{ amperes a.c.}$$

When a.c. circuits contain resistance and either inductance or capacitance, the impedance, Z, is not the same as the resistance, R. The impedance of a circuit is the circuit's total opposition to the flow of current. In an a.c. circuit, this opposition consists of resistance and reactance, either inductive or capacitive, or elements of both.

Resistance and reactance cannot be added directly, but they can be considered as two forces acting at right angles to each other. Thus, the relation between resistance, reactance, and impedance may be illustrated by a right triangle, as shown in figure 8–189.

Since these quantities may be related to the sides of a right triangle, the formula for finding the impedance, or total opposition to current flow in an a.c. circuit, can be found by using the law of right triangles. This theorem, called the Pythagorean theorem, applies to any right triangle. It states that the square of the hypotenuse is equal to the sum of the squares of the other two sides. Thus, the value of any side of a right triangle can be found if the other two sides are known. If an a.c. circuit contains resistance and inductance, as shown in figure 8–190, the relation between the sides can be stated as:

$$Z^2 = R^2 + X_L^2.$$

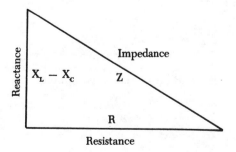

FIGURE 8–188. Applying d.c. and a.c. to a circuit.

FIGURE 8–189. Impedance triangle.

353

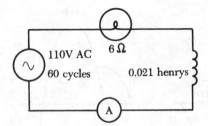

FIGURE 8–190. A circuit containing resistance and inductance.

The square root of both sides of the equation gives

$$Z = \sqrt{R^2 + X_L^2}.$$

This formula can be used to determine the impedance when the values of inductive reactance and resistance are known. It can be modified to solve for impedance in circuits containing capacitive reactance and resistance by substituting X_C in the formula in place of X_L. In circuits containing resistance with both inductive and capacitive reactance, the reactances can be combined, but because their effects in the circuit are exactly opposite, they are combined by subtraction:

$X = X_L - X_C$ or $X = X_C - X_L$ (the smaller is always subtracted from the larger).

In figure 8–190, a series circuit consisting of resistance and inductance connected in series is connected to a source of 110 volts at 60 cycles per second. The resistive element is a lamp with 6 ohms resistance, and the inductive element is a coil with an inductance of 0.021 henry. What is the value of the impedance and the current through the lamp and the coil?

Solution:

First, the inductive reactance of the coil is computed:

$$X_L = 2\pi \times f \times L$$
$$X_L = 6.28 \times 60 \times 0.021$$
$$X_L = 8 \text{ ohms inductive reactance.}$$

Next, the total impedance is computed:

$$Z = \sqrt{R^2 + X_L^2}$$
$$Z = \sqrt{6^2 + 8^2}$$
$$Z = \sqrt{36 + 64}$$
$$Z = \sqrt{100}$$
$$Z = 10 \text{ ohms impedance.}$$

Then the current flow,

$$I = \frac{E}{Z}$$

$$I = \frac{110}{10}$$

$$I = 11 \text{ amperes current.}$$

The voltage drop across the resistance (E_R) is

$$E_R = I \times R$$
$$E_R = 11 \times 6 = 66 \text{ volts.}$$

The voltage drop across the inductance (E_{X_L}) is

$$E_{X_L} = I \times X_L$$
$$E_{X_L} = 11 \times 8 = 88 \text{ volts.}$$

The sum of the two voltages is greater than the impressed voltage. This results from the fact that the two voltages are out of phase and, as such, represent the maximum voltage. If the voltage in the circuit is measured by a voltmeter, it will be approximately 110 volts, the impressed voltage. This can be proved by the equation

$$E = \sqrt{(E_R)^2 + (E_{X_L})^2}$$
$$E = \sqrt{66^2 + 88^2}$$
$$E = \sqrt{4356 + 7744}$$
$$E = \sqrt{12100}$$
$$E = 110 \text{ volts.}$$

In figure 8–191, a series circuit is illustrated in which a capacitor of 200 μf. is connected in series with a 10-ohm lamp. What is the value of the impedance, the current flow, and the voltage drop across the lamp?

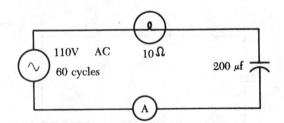

FIGURE 8–191. A circuit containing resistance and capacitance.

354

Solution:

First the capacitance is changed from μf. to farads. Since 1 million microfarads equal 1 farad, then

$$200 \ \mu f. = \frac{200}{1,000,000} = .000200 \text{ farads.}$$

$$X_C = \frac{1}{2\pi fC}$$

$$X_C = \frac{1}{6.28 \times 60 \times .000200 \text{ farads}}$$

$$X_C = \frac{1}{.07536}$$

$$X_C = 13 \text{ ohms capacitive reactance.}$$

To find the impedance,

$$Z = \sqrt{R^2 + X_C^2}$$
$$Z = \sqrt{10^2 + 13^2}$$
$$Z = \sqrt{100 + 169}$$
$$Z = \sqrt{269}$$
$$Z = 16.4 \text{ ohms capacitive reactance.}$$

To find the current,

$$I = \frac{E}{Z}$$

$$I = \frac{110}{16.4}$$

$$I = 6.7 \text{ amperes.}$$

The voltage drop across the lamp (E_R) is

$$E_R = 6.7 \times 10$$
$$E_R = 67 \text{ volts.}$$

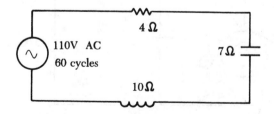

FIGURE 8–192. A circuit containing resistance, inductance, and capacitance.

The voltage drop across the capacitor (E_{XC}) is

$$E_{XC} = I \times X_C$$
$$E_{XC} = 6.7 \times 13$$
$$E_{XC} = 86.1 \text{ volts.}$$

The sum of these two voltages does not equal the applied voltage, since the current leads the voltage. To find the applied voltage, the formula $E_T = \sqrt{(E_R)^2 + (E_{XC})^2}$ is used.

$$E_T = \sqrt{67^2 + 86.1^2}$$
$$E_T = \sqrt{4489 + 7413}$$
$$E_T = \sqrt{11902}$$
$$E_T = 110 \text{ volts.}$$

When the circuit contains resistance, inductance, and capacitance, the equation

$$Z = \sqrt{R^2 + (X_L - X_C)^2}$$

is used to find the impedance.

Example:

What is the impedance of a series circuit (figure 8–192), consisting of a capacitor with a reactance of 7 ohms, an inductor with a reactance of 10 ohms, and a resistor with a resistance of 4 ohms?

Solution:

$$Z = \sqrt{R^2 + (X_L - X_C)^2}$$
$$Z = \sqrt{4^2 + (10 - 7)^2}$$
$$Z = \sqrt{4^2 + 3^2}$$
$$Z = \sqrt{25}$$
$$Z = 5 \text{ ohms.}$$

Assuming that the reactance of the capacitor is 10 ohms and the reactance of the inductor is 7 ohms, then X_C is greater than X_L. Thus,

$$Z = \sqrt{R^2 + (X_L - X_C)^2}$$
$$Z = \sqrt{4^2 + (7 - 10)^2}$$
$$Z = \sqrt{4^2 + (-3)^2}$$
$$Z = \sqrt{16 + 9}$$
$$Z = \sqrt{25}$$
$$Z = 5 \text{ ohms.}$$

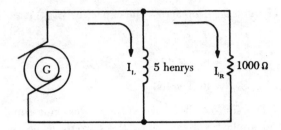

FIGURE 8-193. A.C. parallel circuit containing inductance and resistance.

Parallel A. C. Circuits

The methods used in solving parallel a.c. circuit problems are basically the same as those used for series a.c. circuits. Out-of-phase voltages and currents can be added by using the law of right triangles, but in solving circuit problems, the currents through the branches are added, since the voltage drops across the various branches are the same and are equal to the applied voltage. In figure 8-193, a parallel a.c. circuit containing an inductance and a resistance is shown schematically. The current flowing through the inductance, I_L, is 0.0584 ampere, and the current flowing through the resistance is 0.11 ampere. What is the total current in the circuit?

Solution:

$$I_T = \sqrt{I_L{}^2 + I_R{}^2}$$
$$= \sqrt{(0.0584)^2 + (0.11)^2}$$
$$= \sqrt{0.0155}$$
$$= 0.1245 \text{ ampere.}$$

Since inductive reactance causes voltage to lead the current, the total current, which contains a component of inductive current, lags the applied voltage. If the current and voltages are plotted, the angle between the two, called the phase angle, illustrates the amount the current lags the voltage.

In figure 8-194, a 110-volt generator is connected to a load consisting of a 2-μf. capacitance and a 10,000-ohm resistance in parallel. What is the value of the impedance and total current flow?

Solution:

First, find the capacitive reactance of the circuit:

$$X_C = \frac{1}{2 \pi \, fC}.$$

Changing 2μf. to farads and entering the values

into the formula given:

$$= \frac{1}{2 \times 3.14 \times 60 \times 0.000002}$$

$$= \frac{1}{0.00075360} \text{ or } \frac{10,000}{7.536}$$

$$= 1,327 \Omega \text{ capacitive reactance.}$$

To find the impedance, the impedance formula used in a series a.c. circuit must be modified to fit the parallel circuit:

$$Z = \frac{RX_C}{\sqrt{R^2 + X_C{}^2}}$$

$$= \frac{10,000 \times 1327}{\sqrt{(10,000)^2 + (1327)^2}}$$

$$= 0.1315 \Omega \text{ (approx.).}$$

To find the current through the capacitance:

$$I_C = \frac{E}{X_C}$$

$$= \frac{110}{1327}$$

$$= 0.0829 \text{ ampere.}$$

To find the current flowing through the resistance:

$$I_R = \frac{E}{R}$$

$$= \frac{110}{10,000}$$

$$= 0.011 \text{ ampere.}$$

To find the total current in the circuit:

$$I_T{}^2 = \sqrt{I_R{}^2 + I_C{}^2}$$
$$I_T = \sqrt{(0.011)^2 + (.0829)^2}$$
$$= 0.0836 \text{ ampere (approx.).}$$

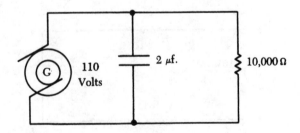

FIGURE 8-194. A parallel a.c. circuit containing capacitance and resistance.

356

Resonance

It has been shown that both inductive reactance ($X_L = 2\pi fL$) and capacitive reactance

$$(X_C = \frac{1}{2\pi fC})$$

are functions of an alternating current frequency. Decreasing the frequency decreases the ohmic value of the inductive reactance, but a decrease in frequency increases the capacitive reactance. At some particular frequency, known as the resonant frequency, the reactive effects of a capacitor and an inductor will be equal. Since these effects are the opposite of one another, they will cancel, leaving only the ohmic value of the resistance to oppose current flow in a circuit. If the value of resistance is small or consists only of the resistance in the conductors, the value of current flow can become very high.

In a circuit where the inductor and capacitor are in series, and the frequency is the resonant frequency, or frequency of resonance, the circuit is said to be "in resonance" and is referred to as a series resonant circuit. The symbol for resonant frequency is Fn.

If, at the frequency of resonance, the inductive reactance is equal to the capacitive reactance, then

$$X_L = X_C \text{, or}$$

$$2\pi fL = \frac{1}{2\pi fC}.$$

Dividing both sides by $2 fL$,

$$Fn^2 = \frac{1}{(2\pi)^2 LC}$$

Extracting the square root of both sides gives

$$Fn = \frac{1}{2\pi \sqrt{LC}}.$$

Where F_n is the resonant frequency in cycles per second, C is the capacitance in farads, and L is the inductance in henrys. With this formula the frequency at which a capacitor and inductor will be resonant can be determined.

To find the inductive reactance of a circuit use

$$X_L = 2 (\pi) fL$$

The impedance formula used in a series ac circuit must be modified to fit a parallel circuit.

$$Z = \frac{R_{XL}}{\sqrt{R^2 = XL^2}}$$

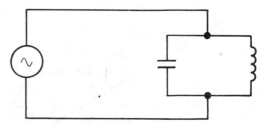

FIGURE 8–195. A parallel resonant circuit.

To find the parallel networks of inductance and capacitive reactors use

$$X = \frac{X_L X_C}{\sqrt{X_L + X_C}}$$

To find the parallel networks with resistance capacitive and inductance use:

$$Z = \frac{R X_L X_C}{X_L^2 X_C^2 + (RX_L - RX_C)^2}$$

Since at the resonant frequency X_L cancels X_C, the current can become very large, depending on the amount of resistance. In such cases, the voltage drop across the inductor or capacitor will often be higher than the applied voltage.

In a parallel resonant circuit (figure 8–195), the reactances are equal and equal currents will flow through the coil and the capacitor.

Since the inductive reactance causes the current through the coil to lag the voltage by 90°, and the capacitive reactance causes the current through the capacitor to lead the voltage by 90°, the two currents are 180° out of phase. The cancelling effect of such currents would mean that no current would flow from the generator and the parallel combination of the inductor and the capacitor would appear as an infinite impedance. In practice, no such circuit is possible, since some value of resistance is always present, and the parallel circuit, sometimes called a tank circuit, acts as a very high impedance. It is also called an antiresonant circuit, since its effect in a circuit is opposite to that of a series-resonant circuit, in which the impedance is very low.

Power in A. C. Circuits

In a d.c. circuit, power is obtained by the equation, $P = EI$, (watts equal volts times amperes). Thus, if 1 ampere of current flows in a circuit at a pressure of 200 volts, the power is 200 watts. The product of the volts and the amperes is the true power in the circuit.

In an a.c. circuit, a voltmeter indicates the effective voltage and an ammeter indicates the

357

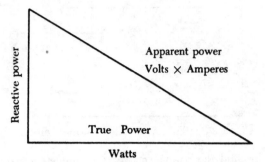

FIGURE 8-196. Power relations in a.c. circuit.

effective current. The product of these two readings is called the apparent power. Only when the a.c. circuit is made up of pure resistance is the apparent power equal to the true power (figure 8–196). When there is capacitance or inductance in the circuit, the current and voltage are not exactly in phase, and the true power is less than the apparent power. The true power is obtained by a wattmeter reading. The ratio of the true power to the apparent power is called the power factor and is usually expressed in percent. In equation form, the relationship is:

Power Factor $(PF) =$

$$\frac{100 \times \text{Watts (True Power)}}{\text{Volts} \times \text{Amperes (Apparent Power)}}.$$

Problem:

A 220-volt a.c. motor takes 50 amperes from the line, but a wattmeter in the line shows that only 9,350 watts are taken by the motor, What is the apparent power and the power factor?

Solution:

Apparent power = Volts × Amperes.
Apparent power = 220 × 50 = 11,000 watts or volt-amperes.

$$PF = \frac{\text{Watts (True Power)} \times 100}{VA \text{ (Apparent Power)}}$$

$$PF = \frac{9,350 \times 100}{11,000}$$

$$PF = 85, \text{ or } 85\%.$$

TRANSFORMERS

A transformer changes electrical energy of a given voltage into electrical energy at a different voltage level. It consists of two coils which are not electrically connected, but which are arranged in such a way that the magnetic field surrounding one coil cuts through the other coil. When an alternating voltage is applied to (across) one coil, the varying magnetic field set up around that coil creates an alternating voltage in the other coil by

mutual induction. A transformer can also be used with pulsating d.c., but a pure d.c. voltage cannot be used, since only a varying voltage creates the varying magnetic field which is the basis of the mutual induction process.

A transformer consists of three basic parts, as shown in figure 8–197. These are an iron core which provides a circuit of low reluctance for magnetic lines of force, a primary winding which receives the electrical energy from the source of applied voltage, and a secondary winding which receives electrical energy by induction from the primary coil.

The primary and secondary of this closed-core transformer are wound on a closed core to obtain maximum inductive effect between the two coils.

There are two classes of transformers: (1) Voltage transformers used for stepping up or stepping down voltages, and (2) current transformers used in instrument circuits.

In voltage transformers the primary coils are connected in parallel across the supply voltage, as shown in A of figure 8–198. The primary windings of current transformers are connected in series in the primary circuit (B of figure 8–198). Of the two types, the voltage transformer is the more common.

There are many types of voltage transformers. Most of these are either step-up or step-down transformers. The factor which determines whether a transformer is a step-up or step-down type is the "turns" ratio. The turns ratio is the ratio of the number of turns in the primary winding to the number of turns in the secondary winding. For example, the turns ratio of the step-down transformer shown in A of figure 8–199 is 5 to 1, since there are five times as many turns in the primary as in the secondary. The step-up

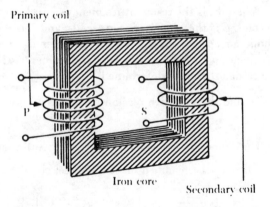

FIGURE 8-197. An iron-core transformer.

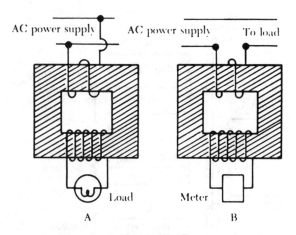

FIGURE 8–198. Voltage and current transformers.

transformer shown in *B* of figure 8–199 has a 1-to-4 turns ratio.

The ratio of the transformer input voltage to the output voltage is the same as the turns ratio if the transformer is 100 percent efficient. Thus, when 10 volts are applied to the primary of the transformer shown in *A* of figure 8–199, two volts are induced in the secondary. If 10 volts are applied to the primary of the transformer in *B* of figure 8–199, the output voltage across the terminals of the secondary will be 40 volts.

No transformer can be constructed that is 100 percent efficient, although iron-core transformers can approach this figure. This is because all the magnetic lines of force set up in the primary do not cut across the turns of the secondary coil. A certain amount of the magnetic flux, called leakage flux, leaks out of the magnetic circuit. The measure of how well the flux of the primary is coupled into the secondary is called the "coefficient of coupling." For example, if it is assumed that the primary of a transformer develops 10,000 lines of force and only 9,000 cut across the secondary, the coefficient of coupling would be .9 or, stated another way, the transformer would be 90 percent efficient.

When an a.c. voltage is connected across the primary terminals of a transformer, an alternating current will flow and self-induce a voltage in the primary coil which is opposite and nearly equal to the applied voltage. The difference between these two voltages allows just enough current in the primary to magnetize its core. This is called the exciting, or magnetizing, current. The magnetic field caused by this exciting current cuts across the secondary coil and induces a voltage by mutual induction. If a load is connected across the secondary coil, the load current flowing through

the secondary coil will produce a magnetic field which will tend to neutralize the magnetic field produced by the primary current. This will reduce the self-induced (opposition) voltage in the primary coil and allow more primary current to flow. The primary current increases as the secondary load current increases, and decreases as the secondary load current decreases. When the secondary load is removed, the primary current is again reduced to the small exciting current sufficient only to magnetize the iron core of the transformer.

If a transformer steps up the voltage, it will step down the current by the same ratio. This should be evident if the power formula is considered, for the power ($I \times E$) of the output (secondary) electrical energy is the same as the input (primary) power minus that energy loss in the transforming process. Thus, if 10 volts and 4 amps (40 watts of power) are used in the primary to produce a magnetic field, there will be 40 watts of power developed in the secondary (disregarding any loss). If the transformer has a step-up ratio of 4 to 1, the voltage across the secondary will be 40 volts and the current will be 1 amp. The voltage is 4 times greater and the current is one-fourth the primary circuit value, but the power ($I \times E$ value) is the same.

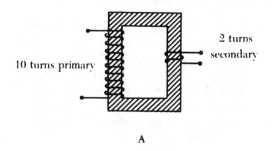

A

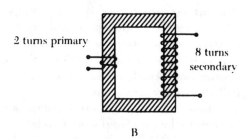

B

FIGURE 8–199. A step-down and a step-up transformer.

359

FIGURE 8–200.   Power supply transformer.

When the turns ratio and the input voltage are known, the output voltage can be determined as follows:

$$\frac{E_2}{E_1} = \frac{N_2}{N_1}.$$

Where E is the voltage of the primary, E_2 is the output voltage of the secondary, and N_1 and N_2 are the number of turns of the primary and secondary, respectively.

Transposing the equation to find the output voltage gives:

$$E_2 = \frac{E_1\,N_2}{N_1}.$$

The most commonly used types of voltage transformers are as follows:

(1) Power transformers are used to step up or step down voltages and current in many types of power supplies. They range in size from the small power transformer shown in figure 8–200 used in a radio receiver to the large transformers used to step down high-power line voltage to the 110–120 volt level used in homes.

In figure 8–201, the schematic symbol for an iron-core transformer is shown. In this case the secondary is made up of three separate windings. Each winding supplies a different circuit with a specific voltage, which saves the weight, space, and expense of three separate transformers. Each secondary has a midpoint connection, called a "center tap," which provides a selection of half the voltage across the whole winding. The leads from the various windings are color-coded by the manufacturer, as labeled in figure 8–201. This is a standard color code, but other codes or numbers may be used.

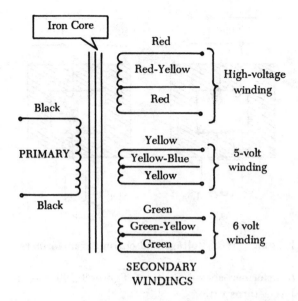

FIGURE 8–201.   Schematic symbol for an iron-core power transformer.

(2) Audio transformers resemble power transformers. They have only one secondary and are designed to operate over the range of audio frequencies (20 to 20,000 c.p.s.).

(3) RF transformers are designed to operate in equipment that functions in the radio range of frequencies. The symbol for the RF transformer is the same as for an RF choke coil. It has an air core as shown in figure 8–202.

(4) Autotransformers are normally used in power circuits; however, they may be designed for other uses. Two different symbols for autotransformers used in power or audio circuits are shown in figure 8–203. If used in an RF communication or navigation circuit (B of figure 8–203), it is the same, except there is no symbol for an iron core. The autotransformer uses part of a winding as a primary; and, depending on whether it is step-up or step-down, it uses all or part of the same winding as the secondary. For example, the autotransformer shown in A of figure 8–203 could use the following possible choices for primary and secondary terminals.

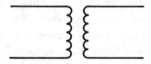

FIGURE 8–202.   An air-core transformer.

360

Current Transformers

Current transformers are used in a.c. power supply systems to sense generator line current and to provide a current, proportional to the line current, for circuit protection and control devices.

The current transformer is a ring-type transformer using a current-carrying power lead as a primary (either the power lead or the ground lead of the a.c. generator). The current in the primary induces a current in the secondary by magnetic induction.

The sides of all current transformers are marked "H1" and "H2" on the unit base. The transformers must be installed with the "H1" side toward the generator in the circuit in order to have proper polarity. The secondary of the transformer should never be left open while the system is being operated; to do so could cause dangerously high voltages, and could overheat the transformer. Therefore, the transformer output connections should always be connected with a jumper when the transformer is not being used but is left in the system.

Transformer Losses

In addition to the power loss caused by imperfect coupling, transformers are subject to "copper" and "iron" losses. Copper loss is caused by the resistance of the conductor comprising the turns of the coil. The iron losses are of two types called hysteresis loss and eddy current loss. Hysteresis loss is the electrical energy required to magnetize the transformer core, first in one di-

rection and then in the other, in step with the applied alternating voltage. Eddy current loss is caused by electric currents (eddy currents) induced in the transformer core by the varying magnetic fields. To reduce eddy current losses, cores are made of laminations coated with an insulation, which reduces the circulation of induced currents.

Power in Transformers

Since a transformer does not add any electricity to the circuit but merely changes or transforms the electricity that already exists in the circuit from one voltage to another, the total amount of energy in a circuit must remain the same. If it were possible to construct a perfect transformer, there would be no loss of power in it; power would be transferred undiminished from one voltage to another.

Since power is the product of volts times amperes, an increase in voltage by the transformer must result in a decrease in current and vice versa. There cannot be more power in the secondary side of a transformer than there is in the primary. The product of amperes times volts remains the same.

The transmission of power over long distances is accomplished by using transformers. At the power source the voltage is stepped up in order to reduce the line loss during transmission. At the point of utilization, the voltage is stepped down, since it is not feasible to use high voltage to operate motors, lights, or other electrical appliances.

Connecting Transformers in A. C. Circuits

Before studying the various means of connecting transformers in a.c. circuits, the differences between single-phase and three-phase circuits must be clearly understood. In a single-phase circuit the voltage is generated by one alternator coil. This single-phase voltage may be taken from a single-phase alternator, or from one phase of a three-phase alternator, as explained later in the study of a.c. generators.

In a three-phase circuit three voltages are generated by an alternator with three coils so spaced within the alternator that the three voltages generated are equal but reach their maximum values at different times. In each phase of a 400-cycle, three-phase generator, a cycle is generated every $\frac{1}{400}$ second.

In its rotation, the magnetic pole passes one

Primary			Secondary
1–2	used with		1–3
1–2	"	"	2–3
1–3	"	"	1–2
1–3	"	"	2–3
2–3	"	"	1–3
2–3	"	"	1–2

FIGURE 8–203. Autotransformers.

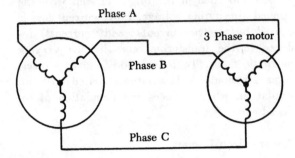

FIGURE 8–204. Three-phase generator using a three conductors.

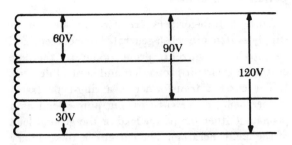

FIGURE 8–206. Tapped transformer secondary.

coil and generates a maximum voltage; one-third cycle ($\frac{1}{1200}$ second) later, this same pole passes another coil and generates a maximum voltage in it; and the next one-third cycle later, it passes still another coil and generates a maximum voltage in it. This causes the maximum voltages generated in the three coils always to be one-third cycle ($\frac{1}{1200}$ second) apart.

The early three-phase generators were connected to their loads with six wires and all six leads in the circuit carried the current. Later, experiments proved that the generator would furnish as much power with the coils connected so that only three wires were needed for all three phases as shown in figure 8–204. The use of three wires is standard for the transmission of three-phase power today. The return current from any one alternator coil always flows back through the other two wires in the three-phase circuit.

Three-phase motors and other three-phase loads are connected with their coils or load elements arranged so that three transmission lines are required for delivery of power. Transformers that are used for stepping the voltage up or down in a three-phase circuit are electrically connected so

that power is delivered to the primary and taken from the secondary by the standard three-wire system.

However, single-phase transformers and single-phase lights and motors may be connected across any one phase of a three-phase circuit, as shown in figure 8–205. When single-phase loads are connected to three-phase circuits, the loads are distributed equally among the three phases in order to balance the loads on the three generator coils.

Another use of the transformer is the single-phase transformer with several taps in the secondary. With this type of transformer, the voltage can be lowered to provide several working voltages, as shown in figure 8–206.

A center tapped transformer, powering a motor requiring 220 volts along with four lights requiring 110 volts, is shown in figure 8–207. The motor is connected across the entire transformer output, and the lights are connected from the center tap to one end of the transformer. With this connection only half of the secondary output is used.

This type of transformer connection is used

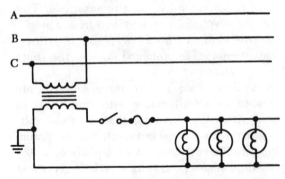

FIGURE 8–205. Step-down transformer using two-wire system.

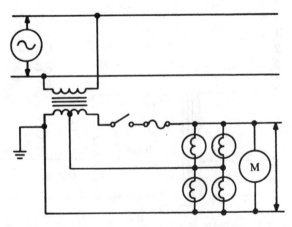

FIGURE 8–207. Step-down transformer using a three-wire system.

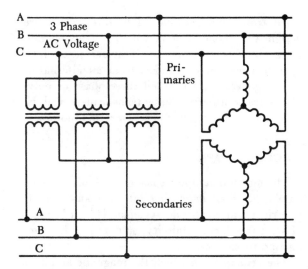

FIGURE 8–208.   Wye-to-wye connection.

extensively on aircraft because of the combinations of voltages that can be taken from one transformer. Various voltages can be picked off the secondary winding of the transformer by inserting taps (during manufacture) at various points along the secondary windings.

The various amounts of voltage are obtained by connecting to any two taps or to one tap and either end.

Transformers for three-phase circuits can be connected in any one of several combinations of the wye (y) and delta (Δ) connections. The connection used depends on the requirements for the transformer.

When the wye connection is used in three-phase

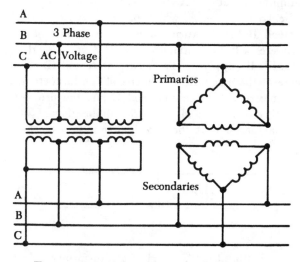

FIGURE 8–209.   Delta-to-delta connection.

transformers, a fourth or neutral wire may be used. The neutral wire connects single-phase equipment to the transformer. Voltages (115v) between any one of the three-phase lines and the neutral wire can be used for power for devices such as lights or single-phase motors.

In combination, all four wires can furnish power at 208 volts, three-phase, for operating three-phase equipment, such as three-phase motors or rectifiers. When only three-phase equipment is used, the ground wire may be omitted. This leaves a three-phase, three-wire system as illustrated in figure 8–208.

Figure 8–209 shows the primary and secondary with a delta connection. With this type of connection the transformer has the same voltage output as the line voltage. Between any two phases the voltage is 240 volts. In this type of connection, wires A, B, and C can furnish 240-volt, three-phase power for the operation of three-phase equipment.

The type of connection used for the primary coils may or may not be the same as the type of connection used for the secondary coils. For example, the primary may be a delta connection and the secondary a wye connection. This is called a delta-wye-connected transformer. Other combinations are delta-delta, wye-delta, and wye-wye.

Troubleshooting Transformers

There are occasions when a transformer must be checked for opens or shorts, and it is often necessary to determine that a transformer is a step-up or step-down transformer.

An open winding in a transformer can be located by connecting an ohmmeter as shown in figure 8–210. Connected as shown, the ohmmeter would read infinity. If there were no open in the coil, the ohmmeter would indicate the resistance of wire in the coil. Both primary and secondary can be checked in the same manner.

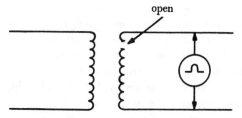

FIGURE 8–210.   Checking for an open in a transformer winding.

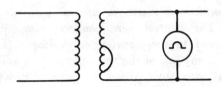

FIGURE 8–211. Checking for shorted
transformer windings.

The ohmmeter may also be used to check for shorted windings, as shown in figure 8–211, however, this method is not always accurate. If, for example, the transformer had 500 turns and a resistance of 2 ohms, and 5 turns were shorted out, the resistance would be reduced to approximately 1.98 ohms, which is not enough of a change to be read on the ohmmeter. In this case, the rated input voltage can be applied to the primary to permit measurement of the secondary output voltage. If the secondary voltage is low, it can be assumed that the transformer has some shorted windings, and the transformer should be replaced. If the output voltage is then normal, the original transformer can be considered defective.

An ohmmeter can be used to determine whether a transformer is a step-up or step-down transformer. In a step-down transformer, the resistance of the secondary will be less than that of the primary, and the opposite will be true in the case of a step-up transformer. Still another method involves applying a voltage to the primary and measuring the secondary output. The voltages used should not exceed the rated input voltage of the primary.

If a winding is completely shorted, it usually becomes overheated because of the high value of current flow. In many cases, the high heat will melt the wax in the transformer, and this can be detected by the resulting odor. Also, a voltmeter reading across the secondary will read zero. If the circuit contains a fuse, the heavy current may cause the fuse to blow before the transformer is heavily damaged.

In figure 8–212 one point on a transformer winding is shown connected to ground. If the external circuit of the transformer circuit is grounded, a part of the winding is effectively shorted. A megger connected between one side of the winding and the transformer case (ground) will verify this condition with a low or zero reading. In such a case, the transformer must be replaced.

All transformers discussed in this section are designed with one primary winding. They operate on a single source of a.c. Transformers which operate from three voltages from an alternator, or a.c. generator, are called three-phase or polyphase transformers. These transformers will be discussed in the study of generators and motors.

MAGNETIC AMPLIFIERS

The magnetic amplifier is a control device being employed at an increasing rate in many aircraft electrical and electronic systems. This is because of its ruggedness, stability, and safety in comparison to vacuum tubes.

The principles on which the magnetic amplifier operates can best be explained by reviewing the operation of a simple transformer. If an a.c. voltage is applied to the primary of an iron core transformer, the iron core will be magnetized and demagnetized at the same frequency as that of the applied voltage. This, in turn, will induce a voltage in the transformer secondary. The output voltage across the terminals of the secondary will depend on the relationship of the number of turns in the primary and the secondary of the transformer.

The iron core of the transformer has a saturation point after which the application of a greater magnetic force will produce no change in the intensity of magnetization. Hence, there will be no change in transformer output, even if the input is greatly increased.

The magnetic amplifier circuit in figure 8–213 will be used to explain how a simple magnetic amplifier functions. Assume that there is 1 ampere of current in coil A, which has 10 turns of wire. If coil B has 10 turns of wire, an output of 1 ampere will be obtained if coil B is properly loaded. By applying direct current to coil C, the core of the magnetic amplifier coil can be further magnetized. Assume that coil C has the proper number of turns and, upon the application of 30 milliamperes, that the core is magnetized to the

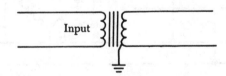

FIGURE 8–212. Part of a transformer
winding grounded.

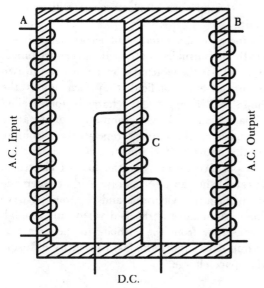

FIGURE 8–213.   Magnetic amplifier circuit.

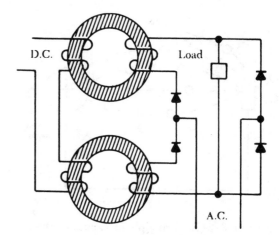

FIGURE 8–215.   Self-saturating, full-wave
magnetic amplifier.

point where 1 ampere on coil A results in only 0.24 ampere output from coil B.

By making the d.c. input to coil C continuously variable from 0 to 30 milliamperes and maintaining an input of 1 ampere on coil A, it is possible to control the output of coil B to any point between 0.24 ampere and 1 ampere in this example. The term "amplifier" is used for this arrangement because, by use of a few milliamperes, control of an output of 1 or more amperes is obtained.

The same procedure can be used with the circuit shown in figure 8–214.

By controlling the extent of magnetization of the iron ring, it is possible to control the amount of current flowing to the load, since the amount of magnetization controls the impedance of the a.c. input winding. This type of magnetic amplifier is called a simple saturable reactor circuit.

Adding a rectifier to such a circuit would remove half the cycle of the a.c. input and permit a direct current to flow to the load. The amount of

d.c. flowing in the load circuit is controlled by a d.c. control winding (sometimes referred to as bias). This type of magnetic amplifier is referred to as being self-saturating.

In order to use the full a.c. input power, a circuit such as that shown in figure 8–215 may be used. This circuit uses a full-wave bridge rectifier. The load will receive a controlled direct current by using the full a.c. input. This type of circuit is known as a self-saturating, full-wave magnetic amplifier.

In figure 8–216 it is assumed that the d.c. control winding is supplied by a variable source, such as a sensing circuit. In order to control such a source and use its variations to control the a.c. output, it is necessary to include another d.c. winding that has a constant value. This winding, referred to as the reference winding, magnetizes the magnetic core in one direction.

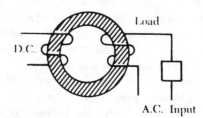

FIGURE 8–214.   Saturable reactor circuit.

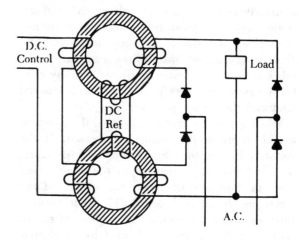

FIGURE 8–216.   Basic preamplifier circuit.

365

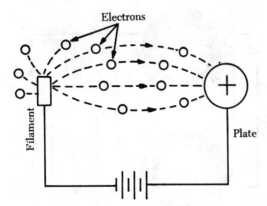

FIGURE 8–217.   Principle of vacuum tube
operation.

The d.c. control winding, acting in opposition to the reference winding, either increases (degenerative) or decreases (regenerative) the magnetization of the core to change the amount of current flowing through the load. This is essentially a basic preamplifier.

VACUUM TUBES

The use of vacuum tubes in aircraft electrical and electronic systems is rapidly declining because of the many advantages of using transistors. On the other hand, some systems still employ vacuum tubes in special applications, and a large number of older model aircraft still in service are equipped with devices that use vacuum tubes. For these reasons a general study of vacuum tubes is still considered a necessary part of the aviation maintenance program.

Originally, vacuum tubes were developed for radio work. They are used in radio transmitters as amplifiers for controlling voltage and current, as oscillators for generating audio and radio frequency signals, and as rectifiers for converting alternating current into direct current. Radio tubes are used for similar purposes in many electrical devices in aircraft, such as the automatic pilot and the turbosupercharger regulator.

When a piece of metal is heated, the speed of the electrons in the metal is increased. If the metal is heated to a high enough temperature, the electrons are accelerated to the point where some of them actually leave the surface of the metal, as shown in figure 8–217. In a vacuum tube, electrons are supplied by a piece of metal, called a cathode, which is heated by an electric current. Within limits, the hotter the cathode the greater the number of electrons it will give off or emit.

To increase the number of electrons emitted, the cathode is usually coated with special chemical compounds. If the emitted electrons are not drawn away by an external field, they form about the cathode into a negatively charged cloud called the space charge. The accumulation of negative electrons near the emitter repels others coming from the emitter. The emitter, if insulated, becomes positive because of the loss of electrons. This establishes an electrostatic field between the cloud of negative electrons and the now positive cathode. A balance is reached when only enough electrons flow from the cathode to the area surrounding it to supply the loss caused by diffusion of the space charge.

Types of Vacuum Tubes

There are many different types of vacuum tubes, most of which fall into four general types: (1) The diode, (2) the triode, (3) the tetrode, and (4) the pentode. Of these, the diode is used almost exclusively for changing a.c. current to d.c. current.

In some vacuum tubes, the cathode is heated by d.c. and is both the electron emitter and current carrying member, while in others the cathode is heated by a.c. Tubes designed for a.c. operation employ a special heating element which heats the electron emitter (cathode) indirectly.

When a d.c. potential is applied between the cathode and another element in the tube called a plate, with the positive side of the voltage connected to the plate, the electrons emitted by the cathode are attracted to the plate. These two elements constitute the simplest form of vacuum tube, which is the diode. In the diode, electrons are attracted to the plate, when it is more positive than the cathode, and are repelled when the plate is less positive than the cathode.

Current flows through the tube when it is connected in a circuit only when the plate is positive with respect to the cathode. Current does not flow when the plate is negative (less positive) with respect to the cathode as illustrated in figure 8–218. This characteristic gives the diode its principle use, that of rectification, or the changing of alternating current into direct current.

Diode rectifiers are used in aircraft electrical systems, especially when high voltage d.c. is desired for light loads. They may be used as either half-wave or full-wave rectifiers; they may be

366

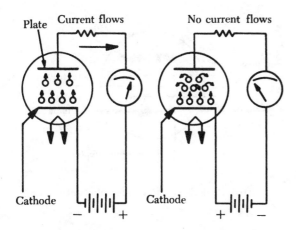

FIGURE 8–218. Diode tube operation.

used singly, in parallel, or in bridge circuits. As shown in figure 8–219, a half-wave rectifier contains two tube elements (plate and cathode). A full-wave rectifier contains three elements (two plates and a cathode).

In the half-wave circuit, current flows only during the positive half of the cycle of the applied voltage (plate positive, cathode negative for electron flow). It flows from the cathode to the plate and then through the load back to the cathode. On the negative cycle of the applied voltage, no current flows through the tube. As a result, the rectified output voltage is d.c., but it consists of pulses, or half cycles, of current.

In a vacuum tube connected as a full-wave rectifier, current flows to the load on both half cycles of the alternating voltage. In the full-wave rectifier, current flows from the top plate through the d.c. load on one alternation, and on the next

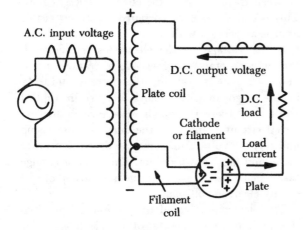

FIGURE 8–219. Half-wave vacuum tube rectifier circuit.

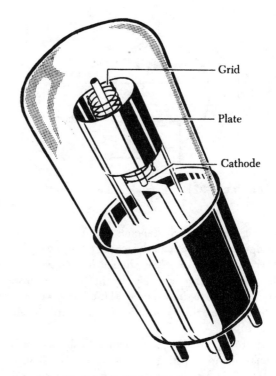

FIGURE 8–220. Triode tube.

alternation, current flows to the lower plate and through the load in the same direction.

Vacuum tube rectifiers have been replaced to a great degree in aircraft systems by dry-disk or semiconductor diodes. In the study of solid state devices the process of rectification is treated in greater detail.

The triode tube is a three-element tube. In addition to the plate and cathode, there is a third element, called the grid, located between the cathode and the plate as shown in figure 8–220. The grid is a fine-wire mesh or screen. It serves to control the electron flow between the cathode and the plate. Whenever the grid is made more positive than the cathode, there is an increase in the number of electrons attracted to the plate, resulting in an increase in plate current flow. If the grid is made negative with respect to the cathode, electron movement to the plate is retarded and plate current flow decreases.

Usually the grid is negative with reference to the cathode. One method of making the grid negative is to use a small battery connected in series with the grid circuit. This negative voltage applied to the grid is called bias.

The most important use of a triode is as an amplifier tube. When a resistance or impedance is connected in series in the plate circuit, the voltage

367

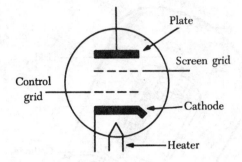

FIGURE 8–221.　Tetrode tube schematic.

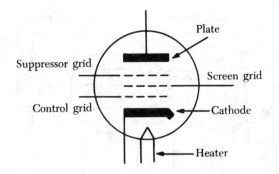

FIGURE 8–222.　Pentode schematic.

drop across it, which depends upon the current flowing through it, can be changed by varying the grid voltage. A small change in grid voltage will cause a large change in the voltage drop across the plate impedance. Thus, the voltage applied to the grid is amplified in the plate circuit of the tube.

A tetrode tube is a four-element tube, the additional element being the screen grid (figure 8–221). This grid is located between the control grid and the plate. The screen grid is operated at a positive voltage somewhat lower than the plate voltage. It reduces the sometimes undesirable effect in tube operation caused by energy fed from the output of a tube back into the input (grid) circuit.

Under certain operating conditions, this feedback action is very pronounced in a triode and causes the tube to act as an oscillator instead of an amplifier. The chief advantages of tetrodes over triodes are greater amplification for smaller input voltages, and less feedback from the plate to the grid circuit.

An undesirable characteristic of the tetrode tube is secondary emission. Secondary emission is the term applied to the condition where electrons are knocked out of the plate into the space between the elements of a tube by rapidly moving electrons striking the plate. In triode tubes, since the grid is negative with respect to the cathode, it repels the secondary electrons and tube operation is undisturbed. In the tetrode, the effect of secondary emission is especially noticeable since the screen grid, which is positive with respect to the cathode, attracts the secondary electrons and causes a reverse current to flow between the screen and plate.

The effects of secondary emission are overcome by adding a third grid, called the suppressor grid, between the screen grid and the plate. This grid

repels the secondary electrons toward the plate. A tube with three grids is called a pentode, which has a high amplification factor and is used to amplify weak signals. The schematic of a pentode is shown in figure 8–222.

Another type of vacuum tube is the gas tube. Gas-filled tubes are primarily diodes and are used mostly as rectifiers. In tubes of this type the gas should be one ten-thousandth as dense as air under normal atmospheric pressure. When an electron meets a gas molecule, the energy imparted by the impact can cause the molecule (or atom) to lose or gain one or more electrons. Consequently, ionization takes place.

Any gas or vapor having no ions is practically a perfect insulator. If two electrodes are placed in such a medium, no current will flow between them. However, gases always have some residual ionization because of cosmic rays, radioactive materials in the walls of the containers, or the action of light. If a potential is applied between two elements in such a gas, the ions migrate between them and give the effect of current flow. This is called the dark current because no visible light is associated with it.

If the voltage on the electrodes is increased, the current starts to rise. At a certain point, known as the threshold, the current suddenly begins to go up without any increase in applied voltage. If there is enough resistance in the external circuit to prevent the current from rising quickly, the voltage immediately drops to a lower value and breakdown occurs. This abrupt change takes place as a result of the ionization of the gas by electron collision.

The electrons released by the ionized gas join the stream and liberate other electrons. The process, then, is cumulative. Breakdown voltage is determined primarily by the type of gas, the materials used for the electrodes, and their size and spacing. Once ionization takes place, the current can rise to 50 milliamperes (ma.), or more, with little change in the voltage applied. If the voltage is increased, the current increases and the cathode is heated by the bombardment of the ions which strike it. When the tube gets hot enough, thermionic emission results.

This emission reduces the voltage loss in the tube, which, in turn, causes more current to flow and increases the rate of emission and ionization. This cumulative action causes a sudden decrease in the voltage drop across the tube and an extremely high rise in current flow. Unless the tube is designed to operate in this manner, it can be damaged by heavy current flow. This is basic to the formation of an arc; therefore, tubes that operate at these high currents are called arc tubes. For currents up to 50 milliamperes, the unit usually is small and is termed a glow tube because of the colored light it emits. An example of such a tube is the familiar neon light.

The principle of grid control can be applied to almost any gas tube, but it is used specifically with cold cathode, hot cathode, and arc types of triodes and tetrodes. The hot cathode type of three-element gas tube is given the general name of thyratron.

The phototube is another special type of vacuum tube. It is basically the same as the simple diode discussed earlier. It has an evacuated glass bulb, a cathode which emits electrons when light is allowed to fall upon it, and a plate which

attracts electrons when a voltage is applied. The sensitivity of the tube depends on the frequency or color of the light used to excite it and is specified in these terms.

For example, some tubes are sensitive to red light, others to blue light. In most phototubes, the cathode resembles a half cylinder. It is covered with multiple layers of the rare metal, cesium, overlaid on cesium oxide, which, in turn, lies on a layer of silver. The plate is shaped like a small rod and is located in the center of the cathode.

Other types of vacuum tubes include those with the characteristics of several tubes incorporated into one, as shown in figure 8–223. Among these, for example, are twin triode tubes containing two triode sections in a single tube envelope, and diode-triode tubes with a rectifier diode and an amplifier triode in the same envelope. There are many other tube combinations.

TRANSISTORS

The transistor is an electronic device that is capable of performing most of the functions of vacuum tubes. It is very small, light in weight, and requires no heater. It is also mechanically rugged and does not pick up stray signals. Transistors have been in general use for more than a decade, but compared to some of the components they are replacing they are relatively new. As research progresses, new discoveries often cause some elements of transistor theory to be modified.

A transistor is a semiconductor device consisting of two types of materials each of which exhibits electrical properties. Semiconductors are materials whose resistive characteristics fall approximately midway between those of good conductors and insulators. The interface between the parts is called a junction. Selenium and germanium diodes (rectifiers) are examples of such devices and are called junction diodes. Most transistors are made of germanium to which certain impurities are added to impart certain characteristics. The impurities used are generally arsenic or indium.

The type of transistor which may be used in some applications in place of the triode tube is the "junction" transistor, which actually has two junctions. It has an emitter, base, and collector which correspond to the cathode, grid, and plate, respectively, in the triode tube. Junction transistors are of two types, the NPN type and the PNP type (see figure 8–224).

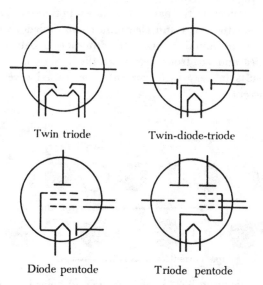

Twin triode   Twin-diode-triode

Diode pentode   Triode pentode

FIGURE 8–223.   Multiunit tubes.

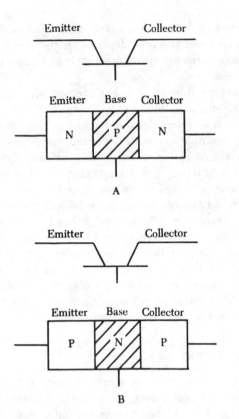

FIGURE 8–224.   NPN and PNP transistors.

Theory of Transistor Operation

Before transistor operation and the meaning of "N" and "P" can be explained, it is necessary to consider the theory of transistor action.

An electron is a negatively charged particle. In any material, there are electrons separated from each other by some minute distance. Whenever there is an electron, there is a negative charge. An atom of the semiconductor material has a specified number of electrons, depending on the type of material. If one of the electrons is removed, the hole from which the electrons moved is more positive than the electron that was removed.

To hole is considered to have a positive charge. If an electron from a neighboring atom moves into the hole, the hole apparently moves to the place from which the electron came. The hole does not really move; it is filled in one place and formed in another. In A of figure 8–225, the electrons are represented as black dots and the holes as dotted circles.

In B of figure 8–225, the electrons have moved one space to the left of their position occupied in A of figure 8–225. In effect, the holes have, therefore, moved one space to the right.

The movement of the electrons is current. In the same sense, the movement of holes is current also. Electron current moves in one direction; hole current travels in the opposite direction. The movement of the charge is a current. In transistors both electrons and holes act as carriers of current.

In transistors, materials referred to as N-materials and P-materials are used. The N-materials are rich in electrons and, therefore, electrons act as the carriers. The P-material is lacking in electrons and, therefore, has holes as carriers.

An NPN transistor is not interchangeable with a PNP transistor and vice versa. However, if all power supplies are reversed, they may be interchanged.

Since temperature is critical in a transistor circuit, there must be sufficient cooling for the transistors. Another precaution to observe which applies to any circuit is: *Power should never knowingly be applied to an open circuit.*

Diodes

Figure 8–226 illustrates a germanium diode and consists of two different types of semiconductor materials. With the battery connected as shown, positive holes and electrons are repelled by the battery toward the junction, causing an interaction between the holes and electrons. This results in electrons flowing through the junction to the holes and to the positive terminal of the battery. The holes move toward the negative terminal of the battery. This is called the forward direction and is a "high" current.

Connecting the battery as shown in figure 8–227 causes the holes and electrons to be pulled away from the junction, and little interaction between holes and electrons occurs at the junction. This results in very little current flow, called reverse current.

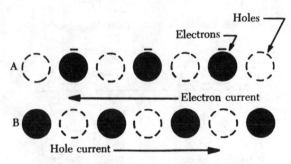

FIGURE 8–225.   Electrons and holes in transistors.

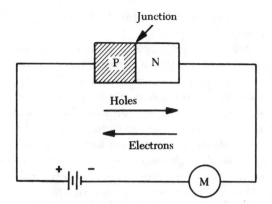

FIGURE 8–226.   Electron and hole flow in a diode with forward bias.

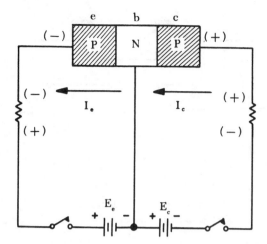

FIGURE 8–228.   Transistor electron flow.

The potential on the electrodes of the transistor diodes applied from the battery is called bias. It may be either forward or reverse bias, that is, in a high-current or a low-current direction.

The N-germanium is manufactured with an impurity, such as arsenic, added to give it an excess of electrons. Arsenic gives up its electrons readily and can be used as a carrier. The P-germanium has an impurity, such as indium, added. This takes the electrons from the germanium and leaves holes, or positive carriers.

Zener Diodes

Zener diodes (sometimes called "breakdown diodes") are used primarily for voltage regulation. They are designed so that they will break down (allow current to pass) when the circuit potential is equal to or in excess of the desired voltage. Below the desired voltage the zener blocks the circuit like any other diode biased in the reverse direction. Because the zener diode allows free flow in one direction when it is used in an a.c. circuit,

two diodes connected in opposite directions must be used. This takes care of both alternations of current.

The zener may be used in many places where a gas-filled vacuum tube cannot be used, because it is smaller in size and can be used in low voltage circuits. The gas-filled tube is used in circuits above 75 volts, but the zener diode may be used in regulating voltages as low as 3.5 volts.

PNP Transistor

Figure 8–228 shows a transistor circuit powered by batteries. The emitter circuit is biased by the battery E_e in the forward or high-current-flow direction. The collector circuit is biased by battery E_c in the reverse or low-current-flow direction.

If the switch in the emitter circuit were closed (collector switch open), a high emitter current would flow since it is biased in the forward direction. If the collector switch were closed (emitter switch open), a low current would flow since it is biased in the reverse direction.

At the same time, a hole current is flowing in the opposite direction in the same circuit, as shown in figure 8–229. Hole current flows from the positive terminal of the battery, whereas electron current originates at the negative terminal.

The operation with both switches closed is the same as with a PNP transistor, except that the emitter now ejects electrons instead of holes into the base, and the collector, being positive, will collect the electrons. There is again a large increase in collector current with the emitter switch closed. With the emitter switch open, the collector current will be small, since it is biased for reverse

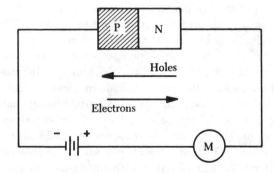

FIGURE 8–227.   Electron and hole flow in a diode with reverse bias.

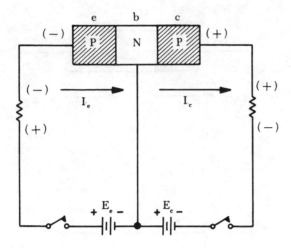

FIGURE 8–229.   Transistor hole current flow.

flow. At first glance it may appear that the transistor cannot amplify, since there is less current in the collector than in the emitter circuit. Remember, however, that the emitter is biased in the forward direction and a small voltage causes a large current, which is equivalent to a low resistance. The collector circuit is biased in the reverse direction, and a large voltage causes a small current, which is the equivalent of a high resistance.

When both switches are closed, a phenomenon known as transistor action occurs. The emitter, biased in the forward direction, has its positive holes ejected through the junction into the "N" region of the base. (The positive battery terminal repels the holes through the junction.) The collector, being biased negatively, will now attract

these holes through the junction from the base to the collector.

This collecting of holes by the collector causes a much greater reverse current than there would be if the emitter switch were open. The large increase of reverse collector current is caused by so-called transistor action, whereby holes from the emitter pass to the collector. Instead of holes flowing through the base and back to the emitter, they flow through the collector, E_c, and E_e to the emitter; the actual base current is very small.

The sum of collector current and base current equals the emitter current. In typical transistors the collector current can be 80–99 percent of the emitter current, with the remainder flowing through the base.

NPN Transistor

In figure 8–230 an NPN transistor is connected into a circuit. Notice that the battery polarities are reversed from those for the PNP transistor. But with the types of transistor material reversed, the emitter is still biased in the forward direction, and the collector is still biased in the reverse direction.

In this circuit a small signal applied to the input terminal causes a small change in both emitter and collector currents; however, the collector, being a high-resistance, requires only a small current change to produce large voltage changes. Therefore, an amplified signal appears at the output terminals.

The circuit in this illustration is called a grounded base amplifier, because the base is common to input and output (emitter and collector) circuits.

Figure 8–231 shows a different type of circuit connection. This is called a grounded emitter amplifier, and is similar to a conventional triode amplifier. The emitter is like a cathode, the base like a grid, and the collector like a plate. The collector is biased for a reverse current flow.

If the input signal swings positive, as shown in figure 8–231, it will aid the bias and increase base and emitter current. This increases collector current, making the upper output terminal more negative. On the next half cycle, the signal will oppose the bias and decrease emitter and collector current. Therefore, the output will swing positive. It is 180° out of phase with the input just as in the conventional triode tube amplifier.

Since the base current is a very small part of

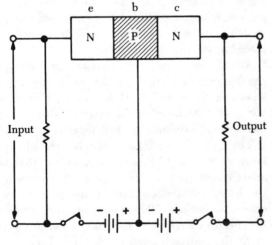

FIGURE 8–230.   NPN transistor circuit.

372

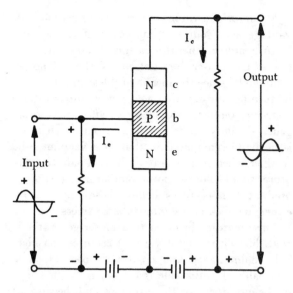

FIGURE 8–231.   A grounded-emitter amplifier circuit.

the total emitter current, it requires only a very small change in base current to cause a large change in collector current. Therefore, it again amplifies the signal. This circuit has the highest gain (output/input) of the various transistor amplifiers. A PNP transistor could also be used if battery polarities were reversed.

Use of Transistors

Transistors can be used in all applications where vacuum tubes are used, within certain limitations imposed by their physical characteristics. The main disadvantage of transistors is their low power output and limited frequency range. However, since they are approximately one one-thousandth the physical size of a vacuum tube, they can be used in compact equipment. Their weight, approximately one one-hundredth that of a vacuum tube, makes the equipment much lighter. Their life is approximately three times that of a vacuum tube, and their power requirement is only about one-tenth that of a vacuum tube.

Transistors can be permanently damaged by heat or by reversed polarity of the power supply. For this reason, care must be exercised when installing them in a circuit to prevent these conditions.

Transistors can be installed in miniature tube sockets, or they can be soldered directly into the circuits. There is no maintenance to be performed on them other than to remove and replace them as necessary.

When first tracing transistor circuits, trouble may be experienced in understanding from the schematic whether a transistor is an NPN or a PNP. Refer to figure 8–232, which shows the schematic symbol for two types of transistors. Notice an arrow in the emitter line. When this arrow is pointing away from the base, it is an NPN; if the arrow is pointing toward the base, it is a PNP transistor.

A simple rule to determine whether the transistor is a PNP or an NPN is as follows: If it is a PNP, the center letter "N" indicates a negative base or, in other words, that the base will conduct more freely on a negative charge. If the transistor is an NPN, the "P" indicates a positive base and the transistor will conduct more freely on a positive base charge.

Since there are different types of transistors based on the method used in their manufacture, there are several means of identifying the transistor in a circuit as either an NPN or a PNP. One method used to identify the type of transistor, called the junction transistor, is illustrated in figure 8–233. In this case, the method used to determine which of the three wires connected to a transistor is the base lead, which is the collector lead, and which is the emitter lead is based on the physical spacing of the leads. Notice that there are two leads close together and one lead further apart. The center lead is always the base. The lead closest to the base is the emitter lead, and the lead further out is the collector lead. The schematic shown in this illustration holds true for all junction-type transistors. For detailed information on any transistor, the applicable manufacturer's publications should be consulted.

RECTIFIERS

Many devices in an aircraft require high-amperage, low-voltage d.c. for operation. This

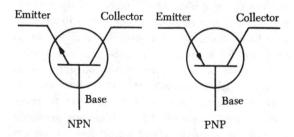

FIGURE 8–232.   Transistor schematic symbols.

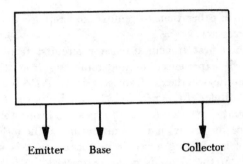

Emitter   Base   Collector

FIGURE 8-233. Junction transistor connections.

power may be furnished by d.c. engine-driven generators, motor-generator sets, vacuum tube rectifiers, or dry-disk or solid-state rectifiers.

In aircraft with a.c. systems, a special d.c. generator is not desirable since it would be necessary for the engine accessory section to drive an additional piece of equipment. Motor-generator sets, consisting of air-cooled a.c. motors that drive d.c. generators, eliminate this objection because they operate directly off the a.c. power system. Vacuum tube or various types of solid-state rectifiers provide a simple and efficient method of obtaining high voltage d.c. at low amperage. Dry-disk and solid-state rectifiers on the other hand are an excellent source of high amperage at low voltage.

A rectifier is a device which transforms alternating current into direct current by limiting or regulating the direction of current flow. The principal types of rectifiers are dry-disk, solid-state, and vacuum tube rectifiers. Solid-state, or semiconductor, rectifiers are rapidly replacing all other types; and, since dry-disk and vacuum tube rectifiers and motor-generators are largely limited to older model aircraft, the major part of the study of rectifiers will be devoted to solid-state devices used for rectification.

Motor-Generator

A motor-generator is an a.c. motor and a d.c. generator combined in one unit. This combination is often called a converter. Converters operate directly on either single-phase or three-phase voltage. Converters used on large aircraft are often operated by a three-phase, 208-volt, a.c. system and develop a direct current of 200 amperes at 30 volts with an approximate 28-ampere current drain on the a.c. system. Units similar to those used in airplanes with d.c. systems are provided for voltage regulation and paralleling of motor-generator sets.

A motor-generator offers a number of advantages as a source of d.c. power in an airplane. With a motor-generator, a momentary interruption of a.c. power does not cut off the d.c. power completely, since the inertia of the armature keeps it turning during the a.c. power interruption. Extreme temperature changes affect a motor-generator only slightly. Failure from overheating is negligible compared to that in a vacuum tube rectifier when it is operated above a safe temperature. In addition, a motor-generator can be operated at temperatures below those required by either dry-disk or vacuum tube rectifiers.

The greatest objection to a motor-generator is that, like all rotary devices, it requires considerable maintenance and creates a noise which is especially objectionable if the set is in the cabin of the airplane. For these reasons and, because of weight, space, and cost consideration, the motor-generator set is rapidly being replaced by various solid-state power sources.

Dry-Disk

Dry-disk rectifiers operate on the principle that electric current flows through a junction of two dissimilar conducting materials more readily in one direction than it does in the opposite direction. This is true because the resistance to current flow in one direction is low, while in the other direction it is high. Depending on the materials used, several amperes may flow in the direction of low resistance but only a few milliamperes in the direction of high resistance.

Three types of dry-disk rectifiers may be found in aircraft: the copper-oxide rectifier, the selenium rectifier, and the magnesium copper-sulfide rectifier. The copper-oxide rectifier (figure 8-234) consists of a copper disk upon which a layer of copper oxide has been formed by heating. It may also consist of a chemical copper-oxide preparation spread evenly over the copper surface. Metal plates, usually lead plates, are pressed against the two opposite faces of the disk to form a good contact. Current flow is from the copper to the copper oxide.

The selenium rectifier consists of an iron disk, similar to a washer, with one side coated with selenium. Its operation is similar to that of the copper-oxide rectifier. Current flows from the selenium to the iron.

The magnesium copper-sulfide rectifier is made of washer-shaped magnesium disks coated with a

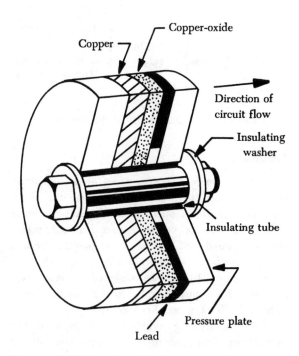

FIGURE 8–234.   Copper-oxide dry-disk rectifier.

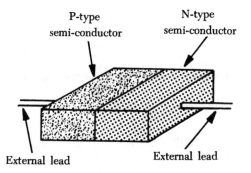

FIGURE 8–235.   Junction diode.

layer of copper sulfide. The disks are arranged similarly to the other types. Current flows from the magnesium to the copper sulfide.

Solid-State Rectifiers

In the study of transistors it was pointed out that the solid-state diode is manufactured from semiconductor material. It consists of N-type and P-type material joined in a single crystal. The point, or junction, where the two materials are in contact is called a P–N junction. This type of semiconductor, regardless of rating or size, is called a junction diode. The first type of semiconductor used was called the point-contact diode. It utilized a single type of semiconductor material, against which a tungsten or phosphor-bronze wire, called a "cat whisker," was pressed or fused. The point-contact diode has been largely replaced by the junction diode because of its limited current-carrying capabilities. The most common semiconductor materials are germanium and silicon. A typical junction diode is shown in figure 8–235.

In figure 8–236, the positive terminal of the battery is connected to the P-type semiconductor material, and the negative terminal is connected to the N-type. This arrangement constitutes forward bias. The holes in the P-type material are repelled from the positive terminal and move toward the junction. The electrons in the N-type

material are repelled from the negative terminal and likewise move toward the junction. This decreases the space charge existing at the junction, and electron current flow is maintained through the external circuit. The current in the P-type material is in the form of holes, and in the N-type material it is in the form of electrons. If the forward bias is increased, current flow will increase. If the forward bias is increased excessively, it will cause excessive current. The excessive current will increase thermal agitation and the crystal structure will break down. One important fact worth remembering is that all solid-state devices are sensitive to heat and will be destroyed if the heat becomes too intense.

If the battery connections shown in figure 8–236 are reversed, the junction diode is reverse-biased. Now the holes are attracted toward the negative terminal and away from the junction. The electrons are attracted toward the positive terminal, also away from the junction. This widens the depletion region, increases the space charge, and reduces current to a minimum condition. It is possible to apply too high a reverse bias. When this happens, the crystal structure will break down.

The symbol for the semiconductor diode is shown in figure 8–237. Note that this is the same

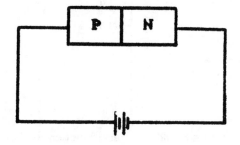

FIGURE 8–236.   Forward bias on a junction diode.

375

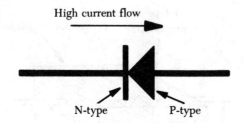

FIGURE 8–237. Semiconductor diode symbol.

symbol used for other types of diodes, such as the copper-oxide and selenium dry-disk rectifiers. The forward-bias, or high-current, direction is always against the arrow of the symbol.

Figure 8–238 shows a typical characteristic curve for a junction diode. As forward bias is increased a small amount, current flow is increased a considerable amount. For this reason, solid-state devices are said to be current-operated devices, since it is easier to measure the relatively large changes in current flow as compared to the small changes in applied voltage. With forward bias applied, the diode displays a low-resistance characteristic. On the other hand, with reverse bias applied, a high-resistance state exists. The most important characteristic of a diode is that it allows current to flow in one direction only. This permits solid-state devices to be used in rectifier circuits.

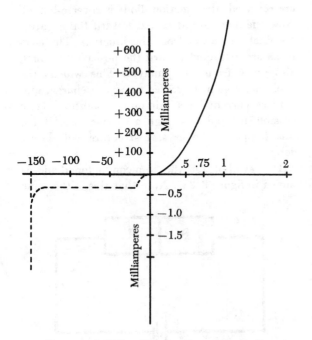

FIGURE 8–238. Typical junction diode characteristic curve.

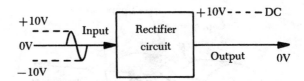

FIGURE 8–239. Rectification process.

Rectification

Rectification is the process of changing alternating current to direct current. When a semiconductor rectifier, such as a junction diode, is connected to an a.c. voltage source, it is alternately biased forward and reverse, in step with the a.c. voltage, as shown in figure 8–239.

In figure 8–240 a diode is placed in series with a source of a.c. power and a load resistor. This is called a half-wave rectifier circuit.

The transformer provides the a.c. input to the circuit; the diode provides the rectification of the a.c.; and the load resistor serves two purposes: (1) It limits the amount of current flow in the circuit to a safe level, and (2) it develops an output signal due to the current flow through it.

Assume, in figure 8–241, that the top of the transformer secondary is positive and the bottom negative. With this polarity, the diode is forward-biased, resistance of the diode is very low, and current flows through the circuit in the direction of the arrows. The output (voltage drop) across the load resistor follows the waveshape of the positive half of the a.c. input. When the a.c. input goes in a negative direction, the top of the transformer secondary becomes negative and the diode becomes reverse-biased.

With reverse bias applied to the diode, the resistance of the diode becomes very great, and current flow through the diode and load resistor becomes zero. (Remember that a very small current will flow through the diode.) The output,

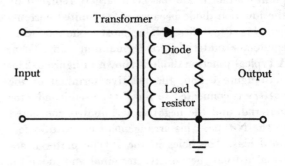

FIGURE 8–240. Half-wave rectifier circuit.

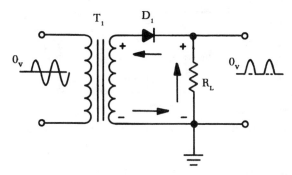

FIGURE 8–241. Output of a half-wave rectifier.

taken across the load resistor, will be zero. If the position of the diode were reversed, the output would be negative pulses.

In a half-wave rectifier, a half cycle of power is produced across the load resistor for each full cycle of input power. To increase the output power, a full-wave rectifier can be used. Figure 8–242 shows a full-wave rectifier, which is, in effect, two half-wave rectifiers combined into one circuit. In this circuit a load resistor is used to limit current flow and develop an output voltage, two diodes to provide rectification, and a transformer to provide an a.c. input to the circuit. The transformer, used in full-wave rectifier circuits, must be center tapped to complete the path for current flow through the load resistor.

Assuming the polarities shown on the transformer, diode D_1 will be forward-biased and current will flow from ground through the load resistor, through diode D_1, to the top of the transformer.

When the a.c. input changes direction, the transformer secondary will assume an opposite polarity.

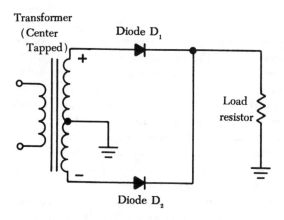

FIGURE 8–242.   Full-wave rectifier.

Diode D_2 is now forward-biased and current will flow in the opposite direction, from ground through the load resistor, through diode D_2, to the bottom half of the transformer.

When one diode is forward-biased, the other is reverse-biased. No matter which diode is forward biased, current will flow through the load resistor in the same direction; so the output will be a series of pulses of the same polarity. By reversing both diodes, the output polarity will be reversed.

The voltage which is felt across a rectifier when reverse bias is being applied is often referred to as "the inverse peak voltage." By definition, this is the peak value of the instantaneous voltage across the rectifier during the half-cycle in which current does not flow or that reverse bias is applied. If an inverse voltage is applied that is too large, the rectifier will be destroyed. The term "breakdown voltage" is often used instead of the term "inverse peak voltage rating," but both terms have the same meaning. Breakdown voltage is the maximum voltage that the rectifier can stand while it is not conducting (reverse-biased); the inverse peak voltage is the voltage actually being applied to the rectifier. As long as the inverse peak voltage is lower than breakdown voltage, there will be no problem of rectifier destruction.

Diode Bridge Rectifier Circuit

An advantageous modification of the full-wave diode rectifier is the bridge rectifier. The bridge rectifier differs from the full-wave rectifier in that a bridge rectifier does not require a center-tapped transformer, but does require two additional diodes.

To illustrate how a bridge rectifier performs, consider a sine wave input which is on its positive alternation as denoted on the schematic of figure 8–243. With the secondary of T_1 functioning as the bridge rectifier's power supply, point A is the most positive point of the bridge, while B is the most negative. Current flow will be from B to A through the forward-biased diodes. As an aid in finding the path of electron flow, consider the redrawn bridge circuit in figure 8–244. The forward-biased diodes, CR_3 and CR_4 are easily recognized. Voltage is dropped across each voltage loop as indicated. Thus, on the positive half-cycle input CR_3 and CR_4 are both forward-biased and CR_1 and CR_2 are reverse-biased.

As long as diode breakdown voltage is not exceeded, current flow will be from point B up and

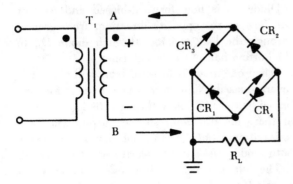

FIGURE 8–243.   Diode bridge rectifier.

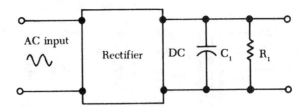

FIGURE 8–245.   A capacitor used as a filter.

FILTERING

across CR_4 down and to the left across R_L. After current crosses R_L, it will flow to point A through CR_3. Notice that current flow across R_L is from right to left, or in respect to polarity, a negative half-cycle output for positive half-cycle input.

Remember that, when tracing current flow for the negative half-cycle, electron flow through a diode is against the symbolic arrow and from negative to a less negative or positive point. Therefore, no confusion should arise when tracing electron flow up to and away from the common point between CR_3 and CR_1. Although it may appear that CR_1 as well as CR_4 is forward-biased, such is not the case. The collector of CR_1 is more negative than its emitter; therefore, it is reverse-biased.

Since, on the negative half-cycle, CR_1 and CR_2 are forward-biased, the output signal on the negative half-cycle is negative.

Since both half-cycles of the input signal result in negative output pulses, the bridge rectifier has accomplished the same goal as the full-wave diode rectifier.

That part of the rectification process which involves the converting of an a.c. voltage into pulses of d.c. voltage has been treated in the discussion of vacuum tube, dry-disk, and semiconductor diodes. To complete the rectification process so that the pulses of voltage are changed to an acceptable approximation of smooth d.c. involves a process called filtering.

Any reactance which opposes a change in voltage (or current) by storing energy and then releasing this energy back to the circuit may be used as a filter.

In the study of capacitors, it was demonstrated that a capacitance opposes a voltage change across its terminal by storing energy in its electrostatic field. Whenever the voltage tends to rise, the capacitor converts this voltage change to stored energy. When the voltage tends to fall, the capacitor converts this stored energy back to voltage. The use of a capacitor for filtering the output of a rectifier is illustrated in figure 8–245. The rectifier is shown as a block, and the capacitor C_1 is connected in parallel with the load R_1.

The capacitor C_1 is chosen to offer very low impedance to the a.c. ripple frequency and very high impedance to the d.c. component. The ripple voltage is therefore bypassed to ground through the low-impedance path, while the d.c. voltage is applied unchanged to the load. The effect of the capacitor on the output of the rectifier can be seen in the waveshapes shown in figure 8–246. Dotted lines show the rectifier output; solid lines show the effect of the capacitor. Full-wave rectifier outputs are shown. The capacitor C_1 charges when the rectifier voltage output tends to increase and discharges when the voltage output tends to decrease. In this manner, the voltage across the load R_1 is kept fairly constant.

An inductance may be used as a filter, because it opposes a change in current through it by storing energy in its electromagnetic field when-

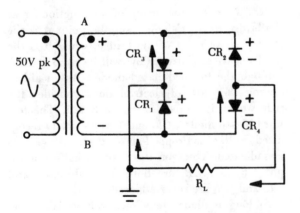

FIGURE 8–244.   Redrawn bridge rectifier circuit.

378

Voltage across C_1 with large load circuit

Voltage across C_1 with small load circuit

FIGURE 8–246.   Half-wave and full-wave rectifier outputs using capacitor filter.

FIGURE 8–248.   Output of an inductor filter rectifier.

ever current tends to increase. When the current through the inductor tends to decrease, the inductor supplies the energy to maintain the flow of current. The use of an inductor for filtering the output of a rectifier is shown in figure 8–247. Note that the inductor L_1 is in series with the load R_1.

The inductance L_1 is chosen to offer high impedance to the a.c. ripple voltage and low impedance to the d.c. component. Therefore, for the a.c. ripple, a very large voltage drop occurs across the inductor and a very small voltage drop across the load R_1. For the d.c. component, however, a very small voltage drop occurs across the inductor and a very large voltage drop across the load. The effect of an inductor on the output of a full-wave rectifier in the output waveshape is shown in figure 8–248. Note that the ripple has been attenuated (reduced) in the output voltage.

Capacitors and inductors are combined in various ways to provide more satisfactory filtering than can be obtained with a single capacitor or inductor. These are referred to collectively as "LC filters." Several combinations are shown schematically in figure 8–249. Note that the L-, or inverted L-type, and the T-type filter sections resemble schematically the corresponding letters of the alphabet. The pi-type filter section resembles the Greek letter pi (π) schematically.

All the filter sections shown are similar in that

the inductances are in series and the capacitances are in parallel with the load. The inductances must, therefore, offer a very high impedance and the capacitors a very low impedance to the ripple frequency. Since the ripple frequency is comparatively low, the inductances are iron-core coils having large values of inductance (several henries). Because they offer such high impedance to the ripple frequency, these coils are called chokes. The capacitors must also be large (several microfarads) to offer very little opposition to the ripple frequency. Because the voltage across the capacitor is d.c., electrolytic capacitors are frequently used as filter capacitors. The correct polarity in connecting electrolytic capacitors should always be observed.

Additional filter sections may be combined to improve the filtering action.

LC filters are also classified according to the position of the capacitor and inductor. A capacitor-input filter is one in which the capacitor is connected directly across the output terminals of the rectifier. A choke-input filter is one in which a choke precedes the filter capacitor.

If it is necessary to increase the applied voltage to more than a single rectifier can tolerate, the usual solution is to stack them. These rectifiers are similar to resistors added in series. Each resistor will drop a portion of the applied voltage rather than the total voltage. The same theory applies to rectifiers added in series, or stacked. Series stacking increases the voltage rating. If, for example, a rectifier will be destroyed with an applied voltage exceeding 50 volts, and it is to be used in a circuit with an applied voltage of 150 volts, stacking of diodes can be employed. The result is shown in figure 8–250.

Identification of Semiconductor Diodes

There are many types of semiconductor diodes in existence today and several methods are used to identify the emitter and collector. The following are the three most common methods used to identify the emitter and collector.

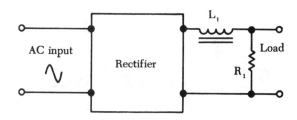

FIGURE 8–247.   An inductor used as a filter.

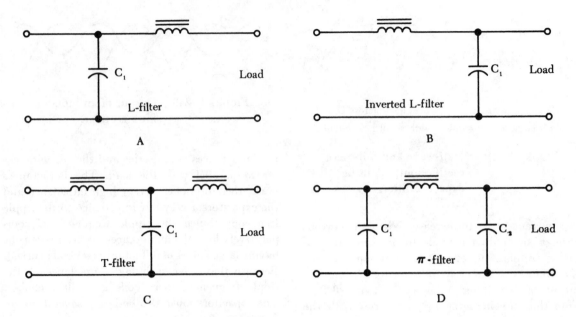

FIGURE 8–249.   LC filters.

One method places a small dot near the emitter lead (A of figure 8–251). A second method stamps the rectifier symbol on the diode case (B of figure 8–251). The third method used quite frequently is the color code method (C of figure 8–251). Frequently the color code used is the same as the color code used for resistors.

One very common diode is the 1N538. The "1N" indicates that there is only one PN junction, or that the device is a diode; the numbers that follow normally indicate manufacturing sequence; that is, a 1N537 was developed before the 1N538, which may be an improved model of the 1N537 or may be an entirely different diode altogether.

A. C. MEASURING INSTRUMENTS

A d.c. meter, such as an ammeter, connected in an a.c. circuit will indicate zero, because the moving ammeter coil that carries the current to be measured is located in a permanent magnet

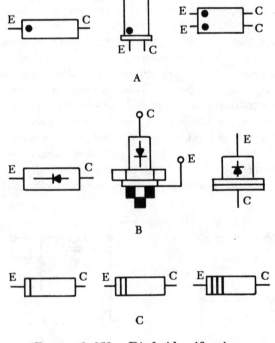

FIGURE 8–251.   Diode identification.

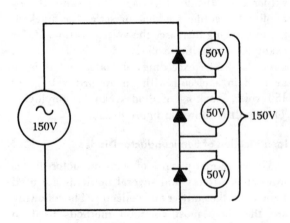

FIGURE 8–250.   Stacking diodes in a circuit.

field. Since the field of a permanent magnet remains constant and in the same direction at all times, the moving coil follows the polarity of the current. The coil attempts to move in one direction during half of the a.c. cycle and in the reverse direction during the other half when the current reverses.

The current reverses direction too rapidly for the coil to follow, causing the coil to assume an average position. Since the current is equal and opposite during each half of the a.c. cycle, the direct current meter indicates zero, which is the average value. Thus, a meter with a permanent magnet cannot be used to measure alternating voltage and current. However, the permanent magnet D'Arsonval meter may be used to measure alternating current or voltage if the current that passes through the meter is first rectified—that is, changed from alternating current to direct current.

Rectifier A. C. Meters

Copper-oxide rectifiers are generally used with D'Arsonval d.c. meter movements to measure alternating currents and voltages; however, there are many types of rectifiers which may be used, some of which are included in the discussion of alternator systems.

A copper-oxide rectifier allows current to flow through a meter in only one direction. As shown in figure 8–252, the copper-oxide rectifier consists of copper-oxide disks separated alternately by copper disks and fastened together as a single unit. Current flows more readily from copper to copper oxide than from copper oxide to copper. When a.c. is applied, therefore, current flows in only one direction, yielding a pulsating d.c. output as shown by the output wave shapes in figure 8–253. This current can then be measured as it flows through the meter movement.

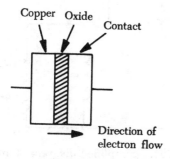

FIGURE 8–252. Copper-oxide rectifier.

In some a.c. meters, selenium or vacuum tube rectifiers are used in place of the copper-oxide rectifier. The principle of operation, however, is the same in all meters employing rectifiers.

Electrodynamometer Meter Movement

The electrodynamometer meter can be used to measure alternating or direct voltage and current. It operates on the same principles as the permanent magnet moving-coil meter, except that the permanent magnet is replaced by an air-core electromagnet. The field of the electrodynamometer meter is developed by the same current that flows through the moving coil (see figure 8–254).

In the electrodynamometer meter, two stationary field coils are connected in series with the movable coil. The movable coil is attached to the central shaft and rotates inside the two stationary field coils. The spiral springs provide the restraining force for the meter and also a means of introducing current to the movable coil.

When current flows through field coils A and B and movable coil C, coil C rotates in opposition to the springs and places itself parallel to the field coils. The more current flowing through the coils, the more the moving coil overcomes the opposition of the springs and the farther the pointer moves across the scale. If the scale is properly calibrated and the proper shunts or multipliers are used, the dynamometer movement will indicate current or voltage.

Although electrodynamometer meters are very accurate, they do not have the sensitivity of D'Arsonval meters and, for this reason, are not widely used outside the laboratory.

Electrodynamometer Ammeter

In the electrodynamometer ammeter, low resistance coils produce only a small voltage drop in the circuit measured. An inductive shunt is connected in series with the field coils. This shunt, similar to the resistor shunt used in d.c. ammeters, permits only part of the current being measured to flow through the coils. As in the d.c. ammeter, most of the current in the circuit flows through the shunt; but the scale is calibrated accordingly, and the meter reads the total current. An a.c. ammeter, like a d.c. ammeter, is connected in series with the circuit in which current is measured. Effective values are indicated by the

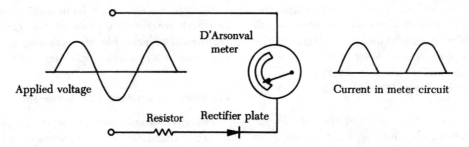

FIGURE 8–253.   A half-wave rectifier circuit.

meter. A schematic diagram of an electrodyna-mometer ammeter circuit is shown in figure 8–255.

Electrodynamometer Voltmeter

In the electrodynamometer voltmeter, field coils are wound with many turns of small wire. Approximately 0.01 ampere of current flow through both coils is required to operate the meter. Resistors of a noninductive material, connected in series with the coils, provide for different voltage ranges. Voltmeters are connected in parallel across the unit in which voltage is to be measured. The values of voltages indicated are effective values. A schematic diagram of an electrodynamometer voltmeter is shown in figure 8–256.

Moving Iron-Vane Meter

The moving iron-vane meter is another basic type of meter. It can be used to measure either a.c. or d.c. Unlike the D'Arsonval meter, which employs permanent magnets, it depends on induced magnetism for its operation. It utilizes the principle of repulsion between two concentric iron vanes, one fixed and one movable, placed inside a solenoid, as shown in figure 8–257. A pointer is attached to the movable vane.

When current flows through the coil, the two iron vanes become magnetized with north poles at their upper ends and south poles at their lower ends for one direction of current through the coil. Because like poles repel, the unbalanced component of force, tangent to the movable element, causes it to turn against the force exerted by the springs.

The movable vane is rectangular in shape and the fixed vane is tapered. This design permits the use of a relatively uniform scale.

When no current flows through the coil, the movable vane is positioned so that it is opposite the larger portion of the tapered fixed vane, and

the scale reading is zero. The amount of magnetization of the vanes depends on the strength of the field, which, in turn, depends on the amount of current flowing through the coil. The force of

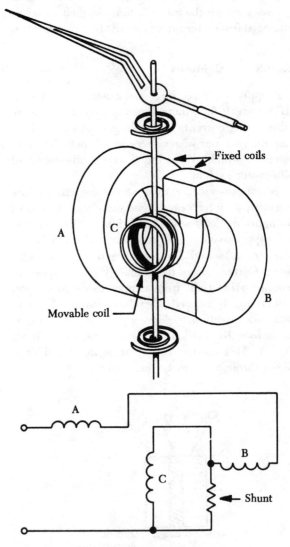

FIGURE 8–254.   Simplified diagram of an electrodynamometer movement.

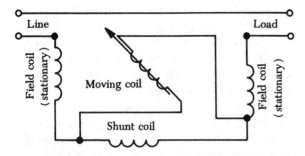

FIGURE 8–255.   Electrodynamometer ammeter circuit.

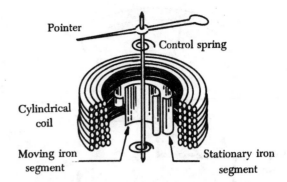

FIGURE 8–257.   Moving iron-vane meter.

repulsion is greater opposite the larger end of the fixed vane than it is nearer the smaller end. Therefore, the movable vane moves toward the smaller end through an angle that is proportional to the magnitude of the coil current. The movement ceases when the force of repulsion is balanced by the restraining force of the spring.

Because the repulsion is always in the same direction (toward the smaller end of the fixed vane), regardless of the direction of current flow through the coil, the moving iron-vane instrument operates on either d.c. or a.c. circuits.

Mechanical damping in this type of instrument can be obtained by the use of an aluminum vane attached to the shaft so that, as the shaft moves, the vane moves in a restricted air space.

When the moving iron-vane meter is designed to be used as an ammeter, the coil is wound with relatively few turns of large wire in order to carry the rated current.

When the moving iron-vane meter is designed to be used as a voltmeter, the solenoid is wound with many turns of small wire. Portable voltmeters are made with self-contained series resistance for ranges up to 750 volts. Higher ranges

are obtained by the use of additional external multipliers.

The moving iron-vane instrument may be used to measure direct current but has an error due to residual magnetism in the vanes. The error may be minimized by reversing the meter connections and averaging the readings. When used on a.c. circuits the instrument has an accuracy of 0.5 percent. Because of its simplicity, its relatively low cost, and the fact that no current is conducted to the moving element, this type of movement is used extensively to measure current and voltage in a.c. power circuits. However, because the reluctance of the magnetic circuit is high, the moving iron-vane meter requires much more power to produce full-scale deflection than is required by a D'Arsonval meter of the same range. Therefore, the moving iron-vane meter is seldom used in high-resistance low-power circuits.

Inclined-Coil Iron-Vane Meter

The principle of the moving iron-vane mechanism is applied to the inclined-coil type of meter, which can be used to measure both a.c. and d.c. The inclined-coil, iron-vane meter has a coil mounted at an angle to the shaft. Attached obliquely to the shaft, and located inside the coil, are two soft-iron vanes. When no current flows through the coil, a control spring holds the pointer at zero, and the iron vanes lie in planes parallel to the plane of the coil. When current flows through the coil, the vanes tend to line up with magnetic lines passing through the center of the coil at right angles to the plane of the coil. Thus, the vanes rotate against the spring action to move the pointer over the scale.

The iron vanes tend to line up with the magnetic lines regardless of the direction of current

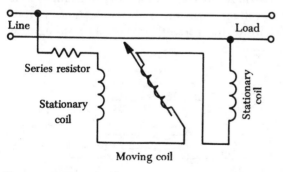

FIGURE 8–256.   Electrodynamometer voltmeter circuit.

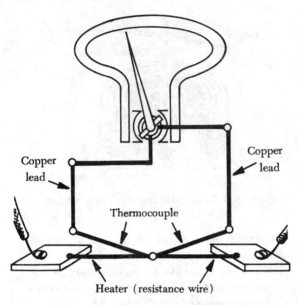

FIGURE 8–258.   Simplified diagram of a
thermocouple meter.

flow through the coil. Therefore, the inclined-coil, iron-vane meter can be used to measure either alternating current or direct current. The aluminum disk and the drag magnets provide electromagnetic damping.

Like the moving iron-vane meter, the inclined-coil type requires a relatively large amount of current for full-scale deflection and is seldom used in high-resistance low-power circuits.

As in the moving iron-vane instruments, the inclined-coil instrument is wound with few turns of relatively large wire when used as an ammeter and with many turns of small wire when used as a voltmeter.

Thermocouple Meter

If the ends of two dissimilar metals are welded together and this junction is heated, a d.c. voltage is developed across the two open ends. The voltage developed depends on the material of which the wires are made and on the difference in temperature between the heated junction and the open ends.

In one type of instrument, the junction is heated electrically by the flow of current through a heater element. It does not matter whether the current is alternating or direct because the heating effect is independent of current direction. The maximum current that can be measured depends on the current rating of the heater, the heat that the

thermocouple can stand without being damaged, and on the current rating of the meter used with the thermocouple. Voltage can also be measured if a suitable resistor is placed in series with the heater. In meter applications, a D'Arsonval meter is used with a resistance wire heater, as shown in figure 8–258.

As current flows through the resistance wire, the heat developed is transferred to the contact point and develops an e.m.f. which causes current to flow through the meter. The coil rotates and causes the pointer to move over a calibrated scale. The amount of coil movement is dependent on the amount of heat, which varies as the square of the current. Thermocouple meters are used extensively in a.c. measurements.

Varmeters

Multiplying the volts by the amperes in an a.c. circuit gives the apparent power: the combination of the true power which does the work and the reactive power which does no work and is returned to the line. Reactive power is measured in units of vars (volt-amperes reactive) or kilovars (kilovolt-amperes reactive, abbreviated KVAR). When properly connected, wattmeters measure the reactive power. As such, they are called varmeters. The illustration in figure 8–259 shows a varmeter connected in an a.c. circuit.

Wattmeter

Electric power is measured by means of a wattmeter. Because electric power is the product of current and voltage, a wattmeter must have two elements, one for current and the other for voltage, as indicated in figure 8–260. For this reason, wattmeters are usually of the electrodynamometer type.

The movable coil with a series resistance forms the voltage element, and the stationary coils constitute the current element. The strength of

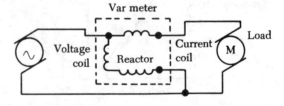

FIGURE 8–259.   A varmeter connected in an
a.c. circuit.

384

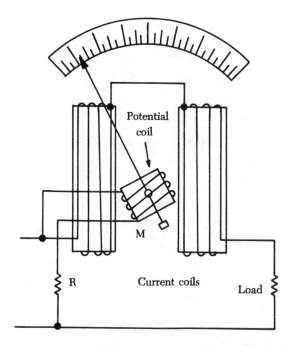

FIGURE 8–260. Simplified electrodynamometer wattmeter circuit.

the field around the potential coil depends on the amount of current that flows through it. The current, in turn, depends on the load voltage applied across the coil and the high resistance in series with it. The strength of the field around the current coils depends on the amount of current flowing through the load. Thus, the meter deflection is proportional to the product of the voltage across the potential coil and the current through the current coils. The effect is almost the same (if the scale is properly calibrated) as if the voltage applied across the load and the current through the load were multiplied together.

If the current in the line is reversed, the direction of current in both coils and the potential coil is reversed, the net result is that the pointer continues to read up-scale. Therefore, this type of wattmeter can be used to measure either a.c. or d.c. power.

FREQUENCY METERS

Alternating-current electrical equipment is designed to operate within a given frequency range. In some instances the equipment is designed to operate at one particular frequency, as are electric clocks and time switches. For example, electric clocks are commonly designed to operate at 60

c.p.s. If the supply frequency is reduced to 59 c.p.s., the clock will lose one minute every hour.

Transformers and a.c. machinery are designed to operate at a specified frequency. If the supply frequency falls more than 10 percent from the rated value, the equipment may draw excessive current, and dangerous overheating will result. It is, therefore, necessary to control the frequency of electric power systems. Frequency meters are employed to indicate the frequency so that corrective measures can be taken if the frequency varies beyond the prescribed limits.

Frequency meters are designed so that they will not be affected by changes in voltage. Because a.c. systems are designed to operate normally at one particular frequency, the range of the frequency meter may be restricted to a few cycles on either side of the normal frequency. There are several types of frequency meters, including the vibrating-reed type, the fixed-coil and moving-coil type, the fixed-coil and moving-disk type, and the resonant-circuit type. Of these types, the vibrating-reed frequency meter is used most often in aircraft systems, and is discussed in some detail.

Vibrating-Reed Frequency Meter

The vibrating-reed type of frequency meter is one of the simplest devices for indicating the frequency of an a.c. source. A simplified diagram of one type of vibrating-reed frequency meter is shown in figure 8–261.

The current whose frequency is to be measured flows through the coil and exerts maximum attraction on the soft-iron armature twice during each cycle (A of figure 8–261). The armature is attached to the bar, which is mounted on a flexible support. Reeds of suitable dimensions to have natural vibration frequencies of 110, 112, 114, and so forth up to 130 c.p.s. are mounted on the bar (B of figure 8–261). The reed having a frequency of 110 c.p.s. is marked "55" cycles; the one having a frequency of 130 c.p.s. is marked "65" c.p.s.; the one having a frequency of 120 c.p.s. is marked "60" c.p.s., and so forth.

In some instruments the reeds are the same lengths, but are weighted by different amounts at the top so that they will have different natural rates of vibration.

When the coil is energized with a current having a frequency between 55 and 65 c.p.s., all the reeds are vibrated slightly; but the reed having a

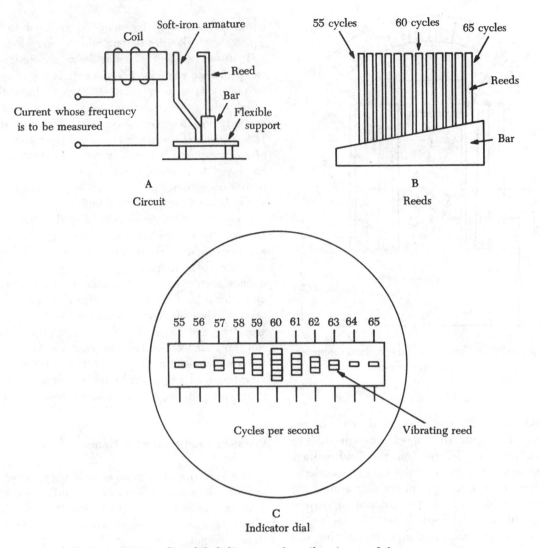

FIGURE 8–261. Simplified diagram of a vibrating-reed frequency meter.

natural frequency closest to that of the energizing current (whose frequency is to be measured) vibrates through a larger amplitude. The frequency is read from the scale value opposite the reed having the greatest amplitude of vibration.

An end view of the reeds is shown in the indicator dial (C of figure 8–261). If the energizing current has a frequency of 60 c.p.s., the reed marked "60" c.p.s. will vibrate the greatest amount, as shown.

CHAPTER 9

AIRCRAFT GENERATORS AND MOTORS

D. C. GENERATORS

Energy for the operation of most electrical equipment in an airplane depends upon the electrical energy supplied by a generator. A generator is any machine which converts mechanical energy into electrical energy by electromagnetic induction. A generator designed to produce alternating-current energy is called an a.c. generator, or alternator; a generator which produces direct-current energy is called a d.c. generator. Both types operate by inducing an a.c. voltage in coils by varying the amount and direction of the magnetic flux cutting through the coils.

For airplanes equipped with direct-current electrical systems, the d.c. generator is the regular source of electrical energy. One or more d.c. generators, driven by the engine, supply electrical energy for the operation of all units in the electrical system, as well as energy for charging the battery. The number of generators used is determined by the power requirement of a particular airplane. In most cases, only one generator is driven by each engine, but in some large airplanes, two generators are driven by a single engine. Aircraft equipped with alternating-current systems use electrical energy supplied by a.c. generators, also called alternators.

Theory of Operation

In the study of alternating current, basic generator principles were introduced to explain the generation of an a.c. voltage by a coil rotating in a magnetic field. Since this is the basis for all generator operation, it is necessary to review the principles of generation of electrical energy.

When lines of magnetic force are cut by a conductor passing through them, voltage is induced in the conductor. The strength of the induced voltage is dependent upon the speed of the conductor and the strength of the magnetic field. If the ends of the conductor are connected to form a complete circuit, a current is induced in the con-

ductor. The conductor and the magnetic field make up an elementary generator. This simple generator is illustrated in figure 9–1, together with the components of an external generator circuit which collect and use the energy produced by the simple generator. The loop of wire (A and B of figure 9–1) is arranged to rotate in a magnetic field. When the plane of the loop of wire is parallel to the magnetic lines of force, the voltage induced in the loop causes a current to flow in the direction indicated by the arrows in figure 9–1. The voltage induced at this position is maximum, since the wires are cutting the lines of force at right angles and are thus cutting more lines of force per second than in any other position relative to the magnetic field.

As the loop approaches the vertical position shown in figure 9–2, the induced voltage decreases because both sides of the loop (A and B) are approximately parallel to the lines of force and

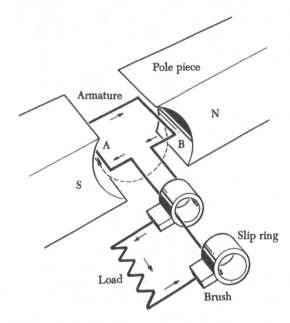

FIGURE 9–1. Inducing maximum voltage in an elementary generator.

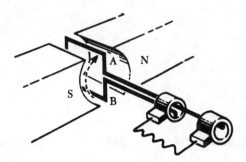

FIGURE 9–2. Inducing minimum voltage in an elementary generator.

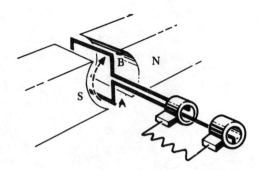

FIGURE 9–4. Inducing a minimum voltage in the opposite direction.

the rate of cutting is reduced. When the loop is vertical, no lines of force are cut since the wires are momentarily traveling parallel to the magnetic lines of force, and there is no induced voltage. As the rotation of the loop continues, the number of lines of force cut increases until the loop has rotated an additional 90° to a horizontal plane. As shown in figure 9–3, the number of lines of force cut and the induced voltage once again are maximum. The direction of cutting, however, is in the opposite direction to that occurring in figures 9–1 and 9–2, so the direction (polarity) of the induced voltage is reversed.

As rotation of the loop continues, the number of lines of force having been cut again decreases, and the induced voltage becomes zero at the position shown in figure 9–4, since the wires A and B are again parallel to the magnetic lines of force.

If the voltage induced throughout the entire 360° of rotation is plotted, the curve shown in figure 9–5 results. This voltage is called an alternating voltage because of its reversal from positive to negative values—first in one direction and then in the other.

To use the voltage generated in the loop for producing a current flow in an external circuit, some means must be provided to connect the loop of wire in series with the external circuit. Such an electrical connection can be effected by opening the loop of wire and connecting its two ends to two metal rings, called slip rings, against which two metal or carbon brushes ride. The brushes are connected to the external circuit.

By replacing the slip rings of the basic a.c. generator with two half-cylinders, called a commutator, a basic d.c. generator (figure 9–6), is obtained. In this illustration the black side of the coil is connected to the black segment and the white side of the coil to the white segment. The segments are insulated from each other. The two stationary brushes are placed on opposite sides of the commutator and are so mounted that each brush contacts each segment of the commutator as the latter revolves simultaneously with the loop. The rotating parts of a d.c. generator (coil and commutator) are called an armature.

The generation of an e.m.f. by the loop rotating in the magnetic field is the same for both a.c. and d.c. generators, but the action of the commutator produces a d.c. voltage. This generation of a d.c. voltage is described as follows for the various

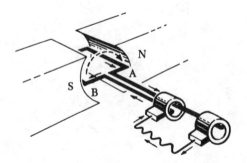

FIGURE 9–3. Inducing maximum voltage in the opposite direction.

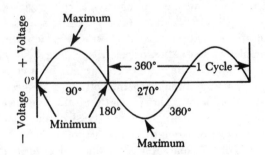

FIGURE 9–5. Output of an elementary generator.

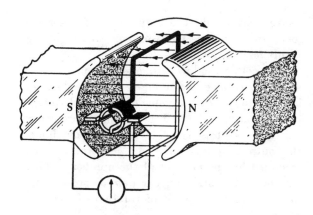

FIGURE 9–6.   Basic d.c. generator.

positions of the loop rotating in a magnetic field, with reference to figure 9–7.

The loop in position A of figure 9–7 is rotating clockwise, but no lines of force are cut by the coil sides and no e.m.f. is generated. The black brush is shown coming into contact with the black segment of the commutator, and the white brush is just coming into contact with the white segment.

In position B of figure 9–7, the flux is being cut at a maximum rate and the induced e.m.f. is maximum. At this time, the black brush is contacting the black segment and the white brush is contacting the white segment. The deflection of

the meter is toward the right, indicating the polarity of the output voltage.

At position C of figure 9–7, the loop has completed 180° of rotation. Again, no flux lines are being cut and the output voltage is zero. The important condition to observe at position C is the action of the segments and brushes. The black brush at the 180° angle is contacting both black and white segments on one side of the commutator, and the white brush is contacting both segments on the other side of the commutator. After the loop rotates slightly past the 180° point, the black brush is contacting only the white segment and the white brush is contacting only the black segment.

Because of this switching of commutator elements, the black brush is always in contact with the coil side moving downward, and the white brush is always in contact with the coil side moving upward. Though the current actually reverses its direction in the loop in exactly the same way as in the a.c. generator, commutator action causes the current to flow always in the same direction through the external circuit or meter.

A graph of one cycle of operation is shown in figure 9–7. The generation of the e.m.f. for positions A, B, and C is the same as for the basic a.c. generator, but at position D, commutator

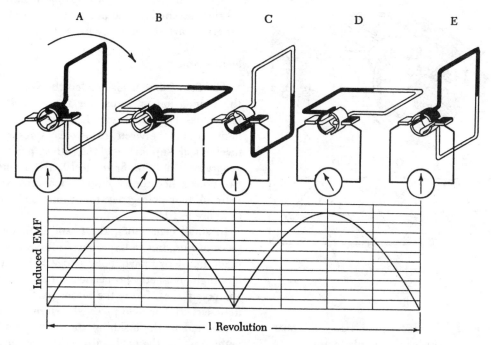

FIGURE 9–7.   Operation of a basic d.c. generator.

action reverses the current in the external circuit, and the second half-cycle has the same waveform as the first half-cycle. The process of commutation is sometimes called rectification, since rectification is the converting of an a.c. voltage to a d.c. voltage.

At the instant that each brush is contacting two segments on the commutator (positions A, C, and E in figure 9–7), a direct short circuit is produced. If an e.m.f. were generated in the loop at this time, a high current would flow in the circuit, causing an arc and thus damaging the commutator. For this reason, the brushes must be placed in the exact position where the short will occur when the generated e.m.f. is zero. This position is called the neutral plane.

The voltage generated by the basic d.c. generator in figure 9–7 varies from zero to its maximum value twice for each revolution of the loop. This variation of d.c. voltage is called "ripple," and may be reduced by using more loops, or coils, as shown in A of figure 9–8. As the number of loops is increased, the variation between maximum and minimum values of voltage is reduced (B of figure 9–8), and the output voltage of the generator approaches a steady d.c. value. In A of figure 9–8 the number of commutator segments is increased in direct proportion to the number of

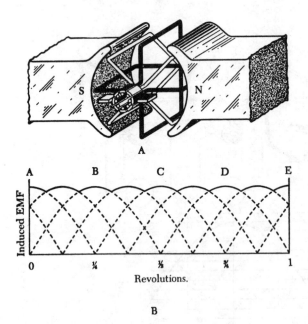

A

B

FIGURE 9–8. Increasing the number of coils reduces the ripple in the voltage.

loops; that is, there are two segments for one loop, four segments for two loops, and eight segments for four loops.

The voltage induced in a single-turn loop is small. Increasing the number of loops does not increase the maximum value of generated voltage, but increasing the number of turns in each loop will increase this value. Within narrow limits, the output voltage of a d.c. generator is determined by the product of the number of turns per loop, the total flux per pair of poles in the machine, and the speed of rotation of the armature.

An a.c. generator, or alternator, and a d.c. generator are identical as far as the method of generating voltage in the rotating loop is concerned. However, if the current is taken from the loop by slip rings, it is an alternating current, and the generator is called an a.c. generator, or alternator. If the current is collected by a commutator, it is direct current, and the generator is called a d.c. generator.

Construction Features of D. C. Generators

Generators used on aircraft may differ somewhat in design, since they are made by various manufacturers. All, however, are of the same general construction and operate similarly. The major parts, or assemblies, of a d.c. generator are a field frame (or yoke), a rotating armature, and a brush assembly. The parts of a typical aircraft generator are shown in figure 9–9.

Field Frame

The field frame is also called the yoke, which is the foundation or frame for the generator. The frame has two functions: It completes the magnetic circuit between the poles and acts as a mechanical support for the other parts of the generator. In A of figure 9–10, the frame for a two-pole generator is shown in a cross-sectional view. A four-pole generator frame is shown in B of figure 9–10.

In small generators, the frame is made of one piece of iron, but in larger generators, it is usually made up of two parts bolted together. The frame has high magnetic properties and, together with the pole pieces, forms the major part of the magnetic circuit. The field poles, shown in figure 9–10, are bolted to the inside of the frame and form a core on which the field coil windings are mounted. The poles are usually laminated to reduce eddy

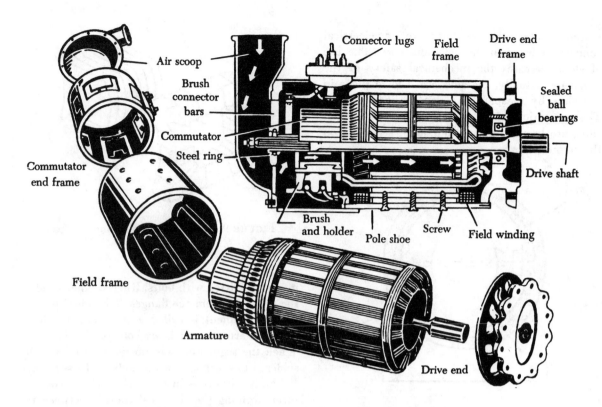

FIGURE 9–9. Typical 24-volt aircraft generator.

current losses and serve the same purpose as the iron core of an electromagnet; that is, they concentrate the lines of force produced by the field coils. The entire frame including field poles, is made from high-quality magnetic iron or sheet steel.

A practical d.c. generator uses electromagnets instead of permanent magnets. To produce a magnetic field of the necessary strength with permanent magnets would greatly increase the physical size of the generator.

The field coils are made up of many turns of insulated wire and are usually wound on a form which fits over the iron core of the pole to which it is securely fastened (figure 9–11). The exciting current, which is used to produce the magnetic field and which flows through the field coils, is obtained from an external source or from the generated d.c. of the machine. No electrical connection exists between the windings of the field coils and the pole pieces.

Most field coils are connected in such a manner that the poles show alternate polarity. Since there is always one north pole for each south pole, there must always be an even number of poles in any generator.

Note that the pole pieces in figure 9–10 project from the frame. Because air offers a great amount of reluctance to the magnetic field, this design reduces the length of the air gap between the poles and the rotating armature and increases the efficiency of the generator. When the pole pieces are made to project as shown in figure 9–10, they are called salient poles.

Armature

The armature assembly consists of armature coils wound on an iron core, a commutator, and associated mechanical parts. Mounted on a shaft, it rotates through the magnetic field produced by the field coils. The core of the armature acts as an iron conductor in the magnetic field and, for this reason, is laminated to prevent the circulation of eddy currents.

There are two general kinds of armatures: the ring and the drum. Figure 9–12 shows a ring-type armature made up of an iron core, an eight-section winding, and an eight-segment commutator. This kind of armature is rarely used; most generators use the drum-type armature.

A drum-type armature (figure 9–13) has coils

placed in slots in the core, but there is no electrical connection between the coils and core. The use of slots increases the mechanical safety of the armature. Usually, the coils are held in place in the slots by means of wooden or fiber wedges. The connections of the individual coils, called coil ends, are brought out to individual segments on the commutator.

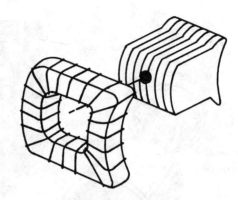

FIGURE 9–11.   A field coil removed from a field pole.

ing flanges fitted with bolts. Rings of mica insulate the segments from the flanges. The raised portion of each segment is called a riser, and the leads from the armature coils are soldered to the risers. When the segments have no risers, the leads are soldered to short slits in the ends of the segments.

The brushes ride on the surface of the commutator, forming the electrical contact between the armature coils and the external circuit. A flexible, braided-copper conductor, commonly called a pigtail, connects each brush to the external circuit. The brushes, usually made of high-grade carbon and held in place by brush holders insulated from the frame, are free to slide up and down in their holders in order to follow any irregularities in the surface of the commutator. The brushes are usually adjustable so that the pressure of the brushes on the commutator can be varied and the position of the brushes with respect to the segments can be adjusted.

The constant making and breaking of connections to the coils in which a voltage is being

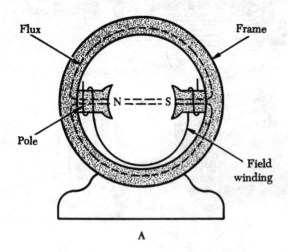

A

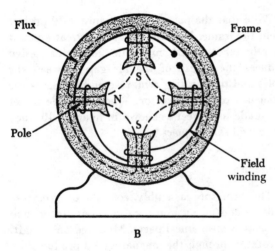

B

FIGURE 9–10.   A two-pole and a four-pole frame assembly.

Commutators

Figure 9–14 shows a cross-sectional view of a typical commutator. The commutator is located at the end of an armature and consists of wedge-shaped segments of hard-drawn copper, insulated from each other by thin sheets of mica. The segments are held in place by steel V-rings or clamp-

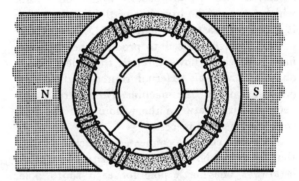

FIGURE 9–12.   An eight-section, ring-type armature.

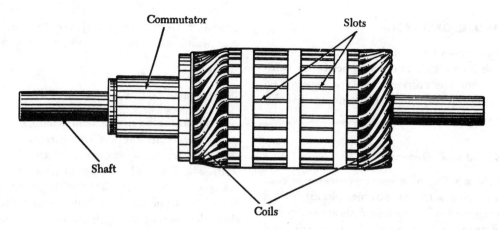

FIGURE 9–13. A drum-type armature.

induced necessitates the use of material for brushes which has a definite contact resistance. Also, this material must be such that the friction between the commutator and the brush is low, to prevent excessive wear. For these reasons, the material commonly used for brushes is high-grade carbon. The carbon must be soft enough to prevent undue wear of the commutator and yet hard enough to provide reasonable brush life. Since the contact resistance of carbon is fairly high, the brush must be quite large to provide a large area of contact. The commutator surface is highly polished to reduce friction as much as possible. Oil or grease must never be used on a commutator, and extreme care must be used when cleaning it to avoid marring or scratching the surface.

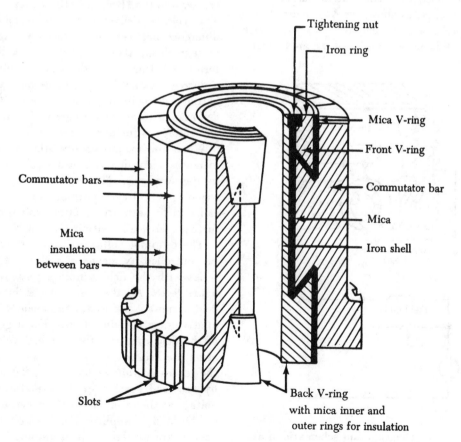

FIGURE 9–14. Commutator with portion removed to show construction.

TYPES OF D. C. GENERATORS

There are three types of d.c. generators: series-wound, shunt-wound, and shunt-series or compound wound. The difference in type depends on the relationship of the field winding to the external circuit.

Series-Wound D. C. Generators

The field winding of a series generator is connected in series with the external circuit, called the load (figure 9–15). The field coils are composed of a few turns of large wire; the magnetic field strength depends more on the current flow rather than the number of turns in the coil. Series generators have very poor voltage regulation under changing load, since the greater the current through the field coils to the external circuit, the greater the induced e.m.f. and the greater the terminal or output voltage. Therefore, when the load is increased, the voltage increases; likewise, when the load is decreased, the voltage decreases. The output voltage of a series-wound generator may be controlled by a rheostat in parallel with the field windings, as shown in A of figure 9–15. Since the series-wound generator has such poor regulation, it is never employed as an airplane

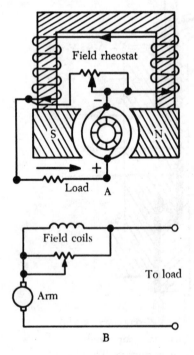

FIGURE 9–15.   Diagram and schematic of a series-wound generator.

generator. Generators in airplanes have field windings which are connected either in shunt or in compound.

Shunt-Wound D. C. Generators

A generator having a field winding connected in parallel with the external circuit is called a shunt generator, as shown in A and B of figure 9–16. The field coils of a shunt generator contain many turns of small wire; the magnetic strength is derived from the large number of turns rather than the current strength through the coils. If a constant voltage is desired, the shunt-wound generator is not suitable for rapidly fluctuating loads. Any increase in load causes a decrease in the terminal or output voltage, and any decrease in load causes an increase in terminal voltage; since the armature and the load are connected in series, all current flowing in the external circuit passes through the armature winding. Because of the resistance in the armature winding, there is a voltage drop (IR drop = current $\times$ resistance). As the load increases, the armature current increases and the IR drop in the armature increases. The voltage delivered to the terminals is the difference between the induced voltage and the voltage drop; therefore, there is a decrease in terminal voltage. This decrease in voltage causes a decrease in field strength, because the current in the field coils decreases in proportion to the decrease in terminal voltage; with a weaker field, the voltage is further decreased.

When the load decreases, the output voltage increases accordingly, and a larger current flows in the windings. This action is cumulative, so the output voltage continues to rise to a point called field saturation, after which there is no further increase in output voltage.

The terminal voltage of a shunt generator can be controlled by means of a rheostat inserted in series with the field windings as shown in A of figure 9–16. As the resistance is increased, the field current is reduced; consequently, the generated voltage is reduced also. For a given setting of the field rheostat, the terminal voltage at the armature brushes will be approximately equal to the generated voltage minus the IR drop produced by the load current in the armature; thus, the voltage at the terminals of the generator will drop as the load is applied. Certain voltage-sensitive devices are available which automatically adjust the field rheostat to compensate for variations in

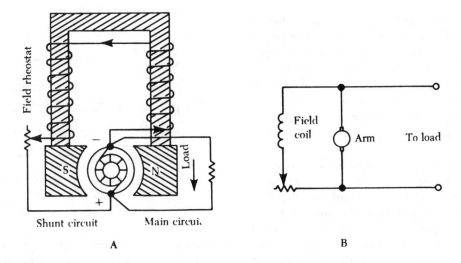

FIGURE 9–16. Shunt-wound generator.

load. When these devices are used, the terminal voltage remains essentially constant.

Compound-Wound D. C. Generators

A compound-wound generator combines a series winding and a shunt winding in such a way that the characteristics of each are used to advantage. The series field coils are made of a relatively small number of turns of large copper conductor, either circular or rectangular in cross section, and are connected in series with the armature circuit. These coils are mounted on the same poles on which the shunt field coils are mounted and, therefore, contribute a magnetomotive force which influences the main field flux of the generator. A diagrammatic and a schematic illustration of a compound-wound generator is shown in A and B of figure 9–17.

If the ampere-turns of the series field act in the same direction as those of the shunt field, the combined magnetomotive force is equal to the sum of the series and shunt field components. Load is added to a compound generator in the same manner in which load is added to a shunt generator, by increasing the number of parallel paths across the generator terminals. Thus, the decrease in total load resistance with added load is accompanied by an increase in armature-circuit and series-field circuit current.

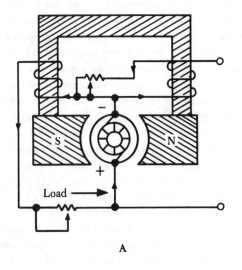

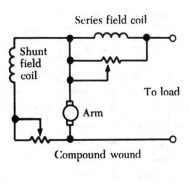

FIGURE 9–17. Compound-wound generator.

The effect of the additive series field is that of increased field flux with increased load. The extent of the increased field flux depends on the degree of saturation of the field as determined by the shunt field current. Thus, the terminal voltage of the generator may increase or decrease with load, depending on the influence of the series field coils. This influence is referred to as the degree of compounding.

A flat-compound generator is one in which the no-load and full-load voltages have the same value; whereas an under-compound generator has a full-load voltage less than the no-load value, and an over-compound generator has a full-load voltage which is higher than the no-load value. Changes in terminal voltage with increasing load depends upon the degree of compounding.

If the series field aids the shunt field, the generator is said to be cumulative-compounded (B of figure 9–17).

If the series field opposes the shunt field, the machine is said to be differentially compounded, or is called a differential generator.

Compound generators are usually designed to be overcompounded. This feature permits varied degrees of compounding by connecting a variable shunt across the series field. Such a shunt is sometimes called a diverter. Compound generators are used where voltage regulation is of prime importance.

Differential generators have somewhat the same characteristics as series generators in that they are essentially constant-current generators. However, they generate rated voltage at no load, the voltage dropping materially as the load current

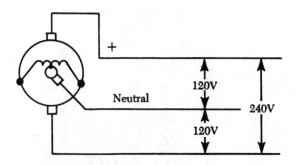

FIGURE 9–19.   Three-wire generator.

increases. Constant-current generators are ideally suited as power sources for electric arc welders and are used almost universally in electric arc welding.

If the shunt field of a compound generator is connected across both the armature and the series field, it is known as a long-shunt connection, but if the shunt field is connected across the armature alone, it is called a short-shunt connection. These connections produce essentially the same generator characteristics.

A summary of the characteristics of the various types of generators discussed is shown graphically in figure 9–18.

Three-Wire Generators

Some d.c. generators, called three-wire generators, are designed to deliver 240 volts, or 120 volts from either side of a neutral wire (figure 9–19). This is accomplished by connecting a reactance coil to opposite sides of the commutator, with the neutral connected to the midpoint of the reactance coil. Such a reactance coil acts as a low-loss voltage divider. If resistors were used, the IR loss would be prohibitive unless the two loads were perfectly matched. The coil is built into some generators as part of the armature, with the midpoint connected to a single slip ring which the neutral contacts by means of a brush. In other generators, the two connections to the commutator are connected, in turn, to two slip rings, and the reactor is located outside the generator. In either case, the load unbalance on either side of the neutral must not be more than 25 percent of the rated current output of the generator. The three-wire generator permits simultaneous operation of 120-volt lighting circuits and 240-volt motors from the same generator.

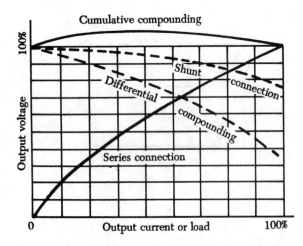

FIGURE 9–18.   Generator characteristics.

396

Armature Reaction

Current flowing through the armature sets up electromagnetic fields in the windings. These new fields tend to distort or bend the magnetic flux between the poles of the generator from a straight line path. Since armature current increases with load, the distortion becomes greater with an increase in load. This distortion of the magnetic

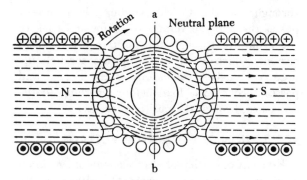

A   Field excited, armature unexcited

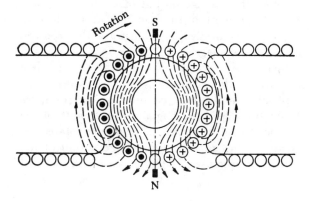

B   Armature excited, field unexcited

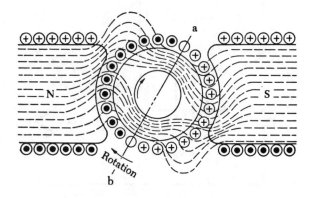

C   Both field and armature excited

FIGURE 9–20.   Armature reaction.

field is called armature reaction and is illustrated in figure 9–20.

Armature windings of a generator are spaced in such a way that, during rotation of the armature, there are certain positions when the brushes contact two adjacent segments, thereby shorting the armature windings to these segments. Usually, when the magnetic field is not distorted, there is no voltage being induced in the shorted windings, and, therefore, no harmful results occur from the shorting of the windings. However, when the field is distorted, a voltage is induced in these shorted windings and sparking takes place between the brushes and the commutator segments. Consequently, the commutator becomes pitted, the wear on the brushes becomes excessive, and the output of the generator is reduced. To correct this condition, the brushes are set so that the plane of the coils which are shorted by the brushes is perpendicular to the distorted magnetic field, which is accomplished by moving the brushes forward in the direction of rotation. This operation is called shifting the brushes to the neutral plane, or plane of commutation. The neutral plane is the position where the plane of the two opposite coils is perpendicular to the magnetic field in the generator. On a few generators, the brushes can be shifted manually ahead of the normal neutral plane to the neutral plane caused by field distortion. On nonadjustable brush generators, the manufacturer sets the brushes for minimum sparking.

Interpoles may be used to counteract some of the effects of field distortion, since shifting the brushes is inconvenient and unsatisfactory, especially when the speed and load of the generator are changing constantly. An interpole is a pole placed between the main poles of a generator. For example, a four-pole generator has four interpoles, which are north and south poles, alternately, as are the main poles. A four-pole generator with interpoles is shown in figure 9–21.

An interpole has the same polarity as the next main pole in the direction of rotation. The magnetic flux produced by an interpole causes the current in the armature to change direction as an armature winding passes under it. This cancels the electromagnetic fields about the armature windings. The magnetic strength of the interpoles varies with the load on the generator; and since field distortion varies with the load, the magnetic field of the interpoles counteracts the effects of the field set up around the armature windings

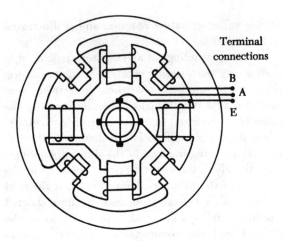

FIGURE 9–21.   Generator with interpoles.

and minimizes field distortion. Thus, the interpole tends to keep the neutral plane in the same position for all loads on the generator; therefore, field distortion is reduced by the interpoles, and the efficiency, output, and service life of the brushes are improved.

Generator Ratings

A generator is rated in power output. Since a generator is designed to operate at a specified voltage, the rating usually is given as the number of amperes the generator can safely supply at its rated voltage.

Generator rating and performance data are stamped on the name plate attached to the generator. When replacing a generator, it is important to choose one of the proper rating.

The rotation of generators is termed either clockwise or counterclockwise, as viewed from the driven end. Usually, the direction of rotation is stamped on the data plate. If no direction is stamped on the plate, the rotation may be marked by an arrow on the cover plate of the brush housing. It is important that a generator with the correct direction of rotation be used; otherwise the voltage will be reversed.

The speed of an aircraft engine varies from idle r.p.m. to takeoff r.p.m.; however, during the major portion of a flight, it is at a constant cruising speed. The generator drive is usually geared to revolve the generator between $1\frac{1}{8}$ and $1\frac{1}{2}$ times the engine crankshaft speed. Most aircraft generators have a speed at which they begin to produce their normal voltage. Termed the "coming-in" speed, it is usually about 1,500 r.p.m.

Generator Terminals

On most large 24-volt generators, electrical connections are made to terminals marked B, A, and E. (See figure 9–22.) The positive armature lead in the generator connects to the B terminal. The negative armature lead connects to the E terminal. The positive end of the shunt field winding connects to terminal A, and the opposite end connects to the negative terminal brush. Terminal A receives current from the negative generator brush through the shunt field winding. This current passes through the voltage regulator and back to the armature through the positive brush. Load current, which leaves the armature through the negative brushes, comes out of the E lead and passes through the load before returning to the armature through the positive brushes.

REGULATION OF GENERATOR VOLTAGE

Efficient operation of electrical equipment in an airplane depends on a constant voltage supply from the generator. Among the factors which determine the voltage output of a generator, only one, the strength of the field current, can be conveniently controlled. To illustrate this control, refer to the diagram in figure 9–22, showing a simple generator with a rheostat in the field circuit. If the rheostat is set to increase the resistance in the field circuit, less current flows through the field winding and the strength of the magnetic field in which the armature rotates decreases. Consequently, the voltage output of the generator decreases. If the resistance in the field

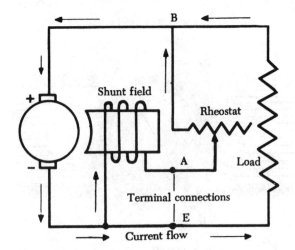

FIGURE 9–22.   Regulation of generator voltage by field rheostat.

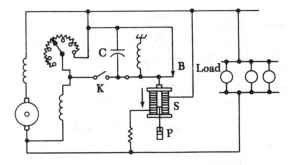

FIGURE 9–23.   Vibrating-type voltage regulator.

circuit is decreased with the rheostat, more current flows through the field windings, the magnetic field becomes stronger, and the generator produces a greater voltage.

With the generator running at normal speed and switch K open (figure 9–23), the field rheostat is adjusted so that the terminal voltage is about 60 percent of normal. Solenoid S is weak and contact B is held closed by the spring. When K is closed, a short circuit is placed across the field rheostat. This action causes the field current to increase and the terminal voltage to rise.

When the terminal voltage rises above a certain critical value, the solenoid downward pull exceeds the spring tension and contact B opens, thus reinserting the field rheostat in the field circuit and reducing the field current and terminal voltage.

When the terminal voltage falls below a certain critical voltage, the solenoid armature contact B is closed again by the spring, the field rheostat is now shorted, and the terminal voltage starts to rise. The cycle repeats with a rapid, continuous action. Thus, an average voltage is maintained with or without load change.

The dashpot P provides smoother operation by acting as a damper to prevent hunting. The capacitor C across contact B eliminates sparking. Added load causes the field rheostat to be shorted for a longer period of time and, thus, the solenoid armature vibrates more slowly. If the load is reduced and the terminal voltage rises, the armature vibrates more rapidly and the regulator holds the terminal voltage to a steady value for any change in load, from no load to full load, on the generator.

Vibrating-type regulators cannot be used with generators which require a high field current, since the contacts will pit or burn. Heavy-duty gener-

ator systems require a different type of regulator, such as the carbon-pile voltage regulator.

Carbon-Pile Voltage Regulator

The carbon-pile voltage regulator depends on the resistance of a number of carbon disks arranged in a pile or stack. The resistance of the carbon stack varies inversely with the pressure applied. When the stack is compressed under appreciable pressure, the resistance in the stack is less. When the pressure is reduced, the resistance of the carbon stack increases, because there is more air space between the disks, and air has high resistance. Pressure on the carbon pile depends upon two opposing forces: a spring and an electromagnet. The spring compresses the carbon pile, and the electromagnet exerts a pull which de-

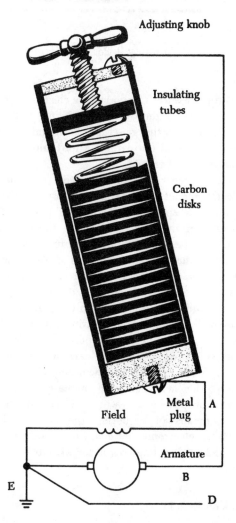

FIGURE 9–24.   Illustrating the controlling effect of a carbon-pile voltage regulator.

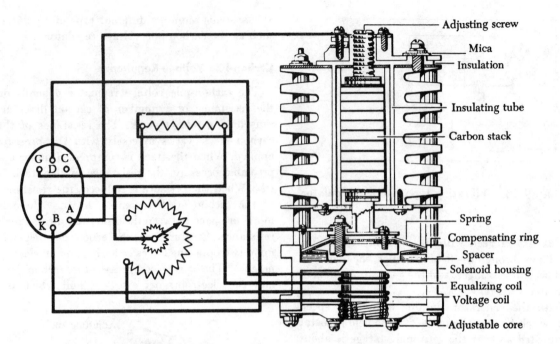

FIGURE 9–25. A 24-volt voltage regulator showing internal circuits.

creases the pressure. The coil of the electromagnet, as represented in the diagram in figure 9–24, is connected across the generator terminal B and through a rheostat (adjustable knob) and resistor (carbon disks) to ground.

When the generator voltage varies, the pull of the electromagnet varies. If the generator voltage rises above a specific amount, the pull of the electromagnet increases, decreasing the pressure exerted on the carbon pile and increasing its resistance. Since this resistance is in series with the field, less current flows through the field winding, there is a corresponding decrease in field strength, and the generator voltage drops. On the other hand, if the generator output drops below the specified value, the pull of the electromagnet is decreased and the carbon pile places less resistance in the field winding circuit. In addition, the field strength increases and the generator output increases. A small rheostat provides a means of adjusting the current flow through the electromagnet coil. Figure 9–25 shows a typical 24-volt voltage regulator with its internal circuits.

Three-Unit Regulators

Many light aircraft employ a three-unit regulator for their generator systems. This type of regulator includes a current limiter and a reverse-current cutout in addition to a voltage regulator.

The action of the voltage regulator unit is similar to the vibrating-type regulator described earlier. The second of the three units is a current regulator to limit the output current of the generator. The third unit is a reverse-current cutout that disconnects the battery from the generator. If the battery is not disconnected, it will discharge through the generator armature when the generator voltage falls below that of the

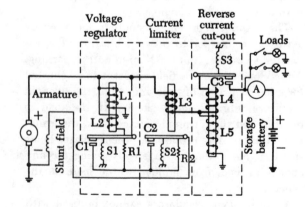

FIGURE 9–26. Three-unit regulator for variable-speed generators.

400

battery, thus driving the generator as a motor. This action is called "motoring" the generator and, unless it is prevented, it will discharge the battery in a short time.

The operation of a three-unit regulator is described in the following paragraphs. (Refer to figure 9–26.)

The action of vibrating contact C1 in the voltage regulator unit causes an intermittent short circuit between points R1 and L2. When the generator is not operating, spring S1 holds C1 closed; C2 is also closed by S2. The shunt field is connected directly across the armature.

When the generator is started, its terminal voltage will rise as the generator comes up to speed, and the armature will supply the field with current through closed contacts C2 and C1.

As the terminal voltage rises, the current flow through L1 increases and the iron core becomes more strongly magnetized. At a certain speed and voltage, when the magnetic attraction on the movable arm becomes strong enough to overcome the tension of spring S1, contact points C1 are separated. The field current now flows through R1 and L2. Because resistance is added to the field circuit, the field is momentarily weakened and the rise in terminal voltage is checked. Also, since the L2 winding is opposed to the L1 winding, the magnetic pull of L1 against S1 is partially neutralized, and spring S1 closes contact C1. Therefore, R1 and L2 are again shorted out of the circuit, and the field current again increases; the output voltage increases, and C1 is opened because of the action of L1. The cycle is rapid and occurs many times per second. The terminal voltage of the generator varies slightly, but rapidly, above and below an average value determined by the tension of spring S1, which may be adjusted.

The purpose of the vibrator-type current limiter is to limit the output current of the generator automatically to its maximum rated value in order to protect the generator. As shown in figure 9–26, L3 is in series with the main line and load. Thus, the amount of current flowing in the line determines when C2 will be opened and R2 placed in series with the generator field. By contrast, the voltage regulator is actuated by line voltage, whereas the current limiter is actuated by line current. Spring S2 holds contact C2 closed until the current through the main line and L3 exceeds a certain value, as determined by the tension of spring S2, and causes C2 to be opened. The

increase in current is due to an increase in load. This action inserts R2 into the field circuit of the generator and decreases the field current and the generated voltage. When the generated voltage is decreased, the generator current is reduced. The core of L3 is partly demagnetized and the spring closes the contact points. This causes the generator voltage and current to rise until the current reaches a value sufficient to start the cycle again. A certain minimum value of load current is necessary to cause the current limiter to vibrate.

The purpose of the reverse-current cutout relay is to automatically disconnect the battery from the generator when the generator voltage is less than the battery voltage. If this device were not used in the generator circuit, the battery would discharge through the generator. This would tend to make the generator operate as a motor, but because the generator is coupled to the engine, it could not rotate such a heavy load. Under this condition, the generator windings may be severely damaged by excessive current.

There are two windings, L4 and L5, on the soft-iron core. The current winding, L4, consisting of a few turns of heavy wire, is in series with the line and carries the entire line current. The voltage winding, L5, consisting of a large number of turns of fine wire, is shunted across the generator terminals.

When the generator is not operating, the contacts, C3 are held open by the spring S3. As the generator voltage builds up, L5 magnetizes the iron core. When the current (as a result of the generated voltage) produces sufficient magnetism in the iron core, contact C3 is closed, as shown. The battery then receives a charging current. The coil spring, S3, is so adjusted that the voltage winding will not close the contact points until the voltage of the generator is in excess of the normal voltage of the battery. The charging current passing through L4 aids the current in L5 to hold the contacts tightly closed. Unlike C1 and C2, contact C3 does not vibrate. When the generator slows down or, for any other cause, the generator voltage decreases to a certain value below that of the battery, the current reverses through L4 and the ampere-turns of L4 oppose those of L5. Thus, a momentary discharge current from the battery reduces the magnetism of the core and C3 is opened, preventing the battery from discharging into the generator and motoring it. C3 will not close again until the generator terminal voltage

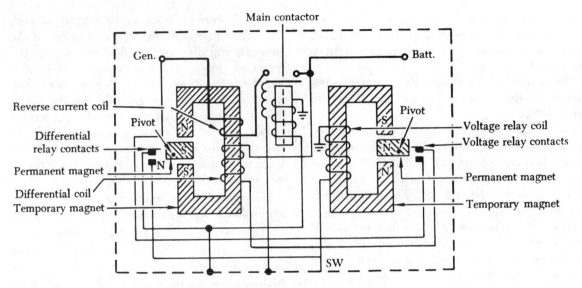

FIGURE 9–27. Differential generator control relay.

DIFFERENTIAL RELAY SWITCH

Aircraft electrical systems normally use some type of reverse-current relay switch, which acts not only as a reverse-current relay cutout but also serves as a remote-control switch by which the generator can be disconnected from the electrical system at any time. One type of reverse-current relay switch operates on the voltage level of the generator, but the type most commonly used on large aircraft is the differential relay switch, which is controlled by the difference in voltage between the battery bus and the generator.

The differential type relay switch connects the generator to the main bus bar in the electrical system when the generator voltage output exceeds the bus voltage by 0.35 to 0.65 volt. It disconnects the generator when a nominal reverse current flows from the bus to the generator. The differential relays on all the generators of a multiengine aircraft do not close when the electrical load is light. For example, in an aircraft having a load of 50 amperes, only two or three relays may close. If a heavy load is applied, the equalizing circuit will lower the voltage of the generators already on the bus and, at the same time, raise the voltage of the remaining generators, allowing their relays to close. If the generators have been paralleled properly, all the relays stay closed until the generator control switch is turned off or until

the engine speed falls below the minimum needed to maintain generator output voltage.

The differential generator control relay shown in the illustration in figure 9–27 is made up of two relays and a coil-operated contactor. One relay is the voltage relay and the other is the differential relay. Both relays include permanent magnets, which pivot between the pole pieces of temporary magnets wound with relay coils. Voltages of one polarity set up fields about the temporary magnets with polarities which cause the permanent magnet to move in the direction necessary to close the relay contacts; voltages of the opposite polarity establish fields that cause the relay contacts to open. The differential relay has two coils wound on the same core. The coil-operated contactor, called the main contactor, consists of movable contacts that are operated by a coil with a movable iron core.

Closing the generator switch on the control panel connects the generator output to the voltage relay coil. When generator voltage reaches 22 volts, current flows through the coil and closes the contacts of the voltage relay. This action completes a circuit from the generator to the battery through the differential coil. When the generator voltage exceeds the bus voltage by 0.35 volt, current will flow through the differential coil, the differential relay contact will close and, thus, complete the main contactor coil circuit. The contacts of the main contactor close and connect the generator to the bus.

When the generator voltage drops below the

bus (or battery) voltage, a reverse current weakens the magnetic field about the temporary magnet of the differential relay. The weakened field permits a spring to open the differential relay contacts, breaking the circuit to the coil of the main contactor relay, opening its contacts, and disconnecting the generator from the bus.

The generator-battery circuit may also be broken by opening the cockpit control switch, which opens the contacts of the voltage relay, causing the differential relay coil to be deenergized.

Overvoltage and Field Control Relays

Two other items used with generator control circuits are the overvoltage control and the field control relay.

As its name implies, the overvoltage control protects the system when excessive voltage exists. The overvoltage relay is closed when the generator output reaches 32 volts and completes a circuit to the trip coil of the field control relay. The closing of the field control relay trip circuit opens the shunt field circuit and completes it through a resistor, causing generator voltage to drop; also, the generator switch circuit and the equalizer circuit (multiengine aircraft) are opened. An indicator light circuit is completed, warning that an overvoltage condition exists. A "reset" position of the cockpit switch is used to complete a reset coil circuit in the field control relay, returning the relay to its normal position.

PARALLELING GENERATORS

When two or more generators are operated at the same time to supply power for a load, they are operated in parallel; that is, each supplies a proportional part of the ampere-load. Successful multigenerator operation requires that each generator share the load equally, since a very small increase in the voltage output of one generator will result in that generator's supplying the greater part of the power needed by the load.

The power supplied by a generator for a load is often referred to as ampere-load. Although power is actually measured in watts—the product of voltage and current—the term "ampere-load" is applicable because the voltage output of a generator is considered constant; therefore, the power is directly proportional to the ampere output of the generator.

Negative Lead Paralleling

To distribute the load equally among generators operated in parallel, a special coil is wound on the same core as the voltage coil of the voltage regulator. This is part of the equalizing system shown in figure 9–28. A calibrated resistor is located in the lead from the generator negative terminal E to ground. The value of the resistance in this lead is such that when the generator is operating at full current output, there is a 0.5-volt drop across the resistor. This resistor may be a special resistor; it may be a ground lead long enough to have the required resistance, or a series winding of the generator.

The equalizing system depends upon the voltage drop in the individual calibrated resistors. If all generators are supplying the same current, the voltage drop in all ground leads is the same. If the current supplied by the generators is unequal, there is a greater voltage drop in the ground lead of the generator supplying more current. Thus, when the No. 1 generator is supplying 150 amperes and the No. 2 generator is supplying 300 amperes, the voltage drop in the negative lead of the No. 1 generator is 0.25 volt and that in the negative lead of the No. 2 generator is 0.5 volt. This means that point E of the No. 1 generator is at a lower voltage than point E of the No. 2 generator, and current will flow in the equalizing circuit from E of the No. 2 generator to E of the No. 1 generator. The equalizing coil will aid the voltage coil in voltage regulator No. 2 and oppose the voltage coil in regulator No. 1. In this way, the voltage of generator No. 2 will be lowered and that of the other will be increased.

Positive Lead Paralleling

The diagram in figure 9–29 shows two generators carrying a total load of 300 amperes. If the generators were sharing this load equally, the ammeters would each indicate 150 amperes. The generators would be "paralleled" and no current would flow in the equalizing coils between the K and D terminals on the regulators. Note, however, that the ammeter for the No. 1 generator indicates only 100 amperes, but the ammeter for the No. 2 generator indicates 200 amperes. This is an unbalanced load and causes current to flow through the equalizing circuit (dotted lines) in the direction indicated by the arrows. The reason is as follows: With 200 amperes of current flowing through the No. 2 equalizing resistor (from Ohm's law, $E =$

403

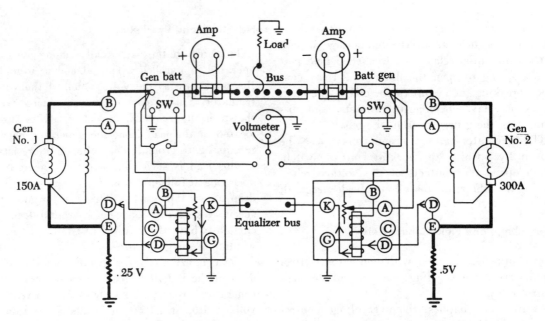

FIGURE 9–28.   Generator equalizer circuits.

$I \times R$), there will be a 0.5 volt drop in voltage across the No. 2 resistor. Since there are only 100 amperes flowing through the No. 1 equalizing resistor, there will be a one-fourth volt drop across that resistor, and a difference in voltage of one-fourth volt will exist between the two resistors. Since current flows from a high pressure (potential) to a lower pressure and from negative to positive, it will be in the direction indicated by the arrows. When the load is equal, there will not be a difference in voltage betweeen the two resistors.

The current can be traced through the equalizing circuit and through the voltage regulator coils to show the effect on the electromagnets. With the current in the direction shown, the equalizing coil and voltage coil of the No. 1 voltage regulator set up magnetic fields opposing each other, thus weakening the electromagnet of the No. 1 voltage regulator. This allows the spring to compress the carbon disks, decreasing their resistance and allowing more current to flow in the field circuit of the No. 1 generator. As a result, the voltage output of that generator increases, but at the same time, the current through the equalizing coil and voltage coil of No. 2 voltage regulator sets up magnetic fields that aid each other, thus increasing the strength of that electromagnet. This decreases the spring pressure on the carbon disks, increasing their resistance and allowing less current to flow in the field circuit of the No. 2 generator. As a result, the voltage output

of this generator will decrease. With the voltage output of the No. 1 generator increased, the voltage drop across No. 1 equalizing resistor increases; and with a decrease in voltage output of the No. 2 generator, the voltage drop across the No. 2 equalizing resistor decreases. When the voltage output of the two generators is equal, the voltage drop across the equalizing resistors will also be equal. No current will flow in the equalizing circuit, the load will be balanced, and the ammeters will read approximately the same. The generators are then paralleled.

The purpose of the equalizing circuit is to help the voltage regulators automatically by lowering the voltage of the high generator and raising the voltage of the low generator, so that the total will be shared equally by the generators.

D. C. GENERATOR MAINTENANCE

Inspection

The following information about the inspection and maintenance of d.c. generator systems is general in nature because of the large number of differing aircraft generator systems. These procedures are for familiarization only. Always follow the applicable manufacturer's instructions for a given generator system.

In general, the inspection of the generator in-

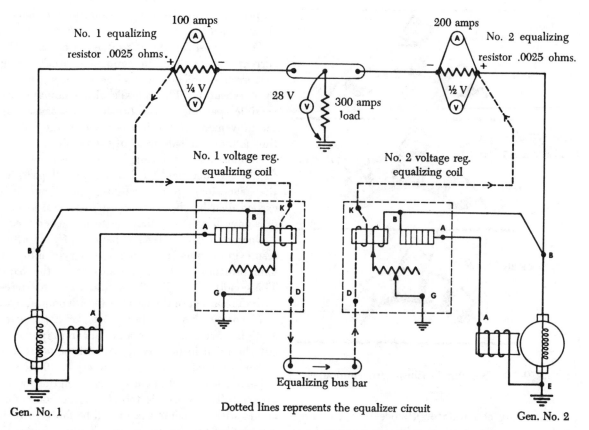

No. 1 equalizing resistor .0025 ohms.

100 amps

No. 2 equalizing resistor .0025 ohms.

200 amps

¼ V

½ V

28 V

300 amps load

No. 1 voltage reg. equalizing coil

No. 2 voltage reg. equalizing coil

Gen. No. 1

Gen. No. 2

Equalizing bus bar

Dotted lines represents the equalizer circuit

FIGURE 9–29. Generator and equalizer circuits.

stalled in the aircraft should include the following items:

1. Security of generator mounting.
2. Condition of electrical connections.
3. Dirt and oil in the generator. If oil is present, check engine oil seal. Blow out dirt with compressed air.
4. Condition of generator brushes.
5. Generator operation.
6. Voltage regulator operation.

A detailed discussion of items 4, 5, and 6 is presented in the following paragraphs.

Condition of Generator Brushes

Sparking of brushes quickly reduces the effective brush area in contact with the commutator bars. The degree of such sparking should be determined. Excessive wear warrants a detailed inspection.

The following information pertains to brush seating, brush pressure, high-mica condition, and brush wear.

Manufacturers usually recommend the following procedures to seat brushes which do not make good contact with slip rings or commutators.

The brush should be lifted sufficiently to permit the insertion of a strip of No. 000, or finer, sandpaper under the brush, rough side out (figure 9–30). Pull sandpaper in the direction of armature rotation, being careful to keep the ends of the sandpaper as close to the slip ring or commutator surface as possible in order to avoid rounding the edges of the brush. When pulling the sandpaper back to the starting point, the brush should be raised so it does not ride on the sandpaper. The brush should be sanded only in the direction of rotation.

After the generator has run for a short period, brushes should be inspected to make sure that pieces of sand have not become embedded in the brush and are collecting copper.

Under no circumstances should emery cloth or similar abrasives be used for seating brushes

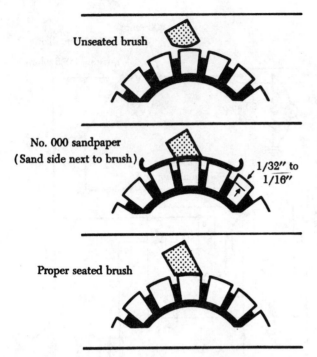

Unseated brush

No. 000 sandpaper
(Sand side next to brush)

1/32" to
1/16"

Proper seated brush

FIGURE 9–30. Seating brushes with sandpaper.

(or smoothing commutators), since they contain conductive materials which will cause arcing between brushes and commutator bars.

Excessive pressure will cause rapid wear of brushes. Too little pressure, however, will allow "bouncing" of the brushes, resulting in burned and pitted surfaces.

A carbon, graphite, or light metalized brush should exert a pressure of 1½ to 2½ p.s.i. on the commutator. The pressure recommended by the manufacturer should be checked by the use of a spring scale graduated in ounces. Brush spring tension is usually adjusted between 32 to 36 ounces; however, the tension may differ slightly for each specific generator.

When a spring scale is used, the measurement of the pressure which a brush exerts on the commutator is read directly on the scale. The scale is applied at the point of contact between the spring arm and the top of the brush, with the brush installed in the guide. The scale is drawn up until the arm just lifts off the brush surface. At this instant, the force on the scale should be read.

Flexible low-resistance pigtails are provided on most heavy-current-carrying brushes, and their connections should be securely made and checked at frequent intervals. The pigtails should never be permitted to alter or restrict the free motion of the brush.

The purpose of the pigtail is to conduct the current, rather than subjecting the brush spring to currents which would alter its spring action by overheating. The pigtails also eliminate any possible sparking to the brush guides caused by the movement of the brushes within the holder, thus minimizing side wear of the brush.

Carbon dust resulting from brush sanding should be thoroughly cleaned from all parts of the generators after a sanding operation. Such carbon dust has been the cause of several serious fires as well as costly damage to the generator.

Operation over extended periods of time often results in the mica insulation between commutator bars protruding above the surface of the bars. This condition is called "high mica" and interferes with the contact of the brushes to the commutator.

Whenever this condition exists, or if the armature has been turned on a lathe, carefully undercut the mica insulation to a depth equal to the width of the mica, or approximately 0.020 inch.

Each brush should be a specified length to work properly. If a brush is too short, the contact it makes with the commutator will be faulty, which can also reduce the spring force holding the brush in place. Most manufacturers specify the amount of wear permissible from a new brush length. When a brush has worn to the minimum length permissible, it must be replaced.

Some special generator brushes should not be replaced because of a slight grooving on the face of the brush. These grooves are normal and will appear in a.c. and d.c. generator brushes which are installed in some models of aircraft generators. These brushes have two cores made of a harder material with a higher expansion rate than the material used in the main body of the brush. Usually, the main body of the brush face rides on the commutator. However, at certain temperatures, the cores extend and wear through any film on the commutator.

Generator Operation

If there is no generator output, follow a systematic troubleshooting procedure to locate the malfunction. The following method is an example. Although this method may be acceptable for most 28-volt, twin-engine or four-engine d.c. generator systems using carbon-pile voltage regulators, the applicable manufacturer's procedures should be followed in all cases.

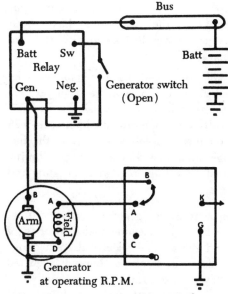

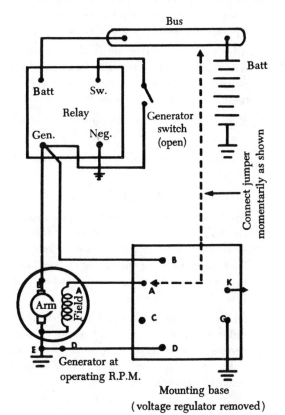

FIGURE 9–31. Checking generator by shorting terminals A and B.

If the generator is not producing voltage, remove the voltage regulator and, with the engine running at approximately 1,800 r.p.m., short circuit terminals A and B at the subbase of the regulator as shown in the diagram of figure 9–31. If this test shows excessive voltage, the generator is not at fault, but the trouble lies in the voltage regulator. If the test fails to produce voltage, the generator field may have lost its residual magnetism.

To restore residual magnetism, flash the generator field by removing the regulator and connect terminal A of the voltage regulator base to the battery at a junction box or a bus bar as indicated by the dotted line in the diagram of figure 9–32, while running the engine at cruising r.p.m. If there is still no voltage, check the leads for continuity shorts and grounds. If the generator is located where the brushes and commutator can be inspected, check each for proper condition as prescribed in the applicable manufacturer's procedures. If necessary, replace the brushes and clean the commutator. If the generator is located so that it cannot be serviced in the airplane, remove it and make the inspection.

VOLTAGE REGULATOR OPERATION

To inspect the voltage regulator, remove it from the subbase and clean all the terminals and con-

tact surfaces. Examine the base or housing for cracks. Check all connections for security. Remember that the voltage regulator is a precision instrument and cannot withstand rough treatment. Handle it with care. To adjust a voltage regulator, a precision portable voltmeter is required. This, too, must be handled with care, since it will not maintain accuracy under conditions of mishandling, vibration, or shock.

Detailed procedures for adjusting voltage regulators are given in applicable manufacturer's instructions. The following procedures are guidelines for adjusting the carbon-pile voltage regulator in a multiengine 28-volt d.c. electrical system:

1. Start and warm up all engines which have installed generators.
2. Turn all generator switches to the "off" position.
3. Connect a precision voltmeter from the B terminal of one voltage regulator to a good ground.

FIGURE 9–32. A method of flashing generator field.

407

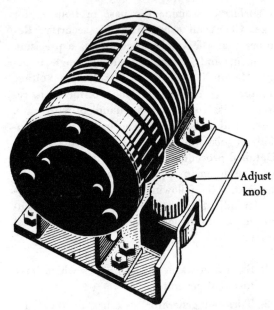

FIGURE 9–33.   Adjustment knob on carbon-pile
voltage regulator.

4. Increase the engine speed of the generator being checked to normal cruising r.p.m. Operate remaining engines at idling speed.

5. Adjust the regulator until the voltmeter reads exactly 28 volts. (The location of the adjustment knob on a carbon-pile voltage regulator is shown in figure 9–33.)

6. Repeat this procedure to adjust all voltage regulators.

7. Increase the speed of all engines to normal cruising r.p.m.

8. Close all generator switches.

9. Apply a load equivalent to approximately one-half full load rating of one generator when checking a two-generator system or a load comparable to the rating of one generator when checking a system that has more than two generators.

10. Observe the ammeters or load meters. The difference between the highest and lowest generator current should not exceed the value listed in the manufacturer's maintenance instructions.

11. If the generators are not dividing the load equally (unparalled), first lower the voltage of the highest generator and slightly raise the voltage of the lowest generator by

adjusting the corresponding voltage regulators. When the generators have been adjusted to share the load equally, they are in "parallel."

12. After all adjustments have been made, make a final check of bus voltage from positive bus to ground, with a precision voltmeter. The voltmeter should read 28 volts, (± 0.25 volt on most 28-volt systems). If the bus voltage is not within the proper limits, readjust all voltage regulator rheostats and recheck.

When inspecting the generator relay switch, examine the relay for cleanness and security of mounting and see that all electrical connections are tightly fastened. Look for burned or pitted contacts. Never close the relay manually by pressing the contacts together; this might severely damage the relay or cause an injury. Never adjust the differential type relay, since it closes when the generator voltage exceeds the system voltage by a specified value and is not checked to close at any set voltage; however, check it for proper closing by noting the ammeter indication with the battery generator control switches turned on while running the engines. It is sometimes necessary to put a slight load on the system before the ammeter will show a positive indication when the engine is run up to cruising speed. If the ammeter does not indicate, the relay is probably defective; therefore, remove it and replace it with a new relay. Check the reverse-current relay for proper opening value. If the relay fails to close when the engine speed is increased or fails to disconnect the generator from the bus bar, the relay is defective.

Troubleshooting

If a generator system malfunctions, there are two general possibilities: (1) The generator itself may be at fault (burned out, damaged mechanically, etc.), or (2) that part of the circuit leading to or from the generator may be at fault. Continuity testing refers to checking for the existence of a complete electrical system between two points. The three main types of continuity testers are:

1. The portable dry cell tester, having a buzzer or a 3-volt lamp to indicate the completed circuit, is used to test circuits with the main circuit power off.

2. An ordinary lamp bulb (24-volt type), with one lead from the center lamp contact and one ground lead attached to the lamp housing, can be used to test circuits with the main circuit power on.

3. A precision voltmeter is used to test circuits with the main circuit power on by placing the positive lead on the circuit point and the negative lead on any convenient ground.

Tests should be made at each terminal of the circuit. Between the last point at which voltage is indicated and the first point at which zero voltage is indicated, there is an open circuit or a voltage drop caused by unit operation or short to ground. If the same voltage reading is obtained on the negative terminal of a unit as was obtained on the positive terminal, an open ground is indicated. If a small voltage reading is obtained on the negative terminal of the unit, a high resistance is indicated between the unit and ground.

The following troubleshooting chart outlines the most commonly encountered malfunctions, a list of probable causes to isolate the malfunction, and the proper corrective action to be taken. This chart is a general guide for troubleshooting a twin-engine d.c. generator system, which utilizes carbon-pile voltage regulators.

TROUBLE	ISOLATION PROCEDURE	CORRECTION
No voltage indication on any one generator.	Check for defective generator switch or field switch.	Replace generator switch or field switch.
	Determine if generator polarity is reversed.	Flash generator field.
	Check for open, shorted, or grounded wiring.	Replace defective wiring.
	Check for defective generator.	Replace generator.
Low voltage on any one generator.	Check voltage regulator adjustment.	Adjust voltage regulator.
	Check for defective voltage regulator.	Replace voltage regulator.
	Check for defective wiring.	Replace defective wiring.
	Check for defective generator.	Replace generator.
Generator cuts out.	Check for defective reverse-current cutout relay.	Replace reverse-current cutout relay.
	Check for defective overvoltage relay.	Replace overvoltage relay.
	Check for defective field control relay.	Replace field control relay.
	Check for defective voltage regulator.	Replace voltage regulator.
	Check for defective wiring.	Replace defective wiring.
Voltage unsteady for any one generator.	Check for defective wiring.	Replace defective wiring.
	Check for defective generator.	Replace generator.
	Check wear of generator bearings.	Replace generator.
No load indication on any one generator. Voltage is normal.	Check for defective reverse-current cutout relay.	Replace reverse-current cutout relay.
	Check for defective generator switch.	Replace generator switch.
	Check for defective wiring.	Replace defective wiring.

TROUBLE	ISOLATION PROCEDURE	CORRECTION
Low d.c. bus voltage.	Check improper voltage regulator adjustment. Check for defective reverse-current cutout relays.	Adjust voltage regulator. Replace reverse-current cutout relays.
Voltage high on any one generator.	Check for improper voltage regulator adjustment. Check for defective voltage regulator. Determine if generator field lead A is shorted to positive.	Adjust voltage regulator. Replace voltage regulator. Replace shorted wiring or repair connections.
Generator fails to build up more than approximately 2 volts.	Check voltage regulator or base. Take precision voltmeter reading between A terminal and ground. No voltage reading indicates trouble in either regulator or base. Reading of about 2 volts indicates regulator and base are OK. Check for defective generator. Low ohmmeter reading indicates current is good and trouble must be within the generator.	Check regulator contacts where they rest on the silver contact bar. Any signs of burning at this point is cause for replacement of regulator. Disconnect generator plug. Place one lead of ohmmeter on A terminal and the other lead on E terminal. High reading indicates that the generator field is open. Replace generator.
Instrument panel voltmeter reading of excessive voltage.	Check for short across A and B terminal of voltage regulator. Check voltage regulator control.	If shorted, change voltage regulator. Replace voltage regulator.
Instrument panel voltmeter reading of zero volts.	Check for defective voltmeter circuit. Check for broken B or E lead. Remove voltage regulator and take ohmmeter reading between B contact finger of regulator	Place positive lead of voltmeter on positive terminal of instrument panel voltmeter and negative lead to ground. Reading should be 27.5 volts. If not, lead from regulator to instrument is defective. Replace or correct lead. Place positive lead of voltmeter on negative terminal of instrument panel voltmeter and negative lead to ground. If voltmeter reading is zero, instrument panel voltmeter is defective. Replace voltmeter. High resistance most likely is caused by oil, dirt, or burning at connector plug or commutator. Replace generator.

TROUBLE	ISOLATION PROCEDURE	CORRECTION
	base and ground. Low reading indicates circuit is OK. High reading indicates that a high resistance is the trouble.	
	Check for loss of residual magnetism.	Place flasher switch in ON position momentarily. Do not hold. *NOTE:* If flasher switch is held ON rather than switched momentarily, damage may be done to generator field coils.
Voltage does not build up properly when field is flashed.	Check for open field. Disconnect generator connector and take ohmmeter reading between A and E terminals of generator connectors. High reading indicates field circuit is open.	Check and repair lead or connectors.
	Check for grounded field. Take ohmmeter reading between A terminal of generator and generator housing. Low reading indicates field is grounded.	Insulation on field winding is broken. Replace generator.
	Check for open armature. Remove generator cover and inspect commutator. If solder is melted and has been thrown off, then armature is open (caused by generator overheating).	Replace generator.

ALTERNATORS

An electrical generator is a machine which converts mechanical energy into electrical energy by electromagnetic induction. A generator which produces alternating current is referred to as an a.c. generator and, through combination of the words "alternating" and "generator," the word "alternator" has come into widespread use. In some areas, the word "alternator" is applied only to small a.c. generators. This text treats the two terms synonymously and uses the term "alternator" to distinguish between a.c. and d.c. generators.

The major difference between an alternator and a d.c. generator is the method of connection to the external circuit; that is, the alternator is connected to the external circuit by slip rings, but the d.c. generator is connected by a commutator.

Types of Alternators

Alternators are classified in several ways in order to distinguish properly the various types. One means of classification is by the type of excitation system used. In alternators used on aircraft, excitation can be affected by one of the following methods:

1. A direct-connected, direct-current generator. This system consists of a d.c. generator fixed on the same shaft with the a.c. generator. A variation of this system is a type of alternator which uses d.c. from the battery for excitation, after which the alternator is self-excited.
2. By transformation and rectification from the a.c. system. This method depends on residual magnetism for initial a.c. voltage buildup,

after which the field is supplied with rectified voltage from the a.c. generator.

3. Integrated brushless type. This arrangement has a direct-current generator on the same shaft with an alternating-current generator. The excitation circuit is completed through silicon rectifiers rather than a commutator and brushes. The rectifiers are mounted on the generator shaft and their output is fed directly to the alternating-current generator's main rotating field.

Another method of classification is by the number of phases of output voltage. Alternating-current generators may be single-phase, two-phase, three-phase, or even six-phase and more. In the electrical systems of aircraft, the three-phase alternator is by far the most common.

Still another means of classification is by the type of stator and rotor used. From this standpoint, there are two types of alternators: the revolving-armature type and the revolving-field type. The revolving-armature alternator is similar in construction to the d.c. generator, in that the armature rotates through a stationary magnetic field. The revolving-armature alternator is found only in alternators of low power rating and generally is not used. In the d.c. generator, the e.m.f. generated in the armature windings is converted into a unidirectional voltage (d.c.) by means of the commutator. In the revolving-armature type of alternator, the generated a.c. voltage is applied unchanged to the load by means of slip rings and brushes.

The revolving-field type of alternator (figure 9–34) has a stationary armature winding (stator) and a rotating-field winding (rotor). The advantage of having a stationary armature winding is that the armature can be connected directly to the load without having sliding contacts in the load circuit. A rotating armature would require slip rings and brushes to conduct the load current from the armature to the external circuit. Slip rings have a relatively short service life and arc-over is a continual hazard; therefore, high-voltage alternators are usually of the stationary-armature, rotating-field type. The voltage and current supplied to the rotating field are relatively small, and slip rings and brushes for this circuit are adequate. The direct connection to the armature circuit makes possible the use of large cross-section conductors, adequately insulated for high voltage.

Since the rotating-field alternator is used almost

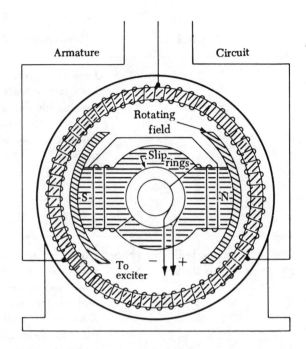

FIGURE 9–34. Alternator with stationary armature and rotating field.

universally in aircraft systems, this type will be explained in detail, as a single-phase, two-phase, and three-phase alternator.

Single-Phase Alternator

Since the e.m.f. induced in the armature of a generator is alternating, the same sort of winding can be used on an alternator as on a d.c. generator. This type of alternator is known as a single-phase alternator, but since the power delivered by a single-phase circuit is pulsating, this type of circuit is objectionable in many applications.

A single-phase alternator has a stator made up of a number of windings in series, forming a single circuit in which an output voltage is generated. Figure 9–35 illustrates a schematic diagram of a single-phase alternator having four poles. The stator has four polar groups evenly spaced around the stator frame. The rotor has four poles, with adjacent poles of opposite polarity. As the rotor revolves, a.c. voltages are induced in the stator windings. Since one rotor pole is in the same position relative to a stator winding as any other rotor pole, all stator polar groups are cut by equal numbers of magnetic lines of force at any time. As a result, the voltages induced in all the windings have the same amplitude, or value, at

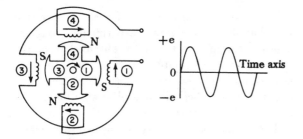

FIGURE 9–35. Single-phase alternator.

any given instant. The four stator windings are connected to each other so that the a.c. voltages are in phase, or "series adding." Assume that rotor pole 1, a south pole, induces a voltage in the direction indicated by the arrow in stator winding 1. Since rotor pole 2 is a north pole, it will induce a voltage in the opposite direction in stator coil 2 with respect to that in coil 1.

For the two induced voltages to be in series addition, the two coils are connected as shown in the diagram. Applying the same reasoning, the voltage induced in stator coil 3 (clockwise rotation of the field) is the same direction (counterclockwise) as the voltage induced in coil 1. Similarly, the direction of the voltage induced in winding 4 is opposite to the direction of the voltage induced in coil 1. All four stator coil groups are connected in series so that the voltages induced in each winding add to give a total voltage that is four times the voltage in any one winding.

Two-Phase Alternator

Two-phase alternators have two or more single-phase windings spaced symmetrically around the stator. In a two-phase alternator there are two single-phase windings spaced physically so that the a.c. voltage induced in one is 90° out of phase with the voltage induced in the other. The windings are electrically separate from each other. When one winding is being cut by maximum flux, the other is being cut by no flux. This condition establishes a 90° relation between the two phases.

Three-Phase Alternator

A three-phase, or polyphase circuit, is used in most aircraft alternators, instead of a single or two-phase alternator. The three-phase alternator has three single-phase windings spaced so that the voltage induced in each winding is 120° out of phase with the voltages in the other two wind-

ings. A schematic diagram of a three-phase stator showing all the coils becomes complex and difficult to see what is actually happening.

A simplified schematic diagram, showing each of three phases, is illustrated in figure 9–36. The rotor is omitted for simplicity. The waveforms of voltage are shown to the right of the schematic. The three voltages are 120° apart and are similar to the voltages which would be generated by three single-phase alternators whose voltages are out of phase by angles of 120°. The three phases are independent of each other.

Rather than have six leads from the three-phase alternator, one of the leads from each phase may be connected to form a common junction. The stator is then called wye- or star-connected. The common lead may or may not be brought out of the alternator. If it is brought out, it is called the neutral lead. The simplified schematic (A of figure 9–37) shows a wye-connected stator with the common lead not brought out. Each load is connected across two phases in series. Thus, R_{AB} is connected across phases A and B in series; R_{AC} is connected across phases A and C in series; and R_{BC} is connected across phases B and C in series. Therefore, the voltage across each load is larger than the voltage across a single phase. The total voltage, or line voltage, across any two phases is the vector sum of the individual phase voltages. For balanced conditions, the line voltage is 1.73 times the phase voltage. Since there is only one path for current in a line wire and the phase to which it is connected, the line current is equal to the phase current.

A three-phase stator can also be connected so that the phases are connected end-to-end as shown in B of figure 9–37. This arrangement is called a delta connection. In a delta connection, the voltages are equal to the phase voltages; the line currents are equal to the vector sum of the

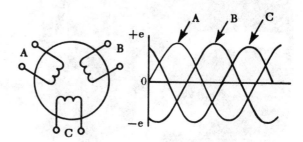

FIGURE 9–36. Simplified schematic of three-phase alternator with output waveforms.

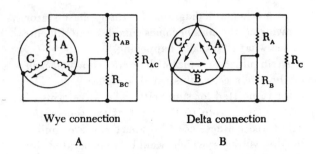

FIGURE 9–37. Wye- and delta-connected alternators.

phase currents; and the line current is equal to 1.73 times the phase current, when the loads are balanced.

For equal loads (equal kw. output), the delta connection supplies increased line current at a value of line voltage equal to phase voltage, and the wye connection supplies increased line voltage at a value of line current equal to phase current.

Alternator-Rectifier Unit

A type of alternator used in the electrical system of many aircraft weighing less than 12,500 pounds is shown in figure 9–38. This type of power source is sometimes called a d.c. generator, since it is used in d.c. systems. Although its output is a d.c. voltage, it is an alternator-rectifier unit.

This type of alternator-rectifier is a self-excited unit but does not contain a permanent magnet. The excitation for starting is obtained from the battery, and immediately after starting, the unit is self-exciting. Cooling air for the alternator is conducted into the unit by a blast air tube on the air inlet cover (figure 9–38).

The alternator is directly coupled to the aircraft engine by means of a flexible drive coupling. The d.c. output voltage may be regulated by a carbon pile voltage regulator. The output of the alternator portion of the unit is three-phase alternating current, derived from a three-phase, delta-connected system incorporating a three-phase, full-wave bridge rectifier (figure 9–39).

This unit operates in a speed range from 2,100 to 9,000 r.p.m., with a d.c. output voltage of 26–29 volts and 125 amperes.

BRUSHLESS ALTERNATOR

One generator now in use is the brushless type. It is more efficient because there are no brushes to wear down or to arc at high altitudes.

This generator consists of a pilot exciter, an exciter, and the main generator system. The necessity for brushes has been eliminated by utilizing an integral exciter with a rotating armature that has its a.c. output rectified for the main a.c. field, which is also of the rotating type. A brushless alternator is illustrated in figure 9–40.

FIGURE 9–38. Exploded view of alternator-rectifier.

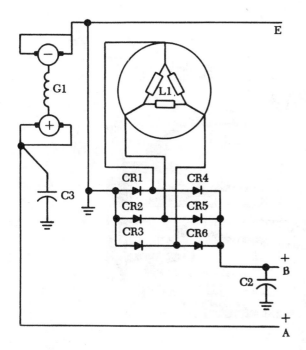

FIGURE 9–39. Wiring diagram of alternator-rectifier unit.

The pilot exciter is an 8-pole, 8,000 r.p.m., 533 c.p.s., a.c. generator. The pilot exciter field is mounted on the main generator rotor shaft and is connected in series with the main generator field (figure 9–40). The pilot exciter armature is mounted on the main generator stator. The a.c. output of the pilot exciter is supplied to the voltage regulator, where it is rectified and controlled, and is then impressed on the exciter field winding to furnish excitation for the generator.

The exciter is a small a.c. generator with its field mounted on the main generator stator and its 3-phase armature mounted on the generator rotor shaft. Included in the exciter field are permanent magnets mounted on the main generator stator between the exciter poles.

The exciter field resistance is temperature compensated by a thermistor. This aids regulation by keeping a nearly constant resistance at the regulator output terminals. The exciter output is rectified and impressed on the main generator field and the pilot exciter field. The exciter stator has a stabilizing field, which is used to improve stability and to prevent voltage regulator over-corrections for changes in generator output voltage.

The a.c. generator shown in figure 9–40 is a 6-pole, 8,000 r.p.m. unit having a rating of 31.5 kilovolt amperes (KVA), 115/200 volts, 400

c.p.s. This generator is 3-phase, 4-wire, wye-connected with grounded neutrals. By using an integral a.c. exciter the necessity for brushes within the generator has been eliminated. The a.c. output of the rotating exciter armature is fed directly into the 3-phase, full-wave, rectifier bridge located inside the rotor shaft, which uses high-temperature silicon rectifiers. The d.c. output from the rectifier bridge is fed to the main a.c. generator rotating field.

Voltage regulation is accomplished by varying the strength of the a.c. exciter stationary fields. Polarity reversals of the a.c. generator are eliminated and radio noise is minimized by the absence of the brushes. Any existing radio noise is further reduced by a noise filter mounted on the alternator.

The rotating pole structure of the generator is laminated from steel punchings, containing all six poles and a connecting hub section. This provides optimum magnetic and mechanical properties.

Some alternators are cooled by circulating oil through steel tubes. The oil used for cooling is supplied from the constant-speed drive assembly. Oil flow between the constant-speed drive and the generator is made possible by ports located in the flange connecting the generator and drive assemblies.

Voltage is built up by using permanent magnet interpoles in the exciter stator. The permanent magnets assure a voltage buildup, precluding the necessity of field flashing. The rotor of the alternator may be removed without causing loss of the alternator's residual magnetism.

COMBINED A.C. AND D.C. ELECTRICAL SYSTEMS

Many aircraft, especially aircraft of more than 12,500 pounds, employ both a d.c. and an a.c. electrical system. Often the d.c. system is the basic electrical system and consists of paralleled d.c. generators with output of, for example, 300 amperes each.

The a.c. system on such aircraft may include both a fixed frequency and a variable frequency system. The fixed frequency system may consist of three or four inverters and associated controls, protective, and indicating components to provide single-phase, a.c. power for frequency sensitive a.c. equipment. The variable frequency system may consist of two or more engine-driven alternators, with associated control, protective, and indicating components, to provide three-phase, a.c. power for such purposes as resistive heating on propellers, engine ducts, and windshields.

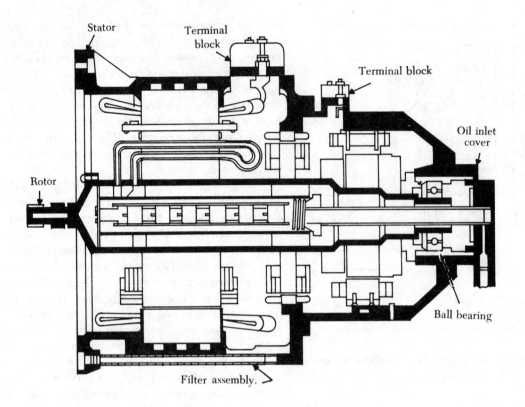

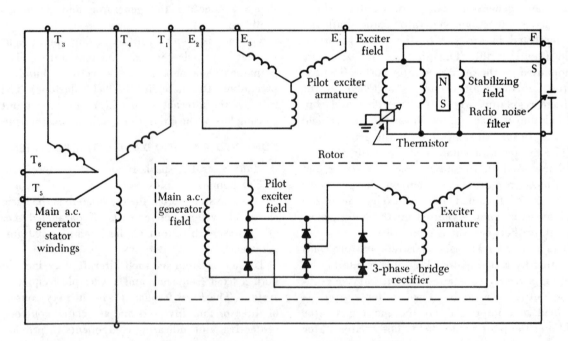

FIGURE 9–40. A typical brushless alternator.

Such combined d.c. and a.c. electrical systems normally include an auxiliary source of d.c. power to back up the main system. This generator is often driven by a separate gasoline or turbine-powered unit.

Alternator Rating

The maximum current that can be supplied by an alternator depends upon the maximum heating loss (I^2R power loss) that can be sustained in the armature and the maximum heating loss that can be sustained in the field. The armature current of an alternator varies with the load. This action is similar to that of d.c. generators. In a.c. generators, however, lagging power factor loads tend to demagnetize the field of an alternator and terminal voltage is maintained only by increasing d.c. field current. For this reason, alternating current generators are usually rated according to KVA, power factor, phases, voltage, and frequency. One generator, for example, may be rated at 40 KVA, 208 volts, 400 cycles, three-phase, at 75 percent power factor. The KVA indicate the apparent power. This is the KVA output, or the relationship between the current and voltage at which the generator is intended to operate.

The power factor is the expression of the ratio between the apparent power (volt-amperes) and the true or effective power (watts). The number of phases is the number of independent voltages generated. Three-phase generators generate three voltages 120 electrical degrees apart.

Alternator Frequency

The frequency of the alternator voltage depends upon the speed of rotation of the rotor and the number of poles. The faster the speed, the higher the frequency will be; the lower the speed, the lower the frequency becomes. The more poles on the rotor, the higher the frequency will be for a given speed. When a rotor has rotated through an angle so that two adjacent rotor poles (a north and a south pole) have passed one winding, the voltage induced in that winding will have varied through one complete cycle. For a given frequency, the greater the number of pairs of poles, the lower the speed of rotation will be. A two-pole alternator rotates at twice the speed of a four-pole alternator for the same frequency of generated voltage. The frequency of the alternator in c.p.s. is related to the number of poles and the speed, as expressed by the equation

$$F = \frac{P}{2} \times \frac{N}{60} = \frac{PN}{120},$$

where P is the number of poles and N the speed in r.p.m. For example, a two-pole, 3,600-r.p.m. alternator has a frequency of $\frac{2 \times 3,600}{120} = 60$ c.p.s.; a four-pole, 1,800-r.p.m. alternator has the same frequency; a six-pole, 500-r.p.m. alternator has a frequency of $\frac{6 \times 500}{120} = 25$ c.p.s.; and a 12-pole, 4,000-r.p.m. alternator has a frequency of $\frac{12 \times 4,000}{120} = 400$ c.p.s.

VOLTAGE REGULATION OF ALTERNATORS

The problem of voltage regulation in an a.c. system does not differ basically from that in a d.c. system. In each case the function of the regulator system is to control voltage, maintain a balance of circulating current throughout the system, and eliminate sudden changes in voltage (anti-hunting) when a load is applied to the system. However, there is one important difference between the regulator system of d.c. generators and alternators operated in a parallel configuration. The load carried by any particular d.c. generator in either a two- or four-generator system depends on its voltage as compared with the bus voltage, while the division of load between alternators depends upon the adjustments of their speed governors, which are controlled by the frequency and droop circuits.

When a.c. generators are operated in parallel, frequency and voltage must both be equal. Where a synchronizing force is required to equalize only the voltage beween d.c. generators, synchronizing forces are required to equalize both voltage and speed (frequency) between a.c. generators. On a comparative basis, the synchronizing forces for a.c. generators are much greater than for d.c. generators. When a.c. generators are of sufficient size and are operating at unequal frequencies and terminal voltages, serious damage may result if they are suddenly connected to each other through a common bus. To avoid this, the generators must be synchronized as closely as possible before connecting them together.

The output voltage of an alternator is best controlled by regulating the voltage output of the d.c. exciter, which supplies current to the alternator rotor field. This is accomplished as shown in figure 9-41, by a carbon-pile regulator of a 28-volt system connected in the field circuit of the exciter. The carbon-pile regulator controls the exciter field current and thus regulates the exciter output voltage applied to the alternator field. The only difference between the d.c. system

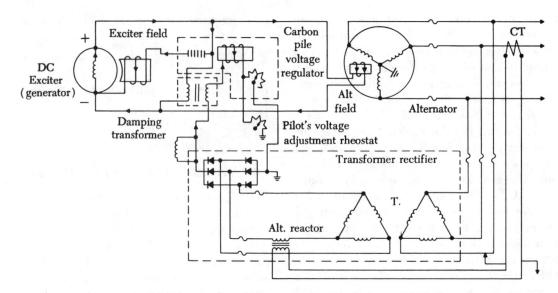

FIGURE 9–41.   Carbon-pile voltage regulator for an alternator.

and the a.c. system is that the voltage coil receives its voltage from the alternator line instead of the d.c. generator. In this arrangement, a three-phase, step-down transformer connected to the alternator voltage supplies power to a three-phase, full-wave rectifier. The 28-volt, d.c. output of the rectifier is then applied to the voltage coil of the carbon-pile regulator. Changes in alternator voltage are transferred through the transformer rectifier unit to the voltage coil of the regulator and vary the pressure on the carbon disks. This controls the exciter field current and the exciter output voltage. The exciter voltage anti-hunting or damping transformer is similar to those in d.c. systems and performs the same function.

The alternator equalizing circuit is similar to that of the d.c. system in that the regulator is affected when the circulating current supplied by one alternator differs from that supplied by the others.

Alternator Transistorized Regulators

Many aircraft alternator systems use a transistorized voltage regulator to control the alternator output. Before studying this section, a review of transistor principles may be helpful.

A transistorized voltage regulator consists mainly of transistors, diodes, resistors, capacitors, and, usually, a thermistor. In operation, current flows through a diode and transistor path to the generator field. When the proper voltage level is reached, the regulating components cause the transistor to cut off conduction to control the alternator field strength. The regulator operating range is usually adjustable through a narrow range. The thermistor provides temperature compensation for the circuitry. The transistorized voltage regulator shown in figure 9–42 will be referred to in explaining the operation of this type of regulator.

The a.c. output of the generator is fed to the voltage regulator, where it is compared to a reference voltage, and the difference is applied to the control amplifier section of the regulator. If the output is too low, field strength of the a.c. exciter generator is increased by the circuitry in the regulator. If the output is too high, the field strength is reduced.

The power supply for the bridge circuit is CR1, which provides full-wave rectification of the three-phase output from transformer T1. The d.c. output voltages of CR1 are proportional to the average phase voltages. Power is supplied from the negative end of the power supply through point B, R2, point C, zener diode (CR5), point D, and to the parallel hookup of V1 and R1. Takeoff point C of the bridge is located between resistor R2 and the zener diode. In the other leg of the reference bridge, resistors R9, R7, and the temperature-compensating resistor RT1 are connected in series with V1 and R1 through points B, A, and D. The output of this leg of the bridge is at the wiper arm of R7.

As generator voltage changes occur, for example, if the voltage lowers, the voltage across

418

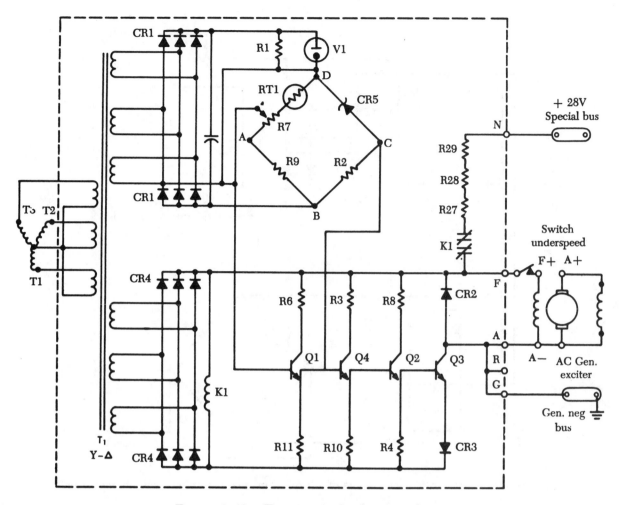

FIGURE 9–42. Transistorized voltage regulator.

R1 and V1 (once V2 starts conducting) will remain constant. The total voltage change will occur across the bridge circuit. Since the voltage across the zener diode remains constant (once it starts conducting), the total voltage change occurring in that leg of the bridge will be across resistor R2. In the other leg of the bridge, the voltage change across the resistors will be proportional to their resistance values. Therefore, the voltage change across R2 will be greater than the voltage change across R9 to wiper arm of R7. If the generator output voltage drops, point C will be negative with respect to the wiper arm of R7. Conversely, if the generator voltage output increases, the polarity of the voltage between the two points will be reversed.

The bridge output, taken between points C and A, is connected between the emitter and the base of transistor Q1. With the generator output voltage low, the voltage from the bridge will be negative to the emitter and positive to the base. This is a forward bias signal to the transistor, and the emitter to collector current will therefore increase. With the increase of current, the voltage across emitter resistor R11 will increase. This, in turn, will apply a positive signal to the base of transistor Q4, increasing its emitter to collector current and increasing the voltage drop across the emitter resistor R10.

This will give a positive bias to the base of Q2, which will increase its emitter to collector current and increase the voltage drop across its emitter resistor R4. This positive signal will control output transistor Q3. The positive signal on the base of Q3 will increase the emitter to collector current.

The control field of the exciter generator is in the collector circuit. Increasing the output of the exciter generator will increase the field strength of the a.c. generator, which will increase the generator output.

419

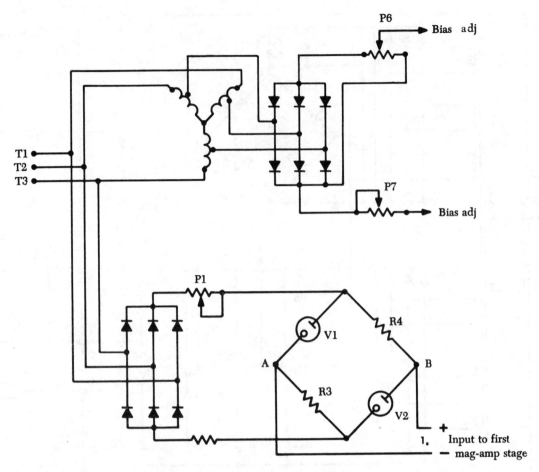

FIGURE 9–43.   Voltage reference circuits of a typical magnetic amplifier voltage regulator.

To prevent exciting the generator when the frequency is at a low value, there is an underspeed switch located near the F+ terminal. When the generator reaches a suitable operating frequency, the switch will close and allow the generator to be excited.

Another item of interest is the line containing resistors R27, R28, and R29 in series with the normally closed contacts of the K1 relay. The operating coil of this relay is found in the lower left-hand part of the schematic. Relay K1 is connected across the power supply (CR4) for the transistor amplifier. When the generator is started, electrical energy is supplied from the 28-volt d.c. bus to the exciter generator field, to "flash the field" for initial excitation. When the field of the exciter generator has been energized, the a.c. generator starts to produce, and as it builds up, relay K1 is energized, opening the "field flash" circuit.

Magnetic Amplifier Regulator

Because of their lack of moving parts, this type of voltage regulator is referred to as a static voltage regulator. Some static regulators employ electron tubes or transistors as amplifiers to achieve the necessary high energy gain, but the most commonly used static regulator utilizes a magnetic amplifier.

The magnetic amplifier voltage regulator is somewhat heavier and larger than a carbon-pile regulator of the same rating. Because of the absence of moving parts, regulators of this type do not require shock or vibration mounts.

This regulator consists of a voltage reference circuit, a two-stage magnetic amplifier, and the associated power transformer and rectifier. The reference circuit consists of a three-phase rectifier, a potentiometer (P1), and a bridge circuit made up of two fixed resistors and two glow tubes.

420

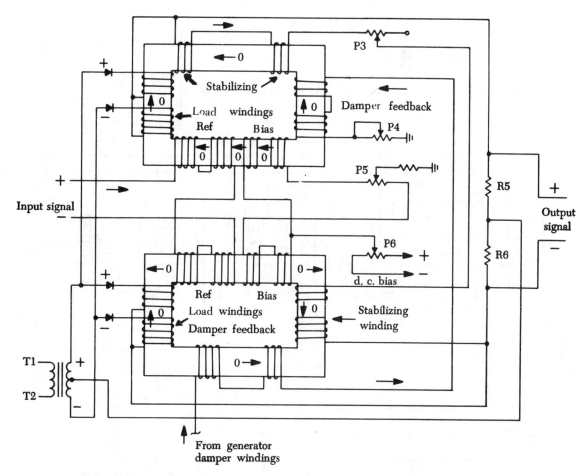

FIGURE 9–44.   First stage of a magnetic amplifier voltage regulator.

These units are shown in figure 9–43. Potentiometer P1 is adjusted so that, at rated bus voltage, there is a zero potential difference between points A and B on the bridge circuit. For any other input voltage, the voltage drop across the glow tubes causes a potential to exist between points A and B.

For example, if the generator voltage is low, the current flow through the arms of the bridge will be reduced. The voltage across R4 will be less than the fixed voltage across V1; consequently, point B will be at a higher potential than point A. This gives an error signal used as an input to the first mag-amp (magnetic amplifier) stage. For high input voltages the error signal polarity is reversed.

The second unit in the system is the magnetic amplifier. The circuitry for the first stage of a typical mag-amp voltage regulator is shown in figure 9–44. This unit consists of two reactors, supply voltage transformers and rectifiers, and the following windings: reference, d.c. bias, damper circuit, load circuit, and feedback circuit. The d.c.

bias winding fixes the operating level of the reactors and is adjusted by potentiometers P5 and P6.

Potentiometer P6 regulates the magnitude of the bias voltage, and P5 regulates the magnitude of biasing current on each reactor to overcome the slight differences in the two cores and the associated rectifiers. If the bias voltage is properly adjusted and if a zero error signal input exists, the voltages developed across R5 and R6 will be equal and the output will be zero.

The damper circuit is connected into the circuit and is used as a stabilizing winding. Its source of power is the damper winding of the generator. The generator damper winding is energized through transformer action by a changing generator excitation current and is, therefore, proportional to the rate of change of excitation. This current is used as a feedback signal in the first magnetic amplifier stage because its polarity always opposes the error signal input.

421

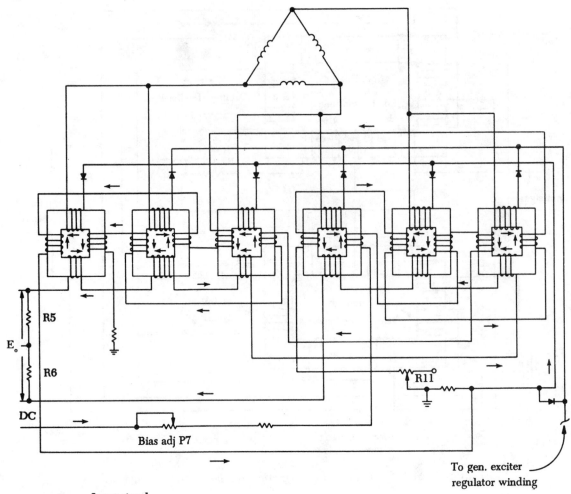

R5

E_o

R6

DC

Bias adj P7

R11

To gen. exciter
regulator winding

E_o = Input signal

FIGURE 9–45.   Second mag-amp stage of voltage regulator.

The magnitude of the damper feedback current is adjusted with potentiometer P4. Its function is to establish the recovery time of the regulator and to provide stable operation. The potentiometer should be adjusted to provide fast voltage recovery during stable operation under normal load conditions.

Next, the feedback winding receives a voltage that is proportional to the output voltage; this provides stability during steady load conditions. A look at the circuit will disclose that the load winding receives its power from transformer-rectifier terminals T1 and T2. The current flow through these windings and load resistors R5 and R6 is regulated by the degree of magnetization of the reactor cores, established by the current flow in the various control windings.

Figure 9–44 also illustrates that, when the input signal is not zero, the currents through R5 and R6

will not be equal. The unequal currents in these resistors provide a potential difference which is the output signal for this stage, the polarity of which depends on the polarity of the error signal input.

All of the units in the regulator have been discussed except the output stage, which is referred to as the second stage of the regulator. This is a three-phase, full-wave, magnetic amplifier, as shown in figure 9–45. The output of the first stage, which we have just discussed, is fed into the control winding of the second stage. The output of this stage is the generator exciter-regulator field voltage. The magnitude of this voltage is established by the magnitude and polarity of the input signal, the bias current which is adjustable by P7, and also by the feedback current which is proportional to the output.

This type of regulator has a distinct advantage

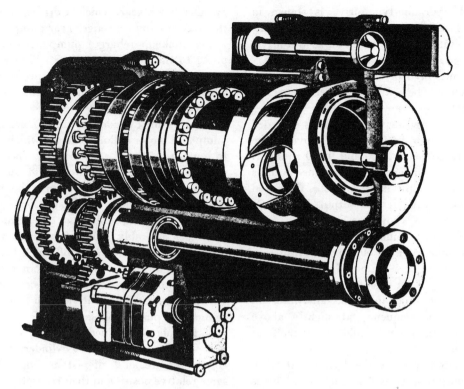

FIGURE 9–46.   Constant-speed drive.

over other types, since it will function on a very small change in voltage. Because of the operating characteristics of this type of regulator, variations in the output voltage will be within 1 percent.

The various adjustments on the unit, with the exception of those on P1, have been discussed. Adjustments on P1 are to be accomplished only on the bench, when the regulator is being calibrated. Potentiometer P1 is located in the center of the front face of the regulator adjacent to the voltmeter jacks. The potentiometer may be adjusted while the regulator is installed on the aircraft to set the bus voltage to the desired value.

The voltage regulator is divided into three main parts: the voltage error detector, the preamplifier, and the power amplifier. These three units work together in a closed-loop circuit with the generator exciter regulator winding to maintain nearly constant voltage at the generator output terminals.

The function of the error detector is to sample the generated voltage, compare it with a fixed standard, and send the error to the preamplifier. The detector includes a three-phase rectifier, a variable resistor for voltage adjustment, and a bridge consisting of two voltage reference tubes and two resistors. In operation, if the generator voltage ranges above or below its rated value, a current will flow either in one direction or the other, depending on the polarity developed in the bridge circuit.

The preamplifier receives an error signal from the voltage error detector. With the use of magnetic amplifiers, it raises the signal to a sufficient level to drive the power amplifier to full output, required for proper excitation.

The power amplifier delivers a signal to the exciter regulator winding; its magnitude depends on the signal from the preamplifier. This will raise or lower the voltage of the exciter regulator winding, which, in turn, will raise or lower the output voltage of the generator.

ALTERNATOR CONSTANT-SPEED DRIVE

Alternators are not always connected directly to the airplane engine like d.c. generators. Since the various electrical devices operating on a.c. supplied by alternators are designed to operate at a certain voltage and at a specified frequency, the speed of the alternators must be constant; however, the speed of an airplane engine varies. Therefore, some alternators are driven by the engine through a constant-speed drive installed between the engine and the alternator.

423

A typical hydraulic-type drive is shown in figure 9–46. The following discussion of a constant-speed drive system will be based on such a drive, found on large multiengine aircraft.

The constant-speed drive is a hydraulic transmission which may be controlled either electrically or mechanically.

The constant-speed drive assembly is designed to deliver an output of 6,000 r.p.m., provided the input remains between 2,800 and 9,000 r.p.m. If the input, which is determined by engine speed, is below 6,000 r.p.m., the drive increases the speed in order to furnish the desired output. This stepping up of speed is known as overdrive.

In overdrive, an automobile engine will operate at about the same r.p.m. at 60 m.p.h. as it does in conventional drive at 49 m.p.h. In aircraft, this principle is applied in the same manner. The constant-speed drive enables the alternator to produce the same frequency at slightly above engine-idle r.p.m. as it would at takeoff or cruising r.p.m.

With the input speed to the drive set at 6,000 r.p.m., the output speed will be the same. This is known as straight drive and might be compared to an automobile in high gear. However, when the input speed is greater than 6,000 r.p.m., it must be reduced to provide an output of 6,000 r.p.m. This is called underdrive, which is comparable to an automobile in low gear. Thus, the large input, caused by high engine r.p.m., is reduced to give the desired alternator speed.

As a result of this control by the constant-speed drive, the frequency output of the generator varies from 420 c.p.s. at no load to 400 c.p.s. under full load.

This, in brief, is the function of the constant-speed drive assembly. Before discussing the various units and circuits, the overall operation of the transmission should be discussed.

Hydraulic Transmission

The transmission is mounted between the generator and the aircraft engine. Its name denotes that hydraulic oil is used, although some transmissions may use engine oil. Refer to the cutaway view of such a transmission in figure 9–47. The input shaft D is driven from the drive shaft on the accessory section of the engine. The output drive F, on the opposite end of the transmission, engages the drive shaft of the generator.

The input shaft is geared to the rotating cylinder block gear, which it drives, as well as to the makeup and scavenger gear pumps E.

The makeup (charge) pump delivers oil (300 p.s.i.) to the pump and motor cylinder block, to the governor system, and to the pressurized case, whereas the scavenger pump returns the oil to the external reservoir.

The rotating cylinder assembly B consists of the pump and motor cylinder blocks, which are bolted to opposite sides of a port plate. The two other major parts are the motor wobbler A and the pump wobbler C. The governor system is the unit at the top of the left side in the illustration.

The cylinder assembly has two primary units. The block assembly of one of the units, the pump, contains 14 cylinders, each of which has a piston and pushrod. Charge pressure from the makeup pump is applied to each piston in order to force it outward against the pushrod. It, in turn, is pushed against the pump wobble plate.

If the plate remained as shown in part A of figure 9–48, each of the 14 cylinders would have equal pressure, and all pistons would be in the same relative position in their respective cylinders. But with the plate tilted, the top portion moves outward and the lower portion inward, as shown in part B of the illustration. As a result, more oil enters the interior of the upper cylinder, but oil will be forced from the cylinder of the bottom piston.

If the pump block were rotated while the plate remained stationary, the top piston would be forced inward because of the angle of the plate. This action would cause the oil confined within the cylinder to be subjected to increased pressure great enough to force it into the motor cylinder block assembly.

Before explaining what the high-pressure oil in the motor unit will do, it is necessary to know something about this part of the rotating cylinder block assembly. The motor block assembly has 16 cylinders, each with its piston and pushrod. These are constantly receiving charge pressure of 300 p.s.i. The position of the piston depends upon the point at which each pushrod touches the motor wobble plate. These rods cause the wobble plate to rotate by the pressure they exert against its sloping surface.

This is how the action works: the piston and pushrod of the motor are pushed outward as oil is forced through the motor valve plate from the pump cylinder. The pushrods are forced against the motor wobble plate, which is free to rotate but

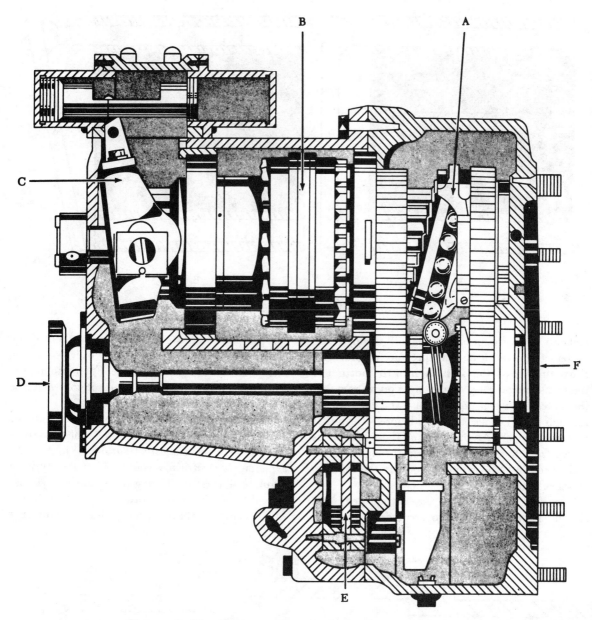

FIGURE 9–47.   Cutaway view of a hydraulic transmission.

cannot change the angle at which it is set. Since the pushrods cannot move sideways, the pressure exerted against the motor wobble plate's sloping face causes it to rotate.

In the actual transmission, there is an adjustable wobble plate. The tilt of the pump wobble plate is determined by the control cylinder assembly. For example, it is set at an angle which causes the motor cylinders to turn the motor wobble plate faster than the motor assembly, if the transmission is in overdrive. The result described is produced by the greater pressure in the pump and motor cylinders.

With the transmission in underdrive, the angle is arranged so there is a reduction in pumping action. The subsequent slippage between the pushrods and motor wobble plate reduces the output speed of the transmission. When the pump wobble plate is not at an angle, the pumping action will be at a minimum and the transmission will have what is known as hydraulic lock. For this condition, the input and output speed will be about the same, and the transmission is considered to be in straight drive.

To prevent the oil temperature from becoming excessively high within the cylinder block, the

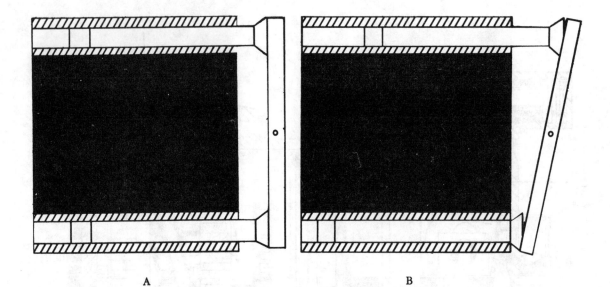

A   B

FIGURE 9–48.   Wobble plate position.

makeup pressure pump forces oil through the center of this block and the pressure relief valve. From this valve, the oil flows into the bottom of the transmission case. A scavenger pump removes the oil from the transmission case and circulates it through the oil cooler and filter before returning it to the reservoir. At the start of the cycle, oil is drawn from the reservoir, passed through a filter, and forced into the cylinder block by the makeup pressure pump.

The clutch, located in the output gear and clutch assembly, is an overrunning one-way, sprag-type device. Its purpose is to ratchet if the alternator becomes motorized; otherwise, the alternator might turn the engine. Furthermore, the clutch provides a positive connection when the transmission is driving the alternator.

There is another unit of the drive which must be covered, the governor system. The governor system, which consists of a hydraulic cylinder with a piston, is electrically controlled. Its duty is to regulate oil pressure flowing to the control cylinder assembly, as shown in figure 9–49.

The center of the system's hydraulic cylinder is

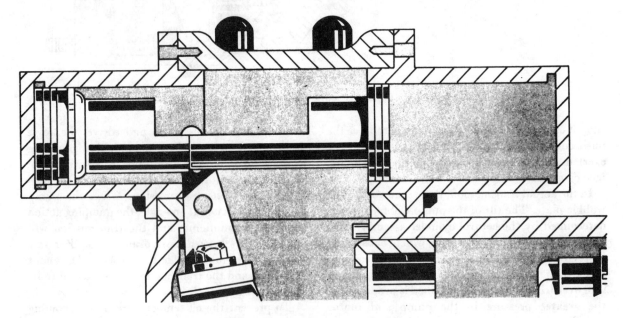

FIGURE 9–49.   Control cylinder.

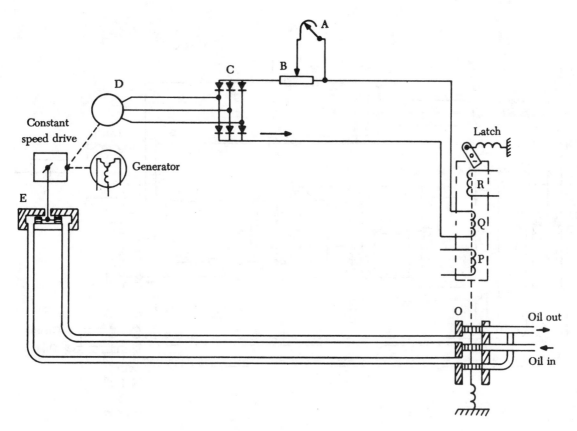

FIGURE 9–50. Electrical hydraulic control circuit.

slotted so the arm of the pump wobble plate can be connected to the piston. As oil pressure moves the piston, the pump wobble plate is placed in either overspeed, underspeed, or straight drive.

Figure 9–50 shows the electrical circuit used to govern the speed of the transmission. First, the main points of the complete electrical control circuit will be discussed (figure 9–50 and 9–51). Then, for simplification, two portions, the overspeed circuit and the load division circuit, will be considered as individual circuits.

Note, then, in figures 9–50, that the circuit has a valve and solenoid assembly O and a control cylinder E, and that it contains such units as the tachometer generator D, the rectifier C, and adjustable resistor B, rheostat A, and the control coil Q.

Since it is driven by a drive gear in the transmission, the tachometer (often called tach) generator, a three-phase unit, has a voltage proportional to the speed of the output drive. Its voltage is changed from a.c. to d.c. by the rectifier. After rectification, the current flows through the resistor, rheostat, and valve and solenoid. Each of these units is connected in series, as shown in figure 9–51.

Under normal operating conditions, the output of the tach generator causes just enough current to enter the valve and solenoid coil to set up a magnetic field of sufficient strength to balance the spring force in the valve. When the alternator speed increases as the result of a decrease in load, the tach generator output increases also. Because of the greater output, the coil in the solenoid is sufficiently strengthened to overcome the spring force. Thus, the valve moves and, as a result, oil pressure enters the reduced speed side of the control cylinder.

In turn, the pressure moves the piston, causing the angle of the pump wobble plate to be reduced. The oil on the other side of the piston is forced back through the valve into the system return. Since the angle of the pump wobble plate is smaller, there is less pumping action in the transmission. The result is decreased output speed. To complete the cycle, the procedure is reversed.

With the output speed reduction, tach generator output decreases; consequently, the flow of current

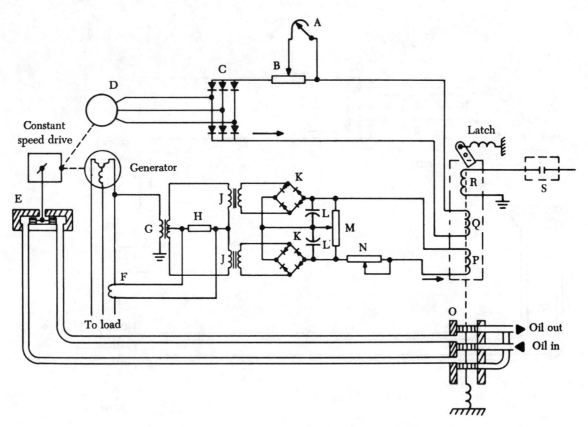

FIGURE 9–51.   Speed control circuit.

to the solenoid diminishes. Therefore, the magnetic field of the solenoid becomes so weak that the spring is able to overcome it and reposition the valve.

If a heavy load is put on the a.c. generator, its speed decreases. The generator is not driven directly by the engine; the hydraulic drive will allow slippage. This decrease will cause the output of the tach generator to taper off and, as a result, weaken the magnetic field of the solenoid coil. The spring in the solenoid will move the valve and allow oil pressure to enter the increase side of the control cylinder and the output speed of the transmission will be raised.

There are still two important circuits which must be discussed: the overspeed circuit and the load division circuit. The generator is prevented from overspeeding by a centrifugal switch (S in figure 9–52) and the overspeed solenoid coil R, which is located in the solenoid and valve assembly. The centrifugal switch is on the transmission and is driven through the same gear arrangement as the tach generator.

The aircraft d.c. system furnishes the power to

operate the overspeed coil in the solenoid and coil assembly. If the output speed of the transmission reaches a speed of 7,000 to 7,500 r.p.m., the centrifugal switch closes the d.c. circuit and energizes the overspeed solenoid. This component then moves the valve and engages the latch which holds the valve in the underdrive position. To release the latch, energize the underdrive release solenoid.

The load division circuit's function is to equalize the loads placed on each of the alternators, which is necessary to assure that each alternator assumes its share; otherwise, one alternator might be overloaded while another would be carrying only a small load.

In figure 9–53, one phase of the alternator provides power for the primary in transformer G, whose secondary supplies power to the primaries of two other transformers, J_1 and J_2. Rectifiers K then change the output of the transformer secondaries from a.c. to d.c. The function of the two capacitors, L, is to smooth out the d.c. pulsations.

The output of the current transformer F depends

428

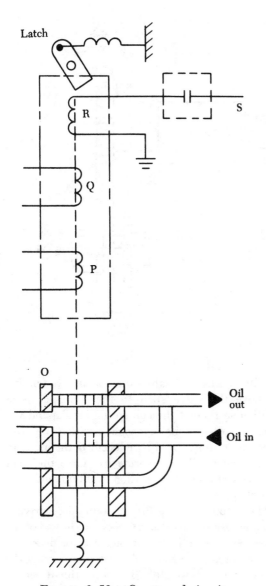

Latch

R

Q

P

O

S

Oil out

Oil in

FIGURE 9-52. Overspeed circuit.

across H, and hence, the greater the difference between the voltages applied to the two primaries of transformer J. The unequal voltages applied to resistor M by the secondaries of transformer J cause a current flow through the control coil P.

The control coil is wound so that its voltage supplements the voltage for the control coil in the valve and solenoid assembly. The resulting increased voltage moves the valve and slows down the generator's speed. Why should the speed be decreased if the load has been increased? Actually, systems using only one generator would not have decreased speed, but for those having two or more generators, a decrease is necessary to equalize the loads.

The load division circuit is employed only when two or more generators supply power. In such systems, the control coils are connected in parallel. If the source voltage for one of these becomes higher than the others, it determines the direction of current flow throughout the entire load division circuit. As explained before, the real load on the generator determines the amount of voltage on the control coil; therefore, the generator with the highest real load has the highest voltage.

As shown in figure 9-54, current through No. 1 control coil, where the largest load exists, aids the control coil of the valve and solenoid, thereby slowing down the generator. (The source voltage of the control coils is represented by battery symbols in the illustration.) The current in the remaining control coils opposes the control coil of the valve and solenoid, in order to increase the speed of the other generators so the load will be more evenly distributed.

On some drives, instead of an electrically controlled governor, a flyweight-type governor is employed, which consists of a recess-type revolving valve driven by the output shaft of the drive, flyweights, two coil springs, and a nonrotating valve stem. Centrifugal force, acting on the governor flyweights, causes them to move outward, lifting the valve stem against the opposition of a coil spring.

The valve stem position controls the directing of oil to the two oil-out lines. If the output speed tends to exceed 6,000 r.p.m., the flyweights will lift the valve stem to direct more oil to the side of the control piston, causing the piston to move in a direction to reduce the pump wobble plate angle. If the speed drops below 6,000 r.p.m., oil is directed to the control piston so that it moves to increase the wobble plate angle. Overspeed

upon the amount of current flowing in the line of one phase. In this way, it measures the real load of the generator. The output voltage of the current transformer is applied across resistor H. This voltage will be added vectorially to the voltage applied to the upper winding of transformer J by the output of transformer F. At the same time as it adds vectorially to the upper winding of transformer J, it subtracts vectorially from the voltage applied to the lower winding of J.

This voltage addition and subtraction depends on the real load of the generator. The amount of real load determines the phase angle and the amount of voltage impressed across resistor H. The greater the real load, the greater the voltage

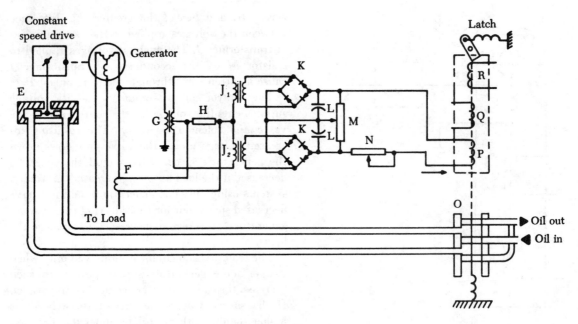

FIGURE 9–53.   Droop circuit.

protection is installed in the governor. The drive starts in the underdrive position. The governor coil springs are fully extended and the valve stem is held at the limit of its downward travel. In this condition, pressure is directed to the side of the control piston giving minimum wobble plate angle. The maximum angle side of the control piston is open to the hollow stem. As the input speed increases, the flyweights start to move outward to overcome the spring bias. This action lifts the valve stem and starts directing oil to the maximum side of the control piston, while the minimum side is opened to the hollow stem.

At about 6,000 r.p.m., the stem is positioned to stop drainage of either side, and the two pressures seek a balance point as the flyweight force is balanced against the spring bias. Thus, a mechanical failure in the governor will cause an underdrive

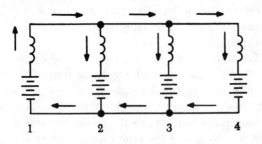

FIGURE 9–54.   Relative direction of current in droop coil circuit with unequal loads.

condition. The flyweight's force is always tending to move the valve stem to the decrease speed position so that, if the coil spring breaks and the stem moves to the extreme position in that direction, output speed is reduced. If the input to the governor fails, the spring will force the stem all the way to the start position to obtain minimum output speed.

The output speed of the constant-speed drive is regulated by an adjustment screw on the end of the governor. This adjustment increases or decreases the compression of a coil spring, opposing the action of the flyweights. The adjustment screws turn in an indented collar, which provides a means of making speed adjustments in known increments. Each "click" provides a small change in generator frequency.

SYNCHRONIZING ALTERNATORS

Two or more alternators may be operated in parallel, with each alternator carrying the same share of the load. However, certain precautions must be taken and various conditions complied with before connecting an alternator to a bus with another alternator.

Synchronizing, or paralleling, alternators is somewhat similar to paralleling d.c. generators, except that there are more steps with alternators. In order to synchronize (parallel) two or more alternators to the same bus, they must have the

430

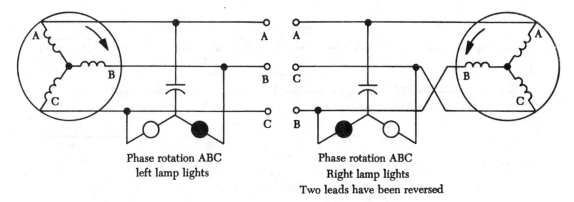

Phase rotation ABC
left lamp lights

Phase rotation ABC
Right lamp lights
Two leads have been reversed

FIGURE 9–55.   Phase sequence indicator.

same phase sequence as well as equal voltages and frequencies.

The following steps are a general guide in synchronizing an alternator and connecting it to a bus system on which one or more alternators are already operating.

1. *Phase sequence check.* The standard phase sequence for a.c., three-phase power circuits is *A*, *B*, *C*. The phase sequence can be determined by observing two small indicator lamps, connected as shown in figure 9–55. If one lamp lights, the phase sequence is *A*, *B*, *C*. If the other lamp lights, the phase sequence is *A*, *C*, *B*. If the light indicates the wrong phase sequence, reverse the two leads to the incoming alternator. To parallel or synchronize two alternators with the wrong phase sequence would be the same as short circuiting two leads and would set up dangerous circulating currents and magnetic disturbances within the alternator system, which could overheat the conductors and loosen the coil windings.

2. *Voltage check.* The voltage of the alternator to be connected to the bus must be equal to the bus voltage. It is adjusted by a control rheostat located on the switch panel. This rheostat controls the current in the voltage regulator coil and causes the alternator magnetic field to increase or decrease, controlling, in turn, the alternator voltage.

3. *Frequency check.* The frequency of an alternator is directly proportional to its speed. This means that the speed of the alternator being connected to the bus must equal the speed of the alternators already connected. By observing the frequency meter

and by adjusting the rheostat on the switch panel, the frequency of the incoming alternator can be brought up to the correct value. By observing the synchronizing lamp, shown in figure 9–56, and by fine adjustment of the speed control rheostat, the frequencies may be brought to almost exact synchronization. The synchronizing lamp will blink as the two frequencies approach the same value; when they are very nearly the same, the lamp will blink slowly. When the blinking decreases to one blink or less per second, close the circuit breaker while the lamp is dark and connect alternator No. 2 to the bus. The dark lamp indicates no voltage between phase *A* of the bus and phase *A* of the incoming alternator. During the period when the lamp is lighted, there is a voltage difference between phase *A* of the bus and phase *A* of the alternator to be connected to the bus. To close the circuit breaker when the synchronizing lamp is lighted would be similar to short circuiting two leads and would cause serious voltage and magnetic disturbances within the alternators.

Alternator Protective Circuits

It is very important that operating alternators be disconnected from the system when harmful electrical faults occur. For an alternator to be removed from the bus when trouble occurs in the circuit, circuit breakers must open rapidly and automatically; otherwise, the alternator could burn up. To provide relays in the circuit breakers, there are a number of protective relays in the circuit. Most of these relays are d.c. energized, since similar a.c. equipment is usually much

431

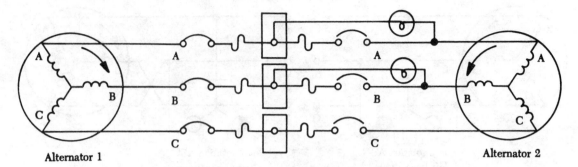

FIGURE 9–56. Synchronizing lamp circuit.

heavier and less efficient. Figure 9–57 contains a diagram showing an alternator control and protective circuit. Included in it are an alternator, circuit breakers, an exciter ceiling relay, and a differential current protection relay.

There are two circuit breakers in this type of airplane alternator control system: (1) The exciter control relay, which opens and closes the exciter field circuits, and (2) the main line circuit breaker, which connects or disconnects the alternator from the bus and also opens or closes the exciter field current.

The main line circuit breaker is latched by a d.c. electromagnet, called a "close" coil. This coil closes the circuit breakers. They are released by a second electromagnet, known as the trip coil, which opens the circuit. Only momentary contact of the closing and tripping circuits is necessary for operation. Once closed, a mechanical latch holds the contactors until the latch is released by the trip coil. The contacts are made of special alloys capable of breaking currents of several thousand amperes without damage to the contacts.

This main line triple-pole circuit breaker has an

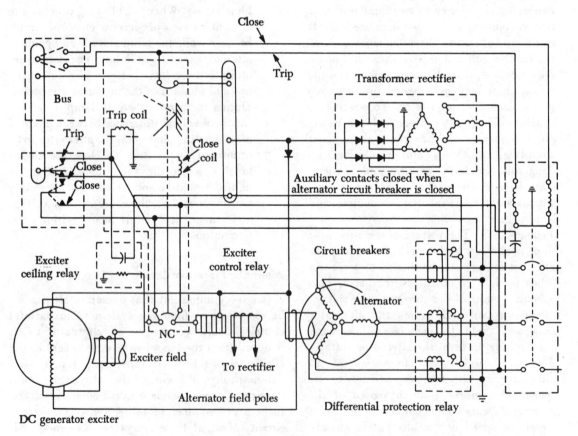

FIGURE 9–57. Alternator control and protective circuit.

432

auxiliary contact which closes the exciter field circuit whenever the main line circuit breakers close and opens it whenever the circuit breakers open. This is desirable because the alternator may be supplying load current when the circuit breakers open; in which case, the exciter field excitation should be decreased or removed. Also, the exciter field circuit is held closed until the main circuit breakers can open, in case the exciter control relay is opened first.

The exciter control relay opens and closes the exciter field circuit. Upon opening, it closes a contact furnishing d.c. power to the main line trip coil and causes the main line circuit breakers to open. The exciter control relay consists of two solenoids, one latching and one tripping. It needs only momentary closing of the switch for operation.

The exciter ceiling relay shown in the protective circuit diagram of figure 9–57 is a thermal-operated relay. It operates whenever the exciter field current increases enough to be dangerous to the operation of the alternator. If at any time the alternator becomes loaded too heavily, either by a short circuit on the line or by the alternator becoming inoperative, the exciter voltage increases to supply the heavy alternator load, and the thermal ceiling relay closes the contacts between the d.c. bus and the trip coil. This opens the exciter field and, at the same time, disconnects the alternator from the line.

The differential current protection relay is much simpler in operation than its name indicates. It is designed to protect the alternator from internal shorts between phases or to ground. As long as there is the same amount of current in each phase going into the alternator as coming out, the differential relay does not operate, no matter how heavy or light these currents may be. However, if a short occurs within the alternator in any one phase, there is a difference in current through the lines; the relay operates, closing the circuit to the exciter trip coil, which, in turn, closes the circuit to the trip coil of the main line circuit breakers. The location of components in a typical relay is shown in figure 9–58.

The two leads from each phase of the alternator are passed through the doughnut-like holes in the relay and act as the primaries of the current transformers. As the current flows in opposite directions in the two leads through each hole, their magnetic fields are cancelled and no current flows in the current-transformer secondary, which

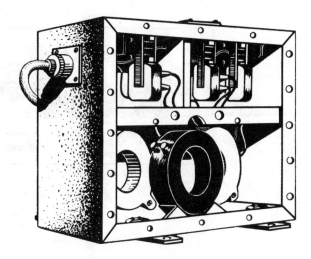

FIGURE 9–58. Differential current protection relay.

energizes the relay. The relay does not operate until a fault occurs that unbalances the currents in these two conductors and causes current to flow in the current-transformer secondary. Failure of the differential current relay would be backed up by the exciter protection relay. Fast clearing of internal faults reduces danger from fire and also reduces system disturbances when the alternators are paralleled improperly. A time-delay action in the exciter protection relay allows overexcitation for short intervals in order to supply d.c. voltage for clearing faults and for brief demands for current beyond the capacity of the alternator. It also opens the main breaker and drops the alternator excitation when other protective devices fail.

ALTERNATOR MAINTENANCE

Maintenance and inspection of alternator systems is similar to that of d.c. systems. Check the exciter brushes for wear and surfacing. On most large aircraft with two or four alternator systems, each power panel has three signal lights, one connected to each phase of the power bus, so the lamp will light when the panel power is on. The individual buses throughout the airplane can be checked by operating equipment from that particular bus. Consult the manufacturer's instructions on operation of equipment for the method of testing each bus.

Alternator test-stands are used for testing alternators and constant-speed drives in a repair facility. They are capable of supplying power to constant-speed drive units at input speeds varying from 2,400 r.p.m. to 9,000 r.p.m. A typical

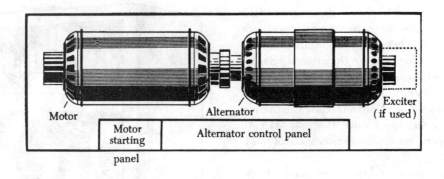

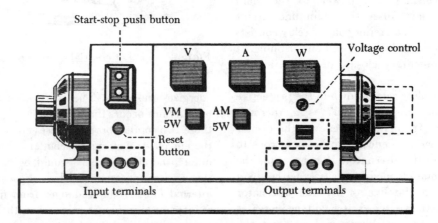

FIGURE 9–59. A.C. motor-generator set for ground testing.

test-stand motor uses 220/440-volt, 60-cycle, 3-phase power. Blowers for ventilation, oil coolers, and necessary meters and switches are integral parts of the test-stand. Test circuits are supplied by a load-bank. An a.c. motor-generator set for ground testing is shown in figure 9–59.

A typical, portable, a.c. electrical system test-set is an analyzer, consisting of a multirange ohm-meter, a multirange combination a.c.-d.c. volt-meter, an ammeter with a clip-on current transformer, a vibrating-reed type frequency meter, and an unmounted continuity light.

A portable load bank unit furnishes a load similar to that on the airplane for testing alternators, either while mounted in the airplane or on the shop test-stand. A complete unit consists of resistive and reactive loads controlled by selector switches and test meters mounted on a control panel. This load unit is compact and convenient, eliminating the difficulty of operating large loads on the airplane while testing and adjusting the alternators and control equipment.

Proper maintenance of an alternator requires that the unit be kept clean and that all electrical connections are tight and in good repair. If the alternator fails to build up voltage as designated by applicable manufacturer's technical instructions, test the voltmeter first by checking the voltages of other alternators, or by checking the voltage in the suspected alternator with another voltmeter and comparing the results. If the voltmeter is satisfactory, check the wiring, the brushes, and the drive unit for faults. If this inspection fails to reveal the trouble, the exciter may have lost its residual magnetism. Residual magnetism is restored to the exciter by flashing the field. Follow the applicable manufacturer's instructions when flashing the exciter field. If, after flashing the field, no voltage is indicated, replace the alternator, since it is probably faulty.

Clean the alternator exterior with an approved fluid; smooth a rough or pitted exciter commutator or slip ring with 000 sandpaper; then clean and polish with a clean, dry cloth. Check the brushes periodically for length and general condition. Consult the applicable manufacturer's instructions on the specific alternator to obtain information on the correct brushes.

Troubleshooting

Use the following table to assist in locating, diagnosing, and correcting alternator troubles:

Trouble	Probable cause	Remedy
Voltmeter registers no voltage.	Voltmeter defective.	Remove and replace voltmeter.
	Voltmeter regulator defective.	Replace regulator.
	Defective exciter.	Replace alternator.
Low voltage.	Improper regulator adjustment.	Adjust voltage regulator.
Erratic meter indication.	Loose connections.	Tighten connections.
	Defective meter.	Remove and replace meter.
Voltage falls off after a period of operation.	Voltage regulator not warmed up before adjustment.	Readjust voltage regulator.

INVERTERS

An inverter is used in some aircraft systems to convert a portion of the aircraft's d.c. power to a.c. This a.c. is used mainly for instruments, radio, radar, lighting, and other accessories. These inverters are usually built to supply current at a frequency of 400 c.p.s., but some are designed to provide more than one voltage; for example, 26-volt a.c. in one winding and 115 volts in another.

There are two basic types of inverters: the rotary and the static. Either type can be single-phase or multiphase. The multiphase inverter is lighter for the same power rating than the single-phase, but there are complications in distributing multiphase power and in keeping the loads balanced.

Rotary Inverters

There are many sizes, types, and configurations of rotary inverters. Such inverters are essentially a.c. generators and d.c. motors in one housing. The generator field, or armature, and the motor field, or armature, are mounted on a common shaft which will rotate within the housing. One common type of rotary inverter is the permanent magnet inverter.

Permanent Magnet Rotary Inverter

A permanent magnet inverter is composed of a d.c. motor and a permanent magnet a.c. generator assembly. Each has a separate stator mounted within a common housing. The motor armature is mounted on a rotor and connected to the d.c. supply through a commutator and brush assembly. The motor field windings are mounted on the housing and connected directly to the d.c. supply. A permanent magnet rotor is mounted at the opposite end of the same shaft as the motor armature, and the stator windings are mounted on the housing, allowing a.c. to be taken from the inverter without the use of brushes. Figure 9–60 shows an internal wiring diagram for this type of rotary inverter. The generator rotor has six poles, magnetized to provide alternate north and south poles about its circumference.

When the motor field and armature are excited, the rotor will begin to turn. As the rotor turns, the permanent magnet will rotate within the a.c. stator coils, and the magnetic flux developed by the permanent magnets will be cut by the conductors in the a.c. stator coils. An a.c. voltage will be produced in the windings whose polarity will change as each pole passes the windings.

This type inverter may be made multiphase by placing more a.c. stator coils in the housing in order to shift the phase the proper amount in each coil.

As the name of the rotary inverter indicates, it has a revolving armature in the a.c. generator section. The illustration in figure 9–61 shows the diagram of a revolving-armature, three-phase inverter.

The d.c. motor in this inverter is a four-pole, compound-wound motor. The four field coils consist of many turns of fine wire, with a few turns of heavy wire placed on top. The fine wire is the shunt field, connected to the d.c. source through a filter and to ground through a centrifugal governor. The heavy wire is the series field, which is connected in series with the motor armature. The centrifugal governor controls the speed by shunting a resistor which is in series with the shunt field when the motor reaches a certain speed.

The alternator is a three-phase, four-pole, star-connected a.c. generator. The d.c. input is supplied to the generator field coils and connected to ground through a carbon-pile voltage regulator. The output is taken off the armature through three slip rings to provide three-phase power.

The inverter would be a single-phase inverter if it had a single armature winding and one slip ring.

The frequency of this type unit is determined by the speed of the motor and the number of generator poles.

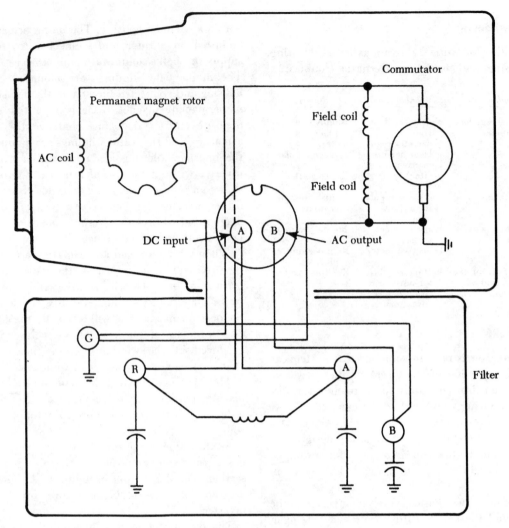

FIGURE 9–60.   Internal wiring diagram of single-phase permanent magnet rotary inverter.

Inductor-Type Rotary Inverter

Inductor-type inverters use a rotor made of soft iron laminations with grooves cut laterally across the surface to provide poles that correspond to the number of stator poles, as illustrated in figure 9–62. The field coils are wound on one set of stationary poles and the a.c. armature coils on the other set of stationary poles. When d.c. is applied to the field coils, a magnetic field is produced. The rotor turns within the field coils and, as the poles on the rotor align with the stationary poles, a low reluctance path for flux is established from the field pole through the rotor poles to the a.c. armature pole and through the housing back to the field pole. In this circumstance, there will be a large amount of magnetic flux linking the a.c. coils.

When the rotor poles are between the stationary poles, there is a high-reluctance path for flux, consisting mainly of air; then, there will be a small amount of magnetic flux linking the a.c. coils. This increase and decrease in flux density in the stator induces an alternating current in the a.c. coils.

The frequency of this type of inverter is determined by the number of poles and the speed of the motor. The voltage is controlled by the d.c. stator field current. A cutaway view of an inductor-type rotary inverter is shown in figure 9–63.

Figure 9–64 is a simplified diagram of a typical aircraft a.c. power distribution system, utilizing a main and a standby rotary inverter system.

Static Inverters

In many applications where continuous d.c. voltage must be converted to alternating voltage,

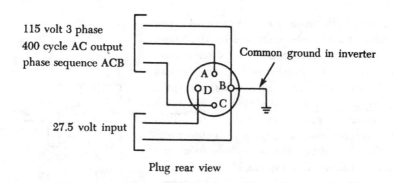

115 volt 3 phase
400 cycle AC output
phase sequence ACB

Common ground in inverter

27.5 volt input

Plug rear view

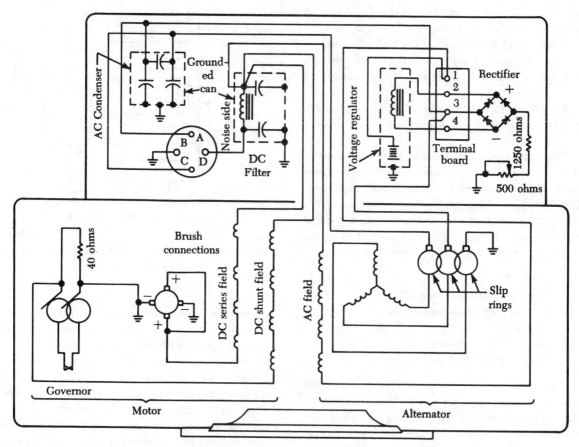

FIGURE 9–61. Internal wiring diagram of three-phase, revolving-armature inverter.

static inverters are used in place of rotary inverters or motor generator sets. The rapid progress being made by the semiconductor industry is extending the range of applications of such equipment into voltage and power ranges which would have been impractical a few years ago. Some such applications are power supplies for frequency-sensitive military and commercial a.c. equipment, aircraft emergency a.c. systems, and conversion of wide frequency range power to precise frequency power.

The use of static inverters in small aircraft also

has increased rapidly in the last few years, and the technology has advanced to the point that static inverters are available for any requirement filled by rotary inverters. For example, 250 VA emergency a.c. supplies operated from aircraft batteries are in production, as are 2,500 VA main a.c. supplies operated from a varying frequency generator supply. This type of equipment has certain advantages for aircraft applications, particularly the absence of moving parts and the adaptability to conduction cooling.

Static inverters, referred to as solid-state inverters, are manufactured in a wide range of types and models, which can be classified by the shape of the a.c. output waveform and the power output capabilities. One of the most commonly used static inverters produces a regulated sine wave output. A block diagram of a typical regulated sine wave static inverter is shown in figure 9–65. This inverter converts a low d.c. voltage into higher a.c. voltage. The a.c. output voltage is held to a very small voltage tolerance, a typical variation of less than 1 percent with a full input load change. Output taps are normally provided to permit selection of various voltages; for example, taps may be provided for a 105-, 115-, and 125-volt a.c. outputs. Frequency regulation is typically within a range of one cycle for a 0–100 percent load change.

Variations of this type of static inverter are available, many of which provide a square wave output.

Since static inverters use solid-state components, they are considerably smaller, more compact, and much lighter in weight than rotary inverters. Depending on the output power rating required, static inverters that are no larger than a typical airspeed indicator can be used in aircraft systems. Some of the features of static inverters are:

1. High efficiency.
2. Low maintenance, long life.
3. No warmup period required.
4. Capable of starting under load.
5. Extremely quiet operation.
6. Fast response to load changes.

Static inverters are commonly used to provide power for such frequency-sensitive instruments as the attitude gyro and directional gyro. They also provide power for autosyn and magnesyn indicators and transmitters, rate gyros, radar, and other airborne applications. Figure 9–66 is a schematic of a typical small jet aircraft auxiliary battery system. It shows the battery as input to the inverter, and the output inverter circuits to various subsystems.

D. C. MOTORS

Most devices in an airplane, from the starter to the automatic pilot, depend upon mechanical energy furnished by direct-current motors. A direct-current motor is a rotating machine which transforms direct-current energy into mechanical energy. It consists of two principal parts—a field

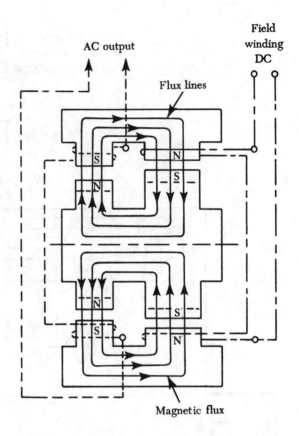

FIGURE 9–62. Diagram of basic inductor-type inverter.

assembly and an armature assembly. The armature is the rotating part in which current-carrying wires are acted upon by the magnetic field.

Whenever a current-carrying wire is placed in the field of a magnet, a force acts on the wire. The force is not one of attraction or repulsion; however, it is at right angles to the wire and also at right angles to the magnetic field set up by the magnet.

The action of the force upon a current-carrying wire placed in a magnetic field is shown in figure 9–67. A wire is located between two permanent magnets. The lines of force in the magnetic field are from the north pole to the south pole. When no current flows, as in diagram A, no force is exerted on the wire, but when current flows through the wire, a magnetic field is set up about it, as shown in diagram B. The direction of the field depends on the direction of current flow. Current in one direction creates a clockwise field about the wire, and current in the other direction, a counter-clockwise field.

Since the current-carrying wire produces a magnetic field, a reaction occurs between the field

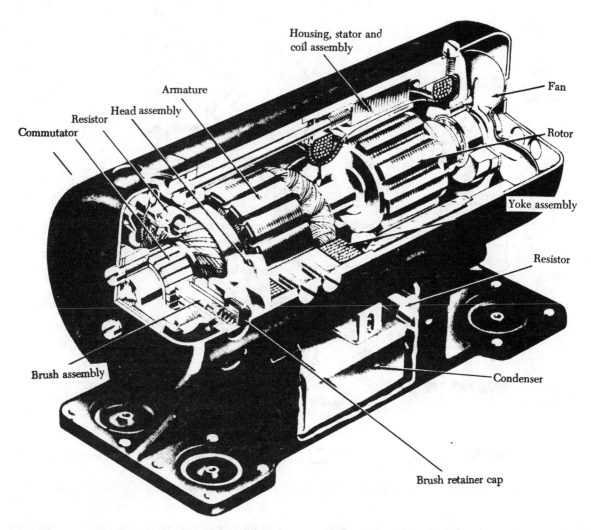

FIGURE 9–63.   Cutaway view of inductor-type rotary inverter.

about the wire and the magnetic field between the magnets. When the current flows in a direction to create a counterclockwise magnetic field about the wire, this field and the field between the magnets add or reinforce at the bottom of the wire because the lines of force are in the same direction. At the top of the wire, they subtract or neutralize, since the lines of force in the two fields are opposite in direction. Thus, the resulting field at the bottom is strong and the one at the top is weak. Consequently, the wire is pushed upward as shown in diagram C of figure 9–67. The wire is always pushed away from the side where the field is strongest.

If current flow through the wire were reversed in direction, the two fields would add at the top and subtract at the bottom. Since a wire is always

pushed away from the strong field, the wire would be pushed down.

Force Between Parallel Conductors

Two wires carrying current in the vicinity of one another exert a force on each other because of their magnetic fields. An end view of two conductors is shown in figure 9–68. In *A*, electron flow in both conductors is toward the reader, and the magnetic fields are clockwise around the conductors. Between the wires, the fields cancel because the directions of the two fields oppose each other. The wires are forced in the direction of the weaker field, toward each other. This force is one of attraction.

In *B*, the electron flow in the two wires is in opposite directions. The magnetic fields are,

439

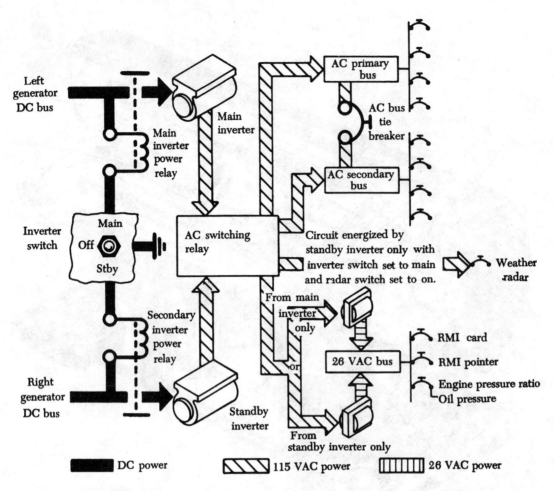

FIGURE 9–64. A typical aircraft a.c. power distribution system using main and standby rotary inverters.

therefore, clockwise in one and counterclockwise in the other, as shown. The fields reinforce each other between the wires, and the wires are forced in the direction of the weaker field, away from each other. This force is one of repulsion.

To summarize: Conductors carrying current in the same direction tend to be drawn together;

conductors carrying current in opposite directions tend to be repelled from each other.

Developing Torque

If a coil in which current is flowing is placed in a magnetic field, a force is produced which will cause

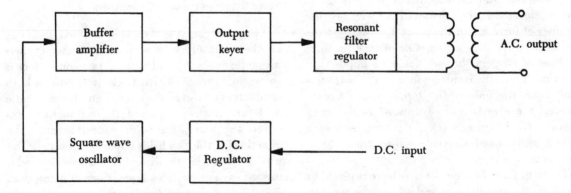

FIGURE 9–65. Regulated sine wave static inverter.

440

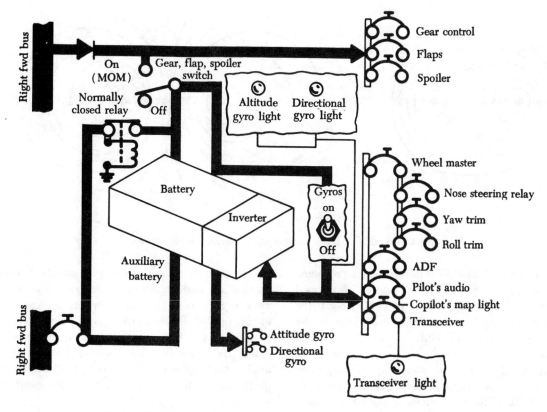

FIGURE 9–66.   Auxiliary battery system using static inverter.

the coil to rotate. In the coil shown in figure 9–69, current flows inward on side *A* and outward on side *B*. The magnetic field about *B* is clockwise and that about *A*, counterclockwise. As previously explained, a force will develop which pushes side *B* downward. At the same time, the field of the magnets and the field about *A*, in which the current is inward, will add at the bottom and

subtract at the top. Therefore, *A* will move upward. The coil will thus rotate until its plane is perpendicular to the magnetic lines between the north and south poles of the magnet, as indicated in figure 9–69 by the white coil at right angles to the black coil.

The tendency of a force to produce rotation is called torque. When the steering wheel of a car is

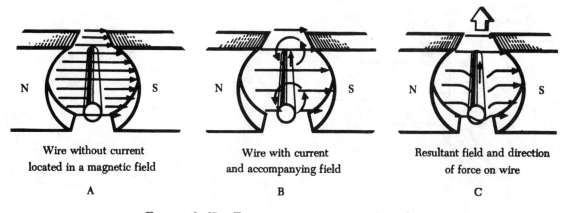

Wire without current located in a magnetic field	Wire with current and accompanying field	Resultant field and direction of force on wire
A	B	C

FIGURE 9–67.   Force on a current-carrying wire

441

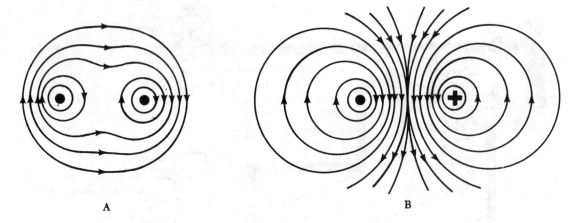

FIGURE 9–68. Fields surrounding parallel conductors.

turned, torque is applied. The engine of an airplane gives torque to the propeller. Torque is developed also by the reacting magnetic fields about the current-carrying coil just described. This is the torque which turns the coil.

The right-hand motor rule can be used to determine the direction a current-carrying wire will move in a magnetic field. As illustrated in figure 9–70, if the index finger of the right hand is pointed in the direction of the magnetic field and the second finger in the direction of current flow, the thumb will indicate the direction the current-carrying wire will move.

The amount of torque developed in a coil depends upon several factors: the strength of the magnetic field, the number of turns in the coil, and the position of the coil in the field. Magnets are made of special steel which produces a strong field. Since there is a torque acting on each turn, the greater the number of turns on the coil, the greater

the torque. In a coil carrying a steady current located in a uniform magnetic field, the torque will vary at successive positions of rotation, as shown in figure 9–71. When the plane of the coil is parallel to the lines of force, the torque is zero. When its plane cuts the lines of force at right angles, the torque is 100 percent. At intermediate positions, the torque ranges between zero and 100 percent.

Basic D. C. Motor

A coil of wire through which the current flows will rotate when placed in a magnetic field. This is the technical basis governing the construction of a d.c. motor. Figure 9–72 shows a coil mounted in a magnetic field in which it can rotate. However, if the connecting wires from the battery were permanently fastened to the terminals of the coil and there was a flow of current, the coil would rotate only until it lined itself up with the magnetic field. Then, it would stop, because the torque at that point would be zero. A motor, of course,

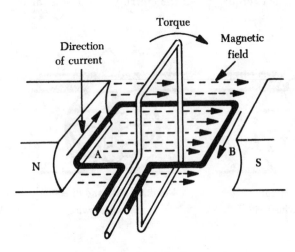

FIGURE 9–69. Developing a torque.

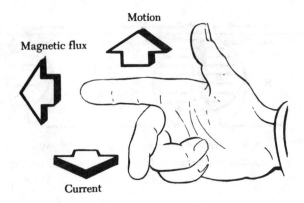

FIGURE 9–70. Right-hand motor rule.

442

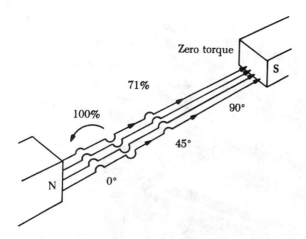

FIGURE 9-71.   Torque on a coil at various angles
of rotation.

must continue rotating. It is necessary, therefore,
to design a device that will reverse the current in
the coil just at the time the coil becomes parallel
to the lines of force. This will create torque again
and cause the coil to rotate. If the current-
reversing device is set up to reverse the current
each time the coil is about to stop, the coil can be
made to continue rotating as long as desired.

One method of doing this is to connect the
circuit so that, as the coil rotates, each contact
slides off the terminal to which it connects and
slides onto the terminal of opposite polarity. In
other words, the coil contacts switch terminals
continuously as the coil rotates, preserving the
torque and keeping the coil rotating. In figure
9-72, the coil terminal segments are labeled A
and B. As the coil rotates, the segments slide onto
and past the fixed terminals or brushes. With this
arrangement, the direction of current in the side
of the coil next to the north seeking pole flows
toward the reader, and the force acting on that side
of the coil turns it downward. The part of the
motor which changes the current from one wire to
another is called the commutator.

When the coil is positioned as shown in A of
figure 9-72, current will flow from the negative
terminal of the battery to the negative $(-)$ brush,
to segment B of the commutator, through the loop
to segment A of the commutator, to the positive
$(+)$ brush, and then, back to the positive terminal
of the battery. By using the right-hand motor rule,
it is seen that the coil will rotate counterclockwise.
The torque at this position of the coil is maximum,
since the greatest number of lines of force are being
cut by the coil.

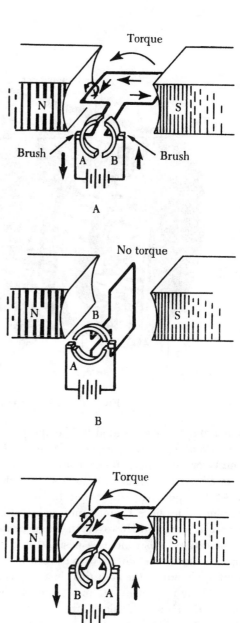

FIGURE 9-72.   Basic d.c. motor operation.

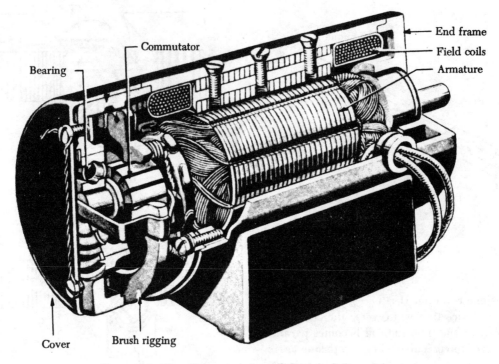

Bearing

Commutator

End frame

Field coils

Armature

Cover   Brush rigging

FIGURE 9–73. Cutaway view of practical d.c. motor.

When the coil has rotated 90° to the position shown in *B* of figure 9–72, segments *A* and *B* of the commutator no longer make contact with the battery circuit and no current can flow through the coil. At this position, the torque has reached a minimum value, since a minimum number of lines of force are being cut. However, the momentum of the coil carries it beyond this position until the segments again make contact with the brushes, and current again enters the coil; this time, though, it enters through segment *A* and leaves through segment *B*. However, since the positions of segments *A* and *B* have also been reversed, the effect of the current is as before, the torque acts in the same direction, and the coil continues its counterclockwise rotation. On passing through the position shown in *C* of figure 9–72, the torque again reaches maximum. Continued rotation carries the coil again to a position of minimum torque, as in *D* of figure 9–72. At this position, the brushes no longer carry current, but once more the momentum rotates the coil to the point where current enters through segment *B* and leaves through *A*. Further rotation brings the coil to the starting point and, thus, one revolution is completed.

The switching of the coil terminals from the positive to the negative brushes occurs twice per revolution of the coil.

The torque in a motor containing only a single coil is neither continuous nor very effective, for there are two positions where there is actually no torque at all. To overcome this, a practical d.c. motor contains a large number of coils wound on the armature. These coils are so spaced that, for any position of the armature, there will be coils near the poles of the magnet. This makes the torque both continuous and strong. The commutator, likewise, contains a large number of segments instead of only two.

The armature in a practical motor is not placed between the poles of a permanent magnet but between those of an electromagnet, since a much stronger magnetic field can be furnished. The core is usually made of a mild or annealed steel, which can be magnetized strongly by induction. The current magnetizing the electromagnet is from the same source that supplies the current to the armature.

D. C. Motor Construction

The major parts in a practical motor are the armature assembly, the field assembly, the brush assembly, and the end frame. (See figure 9–73.)

Armature Assembly

The armature assembly contains a laminated, soft-iron core, coils, and a commutator, all

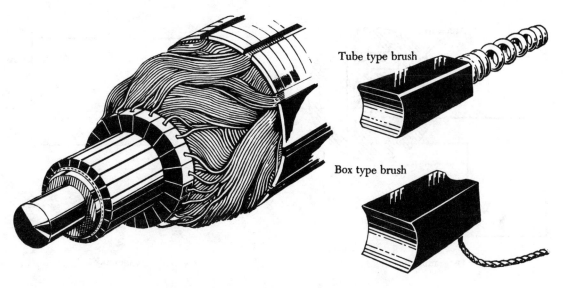

FIGURE 9–74.   Commutator and brushes.

Tube type brush

Box type brush

mounted on a rotatable steel shaft. Laminations made of stacks of soft iron, insulated from each other, form the armature core. Solid iron is not used, since a solid-iron core revolving in the magnetic field would heat and use energy needlessly. The armature windings are insulated copper wire, which are inserted in slots insulated with fiber paper (fish paper) to protect the windings. The ends of the windings are connected to the commutator segments. Wedges or steel bands hold the windings in place to prevent them from flying out of the slots when the armature is rotating at high speeds. The commutator consists of a large number of copper segments insulated from each other and the armature shaft by pieces of mica. Insulated wedge rings hold the segments in place.

Field Assembly

The field assembly consists of the field frame, the pole pieces, and the field coils. The field frame is located along the inner wall of the motor housing. It contains laminated soft steel pole pieces on which the field coils are wound. A coil, consisting of several turns of insulated wire, fits over each pole piece and, together with the pole, constitutes a field pole. Some motors have as few as two poles, others as many as eight.

Brush Assembly

The brush assembly consists of the brushes and their holders. The brushes are usually small blocks of graphitic carbon, since this material has a long

service life and also causes minimum wear to the commutator. The holders permit some play in the brushes so they can follow any irregularities in the surface of the commutator and make good contact. Springs hold the brushes firmly against the commutator. A commutator and two types of brushes are shown in figure 9–74.

End Frame

The end frame is the part of the motor opposite the commutator. Usually, the end frame is designed so that it can be connected to the unit to be driven. The bearing for the drive end is also located in the end frame. Sometimes the end frame is made a part of the unit driven by the motor. When this is done, the bearing on the drive end may be located in any one of a number of places.

TYPES OF D. C. MOTORS

There are three basic types of d.c. motors: (1) Series motors, (2) shunt motors, and (3) compound motors. They differ largely in the method in which their field and armature coils are connected.

Series D. C. Motor

In the series motor, the field windings, consisting of a relatively few turns of heavy wire, are connected in series with the armature winding. Both a diagrammatic and a schematic illustration of a series motor is shown in figure 9–75. The same current flowing through the field winding also flows

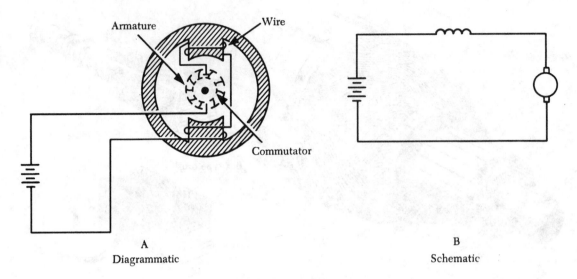

A
Diagrammatic

B
Schematic

FIGURE 9–75. Series motor.

through the armature winding. Any increase in current, therefore, strengthens the magnetism of both the field and the armature.

Because of the low resistance in the windings, the series motor is able to draw a large current in starting. This starting current, in passing through both the field and armature windings, produces a high starting torque, which is the series motor's principal advantage.

The speed of a series motor is dependent upon the load. Any change in load is accompanied by a substantial change in speed. A series motor will run at high speed when it has a light load and at low speed with a heavy load. If the load is removed entirely, the motor may operate at such a high speed that the armature will fly apart. If high starting torque is needed under heavy load conditions, series motors have many applications. Series motors are often used in aircraft as engine starters and for raising and lowering landing gears, cowl flaps, and wing flaps.

Shunt D. C. Motor

In the shunt motor the field winding is connected in parallel or in shunt with the armature winding. (See figure 9–76) The resistance in the field winding is high. Since the field winding is connected directly across the power supply, the current through the field is constant. The field current does not vary with motor speed, as in the series motor and, therefore, the torque of the shunt motor will

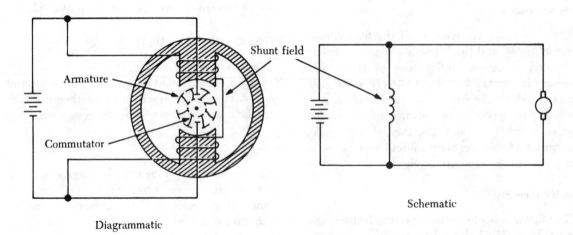

Diagrammatic

Schematic

FIGURE 9–76. Shunt motor.

446

vary only with the current through the armature. The torque developed at starting is less than that developed by a series motor of equal size.

The speed of the shunt motor varies very little with changes in load. When all load is removed, it assumes a speed slightly higher than the loaded speed. This motor is particularly suitable for use when constant speed is desired and when high starting torque is not needed.

Compound D. C. Motor

The compound motor is a combination of the series and shunt motors. There are two windings in the field: a shunt winding and a series winding. A schematic of a compound motor is shown in figure 9–77. The shunt winding is composed of many turns of fine wire and is connected in parallel with the armature winding. The series winding consists of a few turns of large wire and is connected in series with the armature winding. The starting torque is higher than in the shunt motor but lower than in the series motor. Variation of speed with load is less than in a series-wound motor but greater than in a shunt motor. The compound motor is used whenever the combined characteristics of the series and shunt motors are desired.

Like the compound generator, the compound motor has both series and shunt field windings. The series winding may either aid the shunt wind (cumulative compound) or oppose the shunt winding (differential compound).

The starting and load characteristics of the cumulative-compound motor are somewhere between those of the series and those of the shunt motor.

Because of the series field, the cumulative-compound motor has a higher starting torque than a shunt motor. Cumulative-compound motors are used in driving machines which are subject to sudden changes in load. They are also used where a

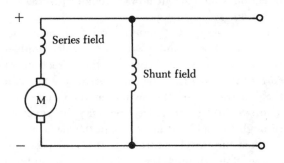

FIGURE 9–77.   Compound motor.

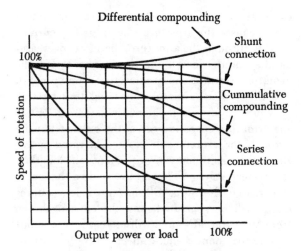

FIGURE 9–78.   Load characteristics of d.c. motors.

high starting torque is desired, but a series motor cannot be used easily.

In the differential compound motor, an increase in load creates an increase in current and a decrease in total flux in this type of motor. These two tend to offset each other and the result is a practically constant speed. However, since an increase in load tends to decrease the field strength, the speed characteristic becomes unstable. Rarely is this type of motor used in aircraft systems.

A graph of the variation in speed with changes of load of the various types of d.c. motors is shown in figure 9–78.

Counter E. M. F.

The armature resistance of a small, 28-volt d.c. motor is extremely low, about 0.1 ohm. When the armature is connected across the 28-volt source, current through the armature will apparently be

$$I = \frac{E}{R} = \frac{28}{0.1} = 280 \text{ amperes.}$$

This high valve of current flow is not only impracticable but also unreasonable, especially when the current drain, during normal operation of a motor, is found to be about 4 amperes. This is because the current through a motor armature during operation is determined by more factors than ohmic resistance.

When the armature in a motor rotates in a magnetic field, a voltage is induced in its windings. This voltage is called the back or counter e.m.f. (electromotive force) and is opposite in direction to the voltage applied to the motor from the external source. Counter e.m.f. opposes the current which causes the armature to rotate. The current flowing through the armature, therefore, decreases as the counter e.m.f. increases. The faster the armature rotates, the greater the counter e.m.f. For this reason, a motor connected to a battery may draw a fairly high current on starting, but as the armature speed increases, the current flowing through the armature decreases. At rated speed, the counter e.m.f. may be only a few volts less than the battery voltage. Then, if the load on the motor is increased, the motor will slow down, less counter e.m.f. will be generated, and the current drawn from the external source will increase. In a shunt motor, the counter e.m.f. affects only the current in the armature, since the field is connected in parallel across the power source. As the motor slows down and the counter e.m.f. decreases, more current flows through the armature, but the magnetism in the field is unchanged. When the series motor slows down, the counter e.m.f. decreases and more current flows through the field and the armature, thereby strengthening their magnetic fields. Because of these characteristics, it is more difficult to stall a series motor than a shunt motor.

Types of Duty

Electric motors are called upon to operate under various conditions. Some motors are used for intermittent operation; others operate continuously. Motors built for intermittent duty can be operated for short periods only and, then, must be allowed to cool before being operated again. If such a motor is operated for long periods under full load, the motor will be overheated. Motors built for continuous duty may be operated at rated power for long periods.

Reversing Motor Direction

By reversing the direction of current flow in either the armature or the field windings, the direction of a motor's rotation may be reversed. This will reverse the magnetism of either the armature or the magnetic field in which the armature rotates. If the wires connecting the motor to an external source are interchanged, the direction of rotation will not be reversed, since changing these wires reverses the magnetism of both field and armature and leaves the torque in the same direction as before.

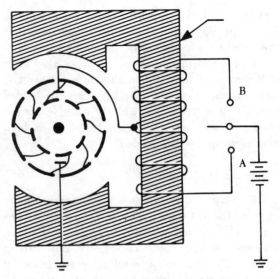

FIGURE 9–79.   Split field series motor.

One method for reversing direction of rotation employs two field windings wound in opposite directions on the same pole. This type of motor is called a split field motor. Figure 9–79 shows a series motor with a split field winding. The single-pole, double-throw switch makes it possible to direct current through either of the two windings. When the switch is placed in the lower position, current flows through the lower field winding, creating a north pole at the lower field winding and at the lower pole piece, and a south pole at the upper pole piece. When the switch is placed in the upper position, current flows through the upper field winding, the magnetism of the field is reversed, and the armature rotates in the opposite direction. Some split field motors are built with two separate field windings wound on alternate poles. The armature in such a motor, a four-pole reversible motor, rotates in one direction when current flows through the windings of one set of opposite pole pieces, and in the opposite direction when current flows through the other set of windings.

Another method of direction reversal, called the switch method, employs a double-pole, double-throw switch which changes the direction of current flow in either the armature or the field. In the illustration of the switch method shown in figure 9–80, current direction may be reversed through the field but not through the armature.

When the switch is thrown to the "up" position, current flows through the field winding to establish a north pole at the right side of the motor and a

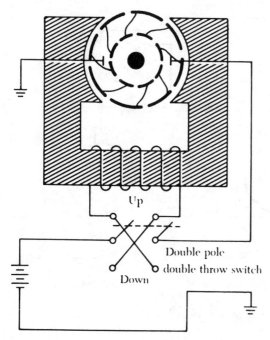

FIGURE 9–80.   Switch method of reversing motor
direction.

south pole at the left side of the motor. When the switch is thrown to the "down" position, this polarity is reversed and the armature rotates in the opposite direction.

Motor Speed

Motor speed can be controlled by varying the current in the field windings. When the amount of current flowing through the field windings is increased, the field strength increases, but the motor slows down since a greater amount of counter e.m.f. is generated in the armature windings. When the field current is decreased, the field strength decreases, and the motor speeds up because the counter e.m.f. is reduced. A motor in which speed can be controlled is called a variable-speed motor. It may be either a shunt or series motor.

In the shunt motor, speed is controlled by a rheostat in series with the field windings (figure 9–81). The speed depends on the amount of current which flows through the rheostat to the field windings. To increase the motor speed, the resistance in the rheostat is increased, which decreases the field current. As a result, there is a decrease in the strength of the magnetic field and

in the counter e.m.f. This momentarily increases the armature current and the torque. The motor will then automatically speed up until the counter e.m.f. increases and causes the armature current to decrease to its former value. When this occurs, the motor will operate at a higher fixed speed than before.

To decrease the motor speed, the resistance of the rheostat is decreased. More current flows through the field windings and increases the strength of the field; then, the counter e.m.f. increases momentarily and decreases the armature current. As a result, the torque decreases and the motor slows down until the counter e.m.f. decreases to its former value; then the motor operates at a lower fixed speed than before.

In the series motor (figure 9–82), the rheostat speed control is connected either in parallel or in series with the motor field, or in parallel with the armature. When the rheostat is set for maximum resistance, the motor speed is increased in the parallel armature connection by a decrease in current. When the rheostat resistance is maximum in the series connection, motor speed is reduced by a reduction in voltage across the motor. For above-normal speed operation, the rheostat is in parallel with the series field. Part of the series field current is bypassed and the motor speeds up.

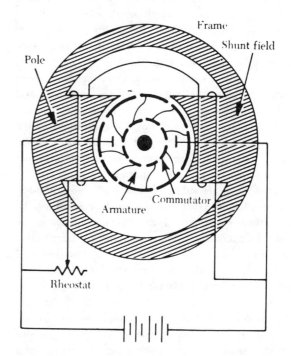

FIGURE 9–81.   Shunt motor with variable speed
control.

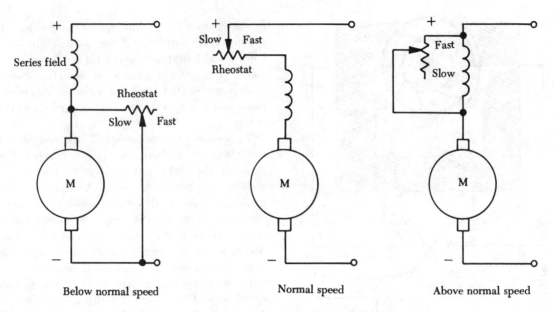

| Below normal speed | Normal speed | Above normal speed |

FIGURE 9–82. Controlling the speed of a series d.c. motor.

Energy Losses in D. C. Motors

Losses occur when electrical energy is converted to mechanical energy (in the motor), or mechanical energy is converted to electrical energy (in the generator). For the machine to be efficient, these losses must be kept to a minimum. Some losses are electrical, others are mechanical. Electrical losses are classified as copper losses and iron losses; mechanical losses occur in overcoming the friction of various parts of the machine.

Copper losses occur when electrons are forced through the copper windings of the armature and the field. These losses are proportional to the square of the current. They are sometimes called I^2R losses, since they are due to the power dissipated in the form of heat in the resistance of the field and armature windings.

Iron losses are subdivided in hysteresis and eddy current losses. Hysteresis losses are caused by the armature revolving in an alternating magnetic field. It, therefore, becomes magnetized first in one direction and then in the other. The residual magnetism of the iron or steel of which the armature is made causes these losses. Since the field magnets are always magnetized in one direction (d.c. field), they have no hysteresis losses.

Eddy current losses occur because the iron core of the armature is a conductor revolving in a magnetic field. This sets up an e.m.f. across portions of the core, causing currents to flow within the core. These currents heat the core and, if they become excessive, may damage the windings. As far as the output is concerned, the power consumed by eddy currents is a loss. To reduce eddy currents to a minimum, a laminated core usually is used. A laminated core is made of thin sheets of iron electrically insulated from each other. The insulation between laminations reduces eddy currents, because it is "transverse" to the direction in which these currents tend to flow. However, it has no effect on the magnetic circuit. The thinner the laminations, the more effectively this method reduces eddy current losses.

Inspection and Maintenance of D. C. Motors

Use the following procedures to make inspection and maintenance checks:

1. Check the operation of the unit driven by the motor in accordance with the instructions covering the specific installation.
2. Check all wiring, connections, terminals, fuses, and switches for general condition and security.
3. Keep motors clean and mounting bolts tight.
4. Check brushes for condition, length, and spring tension. Minimum brush lengths, correct spring tension, and procedures for replacing brushes are given in the applicable manufacturer's instructions.

5. Inspect commutator for cleanness, pitting, scoring, roughness, corrosion or burning. Check for high mica (if the copper wears down below the mica, the mica will insulate the brushes from the commutator). Clean dirty commutators with a cloth moistened with the recommended cleaning solvent. Polish rough or corroded commutators with fine sandpaper (000 or finer) and blow out with compressed air. Never use emery paper since it contains metallic particles which may cause shorts. Replace the motor if the commutator is burned, badly pitted, grooved, or worn to the extent that the mica insulation is flush with the commutator surface.
6. Inspect all exposed wiring for evidence of overheating. Replace the motor if the insulation on leads or windings is burned, cracked, or brittle.
7. Lubricate only if called for by the manufacturer's instructions covering the motor. Most motors used in today's airplanes require no lubrication between overhauls.
8. Adjust and lubricate the gearbox, or unit which the motor drives, in accordance with the applicable manufacturer's instructions covering the unit.

When trouble develops in a d.c. motor system, check first to determine the source of the trouble. Replace the motor only when the trouble is due to a defect in the motor itself. In most cases, the failure of a motor to operate is caused by a defect in the external electrical circuit, or by mechanical failure in the mechanism driven by the motor.

Check the external electrical circuit for loose or dirty connections and for improper connection of wiring. Look for open circuits, grounds, and shorts by following the applicable manufacturer's circuit-testing procedure. If the fuse is not blown, failure of the motor to operate is usually due to an open circuit. A blown fuse usually indicates an accidental ground or short circuit. The chattering of the relay switch which controls the motor is usually caused by a low battery. When the battery is low, the open-circuit voltage of the battery is sufficient to close the relay, but with the heavy current draw of the motor, the voltage drops below the level required to hold the relay closed. When the relay opens, the voltage in the battery increases enough to close the relay again. This cycle repeats and causes chattering, which is very

harmful to the relay switch, due to the heavy current causing an arc which will burn the contacts.

Check the unit driven by the motor for failure of the unit or drive mechanism. If the motor has failed as a result of a failure in the driven unit, the fault must be corrected before installing a new motor.

If it has been determined that the fault is in the motor itself (by checking for correct voltage at the motor terminals and for failure of the driven unit), inspect the commutator and brushes. A dirty commutator or defective or binding brushes may result in poor contact between brushes and commutator. Clean the commutator, brushes, and brush holders with a cloth moistened with the recommended cleaning solvent. If brushes are damaged or worn to the specified minimum length, install new brushes in accordance with the applicable manufacturer's instructions covering the motor. If the motor still fails to operate, replace it with a serviceable motor.

A. C. MOTORS

Because of their advantages, many types of aircraft motors are designed to operate on alternating current. In general, a.c. motors are less expensive than comparable d.c. motors. In many instances, a.c. motors do not use brushes and commutators and, therefore, sparking at the brushes is avoided. They are very reliable and very little maintenance is needed. Also, they are well suited for constant-speed applications and certain types are manufactured that have, within limits, variable-speed characteristics. Alternating-current motors are designed to operate on poly-phase or single-phase lines and at several voltage ratings.

The subject of a.c. motors is very extensive, and no attempt has been made to cover the entire field. Only the types of a.c. motors most common to aircraft systems are discussed in detail.

The speed of rotation of an a.c. motor depends upon the number of poles and the frequency of the electrical source of power:

$$\text{r.p.m.} = \frac{120 \times \text{Frequency}}{\text{Number of Poles}}.$$

Since airplane electrical systems typically operate at 400 cycles, an electric motor at this frequency operates at about seven times the speed of a 60-cycle commercial motor with the same number of poles. Because of this high speed of rotation, 400-cycle a.c. motors are suitable for operating small high-speed rotors, through reduction gears, in lifting and moving heavy loads, such as the wing flaps, the retractable landing gear, and the starting of engines. The 400-cycle induction type motor operates at speeds ranging from 6,000 r.p.m. to 24,000 r.p.m.

Alternating-current motors are rated in horsepower output, operating voltage, full load current, speed, number of phases, and frequency. Whether the motors operate continuously or intermittently (for short intervals) is also considered in the rating.

TYPES OF A. C. MOTORS

There are two general types of a.c. motors used in aircraft systems: induction motors and synchronous motors. Either type may be single-phase, two-phase, or three-phase.

Three-phase induction motors are used where large amounts of power are required. They operate such devices as starters, flaps, landing gears, and hydraulic pumps.

Single-phase induction motors are used to operate devices such as surface locks, intercooler shutters, and oil shutoff valves in which the power requirement is low.

Three-phase synchronous motors operate at constant synchronous speeds and are commonly used to operate flux gate compasses and propeller synchronizer systems.

Single-phase synchronous motors are common sources of power to operate electric clocks and other small precision equipment. They require some auxiliary method to bring them up to synchronous speeds; that is, to start them. Usually the starting winding consists of an auxiliary stator winding.

Three-Phase Induction Motor

The three-phase a.c. induction motor is also called a squirrel-cage motor. Both single-phase and three-phase motors operate on the principle of a rotating magnetic field. A horseshoe magnet held over a compass needle is a simple illustration of the principle of the rotating field. The needle will take a position parallel to the magnetic flux passing between the two poles of the magnet. If the magnet is rotated, the compass needle will follow. A rotating magnetic field can be produced by a two- or three-phase current flowing through two or more groups of coils wound on inwardly

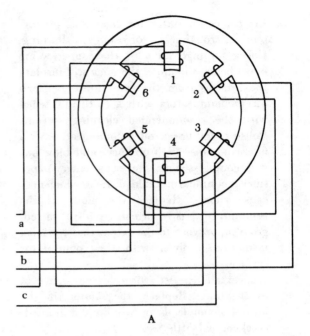

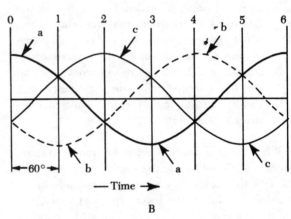

FIGURE 9–83. Rotating magnetic field developed by application of three-phase voltages.

projecting poles of an iron frame. The coils on each group of poles are wound alternately in opposite directions to produce opposite polarity, and each group is connected to a separate phase of voltage. The operating principle depends on a revolving, or rotating, magnetic field to produce torque. The key to understanding the induction motor is a thorough understanding of the rotating magnetic field.

Rotating Magnetic Field

The field structure shown in A of figure 9–83 has poles whose windings are energized by three a.c. voltages, a, b, and c. These voltages have equal

452

magnitude but differ in phase, as shown in *B* of figure 9–83.

At the instant of time shown as 0 in *B* of figure 9–83, the resultant magnetic field produced by the application of the three voltages has its greatest intensity in a direction extending from pole 1 to pole 4. Under this condition, pole 1 can be considered as a north pole and pole 4 as a south pole.

At the instant of time shown as 1, the resultant magnetic field will have its greatest intensity in the direction extending from pole 2 to pole 5; in this case, pole 2 can be considered as a north pole and pole 5 as a south pole. Thus, between instant 0 and instant 1, the magnetic field has rotated clockwise.

At instant 2, the resultant magnetic field has its greatest intensity in the direction from pole 3 to pole 6, and the resultant magnetic field has continued to rotate clockwise.

At instant 3, poles 4 and 1 can be considered as north and south poles, respectively, and the field has rotated still farther.

At later instants of time, the resultant magnetic field rotates to other positions while traveling in a clockwise direction, a single revolution of the field occurring in one cycle. If the exciting voltages have a frequency of 60 c.p.s., the magnetic field makes 60 revolutions per second, or 3,600 r.p.m. This speed is known as the synchronous speed of the rotating field.

Construction of Induction Motor

The stationary portion of an induction motor is called a stator, and the rotating member is called a rotor. Instead of salient poles in the stator, as shown in *A* of figure 9–83, distributed windings are used; these windings are placed in slots around the periphery of the stator.

It is usually impossible to determine the number of poles in an induction motor by visual inspection, but the information can be obtained from the nameplate of the motor. The nameplate usually gives the number of poles and the speed at which the motor is designed to run. This rated, or non-synchronous, speed is slightly less than the synchronous speed. To determine the number of poles per phase on the motor, divide 120 times the frequency by the rated speed; written as an equation:

$$P = \frac{120 \times f}{N}$$

where: *P* is the number of poles per phase, *f* is the frequency in c.p.s., *N* is the rated speed in r.p.m., and 120 is a constant.

The result will be very nearly equal to the number of poles per phase. For example, consider a 60-cycle, three-phase motor with a rated speed of 1,750 r.p.m. In this case:

$$P = \frac{120 \times 60}{1750} = \frac{7200}{1750} = 4.1.$$

Therefore, the motor has four poles per phase. If the number of poles per phase is given on the nameplate, the synchronous speed can be determined by dividing 120 times the frequency by the number of poles per phase. In the example used above, the synchronous speed is equal to 7,200 divided by 4, or 1,800 r.p.m.

The rotor of an induction motor consists of an iron core having longitudinal slots around its circumference in which heavy copper or aluminum bars are embedded. These bars are welded to a heavy ring of high conductivity on either end. The composite structure is sometimes called a squirrel cage, and motors containing such a rotor are called squirrel-cage induction motors. (See figure 9–84.)

Induction Motor Slip

When the rotor of an induction motor is subjected to the revolving magnetic field produced by the stator windings, a voltage is induced in the longitudinal bars. The induced voltage causes a current to flow through the bars. This current, in turn, produces its own magnetic field which combines with the revolving field so that the rotor assumes a position in which the induced voltage is minimized. As a result, the rotor revolves at very nearly the synchronous speed of the stator field, the difference in speed being just sufficient enough to induce the proper amount of current in the rotor to overcome the mechanical and electrical losses in the rotor. If the rotor were to turn at the same speed as the rotating field, the rotor conductors would not be cut by any magnetic lines of force, no e.m.f. would be induced in them, no current could flow, and there would be no torque. The rotor would then slow down. For this reason, there must always be a difference in speed between the rotor and the rotating field. This difference in speed is called slip and is expressed as a percentage of the synchronous speed. For example, if the rotor turns at 1,750 r.p.m. and the synchronous speed is

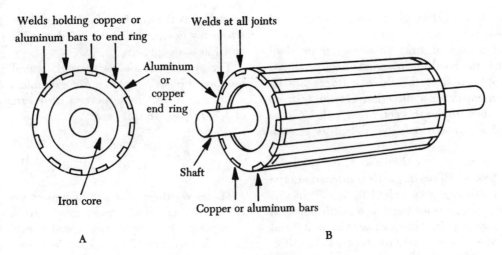

Welds holding copper or
aluminum bars to end ring

Welds at all joints

Aluminum
or
copper
end ring

Shaft

Iron core

Copper or aluminum bars

A

B

FIGURE 9–84.   Squirrel-cage rotor for an a.c. induction motor.

1,800 r.p.m., the difference in speed is 50 r.p.m. The slip is then equal to 50/1,800 or 2.78 percent.

Single-Phase Induction Motor

The previous discussion has applied only to polyphase motors. A single-phase motor has only one stator winding. This winding generates a field which merely pulsates, instead of rotating. When the rotor is stationary, the expanding and collapsing stator field induces currents in the rotor. These currents generate a rotor field opposite in polarity to that of the stator. The opposition of the field exerts a turning force on the upper and lower parts of the rotor trying to turn it 180° from its position. Since these forces are exerted through the center of the rotor, the turning force is equal in each direction. As a result, the rotor does not turn. If the rotor is started turning, it will continue to rotate in the direction in which it is started, since the turning force in that direction is aided by the momentum of the rotor.

Shaded-Pole Induction Motor

The first effort in the development of a self-starting, single-phase motor was the shaded-pole induction motor (figure 9–85). This motor has salient poles, a portion of each pole being encircled by a heavy copper ring. The presence of the ring causes the magnetic field through the ringed portion of the pole face to lag appreciably behind that through the other part of the pole face. The net effect is the production of a slight component of rotation of the field, sufficient to cause the rotor to revolve. As the rotor accelerates, the torque increases until the rated speed is obtained. Such motors have low starting torque and find their greatest application in small fan motors where the initial torque required is low.

In figure 9–86, a diagram of a pole and the rotor is shown. The poles of the shaded-pole motor resemble those of a d.c. motor.

A low-resistance, short-circuited coil or copper band is placed across one tip of each small pole, from which, the motor gets the name of shaded

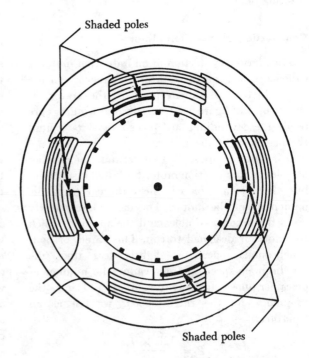

Shaded poles

Shaded poles

FIGURE 9–85.   Shaded-pole induction motor.

454

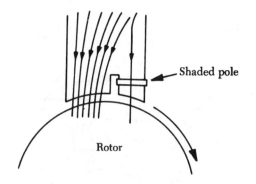

FIGURE 9–86. Diagram of a shaded-pole motor.

pole. The rotor of this motor is the squirrel-cage type.

As the current increases in the stator winding, the flux increases. A portion of this flux cuts the low resistance shading coil. This induces a current in the shading coil, and by Lenz's law, the current sets up a flux which opposes the flux inducing the current. Hence, most of the flux passes through the unshaded portion of the poles, as shown in figure 9–86.

When the current in the winding and the main flux reaches a maximum, the rate of change is zero; thus, no e.m.f. is induced in the shading coil. A little later, the shading coil current, which causes the induced e.m.f. to lag, reaches zero, and there is no opposing flux. Therefore, the main field flux passes through the shaded portion of the field pole.

The main field flux, which is now decreasing, induces a current in the shading coil. By Lenz's law, this current sets up a flux which opposes the decrease of the main field flux in the shaded portion of the pole. The effect is to concentrate the lines of force in the shaded portion of the pole face.

In effect, the shading coil retards, in time phase, the portion of the flux passing through the shaded part of the pole. This lag in time phase of the flux in the shaded tip causes the flux to produce the effect of sweeping across the face of the pole, from left to right in the direction of the shaded tip. This behaves like a very weak rotating magnetic field, and sufficient torque is produced to start a small motor.

The starting torque of the shaded-pole motor is exceedingly weak, and the power factor is low. Consequently, it is built in sizes suitable for driving such devices as small fans.

Split-Phase Motor

There are various types of self-starting motors, known as split-phase motors. Such motors have a starting winding displaced 90 electrical degrees from the main or running winding. In some types, the starting winding has a fairly high resistance, which causes the current in this winding to be out of phase with the current in the running winding. This condition produces, in effect, a rotating field and the rotor revolves. A centrifugal switch disconnects the starting winding automatically, after the rotor has attained approximately 25 percent of its rated speed.

Capacitor-Start Motor

With the development of high-capacity electrolytic capacitors, a variation of the split-phase motor, known as the capacitor-start motor, has been made. Nearly all fractional horsepower motors in use today on refrigerators, oil burners, and other similar appliances are of this type. (See figure 9–87.) In this adaptation, the starting winding and running winding have the same size and resistance value. The phase shift between currents of the two windings is obtained by using capacitors connected in series with the starting winding.

Capacitor-start motors have a starting torque comparable to their torque at rated speed and can be used in applications where the initial load is heavy. Again, a centrifugal switch is required for disconnecting the starting winding when the rotor speed is approximately 25 percent of the rated speed.

Although some single-phase induction motors are rated as high as 2 hp. (horsepower), the major field of application is 1 hp., or less, at a voltage rating of 115 volts for the smaller sizes and 110 to 220 volts for one-fourth hp. and up. For even larger power ratings, polyphase motors generally are used, since they have excellent starting torque characteristics.

Direction of Rotation of Induction Motors

The direction of rotation of a three-phase induction motor can be changed by simply reversing two of the leads to the motor. The same effect can be obtained in a two-phase motor by reversing connections to one phase. In a single-phase motor, reversing connections to the starting winding will reverse the direction of rotation. Most

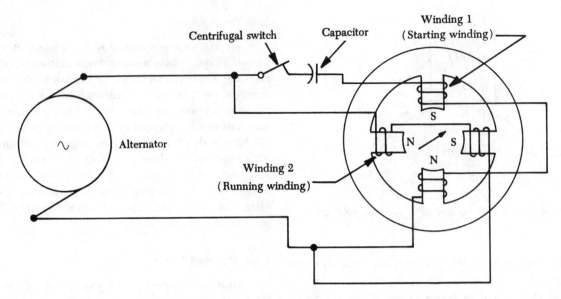

FIGURE 9–87.   Single-phase motor with capacitor starting winding.

single-phase motors designed for general application have provision for readily reversing connections to the starting winding. Nothing can be done to a shaded-pole motor to reverse the direction of rotation because the direction is determined by the physical location of the copper shading ring.

If, after starting, one connection to a three-phase motor is broken, the motor will continue to run but will deliver only one-third the rated power. Also, a two-phase motor will run at one-half its rated power if one phase is disconnected. Neither motor will start under these abnormal conditions.

Synchronous Motor

The synchronous motor is one of the principal types of a.c. motors. Like the induction motor, the synchronous motor makes use of a rotating magnetic field. Unlike the induction motor, however, the torque developed does not depend on the induction of currents in the rotor. Briefly, the principle of operation of the synchronous motor is as follows: A multiphase source of a.c. is applied to the stator windings, and a rotating magnetic field is produced. A direct current is applied to the rotor winding, and another magnetic field is produced. The synchronous motor is so designed and constructed that these two fields react to each other in such a manner that the rotor is dragged along and rotates at the same speed as the rotating magnetic field produced by the stator windings.

An understanding of the operation of the synchronous motor can be obtained by considering the simple motor of figure 9–88. Assume that poles A and B are being rotated clockwise by some mechanical means in order to produce a rotating magnetic field, they induce poles of opposite polarity in the soft-iron rotor, and forces of attraction exist between corresponding north and south poles. Consequently, as poles A and B

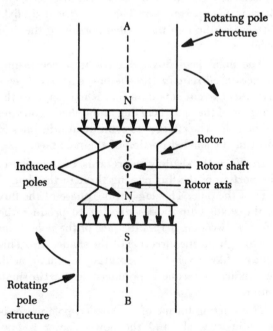

FIGURE 9–88.   Illustrating the operation of a synchronous motor.

456

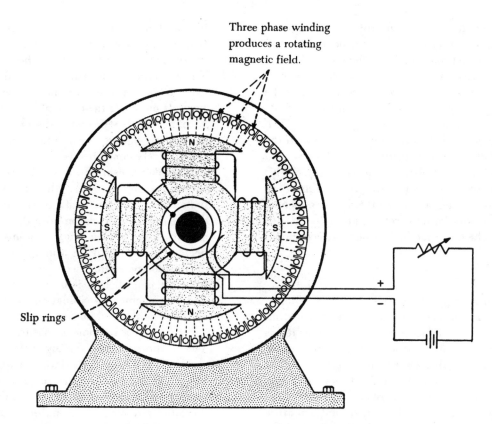

Three phase winding produces a rotating magnetic field.

Slip rings

FIGURE 9–89. Synchronous motor.

rotate, the rotor is dragged along at the same speed. However, if a load is applied to the rotor shaft, the rotor axis will momentarily fall behind that of the rotating field but, thereafter, will continue to rotate with the field at the same speed, as long as the load remains constant. If the load is too large, the rotor will pull out of synchronism with the rotating field and, as a result, will no longer rotate with the field at the same speed. The motor is then said to be overloaded.

Such a simple motor as that shown in figure 9–88 is never used. The idea of using some mechanical means of rotating the poles is impractical because another motor would be required to perform this work. Also, such an arrangement is unnecessary because a rotating magnetic field can be produced electrically by using phased a.c. voltages. In this respect, the synchronous motor is similar to the induction motor.

The synchronous motor consists of a stator field winding similar to that of an induction motor. The stator winding produces a rotating magnetic field. The rotor may be a permanent magnet, as in small single-phase synchronous motors used for clocks and other small precision equipment, or it may be

an electromagnet, energized from a d.c. source of power and fed through slip rings into the rotor field coils, as in an alternator. In fact, an alternator may be operated either as an alternator or a synchronous motor.

Since a synchronous motor has little starting torque, some means must be provided to bring it up to synchronous speed. The most common method is to start the motor at no load, allow it to reach full speed, and then energize the magnetic field. The magnetic field of the rotor locks with the magnetic field of the stator and the motor operates at synchronous speed.

The magnitude of the induced poles in the rotor shown in figure 9–89 is so small that sufficient torque cannot be developed for most practical loads. To avoid such a limitation on motor operation, a winding is placed on the rotor and energized with d.c. A rheostat placed in series with the d.c. source provides the operator of the machine with a means of varying the strength of the rotor poles, thus placing the motor under control for varying loads.

The synchronous motor is not a self-starting motor. The rotor is heavy and, from a dead stop,

457

it is impossible to bring the rotor into magnetic lock with the rotating magnetic field. For this reason, all synchronous motors have some kind of starting device. One type of simple starter is another motor, either a.c. or d.c., which brings the rotor up to approximately 90 percent of its synchronous speed. The starting motor is then disconnected, and the rotor locks in step with the rotating field. Another starting method is a second winding of the squirrel-cage type on the rotor. This induction winding brings the rotor almost to synchronous speed, and when the d.c. is connected to the rotor windings, the rotor pulls into step with the field. The latter method is the more commonly used.

A. C. Series Motor

An alternating-current series motor is a single-phase motor, but is not an induction or synchronous motor. It resembles a d.c. motor in that it has brushes and a commutator. The a.c. series motor will operate on either a.c. or d.c. circuits. It will be recalled that the direction of rotation of a d.c. series motor is independent of the polarity of the applied voltage, provided the field and armature connections remain unchanged. Hence, if a d.c. series motor is connected to an a.c. source, a torque will be developed which tends to rotate the armature in one direction. However, a d.c. series motor does not operate satisfactorily from an a.c. supply for the following reasons:

1. The alternating flux sets up large eddy-current and hysteresis losses in the unlaminated portions of the magnetic circuit and causes excessive heating and reduced efficiency.
2. The self-induction of the field and armature windings causes a low power factor.
3. The alternating field flux establishes large currents in the coils, which are short-circuited by the brushes; this action causes excessive sparking at the commutator.

To design a series motor for satisfactory operation on a.c., the following changes are made:

1. The eddy-current losses are reduced by laminating the field poles, frame and armature.
2. Hysteresis losses are minimized by using high-permeability, transformer-type, silicon-steel laminations.
3. The reactance of the field windings is kept satisfactorily low by using shallow pole pieces, few turns of wire, low frequency (usually 25 cycles for large motors), low flux density, and low reluctance (a short airgap).
4. The reactance of the armature is reduced by using a compensating winding embedded in the pole pieces. If the compensating winding is connected in series with the armature, as shown in figure 9–90, the armature is conductively compensated.

If the compensating winding is designed as shown in figure 9–91, the armature is inductively compensated. If the motor is designed for operation on both d.c. and a.c. circuits, the compensating winding is connected in series with the armature. The axis of the compensating winding is displaced from the main field axis by an angle of 90°. This arrangement is similar to the compensating winding used in some d.c. motors and generators to overcome armature reaction. The compensating winding establishes a counter magnetomotive force, neutralizing the effect of the armature magnetomotive force, preventing distortion of the main field flux, and reducing the armature reactance. The inductively compensated armature acts like the primary of a transformer, the secondary of which is the shorted compensating winding. The shorted secondary receives an induced voltage by the action of the alternating armature flux, and the resulting current flowing through the turns of the compensating winding establishes the opposing magnetomotive force, neutralizing the armature reactance.

5. Sparking at the commutator is reduced by the use of preventive leads P_1, P_2, P_3, and so forth, as shown in figure 9–92, where a ring

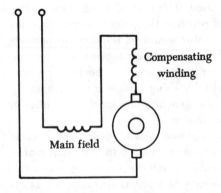

FIGURE 9–90. Conductively compensated armature of a.c. series motor.

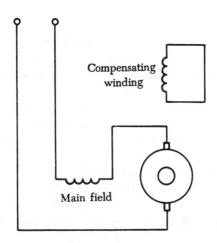

FIGURE 9–91. Inductively compensated armature of a.c. series motor.

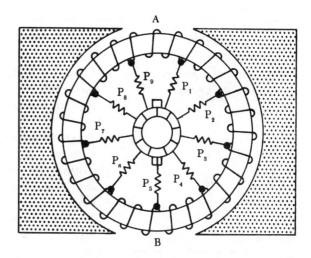

FIGURE 9–92. Preventive coils in a.c. series motor.

armature is shown for simplicity. When coils at *A* and *B* are shorted by the brushes, the induced current is limited by the relatively high resistance of the leads. Sparking at the brushes is also reduced by using armature coils having only a single turn and multipolar fields. High torque is obtained by having a large number of armature conductors and a large-diameter armature. Thus, the commutator has a large number of very thin commutator bars and the armature voltage is limited to about 250 volts.

Fractional horsepower a.c. series motors are called universal motors. They do not have compensating windings or preventive leads. They are used extensively to operate fans and portable tools, such as drills, grinders, and saws.

MAINTENANCE OF A. C. MOTORS

The inspection and maintenance of a.c. motors is very simple. The bearings may or may not need frequent lubrication. If they are the sealed type, lubricated at the factory, they require no further attention. Be sure the coils are kept dry and free from oil or other abuse.

The temperature of a motor is usually its only limiting operating factor. A good rule of thumb is that a temperature too hot for the hand is too high for safety.

Next to the temperature, the sound of a motor or generator is the best trouble indicator. When operating properly, it should hum evenly. If it is overloaded it will "grunt." A three-phase motor with one lead disconnected will refuse to turn and will "growl." A knocking sound generally indicates a loose armature coil, a shaft out of alignment, or armature dragging because of worn bearings.

The inspection and maintenance of all a.c. motors should be performed in accordance with the applicable manufacturer's instructions.

Troubleshooting

The following troubleshooting procedures are not applicable to a particular a.c. motor, but are included as examples of the general troubleshooting procedures provided by various manufacturers of a.c. motors.

Trouble	Possible cause	Correction
Motor speed slow.	No lubrication. Applied voltage low. Motor wiring defective.	Lubricate as necessary. Check motor source voltage. Perform voltage continuity test of motor wiring.
Motor speed fast.	Excessive supply voltage. Motor field windings shorted.	Check and adjust level of motor supply voltage. Repair shorted windings or replace or overhaul motor.

Trouble	Possible cause	Correction
Motor will not operate. No voltage applied to motor.	Loose or broken wiring inside motor.	Perform continuity test of motor circuit.
	Defective motor switch.	Check switch and switch wiring using a continuity tester.
	Armature or field winding open-circuited.	Repair open winding or replace motor.
	Brushes worn excessively.	Replace brushes.
	Brush springs broken or too weak.	Replace brush springs.
	Brushes sticking in brush holders.	Replace or clean and adjust brushes.
Motor vibrates.	Loose or broken motor mountings.	Repair or replace motor mountings.
	Motor shaft bent.	Replace shaft or overhaul or replace motor.
	Motor bearings worn excessively.	Replace bearings or overhaul motor.
Motor arcing excessively at brushes.	Brushes worn excessively.	Replace brushes.
	Brush springs weak.	Replace brush springs.
	Brushes sticking in holders.	Replace or clean brushes.
	Brushes incorrectly located.	Position brushes properly.
	Commutator dirty or excessively worn or pitted.	Clean or repair commutator as necessary.
	Open-circuited armature coil.	Repair open circuit or overhaul or replace motor.
Motor runs but overheats.	Motor bearings improperly lubricated.	Lubricate bearings.
	Excessive applied voltage.	Check voltage and adjust to proper level.
	Field windings short-circuited.	Repair short circuit or overhaul or replace.
	Excessive brush arcing.	Replace and adjust brushes.
Motor will not operate but draws high current.	Shorted circuit to motor.	Locate and repair short circuit.
	Open field winding in shunt motor.	Repair or overhaul or replace motor.
	Motor internal circuit shorted.	Repair short circuit or overhaul or replace motor.
	Mechanical stoppage.	Check for seized motor bearings or binding of mechanism driven by motor. Repair or replace seized components.
	Excessive load on motor.	Reduce load or install motor capable of carrying greater load.

CHAPTER 10

INSPECTION FUNDAMENTALS

GENERAL

Inspections are visual examinations and manual checks to determine the condition of an aircraft or component. An aircraft inspection can range from a casual walkaround to a detailed inspection involving complete disassembly and the use of complex inspection aids.

An inspection system consists of several processes, including: (1) Reports made by mechanics or by the pilot or crew flying an aircraft and (2) regularly scheduled inspections of an aircraft. An inspection system is designed to maintain an aircraft in the best possible condition. Thorough and repeated inspections must be considered the backbone of a good maintenance program. Irregular and haphazard inspection will invariably result in gradual and certain deterioration of an aircraft. The time which must eventually be spent in repairing an aircraft thus abused often totals far more than any time saved in hurrying through routine inspections and maintenance.

It has been proven that regularly scheduled inspections and preventive maintenance assure airworthiness. Operating failures and malfunctions of equipment are appreciably reduced if excessive wear or minor defects are detected and corrected early. The importance of inspections and the proper use of records concerning these inspections cannot be overemphasized.

Airframe and engine inspections may range from preflight inspections to detailed inspections. The time intervals for the inspection periods vary with the models of aircraft involved and the types of operations being conducted. The airframe and engine manufacturer's instructions should be consulted when establishing inspection intervals.

Aircraft may be inspected using flight hours as a basis for scheduling, or on a calendar inspection system. Under the calendar inspection system, the appropriate inspection is performed on the expiration of a specified number of calendar weeks. The calendar inspection system is an efficient system from a maintenance management standpoint. Scheduled replacement of components with stated hourly operating limitations is normally accomplished during the calendar inspection falling nearest the hourly limitation.

In some instances, a flight-hour limitation is established to limit the number of hours that may be flown during the calendar interval.

Aircraft operating under the flight-hour system are inspected when a specified number of flight hours are accumulated. Components with stated hourly operating limitations are normally replaced during the inspection that falls nearest the hourly limitation.

REQUIRED INSPECTIONS

Federal Aviation Regulations (FAR) provide for the inspection of all civil aircraft at specific intervals, depending generally upon the type of operations in which they are engaged, for the purpose of determining their overall condition. Some aircraft must be inspected at least once each 12 calendar months, while inspection is required for others after each 100 hours of flight. In other instances, an aircraft may be inspected in accordance with an inspection system set up to provide for total inspection of the aircraft over a calendar or flight-time period.

In order to determine the specific inspection requirements and rules for the preformance of inspections, reference should be made to the Federal Aviation Regulations which prescribe the requirements for the inspection and maintenance of aircraft in various types of operations.

INSPECTION TECHNIQUES

Before starting an inspection, be certain all plates, access doors, fairings, and cowling have been opened or removed and the structure cleaned. When opening inspection plates and cowling, and before cleaning the area take note of any oil or other evidence of fluid leakage.

CHECKLIST

Always use a checklist when performing the inspection. The checklist may be of your own design, one provided by the manufacturer of the equipment being inspected, or one obtained from some other source. The checklist should include the following:

1. Fuselage and hull group.
   a. Fabric and skin—for deterioration, distortion, other evidence of failure, and defective or insecure attachment of fittings.
   b. Systems and components—for proper installation, apparent defects, and satisfactory operation.
   c. Envelope gas bags, ballast tanks, and related parts— for condition.

2. Cabin and cockpit group.
   a. Generally—for cleanness and loose equipment that should be secured.
   b. Seats and safety belts—for condition and security.
   c. Windows and windshields—for deterioration and breakage.
   d. Instument—for condition, mounting, marking, and (where practicable) for proper operation.
   e. Flight and engine controls—for proper installation and operation.
   f. Batteries—for proper installation and charge.
   g. All systems—for proper installation, general condition, apparent defects, and security of attachment.

3. Engine and nacelle group.
   a. Engine section—for visual evidence of excessive oil, fuel, or hydraulic leaks, and sources of such leaks.
   b. Studs and nuts—for proper torquing and obvious defects.
   c. Internal engine—for cylinder compression and for metal particles or foreign matter on screens and sump drain plugs. If cylinder compression is weak, check for improper internal condition and improper internal tolerances.
   d. Engine mount—for cracks, looseness of mounting, and looseness of engine to mount.
   e. Flexible vibration dampeners—for condition and deterioration.

f. Engine controls—for defects proper travel, and proper safetying.
   g. Lines, hoses, and clamps—for leaks, condition, and looseness.
   h. Exhaust stacks—for cracks, defects, and proper attachment.
   i. Accessories—for apparent defects in security of mounting.
   j. All systems—for proper installation, general condition defects, and secure attachment.
   k. Cowling—for cracks and defects.
   l. Ground runup and functional check—check all powerplant controls and systems for correct response, all instruments for proper operation and indication.

4. Landing gear group.
   a. All units—for condition and security of attachment.
   b. Shock absorbing devices—for proper oleo fluid level.
   c. Linkage, trusses, and members—for undue or excessive wear, fatigue, and distortion.
   d. Retracting and locking mechanism—for proper operation.
   e. Hydraulic lines—for leakage.
   f. Electrical system—for chafing and proper operation of switches.
   g. Wheels—for cracks defects, and condition of bearings.
   h. Tires—for wear and cuts.
   i. Brakes—for proper adjustment.
   j. Floats and skis—for security of attachment and obvious defects.

5. Wing and center section.
   a. All components—for condition and security.
   b. Fabric and skin—for deterioration, distortion, other evidence of failure, and security of attachment.
   c. Internal structure (spars, ribs compression members)—for cracks, bends, and security.
   d. Movable surfaces—for damage or obvious defects, unsatisfactory fabric or skin attachment and proper travel.
   e. Control mechanism—for freedom of movement, alignment, and security.
   f. Control cables—for proper tension, fraying, wear and proper routing through fairleads and pulleys,

462

6. Empennage group.
   a. Fixed surfaces—for damge or obvious defects, loose fasteners, and security of attachment.
   b. Movable control surfaces—for damage or obvious defects, loose fasteners, loose fabric, or skin distortion.
   c. Fabric or skin—for abrasion, tears, cuts or defects, distortion, and deterioration.
7. Propeller group.
   a. Propeller assembly—for cracks, nicks, bends, and oil leakage.
   b. Bolts—for proper torquing, and safetying.
   c. Anti-icing devices—for proper operations and obvious defects.
   d. Control mechanisms—for proper operation, secure mounting, and travel.
8. Communication and navigation group.
   a. Radio and electronic equipment—for proper installation and secure mounting,
   b. Wiring and conduits—for proper routing, secure mounting, and obvious defects.
   c. Bonding and shielding—for proper installation and condition.
   d. Antennas—for condition, secure mounting and proper operation.
9. Miscellaneous.
   a. Emergency and first-aid equipment—for general condition and proper stowage.
   b. Parachutes, life rafts, flares, etc.—inspect in accordance with the manufacturer's recommendations.
   c. Autopilot system—for general condition, security of attachment, and proper operation.

AIRCRAFT LOGS

"Aircraft logs" as used in this handbook is an inclusive term which applies to the aircraft logbook and all supplemental records concerned with the aircraft. The logs and records provide a history of maintenance and operation, control of maintanance schedules, and data for time replacements of components or accessories.

The aircraft logbook is the record in which all data concerning the aircraft is recorded. Information gathered in this log is used to determine the aircraft condition, date of inspections, time on airframe and engines. It reflects a history of all significant events occurring to the aircraft, its components, and accessories, and provides a place for indicating compliance with FAA Airworthiness Directives or manufacturers' service bulletins.

SPECIAL INSPECTIONS

During the service life of an aircraft, occasions may arise when landings are made in an overweight condition or part of a flight must be made through severe turbulence. Rough landings are also experienced for a number of reasons.

When these situations are encountered, special inspection procedures should be followed to determine if any damage to the aircraft structure has occurred. The procedures outlined on the following pages are general in nature and are intended to acquaint the aviation mechanic with the areas which should be inspected. As such, they are not all inclusive. When performing any one of these special inspections, always follow the detailed procedures in the aircraft maintenance manual.

Hard or Overweight Landing Inspection

The structural stress induced by a landing depends not only upon the gross weight at the time but also upon the severity of impact. However, because of the difficulty in estimating vertical velocity at the time of contact, it is hard to judge whether or not a landing has been sufficiently severe to cause structural damage. For this reason, a special inspection should be performed after a landing is made at a weight known to exceed the design landing weight or after a rough landing, even though the latter may have occurred when the aircraft did not exceed the design landing weight.

Wrinkled wing skin is the most easily detected sign of an excessive load having been imposed during a landing. Another indication which can be detected easily is fuel leaks along riveted seams. Other possible locations of damage are spar webs, bulkheads, nacelle skin and attachments, firewall skin, and wing and fuselage stringers.

If none of these areas show adverse effects, it is reasonable to assume that no serious damage has occurred. If damage is detected, a more extensive inspection and alignment check may be necessary.

Severe Turbulence Inspection

When an aircraft encounters a gust condition, the airload on the wings exceeds the normal wingload supporting the aircraft weight. The gust tends to accelerate the aircraft while its inertia acts to resist this change. If the combination of gust velocity and airspeed is too severe, the induced stress can cause structural damage.

A special inspection should be performed after a flight through severe turbulence. Emphasis should be placed upon inspecting the upper and lower wing surfaces for excessive buckles or wrinkles with permanent set. Where wrinkles have occurred, remove a few rivets and examine the rivet shanks to determine if the rivets have sheared or were highly loaded in shear.

Inspect all spar webs from the fuselage to the tip, through the inspection doors and other accessible openings. Check for buckling, wrinkles, and sheared attachments. Inspect for buckling in the area around the nacelles and in the nacelle skin, particularly at the wing leading edge.

Check for fuel leaks. Any sizeable fuel leak is an indication that an area may have received overloads which have broken the sealant and opened the seams.

If the landing gear was lowered during a period of severe turbulence, inspect the surrounding surfaces carefully for loose rivets, cracks, or buckling. The interior of the wheel well may give further indications of excessive gust conditions.

Inspect the top and bottom fuselage skin. An excessive bending moment may have left wrinkles of a diagonal nature in these areas.

Inspect the surface of the empennage for wrinkles, buckling, or sheared attachments, Also, inspect the area of attachment of the empennage to the fuselage.

The above inspections cover the critical areas. If excessive damage is noted in any of the areas mentioned, the inspection should be continued until all damage is detected.

PUBLICATIONS

Aeronautical publications are the sources of information for guiding aviation mechanics in the operation and maintenance of aircraft and related equipment. The proper use of these publications will greatly aid in the efficient operation and maintenance of all aircraft. These include manufacturers' service bulletins, manuals, and catalogs, as well as FAA regulations, airworthiness directives, advisory circulars, and aircraft, engine and propeller specifications.

Bulletins

Service bulletins are one of several types of publications issued by airframe, engine, and component manufacturers.

The bulletins may include: (1) The purpose for issuing the publication; (2) the name of the applicable airframe, engine, or component; (3) detailed instructions for service, adjustment, modification or inspection, and source of parts, if required; and (4) the estimated number of man-hours required to accomplish the job.

Maintenance Manual

The aircraft maintenance manual provided by the manufacturer contains complete instructions for maintenance of all systems and components installed in the aircraft. It contains information for the mechanic who normally works on units, assemblies, and systems, while they are installed in the aircraft, and not for the overhaul mechanic. A typical aircraft maintenance manual contains: (1) A description of the systems such as electrical, hydraulic, fuel, control, etc.; (2) lubrication instructions setting forth the frequency and the lubricants and fluids which are to be used in the various systems; (3) pressures and electrical loads applicable to the various systems; (4) tolerances and adjustments necessary to proper functioning of the airplane; (5) methods of leveling, raising, and towing; (6) methods of balancing control surfaces; (7) identification of primary and secondary structures; (8) frequency and extent of inspections necessary to the proper operation of the airplane; (9) special repair methods applicable to the airplane; (10) special inspection techniques requiring X-ray, ultrasonic, or magnetic particle inspection; and (11) a list of special tools.

Overhaul Manual

The manufacturer's overhaul manual contains brief descriptive information and detailed step-by-step instructions covering work normally performed on a unit away from the aircraft. Simple, inexpensive items, such as switches and relays, on which overhaul is uneconomical, are not covered in the overhaul manual.

Structural Repair Manual

This manual contains information and specific instructions from the manufacturer for repairing primary and secondary structure. Typical skin, frame, rib, and stringer repairs are covered in this manual. Also included are material and fastener substitutions and special repair techniques.

Illustrated Parts Catalog

This catalog presents component breakdowns of structure and equipment in disassembly sequence. Also included are exploded views or cutaway illustrations for all parts and equipment manufactured by the aircraft manufacturer.

Federal Aviation Regulations (FAR)

Federal Aviation Regulations were established by law to provide for the safe and orderly conduct of flight operations and to prescribe airmen privileges and limitations. A knowledge of the FARs is necessary during the performance of maintenance, since all work done on aircraft must comply with FAR provisions.

Airworthiness Directives

A primary safety function of the Federal Aviation Administration is to require correction of unsafe conditions found in an aircraft, aircraft engine, propeller, or appliance when such conditions exist and are likely to exist or develop in other products of the same design. The unsafe condition may exist because of a design defect, maintenance, or other causes. FAR Part 39, Airworthiness Directives, defines the authority and responsibility of the administrator for requiring the necessary corrective action. The Airworthiness Directives (AD) are the media used to notify aircraft owners and other interested persons of unsafe conditions and to prescribe the conditions under which the product may continue to be operated.

Airworthiness Directives are Federal Aviation Regulations and must be complied with, unless specific exemption is granted.

Airworthiness Directives may be divided into two categories: (1) Those of an emergency nature requiring immediate compliance upon receipt and (2) those of a less urgent nature requiring compliance within a relatively longer period of time.

The contents of ADs include the aircraft, engine, propeller, or appliance model and serial numbers affected. Also included are the compliance time or period, a description of the difficulty experienced, and the necessary corrective action.

Type Certificate Data Sheets

The type certificate data sheet describes the type design and sets forth the limitations prescribed by the applicable Federal Aviation Regulations. It also includes any other limitations and information found necessary for type certification of a particular model aircraft.

Type certificate data sheets are numbered in the upper right-hand corner of each page. This number is the same as the type certificate number. The name of the type certificate holder, together with all of the approved models, appears immediately below the type certificate number. The issue date completes this group, which is enclosed in a box to set it off.

The data sheet is separated into one or more sections. Each section is identified by a Roman numeral followed by the model designation of the aircraft to which the section pertains. The category or categories in which the aircraft can be certificated are shown in parentheses following the model number. Also included is the approval date shown on the type certificate.

The data sheet contains information regarding:

1. Model designation for all engines for which the aircraft manufacturer obtained approval for use with this model aircraft.
2. Minimum fuel grade to be used.
3. Maximum continuous and takeoff ratings of the approved engines, including manifold pressure (when used), r.p.m., and horsepower (hp.).
4. Name of the manufacturer and model designation for each propeller for which the aircraft manufacturer obtained approval will be shown together with the propeller limits and any operating restrictions peculiar to the propeller or propeller-engine combination.
5. Airspeed limits in both m.p.h. and knots.
6. Center of gravity range for the extreme loading conditions of the aircraft is given in inches from the datum. The range may also be stated in percent of MAC (Mean Aerodynamic Chord) for transport category aircraft.

7. Empty weight c.g. range (when established) will be given as fore and aft limits in inches from the datum. If no range exists, the word "none" will be shown following the heading on the data sheet.

8. Location of the datum.

9. Means provided for leveling the aircraft.

10. All pertinent maximum weights.

11. Number of seats and their moment arms.

12. Oil and fuel capacity.

13. Control surface movements.

14. Required equipment.

15. Additional or special equipment found necessary for certification.

16. Information concerning required placards.

It is not within the scope of this handbook to list all the items that can be shown on the type certificate data sheets. Those items listed above are merely to acquaint aviation mechanics with the type of information generally included on the data sheets.

A.T.A. Specification No. 100

The Air Transport Association of America (A.T.A.) issued the specifications for Manufacturers Technical Data June 1, 1956.

Quote: "This specification establishes a standard for the presentation of technical data, by an aircraft, aircraft accessory, or component manufacturer required for their respective products."

Quote: "In order to standardize the treatment of subject matter and to simplify the user's problem in locating instructions, a uniform method of arranging material in all publications has been developed."

The A.T.A. Specification 100 has the aircraft divided into systems such as electrical which covers the basic electrical system (ATA 2400). Numbering in each major system provides an arrangement for breaking the system down into several subsystems. Late model aircraft, both over and under the 12,500 dividing line, have their parts manuals and maintenance manuals arranged according to the A.T.A. coded system.

The following table of A.T.A. System, Subsystem, and Titles is included for familiarization purposes.

ATA SPEC. 100—Systems

Sys.	Sub	Title
21		AIR CONDITIONING
	00	General
	10	Compression
	20	Distribution
	30	Pressurization Control
	40	Heating
	50	Cooling
	60	Temperature Control
	70	Moisture/Air Contaminate Control
22		AUTO FLIGHT
	00	General
	10	Autopilot
	20	Speed-Attitude Correction
	30	Auto Throttle
	40	System Monitor
23		COMMUNICATIONS
	00	General
	10	High Frequency (HF)
	20	VHF/UHF
	30	Passenger Address and Entertainment
	40	Interphone
	50	Audio Integrating
	60	Static Discharging
	70	Audio and Video Monitoring
24		ELECTRICAL POWER
	00	General
	10	Generator Drive
	20	AC Generation
	30	DC Generation
	40	External Power
	50	Electrical Load Distribution

Sys.	Sub	Title
25		EQUIPMENT/FURNISHINGS
	00	General
	10	Flight Compartment
	20	Passenger Compartment
	30	Buffet/Galley
	40	Lavatories
	50	Cargo Compartments/AG Spray Apparatus
	60	Emergency
	70	Accessory Compartments
26		FIRE PROTECTION
	00	General
	10	Detection
	20	Extinguishing
	30	Explosion Suppression
27		FLIGHT CONTROLS
	00	General
	10	Aileron and Tab
	20	Rudder/Ruddervator and Tab
	30	Elevator and Tab
	40	Horizontal Stabilizers/Stabilator
	50	Flaps
	60	Spoiler, Drag Devices & Variable Aerodynamic Fairings
	70	Gust Lock and Dampener
	80	Lift Augmenting
28		FUEL
	00	General
	10	Storage
	20	Distribution/Drain Valves
	30	Dump
	40	Indicating

Sys.	Sub	Title

29 HYDRAULIC POWER
- 00 General
- 10 Main
- 20 Auxiliary
- 30 Indicating

30 ICE AND RAIN PROTECTION
- 00 General
- 10 Airfoil
- 20 Air Intakes
- 30 Pilot and Static
- 40 Windows and Windshields
- 50 Antennas and Radomes
- 60 Propellers/Rotors
- 70 Water Lines
- 80 Detection

31 INDICATING/RECORDING SYSTEMS
- 00 General
- 10 Unassigned
- 20 Unassigned
- 30 Recorders
- 40 Central Computers
- 50 Central Warning System

32 LANDING GEAR
- 00 General
- 10 Main Gear
- 20 Nose Gear/Tail Gear
- 30 Extension & Retraction, Level Switch
- 40 Wheels and Brakes
- 50 Steering
- 60 Position, Warning & Ground Safety Switch
- 70 Supplementary Gear/Skis/Floats

33 LIGHTS
- 00 General
- 10 Flight Compartment & Annunciator Panels
- 20 Passenger Compartments
- 30 Cargo and Service Compartments
- 40 Exterior Lighting
- 50 Emergency Lighting

34 NAVIGATION
- 00 General
- 10 Flight Environment Data
- 20 Attitude and Direction
- 30 Landing and Taxiing Aids
- 40 Independent Position Determining
- 50 Dependent Position Determining
- 60 Position Computing

35 OXYGEN
- 00 General
- 10 Crew
- 20 Passenger
- 30 Portable

36 PNEUMATIC
- 00 General
- 10 Distribution
- 20 Indicating

37 VACUUM/PRESSURE
- 00 General
- 10 Distribution
- 20 Indicating

38 WATER/WASTE
- 00 General
- 10 Potable
- 20 Wash
- 30 Waste Disposal
- 40 Air Supply

39 ELECTRICAL/ELECTRONIC PANELS AND MULTIPURPOSE COMPONENTS
- 00 General
- 10 Instrument & Control Panels
- 20 Electrical & Electronic Equipment Racks
- 30 Electrical & Electronic Junction Boxes
- 40 Multipurpose Electronic Components
- 50 Integrated Circuits
- 60 Printed Circuit Card Assemblies

49 AIRBORNE AUXILIARY POWER
- 00 General
- 10 Power Plant
- 20 Engine
- 30 Engine Fuel and Control
- 40 Ignition/Starting
- 50 Air
- 60 Engine Controls
- 70 Indicating
- 80 Exhaust
- 90 Oil

51 STRUCTURES
- 00 General

52 DOORS
- 00 General
- 10 Passenger/Crew
- 20 Emergency Exit
- 30 Cargo
- 40 Service
- 50 Fixed Interior
- 60 Entrance Stairs
- 70 Door Warning
- 80 Landing Gear

53 FUSELAGE
- 00 General
- 10 Main Frame
- 20 Auxiliary Structure
- 30 Plates/Skin
- 40 Attach Fittings
- 50 Aerodynamic Fairings

54 NACELLES/PYLONS
- 00 General
- 10 Main Frame
- 20 Auxiliary Structure
- 30 Plates/Skin
- 40 Attach Fittings
- 50 Fillets/Fairings

Sys.	Sub	Title

55 STABILIZERS

- 00 General
- 10 Horizontal Stabilizers/Stabilator
- 20 Elevator/Elevon
- 30 Vertical Stabilizer
- 40 Rudder/Ruddervator
- 50 Attach Fittings

56 WINDOWS

- 00 General
- 10 Flight Compartment
- 20 Cabin
- 30 Door
- 40 Inspection and Observation

57 WINGS

- 00 General
- 10 Main Frame
- 20 Auxiliary Structure
- 30 Plates/Skin
- 40 Attach Fittings
- 50 Flight Surfaces

61 PROPELLERS

- 00 General
- 10 Propeller Assembly
- 20 Controlling
- 30 Braking
- 40 Indicating

65 ROTORS

- 00 General
- 10 Main Rotor
- 20 Anti-torque Rotor Assembly
- 30 Accessory Driving
- 40 Controlling
- 50 Braking
- 60 Indicating

71 POWERPLANT

- 00 General
- 10 Cowling
- 20 Mounts
- 30 Fireseals & Shrouds
- 40 Attach Fittings
- 50 Electrical Harness
- 60 Engine Air Intakes
- 70 Engine Drains

72 (T) TURBINE/TURBOPROP

- 00 General
- 10 Reduction Gear & Shaft Section
- 20 Air Inlet Section
- 30 Compressor Section
- 40 Combustion Section
- 50 Turbine Section
- 60 Accessory Drives
- 70 By-pass Section

72 (R) ENGINE RECIPROCATING

- 00 General
- 10 Front Section
- 20 Power Section
- 30 Cylinder Section
- 40 Supercharger Section
- 50 Lubrication

73 ENGINE FUEL & CONTROL

- 00 General
- 10 Distribution
- 20 Controlling/Governing
- 30 Indicating

74 IGNITION

- 00 General
- 10 Electrical Power Supply
- 20 Distribution
- 30 Switching

75 BLEED AIR

- 00 General
- 10 Engine Anti-Icing
- 20 Accessory Cooling
- 30 Compressor Control
- 40 Indicating

76 ENGINE CONTROLS

- 00 General
- 10 Power Control
- 20 Emergency Shutdown

77 ENGINE INDICATING

- 00 General
- 10 Power
- 20 Temperature
- 30 Analyzers

78 ENGINE EXHAUST

- 00 General
- 10 Collector/Nozzle
- 20 Noise Suppressor
- 30 Thrust Reverser
- 40 Supplementary Air

79 ENGINE OIL

- 00 General
- 10 Storage (Dry Sump)
- 20 Distribution
- 30 Indicating

80 STARTING

- 00 General
- 10 Cranking

81 TURBINES (RECIPROCATING ENG)

- 00 General
- 10 Power Recovery
- 20 Turbo-Supercharger

82 WATER INJECTION

- 00 General
- 10 Storage
- 20 Distribution
- 30 Dumping & Purging
- 40 Indicating

83 REMOTE GEAR BOXES (ENG DR)

- 00 General
- 10 Drive Shaft Section
- 20 Gearbox Section

MAGNETIC PARTICLE INSPECTION

Magnetic particle inspection is a method of detecting invisible cracks and other defects in ferromagnetic materials, such as iron and steel. This method of inspection is a nondestructive test, which means it is performed on the actual part without damage to the part. It is not applicable to nonmagnetic materials.

In rapidly rotating, reciprocating, vibrating, and other highly stressed aircraft parts, small defects often develop to the point that they cause complete failure of the part. Magnetic particle inspection has proved extremely reliable for the rapid detection of such defects located on or near the surface. In using this method of inspection, the location of the defect is indicated and the approximate size and shape are outlined.

The inspection process consists of magnetizing the part and then applying ferromagnetic particles to the surface area to be inspected. The ferromagnetic particles (indicating medium) may be held in suspension in a liquid that is flushed over the part; the part may be immersed in the suspension liquid; or the particles, in dry powder form, may be dusted over the surface of the part. The wet process is more commonly used in the inspection of aircraft parts.

If a discontinuity is present, the magnetic lines of force will be disturbed and opposite poles will exist on either side of the discontinuity. The magnetized particles thus form a pattern in the magnetic field between the opposite poles. This pattern, known as an "indication," assumes the approximate shape of the surface projection of the discontinuity. A discontinuity may be defined as an interruption in the normal physical structure or configuration of a part such as a crack, forging lap, seam, inclusion, porosity, and the like. A discontinuity may or may not affect the usefulness of a part.

Development of Indications

When a discontinuity in a magnetized material is open to the surface and a magnetic substance in the form of an indicating medium is available on the surface, the flux leakage at the discontinuity tends to form the indicating medium into a path of higher permeability. (Permeability is a term used to refer to the ease with which a magnetic flux can be established in a given magnetic circuit.) Because of the magnetism in the part and the adherence of the magnetic particles to each other, the indication remains on the surface of the part in the form of an approximate outline of the discontinuity that is immediately below it.

The same action takes place when the discontinuity is not open to the surface, but since the amount of flux leakage is less, fewer particles are held in place and a fainter and less sharply defined indication is obtained.

If the discontinuity is very far below the surface, there may be no flux leakage and, therefore, no indication on the surface. The flux leakage at a transverse discontinuity is shown in figure 10–1. The flux leakage at a longitudinal discontinuity is shown in figure 10–2.

Types of Discontinuities Disclosed

The following types of discontinuities are normally detected by the magnetic particle test: cracks, laps, seams, cold shuts, inclusions, splits, tears, pipes, and voids. All these may affect the reliability of parts in service.

Cracks, splits, bursts, tears, seams, voids, and pipes are formed by an actual parting or rupture of the solid metal. Cold shuts and laps are folds that have been formed in the metal, interrupting its continuity.

Inclusions are foreign material formed by impurities in the metal during the metal processing stages. They may consist, for example, of bits of furnace lining picked up during the melting of the basic metal or of other foreign constituents. Inclusions interrupt the continuity of the metal because they prevent the joining or welding of adjacent faces of the metal.

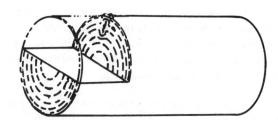

FIGURE 10–1. Flux leakage at transverse discontinuity.

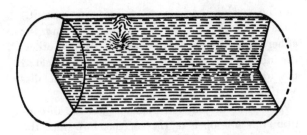

FIGURE 10–2. Flux leakage at longitudinal discontinuity.

Preparation of Parts for Testing

Grease, oil, and dirt must be cleaned from all parts before they are tested. Cleaning is very important, since any grease or other foreign material present can produce nonrelevant indications due to magnetic particles adhering to the foreign material as the suspension drains from the part.

Grease or foreign material in sufficient amount over a discontinuity may also prevent the formation of a pattern at the discontinuity. It is not advisable to depend upon the magnetic particle suspension to clean the part. Cleaning by suspension is not thorough, and any foreign materials so removed from the part will contaminate the suspension, thereby reducing its effectiveness.

In the dry procedure, thorough cleaning is absolutely necessary. Grease or other foreign material would hold the magnetic powder, resulting in nonrelevant indications and making it impossible to distribute the indicating medium evenly over the part's surface.

All small openings and oil holes leading to internal passages or cavities should be plugged with paraffin or other suitable nonabrasive material.

Coatings of cadmium, copper, tin, and zinc do not interfere with the satisfactory performance of magnetic particle inspection, unless the coatings are unusually heavy or the discontinuities to be detected are unusually small.

Chromium and nickel plating generally will not interfere with indications of cracks open to the surface of the base metal but will prevent indications of fine discontinuities, such as inclusions.

Because it is more strongly magnetic, nickel plating is more effective than chromium plating in preventing the formation of indications.

Effect of Flux Direction

In order to locate a defect in a part, it is essential that the magnetic lines of force pass approximately perpendicular to the defect. It is, therefore, necessary to induce magnetic flux in more than one direction, since defects are likely to

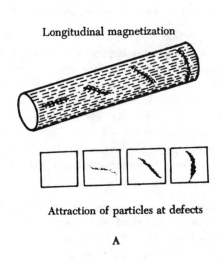

Longitudinal magnetization

Attraction of particles at defects

A

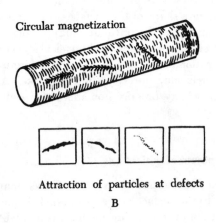

Circular magnetization

Attraction of particles at defects

B

FIGURE 10–3. Effect of flux direction on strength of indication.

470

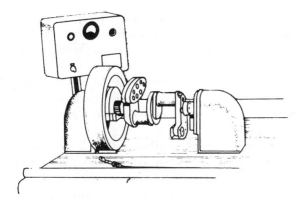

FIGURE 10–4. Circular magnetization of crankshaft.

FIGURE 10–5. Circular magnetization of piston pin with conductor bar.

exist at any angle to the major axis of the part. This requires two separate magnetizing operations, referred to as circular magnetization and longitudinal magnetization. The effect of flux direction is illustrated in figure 10–3.

Circular magnetization is the inducing of a magnetic field, consisting of concentric circles of force about and within the part, by passing electric current through the part. This type of magnetization will locate defects running approximately parallel to the axis of the part.

Circular magnetization of a part of solid cross section is illustrated in figure 10–4. Each head of the magnetizing unit is electrically connected to a pushbutton control, so that when contact is made the magnetizing current passes from one head to the other through the part.

Figure 10–5 illustrates circular magnetization of a hollow part by passing the magnetizing current

through a conductor bar located on the axis of the part.

In longitudinal magnetization the magnetic field is produced in a direction parallel to the long axis of the part. This is accomplished by placing the part in a solenoid excited by electric current. The metal part then becomes the core of an electromagnet and is magnetized by induction from the magnetic field created in the solenoid.

In longitudinal magnetization of long parts, the solenoid must be moved along the part in order to magnetize it. (See figure 10–6.) This is necessary to ensure adequate field strength throughout the entire length of the part.

Solenoids produce effective magnetization for approximately 12 inches from each end of the coil, thus accommodating parts or sections approximately 30 inches in length.

Longitudinal magnetization equivalent to that

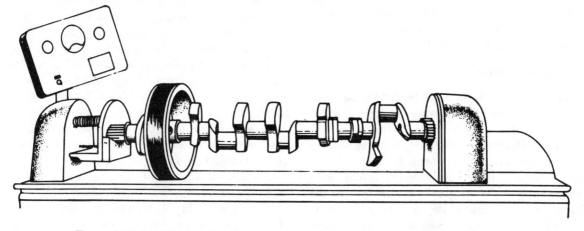

FIGURE 10–6. Longitudinal magnetization of crankshaft (solenoid method).

471

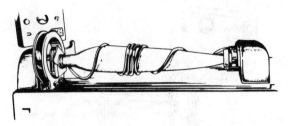

FIGURE 10–7. Longitudinal magnetization of steel propeller blade (cable method).

obtained by a solenoid may be accomplished by wrapping a flexible electrical conductor around the part, as shown in figure 10–7. Although this method is not as convenient, it has the advantage that the coils conform more closely to the shape of the part, thus producing somewhat more uniform magnetization.

The flexible coil method is also useful for large or irregularly shaped parts for which standard solenoids are not available.

Effect of Flux Density

The effectiveness of the magnetic particle inspection also depends on the flux density or field strength at the surface of the part when the indicating medium is applied. As the flux density in the part is increased, the sensitivity of the test increases because of the greater flux leakages at discontinuities and the resulting improved formation of magnetic particle patterns.

Excessively high flux densities, however, may form nonrelevant indications; for example, patterns of the grain flow in the material. These indications will interfere with the detection of patterns resulting from significant discontinuities. It is therefore necessary to use a field strength high enough to reveal all possible harmful discontinuities, but not strong enough to produce confusing nonrelevant indications.

Magnetizing Methods

When a part is magnetized, the field strength in the part increases to a maximum for the particular magnetizing force and remains at this maximum as long as the magnetizing force is maintained.

When the magnetizing force is removed, the field strength decreases to a lower residual value depending on the magnetic properties of the material and the shape of the part. These magnetic characteristics determine whether the continuous or residual method is used in magnetizing the part.

In the continuous inspection method, the part is magnetized and the indicating medium applied while the magnetizing force is maintained. The available flux density in the part is thus at a maximum. The maximum value of flux depends directly upon the magnetizing force and the permeability of the material of which the part is made.

The continuous method may be used in practically all circular and longitudinal magnetization procedures. The continuous procedure provides greater sensitivity than the residual procedure, particularly in locating subsurface discontinuities. The highly critical nature of aircraft parts and assemblies and the necessity for subsurface inspection in many applications have resulted in the continuous method being more widely used.

Inasmuch as the continuous procedure will reveal more nonsignificant discontinuities than the residual procedure, careful and intelligent interpretation and evaluation of discontinuities revealed by this procedure are necessary.

The residual inspection procedure involves magnetization of the part and application of the indicating medium after the magnetizing force has been removed. This procedure relies on the residual or permanent magnetism in the part and is more practical than the continuous procedure when magnetization is accomplished by flexible coils wrapped around the part.

In general, the residual procedure is used only with steels which have been heat treated for stressed applications.

Identification of Indications

The correct evaluation of the character of indications is extremely important but is sometimes difficult to make from observation of the indications alone. The principal distinguishing features of indications are shape, buildup, width, and sharpness of outline. These characteristics, in general, are more valuable in distinguishing between types of discontinuities than in determining their severity. However, careful observation of the character of the magnetic particle pattern should always be included in the complete evaluation of the significance of an indicated discontinuity.

The most readily distinguished indications are those produced by cracks open to the surface. These discontinuities include fatigue cracks, heat-

472

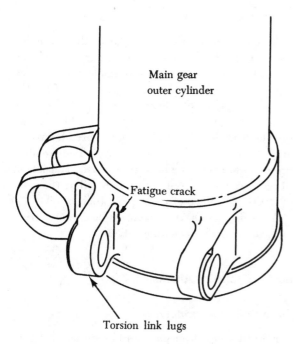

Main gear
outer cylinder

Fatigue crack

Torsion link lugs

FIGURE 10–8. Fatigue crack in a landing gear.

treat cracks, shrink cracks in welds and castings, and grinding cracks.

Fatigue cracks give sharp, clear patterns, generally uniform and unbroken throughout their length and with good buildup. They are often jagged in appearance, as compared with the straight indications of a seam, and may also change direction slightly in localized areas. Figure 10–8 illustrates a fatigue crack.

Fatigue cracks are found in parts that have been in service but are never found in new parts. They are usually in highly stressed areas of the part or where a stress concentration exists for some reason. It is important to recognize that even a small fatigue crack indicates positively that failure of the involved parts is in progress.

Heat-treat cracks have a smooth outline but are usually less clear and have less buildup than fatigue cracks. On thin sections, such as cylinder barrel walls, heat-treat cracks may give very heavy patterns (figure 10–9). These heat-treat cracks have a characteristic form, consisting of short jagged lines grouped together.

Shrink cracks give a sharp, clear pattern and the line is usually very jagged. Since the walls of shrink cracks are close together, their indications generally build up to less extent than do indications of fatigue cracks.

Grinding cracks are fine and sharp but seldom

have a buildup because of their limited depth. Grinding cracks vary from single line indications to a heavy network of lines. Grinding cracks are generally related to the direction of grinding. For example, the crack usually begins and continues at right angles to the motion of a grinding wheel, giving a rather symmetrical pattern. Indications of grinding cracks can frequently be identified by means of this relation.

Indications of seams are usually straight, sharp, and fine. They are often intermittent and sometimes have very little buildup.

Hairlines are very fine seams in which the faces of the seam have been forced very close together during fabrication. Hairline indications are very fine and sharp, with very little buildup. Discontinuities of this type are normally considered detrimental only in highly stressed parts.

Inclusions are nonmetallic materials, such as slag materials and chemical compounds, that have been trapped in the solidifying ingot. They are usually elongated and strung out as the ingot is worked in subsequent processing operations.

FIGURE 10–9. Heat-treat cracks on cylinder barrel wall.

473

Inclusions appear in parts in varying sizes and shapes, from stringers easily visible to the eye to particles only visible under magnification. In a finished part they may occur as either surface or subsurface discontinuities.

Indications of subsurface inclusions are usually broad and fuzzy. They are seldom continuous or of even width and density throughout their length. Larger inclusions, particularly those near or open to the surface, appear more clearly defined. Close examination, however, will generally reveal their lack of definition and the fact that the indication consists of several parallel lines rather than a single line. These characteristics will usually distinguish a heavy inclusion from a crack.

When cavities are located considerably below the surface of a part, the magnetic particle test is not a reliable method of detecting them. If any indication is obtained, it is likely to be an indistinct and inexact outline of the cavity, with the magnetic substance tending to distribute over the whole area rather than to outline clearly the boundary of the discontinuity. Defects of this type are detected more easily by radiographic procedures.

Laps may be identified by their form and location. They tend to occur at the ends or flash line of a forging. The indications are usually heavy and irregular. Islands and short branch indications usually break a lap indication of any length, and the scale included in the lap invariably gives fuzzy or small fernlike patterns stemming from the main indication.

When an ingot solidifies, the distribution of the various elements or compounds, generally, is not uniform throughout the mass of the ingot. Marked segregations of some constituents may thus occur. As the ingot is forged and then rolled, these segregations are elongated and reduced in cross section. Upon subsequent processing, they may appear as very thin parallel lines or bands, known as banding.

Segregation in the form of banding is sometimes revealed by magnetic particle inspection, particularly when high field strengths are used. Banding is not normally considered significant.

The most serious forms of segregation probably occur in castings. Here the basic condition of the metal remains unaltered in the finished part, and any segregations occur as they were originally formed. They may vary in size and will normally be irregular in shape. They may occur on or below the surface.

Magnaglo Inspection

Magnaglo inspection is similar to the preceding method, except that a fluorescent particle solution is used and the inspection is made under black light. Efficiency of inspection is increased by the neon-like glow of defects, and smaller flaw indications are more readily seen. This is an excellent method for use on gears, threaded parts, and aircraft engine components. The reddish brown liquid spray or bath that is used consists of Magnaglo paste mixed with a light oil at the ratio of .10 to .25 ounce of paste per gallon of oil.

After inspection, the part must be demagnetized and rinsed with a cleaning solvent.

MAGNETIZING EQUIPMENT

Fixed Unit (Nonportable)

A fixed general-purpose unit is shown in figure 10–10. This unit provides direct current for wet continuous or residual magnetization procedures. Either circular or longitudinal magnetization may be used, and it may be powered with rectified a.c. as well as d.c.

The contact heads provide the electrical terminals for circular magnetization. One head is fixed in position. Its contact plate is mounted on a shaft surrounded by a pressure spring, in order that the plate may be moved longitudinally. The plate is maintained in the extended position by the spring until pressure transmitted through the work from the movable head forces it back.

The movable head slides horizontally in longitudinal guides and is motor driven. It is controlled by a switch. The spring allows sufficient overrun of the motor-driven head to avoid jamming it and also provides pressure on the ends of the work to ensure good electrical contact.

A plunger-operated switch in the fixed head cuts out the forward motion circuit of the movable head motor when the spring has been properly compressed.

In some units the movable head is hand operated, and the contact plate is sometimes arranged for operation by an air ram. Both contact plates are fitted with various fixtures for supporting the work.

The magnetizing circuit is closed by depressing a pushbutton on the front of the unit. It is set to open automatically, usually after about one-half second.

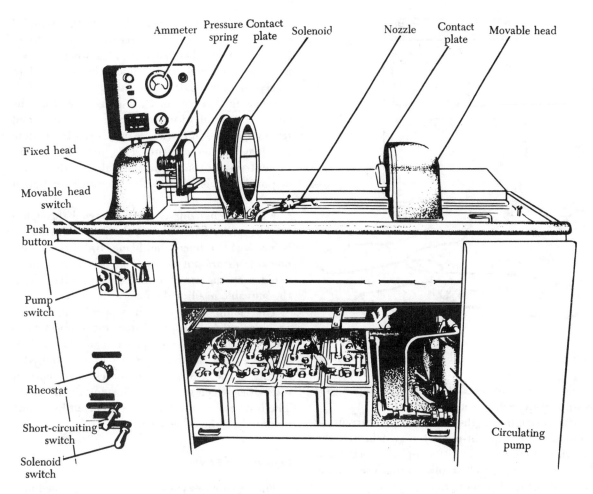

Ammeter Pressure Contact Solenoid   Nozzle Contact Movable head
          spring plate   plate

Fixed head

Movable head
switch

Push
button

Pump
switch

Rheostat

Short-circuiting
switch

Solenoid
switch

Circulating
pump

FIGURE 10–10.   Fixed general-purpose magnetizing unit.

The strength of the magnetizing current may be set manually to the desired value by means of the rheostat or increased to the capacity of the unit by the rheostat short-circuiting switch. The current utilized is indicated on the ammeter.

Longitudinal magnetization is produced by the solenoid, which moves in the same guide rail as the movable head and is connected in the electrical circuit by means of a switch.

The suspension liquid is contained in a sump tank and is agitated and circulated by a pump. The suspension is applied to the work through a nozzle. The suspension drains from the work through the wooden grill into a collecting pan that leads back to the sump. The circulating pump is operated by a pushbutton switch.

General-Purpose Portable Unit

It is often necessary to perform the magnetic particle inspection at locations where fixed general-purpose equipment is not available or to perform an inspection on members of aircraft structures without removing them from the aircraft. This has occurred, particularly on landing gears and engine mounts suspected of having developed cracks in service. Equipment suitable for this purpose, supplying both alternating-current and direct-current magnetization, is available. A typical example is shown in figure 10–11.

This unit is only a source of magnetizing and demagnetizing current and does not provide a means for supporting the work or applying the suspension. It operates on 200-volt, 60-cycle, alternating current and contains a rectifier for producing direct current when required.

The magnetizing current is supplied through the flexible cables. The cable terminals may be fitted with prods, as shown in the illustration, or with contact clamps. Circular magnetization may be developed by using either the prods or clamps.

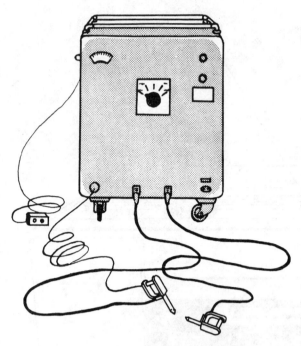

FIGURE 10–11. General-purpose portable unit.

Longitudinal magnetization is developed by wrapping the cable around the part.

The strength of the magnetizing current is controlled by an eight-point tap switch, and the length of time for which it is applied is regulated by an automatic cutoff similar to that used in the standard general-purpose unit.

This portable unit also serves as a demagnetizer and supplies high-amperage, low-voltage, alternating current for this purpose. For demagnetization, the alternating current is passed through the part and gradually reduced by means of a current reducer.

In testing large structures with flat surfaces where current must be passed through the part, it is sometimes impossible to use contact clamps. In such cases contact prods are used.

Prods can be used with the standard general-purpose unit as well as the portable unit. The part or assembly being tested may be suspended above the standard unit and the suspension hosed onto the area; excessive suspension drains into the tank. The dry procedure may also be used.

Prods should be held firmly against the surface being tested. There is a tendency for a high-amperage current to cause burning at contact areas, but with proper care, such burning will usually be slight. For applications where prod magnetization is acceptable, slight burning is normally not objectionable.

When it is desired to use cable with the standard general-purpose unit as a source of power, a contact block is useful. This consists of a wooden block fitted at each end with copper plates spaced to receive the terminals of the cable.

When the contact block is placed between the heads of a standard unit, the regular controls and timing switches of the unit can be used to regulate the magnetizing current. This provides a convenient way of connecting the cable to the source of power and eliminates the necessity for bolted connections.

When magnetizing current is passed through a steel propeller blade for circular magnetization, it is possible to burn the blade tip if necessary precautions are not taken. This possibility can be avoided by the use of a hinged clamp attached to the movable head of the inspection unit.

The clamp is lined with copper braid, which provides good electrical contact by conforming to the curvature of the propeller blade faces. This fixture avoids electrical contact at the thin edge of the blade tip and eliminates high current intensities which may cause burning at the point. The butt end of the blade is supported by a plug mounted on the other head.

Indicating Mediums

The various types of indicating mediums available for magnetic particle inspection may be divided into two general types: wet process materials and dry process materials. The basic requirement for any indicating medium is that it produce acceptable indications of discontinuities in parts.

The contrast provided by a particular indicating medium on the background or part surface is particularly important. The colors most extensively used are black and red for the wet procedure; and black, red, and gray for the dry procedure.

For acceptable operation, the indicating medium must be of high permeability and low retentivity. High permeability ensures that a minimum of magnetic energy will be required to attract the material to flux leakage caused by discontinuities. Low retentivity ensures that the mobility of the magnetic particles will not be hindered; that is, by the particles themselves becoming magnetized and attracting one another.

The magnetic substance for the wet process is usually supplied in paste form. The red paste improves visibility on dark surfaces. Although the exact amount of magnetic substance to be added may vary somewhat, a concentration of 2 ounces of paste per gallon of liquid vehicle has been found generally acceptable. The paste must not be dumped into the suspension liquid in the tank, since the unit agitator and pump cannot be depended on to do the mixing.

The proper procedure for preparing a suspension is to place the correct amount of paste in a container and add small quantities of the suspension liquid, working each addition with a flat paddle until the paste has been diluted to a uniform watery mixture which can then be poured into the tank.

It is important that new magnetic substance always be used in preparing suspensions. When the suspension becomes discolored or otherwise contaminated to the extent that the formation of magnetic particle patterns is interfered with, the unit should be drained, cleaned, and refilled with clean suspension.

DEMAGNETIZATION

The permanent magnetism remaining after inspection must be removed by a demagnetization operation if the part is to be returned to service. Parts of operating mechanisms must be demagnetized to prevent magnetized parts from attracting filings, grindings, or chips inadvertently left in the system, or steel particles resulting from operational wear.

An accumulation of such particles on a magnetized part may cause scoring of bearings or other working parts. Parts of the airframe must be demagnetized so they will not affect instruments.

Demagnetization between successive magnetizing operations is not normally required unless experience indicates that omission of this operation results in decreased effectiveness for a particular application. Previously, this operation was considered necessary to remove completely the existing field in a part before it was magnetized in a different direction.

Demagnetization may be accomplished in a number of different ways. Possibly the most convenient procedure for aircraft parts involves subjecting the part to a magnetizing force that is continually reversing in direction and, at the same time, gradually decreasing in strength. As the decreasing magnetizing force is applied first in one direction and then the other, the magnetization of the part also decreases.

Standard Demagnetizing Practice

The simplest procedure for developing a reversing and gradually decreasing magnetizing force in a part involves the use of a solenoid coil energized by alternating current. As the part is moved away from the alternating field of the solenoid, the magnetism in the part gradually decreases.

A demagnetizer as near the size of the work as practicable should be used; and, for maximum effectiveness, small parts should be held as close to the inner wall of the coil as possible.

Parts that do not readily lose their magnetism should be passed slowly in and out of the demagnetizer several times and, at the same time, tumbled or rotated in various directions. Allowing a part to remain in the demagnetizer with the current on accomplishes very little practical demagnetization.

The effective operation in the demagnetizing procedure is that of slowly moving the part out of the coil and away from the magnetizing field strength. As the part is withdrawn, it should be kept directly opposite the opening until it is 1 or 2 feet from the demagnetizer.

The demagnetizing current should never be cut off until the part is 1 or 2 feet from the opening; otherwise, the part will usually be re-magnetized.

Another procedure used with portable units is to pass alternating current through the part being demagnetized and gradually reduce the current to zero.

DYE-PENETRANT INSPECTION

Penetrant inspection is a nondestructive test for defects open to the surface in parts made of any nonporous material. It is used with equal success on such metals as aluminum, magnesium, brass, copper, cast iron, stainless steel, and titanium. It may also be used on ceramics, plastics, molded rubber, and glass.

Penetrant inspection will detect such defects as surface cracks or porosity. These defects may be caused by fatigue cracks, shrinkage cracks, shrinkage porosity, cold shuts, grinding and heat-treat cracks, seams, forging laps, and bursts. Penetrant inspection will also indicate a lack of bond between joined metals.

The main disadvantage of penetrant inspection is that the defect must be open to the surface in order to let the penetrant get into the defect. For this reason, if the part in question is made of material which is magnetic, the use of magnetic particle inspection is generally recommended.

Penetrant inspection depends for its success upon a penetrating liquid entering the surface opening and remaining in that opening, making it clearly visible to the operator. It calls for visual examination of the part after it has been processed, but the visibility of the defect is increased so that it can be detected. Visibility of the penetrating material is increased by the addition of dye which may be either one or two types—visible or fluorescent.

The visible penetrant kit consists of dye penetrant, dye remover-emulsifier and developer. The fluorescent penetrant inspection kit contains a black light assembly as well as spray cans of penetrant, cleaner, and developer. The light assembly consists of a power transformer, a flexible power cable, and a hand-held lamp. Due to its size, the lamp may be used in almost any position or location.

Briefly, the steps to be taken when performing a penetrant inspection are:

1. Thorough cleaning of the metal surface.
2. Applying penetrant.
3. Removing penetrant with remover-emulsifier or cleaner.
4. Drying the part.
5. Applying the developer.
6. Inspecting and interpreting results.

Interpretation of Results

The success and reliability of a penetrant inspection depends upon the thoroughness with which the part was prepared. Several basic principles applying to penetrant inspection are:

1. The penetrant must enter the defect in order to form an indication. It is important to allow sufficient time so the penetrant can fill the defect. The defect must be clean and free of contaminating materials so that the penetrant is free to enter.
2. If all penetrant is washed out of a defect, an indication cannot be formed. During the washing or rinsing operation, prior to development, it is possible that the penetrant will be removed from within the defect, as well as from the surface.
3. Clean cracks are usually easy to detect. Surface openings that are uncontaminated, regardless of how fine, are seldom difficult to detect with the penetrant inspection.
4. The smaller the defect, the longer the penetrating time. Fine crack-like apertures

require a longer penetrating time than defects such as pores.
5. When the part to be inspected is made of a material susceptible to magnetism, it should be inspected by a magnetic particle inspection method, if the equipment is available.
6. Visible penetrant-type developer, when applied to the surface of a part, will dry to a smooth, even, white coating. As this developer dries, bright red indications will appear where there are surface defects. If no red indications appear, there are no surface defects.
7. When conducting the fluorescent penetrant-type inspection, the defects will show up (under black light) as a brilliant yellow-green color and the sound areas will appear deep blue-violet.
8. It is possible to examine an indication of a defect and to determine its cause as well as its extent. Such an appraisal can be made if something is known about the manufacturing processes to which the part has been subjected.

The size of the indication, or accumulation of penetrant, will show the extent of the defect, and the brilliance will be a measure of its depth. Deep cracks will hold more penetrant and, therefore, will be broader and more brillant. Very fine openings can hold only small amounts of penetrants and, therefore, will appear as fine lines. Figure 10–12 shows some of the types of defects that can be located using dry penetrant.

False Indications

With the penetrant inspection there are no false indications in the sense that such things occur in the magnetic particle inspection. There are, however, two conditions which may create accumulations of penetrant that are sometimes confused with true surface cracks and discontinuities.

The first condition involves indications caused by poor washing. If all the surface penetrant is not removed in the washing or rinsing operation following the penetrant dwell time, the unremoved penetrant will be visible. Evidences of incomplete washing are usually easy to identify since the penetrant is in broad areas rather than in the sharp patterns found with true indications. When accumulations of unwashed penetrant are found on a part, the part should be completely repro-

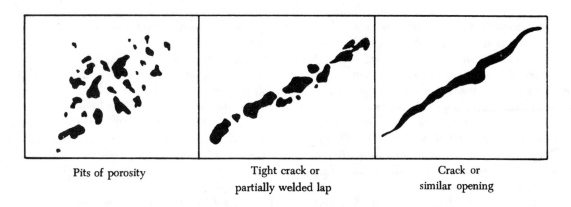

| Pits of porosity | Tight crack or partially welded lap | Crack or similar opening |

FIGURE 10–12. Types of defects.

cessed. Degreasing is recommended for removal of all traces of the penetrant.

False indications may also be created where parts press-fit to each other. If a wheel is press-fit onto a shaft, penetrant will show an indication at the fit line. This is perfectly normal since the two parts are not meant to be welded together. Indications of this type are easy to identify since they are so regular in form and shape.

RADIOGRAPHY

X- and gamma radiations, because of their unique ability to penetrate material and disclose discontinuities, have been applied to the radiographic (X-ray) inspection of metal fabrications and nonmetallic products.

The penetrating radiation is projected through the part to be inspected and produces an invisible or latent image in the film. When processed, the film becomes a radiograph or shadow picture of the object. This inspection medium, in a portable unit, provides a fast and reliable means for checking the integrity of airframe structures and engines.

Radiographic inspection techniques are used to locate defects or flaws in airframe structures or engines with little or no disassembly. This is in marked contrast to other types of nondestructive testing, which usually require removal, disassembly, and stripping of paint from the suspected part before it can be inspected. Due to the nature of X-ray, extensive training is required to become a qualified radiographer, and only qualified radiographers are allowed to operate the X-ray units.

Three major steps in the X-ray process discussed in subsequent paragraphs are: (1) Exposure to radiation, including preparation, (2) processing of film, and (3) interpretation of the radiograph.

Preparation and Exposure

The factors of radiographic exposure are so interdependent that it is necessary to consider all factors for any particular radiographic exposure. These factors include, but are not limited to, the following:

(a) Material thickness and density.
(b) Shape and size of the object.
(c) Type of defect to be detected.
(d) Characteristics of X-ray machine used.
(e) The exposure distance.
(f) The exposure angle.
(g) Film characteristics.
(h) Types of intensifying screen, if used.

Knowledge of the X-ray unit's capabilities should form a background for the other exposure factors. In addition to the unit rating in kilovoltage, the size, portability, ease of manipulation, and exposure particulars of the available equipment should be thoroughly understood.

Previous experience on similar objects is also very helpful in the determination of the overall exposure techniques. A log or record of previous exposures will provide specific data as a guide for future radiographs.

Film Processing

After exposure to X-rays, the latent image on the film is made permanently visible by processing it successively through a developer chemical solution, an acid bath, and a fixing bath, followed by a clear water wash.

The film consists of a radiation-sensitive silver salt suspended in gelatin to form an emulsion. The developer solution converts radition-affected elements in the emulsion to black metallic silver.

479

These black metallic particles form the image. The longer the film remains in the developer, the more metallic silver is formed, causing the image to become progressively darker. Excessive time in the developer solution results in overdevelopment.

An acid rinse bath, sometimes referred to as a stop bath, instantly neutralizes the action of the developer and stops further development. Due to the soft emulsion and the nonabsorbent quality of the base of most negative materials, only a very weak acid bath is required.

The purpose of the fixing bath is to arrest the image at the desired state of development. When a radiation-sensitive material is removed from the developing solution, the emulsion still contains a considerable amount of silver salts which have not been affected by the developing agents. These salts are still sensitive, and if they are allowed to remain in the emulsion, ordinary light will ultimately darken them and obscure the image. Obviously, if this occurs, the film will be useless.

The fixing bath prevents this discoloration by dissolving the salts of silver from the developed free-silver image. Therefore, to make an image permanent, it is necessary to fix the radiation-sensitive material by removing all of the unaffected silver salt from the emulsion.

After fixing, a thorough water rinse is necessary to remove the fixing agent which, if allowed to remain, will slowly combine with the silver image to produce brownish-yellow stains of silver sulfide, causing the image to fade.

> NOTE: All processing is conducted under a subdued light of a color to which the film is not readily sensitive.

Radiographic Interpretation

From the standpoint of quality assurance, radiographic interpretation is the most important phase of radiography. It is during this phase that an error in judgment can produce disastrous consequences. The efforts of the whole radiographic process are centered in this phase; the part or structure is either accepted or rejected. Conditions of unsoundness or other defects which are overlooked, not understood, or improperly interpreted can destroy the purpose and efforts of radiography and can jeopardize the structural integrity of an entire aircraft. A particular danger is the false sense of security imparted by the acceptance of a part or structure based on improper interpretation.

As a first impression, radiographic interpretation may seem simple, but a closer analysis of the problem soon dispels this impression. The subject of interpretation is so varied and complex that it cannot be covered adequately in this type of document. Instead, this chapter will give only a brief review of basic requirements for radiographic interpretation, including some descriptions of common defects.

Experience has shown that, whenever possible, radiographic interpretation should be conducted close to the radiographic operation. It is helpful, when viewing radiographs, to have access to the material being tested. The radiograph can thus be compared directly with the material being tested, and indications due to such things as surface condition or thickness variations can be immediately determined.

The following paragraphs present several factors which must be considered when analyzing a radiograph.

There are three basic categories of flaws: voids, inclusions, and dimensional irregularities. The last category, dimensional irregularities, is not pertinent to these discussions because its prime factor is one of degree, and radiography is not that exacting. Voids and inclusions may appear on the radiograph in a variety of forms ranging from a two-dimensional plane to a three-dimensional sphere. A crack, tear, or cold shut will most nearly resemble a two-dimensional plane, whereas a cavity will look like a three-dimensional sphere. Other types of flaws, such as shrink, oxide inclusions, porosity, etc., will fall somewhere between these two extremes of form.

It is important to analyze the geometry of a flaw, especially for such things as the sharpness of terminal points. For example, in a crack-like flaw the terminal points will appear much sharper than they will for a sphere-like flaw, such as a gas cavity. Also, material strength may be adversely affected by flaw shape. A flaw having sharp points could establish a source of localized stress concentration. Spherical flaws affect material strength to a far lesser degree than do sharp-pointed flaws. Specifications and reference standards usually stipulate that sharp-pointed flaws, such as cracks, cold shuts, etc., are cause for rejection.

Material strength is also affected by flaw size. A metallic component of a given area is designed to carry a certain load plus a safety factor. Reducing this area by including a large flaw weakens the part and reduces the safety factor. Some flaws are often permitted in components because of these safety factors; in this case, the interpreter must determine the degree of tolerance or imperfection specified by the design engineer. Both flaw size and flaw shape should be considered carefully, since small flaws with sharp points can be just as bad as large flaws with no sharp points.

Another important consideration in flaw analysis is flaw location. Metallic components are subjected to numerous and varied forces during their effective service life. Generally, the distribution of these forces is not equal in the component or part, and certain critical areas may be rather highly stressed. The interpreter must pay special attention to these areas. Another aspect of flaw location is that certain types of discontinuities close to one another may potentially serve as a source of stress concentrations; therefore, this type of situation should be closely scrutinized.

An inclusion is a type of flaw which contains entrapped material. Such flaws may be either of greater or lesser density than the item being radiographed. The foregoing discussions on flaw shape, size, and location apply equally to inclusions and to voids. In addition, a flaw containing foreign material could become a source of corrosion.

Radiation Hazards

Radiation from X-ray units and radioisotope sources is destructive to living tissue. It is universally recognized that in the use of such equipment, adequate protection must be provided. Personnel must keep outside the primary X-ray beam at all times.

Radiation produces changes in all matter through which it passes. This is also true of living tissue. When the radiation strikes the molecules of the body, the effect may be no more than to dislodge a few electrons, but an excess of these changes could cause irreparable harm. When a complex organism is exposed to radiation, the degree of damage, if any, depends on which of its body cells have been changed.

The more vital organs are in the center of the body; therefore, the more penetrating radiation is likely to be the most harmful in these areas. The skin usually absorbs most of the radiation and, therefore, reacts earliest to radiation.

If the whole body is exposed to a very large dose of radiation, it could result in death. In general, the type and severity of the pathological effects of radiation depend on the amount of radiation received at one time and the percentage of the total body exposed. The smaller doses of radiation may cause blood and intestinal disorders in a short period of time. The more delayed effects are leukemia and cancer. Skin damage and loss of hair are also possible results of exposure to radiation.

ULTRASONIC TESTING

Ultrasonic detection equipment has made it possible to locate defects in all types of materials without damaging the material being inspected. Minute cracks, checks, and voids, too small to be seen by X-ray, are located by ultrasonic inspection. An ultrasonic test instrument requires access to only one surface of the material to be inspected and can be used with either straight line or angle beam testing techniques.

Two basic methods are used for ultrasonic inspection. The first of these methods is immersion testing. In this method of inspection, the part under examination and the search unit are totally immersed in a liquid couplant, which may be water or any other suitable fluid.

The second method is called contact testing, which is readily adapted to field use, and is the method discussed in this chapter. In this method the part under examination and the search unit are coupled with a viscous material, liquid or a paste, which wets both the face of the search unit and the material under examination.

There are two basic ultrasonic systems: (1) Pulsed and (2) resonance. The pulsed system may be either echo or through-transmission; the echo is the most versatile of the two pulse systems.

Pulse-Echo

Flaws are detected by measuring the amplitude of signals reflected and the time required for these signals to travel between specific surfaces and the discontinuity. (See figure 10–13.)

The time base, which is triggered simultaneously with each transmission pulse, causes a spot to sweep across the screen of the CRT (Cathode ray tube). The spot sweeps from left to right across the face of the scope 50 to 5,000 times per second, or higher if required for high-speed automated scanning. Due to the speed of the cycle of

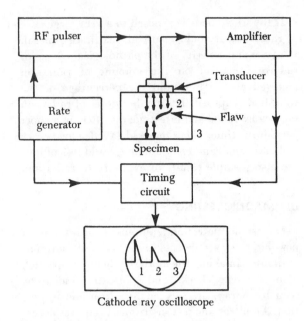

FIGURE 10–13. Block diagram of basic pulse-echo
system.

transmitting and receiving, the picture on the
oscilloscope appears to be stationary.

A few microseconds after the sweep is initiated,
the rate generator electrically excites the pulser
and the pulser in turn emits an electrical pulse.
The transducer converts this pulse into a short
train of ultrasonic sound waves. If the interfaces
of the transducer and the specimen are properly
orientated, the ultrasound will be reflected back
to the transducer when it reaches the internal flaw
and the opposite surface of the specimen. The time
interval between the transmission of the initial
impulse and the reception of the signals from
within the specimen is measured by the timing
circuits. The reflected pulse received by the
transducer is amplified, then transmitted to the
oscilloscope, where the pulse received from the
flaw is displayed on the CRT screen. The pulse is
displayed in the same relationship to the front and
back pulses as the flaw is in relation to the front
and back surfaces of the specimen. (See figure
10–14.)

The Reflectoscope is a pulse-echo type instrument. The Reflectoscope can be used for the
detection of defects such as cracks, folds, inclusions, delaminations, partial welds, voids, shrinks,
porosity, flaking, and other subsurface defects.

The principle of operation is pictured in figure
10–15, where electrical pulses are transformed
by the crystal into ultrasonic vibrations

which are transmitted into the material. The
portion of the electrical pulse delivered to the
cathode-ray tube causes an initial pulse indication,
as shown in figure 10–15, view A. The back
reflection has formed in view B, the vibrations
having traveled to the bottom of the part and
reflected back to the searching unit, which
transforms them back into electrical pulses. The
screen's vertical indication of their return is known
as the "first back-reflection indication." If a defect
is present (figure 10–15, view C), a portion of the
vibrations traveling through the material is
reflected from the defect, causing an additional
indication on the screen. The horizontal-sweep
travel indicates the time elapsed since the vibrations left the crystal.

This type of operation, referred to as straight-
beam testing, is suitable for the detection of flaws
whose planes are parallel to the plane of the part.
By means of angle-beam testing, also referred to
as shear-wave testing, the usefulness of the
Reflectoscope includes the following:

1. Flaws whose planes lie at an angle to the
   plane of the part.
2. Discontinuities in areas that cannot be
   reached with the standard straight-beam
   technique.
3. Some internal defects in plate and sheet
   stock.
4. Some types of internal defects in tubing, pipe
   and bar stock, such as inclusions and small
   cracks near the surface.
5. Cracks in parent metal resulting from
   welding.
6. Some defects in welds.

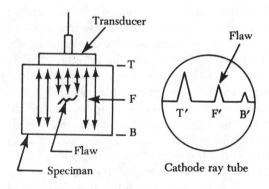

FIGURE 10–14. Oscilloscope display in relationship to flaw location.

482

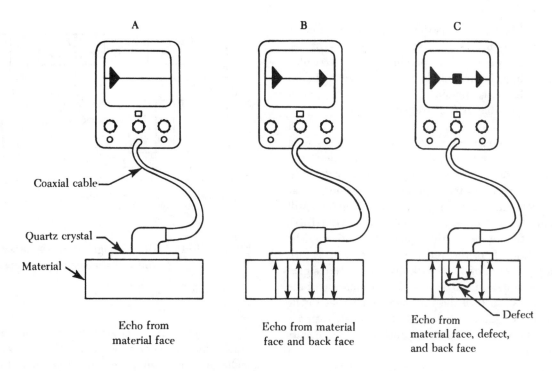

A

B

C

Coaxial cable

Quartz crystal

Material

Echo from
material face

Echo from material
face and back face

Echo from
material face, defect,
and back face

Defect

FIGURE 10–15.   Reflectoscope operation—straight-beam testing.

Angle-beam testing differs from straight-beam testing only in the manner in which the ultrasonic waves pass through the material being tested. As shown in figure 10–16, the beam is projected into the material at an acute angle to the surface by means of a crystal cut at an angle and mounted in plastic. The beam or a portion thereof reflects successively from the surfaces of the material or any other discontinuity, including the edge of the piece. In straight-beam testing, the horizontal distance on the screen between the initial pulse and the first back reflection represents the thickness of the piece; while in angle-beam testing, this distance represents the width of the material between the searching unit and the opposite edge of the piece.

Resonance System

This system differs from the pulse method in that the frequency of transmission is, or can be, continuously varied. The resonance method is principally used for thickness measurements when the two sides of the material being tested are smooth and parallel. The point at which the frequency matches the resonance point of the

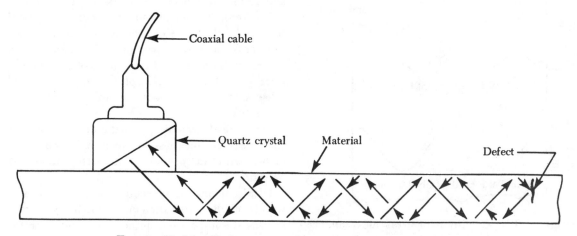

Coaxial cable

Quartz crystal   Material

Defect

FIGURE 10–16.   Reflectoscope operation—angle-beam testing.

483

material being tested is the thickness-determining factor. It is necessary that the frequency of the ultrasonic waves, corresponding to a particular dial setting, be accurately known. Checks should be made with standard test blocks to guard against possible drift of frequency.

If the frequency of an ultrasonic wave is such that its wavelength is twice the thickness of a specimen (fundamental frequency), then the reflected wave will arrive back at the transducer in the same phase as the original transmission so that strengthening of the signal, or a resonance, will occur. If the frequency is increased so that three times the wavelength equals four times the thickness, then the reflected signal will return completely out of phase with the transmitted signal and cancellation will occur. Further increase of the frequency, so that the wavelength is equal to the thickness again, gives a reflected signal in phase with the transmitted signal and resonance occurs once more.

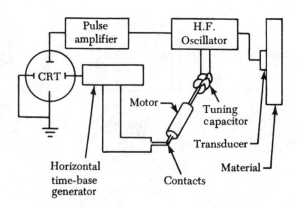

FIGURE 10–18. Block diagram of resonance thickness measuring system.

By starting at the fundamental frequency and gradually increasing the frequency, the successive cancellations and resonances can be noted and the readings used to check the fundamental frequency reading. (See figure 10–17.)

In some instruments, the oscillator circuit contains a motor-driven capacitor which changes the frequency of the oscillator. (See figure 10–18.) In other instruments, the frequency is changed by electronic means.

The change in frequency is synchronized with the horizontal sweep of a CRT. The horizontal axis thus represents a frequency range. If the frequency range contains resonances, the circuitry is arranged to present these vertically. Calibrated transparent scales are then placed in front of the tube, and the thickness can be read directly. The instruments normally operate between 0.25 mc. and 10 mc. in four or five bands.

The resonant thickness instrument can be used to test the thickness of such metals as steel, cast iron, brass, nickel, copper, silver, lead, aluminum, and magnesium. In addition, areas of corrosion or wear on tanks, tubing, airplane wing skins, and other structures or products can be located and evaluated.

Direct-reading, dial-operated units are available that measure thickness between .025 inch and 3 inches with an accuracy of better than ±1 percent.

Ultrasonic inspection requires a skilled operator who is familiar with the equipment being used as well as the inspection method to be used for the many different parts being tested.

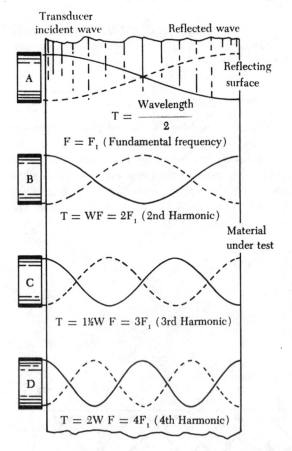

FIGURE 10–17. Conditions of ultrasonic resonance in a metal plate.

484

EDDY CURRENT TESTING

Electromagnetic analysis is a term which describes the broad spectrum of electronic test methods involving the intersection of magnetic fields and circulatory currents. The most widely used technique is the eddy current.

Eddy currents are composed of free electrons, which are made to "drift" through metal, under the influence of an induced electromagnetic field.

Eddy current is used in aircraft maintenance to inspect jet engine-turbine shaft and veins, wing skins, wheels, bolt holes, and spark plug bores for cracks, heat or frame damage. In aircraft manufacturing plants, eddy current is used to inspect castings, stampings, machine parts, forgings, and extrusions.

Basic Principles

When an alternating current is passed through a coil it develops a magnetic field around the coil which in turn induces a voltage of opposite polarity in the coil and opposes the flow of original current. If this coil is placed so that the magnetic field passes through an electrically conducting specimen, eddy currents will be induced into the specimen. The eddy currents create their own field which varies the original field's opposition to the flow of original current. Thus the specimen's susceptibility to eddy currents determine the current flow through the coil (see figure 10–19).

The magnitude and phase of this counter field is dependent primarily upon the resistivity and permeability of the specimen under consideration, and it is this fact that enables us to make a qualitative determination of various physical properties of the test material. The interaction of the eddy current field with the original field results is a power change that can be measured by utilizing electronic circuitry similar to a wheatstone bridge.

The specimen is either placed in or passed through the field of an electromagnetic induction coil, and its effect on the impedance of the coil or on the voltage output of one or more test coils is observed. The process—whereby electric fields are made to explore a test piece for various conditions—involves the transmission of energy through the specimen much like the transmission of X-rays, heat, or ultrasound. In the transmission of X-rays, heat, or ultrasound, the energy flows in beams having a recognizable direction and intensity and obeys the laws of absorption, reflection, diffraction, and diffusion. Receiver elements can be placed into the beams and a direct measurement of energy flow is possible. However, in electromagnetic tests, the energy distributes itself in a vaguely known manner and undergoes a transformation in the process, from magnetic to electric energy, and subsequently, back to magnetic energy. Since the induced currents flow in closed circuits, it is neither convenient nor generally possible, to intercept them at the specimen boundaries.

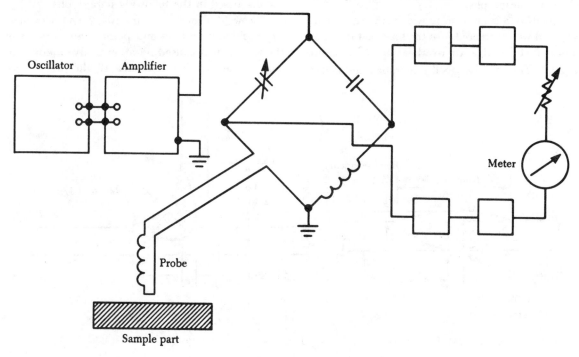

FIGURE 10–19. Eddy current inspection circuit.

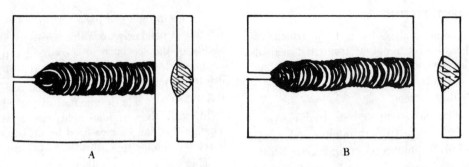

FIGURE 10–20.   Examples of good welds.

VISUAL INSPECTION

Nondestructive testing by visual means is the oldest method of inspection. Defects which would escape the naked eye can be magnified so they will be visible. Telescopes, borescopes, and magnifying glasses aid in performing visual inspection.

A discussion of visual inspection in this chapter will be confined to judging the quality of completed welds by visual means. Although the appearance of the completed weld is not a positive indication of quality, it gives a good clue to the care used in making it.

A properly designed joint weld is stronger than the base metal which it joins. The characteristics of a properly welded joint are discussed in the following paragraphs.

A good weld is uniform in width; the ripples are even and well feathered into the base metal, which shows no burn due to overheating. (See figure 10–20.) The weld has good penetration and is free of gas pockets, porosity, or inclusions. The edges of the bead illustrated in figure 10–20 (B) are not in a straight line, yet the weld is good, since penetration is excellent.

Penetration is the depth of fusion in a weld. Thorough fusion is the most important characteristic which contributes to a sound weld. Penetration is affected by the thickness of the material to be joined, the size of the filler rod, and how it is added. In a butt weld the penetration should be 100 percent of the thickness of the base metal. On a fillet weld the penetration requirements are 25 to 50 percent of the thickness of the base metal. The width and depth of bead for a butt weld and fillet weld are shown in figure 10–21.

To assist further in determining the quality of a welded joint, several examples of incorrect welds are discussed in the following paragraphs.

The weld shown in figure 10–22 (A) was made too rapidly. The long and pointed appearance of the ripples was caused by an excessive amount of heat or an oxidizing flame. If the weld were

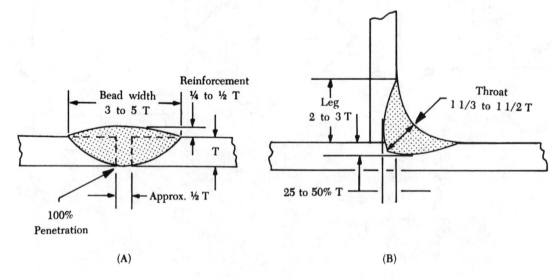

FIGURE 10–21.   (A) Butt weld and (B) fillet weld, showing width and depth of bead.

486

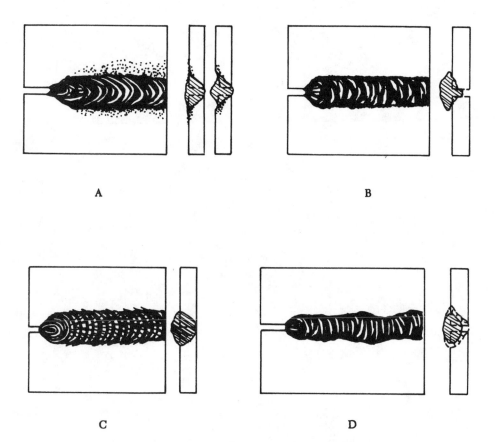

FIGURE 10–22.   Examples of poor welds.

cross-sectioned, it probably would disclose gas pockets, porosity, and slag inclusions.

Figure 10–22 (B) illustrates a weld that has improper penetration and cold laps caused by insufficient heat. It appears rough and irregular and its edges are not feathered into the base metal.

The puddle has a tendency to boil during the welding operation if an excessive amount of acetylene is used. This often leaves slight bumps along the center and craters at the finish of the weld. Cross-checks will be apparent if the body of the weld is sound. If the weld were cross-sectioned, pockets and porosity would be visible. Such a condition is shown in figure 10–22 (C).

A bad weld with irregular edges and considerable variation in the depth of penetration is shown in D of figure 10–22. It often has the appearance of a cold weld.

CHAPTER 11

GROUND HANDLING, SAFETY, AND SUPPORT EQUIPMENT

INTRODUCTION

Aircraft maintenance technicians devote a portion of their aviation career working with ground support equipment and ground handling of aircraft. The complexity of support equipment and the hazards involved in ground handling of expensive aircraft require that maintenance technicians possess a detailed knowledge of safe procedures used in aircraft servicing, taxiing, runup, and in the use of ground support equipment. The information provided in this chapter is intended as a general guide for working on all types of aircraft.

GENERAL

The following instructions cover the starting procedures for reciprocating, turboprop, and turbojet engines. These procedures are presented only as a general guide for familiarization with typical procedures and methods. Detailed instructions for starting a specific type of engine can be found in the manufacturer's instruction book.

Before starting an aircraft engine:

1. Position the aircraft to head into the prevailing wind to insure adequate air flow over the engine for cooling purposes.

2. Make sure that no property damage or personal injury will occur from the propeller or propeller blast.

3. If external electrical power is used for starting, make sure that it can be removed safely.

4. During any and all starting procedures a "fire guard" equipped with a suitable fire extinguisher shall be stationed in an appropriate place. ("Fire guard"—someone familiar with aircraft starting procedures. "Fire extinguisher"—a CO_2 extinguisher at least of 5-lb. capacity. "Appropriate place"—adjacent to the outboard side of the engine, in view of the pilot, and also where he can observe the engine/aircraft for indication of starting problems.)

5. If the aircraft is jet engine powered, the area in front of the jet inlet must be kept clear of personnel, property and/or debris. Also, the exhaust area must be kept clear.

6. These "before starting" procedures apply to all reciprocating, turbo-propeller and turbo-jet powerplants.

STARTING ENGINES

Reciprocating Engines

The following procedures are typical of those used to start reciprocating engines. There are, however, wide variations in the procedures for the many reciprocating engines. *No attempt should be made to use the methods presented here for actually starting an engine.* Instead, always refer to the procedures contained in the applicable manufacturer's instructions.

Reciprocating engines are capable of starting in fairly low temperatures without the use of engine heating or oil dilution, depending on the grade of oil used.

The various covers (wing, tail, cockpit, wheel, etc.) protecting the aircraft must be removed before attempting to turn the engine. External sources of electrical power should be used when starting engines equipped with electric starters. This eliminates an excessive burden on the aircraft battery. All unnecessary electrical equipment should be left off until the generators are furnishing electrical power to the aircraft power bus.

Before starting a radial engine that has been shut down for more than 30 minutes, check the ignition switch for off; turn the propeller three or four complete revolutions with the starter, or it may be pulled through by hand to detect a hydraulic lock if one is present.

Any liquid present in a cylinder is indicated by the abnormal effort required to rotate the propeller, or by the propeller stopping abruptly during rotation. Never use force to turn the propeller when a hydraulic lock is detected.

Sufficient force can be exerted on the crankshaft to bend or break a connecting rod if a lock is present.

To eliminate a lock, remove either the front or rear spark plug from the lower cylinders and pull the propeller through. Never attempt to clear the hydraulic lock by pulling the propeller through in the opposite direction to normal rotation. This tends to inject the liquid from the cylinder into the intake pipe. The liquid will be drawn back into the cylinder with the possibility of complete or partial lock occurring on the subsequent start.

To start the engine, proceed as follows:

1. Turn the auxiliary fuel pump on, if aircraft is so equipped.

2. Place the mixture control to the position recommended for the engine and carburetor combination being started. As a general rule, the mixture control should be in the "idle cutoff" position for pressure type carburetors and in the "full rich" position for float type carburetors.

   Many light aircraft are equipped with a mixture control pull rod which has no detented intermediate positions. When such controls are pushed in flush with the instrument panel, the mixture is set in the "full rich" position. Conversely, when the control rod is pulled all the way out, the carburetor is in the "idle cutoff" or "full lean" position. Unmarked intermediate positions between these two extremes can be selected by the operator to achieve any desired mixture setting.

3. Open the throttle to a position that will provide 1,000 to 1,200 r.p.m. (approximately ⅛ to ½ inch from the "closed" position).

4. Leave the preheat or alternate air (carburetor air) control in the "cold" position to prevent damage and fire in case of backfire. These auxiliary heating devices should be used after the engine warms up. They improve fuel vaporization, prevent fouling of the spark plugs, ice formation, and eliminate icing in the induction system.

5. Energize the starter after the propeller has made at least two complete revolutions, and turn the ignition switch on. On engines equipped with an induction vibrator, turn switch to the "both" position. When starting an engine that uses an impulse coupling magneto, turn the ignition switch to the "left" position. Place the ignition switch to "start" when the magneto incorporates a retard breaker assembly. Do not crank the engine continuously with the starter for more than 1 minute. Allow a 3- to 5-minute period for cooling the starter between successive attempts. Otherwise the starter may be burned out due to overheating.

6. Move the primer switch to "on" intermittently, or prime with one to three strokes of priming pump, depending on how the aircraft is equipped. When the engine begins to fire, hold the primer on while gradually opening throttle to obtain smooth operation.

   After the engine is operating smoothly on the primer, move the mixture control to the "full rich" position. Release the primer as soon as a drop in r.p.m. indicates the engine is receiving additional fuel from the carburetor.

Hand Cranking

If the aircraft has no self-starter, the engine must be started by swinging the propeller. The person who is turning the propeller calls, "fuel on, switch off, throttle closed, brakes on." The person operating the engine will check these items and repeat the phrase. The switch and throttle must not be touched again until the person swinging the prop calls "contact." The operator will repeat "contact" and then turn on the switch. Never turn on the switch and then call "contact."

When swinging the prop, a few simple precautions will help to avoid accidents. When touching a propeller, always assume that the ignition is on. The switches which control the magnetos operate on the principle of short-circuiting the current to turn the ignition off. If the switch is faulty, it can be in the "off" position and still permit current to flow in the magneto primary circuit.

Be sure the ground is firm. Slippery grass, mud, grease, or loose gravel can lead to a fall into or under the propeller. Never allow any portion of your body to get in the way of the propeller. This applies even though the engine is not being cranked.

Stand close enough to the propeller to be able to step away as it is pulled down. Stepping away after cranking is a safeguard in case the brakes fail. Do not stand in a position that requires leaning toward the propeller to reach it. This throws the body off balance and could cause you to fall into the blades when the engine starts.

In swinging the prop, always move the blade downward by pushing with the palms of the hand. Do not grip the blade with the fingers curled over the edge, since "kickback" may break them or draw your body in the blade path.

Excessive throttle opening and intermittent priming after the engine has fired are the principal causes of backfiring during starting. Gradual opening of the throttle while priming continuously will reduce the initial "over rich" mixture to a smooth running, best power mixture as the engine picks up speed. An engine operating on an "over rich" mixture is sluggish but will not backfire.

When starting an engine using a priming pump, move the mixture control into "full rich" position, if not previously placed there, when the engine begins to fire. If the engine fails to start immediately, return the mixture control to "idle cutoff" position. Failure to do so will create an excessive amount of fuel in the carburetor air scoop, constituting a fire hazard.

Avoid priming the engine before it is turned over by the starter. This can result in fires, scored or scuffed cylinders and pistons, and, in some cases, engine failures due to hydraulic lock. If the engine is inadvertently flooded or overprimed, turn the ignition switch off and move the throttle to the "full open" position. To rid the engine of the excess fuel, turn it over by hand or by the starter. If excessive force is needed to turn over the engine, stop immediately. Do not force rotation of the engine. If in doubt, remove the lower cylinder spark plugs. If very serious overloading has occurred, it may be necessary to remove the lower cylinder intake pipes. To reduce the likelihood of damage to the engine due to overpriming on some medium and large aircraft, the engine blower drain valves should be checked frequently for fouling or sticking.

Immediately after the engine starts, check the oil pressure indicator. If oil pressure does not show within 30 seconds, stop the engine and determine the trouble. If oil pressure is indicated, adjust the throttle to the aircraft manufacturer's specified r.p.m. for engine warm-up. Warm-up r.p.m. will usually be in the 1,000 to 1,300 r.p.m. range.

Most aircraft reciprocating engines are air cooled and depend on the forward speed of the aircraft to maintain proper cooling. Therefore, particular care

is necessary when operating these engines on the ground.

During all ground running, operate the engine with the propeller in full low pitch and headed into the wind with the cowling installed to provide the best degree of engine cooling. The engine instruments should be monitored closely at all times. Do not close the cowl flaps for engine warm-up; closing of the cowl flaps may cause the ignition harness to overheat. When warming up the engine, make sure that personnel, ground installations, equipment that may be damaged, or other aircraft are not in the propeller wash.

Extinguishing Engine Fires

In all cases a fireguard should stand by with a CO_2 fire extinguisher while the aircraft engine is being started. This is a necessary precaution against fire during the starting procedure. He should be familiar with the induction system of the engine so that in case of fire he can direct the CO_2 into the air intake of the engine to extinguish it. A fire could also occur in the exhaust system of the engine from liquid fuel being ignited in the cylinder and expelled during the normal rotation of the engine.

If an engine fire develops during the starting procedure, continue cranking to start the engine and blow out the fire. If the engine does not start and the fire continues to burn, discontinue the start attempt. The fireguard should extinguish the fire using the available equipment. The fireguard must observe all safety practices at all times while standing by during the starting procedure.

TURBOPROP ENGINES
Prestart Procedures

The various covers protecting the aircraft must be removed. Engine tailpipes should be carefully inspected for the presence of fuel or oil. A close visual inspection of all accessible parts of the engines and engine controls should be made, followed by an inspection of all nacelle areas to determine that all inspection and access plates are secured. Sumps should be checked for water. Air inlet areas should be inspected for general condition and foreign material. The compressor should be checked for free rotation, when the installation permits, by reaching in and turning the blades by hand.

The following procedures are typical of those used to start turboprop engines. There are, however, wide variations in the procedures applicable to the many turboprop engines, and no attempt should be made to use these procedures in the actual starting of a turboprop engine. These procedures are presented only as a general guide for familiarization with typical procedures and methods. For starting of all turboprop engines, refer to the detailed procedures contained in the applicable manufacturer's instructions or their approved equivalent.

The first step in starting a turbine engine is to provide an adequate source of power for the starter. Where an air turbine starter is used, the starting air supply may be obtained from a gas-turbine compressor(GTC), an external source, or an engine cross-bleed operation. To start the first engine, use a GTC or low-pressure, large-volume tank. Start the remaining engine(s) using bleed air from the running engine.

While starting an engine, always observe the following:

1. Never energize the starter while the engine is rotating.
2. Do not move the power lever of any engine while it is being bled for cross-bleed starting.
3. Do not perform a ground start if turbine inlet temperature is above that specified by the manufacturer.
4. Do not use bleed air from an engine that is accelerating.

Starting Procedures

To start an engine on the ground, perform the following operations:

1. Place the start selector switch to the desired engine and the start-arming switch (if so equipped) to the "start" position.
2. Turn the aircraft boost pumps on.
3. Place the fuel and ignition switch on.
4. Position the low-r.p.m. switch in low or normal (high).
5. Make sure that the power lever is in the "start" position. If the propeller is not at the "start" position, difficulty may be encountered in making a start.
6. Depress the start switch and, if priming is necessary, depress the primer button.
7. Make sure the fuel pump parallel light comes on at, or above, 2,200 r.p.m. and remains on up to 9,000 r.p.m.

8. Check the oil pressure and temperature. Maintain the power lever at the "start" position until the specified minimum oil temperature is reached.
9. Disconnect the ground power supply.

If any of the following conditions occur during the starting sequence, turn off the fuel and ignition switch, discontinue the start immediately, make an investigation and record the findings.

1. Turbine inlet temperature exceeds the specified maximum. Record the observed peak temperature.
2. Acceleration time from start of propeller rotation to stabilized r.p.m. exceeds the specified time.
3. There is no oil pressure indication at 5,000 r.p.m. for either the reduction gear or the power unit.
4. Torching (visible burning in the exhaust nozzle other than normal enrichment) or excessive smoke is observed during initial fire-up.
5. The engine fails to ignite by 4,500 r.p.m. or maximum motoring r.p.m. (whichever is first), and r.p.m. stagnates or begins to decay.
6. Abnormal vibration is noted or compressor surge occurs (indicated by backfiring).
7. There is fuel spewing from the nacelle drain, indicating that the drip valve did not close.
8. Fire warning bell rings. (This may be due to either an engine fire or failure of an anti-icing shutoff valve to close.)

TURBOJET ENGINES

Preflight Operations

Unlike reciprocating engine aircraft, the turbojet-powered aircraft does not require a preflight runup unless it is necessary to investigate a suspected malfunction.

Before starting, all protective covers and air-inlet duct covers should be removed. If possible, the aircraft should be headed into the wind to obtain better cooling, faster starting, and smoother engine performance. It is especially important that the aircraft be headed into the wind if the engine is to be trimmed.

The runup area around the aircraft should be cleared of both personnel and loose equipment.

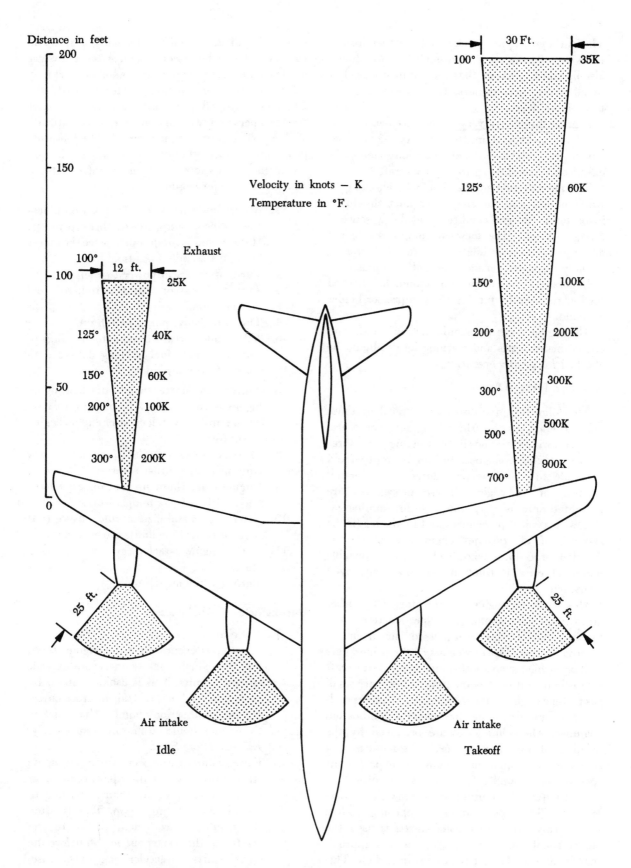

FIGURE 11–1.　Engine intake and exhaust hazard areas.

493

The turbojet engine intake and exhaust hazard areas are illustrated in figure 11–1. Care should also be taken to ensure that the runup area is clear of all items such as nuts, bolts, rocks, rags, or other loose debris.

A great number of very serious accidents occur involving personnel in the vicinity of turbojet engine air inlets. Extreme caution should be exercised when starting turbojet aircraft.

The aircraft fuel sumps should be checked for water or ice, and the engine air inlet should be inspected for general condition and the presence of foreign objects. The forward compressor blades and the compressor inlet guide vanes should be visually inspected for nicks and other damage.

If possible, the compressor should be checked for free rotation by turning the compressor blades by hand.

All engine controls should be operated, and engine instruments and warning lights should be checked for proper operation.

Starting a Turbojet Engine

The following procedures are typical of those used to start many turbojet engines. There are, however, wide variations in the starting procedures used for turbojet engines, and no attempt should be made to use these procedures in the actual starting of an engine. These procedures are presented only as a general guide for familiarization with typical procedures and methods. In the starting of all turbojet engines, refer to the detailed procedures contained in the applicable manufacturer's instructions or their approved equivalent.

Most turbojet engines can be started by either air turbine or combustion-type starters. Air-turbine starters use compressed air from an external source. This source may be a ground cart unit or air bled from another engine on the aircraft that is in operation. Combustion starters are small gas turbine engines that obtain power from expanding gases generated in the starter's combustion chamber. These hot gases are produced by the burning of fuel and air or, in some cases, a slow-burning solid or liquid monopropellant specially compounded for such starter units.

Fuel is turned on either by moving the power-lever to "idle" position or by opening a fuel shutoff valve. If an air-turbine starter is used, the engine should start or "light up" within approximately 20 seconds after the fuel is turned on. This is an arbitrarily chosen time interval that, if exceeded, indicates a malfunction has occurred and the start should be discontinued. After the cause of the trouble has been removed, another start may be made. If a combustion starter is used, the 20-second interval need not be observed, since starter operation will discontinue automatically after a predetermined time interval. The following procedures are useful only as a general guide, and are included to show the sequence of events in starting a turbojet engine.

1. Move power lever to "off" position unless the engine is equipped with thrust reverser. If the engine is so equipped, place the power lever in the "idle" position.
2. Turn on electrical power to engine.
3. Turn fuel system shutoff switch to "fuel on" position.
4. Turn fuel boost pump switch on.
5. A fuel inlet pressure indicator reading of 5 p.s.i. ensures fuel is being delivered to engine fuel pump inlet.
6. Turn engine starter switch on; when engine begins to rotate, check for oil pressure rise.
7. Turn ignition switch on after engine begins to rotate.
8. Move throttle to idle (if engine is not equipped with thrust reverser).
9. Engine start (light up) is indicated by a rise in exhaust gas temperature.
10. After engine stabilizes at idle, ensure that none of the engine limits are exceeded.
11. Turn engine starter switch off after start.
12. Turn ignition switch off.

Unsatisfactory Turbojet Starts

1. *Hot Starts.*

   A hot start occurs when the engine starts, but the exhaust gas temperature exceeds specified limits. This is usually caused by an excessively rich fuel/air mixture entering the combustion chamber. The fuel to the engine should be shut off immediately.

2. *False or Hung Start.*

   False or hung starts occur when the engine starts normally but the r.p.m. remains at some low value rather than increasing to the normal starting r.p.m. This is often the result of insufficient power to the starter, or the starter cutting off before the engine starts self-accelerating. In this case, the engine should be shut down.

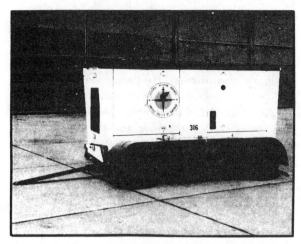

FIGURE 11–2. Mobile ground power unit (towed).

3. *Engine Will Not Start.*

The engine will not start within the prescribed time limit. It can be caused by lack of fuel to the engine, insufficient or no electrical power, or malfunctions in the ignition system. If the engine fails to start within the prescribed time, it should be shut down.

In all cases of unsatisfactory starts the fuel and ignition should be turned off. Continue rotating the compressor for approximately 15 seconds to remove accumulated fuel from the engine. If unable to motor (rotate) the engine, allow a 30-second fuel draining period before attempting another start.

ELECTRICAL POWER

Ground support electrical power units vary widely in size and type. Generally, they can be classified as either towed or self-propelled items of equipment.

The towed power units vary in size and range of available power. The smallest units are simply high-capacity batteries used to start light aircraft. These units are normally mounted on wheels or skids and are equipped with an extra-long electrical line terminated in a suitable plug-in adapter. Larger units (figure 11–2) are equipped with generators. These units provide a wider range of output power.

Such power units are normally designed to supply constant-current, variable-voltage d.c. electrical power for starting jet aircraft engines, and constant-voltage direct current for starting reciprocating aircraft engines. This type of vehicle is normally somewhat top-heavy and possesses a large inertia; consequently, it should be towed at restricted speeds, and sharp turns should be avoided.

Self-propelled power units are normally more expensive than the towed units and in most instances supply a wider range of output voltages and frequencies. For example, the self-propelled power unit shown in figure 11–3 is capable of supplying d.c. power in varying amounts, as well as 115/200-volt, 3-phase, 400-cycle a.c. power continuously for 5 minutes.

When using ground electrical power units, it is important to position the unit carefully. It must be positioned to prevent collision with the aircraft being serviced, or others nearby in the event the brakes on the unit fail. It should be parked a full service cable length away from the aircraft being serviced.

All electrical safety precautions should be observed when servicing an aircraft, and a power unit should never be moved when service cables are attached to an aircraft or when the generator system is engaged.

HYDRAULIC POWER

Portable hydraulic test stands are manufactured in many sizes and cost ranges. Some have a limited range of operation, while others can be used to perform all the system tests that fixed shop test stands are designed to perform. For example, one particular type of portable test unit can perform the following functions:

1. Drain the aircraft hydraulic system.
2. Filter the aircraft system hydraulic fluid.

FIGURE 11–3. Self-propelled ground power unit.

FIGURE 11–4. Air conditioner and heater unit.

3. Refill the aircraft system with clean, micronically filtered hydraulic fluid.
4. Check performance of aircraft systems and subsystems.
5. Check the aircraft hydraulic systems for internal and external leakage.

This type of portable hydraulic test unit is usually an electrically powered unit. It uses a hydraulic system capable of delivering a variable volume of fluid from zero to approximately 24 gallons per minute at variable pressures up to 3,000 p.s.i.g. The test unit and its components are mounted on a metal base enclosed by a removable top cover. The base is usually mounted on four pneumatic rubber tire wheels. It may be self-propelled or provided with a tow bar for towing by hand or vehicle.

AIR-CONDITIONING AND HEATING UNITS

Mobile air-conditioning and heating units are ground support equipment designed to supply conditioned air to heat or cool aircraft. Such units are capable of delivering a large airflow against static pressure at the end of a flexible duct or into an aircraft. Compared to the air-conditioning capability, the heating capability is normally considered an optional accessory, but in some climates the heating capability is often as useful as the cooling.

Figure 11–4 shows a typical mobile air conditioner and heating unit. This unit is capable of delivering up to 3,500 cu. ft. of cooling air per minute. It is capable of dropping the interior temperature of a large aircraft from 115° F. to approximately 76° F. Its heating capability pro-

vides an output of up to 400,000 B.t.u. per hour. A single engine supplies power to the truck and the air-conditioning equipment. This is accomplished by means of power-takeoffs mounted on an auxiliary transmission. By simple shifting of gear handles in various combinations of positions, an operator can drive the truck, operate the blower only, or operate the blower and the refrigeration equipment. All controls and switches for operation are in the cab.

GROUND SUPPORT AIR START UNITS

Air start units provide a supply of compressed air to operate pneumatic starters on turboprop and gas-turbine engines. Air start units may be mounted on trailer units to be towed to the aircraft, or they may be self-propelled units similar to that shown in figure 11–5.

A typical air start unit consists of the following components: A GTC, a high-capacity storage battery, and the necessary fuel, oil and electrical systems, controls, and compressed air lines.

The typical GTC is basically a two-stage centrifugal compressor assembly directly coupled to a radial inward-flow turbine. In addition to compressed bleed air, the compressor supplies compressed air for combustion to drive the turbine wheel. The combustion gas is passed through the combustion chamber to the turbine nozzle assembly. The power extracted by the turbine wheel is transmitted to the compressor, accessory section, and control system components.

FIGURE 11–5. Air start unit.

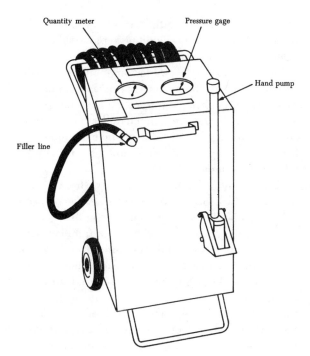

Quantity meter · Pressure gage · Hand pump · Filler line

FIGURE 11–6. Pressure oil unit.

PREOILING EQUIPMENT

Preoiling reciprocating aircraft engines is usually necessary before starting a new or preserved engine, or one which has been idle for a period of time.

Using a preoiler (see figure 11–6) for reciprocating aircraft engines simplifies the job of preoiling. Such units supply preheated oil under pressure to the engine to ensure adequate lubrication before starting.

The conditions for preoiling turbine engines are essentially the same as those for reciprocating engines. In addition, if a lubricating oil line fitting has been disconnected on a turbine engine, the engine must be preoiled before starting again. The portable preoiler tank supplies low-pressure oil to the lubrication system of the turbine engine.

AIRCRAFT FUELING

Strict fire precautions must be adhered to during the fueling process. Smoking is not permitted in or around an aircraft during fueling. Also, open flames such as oil lanterns, candles, or matches are prohibited. Exposed electric switches, sliprings or commutators, dynamos or motors, spark-producing electrical equipment, or any burning material must not be permitted within 100 feet of an aircraft being fueled or defueled. No lights other than approved explosion-proof lights are permitted within 100 feet of these operations, and no light of any sort may be placed where it can come in contact with spilled fuel. Warning signs should be posted as a precautionary measure.

All aircraft fuels or other combustible liquids accidentally spilled should be immediately removed by washing with water or covered with a foam blanket to prevent ignition, or neutralized by other means. The proper fire authorities must be notified if necessary.

If indications of underground leakage of combustible liquids are discovered, areas must be guarded by appropriate means, and the proper fire authorities must be notified immediately.

It is recommended that aircraft fuel tanks be filled before storing aircraft in hangars, since this leaves no space for explosive vapors to form. This practice is also recommended after each flight to prevent water condensation in fuel tanks.

The fuel tanks should not be filled completely to the top when aircraft are stored in hangars, especially if the outside temperature is cooler than the inside temperature. If it is warmer inside the hangar than outside, fuel in the tanks expands and causes overflow through the fuel tank's venting system, creating a fire hazard.

Nonspark tools must be used when working on any part of a system or unit designed for storing or handling combustible liquids.

Use of leaky tanks or fuel lines is not permitted. Repairs must be made on discovery, with due regard to the hazard involved.

All fuel is filtered and passes through water-separating equipment at the tank farm when it is delivered to the mobile refueler; or in the case of island-type refueling stations, as it leaves the supply connections. The mobile refueler also passes the fuel through a system of filters and water-separating equipment before its delivery to the aircraft. These filters and separators are usually checked in the morning for evidence of dirt and water, and each time thereafter that the mobile refueler is reloaded. When the mobile refueler is loaded, it must sit at least 15 minutes and then have the sumps checked for water before any aircraft are refueled from it.

When using fuel which has been stored in cans or barrels, it must be run through a strainer-funnel before being put into aircraft. This practice is necessary as condensation and rust develop inside cans and barrels.

If a chamois is used to filter the fuel, an increase in the static electricity hazard results from the passage of gasoline through the material. The chamois must be grounded and remain grounded until all gasoline has drained through the filter. This can be done by contact with a supporting metal screen which is positively grounded. Never use a plastic funnel, bucket, or similar nonconductive container when servicing from storage cans or barrels.

Aircraft should be fueled in a safe place. Do not fuel or defuel an aircraft in a hangar or other enclosed space except in case of an emergency. Aircraft should be free from fire hazards, and have engine switches off and chocks placed under the wheels prior to fueling or defueling.

A person who functions as a fireguard with a CO_2 extinguisher or other firefighting equipment should possess a thorough knowledge of all fuel-servicing hazards. He should guard against breathing hydrocarbon vapors, which may cause sickness or dizziness, or may even be fatal. Adequate ventilating measures to prevent the accumulation of fumes should be provided.

Because of its high lead content, fuel should not be allowed to come in contact with clothes, skin, or eyes. Fuel-saturated clothing should be removed as soon as possible and the parts of the body exposed to the fuel washed thoroughly with soap and water. Wearing clothing saturated with fuel creates a dangerous fire hazard, and painful blisters (similar to those caused by fire burns) may result from direct contact with fuel. If fuel enters the eyes, medical attention should be sought immediately.

Refueling Crew Duties

When an aircraft is to be overwing fueled by truck, it should be located on the apron or a dispersal site, and should not be in the vicinity of possible sources of fuel-vapor ignition. Consideration must be given to the direction of the wind so that fuel vapors are not carried toward a source of ignition.

The tank truck should be driven to a point as distant from the aircraft as the length of hose permits, and preferably to the windward (upwind) side of the aircraft. It must be parked parallel to or heading away from the wing, or in such a position that it may be driven away quickly in the event of fire (A of figure 11–7). As soon as the fueling operation has been completed, the truck

should be removed from the aircraft's vicinity. The truck fuel tank covers should be kept closed except when a tank is actually being loaded.

Ideally, refueling crews for large aircraft would possibly involve four men. One person stands by with the firefighting equipment; another stays with the truck; the third man handles the fuel hose on the ground; and the fourth man handles the fueling hose at the aircraft and fills the tanks (A and B of figure 11–7).

Care should be taken to identify the aviation fuel and lubricating oil dispensed from each refueling unit before beginning the actual servicing. Aviation technicians should be familiar with the various grades and the aircraft's gasoline requirements so that the appropriate fuel is used. A check should also be made to see that all radio equipment and electrical switches not needed for the fueling operation are turned off, and nonessential outside electrical sources are not connected to the aircraft. A member of the crew then makes sure that both the aircraft and the truck are properly grounded to prevent sparks from static electricity.

Fueling Operations

In the overwing fueling of large aircraft, the man with the CO_2 bottle stands close to the aircraft to be refueled. The fuel hose handler on the truck unreels the hose and passes it up to the man on the aircraft who is to do the fueling. Care should be taken in bringing the hose nozzle up to the filler neck of the fuel tank to avoid excessive marring of the aircraft finish. Attached to the nozzle is a ground wire which is plugged into the receptacle adjacent to the fuel tank to be filled. Another type of ground wire commonly used terminates in an alligator clip connected to a grounding post. This connection is made before the fuel tank cap is removed from the filler neck. This serves as a continuous ground connection for the fuel nozzle (C of figure 11–7). The fuel truck has two ground wires; one is connected to a suitable ground on the apron (A of figure 11–7), and the other is connected to the aircraft (A and B figure 11–7). The aircraft should also be grounded to the apron.

This grounding arrangement may take other forms. In many cases, the fuel truck is grounded by a metal chain that is dragged behind the truck; the aircraft is grounded by a carbon strip embedded in the tires; and the aircraft and fuel truck are held at a common electrical potential by a

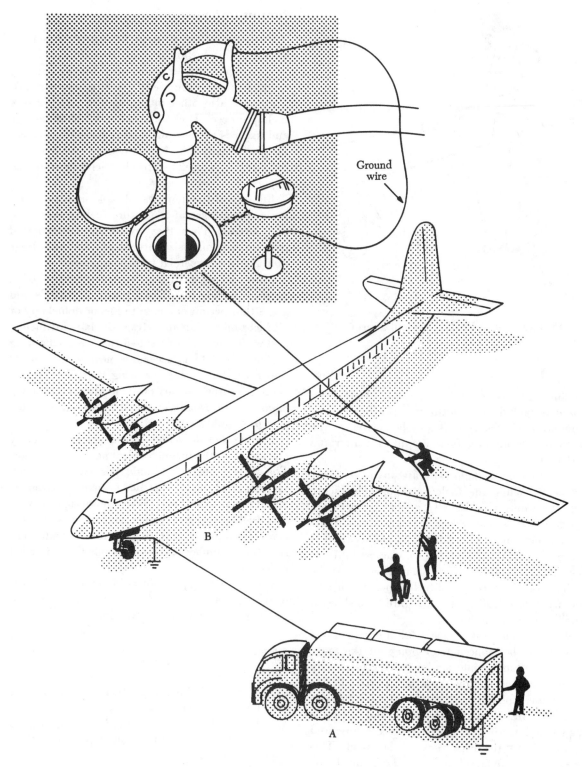

Ground
wire

C

B

A

FIGURE 11–7. Refueling an aircraft.

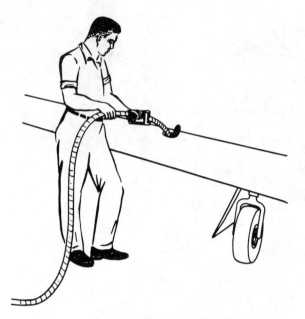

FIGURE 11–8. Fueling a small aircraft.

conducting wire encircling the fuel hose from nozzle to tank fitting. All this is to prevent a spark from static electricity that may be created as the fuel flows through the fuel hose into the aircraft's fuel tank.

The fueling of light aircraft involves fewer problems. While the fueler's responsibilities are still the same, it is usually a one- or two-man operation. The danger of marring the aircraft finish is minimized since the height and location of the fuel tanks usually permit easy accessibility to the filler neck. In addition, small aircraft can be easily pushed by hand to a fueling position near a fuel truck or a fueling island. Figure 11–8 shows a small aircraft being fueled.

When the fuel tank is nearly full, the rate of fuel flow should be reduced for topping off the tank; that is, the tank should be slowly filled to the top without spilling fuel on the wing or ground. The filler cap is replaced on that tank, the ground wire plug removed from its receptacle, and then the man handling the fuel nozzle takes the hose and moves on to the next tank to be filled. This procedure is followed at each tank until the aircraft is completely refueled. Then the ground wires are disconnected from the aircraft, and the hose is rewound onto the hose reel in the truck. During this operation the hose or nozzle should not be allowed to drop to the ground.

Pressure Fueling

Pressure fueling is used on many late-model aircraft. This fueling process, sometimes referred to as single-point or underwing fueling, greatly reduces the time required to service large aircraft. There are also other advantages in the pressure fueling process. It eliminates aircraft skin damage and hazards to personnel and reduces the chances for fuel contamination. Pressure fueling also reduces the chance of static electricity igniting fuel vapors.

Because of the limited fuel tank area, there are fewer advantages of a pressure fueling system in light aircraft. Thus, they are usually incorporated only in medium size executive jets and large military or commercial transport aircraft.

Most pressure fueling systems consist of a pressure fueling hose and a panel of controls and gages that permit one man to fuel or defuel any or all fuel tanks of an aircraft. A single-point fueling system is usually designed so that an in-the-wing fueling manifold is accessible near a wingtip or under the wing near the wing root. The valves connecting the various tanks to the main fueling manifold are usually actuated in response to fuel pressure signals.

Fueling and defueling procedures are normally placarded on the fueling control panel access door. The fueling operator should possess a thorough knowledge of the aircraft fuel system to recognize malfunction symptoms. Since the design of pressure fueling systems varies somewhat with each type of aircraft, the fueling operator should consult the manufacturer's instructions for detailed procedures.

Due to varying procedures in defueling aircraft, it is important to consult the applicable manufacturer's maintenance instructions.

FIRE

Types of Fire

The National Fire Protection Association has classified fires into three basic types:

a. Class A fires—as fires in ordinary combustible materials such as wood, cloth, paper, upholstery materials, etc.

b. Class B fires—as fires in flammable petroleum products or other flammable or combustible liquids, greases, solvents, paints, etc.

c. Class C fires—as fires involving energized electrical equipment where the electrical non-conductivity of the extinguishing media is of importance. In most cases where electrical equipment is deenergized, extinguishers suitable for use on Class A or B fires may be employed effectively.

A fourth class of fire, Class D fire, is defined as fire in flammable metal. Class D fires are not considered a basic type since they are generally caused by a Class A, B, or C fire. Usually these fires involve magnesium in the shop or in aircraft wheels and brakes.

Any one of these types of fires can occur during maintenance or operations. There is a particular type extinguisher which is most effective for each type of fire.

Fire Extinguishment

Three things are required for a fire. Fuel—something that will in the presence of heat combine with oxygen, thereby releasing more heat and as a result reduces itself to other chemical compounds. Heat—can be considered the catalyst which accelerates the combining of oxygen with fuel, in turn releasing more heat. Oxygen—element which combines chemically with another substance through the process of oxidation. Rapid oxidation, accompanied by a noticeable release of heat and light is called combustion or burning (figure 11–9). Remove any one of these things and the fire goes out.

IT TAKES THREE THINGS TO START A FIRE OXYGEN, HEAT, FUEL

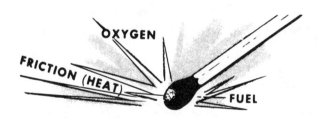

FIGURE 11–9. Three elements for fire.

Types of Fire vs. Extinguishing Agent

Class A fires respond best to water or water type extinguishers which cool the fuel below combustion temperatures. Class B and C extinguishers are effective but not equal to the wetting/cooling action of the Class A extinguisher.

Class B fires respond to carbon dioxide (CO_2), halogenated hydrocarbons (Halons) and dry chemicals, all of which displace the oxygen in the air thereby making combustion impossible. Foam is effective, especially when used in large quantities. Water is ineffective on class B fires and will cause the fire to spread.

Class C fires involving electrical wiring, equipment, or current respond best to carbon dioxide (CO_2) which displaces the oxygen in the atmosphere making combustion improbable. The CO_2 equipment must be equipped with a nonmetallic horn to be approved for use on electrical fires. Two reasons for this must be considered:

1. The discharge of CO_2 as through a metal horn can generate static electricity. The static discharge could reignite the fire.

2. The metal horn if in contact with the electrical current would transmit that current to the extinguisher operator.

Halogenated hydrocarbons are very effective on Class C fires. The vapor reacts chemically with the flame to extinguish the fire. Dry chemicals are effective but have the disadvantage of contaminating the local area with powder. Also, if used on wet and energized electrical equipment, it may aggravate current leakage.

Water, wet water or foam are not acceptable agents for use on electrical equipment fires.

Class D fires respond to application of dry powder, which prevents oxidation and the resulting flame. Application may be from an extinguisher or scoop or shovel. Special techniques are needed in combating fires involving metal. Manufacturers recommendations should be followed at all times. Areas which could be subjected to metal fires should have the proper protective equipment installed. Under no conditions use water on a metal fire. It will cause the fire to burn more violently and can cause explosions.

Fire Extinguisher Periodic Check List

1. Appropriate extinguisher located in proper place.
2. Safety seals unbroken.
3. Remove all external dirt and rust.
4. Gage or indicator in operable range.
5. Check for proper weight.
6. No nozzle obstruction.

Fire Extinguishing Agents

A. Water and water based agents.

Water may be combined with antifreeze compounds or wetting agents (accelerate penetration of materials by water). Water is used on carbonaceous fires. It extinguishes fires by cooling the fuel below the combustion temperature.

1. Soda-acid and foam act on a fire the same as water by lowering the temperature. Foam

501

has some effect on a petroleum base fire by preventing oxygen from getting to the fire.

2. Loaded stream contains an antifreeze as well as a flame retardant.

B. Dry Chemical.

Four types of chemicals are used:

1. Sodium bicarbonate (Formula H). For ordinary risk class B and C fires.
2. Ammonium phosphate (Multipurpose). For multiple risk class B and C fires.
3. Potassium bicarbonate (Purple K). For high risk class B and C fires.
4. Multipurpose dry chemical (ABC). For use on Class A, B, and C fires. The dry chemicals extinguish a fire by smothering it, cutting off oxygen, and the blanket of dry chemicals prevents reflash fires. It also affords the operator some protection from the heat. All dry chemicals are nonconductors of electricity.

C. Gas.

1. Carbon dioxide (CO_2) has a toxicity rating (Underwriter's Laboratory) of 5A especially recommended for use on class B and C fires. Extinguishes flames by dissipating oxygen in the immediate area.
2. Halogenated hydrocarbons (commonly called freon by the industry), are numbered according to chemical formulas with Halon numbers.

Carbon tetrachloride (Halon 104). Chemical formula CCl_4. UL toxicity rating of 3. It is poisonous and toxic. Hydrochloric acid vapor,

chlorine and phosgene gas are produced whenever carbon tetrachloride is used on ordinary fires. The amount of phosgene gas is increased whenever carbon tetrachloride is brought in direct contact with hot metal, certain chemicals, or continuing electrical arcs. It is no longer approved for any fire extinguishing use.

Methyl bromide (Halon 1001). Chemical formula CH_3Br—a liquified gas, UL toxicity rating of 2. Effective but very toxic and also is corrosive to aluminum alloys, magnesium and zinc. Not recommended for aircraft use.

Chlorobromomethane (Halon 1011). Chemical formula CH_2ClBr—a liquified gas, UL toxicity rating is 3. Not recommended for aircraft use.

Dibromodifluoromethane (Halon 1202). Chemical formula CBr_2F_2. UL toxicity rating of 4. Not recommended for aircraft use.

Bromochlorodifluoromethane (Halon 1211). Formula $CBrClF_2$—a liquified gas with a UL toxicity rating of 5. It is colorless, noncorrosive and evaporates rapidly leaving no residue whatever. It does not freeze or cause cold burns and will not harm fabrics, metals, or other materials it contacts. Halon 1211 acts rapidly on fires by producing a heavy blanketing mist that eliminates air from the fire source, but more importantly interferes chemically with the combustion process. It has outstanding properties in preventing reflash after the fire has been extinguished.

Group	Definition	Examples
6 (least toxic)	Gases or vapors which in concentrations up to at least 20% by volume for durations of exposure of the order of 2 hours do not appear to produce injury.	Bromotrifluoromethane (Halon 1301)
5a	Gases or vapors much less toxic than Group 4 but more toxic than Group 6.	Carbon dioxide
4	Gases or vapors which in concentrations of the order of 2 o 2½% for durations of exposure of the order of 2 hours are lethal or produce serious injury.	Dibromodifluoromethane (Halon 1202)
3	Gases or vapors which in concentrations of the order of 2 to 2½% for durations of exposure of the order of 1 hour are lethal or produce serious injury.	Bromochloromethane (Halon 1011), Carbon tetrachloride (Halon 104)
2	Gases or vapors which in concentrations of the order of 1/2 to 1% for durations of exposure of the order of 1/2 hour are lethal or produce serious injury.	Methyl bromide (Halon 1001)

FIGURE 11–10. Toxicity table.

Extinguishing Materials	Classes of fire				Self-generating	Self-expelling	Cartridge of N_2 cylinder	Stored pressure	Pump	Hand
	A	B	C	D						
Water and antifreeze	X						X	X	X	X
Soda-acid (water)	X				X					
Wetting agent	X						X			
Foam	X	X			X					
Loaded stream	X	X+					X	X		
Multipurpose dry chemical	X+	X	X				X	X		
Carbon dioxide		X+	X			X				
Dry chemical		X	X				X	X		
Bromotrifluoromethane – Halon 1301		X	X			X				
Bromochlorodifluoromethane – Halon 1211		X	X					X		
Dry powder (metal fires)				X			X			X

+Smaller sizes of these extinguishers are not recognized for use on these classes of fires.

FIGURE 11–11. Extinguisher operation and methods of expelling.

Bromotrifluoromethane (Halon 1301). Chemical formula CF_3Br is also a liquified gas with a UL toxicity rating of 6. It has all the characteristics of Halon 1211. The significant difference between the two is: Halon 1211 forms a spray similar to CO_2, while Halon 1301 has a vapor spray that is more difficult to direct.

D. Powder.

Dry powder for metal fires. Fires in metal require special handling. If water is used on a magnesium fire the burning is accelerated. Special dry powders are available for use wherever metal fires are possibilities. These are normally applied by scoop or shovel. Multipurpose (ABC) dry chemicals have a limited use on metal fires such as fires in wheel brakes or in magnesium fires. (See figures 11–10 and 11–11).

RECOMMENDED MARKINGS TO INDICATE EXTINGUISHER SUITABILITY

(From NFPA Standard #10)

The following recommendations are given as a guide in marking extinguishers, and/or extinguisher locations, to indicate the suitability of the extinguisher for a particular class of fire.

Markings should be applied by decalcomanias, painting or similar methods having at least equivalent legibility and durability.

Where markings are applied to the extinguisher, they should be located on the front of the shell above or below the extinguisher nameplate. Markings should be of a size and form to give easy legibility at a distance of 3 feet.

Where markings are applied to wall panels, etc., in the vicinity of extinguishers, they should be of a size and form to give easy legibility at a distance of 25 feet. (See figures 11–12 and 11–13).

AIRCRAFT FIRE EXTINGUISHERS

Fire is one of the most dangerous threats to aircraft—either in flight or on the ground. Airborne fixed, powerplant and airframe, detection and extinguishing systems are designed and installed by the manufacturer in compliance with applicable FAR's. The requirement for portable fire extinguishers installed in the crew and passenger compartment says, the extinguisher must be approved, must be appropriate for the kind of fire likely to occur and must minimize the hazard of toxic gases.

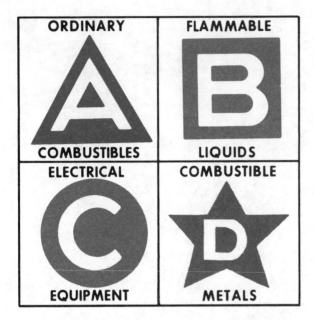

FIGURE 11-12. Identification of fire extinguisher
type location.

The National Fire Protection Association (NFPA) Standard #408, Aircraft Hand Fire Extinguishers, suggests the type, capacity, location and quantity of hand fire extinguishers for the protection of aircraft compartments occupied by passengers and crew. This standard suggests carbon dioxide and water (water solution) as the extinguishing media for hand type extinguishers. Both type extinguishers are suggested for use in the passenger compartment, the number of units being regulated by the number of passengers carried. Carbon dioxide is suggested for the crew compartment. A halogenated hydrocarbon extinguishing agent (Halon 1211 or Halon 1301) having an Underwriter's Laboratory toxicity rating of 5 or higher may be substituted for the carbon dioxide, if there is sufficient free air volume in the immediate area to prevent serious irritating effects on the occupants.

The following extinguishing agents are not recommended for aircraft use:

1. Dry chemical extinguishers are very effective in Class B and C fires but they leave a residual dust or powder. This obstructs vision, is difficult to clean up and causes damage to electronic equipment.

2. Carbon tetrachloride is no longer approved as a fire extinguishing agent. It produces a poisonous gas (phosgene) when in contact with hot metals. Soda acid and foam, these are toxic to a degree and can be corrosive to adjacent materials.

3. Methyl bromide is more toxic than CO_2 and cannot be used in confined areas. It is also very corrosive to aluminum alloy, magnesium and zinc.

4. Chlorobromomethane, although an effective extinguishing agent, is toxic.

TYPICAL EXTINGUISHER MARKINGS

1. Water

2. Carbon Dioxide, Dry Chemical
Bromochlorodifluoromethane and
Bromotrifluoromethane

3. Multipurpose Dry Chemical

4. Multipurpose Dry Chemical (Insufficient Agent for "A" Rating)

5. Dry Powder

FIGURE 11-13. Typical extinguisher markings.

504

Extinguishers

The common aerosol can type extinguishers are definitely not acceptable as airborne hand type extinguishers. In one instance, an aerosol type foam extinguisher located in the pilot's seat back pocket exploded and tore the upholstery from the seat. The interior of the aircraft was damaged by the foam. This occurred when the aircraft was on the ground and the outside temperature was 90° F. In addition to the danger from explosion, the size is inadequate to combat even the smallest fire. In another instance, a dry chemical extinguisher was mounted near a heater vent on the floor. For an unknown reason, the position of the unit was reversed. This placed the extinguisher directly in front of the heater vent. During flight, with the heater in operation, the extinguisher became overheated and exploded filling the compartment with dry chemical powder. The proximity of heater vents should be considered when selecting a location for a hand fire extinguisher.

Additional information relative to airborne hand fire extinguishers may be obtained from the local FAA District Office and from the National Fire Protection Association, 470 Atlantic Ave., Boston, MA 02210.

Ground Type Extinguishers—Hand Type

The selection of a fire extinguisher for ground installation, shop, fueling station, etc., is not restricted as it is for airborne installations. The range of selection for agent and type extinguishers is shown in figure 11–11. (See figures 11–16 and 11–17).

Methods of Extinguisher Operation. The methods of operation of extinguishers are most conveniently arranged by grouping extinguishers according to their expelling means. Six methods are in common use.

Self-generating—actuation causes gases to be generated that provide expellent energy.

Self-expelling—the agents have sufficient vapor pressure at normal operating temperatures to expel themselves.

Gas cartridge or cylinder—expellent gas is confined in a separate pressure vessel until an operator releases it to pressurize the extinguisher shell.

Stored pressure—the extinguishing material and expellent gas are kept in a single container.

Mechanically pumped—the operator provides expelling energy by means of a pump and the vessel containing the agent is not pressurized.

Hand propelled—the material is applied with scoop, pail, or bucket.

Several different extinguishing materials are handled by each of these expelling means.

Discontinued Fire Extinguishers (see figures 11–14 and 11–15)

There are still in use today several million fire extinguishers of a design no longer manufactured. These are the 1½, 2½ and 5 gallon "invert to use" liquid extinguishers. The last of this type were manufactured in the 2½ gallon size. The agents used in these extinguishers are:

1. Soda-acid.
2. Foam.
3. Water cartridge.
4. Loaded stream cartridge.

The reasons which influenced the decision to discontinue manufacturing these extinguishers are:

1. Invert to use—difficult and unorthodox method of activation.
2. Limited to the types of fires for which they are suitable. Mostly Class "A" fires, very limited application of foam on Class "B" fires.
3. None approved for electrical fires.
4. Effective on only minimal size fires.
5. The container does not meet current pressure vessel standards. This is the most significant of all.

Comparison of Safety Factors

Discontinued types of extinguishers use a shell rated at either 350 or 500 p.s.i. However, when these extinguishers are inverted to operate, the pressures generated often are unpredictable, totally unlike the pressures in other extinguisher designs. Pressures may range from 100 to 300 p.s.i for soda-acid extinguishers and from 100 to 350 p.s.i. for the foam extinguishers.

SERVICING AIRCRAFT WITH OIL

Aircraft oil tanks are normally checked at the same time the fuel tanks are filled. There are a few exceptions to this general rule, since some manufacturers recommend that the oil level in certain jet engines be checked within a specified time after engine shutdown. In all cases, the manufacturer's instructions should be followed for the specific aircraft not only for servicing procedures but also for type and grade of oil used.

Aircraft oil tanks should never be filled to capacity or above the labeled full mark on the gage or dipstick. This is because oil expands when it becomes hot, and at high altitude it bubbles and expands. The extra space in oil tanks allows for expansion and prevents overflowing. The aircraft's oil requirements should be checked, and no substitutions should be made for the type of oil to be used unless substitute oils have been approved

Soda-acid fire extinguisher.

Cartridge operated water fire extinguisher.

FIGURE 11–14. . Discontinued types of fire extinguishers #1.

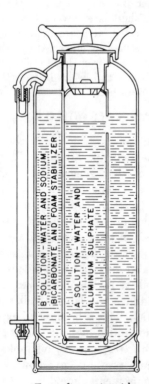

Foam fire extinguisher.

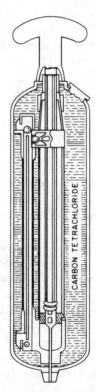

Vaporizing liquid fire extinguisher.

FIGURE 11–15. Discontinued types of fire extinguishers #2.

FIGURE 11–16.   CO₂ fire extinguisher.

for use. When pouring oil into the tanks, be sure that cleaning rags or pieces of rag or other foreign substances do not get into the tanks. Foreign material in the oil system restricts the flow of oil and can cause engine failure.

Lubricating oil is nonexplosive, very difficult to ignite in bulk, and is not normally capable of spontaneous combustion. However, if oil is ignited, a hotter fire results than that from gasoline. The vapor of the oil, however, is explosive when mixed with air in certain proportions. Vapors of many petroleum products are highly toxic when inhaled or ingested. It is therefore necessary to take all precautions when handling lubricating oil.

· FIGURE 11–17.   Dry chemical extinguisher.

MAINTENANCE SAFETY

Good housekeeping in hangars, shops, and on the flight line is essential to safety and efficient maintenance. The highest standards of orderly work arrangements and cleanliness should be observed during the maintenance of aircraft. Where continuous work shifts are established, the outgoing shift should remove and properly store personal tools, rollaway boxes, all workstands, maintenance stands, hoses, electrical cords, hoists, crates, and boxes that are superfluous to the work to be accomplished.

Safety Lanes

Pedestrian walkways or fire lanes should be painted around the perimeter inside the hangars. This should be done as a safety measure to prevent accidents and to keep pedestrian traffic out of work areas.

Power Cords

1. Power cords should be heavy industrial type which are able to resist abrasion and impact.
2. Power cords should not be run over by any equipment.
3. Lights should be explosion proof.
4. Connections should be locking type to prevent accidental disconnection.
5. All lights or equipment should be switched "off", to prevent arching before connecting or disconnecting.
6. Power cords should be straightened, coiled, and properly stored when not in use.

Disregard of the above suggestions may result in explosions and fires with damage into millions of dollars and loss of life.

Compressed Air System

Compressed air is like electricity—an excellent tool as long as it is under control.
1. Air hoses should be inspected frequently for breaks and worn spots. Unsafe hose should be replaced immediately.
2. All connections should be kept in a "no leak condition".
3. In line oilers, if installed, should be maintained in operating condition.
4. The system should have water sumps installed and they should be drained at regular intervals.

5. Air used for paint spraying should be filtered to remove oil and water.
6. Never use compressed air to clean hands or clothing. Pressure can force debris into the flesh leading to infection.
7. Never use compressed air for "horse play".
8. Air hoses should be straightened, coiled, and properly stored when not in use.

Spilled Oil and Grease

Oil, grease, and other substances spilled on hangar or shop floors should be immediately cleaned or covered with an absorbent material to prevent fire or personal injury. Drip pans should be placed beneath engines and engine parts wherever dripping exists. Waste oil and dirty cleaning fluid should be stored in containers for future salvage. Under no circumstances should oil or cleaning fluid be emptied into floor drains. Fumes from this type "disposal" may be ignited and cause severe property damage.

Aircraft Tire Mounting

To prevent possible personal injury, tire dollies and other appropriate lifting and mounting devices should be used in mounting or removing heavy aircraft tires. When inflating tires on wheels equipped with locking rings, tire cage guards should always be used. Where possible, all tires should be inflated in tire cage guards. Because of possible personal injury, extreme caution is required to avoid overinflation of high-pressure tires. Pressure regulators should be used on high pressure air bottles to eliminate the possibility of overinflation of tires.

Tire cages need not be used when adjusting pressure in tires installed on aircraft.

Welding

Welding should not be performed except in designated areas. Any part to be welded should be removed from the aircraft, if possible. Repair would then be accomplished in the welding shop under controlled environment. A welding shop should be equipped with proper tables, ventilation, tool storage, and fire prevention and extinguishing equipment.

Welding on an aircraft should be performed outside if possible. If welding in the hangar is necessary, these precautions should be observed:

1. No open fuel tanks or work on fuel systems should be in progress.
2. No painting in progress.
3. No aircraft within 35 feet.
4. Immaculate housekeeping should prevail around the welding area.

5. Only qualified welders should be permitted to do the work.
6. The area should be roped off and placarded.
7. Fire extinguishing equipment of a minimum rating of 20B should be in the immediate area with 80B rated equipment as a backup.
8. There should be trained fire watches in attendance at the above equipment.
9. Aircraft should be in towable condition, with a tug attached, aircraft brakes off, and a qualified operator on the tug with mechanics available to assist in the towing operation. Hangar doors should be opened.

SERVICING AIRCRAFT OXYGEN SYSTEMS

Before servicing any aircraft, consult the specific aircraft maintenance manual to determine the proper type of servicing equipment to be used. Two persons are required to service an aircraft with gaseous oxygen. One man should be stationed at the control valves of the servicing equipment and one man stationed where he can observe the pressure in the aircraft system. Communication between the two men is required in case of an emergency. Aircraft should not be serviced with oxygen during fueling, defueling, or other maintenance work which could provide a source of ignition. Oxygen servicing of aircraft should be accomplished outside hangars.

Oxygen Hazards

Gaseous oxygen is chemically stable and is nonflammable; however, combustible materials ignite more rapidly and burn with greater intensity in an oxygen-rich atmosphere. In addition, oxygen combines with oil, grease, or bituminous material to form a highly explosive mixture which is sensitive to impact. Physical damage to, or failure of, oxygen containers, valves, or plumbing can result in explosive rupture, with danger to life and property. It is imperative that the highest standard of housekeeping be observed in handling oxygen and that only authorized persons be permitted to service aircraft.

In addition to aggravating the fire hazard, liquid oxygen will cause severe "burns" (frostbite) if it comes in contact with the skin because of its low temperature. (It boils at $-297°$ F.)

Only oxygen marked "Aviators Breathing Oxygen" which meets Federal Specification BB-0-925a. Grade A or equivalent may be used in aircraft breathing oxygen systems.

AIRCRAFT TIEDOWN

Aircraft tiedown is a very important part of aircraft ground handling. The type of tiedown will be determined by the prevailing weather conditions. In normal weather a limited or normal tiedown procedure is used; but when storm conditions are anticipated, a heavy weather or storm condition tiedown procedure should be employed.

Normal Tiedown Procedure

Small aircraft should be tied down after each flight to preclude damage from sudden storms. The direction in which aircraft are to be parked and tied down will be determined by prevailing or forecast wind direction.

Aircraft should be headed, as nearly as possible, into the wind, depending on the locations of the fixed, parking area tiedown points. Spacing of tiedowns should allow for ample wingtip clearance (figure 11–18). After the aircraft is properly located, lock the nosewheel or the tailwheel in the fore-and-aft position.

Tiedown Anchors

All aircraft parking areas should be equipped for three-point tiedowns. This is facilitated at most airports by use of tiedown anchors installed in concrete parking areas. Tiedown anchors, sometimes called "pad eyes," are ringlike fittings installed when the parking area is poured. They are normally set flush with the surface of the concrete or no more than one inch above it. There are several types of tiedown anchors in use. The type selected is usually determined by the material used in aircraft parking areas, since it may be a

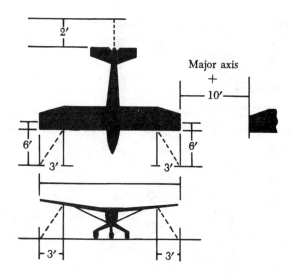

FIGURE 11–18. Diagram of tiedown dimensions.

concrete paved surface, a bituminous paved surface, or an unpaved turf area.

Location of tiedowns is usually indicated by some means such as white or yellow paint markings or by surrounding the tiedown anchor with crushed stone.

Tiedown anchors for small single-engine aircraft should provide a minimum holding power (strength) of approximately 3,000 pounds each. Although this minimum can be achieved when stake-driven tiedowns are used in dry or turfed areas, such stakes will almost invariably pull out

Size (in.)	Manila Minimum tensile strength (lbs.)	Nylon Minimum tensile strength (lbs.)	Dacron (Twist) Minimum tensile strength (lbs.)	Dacron (Braid) Minimum tensile strength (lbs.)	Yellow Polypropylene (Twist) Minimum tensile strength (lbs.)	Yellow Polypropylene (Braid) Minimum tensile strength (lbs.)
3/16	—	960	850	730	800	600
1/4	600	1,500	1,440	980	1,300	1,100
5/16	1,000	2,400	2,200	1,650	1,900	1,375
3/8	1,350	3,400	3,120	2,300	2,750	2,025
7/16	1,750	4,800	4,500	2,900	—	—
1/2	2,650	6,200	5,500	3,800	4,200	3,800
5/8	4,400	10,000	—	—	—	—
3/4	5,400	—	—	—	—	—
1	9,000	—	—	—	—	—

FIGURE 11–19. Comparison of common tiedown ropes.

when the ground becomes soaked from torrential rains which accompany hurricanes and some thunderstorms.

Tiedown Ropes

Tiedown ropes capable of resisting a pull of approximately 3,000 pounds should be used to

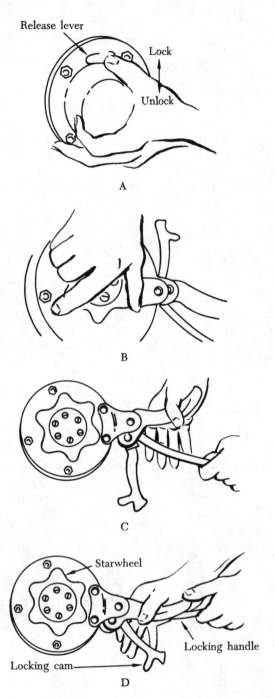

FIGURE 11-20. Operation of a cable tiedown reel.

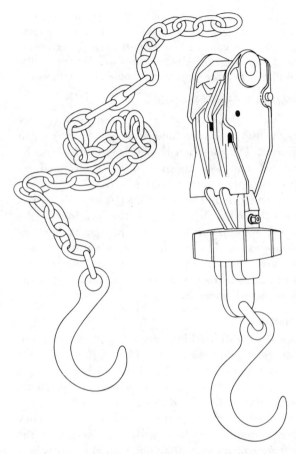

FIGURE 11-21. A multipurpose tiedown chain.

secure light aircraft. Cable or chain tiedown is usually preferred for tying down large aircraft.

Manila ropes should be inspected periodically for mildew and rot. Nylon or Dacron tiedown ropes are preferable to manila rope. The objection to manila rope is that it shrinks when wet, is subject to mildew or rot, and has considerably less tensile strength than either nylon or Dacron. Various types of commonly used tiedown rope are compared in figure 11-19.

Tiedown Cable

Tiedown cables are often used to secure aircraft, especially in the case of large aircraft. Most cable-type tiedowns are accomplished with some form of tiedown reel designed for rapid and reliable securing of all types of aircraft. Figure 11-20 illustrates the operation of a typical cable tiedown reel.

In *A* of figure 11-20 the cable is released by depressing the release lever to provide cable slack. One end of the cable is then attached to the

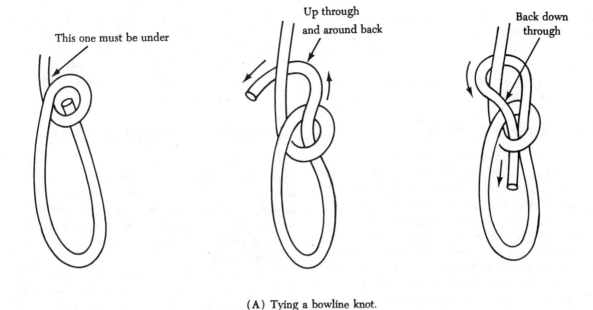

(A) Tying a bowline knot.

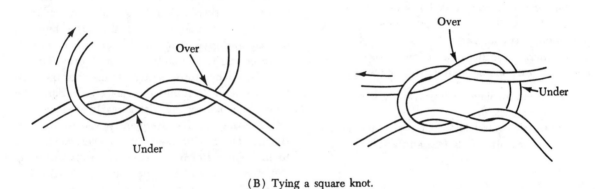

(B) Tying a square knot.

FIGURE 11–22. Knots commonly used for aircraft tiedown.

aircraft tiedown ring and the other end to a tiedown anchor. The starwheel on the reel (B of figure 11–20) is then turned clockwise to remove excess slack from the cable. The locking handle is then secured to the bar when the cable has been adjusted for the desired tautness (C of figure 11–20). Finally, as shown in D of figure 11–20, the locking cam is secured to complete the tiedown procedure.

Tiedown Chains

The chain-type tiedown sometimes is used as a better and stronger tiedown to secure the heaviest aircraft. This tiedown assembly is composed of an all metal quick-release mechanism, a tensioning device, and a length of chain with hooks (figure 11–21).

SECURING LIGHT AIRCRAFT

Light aircraft are most often secured with ropes tied only at the aircraft tiedown rings provided for securing purposes. Rope should never be tied to a lift strut, since this practice can bend a strut if the rope slips to a point where there is no slack. Manila rope shrinks when wet; about 1 inch of slack should be provided for movement. Too much slack will allow the aircraft to jerk against the ropes. Tight tiedown ropes put inverted flight stresses on the aircraft, many of which are not designed to take such loads.

A tiedown rope holds no better than the knot. Antislip knots such as the bowline or square knots are quickly tied and are easy to untie (figure 11–22). Aircraft not equipped with tiedown fittings

511

should be secured in accordance with the manufacturer's instructions. Ropes should be tied to outer ends of struts on high-wing monoplanes, and suitable rings should be provided where structural conditions permit, if the manufacturer has not already provided them.

SECURING HEAVY AIRCRAFT

The normal tiedown procedure for heavy aircraft can be accomplished with rope or cable tiedown. The number of such tiedowns should be governed by anticipated weather conditions.

Most heavy aircraft are equipped with surface control locks which should be engaged or installed when the aircraft is secured. Since the method of locking controls will vary on different type aircraft, check the manufacturer's instructions for proper installation or engaging procedures. In case high winds are anticipated, which may damage the control surfaces or locking devices, control surface battens can also be installed to prevent damage. Figure 11–23 illustrates four common tiedown points on heavy aircraft.

In general, the normal tiedown procedure for heavy aircraft should include the following:

1. Head airplane into prevailing wind whenever possible.
2. Install control locks, all covers and guards.
3. Chock all wheels fore and aft.

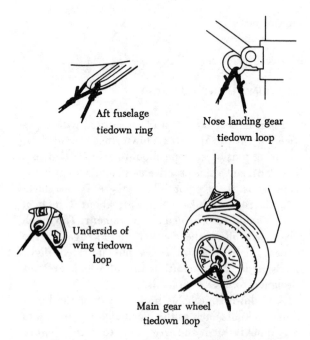

Aft fuselage tiedown ring

Nose landing gear tiedown loop

Underside of wing tiedown loop

Main gear wheel tiedown loop

FIGURE 11–23. Common tiedown points.

4. Attach tiedown reels to airplane tiedown loops and to tiedown anchors or tiedown stakes. Use tiedown stakes for temporary tiedown only. If tiedown reels are not available, $\frac{1}{4}$-inch wire cable or $1\frac{1}{2}$-inch manila line may be used.

AIRCRAFT TIEDOWN FOR STORM CONDITIONS

Each year many aircraft are needlessly damaged by windstorms because of negligence and improper tiedown procedures. A storm can turn a local airport into a junkyard in a matter of minutes. If an aircraft is damaged during a windstorm, the chances are it was improperly secured or was not tied down at all.

Most windstorm damage occurs during the early summer months, but can continue with lessening frequency throughout the year. As a general rule, the large and very severe windstorms cause less damage than the small local ones. This is because there is usually sufficient advance warning for the former, but the latter build up quickly and give little warning of their coming.

According to available weather records, Tampa, Florida, is the storm center of this country, with an average of 94 thunderstorms a year. Santa Fe, New Mexico, is second with a yearly average of 73. Other cities are less frequently visited by such storms. The Pacific Coast States average only one to four such storms a year. Generally speaking, thunderstorms and tornadoes are accompanied by high surface winds which account for most of the damage to aircraft on the ground.

Although most storms are generated in the daytime, many sections of the United States, including the Southwest, the lower Michigan Peninsula, and an extensive area centered in eastern Nebraska, are plagued with night storms during the summer months. Thunderstorms are bothersome in the Central States during the months of July, August, and September. On the other hand, in the winter the greatest storm activity takes place in the lower Mississippi Valley.

The map in figure 11–24 shows the yearly average number of days with thunderstorms based on observations from all U. S. Weather Bureau first-order stations in the United States. A thunderstorm day is considered any day during which one or more thunderstorms occur. It should be realized, however, that there probably are variations which do not show on this map because

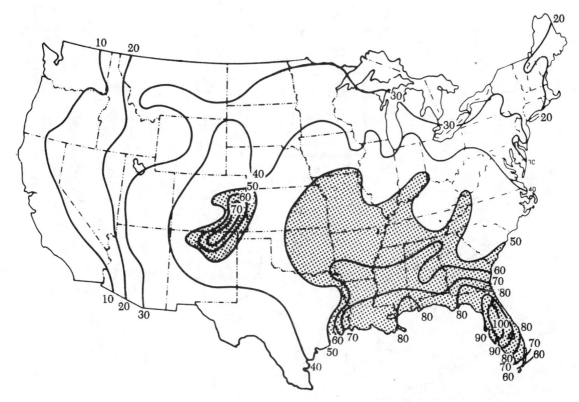

FIGURE 11–24. Map showing average number of thunderstorm days per year.

of the local nature of thunderstorms and the sparsity of observations from some areas. July and August are the months with the greatest number of thunderstorms over most sections of the United States, while December and January have the least number.

Thunderstorms are not the only concern of aircraft owners, fixed-base operators, airport service crews, etc., from a tiedown sense. There are also hurricanes and tornadoes. Figure 11–25 is a map showing the tornado frequency in the various states during a recent 10-year period.

A map showing the principal storm belts in the continental U.S.A. is presented in figure 11–26.

Precautions Against Windstorm Damage

The best protection against windstorm damage is, of course, to fly the aircraft out of the impending storm area when there is sufficient time. The next best protective measure is to secure the aircraft in a stormproof hangar or other suitable shelter. The remaining alternative is to assure that the aircraft is tied down securely. When securing aircraft,

fasten all doors and windows properly to minimize damage inside the aircraft. Engine openings (intake and exhaust) for both reciprocating and gas-turbine type should be covered to prevent entry of foreign matter. Pitot-static tubes should also be covered to prevent damage.

Be prepared for the worst storm conditions; for example, pouring rain, and gusty winds with intermittent sheets of water flowing across the runways, ramps, and parking areas, with perhaps no hangar facilities available. With such conditions in mind, responsible service crews should plan in advance by becoming familiar with their aircraft manufacturer's instructions for the following: (1) Tiedown ropes; (2) installation of tiedown rings for attachment of tiedown ropes; (3) securing nosewheel type aircraft vs. tailwheel type aircraft; and (4) aircraft weights and relative wind velocities that would make varied tiedown procedures necessary for pending weather emergencies.

The following suggestions will materially reduce aircraft damage from windstorms:

1. Partially disassembled aircraft which are outdoors (particularly light aircraft with

513

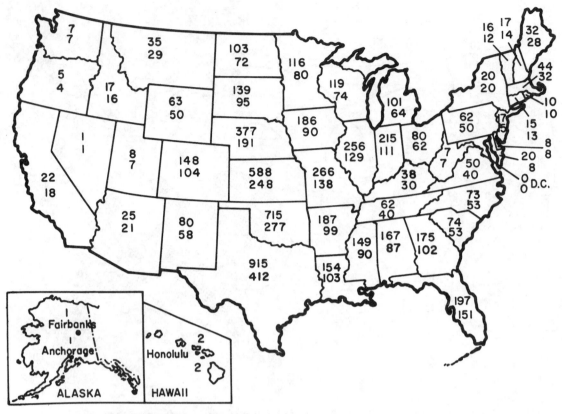

UPPER NUMBER— Number of tornadoes
LOWER NUMBER— Number of tornado days

FIGURE 11–25. Tornado frequency during a recent 10-year period.

engines removed) should be hangared as soon as storm warnings are received. Loose wings should never be tied against a fuselage; they should be stored inside a hangar.

2. Whenever possible, fly aircraft out of anticipated storm danger zones. If impossible, hangar the aircraft in a stormproof hangar.

3. Observe the minimum recommended strength for tiedown ropes.

4. A single row of properly secured sandbags or spoiler boards (2″ × 2′) on the top of a wing's leading edge will serve as an effective spoiler and reduce the lifting tendency of the wings. Do not overload the wings with sandbags. If the anticipated winds will exceed the lift-off speed of the aircraft, the makeshift spoilers should run the entire length of the wings.

Another means for tying down light aircraft (of various types and sizes) utilizes continuous lengths of parallel wire ropes passed through U-bolt anchors secured to ground tiedown points (figures 11–27 and 11–28). Tiedown chains are attached to the wire rope with round-pin galvanized anchor shackles. This allows tiedown chains to "float" along wire rope and gives a variable distance between anchor points so that a variety of aircraft can use a vertical tiedown without loss of space. The vertical anchor significantly reduces impact loads that may occur during gusty wind conditions. The distance between ropes will depend upon the types of aircraft which use the tiedown area.

The diagram in figure 11–28 shows a proper vertical anchor using wire rope tiedown line, straight link coil chain for connection between the wire rope and aircraft wing. One link on the free end is then passed through a link of the taut portion, and a safety snap is used to keep the link from passing back through. Any load on the chain is borne by the chain itself instead of the snap.

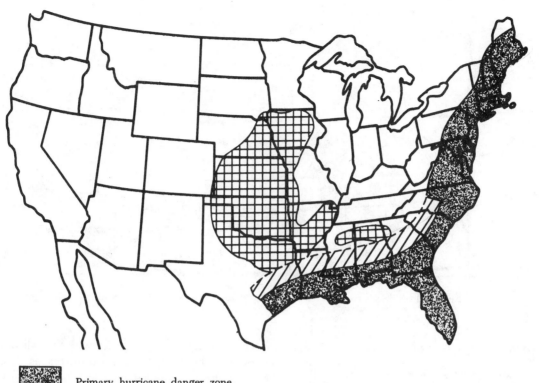

   Primary hurricane danger zone.

   Fringe area.

   Tornado belt.

FIGURE 11–26.   Storm belts in the continental U.S.

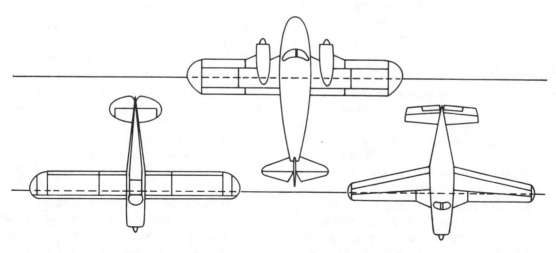

FIGURE 11–27.   Typical aircraft tiedown using a wire rope system.

FIGURE 11–28. Wire rope tiedown line using vertical anchor chain.

Securing Multiengine Aircraft

Multiengine aircraft will obviously require stronger tiedown facilities because of the additional weight of these aircraft. The anchor should be capable of a holding power of 4,000 pounds each for the lighter executive twin-engine aircraft. Much higher load capacity is required for the heavier transport-type aircraft.

Do not depend on the weight of the multiengine aircraft to protect it from damage by windstorms. It is possible for a sudden, severe windstorm to move, damage, or even overturn such aircraft.

Multiengine aircraft should, therefore, always be tied down and chocked when left unattended for any length of time. Gust locks should be used to protect control surfaces. If the landing gear uses downlock safety pins, these pins should be inserted at the time the aircraft is being secured.

Securing Helicopters

Structural damage can occur from high-velocity surface winds. Therefore, if at all possible, helicopters should be evacuated to a safe area if tornadoes or hurricanes are anticipated.

When possible, helicopters should be secured in hangars. If not, they should be tied down securely. Helicopters that are tied down can usually sustain winds up to approximately 65 m.p.h.

For added protection, helicopters should be moved to a clear area so that they will not be damaged by flying objects or falling limbs from surrounding trees.

If high winds are anticipated with the helicopter parked in the open, the main rotor blades should be tied down. Detailed instructions for securing and mooring each type of helicopter can be found in the applicable maintenance manual. Methods of securing helicopters will vary with weather conditions, the length of time the aircraft is expected to remain on the ground, and location and characteristics of the aircraft. Wheel chocks, control locks, rope tiedowns, mooring covers, tip socks, tiedown assemblies, parking brakes, and rotor brakes are used to secure helicopters.

Typical mooring procedures are as follows:

1. Head the helicopter in the direction from which the highest forecasted wind or gusts are anticipated.
2. Spot the helicopter slightly more than rotor-span distance from other aircraft.
3. Place wheel chocks ahead of and behind all wheels (where applicable). On helicopters equipped with skids, retract the handling wheels, lower the helicopter to rest on the skids, and install wheel position lockpins.
4. Install a tiedown assembly on the end of the blade (figure 11–29 and align the blade over the tail boom. Secure the tiedown straps under the structural tubes of the tail boom. Tie the straps snugly without strain. During wet weather, provide some slack to avoid the possibility of the straps tightening.

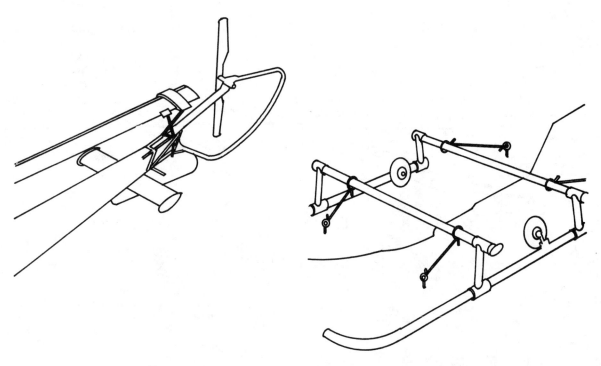

FIGURE 11–29. Securing helicopter blades and fuselage.

5. Fasten the tiedown ropes or cables to the forward and aft landing gear cross tubes and secure to ground stakes or tiedown rings.

Securing Seaplanes and Aircraft on Skis

Aircraft mounted on floats or skis should be secured to tiedown anchors or "deadmen" sunk under the water or ice. When warning of an impending storm is received and it is not possible to fly the aircraft out of the storm area, some compartments of the seaplane can be flooded, partially sinking the aircraft. In addition, the aircraft should be tied down securely to anchors. Seaplanes tied down on land have been saved from high-wind damage by filling the floats with water in addition to tying the aircraft down in the usual manner. Operators of ski-equipped aircraft sometimes pack soft snow around the skis, pour water on the snow, and permit the skis to freeze to the ice. This, in addition to the usual tiedown procedures, aids in preventing damage from windstorms.

MOVEMENT OF AIRCRAFT

General

Movement of large aircraft on an airport and about the flight line and hangar is usually accom-

plished by towing with a tow tractor (sometimes called a "mule or tug"). In the case of small aircraft, most moving is accomplished by hand, by pushing on certain areas of the aircraft surface. Aircraft may also be taxied about the flight line, but usually only by certain qualified persons.

Towing of Aircraft

Towing aircraft can be a hazardous operation, causing damage to the aircraft and injury to personnel, if done recklessly or carelessly. The following paragraphs outline the general procedure for towing aircraft; however, specific instructions for each model of aircraft are detailed in the manufacturer's maintenance instructions and should be followed in all instances.

Before the aircraft to be towed is moved, a qualified man must be in the cockpit to operate the brakes in case the tow bar should fail or become unhooked. The aircraft can then be stopped, preventing possible damage.

Some types of tow bars available for general use (figure 11–30) can be used for many types of towing operations. These bars are designed with sufficient tensile strength to pull most aircraft, but are not intended to be subjected to torsional or twisting loads. Although many have small wheels that permit them to be drawn behind the towing vehicle going to or from an aircraft, they will suffer

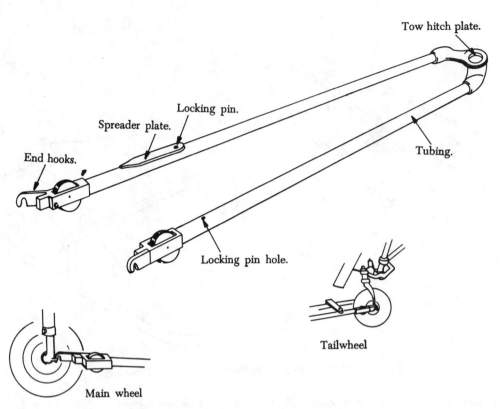

Tow hitch plate.

Locking pin.

Spreader plate.

End hooks.

Tubing.

Locking pin hole.

Tailwheel

Main wheel

FIGURE 11–30. A front or rear tow bar.

less damage and wear if they are loaded aboard the vehicle and hauled to the aircraft. When the bar is attached to the aircraft, all the engaging devices should be inspected for damage or malfunction before moving the aircraft.

Some tow bars are designed for towing various types of aircraft; however, other special types can be used on a particular aircraft only. Such bars are usually designed and built by the aircraft manufacturer.

When towing the aircraft, the towing vehicle speed must be reasonable, and all persons involved in the operation must be alert.

When the aircraft is stopped, the brakes of the towing vehicle alone should not be relied upon to stop the aircraft. The man in the cockpit should coordinate the use of the aircraft brakes with those of the towing vehicle. A typical tow tractor (or tug) is shown in figure 11–31.

The attachment of the tow bar will vary on different types of aircraft. Aircraft equipped with tailwheels are generally towed forward by attaching the tow bar to the tow rings on the main landing gear. In most cases it is permissible to tow the aircraft in reverse by attaching the tow bar to the tailwheel axle. Anytime an aircraft equipped

with a tailwheel is towed, the tailwheel must be unlocked or the tailwheel locking mechanism will be damaged or broken.

Aircraft equipped with tricycle landing gear are generally towed forward by attaching a tow bar to the axle of the nosewheel. They may also be towed forward or backward by attaching a towing bridle or specially designed towing bar to

FIGURE 11–31. Tow tractor.

518

the towing lugs on the main landing gear. When an aircraft is towed in this manner, a steering bar is attached to the nosewheel to steer the aircraft.

The following towing and parking procedures are typical of one type of operation. They are examples, and not necessarily suited to every type of operation. Aircraft ground-handling personnel should be thoroughly familiar with all procedures pertaining to the types of aircraft being towed and local operating standards governing ground handling of aircraft. Only competent persons properly checked out should direct an aircraft towing team.

1. The towing vehicle driver is responsible for operating his vehicle in a safe manner and obeying emergency stop instructions given by any team member.

2. The person in charge should assign team personnel as wing walkers. A wing walker should be stationed at each wingtip in such a position that he can ensure adequate clearance of any obstruction in the path of the aircraft. A tail walker should be assigned when sharp turns are to be made, or when the aircraft is to be backed into position.

3. A qualified person should occupy the pilot's seat of the towed aircraft to observe and operate the brakes as required. When necessary, another qualified person is stationed to watch and maintain aircraft hydraulic system pressure.

4. The person in charge of the towing operation should verify that, on aircraft with a steerable nosewheel, the locking scissors are set to full swivel for towing. The locking device must be reset after the tow bar has been removed from the aircraft. Persons stationed in the aircraft should not attempt to steer or turn the nosewheel when the tow bar is attached to the aircraft.

5. Under no circumstances should anyone be permitted to walk or ride between the nosewheel of an aircraft and the towing vehicle, nor ride on the outside of a moving aircraft or on the towing vehicle. In the interest of safety, no attempt to board or leave a moving aircraft or towing vehicle should be permitted.

6. The towing speed of the aircraft should not exceed that of the walking team members. The aircraft's engines usually are not operated when the aircraft is being towed into position.

7. The aircraft brake system should be charged before each towing operation. Aircraft with faulty brakes should be towed into position only for repair of brake systems, and then only with personnel standing by ready with chocks for emergency use. Chocks must be immediately available in case of an emergency throughout any towing operation.

8. To avoid possible personal injury and aircraft damage during towing operations, entrance doors should be closed, ladders retracted, and gear downlocks installed.

9. Prior to towing any aircraft, check all tires and landing gear struts for proper inflation. (Inflation of landing gear struts of aircraft in overhaul and storage is excluded.)

10. When moving aircraft, do not start and stop suddenly. For added safety, aircraft brakes must never be applied during towing except in emergencies, and then only upon command by one of the tow team members.

11. Aircraft should be parked in specified areas only. Generally, the distance between rows of parked aircraft should be great enough to allow immediate access of emergency vehicles in case of fire, as well as free movement of equipment and materials.

12. Wheel chocks should be placed fore and aft of the main landing gear of the parked aircraft.

13. Internal or external control locks (gust locks or blocks) should be used while the aircraft is parked.

14. Prior to any movement of aircraft across runways or taxiways, contact the airport control tower on the appropriate frequency for clearance to proceed.

15. An aircraft should not be parked in a hangar without immediately being statically grounded.

Taxiing Aircraft

As a general rule, only rated pilots and qualified airframe and powerplant technicians are author-

Lights	Meaning
Flashing green	Cleared to taxi.
Steady red	Stop.
Flashing red	Taxi clear of runway in use.
Flashing white	Return to starting point.
Alternating red and green	Exercise extreme caution.

FIGURE 11–32. Standard taxi light signals.

ized to start, run up, and taxi aircraft. All taxiing operations should be performed in accordance with applicable local regulations. Figure 11–32 contains the standard taxi light signals used by control towers to control and expedite the taxiing of aircraft. Refer to the following section, "Taxi Signals," for detailed instructions on taxi signals and related taxi instructions.

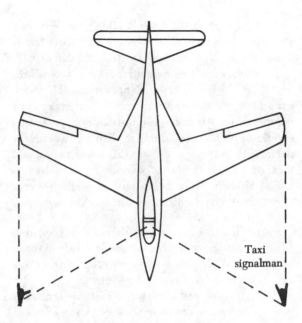

FIGURE 11–34. Position of the taxi signalman.

Taxi Signals

Many ground accidents have occurred as a result of improper technique in taxiing aircraft. Although the pilot is ultimately responsible for the aircraft until the engine is stopped, a taxi signalman can assist him around the flight line. In some aircraft configurations, the pilot's vision is obstructed while he is on the ground. He cannot see obstructions close to the wheels nor under the wings, and has little idea of what is behind him. Consequently, he depends upon the taxi signalman for directions. Figure 11–33 shows a taxi signalman indicating his readiness to assume guidance of the aircraft by extending both arms at full length above his head, palms facing each other.

The standard position for a signalman is slightly ahead of and in line with the aircraft's left wingtip. As the signalman faces the aircraft, the nose of the aircraft is on his left (figure 11–34). He must stay far enough ahead of the wingtip for the pilot to see him easily. He should follow a foolproof test to be sure the pilot can see his signals. If he can see the pilot's eyes, the pilot can see his signals.

Figure 11–35 shows the standard aircraft taxiing signals published in the Airmen's Information Manual by the Federal Aviation Administration. It should be emphasized that there are other standard signals, such as those published by the Armed Forces. In addition, operating conditions in many areas may call for a modified set of taxi

FIGURE 11–33. The taxi signalman.

FLAGMAN DIRECTS PILOT TO SIGNALMAN IF TRAFFIC CONDITIONS REQUIRE

SIGNALMAN'S POSITION

SIGNALMAN DIRECTS TOWING

STOP

COME AHEAD

EMERGENCY STOP

CUT ENGINES

START ENGINES

PULL CHOCKS

INSERT CHOCKS

SLOW DOWN

ALL CLEAR (O.K.)

LEFT TURN

RIGHT TURN

NIGHT OPERATION

FIGURE 11–35. Standard FAA hand taxi signals.

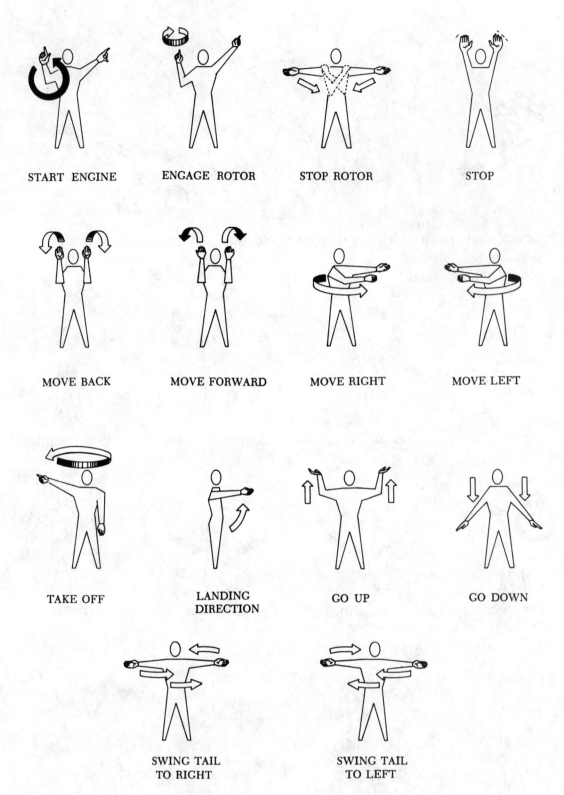

START ENGINE   ENGAGE ROTOR   STOP ROTOR   STOP

MOVE BACK   MOVE FORWARD   MOVE RIGHT   MOVE LEFT

TAKE OFF   LANDING DIRECTION   GO UP   GO DOWN

SWING TAIL TO RIGHT   SWING TAIL TO LEFT

FIGURE 11–36.   Helicopter operating signals.

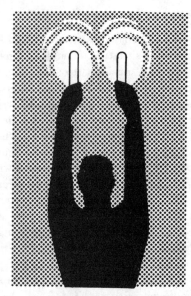

FIGURE 11–37. Night operations with wands.

signals. The signals shown in figure 11–35 represent a minimum number of the most commonly used signals. Whether this set of signals or a modified set is used is not the most important consideration, as long as each flight operational center uses a suitable, agreed-upon set of signals.

Figure 11–36 illustrates some of the most commonly used helicopter operating signals.

The taxi signals to be used should be studied until the taxi signalman can execute them clearly and precisely. The signals must be given in such a way that the pilot cannot confuse their meaning. It should be remembered that the pilot receiving the signals is always some distance away, and must often look out and down from a difficult angle. Thus, the signalman's hands should be kept well separated, and signals should be overexaggerated rather than risk making indistinct signals. If there is any doubt about a signal, or if the pilot does not appear to be following the signals, the "stop" signal should be used and the series of signals begun again.

The signalman should always try to give the pilot an indication of the approximate area in which the aircraft is to be parked. The signalman should glance behind himself often when walking backward to prevent backing into a propeller or tripping over a chock, fire bottle, tiedown line, or other obstruction.

Taxi signals are usually given at night with the aid of illuminated wands attached to flashlights (figure 11–37). Night signals are made in the same manner as day signals with the exception of the stop signal. The stop signal used at night is the "emergency stop" signal. This signal is made by crossing the wands to form a lighted "X" above and in front of the head.

JACKING AIRCRAFT

The aviation technician must be familiar with the jacking of aircraft in order to perform maintenance and inspection. Since jacking procedures and safety precautions vary for different types of aircraft, only general jacking procedures and precautions are discussed. Consult the applicable aircraft manufacturer's maintenance instructions for specific jacking procedures.

Extensive aircraft damage and serious personal injury have resulted from careless or improper jacking procedures. As an added safety measure, jacks should be inspected before use to determine the specific lifting capacity, proper functioning of safety locks, condition of pins, and general serviceability. Before raising an aircraft on jacks, all workstands and other equipment should be removed from under and near the aircraft. No one should remain in the aircraft while it is being raised or lowered, unless maintenance manual procedures require such practice for observing leveling instruments in the aircraft.

The aircraft to be jacked must be located in a

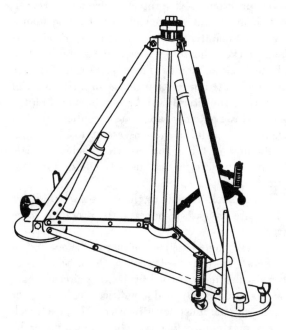

FIGURE 11–38. Typical tripod jack.

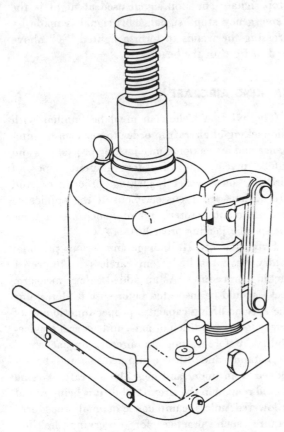

FIGURE 11–39. Typical single-base jack.

Jacking Complete Aircraft

Prior to jacking the aircraft, an overall survey of the complete situation should be made to determine if any hazards to the aircraft or personnel exist. Tripod jacks of the appropriate size for the aircraft being jacked should be placed under the aircraft jacking points and perfectly centered to prevent them from cocking when the aircraft is raised. The legs of the jacks should be checked to see that they will not interfere with the operations to be performed after the aircraft is jacked, such as retracting the landing gear.

At least three places or points are provided on aircraft for jacking purposes; a fourth place on some aircraft is used to stabilize the aircraft while it is being jacked at the other three points. The two main places are on the wings, with a smaller one on the fuselage near either the tail or the nose, depending on the landing gear design.

Most aircraft have jack pads located at the jack points. Others have removable jack pads that are inserted into receptacles bolted in place prior to jacking. The correct jack pad should be used in all cases. The function of the jack pad is to ensure that the aircraft load is properly distributed at the jack point and to provide a convex bearing surface to mate with the concave jack stem. Figure 11–40 illustrates two types of jack pads.

level position, well protected from the wind. A hangar should be used if possible. The manufacturer's maintenance instructions for the aircraft being jacked should be consulted for the location of the jacking points. These jacking points are usually located in relation to the aircraft center of gravity so the aircraft will be well balanced on the jacks. However, there are some exceptions to this. On some aircraft it may be necessary to add weight to the nose or tail of the aircraft to achieve a safe balance. Sandbags are usually used for this purpose.

Tripod jacks similar to the one shown in figure 11–38 are used when the complete aircraft is to be jacked.

A small single-base jack similar to the one shown in figure 11–39 is used when only one wheel is to be raised. The jacks used for jacking aircraft must be maintained in good condition; a leaking or damaged jack must never be used. Also, each jack has a maximum capacity, which must never be exceeded.

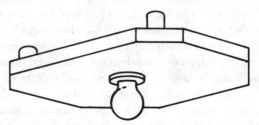

Wing jack pad assembly

Forward jack fitting

FIGURE 11–40. Typical jack pads.

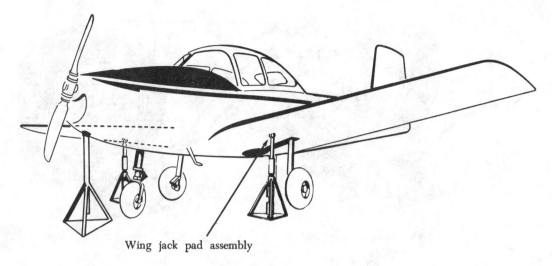

Wing jack pad assembly

FIGURE 11–41. Jacking a complete aircraft.

Prior to jacking, determine if the aircraft configuration will permit jacking. There may be equipment or fuel which has to be removed if serious structural damage is to be avoided during jacking. If any other work is in progress on the aircraft, ascertain if any critical panels have been removed. On some aircraft the stress panels or plates must be in place when the aircraft is jacked to avoid structural damage.

Extend the jacks until they contact the jack pads. A final check for alignment of the jacks should be made before the aircraft is raised, since most accidents during jacking are the result of misalined jacks.

When the aircraft is ready to be raised, a man should be stationed at each jack. The jacks should be operated simultaneously to keep the aircraft as level as possible and to avoid overloading any of the jacks. This can be accomplished by having the crew leader stand in front of the aircraft and give instructions to the men operating the jacks. Figure 11–41 shows an aircraft being jacked.

Caution should be observed, since on many jacks the piston can be raised beyond the safety point; therefore, never raise an aircraft any higher than is necessary to accomplish the job.

The area around the aircraft should be secured while the aircraft is on jacks. Climbing on the aircraft should be held to an absolute minimum, and no violent movements should be made by persons who are required to go aboard. Any cradles or necessary supports should be placed under the fuselage or wings of the aircraft at the earliest possible time, particularly if the aircraft is to remain jacked for any length of time.

On collet-equipped jacks, the collet should be kept within two threads of the lift tube cylinder during raising, and screwed down firmly to the cylinder after jacking is completed to prevent settling.

Before releasing jack pressure and lowering the aircraft, make certain that all cribbing, work-stands, equipment, and persons are clear of the aircraft, that the landing gear is down and locked, and that all ground locking devices are properly installed.

Jacking One Wheel of an Aircraft

When only one wheel has to be raised to change a tire or to grease wheel bearings, a low single-base jack is used. Before the wheel is raised, the remaining wheels must be chocked fore and aft to prevent movement of the aircraft. If the aircraft is equipped with a tailwheel, it must be locked. The wheel should be raised only high enough to clear the concrete surface. Figure 11–42 shows a wheel being raised using a single-base jack.

COLD WEATHER SUGGESTIONS

When an aircraft is to be exposed to extreme cold for any length of time, extra care should be taken to see that the aircraft is prepared for winter. All covers for engines, air-conditioning system intakes, pitot and static system openings, and ram air inlets should be installed to prevent snow and ice accumulations. Small covers should be conspicuously marked or tagged so that they are not likely to be overlooked before flight.

If the aircraft is to be parked in snow or ice

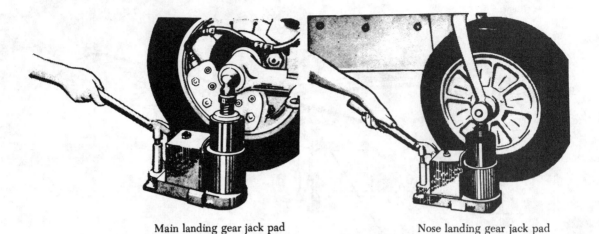

Main landing gear jack pad   Nose landing gear jack pad

FIGURE 11–42. Jacking one wheel.

conditions, it sometimes saves time and man-hours to paint around doors and frequently opened access panels with one of the inhibited glycol antifreeze compounds. The glycol may be painted on surfaces under snow covers to prevent the cover freezing to the surface. It can also be used full strength on wing or tail surfaces themselves to prevent frost. However, if snow is expected, painting exposed surfaces is rarely useful, since the slush that forms will be more troublesome than dry snow.

Another timesaver can be parking the wheels on planking rather than on ice or packed snow, or when sleet or slush may be expected to freeze tires to the ground. Sand can be used for such a purpose but should be confined to wheel areas and not distributed where it may be drawn into the engines on starting.

Flaps and spoilers should be retracted. Aircraft with movable horizontal stabilizers should have them set at approximately zero. All water and waste systems should be drained or serviced with an antifreeze solution when applicable.

If an aircraft is to be parked for a long period of time, leaving a window partially open will permit circulation of the air inside and help prevent frosting of the windows. The best way to remove snow is to sweep off as much as possible. One method is to throw a line over the fuselage and drag the snow off. A brush or broom can be used on wing and tail surfaces. Do not damage vortex generators on aircraft that have them.

A certain amount of snow may freeze to the aircraft surfaces which cannot be brushed off. It is important that all surfaces are entirely free of ice, snow, or frost before takeoff.

Most commercial facilities have spray equipment for applying deicing fluids, which are usually diluted with water and sometimes heated. Glycol antifreeze compounds, often identified by military specification numbers, have been materially improved. The compound recommended for commercial use is MIL-A-8243A. This is ethylene glycol and propylene glycol in approximately 3:1 ratio, with added corrosion inhibitor and a wetting agent. It has low toxicity, causes no damage to aircraft metals, and has no effect on most plastics, paint, or rubber.

If hot air is used for deicing, particularly from a ground starter unit, skin areas should not be overheated. A large flow of warm air is more effective than a blast of hot air. Any temperature under the boiling point of water is safe.

Should the last layer of ice or snow be melted from the fuselage, or from the leading edges of the wing, by internal heating from ground sources, the water will probably run down and refreeze in unheated areas, and must be removed again. Whatever the deicing method, inspect the trailing edge mechanism areas of the wing and tail to be sure that water or slush has not run down inside to refreeze.

When conditions warrant, preheating is used on the following sections or parts of the aircraft: accessory section, nose section, Y-drain valve, all oil lines, oil tank sump, starters, instruments, tires, cockpits, and elevator trim tabs.

Check all drain valves, oil tank sumps, oil drains, fuel strainers, vent lines, and all main and

526

auxiliary control hinges and surfaces, for the existence of ice or hard snow. Thoroughly check all deicing equipment to ensure proper operation. Alcohol tanks must be checked for proper level of deicing alcohol.

The use of an external heater is permissible at temperatures below 0° C. for heating oil and engine(s). If a heater is not available for heating the oil, the oil can be drained, heated, and put back into the system.

When starting a reciprocating engine in cold weather, try to catch the engine on the first starting attempt to prevent ice forming on the spark plugs. If ice should form, remove the spark plugs, bake, and reinstall.

In freezing weather, ice may form on the propellers while the engine is warming up. Using the propeller deicer (if available) during warm-up eliminates this condition. The turbine engine should be easier to start in very bad weather than the average piston engine. Turbine engines do not require oil dilution, priming, or lengthy warm-up.

Turbine engine compressor rotors should be checked to see that ice has not formed inside. This is particularly necessary when an engine has shut down in driving rain or snow. Be very careful when running engines if icy conditions exist. With icy pavement, chocks slide very easily, and once the aircraft is in motion it is difficult to stop.

After a flight, the oil is diluted prior to shutdown of reciprocating engines equipped with an oil dilution system, if temperatures near or below freezing are expected before or at the time of the next start. When it is necessary to dilute the oil, consult the manufacturer's instructions for the applicable aircraft. These instructions should be strictly followed; otherwise the engine can be damaged.

When fueling aircraft, the fuel tanks should be left about 3 to 5 percent below maximum capacity. This allows for expansion in the event the aircraft is brought into the hangar prior to the next flight. Fuel expands approximately 1 percent for each 10° C. increase in temperature. If fuel tanks are filled to the normal levels, at a temperature of approximately 0° C. to 10° C., and later brought into a warm hangar (20° C.), the ensuing expansion will overflow the tanks, causing a fire hazard.

Tires should be inflated to load standards, regardless of possible rise in pressure under warmer conditions. Underinflation quickly causes overheat that would result in more tire damage and more possibility of blowout than a slight amount of overinflation. If a tire is frozen to the ground, it should be thawed with warm air or water and, moved before it re-freezes.

It is easy to exceed nose gear towing load limits in snow or slush. If the airplane must be towed in deep snow, it should be pulled by cables attached to the main landing gear lugs.

The aircraft battery should require no special attention other than the normal routine servicing.

CHAPTER 12

HANDTOOLS AND MEASURING DEVICES

INTRODUCTION

This chapter contains information on some of the handtools used by an aviation mechanic. It outlines the basic knowledge required in using the most common handtools and measuring instruments used in aircraft repair work. This information, however, cannot replace sound judgment on the part of the individual. There are many times when ingenuity and resourcefulness can supplement the basic rules. A sound knowledge is required of these basic rules and of the situations in which they apply. The use of tools may vary, but good practices for safety, care, and storage of tools remain the same.

GENERAL-PURPOSE TOOLS

Hammers and Mallets

Figure 12–1 shows some of the hammers that the aviation mechanic may be required to use. Metal-head hammers are usually sized according to the weight of the head without the handle.

Occasionally it is necessary to use a soft-faced hammer, which has a striking surface made of wood, brass, lead, rawhide, hard rubber, or plastic.

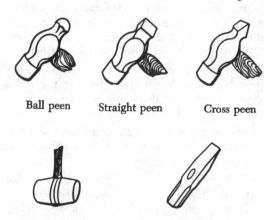

Ball peen   Straight peen   Cross peen

Tinners mallet   Riveting hammer

FIGURE 12–1. Hammers.

These hammers are intended for use in forming soft metals and striking surfaces that are easily damaged. Soft-faced hammers should not be used for rough work. Striking punch heads, bolts, or nails will quickly ruin this type hammer.

A mallet is a hammerlike tool with a head made of hickory, rawhide, or rubber. It is handy for shaping thin metal parts without denting them. Always use a wooden mallet when pounding a wood chisel or a gouge.

When using a hammer or mallet, choose the one best suited for the job. Ensure that the handle is tight. When striking a blow with the hammer, use the forearm as an extension of the handle. Swing the hammer by bending the elbow, not the wrist. Always strike the work squarely with the full face of the hammer.

Always keep the faces of hammers and mallets smooth and free from dents to prevent marring the work.

Screwdrivers

The screwdriver can be classified by its shape, type of blade, and blade length. It is made for only one purpose, i.e., for loosening or tightening screws or screwhead bolts. Figure 12–2 shows several different types of screwdrivers. When using the common screwdriver, select the largest screwdriver whose blade will make a good fit in the screw which is to be turned.

A common screwdriver must fill at least 75 percent of the screw slot. If the screwdriver is the wrong size, it cuts and burrs the screw slot, making it worthless. A screwdriver with the wrong size blade may slip and damage adjacent parts of the structures.

The common screwdriver is used only where slotted head screws or fasteners are found on aircraft. An example of a fastener which requires the use of a common screwdriver is the airlock fastener which is used to secure the cowling on some aircraft.

The two types of recessed head screws in common use are the Phillips and the Reed and Prince.

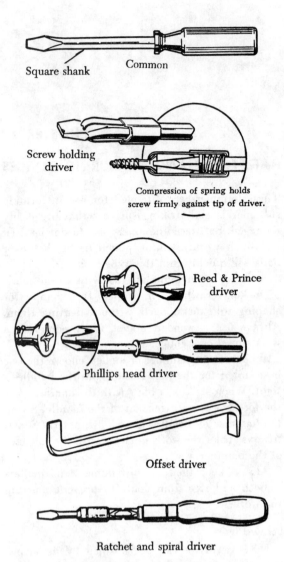

Square shank   Common

Screw holding driver

Compression of spring holds
screw firmly against tip of driver.

Reed & Prince driver

Phillips head driver

Offset driver

Ratchet and spiral driver

FIGURE 12–2. Typical screwdrivers.

Both the Phillips and Reed and Prince recessed heads are optional on several types of screws. As shown in figure 12–2, the Reed and Prince recessed head forms a perfect cross. The screwdriver used with this screw is pointed on the end. Since the Phillips screw has a slightly larger center in the cross, the Phillips screwdriver is blunt on the end. The Phillips screwdriver is not interchangeable with the Reed and Prince. The use of the wrong type screwdriver results in mutilation of the screwdriver and the screwhead. When turning a recessed head screw, use only the proper recessed head screwdriver of the correct size.

An offset screwdriver may be used when vertical space is limited. Offset screwdrivers are constructed with both ends bent 90° to the shank handle. By using alternate ends, most screws can be seated or loosened even when the swinging space is limited. Offset screwdrivers are made for both standard and recessed head screws.

A screwdriver should not be used for chiseling or prying. Do not use a screwdriver to check an electric circuit since an electric arc will burn the tip and make it useless. In some cases, an electric arc may fuse the blade to the unit being checked.

When using a screwdriver on a small part, always hold the part in the vise or rest it on a workbench. Do not hold the part in the hand, as the screwdriver may slip and cause serious personal injury.

The ratchet or spiral screwdriver is fast acting in that it turns the screw when the handle is pulled back and then pushed forward. It can be set to turn the screw either clockwise or counterclockwise, or it can be locked in position and used as a standard screwdriver. The ratchet screwdriver is not a heavy-duty tool and should be used only for light work. A word of caution: When using a spiral or ratchet screwdriver, extreme care must be used to maintain constant pressure and prevent the blade from slipping out from the slot in the screw head. If this occurs, the surrounding structure is subject to damage.

Pliers and Plier Type Cutting Tools

There are several types of pliers, but those used most frequently in aircraft repair work are the diagonal, adjustable combination, needlenose, and duckbill. The size of pliers indicates their overall length, usually ranging from 5 to 12 inches.

The 6-inch slip-joint plier, is the preferred size for use in repair work. The slip-joint permits the jaws to be opened wider at the hinge for gripping objects with large diameters. Slip-joint pliers come in sizes from 5 to 10 inches. The better grades are drop-forged steel.

Flatnose pliers are very satisfactory for making flanges. The jaws are square, fairly deep, and usually well matched, and the hinge is firm. These are characteristics which give a sharp, neat bend.

Roundnose pliers are used to crimp metal. They are not made for heavy work because too much pressure will spring the jaws, which are often wrapped to prevent scarring the metal.

Needlenose pliers have half-round jaws of varying lengths. They are used to hold objects and make adjustments in tight places.

Duckbill pliers resemble a "duck's bill" in that the jaws are thin, flat, and shaped like a duck's bill. They are used exclusively for twisting safety wire.

Water pump (channel locks) pliers are slip-joint pliers with the jaws set at an angle to the handles.

The most popular type has the slip-joint channeled, hence the name channel locks. These are used to grasp packing nuts, pipe, and odd shaped parts.

Diagonal pliers are usually referred to as diagonals or "dikes." The diagonal is a short-jawed cutter with a blade set at a slight angle on each jaw. This tool can be used to cut wire, rivets, small screws, and cotter pins, besides being practically indispensible in removing or installing safety wire. The duckbill pliers and the diagonal cutting pliers are used extensively in aviation for the job of safety wiring.

Two important rules for using pliers are:

1. Do not make pliers work beyond their capacity. The longnosed variety are especially delicate. It is easy to spring or break them, or nick the edges. If this occurs, they are practically useless.
2. Do not use pliers to turn nuts. In just a few seconds, a pair of pliers can damage a nut more than years of service.

Punches

Punches are used to locate centers for drawing circles, to start holes for drilling, to punch holes in sheet metal, to transfer location of holes in patterns, and to remove damaged rivets, pins, or bolts.

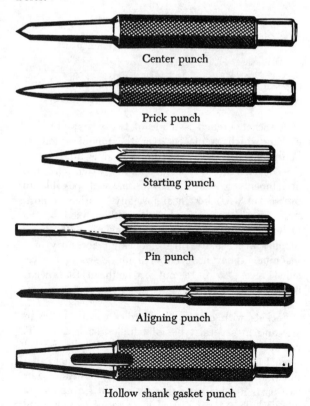

Center punch

Prick punch

Starting punch

Pin punch

Aligning punch

Hollow shank gasket punch

FIGURE 12–3. Punches.

Solid or hollow punches are the two types generally used. Solid punches are classified according to the shape of their points. Figure 12–3 shows several types of punches.

Prick punches are used to place reference marks on metal. This punch is often used to transfer dimensions from a paper pattern directly on the metal. To do this, first place the paper pattern directly on the metal. Then go over the outline of the pattern with the prick punch, tapping it lightly with a small hammer and making slight indentations on the metal at the major points on the drawing. These indentations can then be used as reference marks for cutting the metal. A prick punch should never be struck a heavy blow with a hammer because it may bend the punch or cause excessive damage to the material being worked.

Large indentations in metal, that are necessary to start a twist drill, are made with a center punch. It should never be struck with enough force to dimple the material around the indentation or to cause the metal to protrude through the other side of the sheet. A center punch has a heavier body than a prick punch and is ground to a point with an angle of about 60°.

The drive punch, which is often called a tapered punch, is used for driving out damaged rivets, pins, and bolts which sometimes bind in holes. The drive punch is therefore made with a flat face instead of a point. The size of the punch is determined by the width of the face, which is usually ⅛ inch to ¼ inch.

Pin punches, often called drift punches, are similar to drive punches and are used for the same purposes. The difference in the two is that the sides of a drive punch taper all the way to the face while the pin punch has a straight shank. Pin punches are sized by the diameter of the face, in thirty-seconds of an inch, and range from 1/16 to 3/8 inch in diameter.

In general practice, a pin or bolt which is to be driven out is usually started and driven with a drive punch until the sides of the punch touch the side of the hole. A pin punch is then used to drive the pin or bolt the rest of the way out of the hole. Stubborn pins may be started by placing a thin piece of scrap copper, brass, or aluminum directly against the pin and then striking it with a hammer until the pin begins to move.

Never use a prick punch or center punch to remove objects from holes, because the point of the punch will spread the object and cause it to bind even more.

The transfer punch is usually about 4 inches long. It has a point that tapers, then turns straight for a short distance in order to fit a drill-locating hole in a template. The tip has a point similar to that of a prick punch. As its name implies, the transfer punch is used to transfer the location of holes through the template or pattern to the material.

Wrenches

The wrenches most often used in aircraft maintenance are classified as open-end, box-end, socket, adjustable, and special wrenches. The allen wrench, although seldom used, is required on one special type of recessed screw. One of the most widely used metals for making wrenches is chrome-vanadium steel. Wrenches made of this metal are almost unbreakable.

Solid, nonadjustable wrenches with open parallel jaws on one or both ends are known as open-end wrenches. These wrneches may have their jaws parallel to the handle or at an angle up to 90°; most are set at an angle of 15°. Basically, the wrenches are designed to fit a nut, bolthead, or other object which makes it possible to exert a turning action.

Box-end wrenches are popular tools because of their usefulness in close quarters. They are called box wrenches since they box, or completely surround, the nut or bolthead. Practically all box-end wrenches are made with 12 points so they can be used in places having as little as 15° swing. In figure 12–4, point A on the illustrated double broached hexagon wrench is nearer the center line of the head and the wrench handle than point B, and also the center line of nut C. If the wrench is inverted and installed on nut C, point A will be centered over side "Y" instead of side "X". The center line of the handle will now be in the dotted line position. It is by reversing (turning the wrench over) the position of the wrench that a 15° arc may be made with the wrench handle.

Although box-end wrenches are ideal to break loose tight nuts or pull tight nuts tighter, time is lost turning the nut off the bolt once the nut is broken loose. Only when there is sufficient clearance to rotate the wrench in a complete circle can this tedious process be avoided.

After a tight nut is broken loose, it can be completely backed off or unscrewed more quickly with an open-end than with a box-end wrench. In this case, a combination wrench is needed, which has a box-end on one end and an open-end wrench of

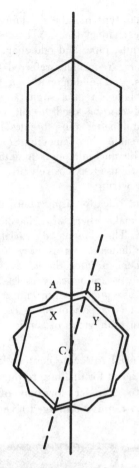

FIGURE 12–4. Box-end wrench use.

the same size on the other. Both the box-end and combination wrenches are shown in figure 12–5.

A socket wrench is made of two parts: (1) The socket, which is placed over the top of a nut or bolthead, and (2) a handle, which is attached to the socket. Many types of handles, extensions, and attachments are available to make it possible to use socket wrenches in almost any location or position. Sockets are made with either fixed or detachable handles. Socket wrenches with fixed handles are usually furnished as an accessory to a machine. They have either a four-, six- or twelve-sided recess to fit a nut or bolthead that needs regular adjustment.

Sockets with detachable handles usually come in sets and fit several types of handles, such as the T, ratchet, screwdriver grip, and speed handle. Socket wrench handles have a square lug on one end that fits into a square recess in the socket head. The two parts are held together by a light spring-loaded poppet. Two types of sockets, a set of handles, and an extension bar are shown in figure 12–6.

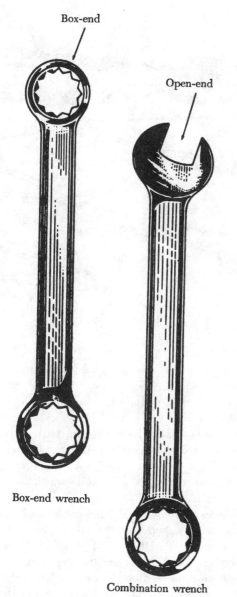

Box-end

Open-end

Box-end wrench

Combination wrench

FIGURE 12–5. Box end and combination wrenches.

The adjustable wrench is a handy utility tool which has smooth jaws and is designed as an open-end wrench. One jaw is fixed, but the other may be moved by a thumbscrew or spiral screwworm adjustment in the handle. The width of the jaws may be varied from 0 to $\frac{1}{2}$ inch or more. The angle of the opening to the handle is $22\frac{1}{2}°$ on an adjustable wrench. One adjustable wrench does the work of several open-end wrenches. Although versatile, they are not intended to replace the standard open-end, box-end, or socket wrenches. When using any adjustable wrench, always exert the pull on the side of the handle attached to the fixed jaw of the wrench.

Special Wrenches

The category of special wrenches includes the spanner, torque, and allen wrenches. The hook spanner is for a round nut with a series of notches cut in the outer edge. This wrench has a curved arm with a hook on the end which fits into one of the notches on the nut. The hook is placed in one of these notches with the handle pointing in the direction the nut is to be turned.

Some hook spanner wrenches are adjustable and will fit nuts of various diameters. U-shaped hook spanners have two lugs on the face of the wrench to fit notches cut in the face of the nut or screw plug. End spanners resemble a socket wrench but have a series of lugs that fit into corresponding notches in a nut or plug. Pin spanners have a pin in place of a lug, and the pin fits into a round hole in the edge of a nut. Face pin spanners are similar to the U-shaped hook spanners except that they have pins instead of lugs.

There are times when definite pressure must be applied to a nut or bolt. In such cases a torque

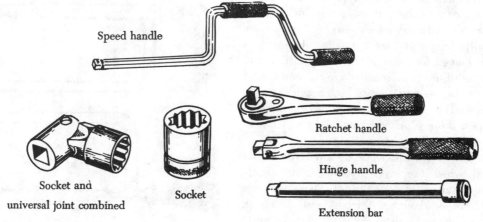

Speed handle

Ratchet handle

Hinge handle

Socket and
universal joint combined

Socket

Extension bar

FIGURE 12–6. Socket wrench set.

wrench must be used. The torque wrench is a precision tool consisting of a torque-indicating handle and appropriate adapter or attachments. It measures the amount of turning or twisting force applied to a nut, bolt, or screw.

The three most commonly used torque wrenches are the deflecting beam, dial-indicating, and micrometer-setting types. When using the deflecting beam and the dial-indicating torque wrenches, the torque is read visually on a dial or scale mounted on the handle of the wrench. The micrometer-setting torque wrench is preset to the desired torque. When this torque is reached, a sharp impulse or breakaway is noticed by the operator.

Before each use, the torque wrench should be visually inspected for damage. If a bent pointer, cracked or broken glass (dial type), or signs of rough handling are found, the wrench must be tested. Torque wrenches must be tested at periodic intervals to ensure accuracy.

Most headless setscrews are the allen type and must be installed and removed with an allen wrench. Allen wrenches are six-sided bars in the shape of an L. They range in size from ³⁄₆₄ to ½ inch and fit into a hexagonal recess in the setscrew.

METAL CUTTING TOOLS
Hand Snips

There are several kinds of hand snips, each of which serves a different purpose. Straight, curved, hawksbill, and aviation snips are in common use (figure 12–7). Straight snips are used for cutting straight lines when the distance is not great enough to use a squaring shear and for cutting the outside of a curve. The other types are used for cutting the inside of curves or radii. Snips should never be used to cut heavy sheet metal.

Aviation snips are designed especially for cutting heat-treated aluminum alloy and stainless steel. They are also adaptable for enlarging small holes. The blades have small teeth on the cutting edges and are shaped for cutting very small circles and irregular outlines. The handles are the compound leverage type, making it possible to cut material as thick as 0.051 inch. Aviation snips are available in two types, those which cut from right to left and those which cut from left to right.

Unlike the hacksaw, snips do not remove any material when the cut is made, but minute fractures often occur along the cut. Therefore, cuts should be made about one-thirty-second inch from the layout line and finished by hand-filing down to the line.

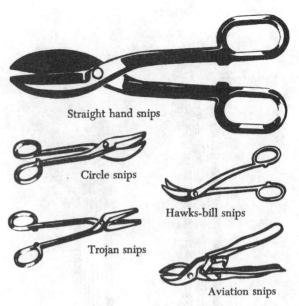

Straight hand snips

Circle snips

Hawks-bill snips

Trojan snips

Aviation snips

FIGURE 12–7. Snips.

Hacksaws

The common hacksaw has a blade, a frame, and a handle. The handle can be obtained in two styles, pistol grip and straight (figure 12–8).

Hacksaw blades have holes in both ends; they are mounted on pins attached to the frame. When installing a blade in a hacksaw frame, mount the blade with the teeth pointing forward, away from the handle.

Blades are made of high-grade tool steel or tungsten steel and are available in sizes from 6 to 16 inches in length. The 10-inch blade is most commonly used. There are two types, the all-hard blade and the flexible blade. In flexible blades, only the teeth are hardened. Selection of the best

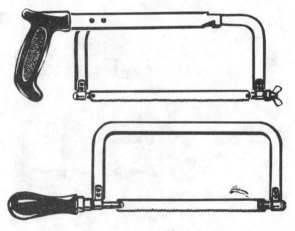

FIGURE 12–8. Hacksaws.

blade for the job involves finding the right type and pitch. An all-hard blade is best for sawing brass, tool steel, cast iron, and heavy cross-section materials. A flexible blade is usually best for sawing hollow shapes and metals having a thin cross section.

The pitch of a blade indicates the number of teeth per inch. Pitches of 14, 18, 24, and 32 teeth per inch are available. A blade with 14 teeth per inch is preferred when cutting machine steel, cold-rolled steel, or structural steel. A blade with 18 teeth per inch is preferred for solid stock aluminum, bearing metal, tool steel, and cast iron. Use a blade with 24 teeth per inch when cutting thick-walled tubing, pipe, brass, copper, channel, and angle iron. Use a 32-teeth-per-inch blade for cutting thin-walled tubing and sheet metal.

When using a hacksaw, observe the following procedures:

1. Select an appropriate saw blade for the job.
2. Assemble the blade in the frame so that the cutting edge of the teeth points away from the handle.
3. Adjust tension of the blade in the frame to prevent the saw from buckling and drifting.
4. Clamp the work in the vise in such a way that will provide as much bearing surface as possible and will engage the greatest number of teeth.
5. Indicate the starting point by nicking the surface with the edge of a file to break any sharp corner that might strip the teeth. This mark will also aid in starting the saw at the proper place.
6. Hold the saw at an angle that will keep at least two teeth in contact with the work at all times. Start the cut with a light, steady, forward stroke just outside the cutting line. At the end of the stroke, relieve the pressure and draw the blade back. (The cut is made on the forward stroke.)
7. After the first few strokes, make each stroke as long as the hacksaw frame will allow. This will prevent the blade from overheating. Apply just enough pressure on the forward stroke to cause each tooth to remove a small amount of metal. The strokes should be long and steady with a

speed not more than 40 to 50 strokes per minute.
8. After completing the cut, remove chips from the blade, loosen tension on the blade, and return the hacksaw to its proper place.

Chisels

A chisel is a hard steel cutting tool which can be used for cutting and chipping any metal softer than the chisel itself. It can be used in restricted areas and for such work as shearing rivets, or splitting seized or damaged nuts from bolts (figure 12–9).

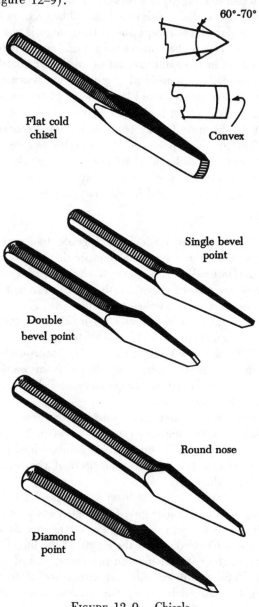

FIGURE 12–9. Chisels.

The size of a flat cold chisel is determined by the width of the cutting edge. Lengths will vary, but chisels are seldom under 5 inches or over 8 inches long.

Chisels are usually made of eight-sided tool steel bar stock, carefully hardened and tempered. Since the cutting edge is slightly convex, the center portion receives the greatest shock when cutting, and the weaker corners are protected. The cutting angle should be 60° to 70° for general use, such as for cutting wire, strap iron, or small bars and rods.

When using a chisel, hold it firmly in one hand. With the other hand, strike the chisel head squarely with a ball-peen hammer.

When cutting square corners or slots, a special cold chisel called a cape chisel should be used. It is like a flat chisel except the cutting edge is very narrow. It has the same cutting angle and is held and used in the same manner as any other chisel.

Rounded or semicircular grooves and corners which have fillets should be cut with a roundnose chisel. This chisel is also used to recenter a drill which has moved away from its intended center.

The diamond point chisel is tapered square at the cutting end, then ground at an angle to provide the sharp diamond point. It is used for cutting B-grooves and inside sharp angles.

Files

Most files are made of high-grade tool steels that are hardened and tempered. Files are manufactured in a variety of shapes and sizes. They are known either by the cross section, the general shape, or by their particular use. The cuts of files must be considered when selecting them for various types of work and materials.

Files are used to square ends, file rounded corners, remove burrs and slivers from metal, straighten uneven edges, file holes and slots, and smooth rough edges.

Files have three distinguishing features: (1) Their length, measured exclusive of the tang (figure 12–10); (2) their kind or name, which has reference to the relative coarseness of the teeth; and (3) their cut.

Files are usually made in two types of cuts, single-cut and double-cut. The single-cut file has a single row of teeth extending across the face at an angle of 65° to 85° with the length of the file. The size of the cuts depends on the coarseness of the file. The double-cut file has two rows of teeth which cross each other. For general work, the angle of the first row is 40° to 45°. The first row is

generally referred to as "overcut," and the second row as "upcut"; the upcut is somewhat finer and not so deep as the overcut.

Files—Care and Use

Files and rasps are cataloged in three ways:

Length. Measuring from the tip to the heel of the file. The tang is never included in the length.

Shape. Refers to the physical configuration of the file (circular, rectangular, or triangular or a variation thereof).

Cut. Refers to both the character of the teeth or the coarseness; rough, coarse and bastard for use on heavier classes of work and second cut, smooth and dead smooth for finishing work.

Most Commonly Used Files (see figure 12–11)

Hand files. These are parallel in width and tapered in thickness. They have one safe edge (smooth edge) which permits filing in corners, and on other work where a safe edge is required. Hand files are double-cut and used principally for finishing flat surfaces and similar work.

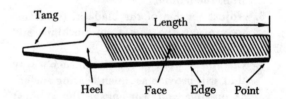

FIGURE 12–10.   Hand file.

Flat files. These files are slightly tapered toward the point in both width and thickness They cut on both edges as well as on the sides. They are the most common files in use. Flat files are double-cut on both sides and single-cut on both edges.

Mill files. These are usually tapered slightly in thickness and in width for about one-third of their length. The teeth are ordinarily single-cut. These files are used for drawfiling and to some extent for filing soft metals.

Square files. These files may be tapered or blunt and are double-cut. They are used principally for filing slots and key seats, and for surface filing.

Round or rattail files. These are circular in cross section and may be either tapered or blunt and single- or double-cut. They are used principally for filing circular openings or concave surfaces.

Triangular and Three-square files. These files are triangular in cross section. Triangular files are single-cut and are used for filing the gullet between saw teeth. Three-square files, which are double-cut, may be used for filing internal angles, clearing out corners, and filing taps and cutters.

Half-round files. These files cut on both the flat and round sides. They may be single- or double-cut. Their shape permits them to be used where other files would be unsatisfactory.

Lead float files. These are especially designed for use on soft metals. They are single-cut and are made in various lengths.

Warding file—Rectangular in section and tapers to narrow point as to width. Used for narrow space filing where other files cannot be used.

Knife file—Knife-blade section. Used by tool and die makers on work having acute angles.

Wood file—Same section as flat and half round files. Has coarser teeth and is especially adaptable for use on wood.

Vixen (Curved tooth files)—Curved tooth files are especially designed for rapid filing and smooth finish on soft metals and wood. The regular cut is adapted for tough work on cast iron, soft steel, copper, brass, aluminum, wood, slate, marble, fibre, rubber, etc. The fine cut gives excellent results on steel, cast iron, phosphor bronze, white brass, and all hard metals. The smooth cut is used where the amount of material to be removed is very slight, but where a superior finish is desired.

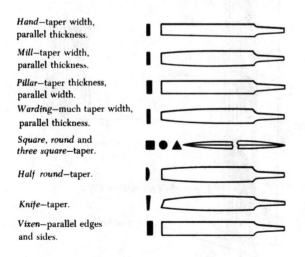

Hand—taper width, parallel thickness.

Mill—taper width, parallel thickness.

Pillar—taper thickness, parallel width.

Warding—much taper width, parallel thickness.

Square, round and three square—taper.

Half round—taper.

Knife—taper.

Vixen—parallel edges and sides.

FIGURE 12–11. Types of files.

The following methods are recommended for using files:

1. *Crossfiling.* Before attempting to use a file, place a handle on the tang of the file. This is essential for proper guiding and safe use. In moving the file endwise across the work (commonly known as crossfiling), grasp the handle so that its end fits into and against the fleshy part of the palm with the thumb lying along the top of the handle in a lengthwise direction. Grasp the end of the file between the thumb and first two fingers. To prevent undue wear, relieve the pressure during the return stroke.

2. *Drawfiling.* A file is sometimes used by grasping it at each end, crosswise to the work, then moving it lengthwise with the work. When done properly, work may be finished somewhat finer than when crossfiling with the same file. In drawfiling, the teeth of the file produce a shearing effect. To accomplish this shearing effect, the angle at which the file is held with respect to its line of movement varies with different files, depending on the angle at which the teeth are cut. Pressure should be relieved during the backstroke.

3. *Rounding Corners.* The method used in filing a rounded surface depends upon its width and the radius of the rounded surface. If the surface is narrow or only a portion of a surface is to be rounded, start the forward stroke of the file with the point of the file inclined downward at approximately a 45° angle. Using a rocking chair motion, finish the stroke with the heel of the file near the curved surface. This method allows use of the full length of the file.

4. *Removing Burred or Slivered Edges.* Practically every cutting operation on sheet metal produces burrs or slivers. These must be removed to avoid personal injury and to prevent scratching and marring of parts to be assembled. Burrs and slivers will prevent parts from fitting properly and should always be removed from the work as a matter of habit.

Lathe filing requires that the file be held against the work revolving in the lathe. The file should not be held rigid or stationary but should be stroked constantly with a slight gliding or lateral motion along the work. A standard mill file may be used for this operation, but the long angle lathe file provides a much cleaner shearing and self-clearing action. Use a file with "safe" edges to protect work with shoulders from being marred.

Care of Files

There are several precautions that any good craftsman will take in caring for his files.

1. Choose the right file for the material and work to be performed.
2. Keep all files racked and separated so they do not bear against each other.
3. Keep the files in a dry place—rust will corrode the teeth points.
4. Keep files clean—Tap the end of the file against the bench after every few strokes, to loosen and clear the filings. Use the file card to keep files clean—a dirty file is a dull file.

Particles of metal collect between the teeth of a file and may make deep scratches in the material being filed. When these particles of metal are lodged too firmly between the teeth and cannot be removed by tapping the edge of the file, remove them with a file card or wire brush (figure 12–12). Draw the brush across the file so that the bristles pass down the gullet between the teeth.

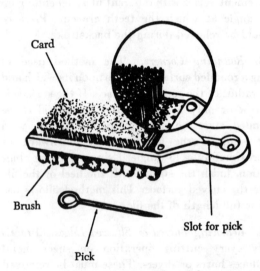

FIGURE 12–12. File card.

Drills

There are generally four types of portable drills used in aviation for holding and turning twist drills. Holes ¼ inch in diameter and under can be drilled using a hand drill. This drill is commonly called an "egg beater." The breast drill is designed to hold larger size twist drills than the hand drill. In addition a breast plate is affixed at the upper end of the drill to permit the use of body weight to increase the cutting power of the drill. Electric and pneumatic power drills are available in various shapes and sizes to satisfy almost any requirement.

Pneumatic drills are preferred for use around flammable materials, since sparks from an electric drill are a fire or explosion hazard.

Twist Drills

A twist drill is a pointed tool that is rotated to cut holes in material. It is made of a cylindrical hardened steel bar having spiral flutes (grooves) running the length of the body, and a conical point with cutting edges formed by the ends of the flutes.

Twist drills are made of carbon steel or high-speed alloy steel. Carbon steel twist drills are satisfactory for the general run of work and are relatively inexpensive. The more expensive high-speed twist drills are used for the tough materials such as stainless steels. Twist drills have from one to four spiral flutes. Drills with two flutes are used for most drilling; those with three or four flutes are used principally to follow smaller drills or to enlarge holes.

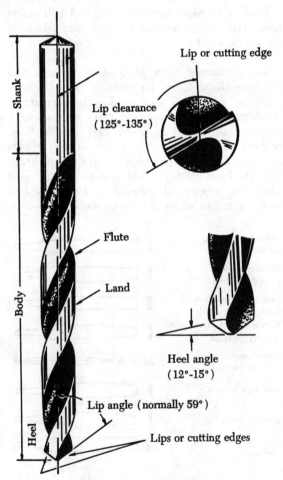

FIGURE 12–13. Twist drill.

538

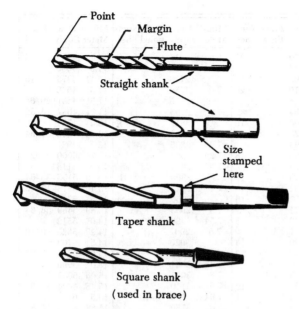

Point
Margin
Flute
Straight shank
Size stamped here
Taper shank
Square shank
(used in brace)

FIGURE 12–14. Drills.

The principal parts of a twist drill are the shank, the body, and the point, illustrated in figure 12–13. The drill shank is the end that fits into the chuck of a hand or power drill. The two shank shapes most commonly used in hand drills are the straight shank and the square or bit stock shank (figure 12–14). The straight shank generally is used in hand, breast, and portable electric drills; the square shank is made to fit into a carpenter's brace. Tapered shanks generally are used in machine shop drill presses.

The metal column forming the core of the drill is the body. The body clearance area lies just back of the margin, slightly smaller in diameter than the margin, to reduce the friction between the drill and the sides of the hole. The angle at which the drill point is ground is the lip clearance angle. On standard drills used to cut steel and cast iron, the angle should be 59° from the axis of the drill. For faster drilling of soft materials, sharper angles are used.

The diameter of a twist drill may be given in one of three ways: (1) By fractions, (2) letters, or (3) numbers. Fractionally, they are classified by sixteenths of an inch (from $\frac{1}{16}$ to $3\frac{1}{2}$ in.), by thirty-seconds (from $\frac{1}{32}$ to $2\frac{1}{2}$ in.), or by sixty-fourths (from $\frac{1}{64}$ to $1\frac{1}{4}$ in.). For a more exact measurement a letter system is used with decimal equivalents: A (0.234 in.) to Z (0.413 in.). The number system of classification is most accurate: No. 80 (0.0314 in.) to No. 1 (0.228 in.). Drill sizes

and their decimal equivalents are shown in figure 12–15.

The twist drill should be sharpened at the first sign of dullness. For most drilling, a twist drill with a cutting angle of 118° (59° on either side of center) will be sufficient; however, when drilling soft metals, a cutting angle of 90° may be more efficient.

Typical procedures for sharpening drills (figure 12–16) are as follows:

1. Adjust the grinder tool rest to a convenient height for resting the back of the hand while grinding.

2. Hold the drill between the thumb and index finger of the right or left hand. Grasp the body of the drill near the shank with the other hand.

3. Place the hand on the tool rest with the center line of the drill making a 59° angle with the cutting face of the grinding wheel. Lower the shank end of the drill slightly.

4. Slowly place the cutting edge of the drill against the grinding wheel. Gradually lower the shank of the drill as you twist the drill in a clockwise direction. Maintain pressure against the grinding surface only until you reach the heel of the drill.

5. Check the results of grinding with a gage to determine whether or not the lips are the same length and at a 59° angle.

Reamers

Reamers are used to smooth and enlarge holes to exact size. Hand reamers have square end shanks so that they can be turned with a tap wrench or similar handle. The various types of reamers are illustrated in figure 12–17.

A hole that is to be reamed to exact size must be drilled about 0.003- to 0.007-inch undersize. A cut that removes more than 0.007 inch places too much load on the reamer and should not be attempted.

Reamers are made of either carbon tool steel or high-speed steel. The cutting blades of a high-speed steel reamer lose their original keenness sooner than those of a carbon steel reamer; however, after the first super-keenness is gone, they are still serviceable. The high-speed reamer usually lasts much longer than the carbon steel type.

Milli-Meter	Dec. Equiv.	Frac-tional	Num-ber	Milli-Meter	Dec. Equiv.	Frac-tional	Num-ber	Milli-Meter	Dec. Equiv.	Frac-tional	Num-ber	Milli-Meter	Dec. Equiv.	Frac-tional	Num-ber	Milli-Meter	Dec. Equiv.	Frac-tional
.1	.0039			1.75	.0689				.1570		22	6.8	.2677			10.72	.4219	27/64
.15	.0059				.0700		50	4.0	.1575			6.9	.2716			11.0	.4330	
.2	.0079			1.8	.0709				.1590		21		.2720		I	11.11	.4375	7/16
.25	.0098			1.85	.0728				.1610		20	7.0	.2756			11.5	.4528	
.3	.0118				.0730		49	4.1	.1614				.2770		J	11.51	.4531	29/64
	.0135		80	1.9	.0748			4.2	.1654			7.1	.2795			11.91	.4687	15/32
.35	.0138				.0760		48		.1660		19		.2811		K	12.0	.4724	
	.0145		79	1.95	.0767			4.25	.1673			7.14	.2812	9/32		12.30	.4843	31/64
.39	.0156	1/64		1.98	.0781	5/64		4.3	.1693			7.2	.2835			12.5	.4921	
.4	.0157			2.0	.0787				.1695		18	7.25	.2854			12.7	.5000	1/2
	.0160		78	2.05	.0807			4.37	.1719	11/64		7.3	.2874			13.0	.5118	
.45	.0177				.0810		46		.1730		17		.2900		L	13.10	.5156	33/64
	.0180		77		.0820		45	4.4	.1732			7.4	.2913			13.49	.5312	17/32
.5	.0197			2.1	.0827				.1770		16		.2950		M	13.5	.5315	
	.0200		76	2.15	.0846			4.5	.1771			7.5	.2953			13.89	.5469	35/64
	.0210		75		.0860		44		.1800		15	7.54	.2968	19/64		14.0	.5512	
.55	.0217			2.2	.0866			4.6	.1811			7.6	.2992			14.29	.5625	9/16
	.0225		74	2.25	.0885				.1820		14		.3020		N	14.5	.5709	
.6	.0236				.0890		43	4.7	.1850		13	7.7	.3031			14.68	.5781	37/64
	.0240		73	2.3	.0905			4.75	.1870			7.75	.3051			15.0	.5906	
	.0250		72	2.35	.0925			4.76	.1875	3/16		7.8	.3071			15.08	.5937	19/32
.65	.0256				.0935		42	4.8	.1890		12	7.9	.3110			15.48	.6094	39/64
	.0260		71	2.38	.0937	3/32			.1910		11	7.94	.3125	5/16		15.5	.6102	
	.0280		70	2.4	.0945			4.9	.1929			8.0	.3150			15.88	.6250	5/8
.7	.0276				.0960		41		.1935		10		.3160		O	16.0	.6299	
	.0292		69	2.45	.0964				.1960		9	8.1	.3189			16.27	.6406	41/64
.75	.0295				.0980		40	5.0	.1968			8.2	.3228			16.5	.6496	
	.0310		68	2.5	.0984				.1990		8		.3230		P	16.67	.6562	21/32
.79	.0312	1/32			.0995		39	5.1	.2008			8.25	.3248			17.0	.6693	
.8	.0315				.1015		38		.2010		7	8.3	.3268			17.06	.6719	43/64
	.0320		67	2.6	.1024			5.16	.2031	13/64		8.33	.3281	21/64		17.46	.6875	11/16
	.0330		66		.1040		37		.2040		6	8.4	.3307			17.5	.6890	
.85	.0335			2.7	.1063			5.2	.2047				.3320		Q	17.86	.7031	45/64
	.0350		65		.1065		36		.2055		5	8.5	.3346			18.0	.7087	
.9	.0354			2.75	.1082			5.25	.2067			8.6	.3386			18.26	.7187	23/32
	.0360		64	2.78	.1094	7/64		5.3	.2086				.3390		R	18.5	.7283	
	.0370		63		.1100		35		.2090		4	8.7	.3425			18.65	.7344	47/64
.95	.0374			2.8	.1102			5.4	.2126			8.73	.3437	11/32		19.0	.7480	
	.0380		62		.1110		34		.2130		3	8.75	.3445			19.05	.7500	3/4
	.0390		61		.1130		33	5.5	.2165			8.8	.3465			19.45	.7656	49/64
1.0	.0394			2.9	.1141			5.56	.2187	7/32			.3480		S	19.5	.7677	
	.0400		60		.1160		32	5.6	.2205			8.9	.3504			19.84	.7812	25/32
	.0410		59	3.0	.1181				.2210		2	9.0	.3543			20.0	.7874	
1.05	.0413				.1200		31	5.7	.2244				.3580		T	20.24	.7969	51/64
	.0420		58	3.1	.1220			5.75	.2263			9.1	.3583			20.5	.8071	
	.0430		57	3.18	.1250	1/8			.2280		1	9.13	.3594	23/64		20.64	.8125	13/16
1.1	.0433			3.2	.1260			5.8	.2283			9.2	.3622			21.0	.8268	
1.15	.0452			3.25	.1279			5.9	.2323			9.25	.3641			21.03	.8281	53/64
	.0465		56		.1285		30		.2340		A	9.3	.3661			21.43	.8437	27/32
1.19	.0469	3/64		3.3	.1299			5.95	.2344	15/64			.3680		U	21.5	.8465	
1.2	.0472			3.4	.1338			6.0	.2362			9.4	.3701			21.83	.8594	55/64
1.25	.0492				.1360		29		.2380		B	9.5	.3740			22.0	.8661	
1.3	.0512			3.5	.1378			6.1	.2401			9.53	.3750	3/8		22.23	.8750	7/8
	.0520		55		.1405		28		.2420		C		.3770		V	22.5	.8858	
1.35	.0531			3.57	.1406	9/64		6.2	.2441			9.6	.3780			22.62	.8906	57/64
	.0550		54	3.6	.1417			6.25	.2460		D	9.7	.3819			23.0	.9055	
1.4	.0551				.1440		27	6.3	.2480			9.75	.3838			23.02	.9062	29/32
1.45	.0570			3.7	.1457			6.35	.2500	1/4	E	9.8	.3858			23.42	.9219	59/64
1.5	.0591				.1470		26	6.4	.2520				.3860		W	23.5	.9252	
	.0595		53	3.75	.1476			6.5	.2559			9.9	.3898			23.81	.9375	15/16
1.55	.0610				.1495		25		.2570		F	9.92	.3906	25/64		24.0	.9449	
1.59	.0625	1/16		3.8	.1496			6.6	.2598			10.0	.3937			24.21	.9531	61/64
1.6	.0629				.1520		24		.2610		G		.3970		X	24.5	.9646	
	.0635		52	3.9	.1535			6.7	.2638				.4040		Y	24.61	.9687	31/32
1.65	.0649				.1540		23	6.75	.2657	17/64		10.32	.4062	13/32		25.0	.9843	
1.7	.0669			3.97	.1562	5/32		6.75	.2657				.4130		Z	25.03	.9844	63/64
	.0670		51						.2660		H	10.5	.4134			25.4	1.0000	1

FIGURE 12–15. Drill sizes.

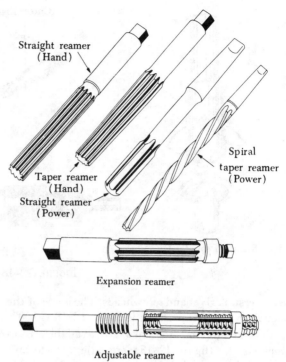

FIGURE 12–17. Reamers.

Reamer blades are hardened to the point of being brittle and must be handled carefully to avoid chipping them. When reaming a hole, rotate the reamer in the cutting direction only. Turn the reamer steadily and evenly to prevent chattering, or marking and scoring of the hole walls.

Reamers are available in any standard size. The straight-fluted reamer is less expensive than the spiral-fluted reamer, but the spiral type has less tendency to chatter. Both types are tapered for a short distance back of the end to aid in starting. Bottoming reamers have no taper and are used to complete the reaming of blind holes.

For general use, an expansion reamer is the most practical. This type is furnished in standard sizes from ¼ inch to 1 inch, increasing in diameter by 1/32-inch increments.

Taper reamers, both hand- and machine-operated, are used to smooth and true tapered holes and recesses.

Countersink

A countersink is a tool which cuts a cone-shaped depression around the hole to allow a rivet or screw to set flush with the surface of the material. Countersinks are made with various angles to correspond to the various angles of the

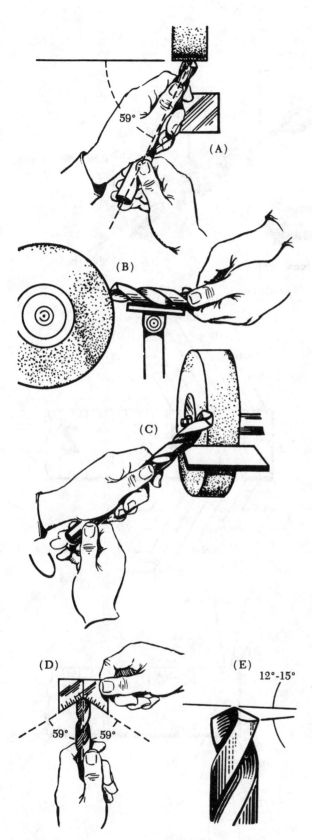

FIGURE 12–16. Drill sharpening procedures.

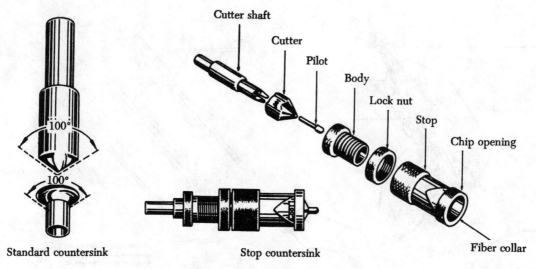

FIGURE 12–18. Countersinks.

countersunk rivet and screwheads. The angle of the standard countersink shown in figure 12–18 is 100°.

Special stop countersinks are available. Stop countersinks (figure 12–18) are adjustable to any desired depth, and the cutters are interchangeable so that holes of various countersunk angles may be made. Some stop countersinks have a micrometer set arrangement (in increments of 0.001 inch) for adjusting the cutting depths.

When using a countersink, care must be taken not to remove an excessive amount of material since this reduces the strength of flush joints.

LAYOUT AND MEASURING TOOLS

Layout and measuring devices are precision tools. They are carefully machined, accurately marked and, in many cases, are made up of very delicate parts. When using these tools, be careful not to drop, bend, or scratch them. The finished product will be no more accurate than the measurements or the layout; therefore, it is very important to understand how to read, use, and care for these tools.

Rules

Rules are made of steel and are either rigid or flexible. The flexible steel rule will bend, but it should not be bent intentionally as it may be broken rather easily.

In aircraft work the unit of measure most commonly used is the inch. The inch may be divided into smaller parts by means of either common or decimal fraction divisions. The frac-

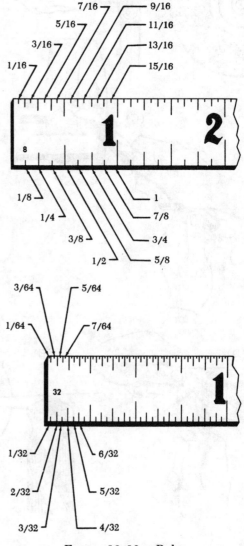

FIGURE 12–19. Rules.

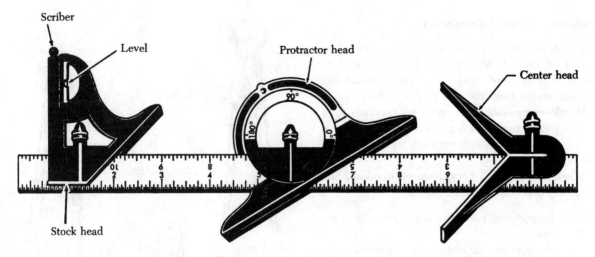

FIGURE 12–20. Combination set.

tional divisions for an inch are found by dividing the inch into equal parts—halves (½), quarters (¼), eighths (⅛), sixteenths (1/16), thirty-seconds (1/32), and sixty-fourths (1/64)—as shown in figure 12–17.

The fractions of an inch may be expressed in decimals, called decimal equivalents of an inch; for example, ⅛ inch is expressed as 0.0125 (one hundred twenty-five ten-thousandths of an inch).

Rules are manufactured in two basic styles, those divided or marked in common fractions (figure 12–19) and those divided or marked in decimals or divisions of one one-hundredth of an inch. A rule may be used either as a measuring tool or as a straightedge.

Combination Sets

The combination set (figure 12–20), as its name implies, is a tool that has several uses. It can be used for the same purposes as an ordinary tri-square, but it differs from the tri-square in that the head slides along the blade and can be clamped at any desired place. Combined with the square or stock head are a level and scriber. The head slides in a central groove on the blade or scale, which can be used separately as a rule.

The spirit level in the stock head makes it convenient to square a piece of material with a surface and at the same time tell whether one or the other is plumb or level. The head can be used alone as a simple level.

The combination of square head and blade can also be used as a marking gage to scribe lines at a 45° angle, as a depth gage, or as a height gage.

A convenient scriber is held frictionally in the head by a small brass bushing.

The center head is used to find the center of shafts or other cylindrical work. The protractor head can be used to check angles and also may be set at any desired angle to draw lines.

Scriber

The scriber is designed to serve the aviation mechanic in the same way a pencil or pen serves a writer. In general, it is used to scribe or mark lines on metal surfaces. The scriber (figure 12–21) is made of tool steel, 4 to 12 inches long, and has two needle-pointed ends. One end is bent at a 90° angle for reaching and marking through holes.

Before using a scriber always inspect the points for sharpness. Be sure the straightedge is flat on the metal and in position for scribing. Tilt the scriber slightly in the direction toward which it will be moved, holding it like a pencil. Keep the scriber's point close to the guiding edge of the straightedge. The scribed line should be heavy enough to be visible, but no deeper than necessary to serve its purpose.

FIGURE 12–21. Scriber.

Dividers and Pencil Compasses

Dividers and pencil compasses have two legs joined at the top by a pivot. They are used to scribe circles and arcs and for transferring measurements from the rule to the work.

Pencil compasses have one leg tapered to a needle point; the other leg has a pencil or pencil lead inserted. Dividers have both legs tapered to needle points.

When using pencil compasses or dividers, the following procedures are suggested:

1. Inspect the points to make sure they are sharp.
2. To set the dividers or compasses, hold them with the point of one leg in the graduations on the rule. Turn the adjustment nut with the thumb and forefinger; adjust the dividers or compasses until the point of the other leg rests on the graduation of the rule which gives the required measurement.
3. To draw an arc or circle with either the pencil compasses or dividers, hold the thumb attachment on the top with the thumb and forefinger. With pressure exerted on both legs, swing the compass in a clockwise direction and draw the desired arc or circle.
4. The tendency for the legs to slip is avoided by inclining the compasses or dividers in the direction in which they are being rotated. In working on metals, the dividers are used only to scribe arcs or circles that will later be removed by cutting. All other arcs or circles are drawn with pencil compasses to avoid scratching the material.
5. On paper layouts, the pencil compasses are used for describing arcs and circles. Dividers should be used to transfer critical measurements because they are more accurate than a pencil compass.

Calipers

Calipers are used for measuring diameters and distances or for comparing distances and sizes. The three common types of calipers are the inside, the outside, and the hermaphrodite calipers, such as gear-tool calipers. (See figure 12–22.)

Outside calipers are used for measuring outside dimensions, for example, the diameter of a piece of

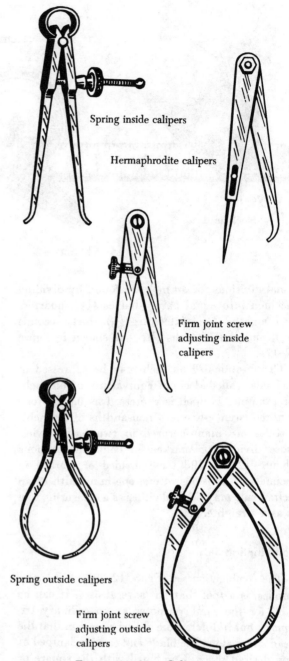

Spring inside calipers

Hermaphrodite calipers

Firm joint screw adjusting inside calipers

Spring outside calipers

Firm joint screw adjusting outside calipers

FIGURE 12–22.   Calipers.

round stock. Inside calipers have outward curved legs for measuring inside diameters, such as diameters of holes, the distance between two surfaces, the width of slots, and other similar jobs. A hermaphrodite caliper is generally used as a marking gage in layout work. It should not be used for precision measurement.

Micrometer Calipers

There are four types of micrometer calipers, each designed for a specific use. The four types are

544

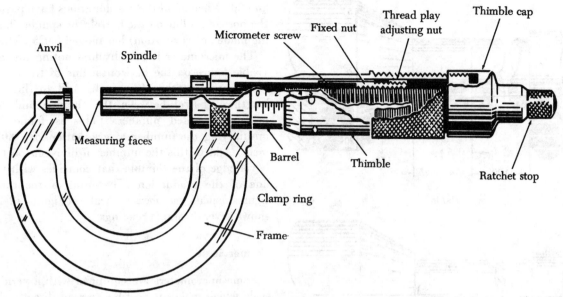

FIGURE 12–23. Outside micrometer.

commonly called outside micrometer, inside micrometer, depth micrometer, and thread micrometer. Micrometers are available in a variety of sizes, either 0 to ½ inch, 0 to 1 inch, 1 to 2 inch, 2 to 3 inch, 3 to 4 inch, 4 to 5 inch, or 5 to 6 inch sizes.

The outside micrometer (figure 12–23) is used by the mechanic more often than any other type. It may be used to measure the outside dimensions of shafts, thickness of sheet metal stock, diameter of drills, and for many other applications.

The smallest measurement which can be made with the use of the steel rule is one sixty-fourth of an inch in common fractions, and one one-hundredth of an inch in decimal fractions. To measure more closely than this (in thousandths and ten-thousandths of an inch), a micrometer is used. If a dimension given in a common fraction is to be measured with the micrometer, the fraction must be converted to its decimal equivalent.

All four types of micrometers are read in the same way. The method of reading an outside micrometer is discussed later in this chapter.

Micrometer Parts

The fixed parts of a micrometer (figure 12–23) are the frame, barrel, and anvil. The movable parts of a micrometer are the thimble and spindle. The thimble rotates the spindle which moves in the threaded portion inside the barrel. Turning the thimble provides an opening between the anvil and the end of the spindle where the work is measured. The size of the work is indicated by the graduations on the barrel and thimble.

Reading a Micrometer

The lines on the barrel marked 1, 2, 3, 4, etc., indicate measurements of tenths, or 0.100 inch, 0.200 inch, 0.300 inch, 0.400 inch, respectively (see figure 12–24).

Each of the sections between the tenths divisions (between 1, 2, 3, 4, etc.) is divided into four parts of 0.025 inch each. One complete revolution of the thimble (from zero on the thimble around to the same zero) moves it one of these divisions (0.025 inch) along the barrel.

The bevel edge of the thimble is divided into 25 equal parts. Each of these parts represents one twenty-fifth of the distance the thimble travels along the barrel in moving from one of the 0.025-inch divisions to another. Thus, each division on the thimble represents one one-thousandth (0.001) of an inch. These divisions are marked for convenience at every five spaces by 0, 5, 10, 15,

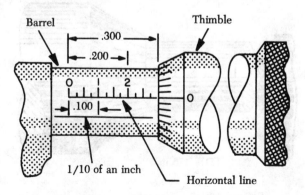

FIGURE 12–24. Micrometer measurements.

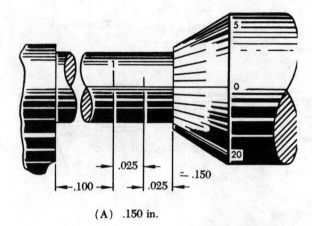

(A) .150 in.

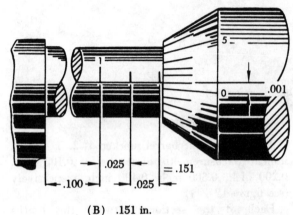

(B) .151 in.

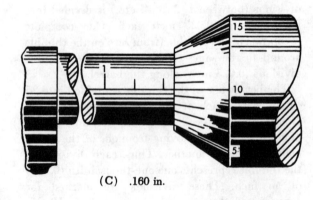

(C) .160 in.

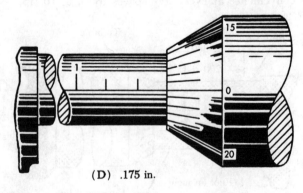

(D) .175 in.

FIGURE 12–25. Reading a micrometer.

and 20. When 25 of these graduations have passed the horizontal line on the barrel, the spindle (having made one revolution) has moved 0.025 inch.

The micrometer is read by first noting the last visible figure on the horizontal line of the barrel representing tenths of an inch. Add to this the length of barrel between the thimble and the previously noted number. (This is found by multiplying the number of graduations by 0.025 inch.) Add to this the number of divisions on the bevel edge of the thimble that coincides with the line of the graduation. The total of the three figures equals the measurement. (Figure 12–25 shows several sample readings.)

Vernier Scale

Some micrometers are equipped with a vernier scale which makes it possible to read directly the fraction of a division that may be indicated on the thimble scale. Typical examples of the vernier scale as it applies to the micrometer are shown in figure 12–26.

All three scales on a micrometer are not fully visible without turning the micrometer; but the examples shown in figure 12–26 are drawn as though the barrel and thimble of the micrometer were laid out flat so that all three scales can be seen at the same time. The barrel scale is the lower horizontal scale; the thimble scale is vertical on the right; and the long horizontal lines (0 through 9 and 0) make up the vernier scale.

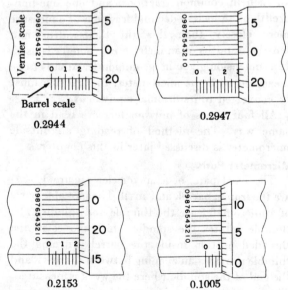

FIGURE 12–26. Vernier scale readings.

In reading a micrometer, an excellent way to remember the relative scale values is to remember that the 0.025-inch barrel scale graduations are established by the lead screw (40 threads per inch). Next, the thimble graduations divide the 0.025 inch into 25 parts, each equal to 0.001 inch; then the vernier graduations divide the 0.001 inch into 10 equal parts, each equal to 0.0001 inch. Remembering the values of the various scale graduations, the barrel scale reading is noted. The thimble scale reading is added to it; then the vernier scale reading is added to get the final reading. The vernier scale line to be read is always the one aligned exactly with any thimble graduation.

In the first example in figure 12–26, the barrel reads 0.275 inch and the thimble reads more than 0.019 inch. The number 1 graduation on the thimble is alined exactly with the number 4 graduation on the vernier scale. Thus, the final reading is 0.2944 inch.

In the second example in figure 12–26, the barrel reads 0.275 inch, and the thimble reads more than 0.019 inch and less than 0.020 inch. On the vernier scale, the number 7 graduation coincides with a line on the thimble. This means that the thimble reading would be 0.0197 inch. Adding this to the barrel reading of 0.275 inch gives a total measurement of 0.2947 inch.

The third and fourth examples in figure 12–26 are additional readings that would require use of the vernier scale for accurate readings to ten-thousandths of an inch.

Using a Micrometer

The micrometer must be handled carefully. If it is dropped, its accuracy may be permanently affected. Continually sliding work between the

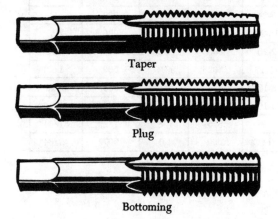

Taper

Plug

Bottoming

FIGURE 12–27. Hand taps.

Adjusting screw

A   Adjustable round split die

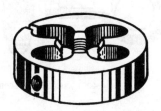

B   Plain round split die

FIGURE 12–28.   Types of dies.

anvil and spindle may wear the surfaces. If the spindle is tightened too much, the frame may be sprung permanently and inaccurate readings will result.

To measure a piece of work with the micrometer, hold the frame of the micrometer in the palm of the hand with the little finger or third finger, whichever is more convenient. This allows the thumb and forefinger to be free to revolve the thimble for adjustment.

TAPS AND DIES

A tap is used to cut threads on the inside of a hole, while a die is for cutting external threads on round stock. They are made of hard-tempered steel and ground to an exact size. There are four types of threads that can be cut with standard taps and dies. They are: National Coarse, National Fine, National Extra Fine, and National Pipe.

Hand taps are usually provided in sets of three taps for each diameter and thread series. Each set contains a taper tap, a plug tap, and a bottoming tap. The taps in a set are identical in diameter and cross section; the only difference is the amount of taper (see figure 12–27).

The taper tap is used to begin the tapping process, because it is tapered back for 6 to 7 threads. This tap cuts a complete thread when it is cutting above the taper. It is the only tap needed when tapping holes that extend through thin sections. The plug tap supplements the taper tap for tapping holes in thick stock.

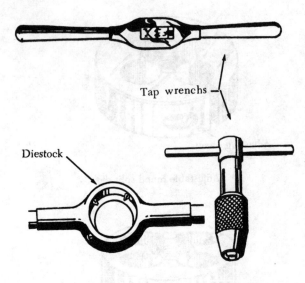

FIGURE 12–29. Diestock and tap wrenches.

The bottoming tap is not tapered. It is used to cut full threads to the bottom of a blind hole.

Dies may be classified as adjustable round split die, and plain round split die (see figure 12–28). The adjustable-split die has an adjusting screw that can be tightened so that the die is spread slightly. By adjusting the die, the diameter and fit of the thread can be controlled.

Solid dies are not adjustable; therefore, a variety of thread fits cannot be obtained with this type.

There are many types of wrenches for turning taps, as well as turning dies. The T-handle, the adjustable tap wrench, and the diestock for round split dies shown in figure 12–29 are a few of the more common types.

Information on thread sizes, fits, types, etc., is shown in figs. 12–30, 12–31 and 12–32.

NATIONAL COARSE THREAD SERIES MEDIUM FIT. CLASS 3 (NC)					NATIONAL FINE THREAD SERIES MEDIUM FIT. CLASS 3 (NF)				
Size and Threads	Dia. of body for thread	Body Drill	Tap Drill		Size and threads	Dia. of body for thread	Body Drill	Tap Drill	
			Pref'd dia. of hole	Nearest stand'd Drill Size				Pref'd dia. of hole	Nearest stand'd Drill Size
					0-80	.060	52	.0472	3/64
1-64	.073	47	.0575	#53	1-72	.073	47	.0591	#53
2-56	.086	42	.0682	#51	2-64	.086	42	.0700	#50
3-48	.099	37	.078	5/64	3-56	.099	37	.0810	#46
4-40	.112	31	.0866	#44	4-48	.112	31	.0911	#42
5-40	.125	29	.0995	#39	5-44	.125	25	.1024	#38
6-32	.138	27	.1063	#36	6-40	.138	27	.113	#33
8-32	.164	18	.1324	#29	8-36	.164	18	.136	#29
10-24	.190	10	.1472	#26	10-32	.190	10	.159	#21
12-24	.216	2	.1732	#17	12-28	.216	2	.180	#15
1/4-20	.250	1/4	.1990	#8	1/4-28	.250	F	.213	#3
5/16-18	.3125	5/16	.2559	#F	5/16-24	.3125	5/16	.2703	I
3/8-16	.375	3/8	.3110	5/16"	3/8-24	.375	3/8	.332	Q
7/16-14	.4375	7/16	.3642	U	7/16-20	.4375	7/16	.386	W
1/2-13	.500	1/2	.4219	27/64"	1/2-20	.500	1/2	.449	7/16"
9/16-12	.5625	9/16	.4776	31/64"	9/16-18	.5625	9/16	.506	1/2"
5/8-11	.625	5/8	.5315	17/32"	5/8-18	.625	5/8	.568	9/16"
3/4-10	.750	3/4	.6480	41/64"	3/4-16	.750	3/4	.6688	11/16"
7/8-9	.875	7/8	.7307	49/64"	7/8-14	.875	7/8	.7822	51/64"
1-8	1.000	1.0	.8376	7/8"	1-14	1.000	1.0	.9072	49/64"

FIGURE 12–30. American (National) screw thread sizes.

Nominal Size Inches	No. of Threads per Inch	Pitch Diameter		Length		Pipe O. D. D Inches	Depth of Thread Inches	Tap Drills for Pipe Threads	
		A Inches	B Inches	L2 Inches	L1 Inches			Minor Diameter Small End of Pipe	Size Drill
1/8	27	.36351	.37476	.2638	.180	.405	.02963	.33388	R
1/4	18	.47739	.48989	.4018	.200	.540	.04444	.43294	7/16
3/8	18	.61201	.62701	.4078	.240	.675	.04444	.56757	37/64
1/2	14	.75843	.77843	.5337	.320	.840	.05714	.70129	23/32
3/4	14	.96768	.98887	.5457	.339	1.050	.05714	.91054	59/64
1	11-1/2	1.21363	1.23863	.6828	.400	1.315	.06957	1.14407	1-5/32
1-1/4	11-1/2	1.55713	1.58338	.7068	.420	1.660	.06957	1.48757	1-1/2
1-1/2	11-1/2	1.79609	1.82234	.7235	.420	1.900	.06957	1.72652	1-47/64
2	11-1/2	2.26902	2.29627	.7565	.436	2.375	.06957	2.19946	2-7/32
2-1/2	8	2.71953	2.76216	1.1375	.682	2.875	.10000	2.61953	2-5/8
3	8	3.34062	3.38850	1.2000	.766	3.500	.10000	3.24063	3-1/4
3-1/2	8	3.83750	3.88881	1.2500	.821	4.000	.10000	3.73750	3-3/4
4	8	4.33438	4.38712	1.3000	.844	4.500	.10000	4.23438	4-1/4

FIGURE 12–31.   American (National) pipe thread
dimensions and tap drill sizes.

Diameter of Drill	Soft Metals 300 F.P.M.	Plastics and Hard Rubber 200 F.P.M.	Annealed Cast Iron 140 F.P.M.	Mild Steel 100 F.P.M.	Malleable Iron 90 F.P.M.	Hard Cast Iron 80 F.P.M.	Tool or Hard Steel 60 F.P.M.	Alloy Steel Cast Steel 40 F.P.M.
1/16 (No. 53 to 80)	18320	12217	8554	6111	5500	4889	3667	2445
3/32 (No. 42 to 52)	12212	8142	5702	4071	3666	3258	2442	1649
1/8 (No. 31 to 41)	9160	6112	4278	3056	2750	2445	1833	1222
5/32 (No. 23 to 30)	7328	4888	3420	2444	2198	1954	1465	977
3/16 (No. 13 to 22)	6106	4075	2852	2037	1833	1630	1222	815
7/32 (No. 1 to 12)	5234	3490	2444	1745	1575	1396	1047	698
1/4 (A to E)	4575	3055	2139	1527	1375	1222	917	611
9/32 (G to K)	4071	2712	1900	1356	1222	1084	814	542
9/16 (L, M, N)	3660	2445	1711	1222	1100	978	733	489
11/32 (O to R)	3330	2220	1554	1110	1000	888	666	444
3/8 (S, T, U)	3050	2037	1426	1018	917	815	611	407
13/32 (V to Z)	2818	1878	1316	939	846	752	563	376
7/16	2614	1746	1222	873	786	698	524	349
15/32	2442	1628	1140	814	732	652	488	326
1/2	2287	1528	1070	764	688	611	458	306
9/16	2035	1357	950	678	611	543	407	271
3/8	1830	1222	856	611	550	489	367	244
11/16	1665	1110	777	555	500	444	333	222
3/4	1525	1018	713	509	458	407	306	204

Figures are for High-Speed Drills. The speed of Carbon Drills should be reduced one-half.
Use drill speed nearest to figure given.

FIGURE 12–32.   Drill speeds.

INDEX

552

Overvoltage relays, 403
Oxygen systems, cleaning compound, 189
Oxygen system, servicing of, 508

P

Packings, 166
  backup, 168
  0-ring, 167
  U-cup, 167
  U-ring, 167, 168
  V-ring, 167, 168
  V-ring adapter, 167
Packing rings, 168
Paper capacitors, 348, 349
Parallel circuit, 336
Parallel D.C. circuits, 290
  a parallel circuit, 290, 291
  current flow, 291
Paralleling generators, 403
Parco lubrizing, 183
Pascal's Law, 231
Pentode tube schematic, 368
Percentage, 9
  expressing as a decimal, 9, 12
  given number, 9
  one number of another, 9, 12
Performance number rating, 75
Phantom lines, 44, 45
Phillips screwdriver, 529, 530
Phosphoric-citric acid, 190
Photoelectric, 321
Physics, 221
  fluids, 222
  general, 221
Pico (10 to the 12th power), 28, 298
Pictograph, 24
Pictorial drawings, 39
Piezoelectric, 322
Pin punch, 531
Pin rivets (hi-shear), 163
Pins, 144
  cotter, 145
  flathead, 145
  roll, 145
  taper, 145
Pipe thread sizes, American National, 549
Plain washers, 130, 131
Plastics, 163
  reinforced, 163
  transparent, 163
Plate (diode tube), 367, 368
Pliers, 530
Plumbing
  assembly precautions, 117
  connectors, 103
  lines, 99
Pneumatic fluid line, 102
Polarity, 52
Positive numbers, 11
  addition of, 12
  subtraction of, 12
Potentiometer, 296, 297
Power, 249, 252, 284
Power in transformer, 361
Powerplant cleaning, 188
Powers, 12
Powers of ten, 14, 15

  added, 15
  subtracted, 15
  their equivalents, 14
Power supply transformer, 361
Precipitation heat treating, 214
  heat treatment of aluminum alloys, 215
  practices, 214
Prefixes (see Metric system), 297, 298
Preoiling equipment, 497
Pressure, 226
  absolute, 227
  acting on a container, 231
  and density relationship, 232
  altitude, 242
  atmospheric, 227
  computing of, 232
  force in fluid power system, 233
  fueling, 500
  relationship with shape, 232
Preventive maintenance corrosion, 173
Prick punch, 531
Primary coil, 358, 359
Print numbers, 37
Prints, 35
Protective paint finishes, 185
Publications, 464-468
Pulley, single fixed, 248
Pull-thru rivets, 156
  countersunk head, 156
  protruding head, 156
Pumps, 85
  engine driven fuel, 86
  hand pump, 85
Punches, 531
Pure nickel, 99
Push-button switch, 318
Push-button type contacts, 52
Push-pull tube assembly, 145

Q

Quick-disconnect couplings, 108
Quick-release fasteners (turnlock type), 141

R

Radiation, 259
Radiography, 479
Rankine scale, 226
Rarefaction of sound, 263
Ratchet screwdriver, 530
Ratchet torque wrench, 133
Ratio, 10
  quantity of first term, 10
  quantity of second term, 11
  two quantities of, 10
Reactance, 355
Reaction of like and unlike charges, 269
Reading drawings, 45
Reading views, 46
Reamers, 539
Reciprocating engine starting, 489, 490
Rectangle, 16
Rectangular, solid, 21
Rectification, 376

Rectifier alternator, 414
Rectifiers, 374-381
  A.C. meters, 381
  bridge rectifier circuit, 378
  copper oxide, 381
  copper oxide dry-disk, 375
  diode bridge circuit, 377
  dry-disk, 374
  forward bias junction diode, 375
  fullwave, 377, 379
  half-wave circuit, 376, 379
  half-wave circuit output, 377
  inductor filter rectifier, output of, 377
  junction diode, 375, 376
  motor generator, 374
  rectification process, 376
  semiconductor diode symbol, 376
  solid state, 375
Rectification, 376
Reed and Prince screwdriver, 529, 530
Reference numbers, 37
Regulators (see Voltage regulators), 398
Reinforced plastics, 163
Relays, 52, 319, 403
  fixed-core, 321
  moveable-core, 321
Removed section, 42, 43
Resistance, 272, 334, 354-356
  circular mil, 274
  factors affecting, 273
  varies with length of conductor, 273
Resistance arm, 247
Resistor, 52, 535
Resistors, 277
  adjustable taps, 278
  black third color band, 281
  carbon, 278
  carbon variable, 279
  coded with body-end-dot system 281, 282
  color code, 279, 280
  color code example, 281
  end-to-center band marking, 281
  fixed, 280
  fixed wire-wound, 278
  gold third band, 281
  precision wire-wound, 278
  silver third band, 281
  unknown resistance, 283
  variable, 280
  wire-wound, 278
  wire-wound variable, 279
Resonance, parallel circuits, 357
Revision block, 38
Revolved sections, 42, 43
Reworked bolt, 122
Rheostat, 52
Rheostat field, 398
Rheostats, 296
Right-hand motor rule, 442
Rigid frame torque wrench, 133
Rigid tubing, installation of, connection torque, 115
Riveting hammer, 529
Rivets (see Self-plugging), 150
  deutsch, 162
  dill lok-skrus, 162
  heating time, 152
  identification, 152
  identification chart, 154
  internally threaded (rivnut), 162
  length of friction lock, 156
  mechanically expanded, 155
  pin, 163